Nursing Leadership

John Daly

Sandra Speedy

Debra Jackson

CHURCHILL
LIVINGSTONE

Sydney Edinburgh London New York
Philadelphia St Louis Toronto

ELSEVIER

WY 122

Churchill Livingstone
is an imprint of Elsevier

Elsevier Australia
30–52 Smidmore Street, Marrickville, NSW 2204

This edition © 2004 Elsevier Australia, reprinted 2005
(a division of Reed International Books Australia Pty Ltd)
ACN 001 002 357

National Library of Australia Cataloguing-in-Publication Data
Daly, John.
Nursing leadership

Bibliography.
Includes Index.
For nursing students and nurse managers.
ISBN 0 7295 3741 2

1. Nursing – Management. 2. Nurse administrators. 3. Leadership – Study
and teaching. I. Speedy, Sandra. II. Jackson, Debra. III. Title.

362.173068

Publisher: Vaughn Curtis
Developmental editor: Rhiain Hull
Publishing Services Manager: Helena Klijn
Edited and proofread by Margaret Trudgeon
Cover design by Trina McDonald
Internal design and typesetting by Egan-Reid Limited
Index by Max McMaster
Printed and bound by Shannon Books, Bayswater, Victoria.

Contents

Nursing Leadership

Preface

This timely book has been created to fill a vital need in the nursing profession and in nursing practice. It represents the current condition of leadership as practised in a wide range of settings, and indicates the challenges that nurse leaders face in ethically fulfilling their various leadership roles, both now and in the future. It points to a future for nursing that is dependent on skilled and informed leadership from within its ranks, whether this be formal or informal leadership. The book rests on the premise that leadership is for everyone, it is not just for the person authorised to hold a position of leadership within the organisation. Equally, we believe that effective leadership is not possible until one has an understanding of self and what motivates others. A diverse range of voices can be found in this collection, representing the global perspectives of nurse leaders specifically selected to contribute their expertise to this volume.

A number of individuals provided vital assistance and support during the preparation of this book. First and foremost, gratitude must go to our families and loved ones for their patience, tolerance, and sacrifice of lost time with us. Our sincere thanks go to Alison Sheppard of the University of Western Sydney for secretarial and administrative support, and Vaughn Curtis and the Elsevier team for seeing us through the project and providing support along the way. Thanks also to Debbie Lee, formerly of MacLennan & Petty, who originally developed this project.

John Daly
Sandra Speedy
Debra Jackson

Sydney
March 2003

Introduction

It should be acknowledged that many contributors to this text have not made a differentiation between management and leadership. It is important to note this, since it may create confusion for beginning as well as continuing leaders and managers. The management literature addresses this issue and there is no doubt that the concept of leadership has become blurred with the more traditional organisational challenge of management. Parry (2001) suggests there are four options that can be considered when addressing the differences (or lack thereof) between leadership and management.

The first option is that leadership and management are two very different constructs, so that management and leadership are obviously different and require particular skills and attributes. The second option is that leadership and management are two overlapping constructs. The third option is that leadership is one part of management: leadership is one of the functions of management, although leaders may not be managers, managers must always be leaders. The fourth and final option is that management is one part of leadership, which implies that there are two types of leadership, namely transformational and transactional leadership. The latter is more often associated with managers, while the former is more often associated with transformational leaders: 'effective leadership comes when managers enact (transactional) management *and* supplement it with (transformational) leadership' (Parry 2001, p.163).

Graetz, et al. (2002) suggest that leadership and management are different and require distinctive skills and attributes, but that one should not be abandoned in favour of the other. A recurring theme of leadership is that it is something that can be learned and applied to leadership challenges as they appear. Thus, leadership is an ability, a style and a process which can be translated into a range of roles, activities, skills and behaviours. Note that management is normally thought of as roles, activities, skills and behaviours. 'Management is *not normally* written up as an ability or a style or a process' (Parry 2001, p.164).

There has long been the view that managers are appointed and that these managers have legitimate power for rewarding and punishing. Their ability to influence is based on the formal authority inherent in their position. On the other hand, according to Robbins et al. (2000), leaders are either appointed or emerge, and can influence others to perform beyond the actions dictated by formal authority. Another view is that managers promote efficiency through negotiations and an eye for detail, whereas leaders stir emotion, provide vision and generate commitment. Thus leadership and management are not merely different entities but diametrical opposites (Yiannis 1998). Sinclair (1998) points out that Kotter distinguishes leaders from managers on the basis of their capacity to envisage change and transform organisations. Consequently, it often takes an outsider to execute a dramatic turnover of leadership when an organisation is on the verge of self-destruction.

INTRODUCTION

For Dubrin and Dalglish (2003), management is more formal and scientific than leadership; it relies on planning, budgeting and controlling, and has explicit tools and techniques which are based on reasoning and testing. Leadership, on the other hand, involves having a vision of what an organisation can become. This requires eliciting co-operation and teamwork, keeping motivational levels high, and ultimately produces change, whereas management is more likely to produce predictability and order. So top level leaders are more likely to transform their organisation, while managers maintain them. The leader creates a vision, while the manager implements that vision.

One view expressed in this text, among others, is that leaders formulate goals from their passion and beliefs about what has to be achieved, while managers, by comparison, adopt the goals of the organisation (Mitchell 2003). Depending on how convincing we find these arguments, we might conclude that the difference between leadership and management is one of emphasis. Effective leaders also manage and effective managers also lead. It is not difficult to move from this position to one that asserts that leadership is a partnership between the leader and group members or followers. In this case, control shifts from the leader to the group, away from authoritarianism and towards shared decision-making. This may not be easy within the nursing practice environment. It requires an exchange of purpose, the right to say no, joint accountability and absolute honesty (Dubrin & Dalglish 2003), characteristics that may be difficult to practise.

Within nursing or other professional workforces, to be effective and credible, senior managers must shift their focus from managing operational tasks which involve planning and budgeting, organising, staffing, controlling and problem-solving, to confronting the challenges involved in leading change. Leading change involves and requires setting a direction and articulating a compelling vision, aligning, motivating and inspiring people. As leaders rather than managers, personal attributes and abilities, not position and status, are the foundations of the personal power of the leader.

It is also conceivable that 'leadership at the top must be "personalised", because it provides the "soft glue", a sense of shared values and purpose that holds the organisational community together' (Graetz et al. 2002, p.211). Ideally, all managers should be leaders, but not all leaders have the capabilities or skills needed in other managerial functions, and therefore should not hold managerial positions. Thus leaders are people who are able to influence others, and possess managerial authority.

It should be noted that there is an ongoing debate on whether leaders make a difference, or whether they do not. While this is quite a fascinating digression, it is beyond the scope of this text. However, readers who wish to pursue this angle are referred to Dubrin and Dalglish (2003).

Leaders, while needing all the skills noted above, must have a strong knowledge base in order to make appropriate judgements within their specific contexts. It is one thing to have the characteristics and authority that facilitate leadership, it is yet another to have the knowledge. This volume is a contribution to that knowledge, examining a range of issues and situations that are pertinent to nurses and other health care practitioners. This book therefore endeavours to provide this knowledge, underpinned by rigorous theoretical perspectives, as it addresses contemporary, ethical nursing practice, governance, research, finance, industrial relations, reflective practice, the working environment and some of the problematic aspects of organisations which impact on leadership.

Accordingly, all chapters have been allocated into three categories. The first category deals with foundational aspects of leadership, and addresses *fundamental issues* such as human behaviour, group dynamics, leadership style, cross–cultural health issues, ethics, law, industrial relations and some of the dysfunctional aspects of organisational leadership. The second category addresses *leadership within the clinical practice context,* and considers the role of motivation, change, research, community practice, quality (of nursing care and of work life), health informatics and reflective practice. The third category describes *leadership in action*, and addresses such issues as contemporary approaches to nursing practice, patient-focused care, management teams, governance, trust and reciprocity. In all, we think that this book will provide you with much to reflect on and incorporate into your professional thinking and lives.

Sandra Speedy
John Daly
Debra Jackson

Contributors

Robert L Anders RN DrPH APRN CS CNAA
Associate Dean, College of Health Science
Professor and Director, School of Nursing
University of Texas at El Paso
El Paso, Texas, USA

Julie Black RN RM BN
Nurse Educator
Director, Royal District Nursing Service Education Centre
Royal District Nursing Service
Glenside, SA

Nicholas Blake BBus
Federal Industrial Officer
Australian Nursing Federation
Canberra, ACT

Sally Borbasi RN PhD
Associate Professor of Nursing
School of Nursing and Midwifery
Flinders University
Adelaide, SA

Esther Chang RN CM BAppSc MEdAdmin PhD
Professor of Nursing and Director, International & Business
School of Nursing, Family & Community Health
College of Social & Health Sciences
University of Western Sydney
Sydney, NSW

Judith Clare RN PhD FRCNA
Professor of Nursing
School of Nursing and Midwifery
Flinders University of SA
Adelaide, SA

Julie Cogin PhD MComm GDip Adult Ed BBus
Adjunct Faculty
Australian Graduate School of Management
A School of both The University of Sydney and
    The University of NSW
Sydney, NSW

Mary Courtney RN PhD
Professor of Nursing, School of Nursing
Queensland University of Technology
Brisbane, Qld

Reta Creegan RN CM RPN BAdmin FCN(NSW)
    FRCNA
Adjunct Professor of Nursing
Centre for Health Services Management
University of Technology
Sydney, NSW

Patrick Crookes RN PhD
Professor of Nursing and Head, Department of Nursing
University of Wollongong
Wollongong, NSW

Kathy Daffurn RN CM BHA MAppSc
Co-Director, Critical Care Services
Conjoint Associate Professor, School of Nursing, Family &
    Community Health
Liverpool Health Service
Liverpool, NSW

John Daly RN PhD FINE FCN(NSW) FRCNA
Professor of Nursing & Foundation Head of School
School of Nursing, Family & Community Health
College of Social & Health Sciences
University of Western Sydney
Sydney, NSW

Patricia Davidson RN PhD
Associate Professor of Nursing
School of Nursing, Family & Community Health
College of Social & Health Sciences
University of Western Sydney and Director, Nursing
    Research Unit
Western Sydney Area Health Service
Sydney, NSW

Christine Duffield RN PhD
Professor of Nursing & Health Services Management
Director, Centre for Health Services Management
University of Technology Sydney
Sydney, NSW

Doug Elliott RN PhD
Professor of Nursing (Critical Care)
Department of Clinical Nursing
Faculty of Nursing
University of Sydney and Prince of Wales Hospital
Sydney, NSW

Kim Forrester RN BA LLB LLM (Advanced)
Barrister-at-Law, Lecturer, Faculty of Nursing and Health
Griffith University, Gold Coast Campus
Southport, Qld

Carol Gaston BAppSc(Nsg) BEd(Admin) GDip Env St
Deputy Chair & Executive Officer
Generational Health Review
Adelaide, SA

Jane Gordon RN BAdmin MHA FCN(NSW)
Executive Director of Clinical Services
Wentworth Area Health Service and Adjunct Associate
    Professor

Jane Gordon *(Continued)*
School of Nursing, Family & Community Health
College of Social & Health Sciences
University of Western Sydney
Sydney, NSW

Genevieve Gray RN CM MSc Dip NEd FRCNA
Professor & Dean
Faculty of Nursing
University of Alberta
Edmonton, Alberta, Canada

Jennifer Greenwood RN CM PhD FRCNA
Nurse Consultant
Edmonton, Alberta, Canada

Rhonda Griffiths RN CM MSc DrPH
Professor of Nursing
School of Nursing, Family & Community Health
College of Social & Health Sciences
University of Western Sydney
Sydney, NSW
and Director, Centre for Applied Nursing Research
UWS/South Western Sydney Area Health Service
Liverpool, NSW

Karen Hancock BSc(Hons) PhD
Research Associate
School of Nursing, Family & Community Health
College of Social & Health Sciences
University of Western Sydney
Sydney, NSW

Jennifer Hardy RN BSc MHP Ed
Senior Lecturer, School of Nursing
Australian Catholic University (ACU National)
North Sydney, NSW

James A Hawkins BA MBA
President
The Directions Corporation
Honolulu, Hawaii, USA

Anne Hofmeyer RN PhD
Lecturer
School of Nursing
Flinders University of SA
Adelaide, SA

Jill Iliffe RN RM BAppSc(N) MIntStuds
Federal Secretary
Australian Nursing Federation
Canberra, ACT

Debra Jackson RN PhD
Associate Professor of Nursing
School of Nursing, Family & Community Health
College of Social & Health Sciences
University of Western Sydney
Sydney, NSW

Megan-Jane Johnstone RN PhD
Professor of Nursing
Department of Nursing and Midwifery
RMIT University
Melbourne, Vic

Jacqueline Jones RN PhD
Senior Lecturer – Professional Services
Australian Nursing Federation (SA Branch)
Flinders University
Adelaide, SA

Tina Koch RN PhD
Adjunct Professor of Nursing
School of Nursing, Family & Community Health
College of Social & Health Sciences
University of Western Sydney
Sydney, NSW
and Director of Research
Royal District Nursing Service
Glenside, SA

Juliene Lipson RN PhD
Professor of Nursing
School of Nursing
University of California, San Francisco
San Francisco, California, USA

Afaf I Meleis RN PhD DrPS(Hon) FAAN
Professor and Margaret Bond Simon Dean of Nursing
School of Nursing
University of Pennsylvania
Philadelphia, Pennsylvania, USA

Gail J Mitchell RN MScN PhD
Nurse Consultant
Formerly Chief Nursing Officer
Sunnybrook Health Sciences Centre
Toronto, Ontario, Canada

Robyn Nash RN MSc
Senior Lecturer in Nursing, School of Nursing
Queensland University of Technology
Brisbane, Qld

Maria O'Rourke RN DScN
O'Rourke & Associates
San Francisco, California, USA

Maree Rogers GDip Mgmt
Director of Human Resources
Royal District Nursing Service
Glenside, SA

Judy Smith RN DipAppSc NsgMgmt BClinNsg MN
FRCNA
Executive Director of Nursing & Client Services
Royal District Nursing Service
Glenside, SA

Sandra Speedy RN BA(Hons) MURP EdD MAPS
Professor and Director
Graduate College of Management
Southern Cross University
Lismore, NSW

David R Thompson RN MBA PhD FRCN FESC
Professor of Clinical Nursing & Director
The Nethersole School of Nursing
The Chinese University of Hong Kong
Shatin, Hong Kong, China

Robert Thornton RN Dip NEd BEd GDip Admin(Ed)
GDip Clinical Nutrition MHPEd PhD
Senior Lecturer, School of Nursing
Queensland University of Technology
Brisbane, Qld

Jill Wiese RN MSc
Executive Assistant Mental Health
Macarthur and South Western Sydney Area Health Service
Liverpool, NSW

PART ONE

Foundational Aspects of Leadership

CHAPTER ONE

Leading and managing in nursing practice: Concepts, processes and challenges

Mary Courtney, Robyn Nash & Robert Thornton

LEARNING OBJECTIVES

At the completion of this chapter, the reader will be able to:

▲ describe the principles of leadership and management theories;

▲ describe old and new paradigms in the management of nursing practice;

▲ discuss challenges and issues in nursing practice;

▲ describe four factors that are essential for transforming and leading change in nursing practice;

▲ understand the essential requirements to become effective leaders and managers; and

▲ understand the leadership role within the health context and describe essential aspects for nurse leaders.

KEY WORDS

Leadership, management, theories, creativity, modelling

INTRODUCTION

This chapter explores leadership and management theories, as well as concepts that underpin current understandings of complex organisations such as health care systems. We give an overview of how such organisations interact with their environments and discuss the challenges and issues that impact upon these organisations. Four factors essential for transforming and leading change in nursing practice are examined. Finally, we look at essential requirements in becoming effective leaders and managers and how to understand the leadership role within the health care context.

PRINCIPLES OF LEADERSHIP AND MANAGEMENT THEORY

Differences between leadership and management

Theorists continue to debate the relationship between leadership and management. Some theorists argue that leadership is simply one of the many functions of management (Tranbarger 1988), while others assert that leadership requires an extended range of complex skills and that management is simply one role of leadership (Gardner 1986).

When examining the literature on both leadership and management it is evident that both concepts have a symbiotic or synergistic relationship with each other. That is, in order for managers and leaders to function effectively, the two concepts must be integrated (Marquis & Huston 1996). Traditionally, strong management skills have been highly valued within health care organisations. However, more recently the demand for leadership skills has gained prominence. We will return to the difference between leadership and management later in this chapter.

Development of management theory

Like nursing science, management science has developed a theoretical base from a wide range of other disciplines, such as business, psychology, sociology and anthropology. Over the last 100 years, theorists' views of what constitutes successful management practices have evolved because of the ever-changing nature of health care organisations and the external and internal environment in which they are located.

In order to understand health care organisations, it is necessary to clarify some of the different theoretical approaches used to describe organisations in general. Systems theory offers a range of insights into the functions of organisations. Sampson and Marthas (1990) describe systems theory as having specialised components that work together interdependently to form an overall balanced framework.

Organisations conduct their everyday activities by taking either an open systems or a closed systems approach (see Table 1.1). The open systems approach places importance on the links between organisations, emphasising the need for ensuring open lines of communication. They must also be adaptive, innovative and flexible (Shortell & Kaluzny 1997). On the other hand, organisations with a closed systems approach tend to function independently from the external environment and have processes and procedures set in place to ensure that the organisation's internal efficiency reaches its full potential.

A brief summary of the various theoretical approaches undertaken during the development of management theory is presented on the following pages.

Table 1.1 Open and closed systems functions

Type of system	Function
Open systems	Links between organisations
	Adaptable
	Innovative
	Flexible
Closed systems	Organisation functions independently of external environment

Scientific management

In the late nineteenth century, Frederick W. Taylor was working as a mechanical engineer in a steel plant in Pennsylvania. At the time, 'systematic soldiering' was rife—workers would undertake the least amount of work possible to achieve minimum standards. Taylor (1911) believed that the introduction of 'one best way to accomplish a task' would ensure workers achieved an agreed-upon standard, which in turn would lead to increased productivity.

Did scientific management achieve results? Yes. Indeed, productivity and profits increased dramatically. However, from a closed systems perspective on organisations, scientific management saw puritan work ethics prevail and indeed some have argued that Taylor was ahumanistic.

Bureaucratic theory

In 1922, Weber expanded upon Taylor's theories and wrote an essay entitled 'Bureaucracy', which espoused the need for more rules, regulations and structure within organisations to further improve efficiency and productivity. This closed systems approach encouraged the establishment of an internal hierarchy with clear lines of responsibility and authority. Professional bureaucratic management strategies have traditionally dominated health care organisations. Indeed, Weber's theories and design for bureaucratic organisation are still largely used today in the majority of health care organisations around the world. The structure includes parallel professional and administrative hierarchies with specific lines of responsibilities and operating rules and procedures.

Identification of management functions

In 1925, Fayol described the management functions of planning, organisation, command, coordination and control. Gulick (1937) extended this work by introducing the 'seven activities of management'—planning, organising, staffing, directing, coordinating, reporting and budgeting. These theorists also took a closed systems perspective on organisations.

Human relations theory

In the 1920s the introduction of the assembly line meant that great numbers of relatively unskilled workers were working in large, complex factories on specific tasks. There was great worker unrest, causing human relations theorists to examine what motivated workers to work. M. P. Follett (1926), in her essay entitled 'The Giving of Orders', asserted that managers should have authority *with*, rather than *over*, employees.

Follett was one of the first theorists in this era to argue for what is known today as 'participative decision-making'.

Other human relations theorists such as Mayo (1953), McGregor (1960) and Argyris (1964) all expanded upon her work. Mayo identified the 'Hawthorne effect'. He found that employees increased their productivity levels when special attention was paid to them, regardless of any other changes in their working environment. He noted that people responded to the fact that attention was being paid to them and that they would continue to display the behaviour needed to continue to gain the attention. McGregor (1960) extended upon these concepts by labelling managers as either Theory X or Theory Y managers, depending upon their views of how employees performed their activities (see Table 1.2). Argyris (1964) reinforced the theories of Mayo and McGregor by arguing that managerial domination leads workers to become discouraged and passive, therefore creating low productivity levels and reduced profits. He believed this would subsequently lead to troublesome employees, and eventually an increased turnover of staff.

Although human relations theory seeks to empower individuals, it still adopts a closed system approach to improving the workplace. Individual worker motivation and involvement are recognised by the organisation; however, to encourage harmonious social relations, appropriate structures are usually institutionalised to suit the type of workforce employed. Managers often espouse the importance of developing interpersonal communication and collaboration with individuals to improve workplace relations, while commonly using systems of performance management to motivate workers.

The human relations theory of organisations is based upon a static environment where structures are organised around the professional disciplines. On its own it is not sufficient to describe complex health care organisational structures. Nor does it adequately provide a means of understanding and managing the changes that are taking place in today's health care organisations (Lloyd & Boyce 1998).

Institutional theory

Institutional theory takes an open systems perspective of organisations. It examines how organisations succeed by ensuring they fit together with the external environment (DiMaggio & Powell 1983; Powell & DiMaggio 1991). Powell & DiMaggio (1991) argued that organisations gain legitimacy from key external stakeholders as they adopt norms, rules and values that reflect the stakeholders' belief systems. By adapting to the external stakeholder environment, organisations signal their congruency with the expectations of stakeholders, such as funding agencies, governments, professional bodies and customers (Daft 1998).

Population ecology theory

Population ecology theory is another open systems approach to organisation theory and is founded on the notion that an organisation's success depends on its relationship to competitors in its external environment (Hannan & Freeman 1977). The theory is similar to that of natural selection in biology, whereby as pressures increase on a population within a similar environment, the stronger and more dominant will survive while the weak will suffer and become extinct. Thus, in organisations subject to similar external environments that are under pressure, the more powerful will survive and prosper and the weaker will not.

Subsequently, a gradual evolution of organisational structural changes will occur within the organisation in order to accommodate the complexities of the external environment. Daft (1998) notes that niche markets are often left open in unexploited environments.

Within health care organisations, unresolved social dilemmas concerning inadequate service provision can become the subject of media campaigns and taken up in the political arena. Organisations that are able to adapt their organisational structures to address the complexity of change will therefore be more likely to survive.

Strategic management theory

Strategic management theory is yet another open systems approach to organisations. The organisations that use this theory seek to incorporate the internal and external environment into their planning process as they strive to meet targeted objectives. Strategic management theory is commonly used in health care organisations because of the need to try and balance limited resources while ensuring that patient care is not threatened. These organisations take an ordered approach to the planning process and define and regularly monitor their chosen organisational goals and objectives to ensure they meet budgetary performance targets (Biscoe & Lewis 1996; Ellis & Brockbank 1993).

An overview of these various theoretical approaches is presented in Table 1.2. More recently, we have seen organisations moving towards more open systems perspectives in an endeavour to adapt to the ever-changing environment. This paradigm shift will be discussed in the following section.

Table 1.2 Historical development of management theory

Systems Perspective	Theory	Explanation	Theorist
Closed	Scientific management	Workers could be taught the the 'one best way to accomplish a task'	Taylor (1911) 'father of scientific management'
Closed	Bureaucracy of organisations	A need to provide rules, regulations, and structure within organisations to increase efficiency	Weber (1922)
Closed	Management functions	Planning, organisation, command, coordination and control	Fayol (1925)
Closed	Seven activities of management	Planning organising, staffing, directing, coordinating, reporting and budgeting	Gulick (1937)
Closed	Participative management	Authority with, rather than over, employees	Follett (1926)
Closed	'Hawthorne effect'	People respond to the fact they are being studied	Mayo (1953)
Closed	Theory X and Theory Y	How managers treat employees directly correlated with employee satisfaction	McGregor (1960)

cont.

Table 1.2 cont.

Systems Perspective	Theory	Explanation	Theorist
Closed (cont.)	Theory X and Theory Y	Theory X managers believe employees are basically lazy, need constant supervision and direction, and are indifferent to organisational needs	McGregor (1960)
		Theory Y managers believe workers enjoy work, are self-motivated and willing to work hard to meet personal and organisational goals	
Closed	Employee participation	Managerial domination causes workers to become discouraged and passive	Argyris (1964)
		Flexibility in workplace required	
		Employee participation in decision-making	
Open	Institutional theory	Success depends on ensuring an organisation and its external environment fit together	DiMaggio & Powell (1983)
		Adaptive and congruent with expectations of external stakeholders	
Open	Population ecology theory	Success depends upon relationship with competitors in external environment	Hannan & Freeman (1977)
		Stronger and more dominant survive Weak become extinct	
Open	Strategic management theory	Success depends upon following logical process to meet chosen goals and objectives	Ellis & Brockbank (1993)
		Adaptive to internal and external environment	Biscoe & Lewis (1996)

OLD AND NEW PARADIGMS IN MANAGEMENT OF NURSING PRACTICE

In examining the functions of leadership within an organisation, Stout–Shaffer and Larrabee (1992) identified five paradigm shifts to transform health care organisations into the new millennium (See Table 1.3). In the past, organisations were characterised by centralised hierarchies, with power vested in the management. Employees were skeptical of management and distrusted it. Health care organisations undertook strategic planning activities in isolation from patients and set benchmarks for planned productivity and efficiency within their own organisations in isolation from the external environment.

Table 1.3 Paradigm shifts transforming health care organisations

Past	Future
Centralised hierarchies	Semi-autonomous work units
Power resting with management	Empowerment of all employees
Distrust of management	Trust
Planning for patients	Planning with patients
Quantitative productivity	Intuition and creativity

Source: Stout-Shaffer & Larrabee (1992, pp.54–8).

In contrast, the future scenario sees a move away from centralised hierarchies to semi-autonomous work units where all employees are empowered to work intuitively and creatively—where strategic planning is undertaken in partnership with patients and where employee skepticism is replaced by trust of management.

CHALLENGES AND ISSUES FOR NURSE LEADERS AND MANAGERS

The world of health care continues to change rapidly. Today's health care system presents challenges to administrators and clinicians that have few or no precedents, and there is no indication that it will be any different in the future. Some years ago, Vaill (1989) coined the term 'permanent white water' to describe the phenomenon of change as a constant rather than discontinuous state. Taking this as an accurate statement about the nature of our current and future environments raises an important question about the factors that are influencing such change. Given the increasing complexity of our personal and professional worlds, it is perhaps not surprising that the answers are to be found in multiple arenas—technological, social, political, economic and scientific—each contributing significantly and cumulatively to the impetus for change (Alderman 2001).

Economic and political issues

The term 'doing more with less' has become familiar to clinicians and administrators alike, both at 'ground level' as well as at 'the top'. The challenges associated with delivering quality patient care within an environment of rising consumer expectations and increasingly constrained human and financial resources are everyday realities for many nurses. Continued downsizing of health care facilities/services, increased acuity and decreasing lengths of stay—the 'high-tech short stay' phenomenon—and increased pressures on community-based service provision add further pressures to the day-to-day delivery of appropriate patient care. In a recent survey of nurse and non-nurse executives in the United States, the number one challenge reported by respondents was the provision of quality care with declining reimbursement (Byers 2001). Other responses related to this issue included the maintenance of financial viability with increased government and managed care constraints, and declining reimbursement.

Social and demographic issues

Social changes, both within and outside of the nursing profession, also present contemporary challenges for nursing leadership and management. For example, Alderman (2001) draws attention to changes in worldwide demographics that are likely to lead to increased cultural diversity at the point of care delivery and the challenges that confront increasingly pluralistic societies. She also highlights a trend towards the development of two 'distinct' social classes based on literacy: the educated and the uneducated, the phenomenon of rising violence in our societies and issues stemming from our increasing capabilities to 'create', extend and/or 'end' life through artificial insemination, cloning, genetic engineering, assisted suicide and euthanasia (Alderman 2001, p.45). Other social changes of significance for nurse leaders and managers include the ageing of populations worldwide, employment/unemployment patterns and trends, increasing risks to health and wellbeing, coupled with the apparent reluctance of many to embrace preventative measures/lifestyles and strong views, while at the same time not wanting to pay more for health care (Friedman 1999), and the increasing tendency toward litigation to resolve issues/conflicts.

Professional issues

Within nursing there are several contemporary issues that present significant challenges for nursing leadership and management. Foremost among these are the changing demographics of the nursing workforce and the shortages of nursing staff being experienced in many areas of clinical practice. In Australia, nursing workers (including registered and enrolled nurses, assistants in nursing and personal care assistants) are older than they were just over a decade ago. The proportion of workers aged 45 years and over increased by 17 per cent between 1987 and 2001, while the proportion of workers under 34 years of age decreased by 24 per cent (Shah & Burke 2001). The average retirement age of nurses in Australia is approximately 55 years, therefore it is expected that the ageing of this workforce will continue for some time, resulting in a significant impact as the numbers of retirements increase (Heath 2001, p.80). In addition, there has been a shift toward part-time work, particularly among registered nurses and midwives and, for nurse workers in general, a trend towards working shorter hours per week (Heath 2001, p.81). It is clear that these changes are not confined to the Australian context. Evidence presented by Huber (2000) suggests that similar trends are occurring in the United States, highlighting the importance of such issues from a global perspective.

Currently there appear to be registered nurse shortages, or predictions of shortages, in many countries around the world, including Australia, the United Kingdom, Canada and the United States (Heath 2001, p.81). Although shortages of registered nurses are not new, the pervasive nature of the current phenomenon, coupled with fluctuating enrolments in nursing courses (Heath 2001; USDHHS 1997), problems with the retention of nursing staff (Aiken et al. 2001), and expanding career opportunities for women (Staiger et al. 2000), suggest that the current situation is going to be difficult to turn around. Nursing shortages are being experienced in a broad range of specialisations, including critical/intensive care, aged care, mental health, midwifery, perioperative nursing, accident/emergency nursing, oncology and palliative care. There are also shortages in rural and geographically remote areas, and in community contexts of practice. These issues raise critical questions for nurse leaders and managers with respect to the deployment of scarce resources and the recruitment and retention of competent staff. How effectively these and other questions are addressed affects nurses, nursing and the delivery of patient care.

TRANSFORMING AND LEADING CHANGE IN NURSING PRACTICE

Like other health professionals, nurses are shaped to some extent by changes in the health care system, but as the single largest group of health care workers, they also have considerable opportunity to shape the system itself. It is suggested that to effectively negotiate these increasingly dynamic health care environments several imperatives will be critical for nurse leaders and managers. These can be seen in Figure 1.1 and are discussed briefly in the following section.

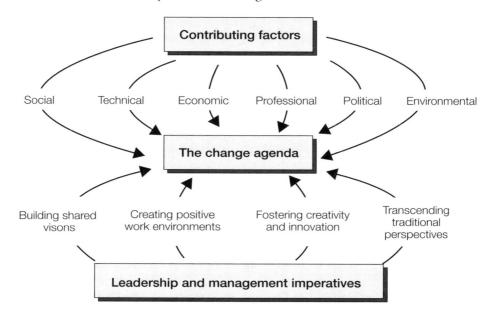

Figure 1.1 Critical leadership and management imperatives

Building shared visions

As put so aptly by Tornabeni (2001), 'to create a new world order in anything that you do, you've got to dare to dream' (p.1). Dreaming, or visioning, has long been considered a key element of leadership, particularly transformational leadership (Bass 1985; Bennis & Nanus 1985). Visioning is about making an assessment of current reality, determining what a desired state would be, and managing the resultant tension between these two states in a manner that is constructive and productive (Yoder-Wise 1999). The ability to conceptualise a vision and communicate it to others is a critical issue for nurse leaders and managers. A clear visualisation of a better or more ideal future state is a powerful means of providing staff with a sense of direction and common purpose (Capowski 1994), guiding and focusing decision-making (Ireland & Hill 1992), creating a balance between the competing interests of various stakeholders (Goffee et al. 2000), and creating forward momentum towards desired goals.

However, it is suggested here that one of the most important elements of visioning is the building of shared visions, that is creating 'dreams' or future states that have 'buy-in' from all relevant staff and/or external stakeholders. Senge (1990) suggests that leadership is really about people working at their best to create the future. Without 'buy-in' even the best vision may never become reality. Thus a crucial challenge for nurse leaders and managers is to be able to work 'top down' as well as 'bottom up'— and with external partners—to define the way forward. Porter-O'Grady (1997b) suggests that 'the leader of tomorrow will be a gatherer of people and a facilitator of the processes that they might use to come to agreement or to find common ground with regard to an issue or direction' (p.18). Being able to foster an 'our' attitude, e.g. 'our' reputation, 'our' organisation, 'our' service, will be an important part of creating and maintaining system-wide continuity of quality care in the face of significant challenges.

Creating positive work environments

From the above discussion it is clear that the creation and maintenance of positive work environments, as characterised by the Bennis and Nanus (1985) concept of a social architecture that provides meaning for employees, will be another significant challenge for nurse leaders and managers. Among other things, this will require, indeed demand, a deep understanding of and abiding respect for others. According to Tornabeni (2001), this is what empowers the building of teams, in her view 'the essential task faced by leaders' (p.9). Murdoch Perra (2001) echoes this sentiment and goes further to highlight the importance of the leader's reflection on their own personal and professional values and sense of self. She puts the view that leaders and managers will only be able to 'reach out to develop trusting and respectful relationships with staff, peers and administrators' (p.70) when they are working from a firm base of personal values that are not in conflict with those of the organisation.

Leadership can be seen as the practice of 'small actions that can engage or alienate, or nourish or deplete those around us' (Kerfoot 2001, p.42). Jack Welch said, 'What we are building is fragile. It's built on trust. The process can be set back in a heartbeat by people at any level who see leadership as a process of intimidation, whose own lack of esteem makes them unable to trust and let go' (cited in Lewin & Regine 2000, p.305). Leaders and managers need to actively cultivate and finely hone the skills of 'listening more, asking more and talking less' (Tornabeni 2001, p.10). Human beings do not react like machines. With the ever-increasing pace of change in our personal and professional lives, staff are likely to be more demanding in terms of work environments that meet their needs efficiently and effectively. In the words of Kerfoot (2001):

> We are leading a journey, not an end product. This journey is better led by a structure that allows everyone to contribute his/her talents to the fullest rather than the leader providing all the direction. The ability to connect with people and to engage their spirit in the noble adventure of patient care is what really matters (p.43).

Fostering creativity and innovation

Creativity is essential for the generation of ideas, options and solutions. According to Bunkers (1999, p.28), the capacity to 'create new order' is one of the four major capacities that are the hallmarks of futuristic leaders. This capacity encompasses the ability to see relationships between unrelated parts or, in other words, relevance and fit between things that have not previously been connected together. Implicit within this is the capacity for systems thinking, described by Senge (1990) as the ability to see the big picture and analyse how things work from a systems perspective. Having a systems understanding facilitates the anticipation and identification of unintended consequences from changes in one or more parts of the system. An important and related skill is that of critical thinking and analysis. Critical analysis enables an individual to see patterns and trends in seemingly unrelated heterogeneous events, thus bringing order to the decision-making process (Alderman 2001, p.47). Not accepting things at face value, being prepared to ask critical questions, challenging assumptions, clarifying conflicting ideas and pursuing the 'what if?' possibilities are essential skills for leaders and managers to develop.

From a nursing perspective, Gilmartin (1999) makes the point that, although a common wisdom exists that nurses are creative when it comes to finding solutions for patient care problems, nursing service has been delivered historically within bureaucratic structures characterised by conformity and regimentation designed to support production efficiency. She comments further that 'in the new era of knowledge-based organisations, responsive strategic actions are driven by imaginative yet feasible solutions that are driven by those who carry out the organisation's primary work' (p.4). The _____ ndency for people to continue to do things in older, more traditiona _____ e ways, especially as increasing energy is required to deal with the c _____ the change agenda. However, the ability to see challenges and o _____ ng old things in new ways can be a path to personal success, as well _____ ribute to improved methods of care (Tushman & O'Reilly 19° _____ nge for nursing leaders and managers will be to capitalise ef _____ nities to 'tap into' the collective wisdom that exists among st _____ ote an environment where new ideas and fresh approach _____ quire risk-taking as well as creativity. But without the cou _____ h the envelope' or try new things, organisational change _____ s will not be realised. The willingness to take risks require _____ ess to persist, particularly in the face of adversity or lack of _____ easy, but 'entering courageously life's turning points' (Bunk _____ ial attribute for contemporary nurse leaders and manag _____ e.

Tran _____ rspectives

According to _____ (_____):

> Effective leaders do not engage themselves in struggles with others. They move out of the control mode and into one of adaptation and change. Their success lies in the ability to clearly specify the outcomes needed, and to nourish and coach others to achieve these outcomes . . . Effective leaders do not try to force people into roles in which they don't fit. They know when to let go (p.42).

One of the issues highlighted by this statement is what can, arguably, be seen as a fundamental distinction between transformational and transactional leadership. Theories of transformational leadership became popular during the 1980s and 1990s as a result of work by people such as Bass (1985), Bennis and Nanus (1985), Kouzes and Posner (1987), and Tichy (1986). In essence, the transformational leader is someone who can motivate others to perform to their full capacity by influencing a change in perceptions and by providing a sense of direction. The notion of performance beyond expectations is a hallmark of transformational leadership. Transactional leadership, on the other hand, is about 'getting the job done'. Transactional leaders identify what needs to be done and, work within the existing culture to ensure that it gets done. Expectations of performance, performance outcomes, contingent reward and management by exception are hallmarks of transactional leadership (Huber 2000).

In a similar fashion, Fedoruk and Pincombe (2000) distinguish between the traditional views of leadership and management, and make the point that the 'old (managerialist, bureaucratically-oriented) competencies required of a nurse executive are no longer appropriate for a constantly changing environment driven by competing demands' (p.6). They go on to suggest that 'the nurse executive has to coalesce the technical demands of a management with the visionary dimensions of leadership if nursing is to survive into the next century as a discrete entity' (p.7).

There is increasing evidence that highlights the role of transformational leadership in terms of achieving positive outcomes (e.g. McDaniel & Wolf 1992; Prenkert & Ehnfors 1997). However, in a brief overview of transformational and transactional leadership, Huber (2000) states that 'the transactional leader is more common' (p.65). The health care organisation of the future will be very different from the institutional models in existence today. It is likely that, in the future, health care service delivery will be described within vertically integrated systems embracing primary care, home health, long-term health and related components of the health care continuum (Shortell et al. 1993). These and other changes will provide important windows of opportunity for nurses in terms of leadership and management. However, in capitalising on these opportunities, a significant challenge for nurse leaders and managers of the future will be to transcend traditional, perhaps more comfortable, ways of thinking and doing in order to move forward with a reflective understanding about what will work best and the courage to make it happen. 'Letting go' is never easy, but the rewards that can potentially be realised through reconfiguring old leadership and management practices to more contemporary integrated approaches will make it worthwhile.

BECOMING A LEADER AND MANAGER
Understanding the difference between leading and managing

The terms leader and manager are often seen as synonymous and used interchangeably in role descriptions. This concept conveys the notion that if one is managing, then one is leading, and vice versa. The popular literature and some conference speakers often use a rather simplistic description by referring to leadership as dealing with people and management as dealing with paper. Although not critical in its approach, this paradigm is a beginning point from which to understand the differences between the two terms.

In the nursing context, the leader is a visionary with a concentration of time and effort who looks outward to how the unit, organisation or profession can go forward. The day-to-day organisation therefore becomes the domain of the manager. Excellence in leadership requires one to see above the plethora of paper, policies and procedures required to maintain the functionality of the workplace. A leader needs to be a negotiator with a broader worldview about how the area of responsibility will grow and develop within overall bureaucratic influences. Often the two roles must be complementary, depending on the size of an organisation. However, without a clear focus, a potential leader can end up spending valuable time dealing with details that should really be delegated. This means that they can never break free of day-to-day responsibilities to provide the staff with the vision and direction essential to maintain a high quality of patient care.

To further emphasise this point, Tappen et al. (2001) indicate that one does not need to be a manager to be a leader—even the most novice practitioner, given the right opportunities, can assume this role.

Knowing oneself as a leader and manager

Paramount to the attainment of any leadership or management role is the ability to be in tune with oneself, or, as stated by Goleman (1998, p.318), to have 'emotional self-awareness'. Despite the above simplistic view of 'paper versus people', all our business involves dealing with people, to a greater or lesser extent. It can be argued that if a role requires you to organise staff and deal with people with a plurality of values, then one firstly needs to have developed an insight into one's emotions and feelings—especially in a conflict situation. This is not to imply the need to undertake psychoanalysis, but rather the need to have a sense of one's strengths and shortcomings. This insight will foster a proactive approach, rather than being reactive to differing opinions as policies and programs are implemented.

The demands of managers and leaders are ever-increasing and self-knowledge about the issues that drive you, and how you respond to others, is important. It is erroneous to think that you have two personas—one for your personal life and the other for your professional life. While many nurses in leadership and management roles claim that they are different people at work compared to at home, one needs to recognise the basic constructs of one's make-up and use this self-awareness to manage situations and lead people. The attainment of 'emotional intelligence' has become an important issue. It refers to 'the capacity for recognising our own feelings and those of others, for motivating ourselves and for managing emotions well in ourselves and in our relationships' (Goleman 1998, p.317). This concept applies equally in one's personal and professional life.

Essential knowledge for leaders and managers

To be effective in either a leadership or managerial role one needs to look beyond the pragmatics of nursing care delivery. Effective nurse leaders and managers need to move from a comfort zone of what one has acquired and learnt through education and clinical experience. They need to be able to deal with high technology changes, rapid throughput of patients, high intensity environments, and ever-changing government policy. It is essential to the role for managers and leaders to be able to make good business decisions based on an understanding of bureaucratic structures. Effective nurse leaders and managers need to be able to internalise and practise skilled application of 'knowledge work'—cognitive activity, analysis of information, and application of specialised expertise in problem-solving, teaching and creation of new ideas or products (Huber 2000, p.144).

Skill elements for leaders and managers

While it is necessary to acquire a base level of operational knowledge as described above, it is also paramount to acquire or enhance skills to convey management and leadership concepts. Three essential skills include:

▲ an ability to communicate decisions and visions to individuals and groups. This is a hallmark of being able to influence peers and others (Huber 2000, p.202);

▲ an ability to discipline oneself regarding time management—working at a fast pace may not equate to achieving a great deal (Tappen et al. 2001, p.76); and

▲ an ability to deal with stress by setting personal and professional goals, establishing priorities, practising good health habits and relaxation techniques, improving self-esteem by obtaining necessary skills, and using support systems (Marriner Tomey 2000, p.27).

Personality traits of leaders and managers

Ineffective managers and leaders are a composite of their habits. Habits are unconscious patterns that express our character, and in the demanding role of quality management, negative traits will not inspire others to follow or be directed. To become effective within and outside an organisation one needs to develop or acquire traits that will result in positive outcomes. Personal traits that others need to acquire will enable one to demonstrate mutual respect, connection, praise and public acknowledgement of colleagues' contributions.

THE LEADERSHIP ROLE

The function of leadership

In nursing today it is becoming evident that autocratic leadership no longer brings staff together to share a common vision. Nursing leaders need to build and develop others to realise their greatest achievement. Grossman and Valiga (2000) argue that leaders need to focus on people, have a long-range perspective, develop innovative ideas and be able to generate a power base from knowledge and credibility to motivate others.

Developing leadership potential

As outlined by Covey (1992), many people live their lives with unused potential and are thus not as effective as they might be. Leaders need to develop the full potential in others, looking for approaches to assist people to improve themselves. Developing potential in others in a nursing context entails building self-directed working teams and mentoring others (Bower 2000).

Modelling leadership behaviour

Nurse leaders need to model behaviour that others wish to emulate. Displayed behaviour that is deemed to be negative or that lacks credibility will cause others to withdraw. Behaviour and reputation clearly demonstrating that one is supportive and willing to listen, will attract people to you and assist them to grow and develop. Decision-making behaviour is a common expectation of nursing leadership, along with the personal qualities of approachability. Leaders who appear unable to make decisions can look ineffective in a situation where an organisation or set of circumstances demands attention. Wheeler (cited in Bower 2000, p.207) suggests further that leaders demonstrating proactive decision-making behaviour are more effective when possessing 'the ability to anticipate the "event" so they act before'. A final recommendation for a potential leader is to avoid becoming known as someone who managed everything, but led nothing.

Encouraging self-assessment for leadership

Self-assessment can be used to monitor one's own actions or behaviour and those of others. In the previous section, the issue of knowing oneself was discussed and remains an important consideration when asking others to undertake self-assessment. Leaders must be confident enough to disclose their own personal weaknesses. Staff will also be less defensive if they are allowed to express their feelings and concerns regarding their own performance, rather than being told of any shortcomings they may have. Leaders in nursing need to also assist others to recognise any perceived weakness when they lack insight. Credibility when facilitating this process will be enhanced if you are prepared to share how you have overcome difficulties in similar circumstances. This approach will not only enhance the development of others but also create an environment that fosters self-assessment.

Delegation to develop leadership potential

Leaders within nursing need to take opportunities to practise delegation. A common reaction to the notion of delegation is to assume that the leader cannot do, or does not want to do, a particular activity. As stated by Arnold (in Bower 2000, p.291), 'Delegation is another form of letting go—it means passing a task from yourself to another'. The manner in which this 'passing' is conducted is very important. A model that creates a positive response can be summarised as follows: when delegating, a leader needs to demonstrate that they have the ability to do the task themselves. The person to whom the activity is delegated needs to be able to undertake this responsibility knowing that the leader is available for support. Once the delegate feels confident in the activity, then they only need to report the outcomes to the leader. This approach can only strengthen the leadership role.

■ CASE STUDY

Building trust and confidence

Deborah was a senior nurse with a long track record of successful management in an intensive care unit. A new staff member, Jeanette, had noticed that a nursing student on clinical placement from the local university was acting in an unprofessional manner towards a patient. Jeanette raised the issue with Deborah and they agreed that the manner of the nursing student was inappropriate. They both counselled the student, the behaviour was recognised and undertakings were made by the student not to repeat the behaviour.

When Deborah and Jeanette met after the meeting with the student, Jeanette expressed admiration that the issue had been resolved and thanked Deborah for her support in dealing with this difficult situation.

A week later Deborah was summoned to the Director of Clinical Services office to be informed that Jeanette had made a complaint about her regarding the manner in which she had dealt with the nursing student incident. Deborah was discouraged by this event, wondering why Jeanette had not bought this issue to her directly and why the Director of Clinical Services had not, in the very least, held a three-way meeting to discuss this issue in-person.

CONCLUSION

This chapter has presented an overview of leadership and management theories and concepts underpinning current understandings of complex organisations. It has provided an overview of how such organisations interact with their environments and examined some of the challenges and issues impacting upon health care organisations. Finally, we looked at some of the essential requirements needed to become an effective leader and manager.

We argued it is important for organisations to clearly understand and evaluate both their internal and external social, economic, political, technological and professional environments. Because of the pace and complexity of change experienced by health care organisations, these issues raise critical questions for nurse leaders and managers with respect to the deployment of scarce resources, and the recruitment and retention of competent staff.

Reflective exercise

1 Reflect on leaders and managers that have had a positive influence on your nursing practice or your nursing career.

   a Reflect on why and how they influenced you.

   b Consider these attributes and compare them with your own.

   The exercise will help you to develop a template to further develop additional skills, attitudes and knowledge and to recognise potential areas for development in the leadership and management role.

2 Discuss the leadership issues and concerns in the Case Study on page 17 regarding the way in which the Director of Clinical Services dealt with this situation.

3 Comment on the appropriateness of a new staff member Jeanette going directly to the Director and circumventing Deborah.

4 If you were Deborah describe how you would react in a similar situation.

5 Reconstruct the case study to result in a more positive leadership outcome.

6 Outline what can be learned from this case study regarding leadership behaviour.

RECOMMENDED READINGS

Bower, F. (2000). *Nurses taking the lead: Personal qualities of effective leadership.* Philadelphia: W. B. Saunders.

Covey, S. (1992). *Principle-centered leadership: Strategies for personal and professional effectiveness.* New York: Simon & Schuster.

Porter-O'Grady, T. (1997b). Quantum mechanics and the future of healthcare leadership. *Journal of Nursing Administration (27),* 15–20.

CHAPTER TWO

Understanding human behaviour and group dynamics

Julie Cogin

LEARNING OBJECTIVES

At the completion of this chapter, the reader will be able to:

- ▲ critique three theories of human behaviour;

- ▲ outline the factors affecting individual behaviour and performance;

- ▲ identify how cultural differences can impact performance at work;

- ▲ list and explain the factors you need to consider when establishing and leading a team; and

- ▲ develop a team-building strategy for a team of which you are a member or leader.

KEY WORDS

Cohesiveness, group dynamics, values, motivation, team composition

An effective leader understands the factors that influence the behaviour of their staff, colleagues and patients, in addition to themselves. In order to lead and manage others it is necessary to know how one's own style is affected by many variables, including personality attributes, cultural background, and the environment we work in.

The health care setting provides an interesting arena in which to study leadership. First, the work environment is made up of a diverse group of people with different personalities, values and ethnic origins. Second, health professionals are presented with many difficulties that alternative professions do not exhibit. Since nurses undertake a career of caring for patients, their duties frequently require them to manage situations where extreme emotions govern behaviour.

This chapter establishes the foundations of human behaviour and group dynamics in a working context. It explores the major theories of human behaviour and factors influencing individual performance at work. The chapter investigates how personal characteristics such as personality, intelligence, values and culture all have an effect on the behaviour of people in the workplace. The second part of the chapter takes a more outward look at work performance. It considers a framework for establishing and leading effective teams, as well as some team-building strategies.

Hellriegal et al. (1998) envision an organisation as an iceberg in order to understand why people behave as they do at work. What sinks ships is not always what sailors can see, but what they cannot see (see Figure 2.1). The overt, formal aspects are really only the tip of the iceberg. It is just as important to concentrate on what you cannot see— the covert, behavioural aspects. These covert behaviours will form the focus of this chapter.

THEORIES OF HUMAN BEHAVIOUR

Theories of human behaviour began to emerge at the beginning of the twentieth century. This section aims to provide a brief sketch of some of the main ideas and criticisms of the most prominent theories of human behaviour.

As indicated in Chapter 1, understanding the make-up of people is important for all who lead others. Since management is sometimes seen as 'getting things done through other people', understanding people is a prerequisite to operating effectively as a manager. Being aware of our own strengths and weaknesses and those of others, and knowing how to develop or use this knowledge is helpful not only in organisations but also in our personal interactions with others.

Lansbury and Spillane (1983) summarise theories of human behaviour into three broad perspectives: psychoanalytical theory, environmental theory and social learning theory.

Psychoanalytical theory

Psychoanalytical theory is based on the work of Sigmund Freud and Carl Jung, and emphasises unconscious motives as a component of personality (Mullins 1999). Psychoanalytical theory proposes that internal processes of the psyche determine human behaviour. Our behaviours are considered to be an interplay between conscious

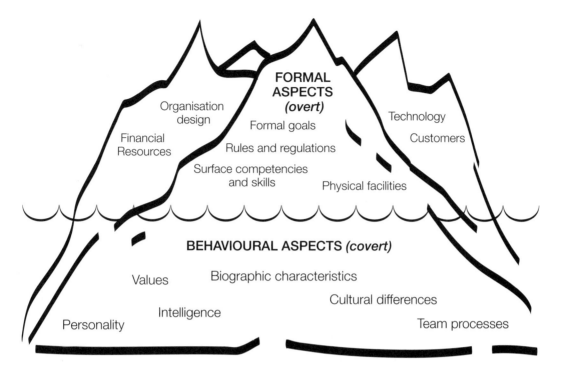

Figure 2.1 The organisational iceberg

Source: Reproduced with permission from Hellriegel et al. (1998, p.6).

and unconscious desires (Lansbury & Spillane 1983). The prescription for mental health, according to psychoanalysts, is self-insight. Understanding the processes of the psyche, including those that we like and do not like, is the basis of much therapy today.

Psychoanalysis has provided many fascinating insights into understanding behaviour, though unconscious psychic processes have proven extremely difficult to objectively verify. Psychoanalysis also has a generally poor track record at both predicting what people will do and assisting them to change their behaviour. People often need more than self-insight to change their behaviour and practical assistance may be required.

Environmental theory

Environmental theory is primarily concerned with reinforcement, imitation and socialisation. This theory contends that a person's development is influenced by their own experiences. Environmental theorists argue that it is stimuli from our environment that generates behavioural responses (Steers 1989). Fashion trends and the influences of peer group pressure on behaviour support environmental theory. Environmental theory has been the basis for understanding how certain aspects of reward and punishment influence human behaviour. A number of popular management schemes of today, for example, reward and bonus incentives, are based on environmental theory.

Even though environmental theory predicts simple human behaviour over short periods and in a structured situation, such as when people are being closely supervised, critics (Chomsky 1959; Locke 1966) believe human behaviour to be more complex, and propose that environmental theory does not account for creative activities, such as the capacity to generate new ideas or paint a picture. There are also employees who do not appear to be influenced by offers of reward or threats of punishment.

Social learning theory

Social learning theory suggests that behaviour is the outcome of an interaction between the environmental stimulus and the personality make-up of the individual (Bandura 1986). Social learning theory asserts that both the environment and personal characteristics such as personality, national culture and intelligence, influence a person's behaviour. The theory is well documented by Bandura (1986), who emphasises the importance of learning from other people and person–situation interaction.

Social learning theory provides a basis for understanding the complex interaction between psychological and environmental factors that culminate in human behaviour. For example, it explains how the impact of certain environments upon a person's behaviour depends upon their values and goals (Bandura 1986). Social learning theory has proven to be effective in predicting what people will do and how long they will persist in the face of setbacks. For managers, it can be a useful tool for influencing others in a desired direction.

The major criticism of social learning theory is that it does not acknowledge that people are driven by unconscious motives. For example, according to social learning theory, people can change their behaviour by altering their environment as well as adopting personal goals. However, such practices have not been completely successful for people trying to break habits, such as smoking.

There are no easy or complete methods for understanding human behaviour, as you may have noticed from the brief critique of three major psychological theories. Further insight into the personal characteristics that affect behaviour, as identified in social learning theory, will assist in gaining a greater insight into factors affecting individual performance.

FACTORS INFLUENCING INDIVIDUAL PERFORMANCE

The amazing feature of humans is their diversity. What is work for one person is pleasure for another (for example, gardening!). What motivates one worker will de-motivate another. Vecchio et al. (1992) propose a simple formula for increased performance—they suggest that people perform better when they work at a job they want to do. It seems so logical doesn't it? But it is more difficult than it sounds. Not only do we need to consider individual work preferences, but many other factors can affect our performance and sense of wellbeing in employment.

Being effective at work as an individual is related to how the personal qualities and characteristics of the individual interact with the requirements of the work environment. Understanding oneself, as well as others, can greatly add to personal effectiveness and the effectiveness of others. Without an understanding of such human traits and characteristics, how they develop and how they can be measured and used at work, organisations will not be as effective as they can be, and morale and satisfaction levels will be lower.

Let us consider the individual performance equation proposed by Wood et al. (2001, p.91) that captures these ideas:

Job performance = Individual attributes × work effort (Motivation) × organisational support

The equation views performance as a result of the personal attributes of individuals, the work effort they make and the organisational support they receive. The multiplication sign indicates that all three factors must be present for high performance to be achieved.

Individual attributes

Four broad categories create individual attributes that need to be considered. These are demographic or biographic characteristics, competency characteristics, personality characteristics and values.

Demographic or biographic characteristics

This includes background variables that help shape what a person has become. Some are current, such as a person's age or socio-economic status, while others are historical, such as where and in how many places a person lived while growing up, size of family, parents' socio-economic status and the like.

Competency characteristics

These can be defined as aptitude/ability, or what a person can do. Different occupations require different skills, competencies and abilities. It is also the case that individuals vary with regard to their mental abilities and the extent to which they apply them at work. The 'happy' scenario is that a match should occur between the individual's abilities and his or her occupation, but reality suggests that this is not always the case. This is evident in the situation where employees are promoted beyond their capacity.

An individual's level of competency and a person's work ability are highly dependent upon his or her intelligence (Behling 1998). Gardener (1993) regarded the simplification of intelligence in terms of an IQ measure as unrealistic in light of different intelligent behaviour that could be observed in everyday life. Although intelligence tests may offer one explanation of why an individual performs better in an academic institution, and may be a legitimate measure of such behaviour, Gardener (1993) states that they fail to take account of the full range of intelligent activity. He suggests that there are multiple intelligences (see Table 2.1) and categorises them into seven varieties (all of which can be divided further).

Table 2.1 Types of intelligence

Verbal intelligence	Ability to understand the meaning of words and comprehend readily what is read or heard
Mathematical intelligence	To be speedy and accurate in arithmetic computations such as adding, subtracting, multiplying, dividing
Spatial capacity	Ability shown by artists and architects
Kinaesthetic intelligence	Abilities of a physical nature
Musical intelligence	Abilities shown by musicians
Personal intelligence—interpersonal skills	Skills for dealing with other people
Personal intelligence—intrapersonal skills	Knowing oneself

Standard IQ tests only examine the first two types, verbal and mathematical intelligence (Behling 1998). Gardener calls personal intelligence (which is comprised of interpersonal and intrapersonal skills) emotional intelligence, or EQ. Leaders need to appreciate that a major influencing factor affecting work performance is the ability of the employee (Goleman 1996, p.34). Ensuring that the right people are selected for work and have an appropriate level of intelligence (IQ and EQ) is a critical human resource management process, now assisted by the appropriate use of psychological tests (see Dakin et al. 1994).

Personality characteristics

These can be defined as the traits that reflect what the person is like and which can influence behaviour in certain predictable ways (Stemberg & Kaufman 1998). Knowledge of personality can help managers understand, predict and even influence the behaviour of other people.

Four dimensions of personality that have special relevance in work settings include problem-solving style, Type A–Type B behaviour, locus of control and Machiavellianism. The latter two concepts are considered in detail in Chapter 3, and should be read in conjunction with this chapter. They will therefore not be addressed in the following material.

As you read on, think about yourself as someone with a particular 'personality' that may well affect what you do and how you respond to things that happen to you at work. Think too about the personalities of other people and how these personality factors may influence their behaviour and accomplishments in the work setting.

1 *Problem-solving style*—this refers to the way in which a person goes about gathering and evaluating information, solving problems and making decisions (Stemberg & Kaufman 1998). In this dimension, information gathering and evaluation are separate activities. Information gathering involves getting and organising data for use. Styles for information gathering vary from sensation to intuition. Stemberg and Kaufman (1998) describe sensation-type individuals as preferring routine and order and as detail oriented in gathering information, while intuition-type people prefer the big picture and like solving new problems. They dislike routine.

   Evaluation involves making judgements about how to deal with information once it has been collected (Stemberg & Kaufman 1998). Styles of information evaluation vary from an emphasis on feeling to an emphasis on thinking. Stemberg and Kaufman (1998) describe feeling-type individuals as being oriented towards conformity and being willing to accommodate other people. They try to avoid problems that might result in disagreements. Thinking-type people use reason to deal with problems. They downplay emotional aspects in the problem situation.

2 *Type A/B Personality*—Type A behaviour is a personality profile characterised by impatience, desire for achievement and perfectionism, while Type B behaviour is a profile of someone more easygoing and less competitive in relation to daily life events (Dakin et al. 1994).

   Individuals with Type A personalities tend to work fast on task performance and in interpersonal relations they tend to be impatient, uncomfortable, irritable and aggressive. Such tendencies indicate 'obsessive' behaviour, however, Type A personalities are fairly widespread among many managers (Stemberg & Kaufman 1998). These are hard-driving, detail-oriented people who have high performance standards and thrive on routine. But when such work obsessions are carried to the extreme, resistance to change, over-control of subordinates and difficulties in interpersonal relationships result. People with Type A personalities create a lot of stress for themselves in situations that Type Bs find relatively stress-free (Stemberg & Kaufman 1998). Type B behaviour is a profile of someone more easygoing and less competitive in relation to daily life events. Type Bs are more casual about appointments and do not feel rushed like Type A personalities. Hence they may not see the urgency in tasks and deadlines. They do things more slowly and tend to express their feelings more openly than Type A, who hold on to their feelings.

A person's personality in respect to locus of control, problem-solving style, Machiavellianism and Type A/B behaviour each have potential managerial implications. Managers should use their knowledge of individual differences to obtain a proper fit between individuals and their jobs. Even though there is no 'best personality type', a person will be more productive and satisfied when there is a fit between their personality and the requirements of the job.

Values

Rokeach (1973) describes values as beliefs that guide actions and judgements across a variety of situations. Parents, friends, teachers and external reference groups can all influence individual values. A person's values develop as a product of learning and experience in the cultural setting in which he or she lives. As learning and experiences vary from one person to the next, value differences are the inevitable result. Consider the values people place on family, religion and personal possessions.

The major implication for leaders when considering an individual's personal attributes is that people are different in their abilities, personality, interests and values. Participation of individuals in work that matches their background, skills and interests will lead to improved performance for the organisation.

Work effort

To achieve high levels of performance, even people with optimal individual attributes must have a willingness to perform; that is, they must display adequate work effort. Think back to your student days—you may have had a group of friends who had similar intellectual abilities, ages and social backgrounds, but the level of performance was different. Some people just work harder than others. Performance will vary because they have a greater willingness to work or are more motivated than others. Work effort and motivation are examined in greater detail in Chapter 10.

Organisational support

Even a person whose individual characteristics satisfy job needs and who is highly motivated to exert work effort may not be a good performer. This could be due to their inability to fulfil their job requirements because they do not receive adequate support in the workplace.

The organisational support factor in the individual performance equation includes all those aspects that help or hinder the achievement of the required performance. Some aspects of organisation support include financial or social rewards, fringe benefits, promotional opportunities, recognition, group and team morale (Wood et al. 2001). Some constraints include a lack of time, inadequate budget, insufficient tools, equipment or supplies, unclear instructions, unrealistic levels of performance, a lack of assistance/help from others and a poorly designed work environment.

Cogin (2002) has identified a number of stressors that affect the performance of nursing students and qualified nurses in Australian hospitals. The most common stressors were associated with emotional trauma related to dealing with sick and terminal patients, overwork and poor job design. Each of these factors can be improved with effective organisational support systems.

Organisational culture

One of the major paradoxes of organisational life is the maintenance of individuality and self-responsibility alongside the requirement for creation of cooperation and conformity. Managers expect their employees to work with others and be willing to follow procedures, but at the same time expect to see evidence of personality, creativity and independence. Balancing individual needs and goals with the organisation's objectives and procedures can be a major cause of tension, and yet is one of the most important tasks of management.

Recognition and management of performance is an essential component of managing. Managing people in organisations requires not only an understanding of the employees but also a recognition of the culture of the organisation; for some organisations, creativity and individuality may be the last thing they would want to see in the workplace, but for others these characteristics are essential. Just as individuals have values that guide their actions and reactions, organisations also have values. Organisational values are expressed in organisational culture. When people work in organisations which have a culture that fits with their values, they are more likely to be satisfied and productive (Posner & Kouzes 1993).

Just as an organisation has a culture that determines acceptable workplace behaviour, each person is influenced by their own ethnic and cultural origins. Like personality, a person's culture is an important determinant of his or her behaviour. In particular, culture helps clarify the relationship between situations and behaviours in terms of the relative importance placed on specific features of a situation.

CULTURAL DIFFERENCES

Culture is a concept that may be usefully conceived as a distinctive pattern of values and beliefs that are characteristic of a particular society or subgroup within that society (Hofstede 1980). These values and beliefs are likely to have been transmitted by previous generations through the process of socialisation such as family influence and/or formal education (Trompenaars 1993).

This section seeks to:

▲ dispel the notion that there is 'one best way' of managing and organising;

▲ give you a better understanding of your own culture and cultural differences; and

▲ provide some strategies or tips for dealing with people from other cultures.

Consider the new breed of international managers—they are educated according to the most modern management philosophies. They know about strategic planning, just-in-time ideals and management by objectives. But just how universal are these management solutions? Can they be applied anywhere, under any circumstance?

Even with experienced international companies, many well-intended 'universal' applications of management theory have had mixed results. For example, pay for performance has had impressive results in the United States, the Netherlands and the United Kingdom (Robbins & Mukerji 1998). According to Hofstede (1980), in more collectivist cultures like France, Germany and large parts of Asia, pay for performance has not been so successful. Employees of collectivist cultures have not universally accepted that individual members of a group should excel in a way that reveals the shortcomings of other members (England 1978).

Globalisation has been presented by some researchers (Robbins & Mukerji 1998) as a vehicle that will create, or at least lead to, a common culture worldwide. McDonald's has been cited as an example of tastes, markets and hence cultures becoming similar everywhere. There are, indeed, many products and services becoming common to world markets. What is important to consider, however, is not what they are and where they are found physically, but what they mean to the people in each culture. The essence of the culture is not what is visible on the surface. It is the shared ways in which groups of people understand and interpret the world (Hofstede 1980). So the fact that we can all eat hamburgers tells us that there are some products that can be sold with a universal message, but it does not tell us what eating hamburgers means in different cultures. Dining at McDonald's is a show of status in Moscow, whereas it is regarded as a cheap meal for a few dollars in New York or Sydney.

Trompenaars (1993) attempted to make a direct link between cultural variance and workplace behaviour. He has identified seven areas in which cultural differences affect behaviour. Each of the seven dimensions below is presented as a continuum, so that rather than categorising societies (or people) into a group, we should consider a range between the two extremes presented by Trompenaars.

Universalism versus particularism

A universalist belief is 'what is good and right can be defined and always applied'. There is rigidity in respect of rule-based behaviour. In particularist cultures, far greater attention is given to the obligations of relationships and unique circumstances. The importance of friendships, for example, may lead to flexibility in the interpretation of situations.

In a busy hospital in North America or Europe, a manager is more likely to award a job to a needy friend or relative over the best-qualified applicant. In Korea or Hong Kong, a manager would probably follow the recruitment and selection guidelines strictly, regardless of their relationship with any of the applicants. Trompenaars (1993) concludes that Australia has a preference towards universalism.

Individualism versus collectivism

Do people regard themselves primarily as individuals or as part of a group? In Canada or the United States, if a hospital is found negligent in the care of a patient due to incorrect dosage of medication, responsibility for this mistake would become known by identifying the person who delivered the medication—they would carry the burden of negligence. In France or Japan, because this person is a member of a team, the whole team would be implicated, possibly without any identification of the actual individual responsible. Trompenaars (1993) categorises Australia as individualistic.

Neutral or emotional

This refers to the nature of our interactions. Should we be objective and detached in our business affairs or is expressing emotion acceptable? Neutral societies favour the 'stiff upper lip', while overt displays of feeling are more likely in emotional societies.

In emotional societies loud laughter, banging your fist on the table or leaving a conference room in anger during a negotiation is all part of business. Trompenaars (1993) suggests Australia has a preference for neutral behaviour.

Specific versus diffuse

This refers to the level at which a person is involved in a business relationship. Deep and personal contact is preferred in a diffuse society, instead of the detached relationship prescribed by a professional contract in specific societies. In many countries a diffuse relationship is not only preferred but also necessary before business can proceed; the whole person (private and professional life) is involved and it takes time to build such relationships. Before building a relationship with a doctor, for example, you would want to know personal information about the doctor and their family. In a specific culture, such as the United States, the basic relationship would be limited to the contractual arrangement. Intrusive questions would be regarded as overstepping the professional relationship. In this dimension Australia rates heavily on the specific side (Trompenaars 1993).

Achievement versus ascription

Achievement-based societies value success or an overall record of accomplishment. You are judged on what you have accomplished. In contrast, in societies relying more on ascription, status could be bestowed on you through such factors as parentage, kinship, age, gender, as well as your connections (who you know). In Australia, the United States, Canada or Norway, the first question is likely to be 'What did you study?', while in a more ascriptive culture (such as Indonesia), the question will more likely be 'Where did you study?' Australia has a preference towards an achievement-based society (Trompenaars 1993).

Attitudes to time

In some societies what a person has achieved in the past is not that important. It is essential to know what they plan for the future. In other societies you can make more of an impression with your past accomplishments than those of today. The American dream is the French nightmare. What matters in the United States is present performance and forward 'strategic' plans. In contrast, the French have an enormous sense of the past and history. Trompenaars (1993) describes Australia as following a future-based preference.

Attitudes to the environment

Some cultures see the major forces affecting their lives and the origins of vice and virtue as residing within the person. These cultures place the power of choice with an individual, so that motivations and values are derived from within. Other cultures see the world as more powerful than individuals. In western societies, there is a perception that individuals are typically in control of their destiny. In other parts of the world, however, the world is more powerful than individuals. In Tokyo many people wear surgical facemasks in the streets. When you inquire why, you are told that when people have colds or a virus, they wear them so they will not pollute or infect other people by breathing on them. In other countries the same facial masks may be worn to protect the individual from the pollution in the environment.

We need to understand cultural differences in order to communicate and work effectively with people from other cultures. This is because practices that are effective within Australia may be inappropriate in other cultures. We also need to avoid the temptation to jump to conclusions about the values or intentions of a particular person or group of people based merely on knowledge of their nation of origin. Cultural insights are best used as a tentative starting point for progressively enhancing your understanding of the values and assumptions that are operating within a particular cross-cultural encounter.

So far in this chapter, we have concentrated on how effective leaders need to have an understanding of individual characteristics and how these influence human behaviour. In the following section we take a more outward look at workplace behaviours and consider groups and teams. The focus is on how a health care professional can capitalise on the use of teams and implement solid strategies for team development.

ESTABLISHING AND LEADING SUCCESSFUL WORK TEAMS

The productivity of a team depends in the first instance on the same factors as the productivity of individuals. That is, the output of a team will depend on the members' individual attributes, work effort and the resources at their disposal in relation to the demands of the task and the environment they face. However, there are other environmental considerations that have an impact on the way a team performs. These factors may add or detract from a team's productivity.

Environmental factors
Size
The size of the team has detectable effects on performance. In larger teams, the potential impact and contribution of each individual is somewhat diminished, but the total resources of the team are increased (Whitfield et al.1995). Although most organisations settle on teams of less than eight to handle most problem-solving tasks, some organisations employ much larger 'spans of control' for simple tasks (Cornel 1998). Hard evidence about an ideal size for teams is sparse, yet several conclusions seem possible.

First, members appear to become more tolerant of authoritarian and directive leadership as team size increases (Mullins 1999). Second, larger teams are more likely to have formalised rules and procedures for dealing with problems (Mullins 1999). Despite this greater formality, larger teams require more time to reach a decision than smaller teams (Pelled et al. 1999). Additionally, sub-teams or cliques are more likely to emerge.

Third, in a review of research on team size, Steers (1989) suggests that job satisfaction is lower in larger teams and cohesiveness and communication diminish with increased team size. In larger teams members may also engage in 'social loafing'. This occurs when an individual feels that the needed effort will be shared by the team's members and that he or she can count on others to take up any necessary slack (Latane et al. 1979). Fourth, as team size increases, productivity reaches a point of diminishing returns because of the rising difficulties of coordination and member involvement.

Steers (1989) suggests that teams should number five or seven as this size is not too intimidating for one member to challenge any decisions made. Wood et al. (2001) also make the point that having the odd number of members means that a tie or split decisions can be avoided when voting.

Composition

Teams composed of highly similar individuals who hold common beliefs and have much the same abilities are likely to view a task from a single perspective. Such solidarity can be productive but it may also mean that the team will lack a critical perspective for looking at certain problems (Dyer 1987). Diversified or heterogenous teams tend to do better on many problem-solving tasks than do homogeneous teams of highly similar individuals. The diverse abilities and experience of the members of a heterogeneous team offer an advantage for generating innovative solutions (Mullins 1999). Thus, merely adding more people to a problem-solving team to broaden the pool of skills and experience will not guarantee a better outcome. Attention must be paid to the appropriateness of the members' attributes and the mix of skills within the team.

Watson et al. (1993) conducted extensive research on teams and found that although management of interpersonal relations is easy in homogeneous teams, the team may suffer performance limitations as result of a narrow range of talents. In most cases they found that strong homogeneity tends to be more beneficial in situations where team tasks are relatively simple and focused. In contrast, team diversity tends to provide better results in situations where team tasks are complex and highly varied. It is important therefore that managers use good judgement when selecting members for work teams, committees and task forces to ensure the most productive mix of people is chosen.

Roles

Membership of a team will create certain expectations. In teams it is common to use the term 'role' to describe a set of expectations of a person holding a particular office or position. Often these expectations are unclear, and such uncertainty creates anxiety and problems (Mullins 1999). This can occur in established teams or newly formed teams, when new members join an existing team.

Roles within teams need to be defined. It is through role differentiation that the structure of work teams and relationships among members are established. Inadequate or inappropriate role definition can result in a number of problems such as role ambiguity or role conflict.

Cotton and Vollrath (1988) found that role ambiguity occurs when a member of a team is unsure about what other members expect of them. This uncertainty raises anxieties and creates problems. Role conflict occurs when a member is unable to respond to the expectations of one or more members of the team (Cotton & Vollrath 1988). This conflict may be due to overload, underload or incompatibility. The classification of roles is important for all members of work teams. Role ambiguities and conflicts create anxiety and stress, and can detract from performance and personal satisfaction.

Norms

Norms are the rules that are established to maintain behavioural consistency of team members (Mullins 1999). They may be written (for example, a uniform code policy) or unwritten (for example, a cake for morning tea on a team member's birthday). An important aspect of any team is the set of norms in which it operates, because they identify the way in which 'loyal' members are supposed to behave. Since norms are rules or standards of member behaviour, they communicate what is appropriate behaviour (Feldman 1984). As such, they can exert a major influence on teams when members adhere to them.

Feldman (1984), in a review of the literature on norms, found that positive performance norms in respect to standards have a significant effect on how teams operate. Positive norms will tend to promote high performance. Consider team norms of safe lifting practices or diligent hygiene standards. Negative norms by contrast can cause poor performance. Consider a team norm to cover up the mistakes of members and not fostering a learning environment. Effective managers are able to help teams acquire the positive norms needed to support long-term team effectiveness.

Cohesiveness

Cohesiveness is the extent to which members are attracted to a team and desire to remain in it (Shaw 1981). Cohesiveness is sometimes described as the sum of all forces acting on individuals to remain in the team. In a highly cohesive team, members value their place in it and are very loyal to it; however, there is the danger of compromise and decisions being made with the 'highest common view' or agreements because one member 'doesn't want to rock the boat' (known as groupthink). Thus, an important rule of thumb in group dynamics is that members of highly cohesive teams conform to team norms (Feldman 1984). Consequently, the combination of the team performance norms and level of cohesiveness can be instructive about its performance potential.

The most favourable situation for any manager or team leader is to lead a highly cohesive team with positive performance norms; the positive norms point behaviour in desired directions, and the high cohesiveness creates desires to live up to the expectations set by these norms.

Team-building strategies

Groups are not static; they change and develop in different stages over time. There are a number of theoretical models that suggest some variation in the exact number, sequence, length and nature of stages. In 1965 Tuckman developed a model suggesting that there are five stages through which groups develop.

In the earliest stage of a group's development, members are concerned with testing each other's reactions to determine which actions are acceptable and unacceptable. In addition, the members depend on each other for cues about what is expected in the way of contribution and personal conduct. Tuckman (1965) calls this initial stage *forming*.

The second stage, *storming*, involves intra-group conflict. Hostility and disagreement arise as the group's members wrestle with how power and status will be divided. Members may resist the formation of a group structure and ignore the desires of the group's leader. Depending on the group size and composition, coalitions or cliques may appear in the form of emergent or informal subgroups.

During the third stage, *norming*, feelings of cohesiveness develop. New standards and roles are adopted and opinions about task accomplishments are freely voiced.

In the fourth stage, *performing*, the group has established a flexible network of relationships that aid task accomplishment. Internal hostility is at a low point as the group directs energies towards the successful performance of valued tasks. The group is now able to deal with complex tasks and handle membership disagreements in a creative way.

The final stage, *mourning*, is a termination stage. It occurs when the task is completed and the group is disbanded for organisational reasons or sometimes when the group's leader leaves. Fundamentally this stage involves the cessation of task-related behaviours and disengagement from relationships with other group members. Some groups have a well-defined termination point; for example, a review team conducting a department evaluation. Others have a more subtle mourning stage, which is experienced when there is a noticeable change of membership.

Not every group goes through all five stages in a fixed sequence. For more formal groups, in which the division of power may be less subject to debate, storming may be virtually eliminated. Also, as a group experiences change, it may return to an earlier stage. For example, if an established group receives a new leader, it may temporarily give up performing and return to storming or norming stage (Shaw 1981).

In practice, it is normal in the beginning for groups to address issues and problems they can manage most easily. Later, the problems become more difficult to solve, and the groups may become disinclined to change the perfect systems they have already worked out. This stage of group development can be difficult to endure. Mature groups may expand or change the group membership and question well-established roles and processes as new problems arise (Shaw 1981).

For leaders and managers, there are two important implications of this model. First, it alerts us to the vulnerability (to failure) of the group at the transition points between stages. For example, a group may be so engrossed with developing cohesive relations in the norming stage that it avoids moving into the more task-directed performing stage. Second, leaders need to recognise the stage of development reached and adjust their leadership style accordingly. Carew et al. (1986) suggest more directive styles may be most appropriate for the earlier stages, while supportive democratic styles may suit the later stages.

Team building is one way for a newly formed group to assess the skills of its members and determine what must be done to maximise this input factor. It includes a sequence of planned action steps designed to gather and analyse data on the functioning of a group, and to implement changes to increase its effectiveness (Dyer 1987). Team building is also a way for ongoing groups to assess themselves periodically and to make the constructive changes necessary for the group to keep up with new developments.

A number of processes (or 'ground rules') need to be established by the leader for teams to be effective. It is imperative that these behaviours become the norms by which the group functions. In a review of the team-building literature (see Coghlan 1994; Cotton & Vollrath 1988; Dyer 1987; Feldman 1984; Shaw 1981; Watson et al. 1993; Wood et al. 2001), the following ground rules for teams and groups are suggested, and summarised in Table 2.2.

Ground rules for teams

1 *Set goals and establish standards:* define problems/tasks/projects/duties, express standards for the group to achieve, apply standards in the evaluating the team.

2 *Encourage positive interpersonal behaviours:* including being friendly, warm and responsive to others, accepting others and their contributions. Encourage input; seek ideas and opinions from others.

3 *Clarify and elaborate:* Interpret or reflect ideas and suggestions; clear up confusion; indicate alternatives and issues before the group; give examples.

4 *Brainstorming and idea generation:* Maximise ideas or suggestions, be creative. Make helpful suggestions, attempt to problem-solve.

5   *Harmonise:* Act as peacemaker, calm things down, compromise, reconcile disagreements, get others to explore differences.

6   *Challenge:* Seek justification, show disagreement in a constructive way.

7   *Regularly summarise:* Link ideas, check progress, and clarify objectives/proposals.

Burleson (1990) makes some additional suggestions for team building:

▲   Set the tone in meetings and create a sense of urgency; set a compelling context for action.

▲   As a team leader, model the expected behaviours.

▲   Continually include new facts and information to the team.

▲   Make sure that team members spend a lot of time together. Ensure each person understands the roles and responsibilities of all members.

▲   Give confirming feedback, reward and recognise high performance results; however, do not tolerate undesirable behaviours, because they will undermine team morale and performance.

▲   Do not allow cliques to develop that will undermine the unity of the team.

▲   Team members should jointly share responsibility for team effectiveness.

▲   The team should have control over decisions that affect the team.

▲   The task–oriented functions of the team are performed not only by the leader but across the entire team through its roles.

Table 2.2 Factors affecting group performance

Problem	Potential pitfall	What managers should do
Ground rules / not established	– Individuals pushing their own agenda – Interrupting – Withdrawal of some members – Biased / uneven decision-making – Destructive criticism – False consensus – Monologues are delivered without being challenged	– Set specific, measurable goals – Break large goals into sub-goals which are easier to achieve – In meetings set time limits per person – Get each person to add to discussion in turn – Ask for quieter members to speak first – Paraphrase previous message before responding – Distinguish between generating ideas and evaluating them – Allow for thinking / reflection time
Large team	– Excessive time to reach a decision – Lowered job satisfaction – Reduced cohesiveness and communication – Social loafing – Difficulties in team coordination	– Consider authoritarian and directive leadership for some tasks – Establish rules for dealing with problems / grievances – Establish smaller teams of five or seven where possible

cont.

Table 2.2 cont.

Problem	Potential pitfall	What managers should do
Composition	– Homogeneous teams may have a narrow range of talents – Heterogeneous teams will require more time for decision-making and resolving interpersonal interactions	– Pay attention to the relevance of the members' attributes and the mix of skills within the team – Consider how the team is 'selected' and, where possible, choose the team members according to the task at hand
Inadequate role definition	– Uncertainty and anxiety – Work overload or underload – Role incompatible with skills / abilities – Duplication of tasks	– Differentiate roles of each team member – Articulate expectations – Induct new members – Watch for overload / underload
Norms not established	– Negative norms may emerge	– Establish and communicate norms – Verbalise unwritten norms – Encourage behaviours that reinforce positive norms, e.g. Covering for team member absenteeism, social functions etc
Cohesion	– In highly cohesive teams there is the danger of compromise and decisions made in line with the 'highest common view' or agreements made because one member 'doesn't want to rock the boat'—groupthink – In teams with low cohesion, there will be frequent conflicts and excess time needed to make decisions.	– Ensure the team spends sufficient time together – Make team smaller – Reward team results, not individuals – Share information with team – Build trust within the team.

CONCLUSION

The complexity of human behaviour makes it difficult to develop one set of ideal characteristics and behaviours which make leaders successful in all situations. An effective leader is not only self-aware but has an understanding of others and considers the different attributes that drive the behaviour of those he or she is influencing.

This chapter has provided a brief overview of three theories of human behaviour as the basis for understanding others. What will motivate one person will not interest another; what one culture finds important or of high value may not be valued by another culture; the skills that one person has will not be the same as another's. The more we understand our employees and colleagues and apply the knowledge, the better the resulting individual and group performance is likely to be.

In groups we need to consider additional factors to establish a high performing team. The size, composition and roles all need attention in addition to creating cohesion and establishing acceptable team norms.

In the process of understanding our employees, showing respect for them as individuals and as members of teams, we will be setting the climate or environment that helps facilitate performance.

Reflective exercise

1 In what situations could Trompenaars' dimensions of culture assist you to become a better leader or manager? How can you apply any of these dimensions to your work setting?

2 Make a list of the personality characteristics and values that you would expect to be associated with a nurse holding a leadership or management position.

3 Describe the basic characteristics of a Type A personality. Discuss the challenges likely to be encountered managing someone with strong Type A tendencies.

4 Imagine you are a consultant. The director of nursing at the local hospital has called you. She is concerned that the seven direct report nursing supervisors do not perform well as a 'team'. The director has heard about your skill with something called the 'team-building process' and asks you to visit to explain it. What will you tell the director about team building as a concept?

5 Assume the director hires you as a consultant. The first job is to undertake team building for the nursing supervisors. You are about to facilitate the first meeting since securing this consultancy contract. What approach would you take in this instance?

RECOMMENDED READINGS

Axtell, R. E. (1990). *Do's and don'ts of hosting international visitors.* Sydney, Australia: John Wiley & Sons.

Burleson, C. W. (1990). *Effective team meetings: The complete guide.* New York, USA: John Wiley & Sons

Cranny, C. J., Smith, P. C., & Stone, E. F. (1992). *Job satisfaction: How people feel about their jobs and how it affects their performance.* New York, USA: Lexington Books.

Davis, E., & Lansbury, R. (1996). *Managing together: Consultation and participation in the workplace.* Melbourne, Australia: Longman.

Goleman, D. (1995*). Emotional intelligence.* New York, USA: Bantam Books.

CHAPTER THREE

Psychological influences on leadership style

Sandra Speedy

LEARNING OBJECTIVES

At the completion of this chapter, the reader will be able to:

▲ gain an overview of the research literature relating to personality as it influences leadership;

▲ be aware of the various factors which influence personality style in relation to leadership behaviour;

▲ consider the role of social, emotional and spiritual intelligence as it impacts on leadership capacity;

▲ understand the role conflict plays in the workplace, and strategies leaders can employ to effectively deal with these; and

▲ consider the potential for gender differences in leadership.

KEY WORDS
Personality, self-efficacy, introversion-extraversion, locus of control, Machiavellianism, self-monitoring, emotional competence

INTRODUCTION

Leadership in professional situations requires a foundation of knowledge and skills that is influenced by a diverse range of factors. These factors include the personalities of leaders, their psychological characteristics and make-up, and the situation or context in which leadership and managerial style is manifest. This chapter examines, in some detail, a range of these characteristics and their influence. It also considers how such characteristics will determine how leaders deal with conflict, and how leaders can enhance their communication techniques to be maximally effective. Finally, the question of differing styles of leadership according to gender is explored.

A historical review of the leadership literature can be found in general management texts and will not be provided here (see, for example: Fulop & Linstead 1999; Hughes et al. 1999; Robbins et al. 2000; Wood et al. 2001). Generally, however, researchers have constructed a range of theories to explain their views of leadership, including trait theory, behavioural theories, reward and punishment theory, situational contingency theories, path–goal theory, and attribution, to name just a few (Wood et al. 2001).

More recently, the focus has been placed on questioning whether leadership itself is a useful concept at all. This has arisen from the question of whether 'followership' explains leadership effectiveness, suggesting that the relationship between the follower and leader impacts on both and has enduring effects. Grossman and Valiga (2000) state that:

> Effective followers . . . actually stimulate and inspire leaders, challenge their creativity, collaborate with them, complement them, give them feedback, and support them (p.54).

Whatever explanations for effective leadership are provided, two vital factors require our focus: the people interacting and being, and the situation or context in which behaviour occurs. This is why this chapter focuses on the role of personality and intelligence, and the way in which personality influences a leader's capacity to handle conflict constructively in the professional setting. First let us consider a typology of leadership styles that takes a macroview of leader characteristics within particular contexts. These leadership styles are autocratic, bureaucratic, participative and *laissez-faire* (Mullins 1993).

In the autocratic style, leader behaviours range from the 'do as I say or else' style to the paternalistic style of 'father/mother knows best'. When leaders have this style, subordinates are left with little freedom and autonomy and no opportunity to participate in problem-solving or decision-making. The advantages of this style are its appropriateness in emergency or crisis situations, since it is the most efficient way to get action. It is also useful when subordinates have low tolerance for ambiguity, are immature or insecure. The disadvantages include the lack of allowance for personal growth and development of potential because it assumes there is no likelihood of this happening; it places great responsibility on the leader, who must be competent and knowledgeable in every situation.

The bureaucratic style, on the other hand, requires the leader to tell subordinates what to do, but in a way that is 'by the book'. Procedure and policy manuals, rules and regulations support the bureaucrat. Traditional hospital settings use this approach abundantly. There are certain advantages in this style because technically it guarantees consistency in the performance of procedures, in the treatment of personnel and in setting standards. The disadvantages include the lack of recourse when commonsense dictates that there should be an exception to the rule. When we are personally frustrated by this, we call it 'red tape'. Furthermore, if rules are ambiguous, productivity decreases, morale drops, and subordinates may become frustrated and resentful.

The participative leadership style allows subordinates to take part in problem-solving and decision-making. This style can range from democratic involvement to simple consultation. Its advantage is that it allows staff to feel committed to implementing a decision they help to make, and provides the opportunity for creativity.

The disadvantages include that decision-making can take a long time; it may not result in effective and efficient attainment of goals; that participation may be compromised by group pressures and dynamics so that the decision is 'watered down' to the lowest common denominator (Mullins 1993; Robbins et al. 2000).

Typically, a leader who uses the *laissez-faire* style sets the goal to be achieved, provides the rules of the game, and becomes accessible to the group for guidance and clarification if and when required. The advantages of this style are that it allows for full utilisation of the talents and energies of group members who have been delegated full responsibility for decision-making and problem-solving. The disadvantages include a high level of risk because the leader must have thorough knowledge of the level of competence and personal integrity of group members in order for this mode of leadership to be successful. Note that there is no recognition of the potential for followership within these leadership styles (Mullins 1993).

PERSONALITY AND LEADERSHIP

There are several factors considered to shape leadership functioning and style. Researchers have established relationships between personality and key aspects of organisational behaviour, including leadership and managerial style (Wood et al. 2001). While different situations may require different styles of leadership (as indicated above), there are also other influential factors, including age, experiences, gender, marital status, number (if any) of dependents, seniority in the organisation, intellectual abilities, values, physical abilities and the ability/job fit.

Personality refers to the unique and relatively stable patterns of behaviour, thoughts and emotions shown by individuals, or 'the overall profile or combination of traits that characterise the unique nature of the person' (Wood et al. 2001, p.98). These are responsible for how we behave in our professional settings, because they affect the way we interact with others, and the situations encountered. While personality is generally persistent and resistant to change, it can be shaped by external pressures and may therefore vary across situations. Behaviour, however, is the result of both personality and nature of the situation experienced, known as an interactionist perspective of organisational behaviour (Ivancevich et al. 1997).

Factors affecting personality

There are three major factors affecting personality, although there is controversy about the degree to which each factor may be influential. These include heredity—factors determined at conception; environment, for example, culture, social conditioning, birth order and gender; and the situation, since different demands in different situations may call forth different aspects of personality.

Personality traits

Much research has gone into what determines personality and how it is expressed (Robbins et al. 1998). These include personality traits such as being shy, aggressive, lazy or ambitious. Research suggests that personality traits must be considered in their situational context (Greenberg & Baron 1995). A whole range of personality traits are said to exist, for example, in charismatic or transformational leaders, or effective managers. Another aspect is the personality type, such as extroversion, where we attend to the world of objects, people, or external ideas, or introversion, where we focus on our inner thoughts, feelings and ideas. Extroverts are generally considered effective salespeople, public relations professionals and teachers, while introverts are more likely to be research scientists, academics or librarians (Robbins et al. 1998).

The 'Big Five' personality dimensions

Another theory is that there are five dimensions of personality, sometimes referred to as the 'Big Five' personality dimensions (Greenberg & Baron 1995; Hughes et al. 1999). These include:

▲ *introversion and extroversion*: a dimension ranging from being sociable, talkative assertive and active at one end, to retiring, sober, reserved and cautious at the other;

▲ *agreeableness*: a dimension ranging from good-natured, gentle, cooperative, forgiving and hopeful at one end, to irritable, ruthless, suspicious, uncooperative and inflexible at the other;

▲ *conscientiousness*: a dimension ranging from being careful, thorough, responsible, organised, self-disciplined and scrupulous at one end, to irresponsible, disorganised, lacking in self-discipline and unscrupulous at the other;

▲ *emotional stability*: a dimension ranging from being anxious, depressed, angry, emotional, insecure and excitable at one end, to being calm, enthusiastic, poised and secure at the other; and

▲ *openness to experience*: a dimension ranging from being imaginative, sensitive, intellectual and polished at one end, to being down-to-earth, insensitive, narrow, crude and simple at the other.

Research has found that conscientiousness is a good predictor of work performance in all types of jobs; emotional stability, however, is not related to performance and extroversion is highly related to job success for people in managerial and sales positions (Robbins et al. 2000). Barrick and Mount (1993) explored the extent to which autonomy in the job influences the relationship between personality dimensions and performance in managerial jobs. The opposite ends of the autonomy continuum would include an assembly-line worker versus a mobile district nurse, whose position is individually paced, with little job structuring and minimal supervision. The position of district nurse would provide more scope for the expression of personality.

The major finding of McCrae and Costa's (1997) study was that managers with higher scores of conscientiousness and extroversion performed better in jobs with high autonomy when compared with those managers in jobs that were low in autonomy. Managers with lower scores in agreeableness performed better in jobs with high autonomy when compared with those managers low in autonomy. Autonomy therefore appears to be an important moderating variable in the relationship between personality and performance.

As a predictor of behaviours at work, the 'Big Five' model has received some endorsement from researchers in recent years, although some disagreement exists. Robertson (1998) argues that while the 'Big Five' structure has created remarkable consensus among psychologists, there is no particular theory to account for or support its existence. He concluded that research has not demonstrated that the model can be viewed as an adequate taxonomy. Hough (1992), on the other hand, suggests that the 'Big Five' model needed to be expanded and proposed a nine factor structure. The debate continues.

Myers-Briggs personality types

Another theoretical approach, known as the Myers-Briggs approach, is derived from the work of analyst, Carl Jung, as well as Myers and Briggs. It is a system that describes different patterns of behaviour based on personality differences, all of which affect and determine how we function in the world. This approach suggests that we are born with four preferred ways of behaving, each having an opposite 'preference'. These include:

▲ extraversion/introversion (E) and (I), which refers to how we focus our attentions and what gives us energy;

▲ 'becoming aware', which refers to sensing (S) and intuition (N), and indicates how we prefer to take in the information around us;

▲ ways of deciding, thinking (T) and feeling (F), which refers to how we evaluate information and make decisions; and

▲ the amount of control, judgement (J) and perception (P) we have, which refers to our lifestyle orientation (Wood et al. 2001; Robbins et al. 1998).

With respect to this theory, personality 'style' has been shown to be a significant factor in the strategic decision-making of leaders and managers. For example, 'sensing–feeling' types want hard data and are less willing to take risks; 'intuitive–feeling' types are more likely to make a decision without considering all facts in the situation; and 'intuitive–thinking' types test the logic of the decision and often require more hard data on which to base their decisions. Kummerow et al. (1997) suggest that 'leaders and followers have different styles and needs based in part on their personality preferences' (p.52). As a leader with a preferred style, it is important to be aware of the strengths and limitations of that style, and take into account the needs of your followers in order that they work most effectively with you, and you with them. Kummerow et al. (1997) note that:

> Type can provide a tool for recognizing and negotiating different communication styles. Using this information can add balance to the communication process, as well as helping avoid the frustration of communications that do not meet your and others' needs (p.52).

Exploration of the Myers-Briggs typology as an explanation of your personality can be an insightful exercise for those who hold nursing leadership positions, or who aspire to them.

Locus of control

Locus of control refers to the degree to which leaders believe they are in charge of their own fate and are able to affect their own lives (Behling 1998). Leaders who believe they can control their own lives or their fate are said to have an 'internal orientation', as they demonstrate internal control. Those who believe that what happens to them is out of their control, or controlled by outside forces, are labelled as 'externals', having an external orientation.

Some interesting findings about the two types are that those who have an external locus of control are:

▲ less satisfied with their jobs;

▲ absent more often from work;

▲ alienated from work;

▲ less involved with work (all probably due to the fact that they perceive they have less control over the organisation and their work life in general);

▲ more compliant and willing to follow directions; and

▲ need structure and routine (Robbins et al. 1998).

Those who have an internal locus of control:

▲ are more likely to take responsibility for their behaviour;

▲ have lower absenteeism rates;

▲ can cope with higher levels of stress;

▲ hold higher-level jobs;

▲ are promoted more quickly; and

▲ are motivated to achieve and make greater attempts to control their environment (Robbins et al. 1998).

Leaders with an internal orientation do well in managerial and professional jobs which require complex information processing and learning, and are suited to jobs requiring initiative and independence of action (Robbins et al. 1998).

It is important to note that if you want to be an effective nursing leader or want to develop others for nursing leadership roles, locus of control can be modified over time by individuals, and be significantly enhanced by a supportive organisation. This can be done by using rewards and recognition for individual initiatives and performance which can be related to individual performance.

Machiavellianism

Another personality attribute reputed to influence leadership style is Machiavellianism, named after Niccolo Machiavelli, an Italian philosopher, who wrote *The Prince* (1513), about the acquisition and manipulation of power. He outlined a ruthless strategy for seizing and holding political power, which has been translated into a personality attribute useful for leaders who seek to control others. Machiavelli believed that people could be readily used or manipulated by applying a few basic rules, including:

▲ never show humility;

▲ be arrogant, as it is far more effective when dealing with others;

▲ morality and ethics are for the weak;

▲ to be powerful you need to feel free to lie, cheat and deceive, whenever it suits your purpose; and

▲ it is much better to be feared than loved (Greenberg & Baron 1995).

Machiavellianism is a measure of the degree to which people are pragmatic, maintain emotional distance and believe that 'the ends justifies the means'; 'if it works, use it' is the approach, and may often be of questionable ethics. So leaders who are high in Machiavellianism (known as 'high Machs') tend to manipulate others and 'win' more, are less persuaded by others, are pragmatic and emotionally distant, and have a greater influence over others than do 'low Machs'. They work best when there are a minimum number of rules and regulations, as they can improvise and be less constrained by existing rules (Ivancevich et al. 1997).

Research using instruments to measure a person's Machiavellian orientation suggests that a 'cool' or 'detached' high-Mach personality can be expected to take control and try to exploit loosely structured situations, but will perform in a perfunctory, even detached manner in highly structured situations. Low Machs, on the other hand, tend to accept direction imposed by others in loosely structured situations, and work hard to perform well in highly structured situations (Dakin et al. 1994).

High Machs can be very difficult to contend with in the work setting. It is wise to protect yourself and others from them by exposing them to others wherever possible, since they often get away with breaking promises or lying because their victims remain silent (typically victims remain silent as they may be too embarrassed to confess that they have been manipulated or cheated). Another strategy is to pay attention to what they do, not what they say: high Machs excel at deception. They often succeed in convincing others that they have others' best interests at heart, and are at their most convincing when they are busy cutting the ground out from under the unsuspecting person. If their actions suggest that they are cold-bloodedly manipulating the people around them, even while they loudly proclaim commitment to such principles as loyalty and fair play, chances are that they are Machiavellian in orientation and should be carefully avoided. Avoid situations that give high Machs an advantage; they prefer to operate in situations where emotions run high, in which others are uncertain of how to proceed. They know that under these conditions many people will be distracted and less likely to recognise that they are being manipulated for someone else's gain (Robbins et al. 1998).

Rubin (1997) takes an interesting gender lens to Machiavellianism. She states that today's women who are struggling to succeed in a man's world must learn that men and women are not equal, but that this difference should be viewed as a strength. Women should claim what they want and deserve using passion, intuition, sensitivity and cunning—subtle weapons that women are reputed to have in abundance.

> They should not rely on 'feminine' tactics such as nurturing, compromise and negotiation, but should welcome and use conflict to establish their authority and make an impact in pursuit of their goals (Buchanan & Badham 1999a, p.195).

This is in contrast to 'playing by the rules of the game'. Princessas, the female variant of the male, the Prince, therefore have to mark themselves as different from others; should not consider themselves brave; treat destiny as their mentor; revel in their emotional lives (rather than viewing emotionality as a liability); and finally, reject the belief that life requires them to choose between love and power (Rubin 1997, pp.12–17).

Self-esteem

Another factor that impacts on leadership style is level of self-esteem—the degree to which you like or dislike yourself, or the extent to which you have a positive or negative view of self. Those with low self-esteem are more likely to need others' approval, are less successful in job searches, and more likely to be dissatisfied with their job because they are not confident at solving problems that confront them (Robbins et al. 1998).

Low self-esteem can be minimised by making people feel uniquely valuable, so that they recognise everyone has a special contribution to make. This encourages constructive ideas and behaviours. When people are appropriately praised and credited with their ideas and achievements they feel more competent, appreciated and accepted. This enhances feelings of empowerment, connectedness and belonging (Robbins et al. 2000). Self-esteem can be a valuable resource and has great potential for the organisation. Building and maintaining the self-esteem of nurses and patients can provide enormous payoffs.

Self-monitoring

Self-monitoring refers to the ability to adjust behaviour to external, situational factors, thus requiring social perceptiveness. It has also been defined as a sensitivity to social cues (Pierce & Newstrom 2000). Normally we 'self-monitor' in order to produce a positive reaction in others. Those who are described as 'high self-monitors' are sensitive to external cues; they pay close attention to the behaviour of others and can modify their own behaviour readily if necessary. In this way, they can present a public persona quite different from their private image of self.

High self-monitors are more successful in leadership and managerial roles when this requires a subset of multiple and even contradictory roles (Robbins et al. 2000). High self-monitors are often very good communicators and effective in jobs that require 'boundary spanning'—communicating and interacting with different groups of people from different professional or occupational groups. They are also more likely to be effective at creating a favourable impression, having the capacity to conceal their true feelings when they consider it inappropriate to reveal them.

In addition, high self-monitors are often more concerned with others' feelings (Ivancevich et al. 1997). In conflict situations they therefore tend to find resolution through collaboration or compromise rather than through avoidance or competition. They tend to be more conciliatory in their approach, and more concerned with long-range solutions, compared with low self-monitors.

Low self-monitors cannot disguise their behaviour; they 'let it all hang out' and therefore will not conform to the situation in which they find themselves. They use their own moods and preferences to decide how to behave in any situation. Low self-monitors are more tolerant of unsatisfactory working conditions and less likely to think of resigning. In general, low self-monitors are less aware of, or less concerned about, their impact on others; they just act according to their inner feelings without changing them in each new context. This makes their behaviour quite predictable within specified situations (Robbins et al. 1998).

Self-efficacy

Self-efficacy is the belief in one's own ability to perform a specific task well and can thus influence leadership style. It is a learned belief, and is derived from life experiences, socialisation within the family group, and/or treatment in the work setting. High self-efficacy develops when specific tasks are performed, with subsequent positive feedback on performance (Robbins et al. 1998). People with high self-efficacy will respond to negative feedback with increased motivation and effort, while those with low self-efficacy will give up and reduce their efforts (Ivancevich et al. 1997). Nursing leaders need to be aware that training, constructive feedback, coaching, and rewards for gradual improvement all increase levels of self-efficacy, while destructive feedback can reduce feelings of self-efficacy.

Risk-taking

Risk-taking or willingness to gamble is another personality characteristic that is usually demonstrated in rapid decision-making when all the information is not available to make that decision. This is probably not a characteristic that should be in abundance in leaders in certain types of organisations, such as nursing organisations. Share-broking firms, on the other hand, benefit from employing people comfortable with a high degree of risk-taking.

SOCIAL AND EMOTIONAL INTELLIGENCE

It has become increasingly apparent in management and leadership literature that intelligence and task competency are insufficient for optimal performance as a leader. Consequently, the concepts of emotional intelligence (EQ), and emotional capital have been developed. While the research is in its formative stages, there is some emerging evidence that the recipe for excellence in leadership gives far more weight to emotional competencies than to cognitive abilities; in fact, emotional competence matters twice as much as cognitive ability (Goleman, 1998, p.36). This is particularly so in the 'new workplace', with its emphasis on flexibility, teamwork and strong 'client' or service orientation. Goleman suggests that the higher one goes in the hierarchy of the organisation, the more important it is to have a high emotional intelligence score (Goleman 1998, p.39). The implications for leaders are obvious.

Emotional competence has been defined as a learned capability based on emotional intelligence, which results in outstanding performance (Goleman 1998). Our emotional competence indicates how much of our potential we translate into on-the-job capabilities. EQ, on the other hand, determines our potential for learning the practical skills that are based on its five elements, including self-awareness, motivation, self-regulation, empathy and adeptness in relationships.

In acknowledging the importance of EQ to managerial and leadership success, Goleman (1998) developed an emotional competence framework. This consists of:

▲ personal competence, which determines how we manage ourselves, and includes self-awareness, self-regulation, motivation; and

▲ social competence, which determines how we handle relationships, and includes empathy and social skills (pp.32–4).

Not only does Goleman provide a detailed analysis of the characteristics and requirements of these skills, he elaborates how they may be taught in order to improve individual performance. In terms of leadership, which results in inspiring and guiding individuals and groups, Goleman suggests that leaders with this competence share a range of characteristics, including the capacity to:

> articulate and arouse enthusiasm for a shared vision and mission; step forward to lead as needed, regardless of whether you are classified as a 'leader', i.e. your position; guide the performance of others while holding them accountable; lead by example (Goleman 1998, p.217).

Goleman suggests that the art of leadership lies in how change is implemented, rather than the change itself. If you are a mirror to your group's emotional state, then you, in turn, can give energy back. Successful nursing leaders will exhibit a high level of positive energy that spreads throughout the organisation. Note that, on the other hand, Goleman uses the term 'emotional incontinence' to refer to the leakage of destructive emotions from the top down, which results in sapping people's energy, often making them anxious, depressed and angry (1998, p.221).

Emotional competence seems therefore to be particularly central to leadership, a role whose essence is getting others to do their jobs more effectively. Effective leadership requires three main clusters of competence: personal competencies, including those commonly referred to as technical skills; social competencies, including the ability to influence others, be empathetic and have political awareness; and cognitive competencies, which involve thinking strategically, seeking out information and strong conceptual thinking. Leadership demands toughness, but this means knowing when to be tough and when to be collegial, and when to use more indirect ways to guide or influence others.

Spiritual intelligence

Zohar and Marshall (2000) suggest the existence of a third type of intelligence (human and emotional intelligence being the other two), known as spiritual intelligence (SQ), which is essential for leadership success. They define spiritual intelligence as:

> the intelligence with which we address and solve problems of meaning and value, the intelligence with which we can place our actions and our lives in a wider, richer, meaning-giving context, the intelligence with which we can assess that one course of action or one life-path is more meaningful than another. SQ is the necessary foundation for the effective functioning of both IQ and EQ. It is our ultimate intelligence (2000, pp.3–4).

Zohar and Marshall argue that IQ and EQ, either separately or in combination, cannot explain the full complexity that is potentially human intelligence. They suggest that, while Goleman's emotional intelligence concept allows us to judge the situation in which we work, and hence how to behave appropriately *within* its boundaries, our spiritual intelligence will allow us to ask if we want to be in this situation at all. The question for us then becomes, would I rather change the situation to create a better one? Here we are working *with* boundaries, so that we guide the situation rather than be guided by it. Zohar and Marshall refer to this as the transformation of SQ (p.5). For them, SQ provides:

> an understanding of who we are and what things mean to us, and have these give others and their meanings a place in the world . . . it helps us live life at a deeper level of meaning (p.14).

For Zohar and Marshall, individuals with high SQ tend to be servant leaders who bring vision and values to others, and show them how to use it. Such leadership is inspirational and includes, for example, Ghandi, Nelson Mandela and the Dahlai Lama. Leaders with highly developed SQ exhibit flexibility, self-awareness, and a capacity to face and use suffering and pain. They are inspired by vision and values, eschew unnecessary harm, are holistic, tend to ask 'why' or 'what if' questions, and are 'field independent'; that is, they readily work against convention.

LEADERSHIP AND CONFLICT

Conflict is a process that begins when one party perceives that another party has negatively affected, or is about to negatively affect, something that the first party cares about (Robbins et al. 1998). This definition acknowledges that there must be an awareness or perception that there is conflict; two or more parties whose interests or goals appear to be incompatible; and limited resources, be they money, power or prestige. Scarcity of resources often creates blocking behaviour. When one party is perceived to block the goal achievement of another, a conflict state exists. Kummerow et al. (1997) suggest that 'people will have different views of what's important, and that may lead to conflict in and of itself' (p.53).

Views of conflict

Over the years a number of views relating to conflict have been proposed. These include the traditional view, the human relations view and the interactionist view. The traditional view, held in the 1930s and 1940s, considered that all conflict is bad, harmful and should be avoided at all costs. Conflict was thought to be a measure of the dysfunction of a group which resulted from poor communication, lack of openness and trust between people, and failure of managers to be responsive to the needs of employees.

From the 1940s to the 1970s the human relations view was developed, arguing that conflict is a natural occurrence in all groups and organisations, and that workplace conflict should be accommodated without too much disruption to the lives and careers of all. More recently, the interactionist view encourages conflict on the grounds that a harmonious, peaceful, tranquil and cooperative group is prone to becoming static, apathetic and non-responsive to needs for change and motivation (Robbins et al. 1998).

Levels of conflict

There are four identified levels of workplace conflict: intrapersonal (conflict within the individual), interpersonal (individual-to-individual conflict), intergroup conflict, and inter-organisational conflict.

Intrapersonal conflict occurs within the individual due to actual or perceived pressures from incompatible goals or expectations. This can result in an approach conflict, when a person must choose between two positive and equally attractive alternatives (a promotion or a new job); avoidance conflict occurs when a person must choose between two negative and equally unattractive alternatives, such as accepting a transfer to an undesirable location or having one's position terminated; while an approach–avoidance conflict occurs when a person must decide to do something that has both positive and negative consequences, such as being offered a higher paying job (positive consequence), but which is potentially very stressful (negative consequence).

Interpersonal conflict occurs between two or more individuals who are in opposition to each other, while intergroup conflict occurs among groups in an organisation. Interorganisational conflict is that which occurs between organisations, when competition and rivalry are manifested as a result.

Constructive and destructive conflict

It should be acknowledged that all conflicts are not necessarily good. Conflict can be dangerous and impact significantly on performance. Destructive conflict is that which works to the group's or organisation's disadvantage. It can occur when two people are unable to work together due to interpersonal hostilities or when a committee fails to act because it cannot agree on group goals. Destructive conflict decreases work productivity, job satisfaction, and can contribute to absenteeism and job turnover.

However, some conflict is beneficial. Constructive conflict is that which results in positive benefits to the group or organisation and has been termed 'creative abrasion' (Leonard and Strauss 1997). It offers the opportunity to identify problems, opportunities, and can prevent stagnation while fostering creativity.

Managing conflict

Because conflict in organisations is inevitable, managing it to advantage is vital. What organisations aim for is conflict resolution, with removal of the underlying reasons for a given conflict. While it is not always possible, the aim is for as much 'winning' as possible for all participants within the situation.

Different individuals have different and preferred ways of handling conflict. Pace and Faules (1994) developed a model that accounts for the following: the competitive or tough battler, the collaborator or problem-solver, the compromiser or manoeuvring conciliator, the accommodator or friendly helper, and the avoider or impersonal complier.

Competitive or tough battlers pursue their own concerns ruthlessly and often at the expense of others in the group. Losing is viewed as a serious weakness, giving reduced status and a negative self-image. Winning is seen as the only worthwhile goal. The strategy here is clearly 'win-lose'.

Collaborators or problem-solvers, on the other hand, seek to create a situation in which the goals of all parties can be accomplished. They examine mutually acceptable solutions and work with a strategy for 'win-win'.

Compromisers or manoeuvering conciliators begin from the premise that everyone stands to lose, so it is best to work out a desirable solution to the conflict. This may mean that there is only partial satisfaction of everyone's concerns, resulting in acceptable rather than optimal outcomes. Using this strategy, no one totally wins or loses.

Accommodators or friendly helpers are usually non-assertive, neglecting their own concerns in favour of those of others. They feel that harmony is vital and that anger and confrontation are bad. Unfortunately they may later wish that the outcome was different, and they may harbour resentment which is bound to find expression at a later time.

Avoiders or impersonal compliers view conflict as unproductive and punitive, so they will try to move away from the situation. There is usually no commitment to future actions, so this strategy may be self-defeating (Pace & Faules 1994).

Quite clearly, it may be more productive in the long term to adopt the collaborative 'win-win' style of approaching conflict. However, this requires effective communication and assertive behaviours, which the avoider or complier may not have.

Kummerow et al. (1997) suggest 'that people will have different views of what is important, and that may lead to conflict in and of itself' (p.53). Using the Myers-Briggs typology, the authors point out that:

> Thinking types typically focus more on the issues to be resolved, whereas Feeling types typically focus more on maintaining the relationships with the people involved. There are some conflicts in which the issues are more important . . . and some in which the relationships are more important . . . there is no one best way to resolve every conflict. We also know that type can influence the timing of dealing with a conflict. Often Extraverts want to talk about a problem (now), and Introverts prefer to withdraw from it and think it over. Respecting one another's needs to think through and talk through conflict (or to compromise and do both) may be helpful (p.53).

Effective communication with others is something we all seek, as it provides us with the potential to meet basic human needs. It requires us to take responsibility for our own behaviour and not of others. In addition, effective communication may develop self-understanding and self-acceptance, and develop qualities for effective relationships, such as trust vs. defensiveness, empowerment vs. control, understanding vs. judging, genuineness vs. dishonesty. Part of effective communication is being able to deal with conflict. For some of us this is easy; for others it is much more difficult. Often we have learned through our socialisation to fear, or at least avoid, conflict. Sometimes we have had ineffective behaviour patterns modelled for us, and we use these as unsuccessfully as those we seek to imitate. Or we may have been taught a range of messages about conflict and our reactions to it, such as: 'If you can't say anything nice, don't say anything at all', which can be a way of controlling anger, and is a message to which women, in particular, are exposed. There are many interesting gender lessons here: women in conflict situations may be intimidated into submission by being told that they are 'aggressive', 'bitchy', 'castrating' and the like. Being described in this way can be intensely insulting to some women, often resulting in rapid compliance.

There are a range of responses to conflict situations. These include: avoidance, defusion (which involves delaying action and/or keeping issues unclear), confrontation, use of power, whether it be covert or overt, and negotiation.

Assertive interpersonal style

Another productive method of handling conflict is by developing an assertive interpersonal style. Assertion involves standing up for your own personal rights and expressing your thoughts, feelings and beliefs in direct and honest ways that do not violate the other person's rights. This may take the form, for example, of: 'This is what I think. This is what I feel. This is how I see the situation.' It is said without dominating, humiliating or degrading the other person, and takes personal responsibility. People who are assertive recognise their rights as well as their responsibilities.

Assertion involves respect for yourself, demonstrated by expressing your needs and defending your rights; and respect for others' needs and rights. It does not require deference, which involves acting in a subservient manner as though the other person is 'right' or superior. You are deferring when you are self-effacing, appeasing and over-apologetic.

Assertiveness is a most desirable behaviour for nursing leaders, and can take a number of forms. Basic assertion can be practised when you are being asked an important question for which you are not prepared. Your response might be: 'I'd like to take a few moments to think about that'.

Empathic assertion involves making a statement that conveys recognition of the other person's feelings/situation, e.g. 'You may not realise it, but when you talk I cannot concentrate on what I was trying to tell you. Would you please wait for me to finish?' Escalating assertion, on the other hand, involves starting with minimal assertive response to increasingly firm assertion. If you start with the latter first, it might be perceived as aggressive because your assertive response is very direct, and hence may elicit a defensive, aggressive response.

Confrontive assertion can be used when a person's words contradict their deeds. It could involve a situation such as: 'I said you could borrow our trolley, as long as you checked with me first. Now you are using it without asking me, and I would like to know why.' This is a matter of fact statement, and is non-evaluative. Contrast an aggressive response, which might be: 'What are you doing with our trolley? I thought you were going to check with me first before you used it. Obviously your word means nothing! Don't even think about using it again!!'

'I–language assertion' involves an objective description of the other person's behaviour; a description of how that behaviour affects you; a description of your subsequent feelings about that behaviour; and finally, describing what you want. For example, to the person who constantly interrupts you, you might say: 'When I am constantly interrupted I lose my train of thought and begin to feel that my ideas are not important to you. I start feeling hurt and angry. I would like you to make a point of waiting until I have finished speaking.'

Non-assertive interpersonal style

Non-assertion, on the other hand, involves violating your own rights by failing to express yourself honestly. The message you are conveying is: 'I don't count. You can take advantage of me. My feelings don't matter—yours do. My thoughts don't matter—yours are the only ones worth listening to.' The goal of non-assertion is to appease others and avoid conflict at any cost. And there is likely to be a cost in long-term non-assertion.

A non-assertive interpersonal style can exist for a number of reasons, including:

▲ a fear of being thought aggressive, and mistaking firm assertion for aggression (which is deemed unacceptable);

▲ mistaking non-assertion for helpfulness and politeness ('good women are polite and respectful' which is acceptable, and sometimes expected behaviour);

▲ failure to accept your own personal rights, which can be reflective of low self-esteem;

▲ anxiety about the negative consequences that may occur, for example, loss of approval, or making others angry; and

▲ the simple lack of assertiveness skills.

Aggressive interpersonal style

Aggression, in contrast, involves standing up for your rights, and expressing thoughts, feelings and beliefs in ways that may be dishonest, inappropriate and always violates the rights of the other person. The usual goal of aggression is domination, winning and forcing the other person to lose. It is ensured by humiliating the other person, degrading and belittling, or overpowering others, expressed both verbally and non-verbally. Much nursing workplace bullying is the work of aggressive individuals.

Indirect approaches to conflict management

Notice in the examples provided above that the assertive leader uses direct conflict management techniques. There are also indirect approaches, including:

▲ appealing to common goals, which requires focusing the attention of conflicting parties on mutually desirable solutions;

▲ using 'hierarchical referral', which requires the use of the chain of command, usually upwards, for conflict resolution; and

▲ organisational redesign, in order to avoid the conflict or reduce its intensity. This can involve what is known as 'decoupling', separating groups, reducing contact or having two people act as 'link pins' within the conflict situation (Wood et al. 2001).

Goleman (1998) suggests that emotionally intelligent leaders who are adept at nego-tiating and resolving disagreements are typically able to mange difficult people and tense situations with diplomacy and tact. They have the competence to identify potential conflict and bring disagreements into the open before too much damage is done. This assists in de-escalating the situation, encourages debate and open discussion, and facilitates the potential for 'win-win' solutions.

The potential value of using the Myers-Briggs psychological type is the capacity to use differences constructively. Recognition and understanding of your type and its strengths and limitations may therefore be important for leadership success. Avoiding attributing your own motives to others is also vital, so listening to and understanding other people from their specific framework, recognising and valuing their goals, will contribute to leadership effectiveness on your part.

LEADERSHIP STYLE: A GENDER DIFFERENCE?

The research literature does not provide clear answers to the question of differing styles of leadership for women and men. Some researchers find that leadership style does vary between women and men, while others can find few or no differences (Bourantas & Papelexandris 1990; Davidson & Cooper 1987; Fierman 1990; Vilkinas & Cartan 1993). The reason for this may have little to do with leadership style, but might be explained by the context of the research, the methodology, and the complexity of measuring leadership itself. There are also cultural stereotypes that permeate gender relationships, as they can obscure real individual differences, but these can become self-fulfilling. Gender stereotypes typically are generalisations and are often over-inclusive.

As Wolpe et al. (1997) suggest:

In the same way as women are not a homogenous group, women managers are also not a homogenous group and may operate using a variety of styles depending on the various situations in which they find themselves. Many women, in order to succeed in male environments, are forced to adopt the hegemonic *modus operandi*. While there are very different leadership and management styles and women have often been associated with particular styles of management, any one style cannot be neatly defined as being totally male or totally female (p.204).

However, some research finds that there are crucial gender differences, including degrees of cooperativeness, collaboration and style of problem-solving (Bass & Avolio 1994; Reardon 1995; Stephenson 1997). Rosenser (1990) suggests that female leaders are more likely to structure flatter organisations and to emphasise frequent contact and sharing of information in 'webs of inclusion'. She believes that women's leadership style is highly interactive, involving participation, sharing of power and information, enhancing the self-worth of others and energising them, in contrast to a more traditional style of 'command and control' (p.120).

One of the major differences between women and men that has been established is in the area of communication (Tannen 1986; 1990). Reardon (1995) suggests that women tend to talk about what they feel, while men talk about what they do. Further, she suggests that women process information differently, and that, 'despite years of trying, few women have become truly fluent in worksite male-speak' (p.6).

Given the lack of agreement regarding differences (if any) of leadership styles between and among women and men, it is probably most prudent to keep an open mind on the question. However, it might be useful to reflect for a moment on your observations of leadership style as expressed by both women and men. Have you found any generalisable differences?

CONCLUSION

This chapter has established that distinctive aspects of individuals, referred to as personality attributes, the 'intelligences', genetic make-up and socialisation practices, have important effects on the way they behave in organisations. The situation in which leaders find themselves also plays a vital part in influencing leadership style. Therefore it is obviously important to develop an awareness of the impact of these factors and variables if nursing leadership is to be optimally effective. Otherwise, such leadership can fail to produce desired outcomes.

Failure can occur because of rigidity within the individual leader, resulting in an inability to adapt leadership style to changes in the organisational culture. To be adaptive, nursing leaders need to take in or respond to feedback about the traits they need in order to change or improve their leadership style. They need to listen and learn, and be agile in working with different styles and with people at all levels of the organisation. This demands empathy and emotional self-management of leaders.

A single most other frequently mentioned reason for failed leadership is poor relationships with others, especially followers. Being too harshly critical, insensitive and demanding can alienate followers. These are fatal handicaps that nursing cannot afford. High levels of insight and awareness of one's psychological make-up are essential. Additionally, knowledge of values and meanings within diverse cultural groupings can provide sensitivity to others that can only enhance leadership behaviour (see Chapter 2). Above all,

> knowing and understanding yourself as a thinking, feeling being interacting with an ever-changing world . . . means being in touch with your aspirations, fears, values and principles (Tappen 2001, p.57).

Reflective exercise

1 Consider the characteristics listed for individuals with both external and internal loci of control.

   a Can you identify your own orientation?

   b How does this orientation affect your leadership style?

   c Can you identify the orientation of nursing staff you lead or manage?

   d Now turn your sights in a different direction. Can you identify the orientation of nursing (and other) leaders within your organisation, and how this orientation affects their leadership?

2 Can you identify your mode of reaction to conflict?

3 Are there differences in your dealing with conflict in personal situations with your friends and family?

   a Do these differ from your reactions within the clinical setting?

   b Why do you think there are differences, if any?

RECOMMENDED READINGS

Buchanan, D., & Badham, R. (1999a). *Power, politics and organizational change: Winning the turf game*. London: Sage.

Dubrin, A. J., & Dalglish, C. (2003). *Leadership: An Australian focus*. Brisbane: John Wiley & Sons.

Goleman, D. (1998). *Working with emotional intelligence*. New York: Bantam Books.

Grint, K. (1997). *Leadership: Classical, contemporary, and critical approaches*. Oxford: Oxford University Press.

Grossman, S., & Valiga, T. M. (2000). *The new leadership challenge: Creating the future of nursing*. Philadelphia: FA Davis Company.

Hall-Taylor, B. (1997). The construction of women's management skills and the marginalization of women in senior management. *Women in Management Review, 12*(7), 255–63.

CHAPTER FOUR

Power, politics and gender: Issues for nurse leaders and managers

Sandra Speedy & Debra Jackson

LEARNING OBJECTIVES

At the completion of this chapter, the reader will be able to:

▲ describe how gender polarisation of the workplace affects nurses;

▲ list sources of power and describe where they come from;

▲ discuss the misuse of power and how it can affect the work environment;

▲ describe the role that language plays in perpetuating images of nursing and nursing leaders; and

▲ list the traits that will enhance political effectiveness of nurse leaders.

KEY WORDS

Power, language, gender polarisation, empowerment, political effectiveness

INTRODUCTION

Nursing is the most strongly gender segregated of all occupational groups. The beginnings of modern nursing were strongly feminine and the traditional view of nursing work has been that it is women's work, and that the knowledge associated with it is somehow innate to women (Evans 1997). Though nursing has also attracted men, it remains strongly female dominated. This means that one of the key features of the health care industry is its strongly polarised occupational segregation (Kaye 1996). This polarisation positions gender, politics and power as central to nurses and nursing. The effects of this polarity are seen in aspects of workplace culture, such as occupational violence, workplace oppression, and in current debates such as those addressing the education of nurses and recruitment into the profession. Occupational segregation also has an effect on nurses' pay and potential for career advancement, especially for female nurses (Clare et al. 2001). Men are greatly over-represented in leadership positions (Brown 1998; Sharman 1998). This means that gender, particularly aspects pertaining to disadvantage and privilege, needs to remain firmly on the nursing agenda.

If we consider the structure of health care organisations such as hospitals, it is evident that nurses represent a high proportion of employees. However, this dominance does not transform into significant organisational power. Nurses are not necessarily appropriately represented in political processes. For example, Robinson-Walker (1999) points out that though nearly one-third of management roles are filled by women, most of these roles are positions of little power or authority. Furthermore, though nurses are active on committees, they tend to be well represented in labour-intensive committees, such as quality improvement committees, which focus on collection and analysis of data (Clare et al. 2001). They are less well represented in powerful decision-making forums such as financial committees. One of the effects of this is that nurses are subject to imposed change, as important decisions may be made with little regard for their effects on nurses and nursing. Imposed change is recognised as a contributing factor to nurses' job dissatisfaction and ultimately to retention of nurses, especially where the change impacts on nurses' workloads and their ability to provide adequate care (Jackson, Mannix & Daly 2001). This chapter considers the concepts of power, politics and gender within the context of nursing practice, management and leadership, and the continued development of the discipline of nursing.

GENDER AND LEADERSHIP IN NURSING

Female nurse leaders are confronted with many barriers (Graybill-D'ercole 1998). Notwithstanding the influence of feminism on nursing, female nurses still earn less than male nurses (Dale 1998; Gray 1995), and are still under-represented in leadership positions in nursing (Brown 1998; Evans 1997; Sharman 1998). Despite the female dominated nature of nursing, 'patriarchal gender relations which reflect a high valuation of all that is male and masculine, play a significant role in situating a disproportionate number of men in administrative and elite speciality positions' (Evans 1997, p.226). It is noteworthy that women have slower rates of achieving promotion than men (Brown 1998; Graybill-D'ercole 1998; Sharman 1998), with some findings suggesting that attainment of a senior position in nursing takes an average of five years longer for women than it does for men (Gray 1995).

The literature suggests that this differential is due to male privilege, particularly in domestic matters (Evans 1997; Gray 1995), as well as the fact that feminine characteristics are seen as undesirable and inappropriate in leaders, while male characteristics are highly valued (Evans 1997). Findings by Dale (1998) indicate that male and female nurse executives are similar in terms of attributes, but he makes the comment that 'executive characteristics are generally associated with masculine characteristics'. This view is also evident in the general management literature (Fulop & Linstead 1999; Robbins et al. 2000; Sinclair 1998). These characteristics include 'aggression, competition, dominance, ambition, decisiveness', whereas women supposedly value quite different qualities, including connectedness, inclusivity and relationships (Robinson-Walker 1999, p.30). This perceived focus on relationships is supported by Gilloran (1995), who noted that women seemed to form closer relationships with subordinates than men. This was seen to cause some difficulties in disciplinary matters (Gilloran 1995). There is also evidence in the literature to suggest that women leaders and managers in nursing may feel they are judged against male or 'macho' values (Markham 1996).

Evans (1997) presents evidence to suggest that although men represent a minority in nursing, they do not experience the hostility and lack of support that women can encounter in male-dominated professions. Rather, she suggests that men are advantaged, with their minority status according them special power and privileges, and this is why they are over-represented in elite power positions in nursing (Brown 1998; Evans 1997; Sharman 1998). Though it is sometimes postulated that attracting greater numbers of men into nursing would elevate the prestige and status of nursing, Evans (1997) suggests that there is the possibility that female nurses might become increasingly subordinate to yet another layer of male dominance. Increased numbers of men in nursing could merely make it more difficult for women to achieve leadership roles. The literature also suggests that a lack of role-modelling and mentoring for potential female nurse leaders may contribute to the under-representation of women in leadership positions (Graybill-D'ercole 1998; Robinson-Walker 1999).

Discrimination against women as leaders can be subtle, with stereotypes and insinuation being used to devalue women and make it more difficult for them to move to leadership positions (Simmons 1996). Furthermore, Robinson-Walker (1999) suggests that women may feel it inappropriate to be openly ambitious. Phrases describing nurse managers as 'petticoat governments' (Gilloran 1995) or similar, devalue the skills of women nurse leaders, and imply that women are frivolous and not fit to lead. Moreover, stereotypes that portray women as domineering and controlling, and dismiss women's talk as whining, gossipmongering or bitching, also perpetuate the idea that women are not appropriate for leadership positions (Evans 1997; Robinson-Walker 1999). The effects of stereotyping were also found to be evident, as men were perceived to be more logical, rational, intellectual and ready to take responsibility than women, and thus more suited to supervisory and leadership roles (Gilloran 1995).

In addition to stereotype advantages, social institutions such as heterosexual marriage also represent career advantage to men (Evans 1997), and there is evidence that women who reach leadership positions are more likely to be single and not responsible for the care of children (Gilloran 1995). This implies that women who have family responsibilities are disadvantaged when aspiring to leadership positions, which is supported by evidence that women consider family responsibilities a barrier to career progression. Female leaders are under scrutiny, and Graybill-D'ercole (1998: 1152) advises that gender politics means 'there is a narrow band of acceptable behaviour for women'. In this case, behaviour includes personal presentation such as dress, accessories, make-up and hair style. Many women are quite used to having aspects of their appearance commented on and criticised in their professional lives, whereas male managers are not subjected to the same level of personal scrutiny. Women's ways of interacting with others may also be the subject of comment in the workplace; for example, women may be accused of being flirtatious or using their femininity to unfair advantage (Sinclair 1998).

POWER

Power is a necessary aspect of management and leadership (Marquis & Huston 1996), and can be defined as the capacity to produce effects on others, change their behaviour, or influence others. There is a difference between power and influence, in that power has the capacity to cause change, whereas influence is the degree of actual change that occurs in the person over whom we have either power or influence. Power can exist in leaders, followers and in situations, and is an important aspect of the working landscape, although the literature suggests women may be ambivalent about power (Robinson-Walker 1999). Leaders can influence their followers, and conversely, followers can affect the leaders' behaviours, as well as their attitudes.

Power may hold negative associations for women, 'for women, power is viewed as dominance versus submission; is associated with personal qualities, not accomplishment; and is dependent on personal or physical attributes, not skill' (Marquis & Huston 1996, p.167). They also point out that many of the attributes associated with holding and using legitimate power—for example, assertiveness, decisiveness and autonomy—are more commonly associated with male than female socialisation (Marquis & Huston 1996).

To be informed is necessarily to be empowered and maintains professional credibility—no one would argue with the assertion that effective leadership requires a sound knowledge base. To be uninformed is to necessarily be disempowered and threatens professional credibility. Lack of knowledge of the total context in which nursing occurs will jeopardise decision-making, planning and service delivery. Despite the time pressures nurse managers face, the importance of remaining well-informed and cognisant of current policies and relevant research cannot be overstated. Strategies for knowledge enhancement may include membership and participation in professional organisations, reading current relevant journals, regular involvement in professional development activities and a commitment to lifelong learning. Such strategies are not only crucial to enhance current knowledge, but also provide opportunities for networking and support.

Sources of power

While there has long been an assumption that leaders have power, the question is now being asked: do leaders have power or do followers give it to them? This is an interesting question because the answer is yes on both accounts. Power is not evenly distributed among individuals or groups; everyone has some power which originates from varying sources.

Power relationships can be observed between individuals by non-verbal behaviours or what is called 'dominance/submission' behaviour (Hughes et al. 1999; Reardon

1995). These behaviours consist of stylised rituals, including staring, which typically dominant individuals do, while submissive individuals do not; pointing, where again, powerful individuals point, while those without power do not; touching is often done by the more powerful to demonstrate the power differential; and interrupting is more often done by powerful individuals, while less powerful individuals are those who are interrupted. Research indicates that women tend to be interrupted more often than men (Tannen 1994). Does this mean that men are more powerful, generally speaking, than women?

Other rituals or non-verbal messages of power in the workplace include placement of furniture, size of office space, displaying symbols of achievement or power (diplomas, awards, etc). Choice of clothing can also affect power and influence. Uniforms are a classic example, as they have been shown to influence people who are in crisis, which results in instructions being more likely to be followed. A person's appearance is an important aspect of leadership, and has led to the 'power dressing' phenomenon that is evident, especially in the business world (Brewis et al. 1997; Hughes et al. 1999). Technology has created the capacity of 'virtual politicking' within organisations—political players increasingly use email for political means, creating significant new challenges and risks for the organisation (Waters–Marsh 2001). Other sources of power by which an individual can potentially influence others are expert, referent, legitimate, reward and coercive power (after French & Raven 1960—see Table 4.1).

Table 4.1 Sources of power

Expert power	Represents the power of knowledge such as the nurse, surgeon or medical specialist may have. This has implications for leadership that is based on the value of followership, because increased knowledge in general means that followers have much expert power to contribute. Leaders in this situation will respect and listen to followers.
Referent power	The political influence a leader has due to the strength of the relationship between the leader and followers. This power is demonstrated in loyalty towards the powerful person, who may be considered charismatic. If you admire, respect or like someone, you will be favourably disposed towards doing what they want; you will be influenced by them. Ask yourself: who has the referent power in your ward/nursing group/organisation?
Legitimate or positional power	Depends on a person's organisational role, rather than on the person in that role. It usually follows formal or official authority—the higher the rank, the more power that can wielded. While the role is an important component of this type of power, followers also grant power to the person occupying the role.
Reward power	Involves the potential to influence others due to one's control over both intrinsic and extrinsic resources. These resources can include the power to give raises, bonuses, promotions, tenure or to select people for special assignments or desirable activities. Reward power can produce compliance, but does not necessarily produce commitment. Overuse of reward power may lead to resentment building up in subordinates, who might begin to feel manipulated, particularly when inconsistencies of reward occur on a regular basis.
Coercive power	That power which is founded on punishments, rather than rewards. It has the potential to influence others, often through the administration of negative sanctions, such as refusing a promotion, or the removal of positive ones, such a desired transfer to another part of the organisation. Coercive power is therefore the opposite of reward power. Some other examples include speeding tickets, punitive behaviour you direct at your children and the coercive power built into legislation, such as that of wearing seatbelts, and preventing or punishing sexual harassment.

Source: French & Raven 1960

Note that leaders and followers can use all of these types of power and that effective leaders generally work to increase their sources of power. In addition, Marquis and Huston (1996) describe charismatic power, which, as the name suggests, comes from personal dynamism and charisma; information power, which comes from having information needed by others; and, feminist or self-power, which comes from personal maturity and self-confidence.

Leaders vary in the degree to which they share power with subordinates. Some leaders view power as a fixed amount, so the more they give away, the less they have. Leaders who subscribe to this view are less likely to share power because it makes them nervous (Bradford & Cohen 1998). However, there is an argument for increasing one's power by delegating it to others and encouraging more participative approaches in the work setting.

Empowerment is an essential aspect of transformational leadership (Marquis & Huston 1996), and gives responsibility, accountability and authority to others to undertake the work that needs to be done (Naish 1995). Empowerment is thus an abstract concept that is fundamentally positive, referring to solutions rather than to problems (Kuokkanen & Leino-Kilpi 2000). Empowerment of staff also helps to develop them and build their skill base (Morrison et al. 1997), which, in providing wellbeing at both the individual and organisational level, will reinforce staff self-image and cooperation networks (Kuokkanen & Leino-Kilpi 2000). However, empowerment will not work in every setting, as it requires the professional to have capability, initiative, commitment and independence in decision-making, which organisational structures may impede. Using empowerment as a leadership strategy is more democratic and participative than using power-based strategies (Tappen 2001). Leaders who rely on power-based strategies to achieve their own ends will generally work to increase their sources of power, be they referent, expert, reward or legitimate.

Leaders who rely most on referent and expert power have teams that are more motivated and satisfied, and who perform better (Wood et al. 2001). In general, this suggests that leaders who take advantage of all their sources of power and influence are the most effective; the type of power they use depends on the situation in which they are placed. Further, while leaders have strong influence and power over their staff, those who are in turn influenced by their team tend to be most successful (Hughes et al. 1999). This type of reciprocity provides opportunities for optimum functioning of their organisation because it requires participation based on empowerment.

Individual personality and power

There are other forms of power, derived from the personalities of individuals. Individuals vary in their motivation to control or influence others. This is known as the 'need for power' (n Power). Those with high 'n Power' derive psychological satisfaction from influencing others (McClelland 1975). They seek positions where they can influence others. Two ways of expressing n Power have been identified: personalised power and socialised power (McClelland & Boyatzis 1982).

Individuals who have a high need for personalised power are said to be selfish, impulsive, uninhibited and lacking in self-control. They aim to exercise power for their own ends and needs. Individuals who have a high need for socialised power demonstrate service of higher goals to others or to organisations, which may involve self-sacrifice toward those ends. This often requires an empowering rather than an autocratic style of management and leadership. Note too, that some followers also have high needs for power. This can lead to tension between leaders and followers when followers are directed to do something they may not wish to do; one of the reasons why it is useful for each of us to be aware of our own power needs, and further, whether our preference is to be leader or follower (Hughes et al. 1999).

People with high needs for power often demonstrate a number of capacities and attributes, including the maintenance of good relationships with authority figures; competition for recognition and advancement; enhanced knowledge and information; personal charisma, such as pleasant personality characteristics, agreeable behaviour, creativity, honesty and integrity and appropriate personal appearance (Greenberg & Baron 1995). They also tend to demonstrate a capacity for sheer hard work; active and assertive behaviours; readiness to exercise influence over subordinates; are visibly different from followers; and are willing to do routine administrative tasks (Hughes et al. 1999; Wood et al. 2001).

MISUSE OF POWER: CAUSES AND CONSEQUENCES

It is important to understand the dynamics of power because power can be used inappropriately, and can become abusive and oppressive. Power implies physical force, such as may be used to restrain patients who are in danger of harming themselves. Inappropriate use and abuse of power is relatively commonplace in the nursing workforce, and this is evidenced by the alarmingly high incidence of work-related violence and harassment experienced by nurses (Jackson, Clare & Mannix 2001). Power gives the ability to harm and this is not limited to those in authority, as is evidenced by the large body of literature on horizontal violence that occurs between nurses (Ashley 1980; David 2000; Duffy 1995; Speedy 2000).

Bullying is increasingly recognised as a workplace issue for nurses (Taylor et al. 1999). McMillan (1995) contends that nurses of all levels, in all specialties, in public and private sectors, are prone to bullying and being bullied. Bullying can vary from open aggression and hostility, to covert rumour-mongering and exclusion, and can involve excessive criticism, intimidation, threats, ridicule, making excessive and impossible demands, withholding information, inequitable rostering practices, blocking opportunities for promotion or training, removing responsibility, and misuse of power to incite others to marginalise or exclude the victim (Paterson et al. 1997). It is generally accepted in the literature that bullying involves a series of incidents, not an incident in isolation. One out of three of respondents in McMillan's (1995) study revealed they had been subject to bullying for two years or more.

The most common perpetrators who bully nurses are other nurses. Paterson et al. (1997) suggest that most bullying is carried out by line managers to their subordinate staff. It is of concern that non-nurse managers are said to be the least responsible for workplace aggression to nurses, compared to nurse-managers who, with the exception of those in accident and emergency, were found to consistently use aggression towards nurses (Farrell 1999). A British study of bullying in nursing found that 61 per cent of nurse respondents identified line managers as being a continual source of violence and bullying (McMillan 1995).

Many nurses and organisational cultures foster an environment which supports violent behaviour (Clare 1991; McMillan 1995; Thomas 1995). Indifference and an unwillingness to intervene are also evident in the literature. For example, McMillan (1995) describes senior nurses witnessing bullying and victimisation of individual nurses, turning a blind eye to it, and doing nothing to intervene to protect those being targeted. These concepts are discussed in detail in Chapter 9.

STRATEGIES TO ENHANCE POWER AND INFLUENCE

Individuals who acquire managerial power seek to maintain or enhance their power by using a number of strategies. These may include:

▲ increasing their centrality and criticality to the organisation;

▲ augmenting their personal discretion and flexibility in their job;

▲ building into their job tasks that are difficult to evaluate, and

▲ expanding the visibility of their job performance, resulting in increased contact with the senior people they seek to impress (Marquis & Huston 1996; Wood et al. 2001).

Humour can be useful in helping people to see the possibilities in a situation, and in gaining support (Marquis & Huston 1996; Naish 1995). There are a number of other common strategies used to enhance one's power and influence. These include:

▲ building and developing personal resources;

▲ the use of reason (using facts and data to support a logical argument);

▲ being friendly and flattering in order to create favourable impressions;

▲ developing coalitions, in which relationships with other people are used for gaining support;

▲ bargaining with others, which involves using the exchange of benefits as a basis for negotiation;

▲ assertiveness, which requires a direct and forceful personal approach;

▲ appealing to a higher authority, which results in high-level support for requests;

▲ continually increasing one's own skills and knowledge; and

▲ the use of sanctions, which are organisationally derived rewards and punishments (Marquis & Huston 1996, Wood et al. 2001).

POLITICS IN NURSING PRACTICE ORGANISATIONS

Politics in organisations refers to political behaviour that is used to affect decision-making. Political behaviour involves those activities that are not required as part of one's formal role in the organisation but that influence or attempt to influence the distribution of advantages and disadvantages within the organisation. Organisational politics is the management of influence to obtain ends not sanctioned by the organisation or to obtain sanctioned ends through non-sanctioned means of influence (Wood et al. 2001). Nursing organisations are not exempt from political behaviour.

Nursing has a history of political activism (Rubotzky 2000), despite what many nurses would prefer to think. Politics is a fact of life for nurses, nursing and health care organisations. Politics occurs because organisations are made up of individuals who have different needs, values, goals, interests, and where there is competition for finite resources. Furthermore, the 'facts' that are used for decision-making are often open to interpretation, and there can be many interpretations of these 'facts'. Politics also occurs because organisations exist in a climate of ambiguity, leading to uncertainty, conflict and concern for one's wellbeing in the organisation (Waters-Marsh 2001).

Political behaviour

Any organisational chart you examine will indicate who is the boss and who reports to whom. It will not, however, reveal the political behaviours and politics of the organisation. To harness the true power in an organisation and work the politics of that organisation, a number of networks can be used. These include:

▲ the advice network, which reveals the people to whom others turn to get the work done;

▲ the trust network, which tends to uncover who shares delicate information with whom; and

▲ the communication network, which shows who talks to whom about work-related matters (Wood et al. 2001).

Language and power

Language is very powerful. It is the principal means by which reality is constructed and mediated. In other words, 'language creates meaning' (Tong 1998, p.198). It conjures up images and sends powerful messages about how things are positioned and where they sit in terms of power, status and prestige. To illustrate this, consider a recent debate in Britain about the possible return of a team of modern 'matrons', who would oversee cleanliness and care standards across ward areas and whole hospitals (Duffin 2001). Although some British nurses welcomed government moves to empower and increase the visibility of nurses, the proposed title of 'matron' caused considerable and heated discussion. The term was said to be 'gender-oriented and specific to women', 'outdated', and to conjure up images of 'fearsome' women, 'housekeeper and surrogate mother' women, and women who lead through 'bullying and harassment' (Duffin 2001, p.7). Clearly these are not images nursing wishes to perpetuate about itself, and one can see that a nurse with a title such as nurse manager, nurse executive, or director of nursing, could carry out the same activities, but without the connotations implicit in the word 'matron'. Thus it can be seen that the word, or the language, has created a set of understandings that may not have been intended, and which has then created enormous controversy.

The ways that nurses use language has changed over the years; for example, changes in the ways nurses refer to patients at handover is noted in the literature (Reed & Ground 1997). Reed and Ground (1997, p.132) point out that language 'is not just a matter of matching objects with words, but it carries a moral and political dimension in the way that we use it'. Like the example above, nurses need to use language that accurately conveys meaning, but that is not denigrating and does not foster stereotypes or negativity about individuals or particular groups of people. The connotation or attitudes that people develop can be directly related to the language used to introduce or describe it. Take a look at the following 'light-hearted' list which uses very different language to describe the same phenomenon:

Table 4.2 How language can be used to manipulate meaning

Effective management label	Can be labelled as. . .
Fixing responsibility	Blaming others
Developing relationships	Kissing up
Demonstrating loyalty	Apple polishing
Delegating authority	Passing the buck
Documenting decisions	Covering your rear
Encouraging change/innovation	Creating conflict
Facilitating teamwork	Forming coalitions
Improving efficiency	Whistle blowing
Planning ahead	Scheming
Competent and capable	Overachieving
Career-minded	Ambitious
Astute	Opportunistic
Practical minded	Cunning
Confident	Arrogant
Attentive to detail	Perfectionistic

It is clear from this listing that one's perception of the occurring behaviour is dependent on the situation in which the behaviour is manifest. Further, description of the behaviour is also dependent on the situation.

Contributions to political behaviour

There are many factors that contribute to political behaviour. These can be described as those that are individual and those that are organisational (see Chapter 3 for further discussion of individual personality characteristics as they relate to leadership). Whether we choose to be political or not, and the degree to which we are political, depends on a number of factors. Within the individual domain, researchers have identified certain traits that will enhance one's political effectiveness. These include:

▲ self-monitoring—a personality trait that measures our ability to adjust our behaviour to external situations (Snyder 1987). High self-monitors can present quite a different public persona to their private selves as they monitor and then adapt to the situation. In this way they can create a good impression and minimise damage to themselves in the event of a threatening situation (Greenberg & Baron 1995).

▲ locus of control—the extent to which people believe they can control their own lives (Robbins et al. 2000). Successful political players typically have an internal locus of control that results in controlling and manipulating the environment to work in their best interests.

▲ the capacity to manipulate others effectively—indicative of a high desire for power. Such individuals are known as 'high Machs', as they view and manipulate people for their own gain (Buchanan & Badham 1999; Vleeming 1979).

▲ high self-esteem, or positive self-regard. This includes confidence, competence, independence and freedom to act (Grossman & Valiga 2000). Nurses are not generally regarded as having an abundance of high self-esteem, which can reduce their political effectiveness in organisations; and

▲ damage control techniques—an essential part of leadership. Organisational politics requires players to protect themselves, as well as to promote their own interests. Behaving in a political manner requires reactive and protective 'defensive' behaviours to avoid action, avoid blame or avoid change.

Extensive use of defensive behaviour will promote the political player's self-interest. In the longer term, however, it may become a liability. Defensive behaviour may become chronic, so that learned defensiveness becomes the only way one can behave. Eventually, this may lead to loss of support of peers, bosses and subordinates, who become aware of the limitations of this type of behaviour. When used in moderation, defensive behaviour can be an effective device for surviving in organisations. However, frequent use tends to reduce effectiveness, delay decisions, increase interpersonal and intergroup tensions, reduce risk-taking, make attributions and evaluations unreliable, and can restrict organisational change. If defensive behaviour is used often and for long periods of time, it can lead to organisational rigidity and stagnation, detachment from the organisational environment, and low employee morale (Wood et al. 2001).

Within the organisational domain, the individual who is highly adept politically will be well served by:

▲ an organisation in which there are finite resources and a win–lose approach to resource allocation;

▲ a culture of low trust and role ambiguity;

▲ an unclear performance evaluation system;

▲ 'supposed' democratic decision-making that subverts power of individuals;

▲ high performance pressures, where the greater the pressure, the more likely is the need to bend the rules; and

▲ a self-serving culture and politicking of seniors who role-model acceptability of 'playing politics' to those below them (Greenberg & Baron 1995; Wood et al. 2001).

THE ETHICS OF BEHAVING POLITICALLY

Apart from personal and organisational contributions to political behaviour, there are a number of processes that can be used to enhance one's power in an organisation. Many people are not comfortable with talk of 'being political', and certainly are distinctly uncomfortable with behaving in political ways. Nurses are no exception. But politics is a fact of life in organisations; to avoid it is to reduce your own effectiveness. It is important that nurses can operate in ways that are politically astute, for as Rubotzky (2000) states, some degree of political savvy is expected in today's nurses (similarly, Hancock 2001). On the other hand, some people enjoy the 'cut and thrust' of politics, while some are significantly more politically astute than others, regardless of their level in the organisation. The politically naive and inept tend to feel continually powerless to influence those decisions that most affect them. They look at actions around them and are perplexed when they are regularly shafted by colleagues, bosses and the so-called 'system'.

Powerful and political people can be very successful at justifying or explaining their self-serving interests. They can, and often do, argue that unfair actions are really fair and just. Immoral people can justify almost any behaviour. They can be influential, articulate and persuasive, and sometimes get away with unethical practices because of these characteristics (Buchanan & Badham 1999).

As Wood et al. (2001) state:

To survive in a highly political environment requires particular skills, including the ability to recognise those who are playing political games despite surface appearances of openness and cooperation. It also requires the ability to identify the power sources of the key players, and to build one's own alliances and connections (p.435).

Recognising that you need to behave politically, but also wanting to behave ethically, there are some guidelines that might be helpful. For example, you can use three types of criteria to judge the ethics of your proposed behaviour.

▲ The first is the criterion of utilitarian outcomes, which indicates that the behaviour should produce the greatest good for the greatest number of people. In this way, everyone inside the organisation and outside it would derive some satisfaction or value.

▲ The second is the criterion of individual rights, where the behaviour respects the basic rights of all affected parties, including the rights of free consent, free speech, freedom of conscience, privacy and due process.

▲ The third criterion is that of distributive justice, where the political behaviour respects the rules of justice and treats people equitably and fairly, not arbitrarily (Wood et al. 2001).

It is important to keep in mind that we may use rationalisations to justify unethical behaviour. For example, we might tell ourselves that some behaviour is not really illegal and thus could be moral, when by the judgement of others it is illegal (and immoral); or we might tell ourselves that the actions we have taken or are about to take are in the organisation's best interests, when a neutral judge might perceive otherwise; or we may convince ourselves that the behaviour/action is unlikely to be detected; or finally, we may convince ourselves that a particular action demonstrates loyalty to the boss or the organisation, and is thus justifiable. In essence, 'organisational politics is . . . about the use of power to develop socially acceptable ends and means that balance individual and collective interests' (Wood et al. 2001, p.435).

CONCLUSION

It is clear that nursing and health care take place in dynamic and highly policitised environments. A strong understanding of political processes is essential to ensure that nurses' interests are brought to attention and that their voices are heard in key decision-making forums. Nurses have a well-established role as client/patient advocates, and it is essential that this advocacy role is maintained at all levels of political influence. It is also important to recognise the contribution that nurses make to political processes within organisations, even though this contribution may not be currently acknowledged or valued.

Gender remains an issue of key interest to nurses, both collectively and individually. Like other professions, research clearly shows that gender is a variable that will affect career development and progression in nursing, and that male nurses are advantaged in terms of career achievement in comparison to female nurses. There is still much to be done to redress gender-related advantage and disadvantage in nursing, and it is a task of nurse managers and leaders to recognise the existence of this and to work to ensure equity in workplace practices.

As we move further into the twenty-first century it is crucial to acknowledge the complex nature of power and to appreciate that men and women may have totally different attitudes to, and understandings of, power. Misuse of power has the potential to impact strongly and negatively on the workplace and contribute to the oppression of nurses and nursing. It is essential that the use of power in nursing is accompanied by integrity and veracity, and that it reflects the values nurses espouse—values such as care, compassion and social justice. Collectively and individually, nurses have the potential to further develop the concept of professional autonomy. A full understanding of the nature of power can only help us to move ahead and improve nursing as a career choice, and further develop practice so as to better meet the needs of the communities we serve.

Reflective exercise

There are some questions that you can ask yourself when you feel uncomfortable about political behaviour. These include:

1 Am I behaving in the best interests of myself or my organisation?

2 What about the other parties involved? What are their rights?

3 Does the political activity conform to standards of equity and justice?

Working through these questions may be helpful in deciding how to behave.

RECOMMENDED READINGS

Grossman, S., & Valiga, T. M. (2000). *The new leadership challenge: Creating the future of nursing.* Philadelphia: F. A. Davis Company.

Hughes, R. L., Ginnett, R. C., & Curphy, G. J. (1999). *Leadership: Enhancing the lessons of experience.* Boston: Irwin McGraw-Hill.

Kramer, R. M., & Neale, M. A. (eds). (1998). *Power and influence in organizations.* Thousand Oaks: SAGE Publications.

Marquis, B., & Huston, C. (1996). *Leadership roles and management functions in nursing: Theory and application.* (2nd edn). Philadelphia: Lippincott.

Robinson-Walker, C. (1999). *Women and leadership in health care: The journey to authenticity and power.* San Fransisco: Jossey-Bass Publishers.

Sinclair, A. (1998). *Doing leadership differently: Gender, power and sexuality in a changing business culture.* Melbourne: Melbourne University Press.

CHAPTER FIVE

Cross-cultural health and strategies to lead development of nursing practice

Afaf Meleis & Juliene Lipson

LEARNING OBJECTIVES

At the completion of this chapter, the reader will be able to:

- ▲ critically define culturally competent care and identify components and policies for its delivery;

- ▲ discuss major models that describe diversity and culturally competent care;

- ▲ critically discuss major principles essential in developing culturally competent skills and attitudes;

- ▲ identify, utilise and evaluate a framework for assessing issues in patient care situations that are based on diversity in nurse–patient pairs; and

- ▲ develop research priorities that could enhance the knowledge base for cultural diversity and culturally competent care.

KEY WORDS

Enthnocentrism, biculturalism, diversity, individuals, cultural competence

INTRODUCTION

Although this chapter has been written from an American perspective and mainly cites literature from the United States, we believe that the concepts discussed are relevant to nursing in many multicultural societies. First, we briefly describe several conceptual frameworks now being used in the United States and then discuss some common issues in cross-cultural nursing. Generic skills are then described, as well as the types of knowledge that support such skills. Finally, we suggest strategies to help nurse leaders foster culturally competent care in practice and educational settings.

LEADERSHIP AND CULTURALLY COMPETENT HEALTH CARE

Because we live in such diverse societies where populations are increasingly mobile, strong nursing leadership is needed to develop and guide culturally competent health care. In particular, nursing leaders must work toward organisational goals that address issues related to diversity and to institute policies for healthy approaches to dealing with and maximising the rewards that are gained from diversity.

Definitions of culturally competent nursing

An American Academy of Nursing monograph defines culturally competent nursing care as being sensitive to issues related to culture, race, gender, sexual orientation, social class and economic situation (Davis et al. 1992; Meleis et al. 1992). In reconsidering this definition we would add disability as an aspect of diversity (Lipson & Rogers 2000). Recently, the US Office of Minority Health (2000) developed a national definition:

> Cultural and linguistic competence is a set of congruent behaviors, attitudes, and policies that come together in a system, agency, or among professionals that enables effective work in cross-cultural situations. 'Culture' refers to integrated patterns of human behavior that include the language, thoughts, communications, actions, customs, beliefs, values, and institutions of racial, ethnic, religious, or social groups. 'Competence' implies having the capacity to function effectively as an individual and an organisation within the context of the cultural beliefs, behaviors, and needs presented by consumers and their communities (Based on Cross et al. 1989).

How does culturally 'competent' care differ from nursing care that is culturally compatible, culturally appropriate, culturally sensitive, culturally responsive or culturally informed? Most of these phrases may or may not imply knowledge, interpretation of behaviour, attitudes, communication or other skills, nursing roles and actual interventions. Some argue that 'culturally competent care' is used too loosely—a health provider cannot be culturally 'competent' in a second culture unless he or she grew up in it or is at least fluent in the language. However, the advantage of the word 'competence' over terms like sensitivity is that it implies more than awareness, it implies the ability to intervene.

Another definitional issue is transcultural nursing versus cross-cultural nursing. Based in anthropology, Brink (1999) describes transcultural as referring to concepts that transcend cultural boundaries, that are universal, and found in all cultural groups, e.g. healing and caring. Cross-cultural refers to describing cultural groups that are first examined as case studies, focusing on similarities and contrasts. She cautions nurses to be careful about using definitions of such topics as caring or social support that apply only to North American cultures without first validating them with cross-cultural information.

COMPONENTS OF CULTURALLY COMPETENT CARE

Cultural competence in health care requires far more than simply acquiring knowledge about another ethnic/cultural group. It is a complex combination of knowledge, attitudes and skills (Campinha-Bacote 1994). For example, attitudes include ethnocentrism, bias, respect and empathy. Skills include such things as flexibility, effective cross-cultural communication and cultural brokerage. This concept is used in two ways, from an organisational perspective and an individual perspective.

The organisational perspective

Culturally competent care in a health care organisation or agency includes:

▲ accessibility—being free of barriers due to geography, administration, money, culture and language;

▲ accountability—high quality and satisfying care delivered ethically with an efficient use of resources;

▲ sustained partnership—based on a trusting, continuing, respectful and responsible relationship between the patient and clinician;

▲ a family context—provided in the context of the patient's living conditions, family background, and cultural values; and

▲ a community context—provided within the context of shared values, e.g. culture, ethnic heritage, religion, neighbourhood, geopolitical boundaries (Rorie et al. 1996).

Multicultural California developed criteria for publicly-funded, managed care that included guaranteed language access through telephone language services or on-site interpreters in areas where there are at least 3000 eligible patients indicated a preferred language other than English; community advisory committees of consumers, advocates and traditional 'safety net' providers; and needs assessment to identify the language and cultural needs of small groups of individuals who speak a primary language other than English. These were used as a model to develop national guidelines recently finalised by the Office of Minority Health. (See Appendix A.)

A cultural competence continuum (Cross et al. 1989) can be applied to either agencies or individual nurses. It includes the following levels:

▲ cultural destructiveness: incidents reflecting negative attitudes such as *prejudice*, (e.g. remarks, shunning) or *discrimination* (e.g. behaviour that blocks opportunities);

▲ cultural incapacity: a biased authoritarian system that cannot foster growth in culturally diverse groups;

▲ cultural blindness: based on the belief that culture and race make no difference in how services are provided (e.g. 'we are all human');

▲ cultural precompetence: 'cultural sensitivity' is the desire and attempt to deliver services in a manner respectful of cultural diversity. Awareness of cultural beliefs and behaviour of a particular group may be evident;

▲ cultural competence: acceptance of and respect for cultural norms, beliefs and differences. Self-assessment regarding degree of cultural competence, adaptation of services, and interplay between policy and practice; and

▲ cultural proficiency: motivation to add to the knowledge base of culturally competent practice, develop culturally therapeutic approaches and hire staff who are specialists in cultural competence.

The individual perspective

There has always been an overemphasis on cultural knowledge as underlying culturally competent care. However, early studies of nurse characteristics facilitating competence focused on ethnicity, attitudes and/or personality variables, e.g. open-mindedness, prejudice, authoritarianism, cultural relativism or intolerance of ambiguity. Such studies assumed that attitudes towards other groups are central to cultural sensitivity and that knowledge is connected to behaviour, e.g. skills in applying this knowledge. Meleis (1999) stated that culturally competent individuals value diversity at all levels and in all areas of their lives, being 'energised' by variations and challenged by teaching, researching or caring for people who are different from themselves, as well as awareness of how being different from the norm can be marginalising.

Cultural competence of nurses as individuals is the effect of our own cultural and socioeconomic backgrounds. There is a common assumption that nurses who represent ethnic minorities are naturally better equipped to give good care to patients of that group than nurses who do not. Indeed, in the mid-1970s to the early 1980s, there was disagreement between 'ethnic nurses of colour' and nurse-anthropologists about whether we should focus on people who are 'visibly' part of a politically or economically marginalised group, e.g. African-Americans, American Indians, or on the 'cultural' backgrounds of all patients, including 'privileged' European-Americans. Despite having moved beyond this issue to 'valuing diversity', nurses bring to patient care their own values, biases and communication styles, which may strongly affect quality of care. Nurses as individuals vary widely in the strength of their ethnic identity, commitment to their communities and respect for differences. Indeed, just as nurses from the dominant culture vary, ethnic minority nurses range from the most competent to the least competent, e.g. judgmental towards ethnic peers who represent a different social class. We must examine our own cultural baggage to see whether and how it may be offending our patients or otherwise interfering with good care.

FRAMEWORKS FOR UNDERSTANDING CROSS-CULTURAL PRACTICE ISSUES IN NURSING

Cross-cultural nursing care is a highly complex art and science. Models help us to organise our thinking about a very complex field. The frameworks described below tend to guide thinking in rational terms and are based in US mainstream culture, which too often focuses on individuals rather than families and communities. Some currently used frameworks were developed by Leininger (1991), Giger and Davidhizar (1999), Campinha-Bacote (1998), Purnell (2000), and Lipson (Lipson & Steiger (1996).

Leininger

Any discussion of transcultural nursing must start with Madeleine Leininger, who began developing her theories in the 1970s and has been the most prolific writer in this area since then. She calls her theory 'Culture care diversity and universality' (Leininger 1991). She published the Sunrise model, which contains nine domains of culture and relates them to client actions. These domains, arranged in a half-circle under cultural and social structure dimensions, include technological factors, religion and philosophical factors, kinship and social factors, cultural values and life paths, political and legal factors, economic factors, and educational factors. These are influenced by care expressions, patterns, practices, wellbeing and nursing care decisions and actions. A very useful part of the Sunrise model is the three major modalities that guide nursing decisions and actions to provide cultural congruent care: cultural care preservation and/or maintenance; cultural care accommodation and/or negotiation; and cultural care re-patterning or restructuring.

Giger and Davidhizar

Giger and Davidhizar's framework is similar to the Leininger model in that it includes a number of domains that are important for client and family assessment (Giger & Davidhizar 1999). One of its strengths is its emphasis on both the uniqueness of individual clients and potential similarities due to their cultural backgrounds. In the centre of this somewhat bull's eye-shaped model is a circle depicting the 'client: unique cultural being'. Surrounding the inner circle is another circle containing three segments: culture, religion and ethnicity. The outer circle contains six segments: communication, space, time, biological variations, environmental control and social organisation.

The focus is on knowledge in each of these major domains, based on the assumption that if nurses have this knowledge they can use it to provide culturally competent care. This popular book includes chapters on many groups that have not been described in other cultures and nursing books in the past, such as East Indian Americans, Irish Americans, Jewish Americans, and French Canadians.

The Purnell model

Purnell's (2000) model is the newest of the popular models used in the United States. Originally devised as an organising framework for cultural assessment, it resembles the previous two models in that it includes important domains of culture and health, contained in a diagram. Arranged in a series of concentric circles, the outermost circle represents the global society, followed by the community, then the family, and people in the centre. Within the inner circle are twelve pie-shaped divisions representing multiple concepts in the following areas: heritage, communication, family roles and organisation, workforce issues, biocultural ecology, high-risk behaviours, nutrition, pregnancy/childbearing practices, death rituals, spirituality, health care practices, and health care practitioner concepts. At the bottom is a continuum often used in diversity training, ranging from 'unconsciously incompetent, consciously incompetent, consciously competent, to unconsciously competent' (p.42). While Purnell asserts that culturally competent health care providers must be aware of their own existence, thoughts and environment, the emphasis is mainly on knowledge to allow providers to adapt care to be congruent with the client's culture. Purnell has included an even wider array of cultural groups in his book (Purnell & Paulanka 2002), including Iranian-Americans, Turkish Americans, Polish-Americans, and so on.

Campinha-Bacote

Campinha-Bacote's model proceeds beyond knowledge about the culture of a patient or community to health provider skills and the ability to act on this knowledge. She conducts training workshops based on three objectives: defining cultural competence, discussing five components of this concept, and identifying cultural interventions. The five components are cultural awareness (e.g. recognising ethnocentric beliefs about health care delivery), cultural knowledge (beliefs and practices of a variety of groups), cultural skill (e.g. culturological assessment), cultural encounters (emphasising face to face interactions), and cultural desire (motivation to achieve cultural competence). She views competence as a journey, not a state to be achieved (Campinha-Bacote 1998).

Lipson

Lipson's framework (Lipson & Steiger 1996) is a guiding perspective rather than a model, a way to think through the complexity of any cross-cultural nursing care encounter. Like Campinha-Bacote, she insists that culturally competent nursing care is more than focusing on knowledge about a patient or group. To capture the complexity, this perspective views care in three different ways:

▲ the context—a focus on the culture of the health care system and the social, political and economic systems and how they affect health care providers, patients, families and communities;

▲ the 'objective' component—a focus on patient/community cultural and socioeconomic characteristics, as well as how any individual or family expresses them, including variations; and

▲ the subjective component—a focus on nurses themselves based on the premise that we must examine our own cultural values, biases and communication patterns in order to recognise their influence on nursing care, and to be able to shift our communication to improve care.

A simple version to guide nursing interventions is similar to Leininger's suggestions to evaluate the benefits or risks of supporting the patient's cultural practices. If the belief or practice is beneficial for health and wellbeing, or at least neutral, it can and should be reinforced. If the belief or practice is potentially risky, the patient and nurse need to discuss their different views on the practice and negotiate a compromise. The nurse might support the patient's belief but suggest a more beneficial practice related to that belief. If a health practice is clearly potentially harmful, the nurse might take a stronger stand in explaining the risks and help the patient to substitute a healthier practice. Of course, we must always acknowledge that it is ultimately the patient's choice.

Strengths and limitations of frameworks

In summary, these frameworks focus on different elements of culturally competent care. All include the importance of cultural knowledge in a broad variety of areas to improve care. Some focus on obtaining a large amount of culturally specific information seems to assume that knowing cultural details leads to the ability to act on this knowledge. Campinha-Bacote and Lipson emphasise a more general approach that includes skills as well as knowledge. Both focus on nurses as cultural beings whose identities and values impact on relationships with patients and families. They also emphasise working in partnership with patients, families and communities, rather than dictating care. These assumptions depend heavily on self-awareness and recognition of the social, economic and political environment.

Each framework has strengths and limitations, but none manages to capture the whole complexity of the cultural, socioeconomic and political reality context within which nursing care is practised. None adequately handles bi-culturalism or diversity within cultural groups. At issue here is whether a general model, relatively devoid of cultural group description, is more or less effective than a model which asks nurses to consider specific cultural group information. While knowledge-based models can provide rich guidelines for culturally competent care, they may tempt culturally unsophisticated nurses to 'fill in the blanks' or stereotype their patients, the so-called 'laundry list' or reductionist approach. The general models provide a context for interpreting what one sees in a patient or family in order to allow them to ask the right questions. Specific cultural facts are very important as a starting point, as long as they are used with the understanding that every belief and behaviour has both a cultural and an individual base.

ISSUES

Stereotyping or generalising

Stereotyping is an outcome of having some information about a cultural group and using it in a 'cookbook' manner. It is applying cultural 'facts' indiscriminately to a patient of a particular cultural group. Publishers' space limitations and reader time often result in brief descriptions of cultural groups that do not emphasise variation within the group. Readers with little familiarity with intragroup variation may tend to assume that individuals will match the description, and end up depersonalising a patient/client. Stereotyping is making an assumption based on group membership without critically assessing whether or not the individual fits all of the assumptions and patterns of response. In generalising without stereotyping, one begins with a cultural pattern, then seeks further information to see whether the assumptions and patterns of responses fit the individual, e.g. whether the patient considers himself or herself to be typical or different from others in their cultural group and/or the effects of age, education, personality or geographic origin on how individuals express their culture.

Ethnocentrism versus cultural relativism

Ethnocentrism is the conviction that the way one does things in one's own cultural group is the best or only correct way. Everyone exhibits some degree of ethnocentrism in the context of group identity. It is usually unquestioned until one confronts a situation that forces them to think differently with regard to one or more groups of people. For example, nurses commonly exhibit ethnocentrism with regard to the biomedical model, assuming that we know more about what is good for patients' health than patients do. We are not always right, of course. With regard to other cultural groups, an ethnocentric stance is usually based on believing that one's world view is the only reality because it has not been challenged by familiarity with other cultural systems. Sometimes it is based on feelings of superiority. Ethnocentrism can be expressed verbally, or non-verbally in facial expressions or posture, either of which can demonstrate bias or condescension.

Cultural relativism, a concept from anthropology, is the ability to view each cultural group as unique, with its own set of values and practices that should not be judged against one's own culture as being either 'good' or 'bad.' In other words, what is 'good' is what is 'socially approved' in a given culture. Because there is no universal set of morals or laws against which to measure those of any particular culture, cultural relativists attempt to appreciate other cultural practices not as 'wrong' but simply different.

The question is where culturally competent care lies along the continuum from ethnocentrism to cultural relativism. Either extreme is potentially damaging, and each specific situation needs to be considered in its sociocultural and political/economic contexts. However, 'Ultimately, culturally competent care is about acknowledging difference, advocacy for the marginalised, and intolerance of inequity and stereotyping' (Meleis 1999, p.12) while, at the same time, refusing to go along with a cultural group's potentially damaging health practices or beliefs as being simply 'part of their culture' in the name of cultural relativism.

Matching versus diversity

A third issue is whether we expect all nurses to work effectively with patients from any cultural group. Many nurses believe that good nursing care means that one can surpass cultural barriers and biases, but that is not necessarily so. Instead, good care may recognise that the barriers are too great—that the nurse and patient or his family just *cannot* work together effectively. Barriers may stem from a strong bias on either side that interferes with communication. It is far better to acknowledge the bias than just blundering through and alienating the patient or being completely ineffective. Nurses tend to think that we should be able to care for all clients, but we are human too. Recognising our own biases and how they may affect our communication is part of culturally competent care. It may be that finding someone else to care for a patient or family member who makes one angry or who one greatly dislikes for some reason is the most sensitive thing to do. Or the family may not tolerate a nurse who is the wrong gender or age.

PRINCIPLES AND SKILLS

Among a number of principles and skills inherent to culturally competent care we describe the following:

▲ meaningful exposure to other cultures;

▲ values clarification;

▲ cross-cultural communication;

▲ integrating the context and culture into the nursing process; and

▲ developing community resources.

Exposure to other cultures

It is impossible to grow up without internalising one's own culture, which tends to be invisible to oneself until confronted by very obvious cultural differences. Significant exposure and integration of the experience is critical to developing a real understanding that cultures fundamentally differ in the way they create and maintain world views. Without exposure, it is difficult to even imagine how differently the world looks through the lens of another culture. Culture directs us to respond to things in our environment that might not even be noticed by people from a different culture. The ideal type of exposure is living for a while in another culture and gaining competence in its language. Language both reflects and shapes one's world view, helping to determine how a cultural group cuts the pie of the world. For example, language reflects the structure of social relationships—while English has one form of the pronoun 'you', Spanish, Farsi and many other languages have formal and familiar forms; addressing another person by the wrong form is a major social gaffe.

Values clarification

Critical to culturally competent nursing care is awareness of one's values about life, health and how to behave with others. All the other skills may not be very useful unless we confront our own biases because these biases, based on our own values and world view, shape our interactions with clients and with other nurses. We need to both recognise our own values and how different patients' values may be. A classic theoretical tool is Kluckhohn and Strodbeck's (1961) framework of value orientations to profile different cultural groups. They stated that human groups are faced with a finite number of problems for which there are a finite number of solutions. They posed four major problems in their Value Orientation Profile with three basic solutions to each question:

▲ What is the relationship of humans to nature? The choices are: (1) mastery over nature; (2) subjugation to nature; and (3) harmony with nature.

▲ What is the nature of time in life? The choices are: (1) past orientation; (2) present orientation; and (3) future orientation.

▲ What is human activity for? The choices are: (1) doing; (2) being; and (3) being in becoming.

▲ How should people relate to other people? The choices are: (1) individualism; and (2) family/community focus (collateral relationships).

An example of a potential conflict in the humans and nature problem is that the biomedical system illustrates 'mastery over nature', the belief that everything is potentially in our control if we just develop the knowledge and technology. However, a family may be oriented to the 'subjugation to nature' and believe that humans can do little to counteract the forces of nature, that disease and death are inevitable; one simply accepts them and goes on living. This so-called 'fatalism' is often seen in Muslims and strict Catholics. Harmony with nature, a sense of oneness among humans, nature, and the supernatural or God, is dominant among many indigenous peoples.

A potential conflict in time orientation occurs when future-oriented nurses encounter ethnic or immigrant patients who are late or miss appointments altogether, because their approach to time is different. It is easy to discuss prevention with future-oriented people, but it does not make sense to those who are present or past-oriented. Even knowing how long a particular symptom has been a problem may be difficult for people who do not think in terms of chunks of time or calendars.

One example of a conflict is nurses whose orientation is 'doing', whereby one is measured by what one accomplishes or achieves according to standards set by the workplace or the family. Such nurses may be perplexed by patients who consider *who* people are as persons, e.g. loving, spontaneous, poetic, a good parent, to be of more importance than what they can accomplish, and consequently evaluate such people as lacking in motivation.

A potential relationship conflict occurs when individually-oriented health providers, who value autonomy and self-direction, attempt to force collaterally-oriented patients to do self-care or make decisions about treatment, when indeed, the collateral alternative demands responsibility to the group, such as the extended family, the tribe or village. Decisions, therefore, are family or group decisions, and patients are to be 'cared for' when sick instead of being expected to get up and walk, or take care of the new baby.

There are various tools for values clarification. One example is a contrast list such as the one provided in Table 5.1 of value differences between Middle Eastern immigrants and the US dominant culture. This type of tool could be used to further clarify the bases for responses in a health/illness situation.

Cross-cultural communication

In order to provide culturally competent care, nurses must be aware of the range of variations in verbal and non-verbal communication, of their own communication style, and be able to be flexible in shifting their own style to better match that of the patient.

Verbal styles

Many clients who appear silent in health care encounters are not accustomed to the biomedical model of communication based on short answers to short questions; they are often able to tell a story that illuminates their situation and symptoms but time limitations do not allow it. For example, if women cannot relate their stories, health care providers may have incomplete information on which to base diagnoses and treatment. Staff in such programs need to examine their own values and communication styles so they can be alert to and respect different ways of communicating, including the importance and various meanings of silence (Goold 2001).

Translation and interpretation

When an interpreter is needed, we caution against using family members because they often do not understand medical terminology or they have inadequate English skills. Children or spouses of immigrants are extremely protective of the pride of their family member and try to avoid embarrassment at all costs, including hiding important medical information. This is particularly important in women's health care. In many immigrant groups, people avoid talking about any topic that has to do with the reproductive system, most particularly across gender.

Style of conversation and tone of voice

European-Americans tend to be blunt and to the point, and tend to get irritated with clients who do not answer directly, ramble, or tell stories. However, many East Asian cultures emphasise care about others' feelings through indirectness and courtesy, particularly with a person considered to be in authority, and consider 'directness' to be rude and insensitive. Middle Easterners will say something loudly when it is important, and may repeat it several times for emphasis.

Ethical conflicts between health providers and patients arise because of what can be discussed openly and what cannot. A frequent clinical problem arises when family members refuse to inform a patient about 'bad news' (Gillotti et al. 2002). This is quite common among Muslims from the Middle East, who prefer to protect patients from bad news or anything that may upset them. This is based partly on the belief that patients should be kept optimistic and relaxed so that they can recover, and partly on a common cultural characteristic in which Muslims do not plan for death or ever give up hope. If the health provider insists on informing a religious patient about a terminal prognosis so she can 'prepare for death', it could be interpreted as attempting to defy the will of Allah or 'what is written' (Meleis & Jonsen 1983).

Table 5.1 Value differences between Middle Eastern immigrants and US dominant culture

US Anglo	Middle Eastern
Curiosity and competitiveness encouraged in relation to education, work, money	Autonomy is not encouraged Emphasis on family group
Promptness valued	Time is not money. Relationships more important than schedules. However, immigrants may be irritated with American professionals who are late.
Privacy valued; e.g. child's own room	Spatial privacy is not that important except between unrelated men and women.
Personal information shared with strangers	Personal information shared only with family and close friends.
Appointments made for socialising	People drop by each other's houses spontaneously, no previous phone call required. Socialisation patterns differ by country, social class, and gender.
Emphasis on achievement, profession, money	Emphasis on personal characteristics, social status, family relationships, and education. Social status is determined by family background rather than solely through economic achievement.
Religion may be separate from other realms	Religious faith permeates life: 'Do your part, and let God do His.'
Ideal: male/female equality	Traditional male/female roles, in which men provide shelter and control women who depend on them and obey them, are beginning to break down.
Friends, acquaintances, obligations vary	True friendship means complete loyalty and commitment. Expectations of friends are almost as high as those of family members.
Virginity a personal choice	Virginity before marriage is expected. Women's modesty is important and should be respected by health care professionals.
Peer groups important	Relationships are formed with people one likes. Social activities usually include family members of various age groups.
Youth is valued	Elders are more important, as is the past and tradition.
Touch varies, OK between genders	Touching is important in human relationships. Middle Easterners often touch each other to emphasise a point. Touching members of the opposite sex, unless married, is frowned upon. (varies)
Bluntness, openness	Some things are better left unsaid; frankness may be considered rude; politeness and tact are very important.
Disagreement expressed	Respect and outward agreement are shown to authority figures; people may not show disagreement or lack of understanding.

Source: Mid-East S. I. H. A. Project, UCSF School of Nursing, 1984.

Personal space

Edward T. Hall (1966) described cultural influences on how people interact with each other in terms of space:

▲ Intimate distance (0–45 cm) is maintained between intimates and close associates, in which people experience each other's smell, heat, touch and rich visual detail.

▲ Personal distance (45 cm–1.2 m) allows rich communication.

▲ Social distance (1.2 m–3.5m) is used for business and general public contact.

People usually experience subtle discomfort with discordant conceptions of space. For example, a Colombian who stands close in order to communicate may cause an Austrian to back away. The Colombian may perceive the Austrian as 'cold', while the Austrian may perceive the Colombian as 'aggressive'.

Eye contact varies from intense to fleeting, depending not only on the cultural group but on gender and social status. For example, while Arabs generally tend to make direct and sustained eye contact, unrelated women and men tend not to sustain eye contact with each other, and in many groups it is considered rude to sustain eye contact with one's 'superiors'. People from many indigenous groups, including Aborigines (Goold 2001) and American Indians tend to avoid direct eye contact because it is perceived as rude and an invasion of privacy. Sustained eye contact has many different meanings, e.g. intimacy, showing one's power. Respecting a patient's style by mirroring it often reduces their discomfort.

Expression of emotions

In some cultural groups, people show their emotions not only on their faces but all over their bodies; in others it is inappropriate to reveal one's feelings to anyone outside the family. Some groups, such as traditional Vietnamese, convey negative emotions with silence or a reluctant smile; but the smile can also express joy, being stoic in adversity, an apology or a response to being scolded.

Conceptions of touch, modesty and gestures

Patients from traditional paternalistic groups may require gender-matched nurses; in actuality, unrelated men and women may not touch or see each other in the most traditional Muslim societies and women are veiled in Saudi Arabia and were in Afghanistan under the Taliban regime. Touching certain parts of the body may also be problematic, e.g. older Vietnamese consider the head sacred and it should not be touched by others; the feet, the lowest part of the body, should not be pointed toward others. It is sometimes considered an insult for a man to touch a woman in the presence of others. Among the Roma, the body below the waist is considered to be highly polluted, and a nurse should never touch the lower part of the body before the upper body; it is a good idea to provide two towels (Lipson et at.1996). The same gesture can mean very different things in different groups. In the United States, the thumb and forefinger in a circle means OK, whereas in Italian or Latin cultures, it may be seen as obscene.

Knowledge of variations and ability to flexibly adjust one's communication to better match that of the patients is an important skill in culturally competent care.

Integrating culture and context into the nursing process

An important skill in providing culturally competent care is integration into the nursing process. A useful model uses a theoretical framework of cultural constructivism in which Engebretson and Littleton (2001) recast the nursing process to frame the interdependence of client–nurse interactions within the social and cultural contexts of the health care system and community. A very important part of this model is that it accommodates the beliefs, values and experiences of both clients and nurses.

Developing coalitions, community empowerment, and resources

Integral to culturally competent care is the ability and commitment to form coalitions with individuals in the ethnic and immigrant communities most represented in one's health care agency or system. Working with key individuals may be the only way in which dominant culture nurses can learn why some community members avoid health care, how they respond to health providers or what they do to maintain their health or place themselves at risk. When key community members are invited to teach health providers and perceive that their knowledge is respected and valued, care can be markedly improved. Indeed, empowering one's clients also empowers oneself.

Involving family and community members in planning and/or providing services can enable nurses to communicate with even 'hard to reach' populations. For example, a clinic-based program could include non–clinical gatherings with peers led by primary care nurses; culturally competent programs should be housed in the neighbourhood and rely on innovative outreach strategies (Meleis et al. 1998).

Finally, developing community resources, both within communities as mentioned above, and through advocating for communities with governmental agencies and funders is a very important part of culturally competent care, e.g. helping to write grant proposals. In this light, participatory action research or working with community members to develop their own communities is a powerful means of obtaining outside resources, as well as fostering empowerment.

KNOWLEDGE TO INFORM CULTURALLY COMPETENT NURSING PRACTICE

There are two types of knowledge that underlie practice: academic knowledge and experiential knowledge. Academic knowledge is generally 'about' various cultural groups served by the health care systems in which nurses work, such as the areas mentioned in the description of models above, with special emphasis on cultural and social influences on health, illness and health care in general. It is also important to be aware of historical treatment that has led to marginalisation of some ethnic groups, such as periods of xenophobia, legislation or a history of colonisation. Nurses should also know something about immigration history and the homeland situation of groups of immigrants and refugees to understand the context of their experiences in the health care system.

This knowledge is available in books, journals and through the Internet, but nurses can also seek it through oral histories or by consulting with spokespeople from various ethnic or immigrant communities, knowledgeable older community members or through interpreters who work in health care agencies.

The second type of knowledge is experiential. One important source is firsthand, personal, lived experience, e.g. being an immigrant; minority group origins or living for an extended time in another country, particularly in a country where one struggles with the language. It is difficult for mainstream nurses to grasp the meaning of being 'a minority' or socially marginalised without firsthand experience, to know what it is like to struggle with being understood, particularly in health care situations (Caver & Livers 2002). A second source is 'close to the heart' vicarious experience, such as having very close friends or a spouse from another culture. Discussions about 'what it is like' can be invaluable. Another source is excellent films, autobiographies and novels that draw the reader into the world of those who do not fit well or are not accepted into the mainstream. For example, a riveting example in health care is *The spirit catches you and you fall down* (Fadiman 1997), an account of a Hmong family's experiences in a California health care system.

Practice-based knowledge is also important, such as how to do a cultural assessment, which can be extensive or relatively brief, given the amount of time available and the setting. For example, there is little time to do a cultural assessment in the emergency room, but home care or public health nursing can allow more extensive information gathering. At a minimum, we suggest obtaining information on the following topics (Lipson & Meleis 1985):

▲ family background. If immigrant, how long has the family been here?

▲ primary and secondary language, non-verbal style;

▲ religion: practices needed in hospital;

▲ ethnic affiliation and strength of identity;

▲ food preferences and prohibitions; and

▲ health and illness beliefs and practices, including family and provider roles in the health care system.

In addition to knowing how to do a cultural assessment, it is important to have a sense of how to intervene. What does one do with cultural knowledge? Such examples as reinforcing neutral or positive health beliefs and practices or negotiation around those who are potentially harmful were mentioned earlier, as well as knowing how to tailor health or patient education so that it can be understood and used by patients. For example, information for people who do not read English, health promotion or prevention information can be videotaped or audiotaped, or written into 'novellas' on health topics, a format very popular among Spanish speakers.

STRATEGIES TO EFFECT DELIVERY OF CULTURALLY APPROPRIATE NURSING CARE

Policy changes

Developing and enhancing sensitivity to difference, respect for diversity, and progressive competencies in dealing effectively with cultural differences are not possible without nursing leadership that has a clear strategic plan and goals. Policies on diversity, supporting diversity, mastering competencies to respond to diversity, and dealing with attitudes toward diverse responses of workers and patients should be systematically developed in institutions. All staff members in institutions should be expected to participate in efforts to clarify values, develop strategic plans, and identify critical questions and policy issues. Policies ranging from recruitment and retention, attendance in cultural training programs, rewards and grievances related to racism, sexism, and culturally inappropriate behaviours should be discussed and instituted.

Examples of changes in existing policies in organisations and/or of instituting new policies range from the simple to the most comprehensive: required readings for all, revising patient and health assessment tools, and overhauling curricula to make them congruent with diverse cultures.

Although the ideals of culturally competent care are becoming increasingly valued in multicultural societies, they may remain simply 'lip service' without policy changes to assure that they are implemented. Currently, some health care agencies provide excellent care because they have bicultural and other staff who are committed to culturally competent programs. It is our impression that the majority of health care agencies do not voluntarily institute policies unless required to do so by federal or local governments. Examples of policy changes might be guided by the guidelines in Appendix A. One example is a policy that ensures language access for patients who do not speak the dominant language, but the policies must be backed up with funding, for example, a dedicated interpreter program, rather than simply 'borrowing' bilingual staff. The Johnson et al. study (1999) pointed out a lack of clarity about what was official policy about using language resources.

Interpreters and cultural brokers
Interpreters

Interpreters are a critical component of culturally competent care, but their roles and utilisation vary. The study by Johnson et al. (1999) found a matrix of types of interpretation based on continua of language fluency (cultural understanding without fluency, social fluency and complex verbalisation) and situations requiring decisions on how language skills are used (greetings and social conversation to transfer complex health and medico-legal information). Particular issues pointed out by participants were inappropriate use of staff at the wrong level, e.g. support staff who were not fluent in English for complicated communication, such as obtaining consent or a drain on bilingual nursing and administrative staff called to other areas to interpret.

Culture brokers

Culture brokers are usually bilingual and bicultural, and may represent immigrant communities who receive services in the health care system. A culture broker helps health care providers shape their care of patients in ways that should lead to greater success and better patient outcomes. Tasks include assessing health beliefs that influence patients' behaviour, identifying areas of difference or incompatibility with those of the provider, and initiating mediation or negotiation. A culture broker may serve as a liaison between patients and their families, between the patient and the milieu, and the patient/family and staff in order to facilitate communication and mutual education. Tripp-Reimer and Brink (1985) consider cultural brokerage a nursing intervention that bridges, negotiates between or links the orthodox health care system with clients of different cultures. Culture brokers interpret both language and culture (Jezewski 1993).

A variation on the culture broker is a cultural consultant, who takes more responsibility than cultural interpretation by helping to direct care for specific patients. The consultant can be a direct care provider or perhaps an anthropologist who acts as a therapy facilitator (Nichter et al. 1985) to interpret patient behaviour in socio-cultural context and make suggestions to improve care. An important role is helping the staff answer the question, 'Is this behaviour normal?' For example, in Budman et al. (1992), Meleis described participating in family meetings to interpret between an Arab patient's parents and staff, attending team conferences, and helping the therapists interpret what they observed in cultural context. She encouraged the staff to appreciate immigrant transition stress and alerted them to Arab culture with regard to normal family interaction, the place of the youngest son in the family and the propensity to sacrifice everything for the children.

Whatever the background or discipline, the cultural consultant needs an in-depth knowledge of the world views of both the health care providers and the patient and family, including values, communication and problem-solving styles, with the goal of helping each understand the other's framework without favouring or alienating either. Ideally bi-cultural and bi-lingual, the consultant should be aware of his or her own identity, behaviour and biases. These can help the consultant go beyond translation and include interpretation of symbols and values within a cultural context.

Training

Training programs need to be instituted to raise consciousness of issues, help staff develop culturally sensitivity and competence, clarify their values, gain skills and troubleshoot issues. We propose two types of training programs, workshops and case-focused review through grand rounds in hospitals, agencies, or issue-focused discussions in institutions of higher education. Both will require continuous planning for initial workshops and systematic, periodic follow-up to support emerging competencies and help participants deal with higher level questions as they emerge.

Workshops

Workshops can be used to teach the basics of culturally competent care, such as cross-cultural communication and cultural assessment. However, it cannot be assumed that a one-hour lecture or one-day workshop will do more than alert nurses to the issues. Unless workshops are required, they are usually attended only by those who do not need convincing of the importance of this topic. How much one learns in a workshop depends on one's readiness to integrate the material and the reason for attending. Nurses may be more willing to attend in the wake of cross-cultural difficulties, either between nurses and patients or between nurses from different backgrounds.

Typical half-day or full-day workshops often begin with a keynote speaker followed by speakers on different topics or perhaps different ethnic groups. Some workshops are mainly presentations while others include experiential learning as well. There is often an attempt to include a panel of representatives from the most populous ethnic or immigrant groups served by the agency. Individuals telling their own stories often have more impact on practising nurses than more academically-oriented speakers. Simply presenting information, however, usually has less impact than involving the audience in experiential work that pushes them to examine their own backgrounds and values. Diversity training often uses such an approach, focusing on the participants themselves rather than focusing on 'the other'.

Case conferences

Problematic patient situations can be used effectively to improve cultural competence because they ground generalities in a specific situation and require that staff use it to improve care. A conference could begin with presenting the cultural context of the patient situation, discussion of the specific patient/family and problems, and end with deciding on potentially more effective interventions.

Grand rounds or case conferences

Planning case- or issue-focused conferences on a regular basis in institutions of higher education, as well as health care organisations, are vital for developing skills and compliance. Modelling culturally competent behaviour by grounding it in presenting problematic patient responses, inappropriate health care responses, interventions, models of excellence in cultural sensitivity, ethical dilemmas, and students' responses in diversity environments are essential for growth in organisations. These approaches are usually very effective methods in clarifying values, providing strategies and enhancing skills.

Administrative issues

Supporting culturally competent care may be difficult without cooperation between nursing leadership and nurses providing direct care. There may be individual enthusiastic staff members who work to improve cultural competence in their agencies or units, but the entire agency will not be involved without support from the top. For example, UCSF had a longstanding Cultural Diversity Enhancement Committee that began with a small group of ethnic minority nurses getting together to discuss common issues. It would have remained only an interest group, had the director of the nursing service not acknowledged the importance of the topic and staff involvement by providing financial support for the committee. With funding, the committee held continuing education workshops for hospital staff, conducted a survey of diversity staff and patient issues, and developed a resource book on the cultural groups most served by the hospital. It also became a resource for staff who had experienced racial or ethnic discrimination.

Role modelling is a second area in which agency nursing leadership can encourage cultural competence. Nurse leaders who demonstrate cultural competence in their interactions with other nurses and patients/families provide a powerful message about the importance of this topic. They are leading by demonstrating. An example is a clinical nurse specialist in cardiology who scheduled case conferences on Arabic-speaking patients who needed frequent admittance to the hospital because of medication noncompliance. She also worked with the patients in a culturally appropriate way, and her success with these patients is an example of leading by demonstrating.

CONCLUSION

There is a growing commitment among nurses to provide culturally competent care in culturally diverse countries, as evidenced in the attention given to diversity in nursing education, program development and the establishment of clinics or health care teams that can address the needs of immigrant or non-English speaking patients, or to those who have been historically marginalised. These efforts need to be theory driven, have better documentation and, in particular, be driven by studies to determine whether improving the cultural competence of health care makes a difference to such outcomes as reducing disease, improving health promotion, increasing the satisfaction of patients and providers and reducing costs. Predictive studies may also provide support for outcomes of providing culturally competent care on the number of incidents that interfere with the healing process and/or prolong illness or hospital stays.

Areas that need work include developing and evaluating culturally appropriate interventions and increasing access to culturally competent care based on cumulative knowledge that is theoretically sound and methodologically valid (Meleis et al. 1995).

Research is needed, for example, on the transition experience of immigrants, to provide an opportunity for comparison and address the issues surrounding language, accuracy, symbolic interpretation and competence in uncovering culturally contexted meanings. More published knowledge is needed on cultural groups about which little has been written, such as South Americans, Africans, Eastern Europeans and Middle Easterners, as well as the elderly or the disabled in all ethnic and immigrant groups. We need to develop and test nursing interventions to decrease structural barriers in accessing health care, such as language, non-biomedical treatment modalities, and use of indigenous healers, among others. Another major need is developing understanding of culturally appropriate health promoting behaviours.

Nurse leaders can promote such efforts in hospital and community settings through proposing and supporting policy changes that are committed to culturally competent care, supporting clinical research, and lobbying for cultural content throughout all levels of educational programs for nurses.

Reflective exercise

1   Reflect on the organisation in which you work. What policies are in place to promote diversity?

2   How have your cultural background and life experiences prepared you for understanding the perspectives and concerns of other people?

3   How does your organisation protect the rights of patients and staff from minority groups?

RECOMMENDED READINGS

Campinha-Bacote, J. (1998). The process of cultural competence in the delivery of health care services. *Journal of Transcultural Nursing, 10,* 290–1.

Giger, J. N., & Davidhizar, R. (1999). *Transcultural nursing: Assessment and intervention.* 3rd edn, St. Louis, MO: Mosby.

Lipson, J., & Meleis, A. (1985). Culturally appropriate care: The case of immigrants. *Topics in Clinical Nursing, 7,* 48–56.

Purnell, L., & Paulanka, B. (2002). *Transcultural health care: A culturally competent approach.* 2nd edn. Philadelphia, PA: F. A. Davis.

Rorie, J., Paine, L., & Berger, M. (1996). Primary care for women: Cultural competence in primary care issues. *Journal of Nurse Midwifery, 41* (2), 92–100.

APPENDIX A

ASSURING CUTURAL COMPETENCE IN HEALTH CARE: RECOMMENDATIONS FOR NATIONAL STANDARDS AND AN OUTCOMES-FOCUSED RESEARCH AGENDA

Federal Register: December 22, 2000 (Volume 65, Number 247) [Page 80865–80879]
Produced for the Office of Minority Health, Public Health Service, U.S. Department of Health and Human Serivices

This project makes recommendations for national standards for culturally and linguistically appropriate services (CLAS) in health care. Based on an analytical review of key laws, regulations, contracts and standards currently in use by federal and state agencies and other national organisations, these standards were developed with input from a national advisory committee of policymakers, health care providers and researchers. Each standard is accompanied by commentary that addresses the proposed guideline's relationship to existing laws and standards, and offers recommendations for implementation and oversight to providers, policymakers and advocates.

1   Health care organizations should ensure that patients/consumers receive from all staff members effective, understandable, and respectful care that is provided in a manner compatible with their cultural health beliefs and practices and preferred language.

2   Health care organizations should implement strategies to recruit, retain, and promote at all levels of the organization a diverse staff and leadership that are representative of the demographic characteristics of the service area.

3   Health care organizations should ensure that staff at all levels and across all disciplines receive ongoing education and training in culturally and linguistically appropriate service delivery.

4   Health care organizations must offer and provide language assistance services, including bilingual staff and interpreter services, at no cost to each patient/ consumer with limited English proficiency at all points of contact, in a timely manner during all hours of operation.

5   Health care organizations must provide to patients/consumers in their preferred language both verbal offers and written notices informing them of their right to receive language assistance services.

6 Health care organizations must assure the competence of language assistance provided to limited english proficient patients/consumers by interpreters and bilingual staff. Family and friends should not be used to provide interpretation services (except on request by the patient/consumer).

7 Health care organizations must make available easily understood patient-related materials and post signage in the languages of the commonly encountered groups and/or groups represented in the service area.

8 Health care organizations should develop, implement, and promote a written strategic plan that outlines clear goals, policies, operational plans, and management accountability/oversight mechanisms to provide culturally and linguistically appropriate services.

9 Health care organizations should conduct initial and ongoing organizational self-assessments of CLAS-related activities and are encouraged to integrate cultural and linguistic competence-related measures into their internal audits, performance improvement programs, patient satisfaction assessments, and outcomes-based evaluations.

10 Health care organizations should ensure that data on the individual patient's/consumer's race, ethnicity, and spoken and written language are collected in health records, integrated into the organization's management information systems, and periodically updated.

11 Health care organizations should maintain a current demographic, cultural, and epidemiological profile of the community, as well as a needs assessment to accurately plan for and implement services that respond to the cultural and linguistic characteristics of the service area.

12 Health care organizations should develop participatory, collaborative partnerships with communities and utilize a variety of formal and informal mechanisms to facilitate community and patient/ consumer involvement in designing and implementing CLAS-related activities.

13 Health care organizations should ensure that conflict and grievance resolution processes are culturally and linguistically sensitive and capable of identifying, preventing, and resolving cross-cultural conflicts or complaints by patients/consumers.

14 Health care organizations are encouraged to regularly make available to the public information about their progress and successful innovations in implementing the CLAS standards and to provide public notice in their communities about the availability of this information.

CHAPTER SIX

Leadership ethics in nursing and health care domains

Megan-Jane Johnstone

LEARNING OBJECTIVES

At the completion of this chapter, the reader will be able to:

▲ describe the nature of leadership ethics in nursing and health care domains;

▲ discuss seven key characteristics of ethical leadership;

▲ outline six undesirable moral consequences of unethical leadership;

▲ explore three key processes for improving ethical practices and standards in nursing and health care domains; and

▲ evaluate their own capacity for ethical leadership.

KEY WORDS
Ethical leadership, moral conduct, power, role modelling, organisations

INTRODUCTION

Nursing leaders at all levels and in all areas of practice have to deal on a daily basis with a range of ethical issues associated with the management and provision of high quality health care to various individuals, families and groups, as well as to entire populations across the continuum of care. One of the greatest challenges (and perhaps also one of the greatest dilemmas) facing nursing leaders today is how best to lead the continual development, improvement and provision of high quality health care services to diverse populations in diverse settings, while also ensuring that they remain economically viable in the face of ever dwindling and often severely reduced health care resources.

The primary mission of health care organisations today is to deliver safe, appropriate, high quality and viable health care serves to individuals and groups in the communities they serve. Whether a health care organisation will be able to fulfil its mission and remain economically viable (as well as accessible to its target patient populations) in today's rapidly changing social–cultural climate, and whether it will be able to 'plan for and respond appropriately to marketplace forces, while maintaining a coherent vision of its values and their meaning', will depend ultimately on the ethics of its leadership (Spencer et al. 2000, p.10). Indeed, there is an emerging consensus that ethical leadership is crucial for the future survival, viability and flourishing of health care (Spencer et al. 2000) and, it should be added, the nursing services upon which health care depends.

Although leadership ethics is of obvious importance to those working in the fields of nursing and health care, curiously little has been written on the topic in the nursing, health professional or bioethics literature. One reason for this might be that many think that ethics in general, and leadership ethics in particular, is a matter of 'practical knowledge, not theoretical knowledge [and] that practical knowledge and common sense (and exemplary moral character) are adequate for discussion on ethics in their particular field' (Ciulla 1998c, p.5). However, leadership ethics in general and nursing leadership ethics in particular requires much more than practical know-how and commonsense. While these things are necessary and important to the realisation of the means and ends of ethical leadership in nursing and health care domains, they are not sufficient. Other characteristics, knowledge and behaviours are also required, as this chapter will attempt to show.

In the discussion to follow, brief attention will be given to:

▲ clarifying the nature of leadership ethics in nursing and health care domains, and the relationship between ethical leadership and effective leadership;

▲ discussing seven key characteristics of ethical leadership; and

▲ exploring strategies for improving ethical practices and standards in nursing and health care domains.

LEADERSHIP ETHICS IN NURSING AND HEALTH CARE DOMAINS

In beginning this discussion, it is important to clarify that leadership ethics is distinct from—and ought to be distinguished from—other (albeit related) sub-fields of ethics such as business ethics, management ethics, health care ethics, medical ethics and nursing ethics. In contradistinction to these other sub-fields, leadership ethics is a relatively new field of inquiry that has as its focus a set of ethical issues that are distinctive to the field of leadership, hence the notion 'leadership ethics'. According to Ciulla (1998c), leadership ethics may be defined as:

> The study of ethical issues related to *leadership* and the *ethics of leadership*. The study generally consists of the examination of right, wrong, good, evil, virtue, duty, obligation, rights, justice, fairness, and so on, in human relationships with each other and other living things (Ciulla 1998c, p.4). [emphasis added]

A distinguishing feature of leadership ethics is the profound relationship that exists between *ethical* leadership and *effective* leadership. One author has even suggested that 'ethics lies at the very heart of leadership' and that without ethics there can be no leadership, only 'mis-leadership' of the kind exemplified by Adolf Hitler (Ciulla 1998b, p. xv). Ciulla explains:

> Managers and generals can act like playground bullies and use their power and rank force to force their will on people, but this is *coercion* [tyranny], not *leadership*. Leadership is not a person or a position. It is a complex moral relationship between people, based on trust, obligation, commitment, emotion, and a shared vision of the good (Ciulla (1998b, p. xv). [emphasis added]

In several respects, ethical leadership is synonymous with effective leadership. This is because many of the key characteristics of ethical leadership (to be discussed in more detail in the next section) are also the characteristics of effective leadership. As discussed in the previous chapters of this book, leadership is first and foremost about vision and transformation. Improvement in any organisation or system requires transformation or change since the very nature of improvement involves 'departure from the status quo' (DuBrin 2000, p.5). A key and critical goal of any leader is to guide the people they work with (otherwise known as their constituents) to develop robust adaptation to new challenges and to foster in them an enduring resilience that will enable them to deal effectively (not merely cope) with other future challenges (Heifetz 1994).

In order to be able to influence and guide others to respond effectively to adaptive challenge and to work collaboratively to achieve a moral vision, leaders must first establish and develop a genuine partnership with the people they are working with. Developing partnerships, in turn, requires the building of meaningful and constructive relationships. Building relationships, in turn, involves the leader working *with*, not *against* his or her constituents, and consistently upholding two top leadership qualities:

▲ integrity (being strongly committed to doing what he or she knows is right); and

▲ trustworthiness (worthy of being trusted; that is, honest, reliable, and dependable) (adapted from DuBrin 2000, p.70; Ciulla 1998a).

Effective leadership involves the ethical influence of other people to realise a vision and achieve positive and constructive change that is of moral benefit to stakeholders. In many important respects (on account of the moral importance of health itself), nursing and health care leaders have a special and perhaps greater obligation to influence transformational change in the organisations and systems in which they work, and thereby challenge and change the status quo—especially in regard to the provision of high quality health care services to the individuals, groups and communities they serve (Johnstone 2002a; 2002c).

SEVEN KEY CHARACTERISTICS OF ETHICAL LEADERSHIP

According to DuBrin (2000), most people want their leaders to be ethical. An important question to be raised here is: What are the characteristics of ethical leadership?

There are at least seven key characteristics of ethical leadership. In summary, these are:

▲ moral conduct and adherence to ethical standards;

▲ moral purpose (moral vision and commitment to achieving moral ends);

▲ moral accomplishment (achieving desirable moral outcomes);

▲ moral duty/responsibility and obligations;

▲ moral knowing (knowing that/knowing how);

▲ moral cooperation and the just exercise of power; and

▲ moral role modelling (leading by example).

Moral conduct and adherence to ethical standards

The first key characteristic of ethical leadership to be considered here is the exemplification of moral character via moral conduct and adherence to ethical standards.

Conduct is literally the manner in which a person behaves or, to put it more simply, a person's behaviour. Moral conduct, by this view, refers to moral behaviour; that is, behaviour which accords with sound standards of ethics. Moral conduct thus presupposes the existence of—and the personal adoption of and strict adherence to—certain ethical standards of behaviour (Beauchamp & Childress 2001; Johnstone 1999).

Moral leaders conduct themselves in accordance with the moral standards they deem to be appropriate, both for themselves and their constituents. Moreover, they uphold the moral standards they have adopted *consistently*—that is, they are consistently moral in their behaviour and endeavours towards others, irrespective of the situation at hand. Moral leaders do not have to be manipulated, coerced or cajoled into conducting themselves morally. Their moral conduct is motivated largely by their own personal moral commitment to and integrity in regard to achieving desirable moral ends, and to literally 'leading the moral life' in the contexts in which they live and work.

Moral purpose (moral vision and commitment to achieving moral ends)

A second key characteristic of ethical leadership is moral purpose, encompassing moral vision and an intense commitment to achieving desirable moral ends or goals. But what is moral purpose?

Purpose may be defined as the intention and determination to do something. Moral purpose, in turn, may be defined as the moral intention to achieve something moral;

in this instance, a moral vision keyed to the achievement of certain desirable moral ends. According to Krause (1997):

> A leader develops intense determination to achieve his [or her] vision and his [or her] objectives. Intense determination creates high morale and spirit among constituents. This allows the leader to effectively employ both personal and organizational power to accomplish goals. The leader uses this power to direct and control the efforts of his [or her] followers (p.37).

Similarly, the moral leader develops 'intense determination', notably, to achieve specific moral ends and associated moral objectives. The intense determination in this instance not only inspires high morale and spirit among constituents, but trust and a sense of moral safety as well. The moral leader uses his or her power 'ethically' to motivate and empower his or her constituents to realise the moral vision at issue and to fulfil the moral objectives associated with the vision.

In working to achieve his or her vision, the moral leader:

▲ resolves to do his/her best for those to whom she/he owes a duty;

▲ strives to do what is 'right', rather than what is easy or expedient;

▲ avoids actions that can create injustice;

▲ develops an empathic understanding of his/her constituents in order to bring the best out of them; and

▲ demonstrates depth of purpose by way of:
   - tact and diplomacy
   - tolerance for ambiguity
   - reliability and loyalty
   - diligence and quality
   - regard for others (adapted from Krause 1997, pp.37, 40, 42 & 47).

Moral accomplishment (achieving desirable moral outcomes)

A third key characteristic of ethical leadership is moral accomplishment and the achievement of desirable moral outcomes. Indeed, moral leadership would not be evident without moral accomplishment and the achievement of desirable moral ends. The successful achievement of moral ends is the foundation of ethical leadership. Whether a given achievement can be judged as 'successful', all things considered, will depend on: (i) the means used to achieve them (notably whether the means used were themselves ethical); and (ii) whether the genuine moral interests of constituents (notably their welfare and well-being) were maximised.

It is important to clarify that moral conduct is not a passive behaviour. For instance, merely *thinking* about moral conduct, or supporting its causes intellectually, is not the same as moral conduct in and of itself. By its very nature, moral conduct is synonymous with moral action and the accomplishment of desirable moral goals. This raises the question: what is moral action?

Action may be defined as the state or process of doing something. Moral action, in turn, may be defined as something (that is, some physical process, preceded by an act of moral will; an occurrence effected by the volition of a human agent) that someone does in order to achieve a desirable moral outcome.

As stated above, moral action is not merely a thought about doing something. For instance, thinking that such-and-such is the right thing to do is not the same as actually doing it. Merely thinking: 'I should develop a policy on conscientious objection to be implemented in my workplace' is not the same as actually drafting a policy on conscientious objection, submitting it to the relevant authorities for approval, and overseeing its implementation in the workplace once approved. Moral action, in contrast to a mere thought of moral action, is the 'deed done'. It is the physical process that occurs as a direct consequence of a given thought-to-action. Although moral action and moral thought are closely connected, it is the deed done that ultimately distinguishes a moral action from the mere thought of moral action (Johnstone 2002c).

Moral accomplishment (and the achievement of desirable moral ends) requires knowledge and skill. Not only must a moral leader know that (e.g. that a certain moral action is required) but also know how (e.g. how to go about achieving the desirable moral end). Knowing how, in turn, requires practical knowledge of applied ethics (see, for example, Beauchamp & Childress 2001; Johnstone 1999), not merely knowledge about leadership.

Moral duty/responsibility and obligations

A fourth key characteristic of ethical leadership is moral duty and the fulfilment of certain 'special' moral responsibilities and obligations associated with the role. In several important respects, leadership is itself a moral duty in the sense that it involves a moral imperative to achieve desirable moral ends/goals. By this view, ethical leadership is not, as might be assumed by some, a moral right (i.e. a special entitlement or privilege one is owed and which ought to be protected for moral reasons).

As can be readily demonstrated, people who do not take seriously the moral duty of leadership (or the complex responsibilities and obligations associated with the role) can cause enormous harm to individuals, groups and communities, as well as to the organisations and institutions in which they work. It is the potential to cause otherwise avoidable harm to others that imposes on nurse leaders a 'special' responsibility to ensure that they know and understand:

▲ the moral duties, responsibilities and obligations inherent in the leadership role generally;

▲ the moral duties, responsibilities and obligations inherent in their specific leadership roles; and

▲ how best to fulfil the duty of leadership overall.

According to Krause (1997):

A leader embraces the duties and obligations that grow from the trust and power given him [or her]. The most critical of these obligations are clear perception, determined action, and an overriding concern for the best interests of his [or her] constituents. A true leader owns up to the results of his [or her] decisions and actions and shares their consequences along with his [or her] constituents (p.59).

Krause then goes on to list what he believes are the nine responsibilities of effective leaders:

▲ To see clearly when he [or she] looks.

▲ To hear correctly when he [or she] listens.

- To think carefully when he [or she] speaks.

- To inquire critically when he [or she] doubts.

- To show respect when he [or she] serves.

- To maintain calm when he [or she] is challenged.

- To consider the consequences when he [or she] decides.

- To create desirable results when he [or she] works.

- To do what is right when he [or she] acts (1997, p.60).

Moral knowing (knowing that/knowing how)

A fifth key characteristic of ethical leadership is moral knowing (also referred to as moral competence). Ethical leaders are, by virtue of their position, also ethical decision-makers. As such, it is important that they have:

- mastery of the requisite moral knowledge and skills necessary for competent moral decision-making; and

- soundness of judgement otherwise necessary for making sound *moral* judgements and decisions (Johnstone 1999, p.186).

Leaders as moral decision-makers must know not just *that* something is the right thing to do in such-and-such a case (moral knowing that), but also to know *how* (in a performative sense) best to do it. Merely having an epistemology (theoretical knowledge) of ethics may not be sufficient in a given scenario to resolve the moral problem at hand; leaders also need 'practical know-how' in regard to applying the theoretical knowledge they have (Johnstone 1999, pp.186–7). This practical know-how may need to include skills for dealing with interpersonal conflicts (akin to family therapy), such as: 'reframing, reconstructing narratives, and shifting from conflict to meta-reflective postures' (Gergen 1994, p.112).

Keys to successful ethical leadership are the following kinds of moral knowing:

- fundamental moral knowing (the art of recognising and responding effectively to ethical issues);

- strategic moral knowing (understanding the significant moral interests, needs, motivations and goals of constituents); and

- tactical moral knowing (taking appropriate and justifiable moral action to avoid harm/promote benefits) (Johnstone 1998).

Ethical leaders who lack moral knowing (moral competence) risk a number of undesirable moral consequences, such as:

- unsound moral decision-making;

- unsound moral action;

- causing hurt and moral harm;

- creating moral conflict;

- perpetrating injustice (including the unjust imposition of their own values on others, *viz.* 'moral bullying'); and

▲ the abdication of their broader moral responsibilities ('moral buck-passing') (Johnstone 1999, p.197).

Moral cooperation and the just exercise of power

A sixth key characteristic of ethical leadership is moral cooperation and the just exercise of power. A fundamental challenge facing ethical leaders is how to lead and achieve robust adaptation and transformational change without destroying his or her constituents in the process. Critical to the success of transformational change, dealing with adaptive challenge and the maximisation of constituent welfare is securing the moral cooperation of constituents and the creative power that comes with it.

It will be recalled that a key goal of leadership is to 'accomplish [morally] useful and desirable things' (Krause 1997, p.8). An unjust exercise of power by a leader may not only fail to achieve this key goal, but may cause otherwise avoidable harm to constituents in the process. As can be widely demonstrated, power that is exercised without moral constraint (unjustly) can be extremely harmful—sometimes irreversibly so. Let us explore this idea further.

Power (from the Vulgar Latin *potére*, meaning unattested, and from Latin *posse*, meaning to be able) is the ability or capacity to do something. In the case of leadership, DuBrin (2000) suggests that power is about having the ability or capacity to help others. He writes: 'Power gives a person the resources to help others. A powerful person, for example, might be able to find a job for someone in need of employment' (p.22).

Leaders are often in an optimal position to help others achieve worthy ends and, more specifically, to help people 'change for the better and make their lives better' (Ciulla 1998b, p. xvi). Helping others, in turn, can improve the status quo by contributing in beneficial ways to the respective contexts in which people live and work. Power that is exercised in a just and beneficial way—and which is used to achieve desirable moral ends—can be justifiably characterised as a virtue, that is, as a morally excellent quality or capacity.

Not all power is exercised in a just and beneficent way. Indeed, there are many historical examples of power being exercised viciously (the deeds of Nazis doctors and Nazi health administrators being a case in point. See, for example, Caplan 1992; Lifton 1986). Vicious (that is, cruel and wicked) acts of power are unethical, and contrary to the tenets of effective leadership. As Hollander (1998, p.50) correctly points out, 'Hurting people is usually not the way to get the best from them'.

Health care leaders who use their power in vicious ways often hurt stakeholder organisations and the people who are associated with them; they also fail to achieve positive and constructive (transformational) change. Power that is used in an unjust and harmful way—and which is used to achieve destructive ends—can be justifiably characterised as a vice; that is, as an immoral, wicked, or evil quality or capacity.

Moral role modelling (leading by example)

A seventh and final key characteristic of ethical leadership to be considered here is moral role modelling and leading by example. Ethical leaders must not only 'preach ethics', they must also practise it. After all, how can leaders credibly claim to be an example for others to follow if they ignore or violate their own ethical standards of conduct—even if only for a moment. As Krause (1997, p.98) challenges, leaders must 'encourage people to strive for excellence by striving for excellence themselves. Lead by example!'

The requirement to be a moral example to others has a rich history dating back to the ancient Greek philosophers (for example, Socrates and Plato), who not only taught ethics to their followers, but 'led the moral life' as well. These and other moral philosophers of the time held the view that it was not possible to both *claim to be moral* and yet not *lead a moral life*. To claim to be moral and yet not lead a moral life was, in their view, inconsistent and dishonourable. If a person really was 'morally upright', this needed to be evident in the way he or she conducted their lives, not merely their speech (rhetoric).

Krause (1997) summarises the demand and its implications for ethical leaders to lead by example as follows:

A leader's actions become a model for the actions of his [or her] constituent group. Further, the leader's character sets the moral tone of leadership. The standards he [or she] sets become the benchmark for the group. The people he [or she] favors become his [or her] flag-bearers. In all situations, the leader is observed and copied: at all times, the leader demonstrates preferred behaviour by his [or her] own actions. The leader sets the example whether he [or she] intends to or not! (p.97).

Before concluding this discussion, a brief word should be said about the importance of emotional intelligence and its relationship to ethical conduct. DuBrin (2000) makes the important point that:

How well a person manages his or her emotions and those of others make an impact on leadership effectiveness. For example, recognizing anger in yourself and others and being able to empathize with people can help you influence others more effectively (p.25).

Leaders who are not able to control their emotions, or who express them inappropriately, undermine their ability to be inspiring, persuading, influencing and motivating—in sum, their ability to be effective leaders. One reason for this is that an inappropriate expression of emotion risks undermining both their trustworthiness and credibility (the 'once bitten, twice shy' phenomenon). Successful change leaders, on the other hand, not only master and control their emotions but 'master the emotional dimension of change through the behaviours they display' (Hooper & Potter 2000, p.9).

IMPROVING ETHICAL PRACTICES AND STANDARDS IN NURSING AND HEALTH CARE DOMAINS*

Nursing and health care leaders have a pivotal role to play in establishing and improving ethical practices and standards in the contexts in which they have a leadership role. Leaders can facilitate the development and maintenance of ethical practice standards in at least three key ways, namely by leading:

▲ the formulation, application and evaluation of meaningful standards of ethical practice;

▲ improvements in the moral culture of the health care organisations in which constituents work; and

▲ the development of organisation ethics.

Formulation, application and evaluation of meaningful standards of ethical practice

Crucial to preventing breaches of the agreed standards of ethical professional conduct in nursing and health care domains is the formulation and enactment of meaningful ethical standards of conduct.

In order for ethical standards to be 'meaningful', a number of conditions must be met:

(a) The standards in question must be part of a larger moral schema that has for its community of users (in this instance, nurses and allied health professionals):

▲ significance (is relevant and will make a material difference to the realisation of morally desirable outcomes in the world);

▲ purpose (offers reasons why moral conduct is imperative);

▲ intention (articulates clearly its moral ends or *telos*); and

▲ value (demonstrates a worthy relation between its significance, purpose and intention) (adapted from Bohm 1989; see also Johnstone 1999, pp.430–2).

(b) The standards in question must have emerged from within and be reflective of the lived moral realities experienced by the community of users (e.g. nurses, allied health professionals), as opposed to being imposed from outside (e.g. moral philosophers). (As a point of clarification, ethical standards emerging from a group's lived reality are an essential part of the fabric of that group's lived moral experience; among other things, they serve the vital function of providing a set of 'common moral perceptions' that can be drawn upon to 'reality test' (objectify) and 'validate' group members' day-to-day moral judgements and interventions) (Johnstone 1998, 1999).

(c) The community of users (e.g. nurse constituents) must feel they have a place in the larger moral scheme of things: that is, they must feel connected with (as opposed to isolated from) other members in the community of users, have a coherent and harmonious relationship with other members in the community of users, and, importantly, feel they have something to offer (even if this something is 'small') to and in this larger moral scheme of things (adapted from Pylkkanen 1989).

Once formulated, it is essential that ethical standards of practice are 'kept before the community of users', internalised as a way of life, and, more importantly, enacted. As is exemplified in the case of codes of ethical conduct, it is very easy for the documented ethical standards of a profession or organisation to sit 'gathering dust on shelves' (Derry 1991). In addition, a community of users might fall into the trap of erroneously thinking that just because they have personally endorsed a formally stated code of ethics or have 'done ethics' (i.e. studied a subject or a course on ethics), they have discharged their moral responsibilities as ethical professionals and do not need to do anything more.

It is crucial that ethical standards are seen to be more than just a list of statements which members can and have endorsed. Rather, they must be seen as means for accomplishing shared ethical goals—as a way of life, and not merely as a set of the ideas about a way of life. One way of achieving this is through the effective communication of agreed ethical standards of conduct. To be effective, the communication of ethical standards must happen repeatedly and more frequently through *actions*, rather than through the mere distribution of documents (codes of ethics), such as through the mail or by displaying wall posters (Derry 1991).

Improving the moral culture of organisations

The culture of health care organisations can make it extremely difficult for practitioners (especially nurses) to function as morally accountable and responsible professionals. As discussed elsewhere (Johnstone 1998, 2002a), some health care organisations are 'morally impaired' and even hostile to moral excellence. Practitioners can lose their jobs and be publicly vilified for taking a moral stand and/or upholding ethical standards of practice and the agreed ethical standards of their profession (Johnstone 1994, 1998, 1999).

Organisations can support ethical behaviour in at least two ways: (i) by removing the disincentives to behaving ethically; and (ii) by providing positive incentives for behaving ethically (Derry 1991). One of the greatest disincentives facing constituents is a reasonably founded fear of being punished for questioning and challenging the moral status quo (see, for example, Johnstone 1994, 1999). Obviously, if constituents fear being punished then they may not come forward when the need arises. This, in turn, could risk otherwise avoidable and preventable moral harms from occurring. Were such harms to occur, this would be an undesirable, unsatisfactory and indefensible moral outcome for all concerned.

In contrast, positive incentives for moral conduct could encourage constituents to 'come forward'. Borrowing from Derry (1991), incentives for moral conduct can include:

> listening, responding on the basis of others' needs rather than on the basis of one's own needs, building strong relationships, making decisions on the basis of responsibility to others, giving feedback, nurturing, building cooperation rather than confrontation (Derry 1991, pp.121–36).

Leading the development of organisation ethics

Key to improving a health care organisation's moral culture is the development, promotion and maintenance of organisation ethics. Organisation ethics is a relatively new concept and is defined here as:

> the study of institutional moral agency, the analysis of institutional culture, and the explanation of how institutions make decisions that may or may not create a balance of benefits over harms, that respects its members and other institutions, that are or are not fair, or that manifest a good (or questionable) moral character (Spencer et al. 2000, p.17).

A primary aim of organisational ethics is to develop and foster an organisation's 'ethical climate'; that is:

▲ its organisational culture—'where the missions and visions of the organization are consistent with its expectations for professional and managerial performance and consistent with the goals of the organization as they are actually practiced'; and

▲ the shared perceptions 'of how ethical issues should be addressed and what is ethically correct behaviour for the organization' (Spencer et al. 2000, pp.6, 27).

In regard to 'shared perceptions', proponents of organisation ethics argue that even though organisations are typically comprised of people (constituents) from diverse backgrounds who hold diverse and sometimes conflicting moral values and beliefs, it is nevertheless possible for an organisation (and its 'placeholders') to share, agree on, and commit to a set of 'minimum standards'. Such standards include:

> what most, if not all, would agree are the 'bads'. They include gratuitous harm, unfair practices, processes, or outcomes; lying; breaking promises and contracts; and not respecting individuals and their rights (Spencer et al. 2000, p.29).

To be effective and to have an impact (that is, 'to work'), an organisation ethics program cannot exist merely in the minds of those who support it. To work, it must:

▲ be visible throughout the organisation; and

▲ be vested with some degree of authority, else risk cynical criticism that it is 'all very well in theory, but no good in practice'.

To be both meaningful and effective, programs designed to advance organisation ethics must aim to:

▲ develop and evaluate the organisation's mission;

▲ create a positive ethical climate within the organisation that perpetuates the mission;

▲ develop decision models for ensuring this perpetuation as reflected in organisational activities; and

▲ serve as a 'cheer leader', evaluator, and critic of organisational, professional, and managerial behaviour (Spencer et al. 2000, pp.3–4).

It is perhaps important to point out here that responsibility and accountability for the success or failure of an organisation ethics programs does not lie solely or even predominantly with organisation leaders: constituents (alias 'placeholders') are also responsible and accountable. Spencer et al (2000) explain:

> Each individual, while working in the formal organization, is a placeholder who is expected to carry out her [or his] role obligations in her official capacity as defined by the organization, rather than consider her own interests values, or professional commitments (pp.21–2).

CONCLUSION

An organisation's moral culture and organisation ethics can be improved by leaders (and constituents) championing the following activities:

▲ formulating and articulating, through democratic processes, an organisation's own ethical standards of conduct (for example, in the form of an organisational code of ethics, position statements and policies);

▲ facilitating repeated, regular and effective communication of ethical standards and policies through printed information, stakeholder access to resource people, and role modelling of ethical conduct;

▲ supporting the establishment of institutional ethics committees and other forums (for example, nursing ethics forums/committees) for the purposes of enabling the discussion of ethical issues in a 'safe place' outside of the usual hierarchy of power and authority characteristic of institutions (see also Johnstone 1998);

▲ supporting 'moral quality assurance' programs and the monitoring of 'key moral performance indicators' (KMPIs) (see also Johnstone 1996); and

▲ rewarding moral conduct; this can include: 'praise, recognition, action on suggestions, responsiveness, setting examples, making positive examples of people for desired ethical actions' (adapted from Derry 1991, pp.121–36).

Nursing and health care leaders have a stringent responsibility to be ethical and to lead developments and improvement in organisation ethics. Being ethical and leading moral challenge and change is not, however, the responsibility only of leaders. Constituents (placeholders) also have a stringent responsibility to be ethical and to lead moral change. This is because, ultimately, all individuals (including constituents) are independently morally accountable and responsible for their own actions, not just an excellent few. Furthermore, as part of their responsibility as moral stakeholders, it is beholden on constituents to question and call into question the moral status quo and to challenge the 'taken-for-granted' moral assumptions that underpin the practices and standards of the organisations in which they work.

In the opening paragraph of this chapter it was suggested that one of the greatest challenges facing nursing leaders today is how best to lead the continual development, improvement and provision of high quality health care services to diverse populations in diverse settings, while also remaining economically viable in the face of ever dwindling and often severely reduced health care resources. Perhaps an even greater challenge facing nursing leaders today is how to lead these processes with integrity and in a manner that upholds the ultimate standards of leadership ethics. It is hoped that the discussion presented in this chapter will assist both leaders and constituents to reflect on how they might best meet this challenge collectively and collaboratively both now and in the future.

Reflective exercise

1 What is the relationship between ethical leadership and effective leadership in nursing and health care domains?

2 How might the principles of leadership ethics be applied by individual nurses when caring for patients and promoting patient health outcomes?

3 In what ways might the moral culture of health care organisations be improved through ethical leadership?

RECOMMENDED READINGS

Ciulla, J. B. (1998a). *Ethics, the heart of leadership.* Westport, Connecticut: Praeger.

Johnstone, M. (2002a). Poor working conditions and the moral capacity of nurses. *Contemporary Nurse, 12*(3), 213–24.

Johnstone, M. (2002b). The changing focus of health care ethics: Implications for health care professionals. *Contemporary Nurse, 12*(3), 213–24.

Johnstone, M. (2002c). Taking moral action. In S. Fry, & M. Johnstone. *Ethics in nursing practice: A guide to ethical decision making* (rev. edn) (pp.173–9). London, UK: Blackwell Science/ International Council of Nurses, London UK/Geneva.

Johnstone, M. (1999). *Bioethics: A nursing perspective* (3rd edn). Sydney: Harcourt Australia.

Murray, D. (1997). *Ethics in organizations.* London, UK: Kogan Page.

Spencer, E., Mills, A., Rorty, M., & Erhane, P. (2000). *Organization ethics in health care.* New York: Oxford University Press.

ENDNOTE

★   The discussion under this subheading has drawn extensively from and has used substantial excerpts from the following previously published work: Johnstone, M. 1998. Determining and responding effectively to ethical professional misconduct in nursing: a report to the Nurses Board of Victoria, Melbourne.

CHAPTER SEVEN

Leadership, the law and management of nursing practice

Kim Forrester

LEARNING OBJECTIVES

At the completion of this chapter, the reader will be able to:

▲ identify the sources of the law and the hierarchy of the courts;

▲ identify and describe the elements of an action in negligence and the requirements necessary for a valid consent;

▲ identify legislative options available to redress discrimination or harassment in the workplace;

▲ understand the obligations imposed under the occupational health and safety legislation; and

▲ understand the significance of documentation and the obligation of confidentiality.

KEY WORDS

jurisdiction, negligence, consent, workplace health and safety, confidentiality

INTRODUCTION

The law is a 'man-made' set of rules that control not only what we are compelled to do, but also what we are prohibited from doing. As an example, the law controls contractual arrangements in purchasing good and services, our working conditions and rates of pay; it requires the registration of marriages, births and deaths; it determines how, and at what speed we drive, when and where we can consume alcohol, where we can walk our dogs, dispose of our rubbish, send our children to school, make loud noise and park our car. These are but a few examples of how the law in a very real way regulates the society in which we live and work. In the health care context, the laws control and regulate the boundaries of our practice (for example, who is legally capable of prescribing medications), the standard of our practice (which is enforced through legal actions such as negligence and trespass to the person), and the employment relationships into which we enter (through enterprise agreements or industrial awards). Clearly, in making decisions about how health professionals care for others, they are required to consider the relevant legal principles and the legislative provisions.

Health professionals employed in leadership and management roles are frequently required to have an in-depth knowledge of the legal responsibilities and obligations that attach to their particular level of employment. It will frequently be the case that those in leadership positions will be required to make significant decisions on behalf of either the employing institution, or those they manage or supervise. Regardless of the particular clinical context, the expectation is that when health professionals place themselves in positions of leadership they will have a broad knowledge of the legislative and common law requirements necessary to ensure a safe and appropriate environment for the delivery of health care services. Though many areas of the law impact either directly or indirectly on the day-to-day practices of all heath professionals, the following will address the major legal issues relevant to nursing practice.

LEGAL ISSUES AND CONCEPTS

Sources of the law

An in-depth discussion of the history of the Australian legal system is beyond the scope of this chapter; however, it is important that nurses have an understanding of the relevant legal concepts and structures. The Australian legal system was initially inherited from the British as a function of colonisation. Until federation in 1901, each of the colonies operated as an individual entity with its own constitution, parliament and courts. Upon federation, however, the six States and two Territories joined to form the Commonwealth of Australia, thereby incorporating into the sources of the law not only the State and Territory parliaments and courts, but also legislation passed through the Commonwealth Parliament and the decisions from courts within the federal jurisdiction.

Legislation

Legislation, statutes or Acts, are the names given to laws enacted through the parliamentary process. State and Territory parliaments, and the Commonwealth

Parliament, pass legislation which, in addition to directing and influencing other areas of Australian life, impacts significantly on the provision of health care services. While an Act of Parliament is a primary source of law and therefore takes priority over decisions from the courts, it may also be open to interpretation by judges as part of legal proceedings. That is, particular sections of an Act may require interpretation by the court and, therefore, those interpretations become relevant as to how the Act will be read and applied in the future. In some jurisdictions, however, the law may be codified. This means that the code itself is a complete statement of the law in that particular area. For example, in Queensland, the criminal law is codified into the *Criminal Code 1995* (Qld). The *Criminal Code 1995* (Qld) therefore contains all the laws relevant to the offences created by the code.

The Australian Constitution allows for both the Commonwealth and State parliaments to pass laws on the same area. These are referred to as 'concurrent powers'. However, should there be an inconsistency between the two pieces of legislation, the Commonwealth legislation prevails to the extent of that inconsistency.[1]

Legislation may also provide for the delegation of power to a specified person or body, to make rules, regulations, by-laws or ordinances that are consistent with the Act. This is referred to as delegated legislation and facilitates the practical application of the provisions of the Act. As an example, most professional regulatory authorities have the delegated power to make regulations that detail more precisely their administrative or disciplinary processes. The obligations and rights contained in delegated legislation are as binding as those contained in the parent Act. However, it must be remembered that they are to be interpreted in conjunction with the content of the Act in total and have no force standing alone.

There are many pieces of legislation at both State and Federal levels that apply to, and control, the practice of nurses and the provision of health care services. Nurses must be familiar with legislation that applies within their jurisdiction and be aware that it may differ from the laws as they apply elsewhere.

Common law

Common law is judge-made law. It is the accumulation of legal principles contained in individual judgements that are applied in similar cases that come before the courts. Where cases of comparable circumstances come to court for determination, judges are bound to follow their own decisions or the decisions of courts at the same level or a superior level in the hierarchy. The basic premise is that if a court determines a matter in a particular way today then a similar case should be interpreted in the same way tomorrow.[2] This is the doctrine of precedent, whereby the recording of judicial decisions over many centuries provides a level of certainty and predictability in the legal system. The largest body of case law relevant in a health care context is that pertaining to civil actions in negligence. There being no legislation on this area of health law, nurses must become familiar with the relevant case law to gain an understanding of the principles that guide their practice. For example, the answers to the questions of: 'To whom do I owe a duty of care?' or 'What conduct amounts to a breach of the duty of care?' are to be found in the decisions of judges who have determined these issues in cases that have come before them.

Court hierarchy

The Australian court hierarchy exists at both the State and Commonwealth levels. That is, within the individual States and Territories there is a hierarchy of courts extending from the lower courts, commonly referred to as Local Courts, Magistrates Courts or Courts of Summary Jurisdiction, through to the District or County Courts, Supreme Court and the Full Court, or Court of Appeal of the Supreme Court. The courts outside the State and Territory systems include the Family Courts, Federal Courts and the High Court of Australia. The courts, through their respective legislation, are empowered to hear and determine certain types of cases, and make certain determinations as to penalties and amounts of compensation. This is referred to as the jurisdiction of the court. Should a person be involved in legal proceedings, the type of case and the outcome sought determines which of the courts they would attend. The Australian High Court has the jurisdiction to hear matters involving the interpretation of the Constitution of the Commonwealth of Australia, disputes between States and the Commonwealth and disputes between residents of different States. The High Court may also hear and determine matters on appeal from other courts in the hierarchy. However, this appellate jurisdiction is only available with leave (or permission) from the High Court.

The development of health law within the Australian legal system is based, to a large extent, on the recognition of the rights of the patient, or client, their family and significant others. The following discussion, therefore, is directed to providing information on the common law and legislation that frame the provision of nursing services. It is important to recognise that the scope of the chapter does not permit an extensive examination of all relevant areas of health law. Therefore, a list of recommended readings is provided at the conclusion of the chapter.

CONSUMER RIGHTS

Patients and clients, as the consumers of health care services, have rights and obligations associated with that status. Wallace defines a 'right' as being an entitlement or benefit belonging to a particular person which is recognised by society and can be demanded from others.[3] While there is no formal, nationally recognised 'Bill of Rights' for patients or clients, many individual health care institutions, organisations and government agencies have developed statements of consumer rights[4] that operate in relation to those individuals, and families, under their care. These documents often contain a combination of legally enforceable rights, rights developed through common practices and rights that arise from the goals and aims of the particular institution or group. It is appropriate, therefore, to consider the broad categories of rights that attach to the receipt of health care services by health care consumers.

On the international stage, Australia is a signatory to a number of Declarations, Treaties and Conventions recognising the basic rights of human beings.[5] These include the right of each person to physical security, self-fulfilment, to be treated with dignity and have access to justice. While an individual is unable to pursue a legal action in an Australian court in relation to these rights, they underpin and guide domestic laws. In relation to the rights of consumers of health care in Australia, these are derived from the *International Covenant on Civil and Political Rights*, the *International Covenant on Social, Economic and Cultural Rights*, the *Declaration of the Rights of the Child*, the *Convention on the Rights of the Child*, the *Declaration on the Rights of Mentally Retarded Persons*, and the *Principles for the Protection of Persons with Mental Illnesses and for the Improvement of Mental Health Care*.[6]

Within the Australian legal system, legislation and common law decisions create the following rights within a health care context that are enforceable by law:

▲ The right to reasonable care.

▲ The right not to be abandoned.

▲ The right to prompt treatment.

▲ The right to be informed of the treatment options.

▲ The right to confidentiality.

▲ The right to access their medical files.

▲ The right not to be discriminated against.

▲ The right to lodge a complaint.

▲ The right to refuse treatment.

These rights are protected through specific legislation or legal principles and therefore impose on nurses, and other health care providers, obligations as to how services required by consumers are to be met. As an example, the right of the patient to reasonable care is protected by the civil action in negligence. The right of the patient or client to be informed of treatment options is enforced not only through the common law actions of trespass to the person (civil assault), but also through legislation such as the *Disability Services Act 1986* (Cth). Legislation at both the State and Federal levels protect patients and clients from being discriminated against in the provision of health care services,[7] and legislation in all jurisdictions provides for the lodgement of complaints in relation to the provision of health care services to consumers.[8]

In addition to the above, there are rights that have been established by common practice that include, among others:

▲ The right to access qualified professionals.

▲ The right to a second opinion.

▲ The right to an interpreter.

▲ The right to know the costs of services.

▲ The right to know the available services.

▲ The right to privacy.

▲ The right to seek legal advice.

While litigation, in response to a breach of a legally recognised right, is an option, consumers of health care services may also choose to pursue an alternative means by which to resolve their complaints. All Australian States and Territories have established health consumer complaint mechanisms as part of the national Medicare funding arrangement. These are independent statutory bodies[9] that have the power to assess, investigate, conciliate and report complaints related to the provision of health services as determined by the legislation in the relevant jurisdiction. As an example, under the *Health Rights Commission Act 1992* (Qld), the Health Rights Commission was established with the mandate to investigate complaints and increase the quality of health care services in Queensland. Complaints to the Health Rights Commission come from the consumers of health care services (this could be the patient or their relatives) or from the professional regulatory authorities (for example, the Queensland Nursing

Council). For the period 2000–01, the Queensland Health Rights Commission received 2520 complaints in relation to the provision of health care services. Of those, 938 were related to the provision of medical services, seven in relation to nursing services, and 781 in relation to services provided by public hospitals.[10]

NEGLIGENCE

Negligence is a civil action in which one person (the plaintiff) sues another person (the defendant), seeking compensation for injuries they have sustained as a result of what they allege has been negligent conduct. The concept of 'person' may include not only an individual citizen but also a company or government department. In the health care context, a negligence action is most frequently initiated by a patient, or their relatives, against a health care professional or health care facility. As an example, the patient may allege that the nurse was negligent in administering an incorrect dose of a medication which resulted in the patient sustaining an injury. The elements of a negligence action are as follows:

▲ duty of care;

▲ breach of the duty of care;

▲ damage; and

▲ causation.

The plaintiff must prove each one of the elements on the 'balance of probabilities'. The failure to do so in relation to any one of the above elements will result in the failure of the action. Therefore, the patient or client will be required to prove, on the 'balance of probabilities', that the nurse owed them a duty of care, that the nurse conducted themselves in a manner that amounted to the breach of the duty and that as a result, the patient sustained damage. It is appropriate to discuss each of these concepts in more depth.

Duty of care

Where a person is responsible for the care of others they will owe those individuals a duty of care. This 'duty' exists in relation to those whom they can reasonably foresee are likely to be injured by what they do or do not do. In the health care context, therefore, the nurse will owe a duty of care to all those patients or clients he or she is able to reasonably foresee as likely to be injured by what the nurse does, or does not do, while undertaking their care. At law, such a patient or client is considered to be the nurse's 'neighbour',[11] and to such a person they have a legally recognised relationship, which gives rise to the ability to sue. The nature and extent of the health professional's duty of care to a patient or client is 'a duty to exercise reasonable care and skill in the provision of professional advice and treatment. That duty is a single comprehensive duty covering all the ways in which a doctor is called upon to exercise his skill and judgement: it extends to the examination, diagnosis and treatment of the patient and the provision of information in the appropriate case'.[12] Though this quote from the High Court refers to 'doctors', it can be taken to apply to all health professionals working within the health care sector. Where there is no such relationship, there will be no duty of care. However, the New South Wales cases of *Lowns v Wood*[13] and *BT (as Administratix of the Estate of the Late AT) v Oei*[14] are examples of the development and expansion of the legal interpretation of the relationship.

Health care institutions, in holding themselves out to the public as the providers of health care services, have a 'non-delegable' duty of care to the health care consumer. This duty is not able to be delegated to the employee and is resultant upon the relationship which exists between the patient and the institution.[15] The duty imposes on the institution the obligation to provide, as an example, adequate numbers of appropriately trained staff, safe plant and equipment and uncontaminated products. This duty is separate from the legal position of the employer as being vicariously liable for an employee who negligently injures a patient during the course and scope of their employment.

Breach of the duty of care

For a nurse to be held liable in a negligence action the plaintiff must prove that the nurse's conduct fell below that considered as *reasonable*. This is an objective standard and is distinct from the standard that applies in everyday life. As a person becomes more skilled, so the assessment of what amounts to *reasonable* conduct changes. The standard of care for a health professional has been identified by the High Court of Australia in *Rogers v Whitaker*[16] as:

> The standard of reasonable care and skill required is that of the ordinary skilled person exercising and professing to have that special skill . . .

While there is a basic concept of the standard for the skilled professional, as a general proposition it will be determined by an examination of the level of knowledge and skill a person ought to have in carrying out a particular activity. As an example, an enrolled nurse working in an aged care facility would be anticipated to have a level of skill and knowledge consistent with that position. It would not be the case that the conduct of the enrolled nurse would be considered in relation to what the registered nurse or medical practitioner would have done, or should have done, in similar circumstances. In relation to liability, it is important that registered nurses understand the level of competency of those to whom they are delegating tasks. Where the registered nurse delegates tasks requiring a particular level of skill and knowledge, to a person they know lacks the requisite level of competency, it is likely that they will also be liable for any damage that results.

Some of the significant factors taken into account by the court in making determinations as to whether there has been a breach of the duty of care are as follows:

▲ *The standard at the time*: Court will consider the conduct at the time the alleged incident occurred and not with hindsight.[17] On the one hand, this is a safeguard for health professionals in that they will not be judged to have known that a particular practice was potentially harmful when it was not known at the time the event occurred.[18] However, the rule does presume that health professionals will be up-to-date in their area of clinical expertise. The practice implication is that health professions must keep up with current practices through their attendance at conferences, reading relevant clinical journals and being familiar with the relevant research in their area of practice.

▲ *The determination of the standard*: The High Court of Australia clearly identified that it was the role of the court and not the experts to determine the standard of care. While expert evidence is of significance, it does not set the standard. In the case of *Albrighton v Royal Prince Alfred Hospital*,[19] the court held:

[I]t is not the law that, if all of the medical practitioners in Sydney habitually fail to take an avoidable precaution to avoid a foreseeable risk of injury to their patient, then none can be found guilty of negligence.

▲ *The form of the breach of the duty*: The breach of the duty of care may take the form of either a technical blunder or the failure to disclose risks.

▲ *Failure to warn cases*: In a failure to disclose risk case, the court will examine what the reasonable patient would have wanted to know prior to giving consent. The obligation on the health professional is to disclose all risks that are material and significant to the patient, or those risks which the health professional ought to have known were material and significant.[20]

▲ *Evidence of standard*: Evidence produced in court going to the determination of whether the nurse has breached the standard of care will take the form of expert testimony, research findings, journal articles and institution and Department of Health policies and procedures. Though policy and procedure documents are not legally binding, they are of great significance in considering whether the conduct of a nurse has fallen below a standard considered as *reasonable*. It is therefore important that such documents are kept up-to-date and reflective of the particular specialty area to which they apply.

Damage

The court will compensate the plaintiff only for damages that are recognised by the court (nervous shock, pure economic loss, physical injury or property damage). The damage must have been reasonably foreseeable. As the damage is the 'gist' of the action, where there is no damage there can be no compensation and the action will fail. Regardless of whether there has been a breach of the duty, if there is no damage that is recognised by the court there will be no negligence. Where a patient is identified as being more susceptible to an injury than an ordinary person, the defendant will still be liable for the damage. This is referred to as the 'eggshell skull' principle.

Causation

A defendant will only be liable for damage that is causally linked to the breach of the duty of care. The test is 'but for'. Can it be said that 'but for' the conduct of the health professional the patient would not have sustained the injury: *Barnett v Chelsea and Kensington Hospital Management Committee*.[21] This, however, is not the exclusive test and the case of *March v E and MH Stramare Pty Ltd and Anor*[22] imposed the rider as to whether the causal connection made 'commonsense'.

THE DEFENCE OF CONSENT

All persons who are involved in the care and treatment of others have a legal obligation to obtain the consent of a patient or client before initiating any procedure or treatment. As a broad principle, obtaining the consent of a person prior to undertaking a procedure or treatment is respectful and therefore should be attended to as a matter of course by all health professionals. It is also the case that the patient or client has a legally enforceable right not to be touched by health care workers without either lawful justification or a valid consent. Obtaining a valid consent from a patient or client prior to touching them converts what would otherwise be assault or battery into lawful touching.[23] This area of the law is changing rapidly with the increase in medical technology and the awareness of health care consumers and health providers of their legal rights and obligations. The legal requirement for obtaining a valid consent from a patient or client, prior to any interference with their person, applies regardless of whether or not the patient or client would benefit from the treatment or be harmed by refusing the procedure.[24]

What is 'assault'?

Strictly speaking, assault refers to the action of intentionally engendering in another the fear of imminent physical violence or harm. Battery refers to the actual physical contact. Within the health care setting, however, the actions of assault and battery are often referred to merely as 'assault'. Assault in this context is a civil action, as the conduct of the defendant (in a health care context this may be the nurse, doctor, physiotherapist or other allied health professionals) will be driven, in the majority of cases, by kindness and concern as opposed to malice, which is necessary for criminal assault to occur. Assault therefore, in the clinical and health area, refers to the intentional touching of another person without their prior consent. In the majority of Australian jurisdictions the definition of civil assault is to be found in the case law, however, in Queensland the *Criminal Code 1995* defines 'assault' for both civil and criminal purposes.

While the actual touching of the patient must be intentional, the intention of the health professional in undertaking the health care treatment or procedure will not be relevant. Therefore, that the nurse, doctor or physiotherapist had the intention of doing something aimed at benefiting the patient or client will not exempt their conduct from amounting to a civil assault where the adult patient or client is of sound mind and has refused.[25] The 'intention', in relation to an action in assault, is referring to whether the health professional intentionally touched the patient or client rather than accidentally touched them. It is also significant that in an action for civil assault the patient or client does not need to have suffered damage in the form described in relation to negligence. In an action for civil assault the person bringing the action is claiming that the actual touching without their consent is in fact the damage.

Types of consent

There are a number of different types of consent accepted as evidence that the patient or client has consented. The following are three examples:

Written consent

There is no legal requirement for a consent to be in writing. However, particular institutions and the health departments have clear policies and guidelines which compel the use of consent forms for certain prescribed procedures and treatments. The reason written consents are generally demanded is to provide documentary evidence of the fact that the consent has been given. The issue in legal proceeding, however, will now often hinge not on whether the patient or client consented to the procedure but rather what they understood the procedure actually entailed. As an example, in the case of *Rogers v Whitaker* (1992) 175 CLR 479, Mrs Whitaker had given the consent to the surgery, but had done so without being told by Dr Rogers of the risks involved.

Verbal consent

Here the patient or client and the health care professional discuss and agree on the particular treatment or procedure which is considered appropriate. This is the most common form of consent, and provided that both parties are clear and understand what is going to occur, the verbal consent will not give rise to any difficulties. Actions that arise from this form of consent relate to a lack of information as to what actual treatment or procedure was consented to.

Implied consent

Where the patient or client, through their actions or behaviour, indicates a willingness to undergo a procedure, the consent is said to be implied. For example, rolling up a sleeve when approached with an injecting needle or assuming some posture appropriate to an exercise routine.[26] The issue of implied consent can, however, cause difficulties where the persons involved do not have the same understanding of what is implied by the conduct.

What constitutes a valid consent?

The consent must:

- ▲ be informed;
- ▲ cover the actual procedure;
- ▲ be voluntarily given by the patient; and
- ▲ be obtained by a patient or client with the legal capacity to give a valid consent.

The following is a brief overview of the elements necessary to ensure a consent is valid.

The patient or client must be informed

The patient or client must be given, 'in broad terms',[27] the information relevant to the care they are about to receive. If the nurse describes the nature of the procedure, it would appear that this is sufficient to fulfil the requirements for obtaining a valid consent for the purpose of defending the action in civil assault. It is important to note that all health professionals are responsible for obtaining a consent for the procedures they themselves are to carry out. However, where the care and treatment is directed by the medical practitioner, that individual controls the information given to their patients. Nurses, and other health professionals, must exercise extreme care to ensure that they are not interfering with the therapeutic relationship between doctor and patient by giving information to the patient that the doctor has determined to withhold on the grounds of 'therapeutic privilege'.

The consent must cover the procedure

The consent given by the patient or client must cover the procedure or treatment. Therefore, if the client is asked, 'Will you have the injection?', then giving the injection is all they have consented to. It is not the case that after the nurse has administered the injection they can then continue on to insert a cannula and commence intravenous therapy. The cannulation and initiation of I.V. therapy has clearly not been consented to by the client.[28] The only exception to this proposition is where the procedure is necessary to save the patient's life. That it is convenient to carry out a procedure unrelated to that which is consented to, at the same time, will not provide a legal excuse where the client is suing the health professional in civil assault.

The consent must be voluntarily given by the patient

A patient must give their consent freely and voluntarily. That means there can be no duress, coercion, or misrepresentation in the process of obtaining the patient or client's consent.

The consent must be obtained from a patient with the legal capacity to give a valid consent

The capacity of a patient or client to consent raises the issues of age and mental and intellectual capacity.

Age

In relation to the provision of health care services, the age of the health care consumer is most likely to be raised as an issue in relation to their ability to give a valid consent. As a general principle, a parent or legal guardian is capable of consenting to the medical and dental treatment of their child. Where an adult is caring for a child on a casual basis, however, such as babysitters, friends, relatives and school teachers, they have no authority. The authority of the parent is not absolute and may be overridden by the courts or through legislative provisions.

When the treatment is necessary to save the life of the child, it can be initiated without consent (for example, where a child has drowned in a swimming pool, CPR can be given without consent of the parent or guardian). In most cases the legislation applies to treatment which is 'necessary to save the child's life' or is required as 'a matter of urgency', or specifically applies to the transfusion of blood. Nurses must familiarise themselves with the law relevant to the jurisdiction in which they practice. In all other situations it would be prudent to wait for the return of the parents or legal guardian to obtain a consent.

Each jurisdiction will have legislation that determines the age at which a person may give a valid consent. The common law is silent on a specified age at which a child (also referred to as a minor) is competent to give a valid consent. The common law incorporates the notion of understanding and comprehension. Is the individual of sufficient intelligence, and at an age, where they are able to understand the consequences of their decision? Are they legally competent for the purposes of consent? This is referred to as 'Gillick competency' and is based on the English House of Lords decision in *Gillick v West Norfolk and Wisbech Area Health Authority*.[29] The majority of the House of Lords held that the rights of the parent declined as the child became increasingly competent. Lord Scarman stated at 188–9:

> I would hold that as a matter of law the parental right to determine whether or not their minor child below the age of 16 will have medical treatment terminates if and when the child achieves a sufficient understanding and intelligence to enable him or her to understand fully what is proposed. It will be a question of fact whether a child seeking advice has sufficient understanding of what is involved to give a consent valid in law. Until the child achieves the capacity to consent, the parental right to make the decision continues save only in exceptional circumstances.

The High Court of Australia approved the Gillick test as to capacity in *Secretary,*

Department of Health and Community Services v JWB and SMB (Marion's case) 175 CLR 218 at 238. The child's capacity to consent does not mean that the parent has lost the power to refuse to consent. In some circumstances there may well be a disagreement between the parent and the child as to the treatment that the child is, or is not, going to undertake. In the event of conflict between parents or guardians and a child, the courts may exercise a general supervisory role to act to protect the best interests of the child.[30]

Intellectual and mental incapacity

Consent must not only be freely given; it must also be given by the person who has an intellectual and mental ability to understand what it is they are consenting to. This includes that they have an understanding of the nature of the procedure or treatment, the risks and benefits associated with undergoing the treatment or procedure and the alternatives and limitations associated with the treatment or procedure proposed. As previously stated, the legislation in each of the States and Territories will determine, to a large extent, the issue of consent to medical and dental treatment, or health and lifestyle decisions, for persons with an intellectual disability.[31]

It is important to recognise that the legislation only applies when the person has lost their capacity. In many of the jurisdictions the legislation expressly provides for the situation where the incapacity of the patient is transient.

It is not the case that all persons with an intellectual disability or a mental illness lack the capacity to consent to medical and dental treatment. Their ability to give a legally valid consent will vary depending on their ability to comprehend the information and make a decision as to what is in their best interests. The legislation, applicable where an adult with an intellectual disability or mental illness is required to give a consent, only comes into force when the person is not capable of understanding what it is they are being asked to consider in terms of treatment or care.

Consent in research

The legal requirement to obtain a consent prior to treatment also applies to the carrying out of research projects. The requirement of a valid consent in relation to research is rigorously applied and must be complied with prior to submitting an application for ethical clearance. The concept of 'therapeutic privilege' does not apply and research participants must have 'full and frank' disclosure of all risks, benefits and alternatives. It must be made clear to prospective participants, particularly in a health care context, that their consent is voluntarily and freely given and that their medical care will not be compromised by their decision as to whether they will, or will not, participate in a clinical research study: *Halushka v University of Saskatchewan* (1965) 53 DLR 74 (2d) 436.

OCCUPATIONAL HEALTH AND SAFETY

Under the common law, employers have an obligation to provide a safe system of work. Failure to do so may amount to a breach of the employer's duty of care and result in the employer being held liable in negligence for the injuries sustained by the employee in their place of work. Occupational health and safety legislation seeks to impose on employers and employees an obligation to ensure that workplaces are healthy and safe, thereby minimising the possibility of a work-related injury. At Commonwealth, State and Territory levels, legislation, regulations and codes have been enacted addressing occupational health and safety.[32] The legislation was introduced into Australia in response to the high rate of industrial accidents.[33] While the main objective of the legislation is to promote safe and healthy workplaces, and prevent occupational injury and disease, it also provides for participatory and joint consultative arrangements whereby employers and employees assume responsibility for establishing and maintaining safe working environments.[34]

The Commonwealth legislation, the *Occupational Health and Safety (Commonwealth Employment) Act 1991* (Cth) is limited to the promotion of occupational health and safety of Commonwealth employees and therefore has little or no application within the States and Territories.[35] The *National Occupational Health and Safety Commission Act 1985* (Cth), however, provides for the setting up of a forum at which government, employer and employee representatives formulate policies applicable to workplace safety. While the legislation in the States and Territories may differ, the *Workplace Health and Safety Act 1995* (Qld), as an example, states the objective of the legislation as being:

> To ensure freedom from disease or injury to persons caused, and risk of disease or injury to persons created, by workplace, workplace activities or specified high risk plants.[36]

Occupational health and safety legislation extends in its application to include occupiers, importers, suppliers, manufacturers and independent contractors. The breadth of the legislation is evidenced in section 6 of the *Workplace Health and Safety Act 1995* (Qld) to include:

▲ everyone who may affect the health and safety of others because of workplaces, workplace activities or specified high–risk plant; and

▲ everyone whose health and safety may be affected by workplaces, workplace activities and specified high–risk plant.

While a breach of occupational health and safety laws may result in the criminal prosecution of the employer or the imposition of a fine, the worker is not able to seek compensation under this legislation. Therefore, all jurisdictions have made separate provision for the insurance of workers, should they be injured at their place of employment.[37] The legislation, as distinct from the common law, establishes a 'no fault' system of insurance for the financial compensation of workers. Workers' compensation legislation imposes on employers the obligation to insure workers for injuries or diseases that arise out of, or in the course and scope of, their employment. As the legislative provisions differ between jurisdictions it is important that all employers and employees are familiar with the particular legislation in the jurisdiction in which they work.

EQUITY LEGISLATION AND POLICY

The *Workplace Relations Act 1996* (Cth) highlights the importance of equal opportunity issues within the workplace, with particular reference to:

▲ unlawful termination of employment;

▲ the inclusion of model anti–discrimination clauses in awards; and

▲ equal remuneration provisions for employees.

The object of the *Workplace Relations Act 1996* (Cth), as stated in section 3 (j), is to:

prevent and eliminate discrimination on the basis of race, colour, sex, sexual preference, age, physical or mental disability, marital status, family responsibilities, pregnancy, religion, political opinion, national extraction or social origin.

Anti-discrimination legislation enacted in all States and Territories operates concurrently with the Federal legislation[38] in prohibiting discrimination in all aspects of Australian life. Within the health care context, anti-discrimination laws apply not only in relation to the employment relationship but also, and significantly, in relation to the provision of health care services. All anti-discrimination laws prohibit the treatment of one person less favourably than another on any of the grounds prescribed in the legislation. This is referred to as 'direct discrimination'. 'Indirect discrimination' is also prohibited by the legislation but is often more difficult to detect as it is less obvious and tends to be the result of 'policies and practices which form the structures and patterns of an organisation in particular, and society as a whole'.[39]

DOCUMENTATION AND THE LEGAL OBLIGATION OF CONFIDENTIALITY

The patient's medical records serve a number of functions and it is with these in mind that nurses should record the patient or client's care and treatment. The records are used to provide an account of the ongoing care, as a method by which health professionals communicate with one another, as a source of information for research, and as evidence for court hearings and coroners' inquests. While the procedure for recording patient information in their medical records will differ from one health care institution to another, the following provides a general overview of some of the relevant issues:

▲ Reports must be written in ink with the date and time recorded. It is advisable to use a 24-hour time clock.

▲ The patient or client must be identified by full name and hospital admission number.

▲ The notes must be sequential and written contemporaneously with the treatment and care of the patient.

▲ The writing must be legible, and the record clear, concise and accurate. Nurses must ensure that they do not write any information in the medical records that they have not attended to or witnessed themselves.

▲ Only the abbreviations accepted by the employing institution should be included in a report. The language used by health professionals is very accurate and it is important that nurses become familiar with this language and use it appropriately.

▲ At the completion of the entry the nurse should sign the report and print their name and designated position. In some institutions the nurse may be required to write their employee number.

▲ If, when writing a patient's report, the nurse makes an error, the correct procedure is to draw a line through the error, write: 'written in error', and sign and date it.

Electronic health records

The issues of confidentiality of information and protection of privacy are the major concerns in relation to the recording of health information on electronic databases. Health care institutions, therefore, must develop policies ahead of the introduction of patient data bases. For health professionals who are responsible for recording information on these databases, it is important to understand that the computer will recognise the writer by their pin number only. Therefore, the nurse, as with other health professionals, must never disclose this number to others. It is important also to ensure that the records are complete prior to logging out, as additional information cannot be added at a later time.

Access

Access to the content of the medical records may become available via a number of mechanisms, for example, under the relevant legislation, and/or through the Department of Health or institution administrative access policies. In both the State and Federal jurisdictions, legislation provides that every person has a legally enforceable right to obtain access to their own health care records.[40] In circumstances where the disclosure of the patient's information may be prejudicial to their medical and/or psychiatric wellbeing, the access may be directed to the patient's medical practitioner. The freedom of information legislation at both State and Federal levels applies only to the provision of public health care services. The legislation has no impact on the private sector. The private sector of health care is now amenable to the *Privacy Act 1998* (Cth) and the *Privacy Amendment (Private Sector) Act 2000* (Cth). This legislation provides for the development of codes consistent with the National Privacy Principles, setting out how the private sector should collect, use, keep and secure personal information. It also provides for the right of individuals to know what information an institution holds about them.

Confidentiality

The general principle is that health professionals do not disclose patient information without the patient's consent. From the patient's perspective, this obligation provides the necessary basis upon which they can safely confide information of a very sensitive nature.[41] This information will often include details not only about themselves, but also about their parents, spouse, children and siblings. It is not unusual for health records to contain quite detailed accounts of illnesses and incidents which may be irrelevant to the present condition but necessary for an assessment of the overall health of the patient. The patient's right to have their information kept confidential is protected through the following legal mechanisms and actions:

▲ Negligence;[42]

▲ Breach of Contract;

▲ Equity;[43]

▲ Defamation;

▲ Professional Codes of Ethics;[44] and

▲ Legislation.

Disclosure of patient information may be permitted through legislation and/or in the public interest. As an example, under the *Health Act 1937* (Qld), identified categories of health professionals are compelled to disclose suspected child abuse and notifiable diseases to the relevant authorities. There is also, at common law, the presumption that health professionals will disclose information which is in the public interest. For example, where the patient tells the nurse that they intend to kill a relative or friend after discharge, the nurse would notify the relevant authorities on the basis that it was in the interests of the public that he or she disclosed the information. The general rule is that the patient's right to have the information kept confidential is overridden where it is in the public interest that the information is disclosed. The cases of *W v Edgell*[45] and *Tarasoff v Regents of the University of California*[46] illustrate this issue. There is obviously an exception to the duty to keep information confidential where the patient or client expressly consents to the health professional disclosing.

CONCLUSION

The law, to a significant extent, regulates and controls the provision of health care services. This occurs not only through the application of the obligations, responsibilities and rights imposed by the relevant Acts of Parliament, but also in response to the decisions handed down by courts in making determinations related to the provision of health care. This chapter has raised for discussion the major legal issues relevant to nursing practice. It is imperative that those employed in leadership positions, within the health system, maintain an in-depth and up-to-date knowledge and understanding of the legal principles and legislative provisions that impact on both the consumers and providers of health care services.

Reflective exercise

1   Identify the rights of patients and clients within a health care context that are created through legislation, judicial decisions or common practice.

2   Identify the elements to be satisfied in obtaining a valid consent.

3   Identify the rights and obligations imposed on both employers and employees under both State and Federal workplace health and safety laws.

RECOMMENDED READINGS

Forrester, K. & Griffiths, D. (2001). *Essentials of law for health professionals*. Sydney: Harcourt Australia.
Freckelton, I. & Petersen, K. (1999). *Controversies in health law.* Sydney: Federation Press.
Health and Medical Law Reporter. CCH Australia.
Johnstone, R. (1997). *Occupational health and safety law and policy, text and materials*. Sydney: LBS.
Wallace, M. (2001). *Health care and the law* (3rd edn). Sydney: Law Book Co.

ENDNOTES

1 Section 109 of the Commonwealth Constitution.

2 Forrester, K. & Griffiths, D. (2001). *Essentials of law for health professionals*, Sydney: Harcourt Australia.

3 Wallace, M. (2001). *Health care and the law* (3rd edn) Sydney: Law Book Co., p. 591.

4 *'Charter of Resident's Rights and Responsibilities'* Queensland Aged and Disability Advocacy Inc. Qld.

5 United Nations, *Universal Declaration of Human Rights*.

6 Wallace, op.cit. p. 595.

7 *Human Rights and Equal Opportunity Commission Act 1986* (Cth), *Sex Discrimination Act 1984* (Cth), *Racial Discrimination Act 1975* (Cth), *Disability Discrimination Act 1992* (Cth), *Anti-Discrimination Act 1977* (NSW), *Equal Opportunity Act 1995* (Vic), *Anti-Discrimination Act 1991* (Qld), *Equal Opportunity Act 1984* (SA), *Racial Vilification Act 1996* (SA), *Equal Opportunity Act 1984* (WA), *Anti-Discrimination Act 1998* (Tas), *Anti-Discrimination Act 1992* (NT), *Discrimination Act 1991* (ACT).

8 *Health Complaints Act 1993* (ACT), *Health Care Complaints Act 1993* (NSW), *Health Services (Conciliation and Review) Act 1987* (Vic), *Health Services (Conciliation and Review) Act 1995* (WA), *Health Complaints Act 1995* (Tas), *Health and Community Services Complaints Act 1998* (NT), *Health Rights Commission Act 1991* (Qld), *The Ombudsman Act 1972* (SA).

9 *Health Complaints Act 1993* (ACT), *Health Care Complaints Act 1993* (NSW), *Health Services (Conciliation and Review) Act 1987* (Vic), *Health Services (Conciliation and Review) Act 1995* (WA), *Health Complaints Act 1995* (Tas), *Health and Community Services Complaints Act 1998* (NT), *Health Rights Commission Act 1991* (Qld), *The Ombudsman Act 1972* (SA).

10 Health Rights Commission 2000/2001, 9th Annual Report, p. 27.

11 *Donoghue v Stevenson* (1932) AC 562.

12 *Rogers v Whitaker* (1992) CLR 479.

13 (1996) Aust Torts Reports 81–376.

14 [1995] NSWSC 1082.

15 *Albrighton v Royal Prince Alfred Hospital* (1980) 2 NSWLR 542, *Kondis v State Transport Authority* (1984) 154 CLR 672.

16 (1992) 175 CLR 479.

17 *Roe v Minister of Health* [1954] 2 QB 66.

18 *H v Royal Alexandra Hospital for Children* (1990) Aust Torts Reports 81–000.

19 [1980] 2 NSWLR 452.

20 *Rogers v Whitaker* (1992) CLR 479.

21 [1969] 1 QB 428.

22 (1991) Aust Torts Reports 81–095.

23 Forrester, op.cit. p. 132.

24 *Malette v Shulman* (1990) 2 Med LR 162.

25 *Mohr v Williams* 104 NW 12 (1905)., Forrester, op.cit. p. 134.

26 *O'Brien v Cunard* SS Co 28 NE (1891).

27 *Chatterton v Gerson* [1980] 3 WLR 1003.

28 *Murray v McMurchy* [1949] 2 DLR 442.

29 [1986] AC 112.

30 *Dalton v Skuthorpe (McLelland J. Supreme Court of New South Wales, 17 November 1989)*, *Secretary, Department of Health and Community Services v JWB and SMB (Marion's case)* (1992) 175 CLR 218.

31 *Powers of Attorney Act 1998* (Qld), *Guardianship and Administration Act 2001* (Qld), *Disabilities Services and Guardianship Act 1987* (NSW), *Guardianship and Administration Act 1990* (WA), *Adult Guardian Act 1991* (NT), *Guardianship and Management of Property Act 1991* (ACT), *Guardianship and Administration Act 1995* (Tas), *Guardianship and Administration Board Act 1993* (SA), *Guardianship and Administration Act 1986* (Vic), *Family Law Act 1975* (Cth).

32 *Occupational Health and Safety (Commonwealth Employment) Act 1991* (Cth), *National Occupational Health and Safety Commission Act 1985* (Cth), *Occupational Health and Safety Act 1985* (Vic), *Workplace Health and Safety Act 1995* (Tas), *Occupational Health and Safety Act 2000* (NSW), *Workplace Health and Safety Act 1995* (Qld), *Occupational Health and Safety Act 1984* (WA), *Safety and Welfare Act 1986* (SA), *Occupational Health and Safety Act 1989* (ACT), *Work Health Act 1986* (NT).

33 Wallace-Bruce, N.L., (1999) *Outline of employment law* (2nd edn). Sydney: Butterworths, p. 122.

34 Forrester, op.cit. p. 292.

35 Wallace-Bruce, op.cit. p. 122.

36 Section 7 (1).

37 *Workers Compensation and Rehabilitation Act 1981* (WA), *Workers Rehabilitation and Compensation Act 1986* (SA), *Work Health Act 1986* (NT), *Workcover Queensland Act 1996* (Qld), *Workers Compensation Act 1988* (NSW), *Accident Compensation Act 1985* (Vic), *Workers Rehabilitation and Compensation Act 1988* (Tas), *Workers Compensation Act 1951* (ACT), *Safety, Rehabilitation and Compensation Act 1988* (Cth).

38 *Human Rights and Equal Opportunity Commission Act 1986* (Cth), *Sex Discrimination Act 1984* (Cth), *Racial Discrimination Act 1975* (Cth), *Disability Discrimination Act 1992* (Cth), *Anti-Discrimination Act 1977* (NSW), *Equal Opportunity Act 1995* (Vic), *Anti-Discrimination Act 1991* (Qld), *Equal Opportunity Act 1984* (SA), *Racial Vilification Act 1996* (SA), *Equal Opportunity Act 1984* (WA), *Anti-Discrimination Act 1998* (Tas), *Anti-Discrimination Act 1992* (NT), *Discrimination Act 1991* (ACT).

39 Ronalds, C. (1987) in Wallace, op.cit. p. 601.

40 *Freedom of Information Act 1982* (Cth), *Freedom of Information Act 1982* (Qld), *Freedom of Information Act 1989* (NSW), *Freedom of Information Act 1989* (ACT), *Freedom of Information Act 1982* (Vic), *Freedom of Information Act 1991* (Tas), *Freedom of Information Act 1992* (WA), *Freedom of Information Act 1991* (SA).

41 *X v Y* [1982] 2 All ER 648.

42 *Furniss v Fitchett* (1957) NZLR 396

43 *Coco v AN Clark (Engineers) Ltd* [1969] RPC 41 at 47 per Megarry J., *Commonwealth of Australia v John Fairfax and Sons Ltd* (1980) 147 CLR 39 at 51 per Mason J:

44 Australian Nursing Council Inc., *ANCI Code of Ethics for Nurses in Australia.*

45 [1990] 1 All ER 835.

46 555 P2d 334 (1976).

CHAPTER EIGHT

Nursing leadership in industrial relations

Jill Iliffe & Nicholas Blake

LEARNING OBJECTIVES

At the completion of this chapter, the reader will be able to:

- ▲ briefly describe the history of industrial relations in Australia;
- ▲ discuss the current industrial relations environment in Australia;
- ▲ name the industrial relations instruments currently in use;
- ▲ explain how industrial instruments support the nursing profession; and
- ▲ describe the leadership skills required to effectively manage industrial relations issues.

KEY WORDS

Industrial relations, union, legislation, arbitration, conciliation, enterprise bargaining

INTRODUCTION

Industrial relations, like nursing, is both an art and a science. There are compelling and practical reasons why knowledge, understanding and expertise in industrial relations are essential attributes for nurse leaders and nurse managers. Knowledge provides confidence, and understanding facilitates cooperation in identifying and addressing industrial issues so that disputes can be avoided or resolved promptly. Disputes cost money, both in economic terms and in terms of lost productivity. They are also a distraction from the core business of nursing, and a drain on scarce resources. Effective leadership involves creating an employment environment, which promotes industrial harmony.

This chapter provides a brief history of industrial relations in Australia, an overview of the current industrial relations environment, and information about nursing awards and agreements. Finally the management of industrial issues is addressed, including matters such as settling disputes, grievance procedures and unfair dismissal.

INDUSTRIAL RELATIONS IN AUSTRALIA

Industrial relations in Australia are governed by both Federal and State legislation. Where there is inconsistency between Federal and State legislation, Federal legislation prevails.[1] The major industrial relations power available to the Federal Government is Section 51 of the Australian Constitution. This allows the Federal Government to make laws about industrial relations in respect to:[2]

▲ preventing and settling industrial disputes that cross State boundaries;

▲ foreign corporations and trading or financial corporations formed within Australia;

▲ Federal Government agency employees;

▲ interstate trade and commerce;

▲ employees in the Australian Capital Territory and Northern Territory; and

▲ external treaty obligations.

The Federal Government has other related powers under the Constitution, which it uses from time to time, such as the 'Referral by States Power' under Section 51 (xxxvii); the 'External Affairs Power' under Section 51 (xxix); the 'Corporations Power' under Section 51 (xx); and the 'Trade and Commerce Power' under Section 51 (i).[3] While the Federal Government does not have the power to legislate directly on such matters as wages and conditions, it exercises its industrial relations power under the Constitution to establish courts and tribunals that regulate industrial relations at the Federal level.

The *Australian Conciliation and Arbitration Act 1904* established the central principles of industrial relations and the central role of industrial tribunals in Australia in the prevention and settlement of industrial disputes. The Act also established the Commonwealth Court of Conciliation and Arbitration.[4] The Court, which initially consisted of a single High Court judge, exercised both judicial and arbitral powers; that is, it could make an award specifying wages and conditions of employment in settlement of a dispute, and it could interpret and enforce the award, if necessary imposing penalties on any party to the award who did not comply with its provisions. The Act also provided for the registration of organisations of employers and employees (unions).[5]

The Court was reconstituted in 1926 to comprise a Chief Judge and other judges. The legislation also provided for the appointment of Conciliation Commissioners and for the Attorney General to intervene 'in the public interest' in basic wages and hours of work applications.[6] In 1956, following a High Court decision determining that it was unconstitutional for an arbitral body to also exercise judicial power, the Court was restructured as two separate bodies, with the establishment of the Commonwealth Conciliation and Arbitration Commission, with a responsibility for conciliation and arbitration; and the Commonwealth Industrial Court, with judicial responsibility (the title 'Commonwealth' was changed to 'Australian' in 1973).[7] The Industrial Division of the Federal Court of Australia subsumed the functions of the Australian Industrial Court in 1978.[8] In 1988 the *Australian Conciliation and Arbitration Act 1904* was repealed and replaced by the *Industrial Relations Act 1988*. The Australian Industrial Relations Commission (AIRC), with a responsibility for arbitration, replaced the Australian Conciliation and Arbitration Commission.[9]

The next major change was the introduction of the *Industrial Relations Reform Act 1993* by the then Federal Labor Government. The primary emphasis of this Act was the introduction of enterprise agreements negotiated at the workplace with awards and arbitrated wage increases acting only as a 'safety net'.[10] Both the AIRC and the unions initially opposed the introduction of enterprise agreements, the AIRC considering that enterprise bargaining had the potential to destroy the orderly system which had been in place since 1967, while the unions believed that their capacity to represent their members would be diminished in a decentralised system and their power to influence outcomes reduced.[11] The Act also established a specialist labour court, the Industrial Relations Court of Australia, to take over the functions previously exercised by the Industrial Division of the Federal Court of Australia.[12]

When the Liberal Coalition Government gained office in 1996, they introduced the *Workplace Relations Act 1996*. The Act maintained the award system as a 'safety net' of fair and enforceable minimum wages and conditions, but set limits on the role of the AIRC in arbitration, restricted the capacity of unions to represent employees and be involved in the bargaining process, introduced individual agreements, and replaced the unfair dismissal provisions with a system based on 'a fair go all round'. The judicial functions of the Australian Industrial Court were transferred to the Federal Court.[13]

A system of conciliation and arbitration

Industrial tribunals established at both a Federal and State level are empowered to conciliate or arbitrate industrial disputes between employers and employees or their representatives; that is, trade unions and employer associations. The system of industrial relations in Australia is commonly referred to as a system of conciliation and arbitration.

Conciliation, as the name suggests, requires discussion, negotiation and, if successful, agreement between the parties about the settlement of the dispute. Arbitration requires the industrial tribunal to make a decision or order settling the dispute, which is then reflected in an industrial instrument (award or agreement).

The main functions of industrial tribunals are to:[14]

▲ prevent and settle industrial disputes, as far as possible by conciliation, and where appropriate, by arbitration;

▲ ensure that a safety net of fair minimum wages and conditions of employment is established and maintained;

▲ facilitate equal remuneration for work of equal value;

▲ facilitate agreements between employers and employees or organisations of employers and employees about wages and conditions of employment; and

▲ determine whether a termination of employment is harsh, unjust or unreasonable.

Industrial awards

Since the introduction of the Federal conciliation and arbitration system in Australia in 1904, part of the wages received by employees has been determined against a standard of what constitutes a fair or living wage. Wage levels have also been set on the basis of comparability between occupations according to the principle of fair relativity. Adjustments to wages were not based on the employers' capacity to pay, nor were they based on productivity outcomes achieved by different industry sectors.[15]

Awards of the AIRC are decisions or determinations establishing the wages and conditions of workers employed by the particular employer or employers named in the award. The making of an award usually follows the serving of a log of claims or demands by a trade union on an employer. If the log of claims, either in part or in whole, is rejected by the employer(s), the AIRC exercises its conciliation and arbitration powers to settle the dispute and make the award. In some instances when the dispute comes before the AIRC for conciliation, the parties, with the assistance and guidance of the AIRC, will agree on the terms of the award. Where there is such agreement, the award is referred to as a consent award. Where there is no agreement from conciliation, the AIRC will arbitrate the outcome.

Awards are periodically reviewed and amended subject to the AIRC's powers at that particular time. For example, the award-making power of the AIRC under the *Workplace Relations Act 1996* (the Act) is far more restrictive than was the case under previous legislation. The AIRC's power in relation to awards is outlined in section 89A of the Act.[16] All the decisions of industrial tribunals, at both Federal and State level, can be appealed to a higher court, such as the Federal Court or the High Court of Australia. This includes the making or amending of an award.

The system of awards established and maintained by the AIRC allowed the majority of employees in a particular industry to enjoy standard employment conditions. For example, in nursing, the award(s) provided standard employment benefits for nurses, such as four weeks annual leave, payment of annual leave loading, and shift or overtime penalties, regardless of the employment setting in which the nurse is employed, e.g. public or private sector, community health or aged care. In nursing, awards also sought to provide consistency in wages across sectors based on educational qualifications, skill levels, and length of service, rather than on a particular employer's capacity or willingness to meet industry standards. This promoted commonality of conditions for nurses between the public, private and non-government sectors, enhancing employment mobility between sectors.

For an occupation such as nursing, industrial arrangements are broader than remuneration and working conditions. The classifications reflect the nursing career path, with remuneration linked to experience and qualifications, with clauses on such things as occupational health and safety, workloads, and access to education and training. Awards have been a very important mechanism in maintaining the professional status of nursing. To some extent, the introduction of enterprise agreements fragmented nursing industrial outcomes; however, nursing unions in Australia have been reasonably successful in achieving and maintaining common conditions in agreements across sectors and in flowing on many of the benefits of agreements made in the public sector to other sectors where nurses work.

One criticism of the award system is that over-award bargaining outcomes by some workers in an industry were flowed on to all workers in that industry, and to secondary awards, as a result of the AIRC using the award-setting standards of comparative wage justice and fair relativities. This pattern of award determination produced a compressed wage structure where increases in wages for one group of workers inevitably translated into increases in wages for the majority of workers.[17]

The introduction of enterprise bargaining

The process of change in Australia's industrial relations environment began with a series of agreements, known as the Prices and Incomes Accords, negotiated between the Australian Labor Party (ALP) and the Australian Council of Trade Unions (ACTU), following the election of a Federal Labor Government in 1983.[18] Under the Federal Labor Government, industrial relations became a tripartite process between government, unions and employers. A broad social agenda was adopted, which saw the introduction of worker entitlements such as maternity leave, occupational superannuation, family leave; and a major focus placed on industry education and training.[19] These entitlements, together with the employee's wages, were commonly referred to as the Living Wage, a doctrine originally developed by the Australian Conciliation and Arbitration Commission in a 1907 decision, which defined a living wage in terms of the needs of a family.[20]

The first Prices and Incomes Accord (Accord Mark I 1983–85) used a centralised wage fixing system based on awards as the primary industrial instrument for delivering wage increases.[21] Accord Mark II (1985–86) continued the centralised wage fixing principle and the wage restraint objective, and included trading a percentage of wage increases for tax cuts and increases in occupational superannuation.[22] In Accord Mark III (1987–88), the ALP and the ACTU abandoned a centralised wage fixing strategy and began the move towards productivity bargaining at the enterprise level. All wage increases above National Wage Case increases (first tier living wage increases) were tied to productivity offsets at the workplace level (second tier fair relativity increases), such as addressing restrictive work and management practices, multi-skilling, broad banding, removing demarcation barriers and streamlining award classifications.[23]

This approach was reinforced in Accord Mark IV (1988–89), when wage increases and tax cuts were linked to further restructuring, greater productivity offsets and efficiency gains at industry and enterprise level, such as adjustments to award relativities, flexible employment practices, and the establishment of minimum award rates of pay consistent across workers with similar skills and experience. Accord Mark IV also sought to establish workplace or enterprise agreements as the principal vehicle for wage movements, with awards providing a 'safety net' of minimum wages and conditions.[24]

The Commission initially opposed the introduction of enterprise agreements as it was concerned that changes to the orderly system of awards supported by National

Wage Case decisions would result, not in a flexible labour market or industrial harmony, but a distorted wage structure, inequity in the labour market and industrial chaos.[25] The *Industrial Relations Act 1988* facilitated the introduction of enterprise agreements, and established the Australian Industrial Relations Commission (AIRC) to replace the Australian Conciliation and Arbitration Commission. In this process, the power of the AIRC was reduced.[26] Accord Mark V (1989–90) incorporated the structural efficiency principle, which had been introduced in the 1988 National Wage Case. The fundamental purpose of the structural efficiency principle was to modernise awards. Wage increases and tax cuts were linked to award simplification and restructuring.[27]

In 1993, with the passage of the *Industrial Relations Reform Act 1993*, an industrial relations system was created which had distinct award and enterprise bargaining streams. This was a significant change to the industrial relations system in Australia. The bargaining stream provided for two types of enterprise agreements: certified agreements which required union involvement and were subject to a 'no disadvantage' test in relation to the relevant award; and enterprise agreements which did not require union involvement and were subject to a more stringent 'public interest' test. The award stream provided 'safety net' increases for those employees who did not have access to enterprise agreements. Accords Mark VI (1990–92) and Mark VII (1993–95) maintained this approach, linking wage increases to productivity gains, and inserting mechanisms to protect the 'safety net' function of awards.[28]

The 1994 ALP *Working Nation* White Paper outlined further structural industrial relations changes, such as restricting AIRC scrutiny of agreements to an assessment against the 'no disadvantage test', limiting awards to a 'safety net' of core conditions, and confirming enterprise agreements as the principal industrial relations instrument.[29] However, Accord Mark VIII (1996–99), incorporating the ideas of *Working Nation*, was abandoned when the ALP lost government at the 1996 Federal elections.[30]

Australia's international industrial relations obligations

The International Labor Organisation (ILO) has criticised Australia's 1993 and 1996 industrial relations legislation for breaching ILO conventions. The Australian legislation restricts the right to strike, limits redress and compensation in cases of unfair dismissal and, according to the ILO, constitutes a clear contravention of Convention No.98.[31] Of the eight conventions considered 'fundamental' by the ILO, Australia has ratified only six—those relating to forced labour, freedom of association, and discrimination. Australia has not ratified the two conventions relating to child labour, nor have they ratified the most recent maternity protection convention.[32]

THE CURRENT INDUSTRIAL RELATIONS ENVIRONMENT IN AUSTRALIA

The first wave industrial reforms of the Liberal Coalition Government

In 1996, a Federal Liberal Coalition Government was elected. One of their first priorities was the introduction of further change to the industrial relations system of the country. The *Workplace Relations Act 1996* was proclaimed on 1 December 1996 and was the vehicle for delivering the Federal Government's industrial relations agenda. The Act aims to ensure that 'the primary responsibility for determining matters affecting the relationship between employers and employees rests with the employer and employees at the workplace'.[33] The motive of the new government was as much ideological as it was a desire to reduce perceived inefficiency, with a move away from reliance on third parties and towards workplace agreements negotiated directly between employers and employees.[34]

The changes actively promoted enterprise-based agreements as the primary mechanism for delivering wage increases, reduced the role of the AIRC by introducing individual agreements that were put outside AIRC jurisdiction with the establishment of the Office of the Employment Advocate, limited awards to 20 specified, allowable matters while maintaining awards as 'a safety net of fair minimum wages and conditions of employment', and restricted the capacity for unions to represent employees in the collective bargaining process.[35] Under the Act, the status of unions was altered from 'interest representation' to 'agency representation', which requires unions to demonstrate that a 'valid majority' of workers want the union to bargain on their behalf prior to negotiation and that a 'valid majority' accepts the outcome of the bargaining.[36]

The Act allows industrial parties to negotiate agreements between industrial organisations or directly between employer and employees. The Act also allows individual employers to negotiate agreements directly with individual employees. These agreements are referred to as Australian Workplace Agreements (AWAs).[37]

Collective agreements (both union and non-union) can cover a single employer, a geographically distinct part of an employer's operation—e.g. an operating theatre—or be made with respect to a number of employers.[38] The AIRC is required to certify collective agreements negotiated between employers and employees, whether or not a union is party to the agreement. Multi-employer agreements are subject to a 'public interest test' conducted by a Full Bench of the Commission. Single employer enterprise agreements are subject to a 'no disadvantage test' conducted by a single Commissioner.[39]

As a result of the changes introduced under the Act, awards have been streamlined so that they only cover specified allowable matters and act as a safety net of minimum wages and conditions of employment. The Act, in fact, stipulates that awards must not include details or processes that would be more appropriately dealt with by agreement at the workplace or enterprise level.[40]

The second wave industrial changes of the Liberal Coalition Government

In 1999, the Liberal Coalition Government introduced the *Workplace Relations Legislation Amendment (More Jobs, Better Pay) Bill*. The Bill had 18 parts which sought to further reduce the scope of awards, introduce another round of award simplification, limit access to the AIRC's arbitral powers, reduce the vetting of enterprise agreements by the AIRC, restrict access to industrial action, and limit the ability of unions to organise, recruit and represent members.[41]

The Government withdrew the legislation when the ALP and the Australian Democrats announced their intention to vote against the Bill in the Senate. The November 1999 Australian Democrats *Supplementary Report* on the Bill outlines the Democrats' objections in detail. Although agreeing that the changes introduced in the *Workplace Relations Act 1996* had been successful in delivering better economic outcomes evidenced by higher real wages, employment and productivity, the Democrats considered that 'a strong or compelling case'[42] had not been made on the need for further major reform, that the changes introduced by the Act had not had a chance to bed down, and that many important provisions of the new Act had not yet been tested in the courts or by a Full Bench of the Commission. The report describes the Bill as 'too harsh, too regressive and too unfair'.[43]

The third wave industrial changes of the Liberal Coalition Government

Following the re-election of the Liberal Coalition Government in 1999, the *Workplace Relations Legislation Amendment (More Jobs, Better Pay) Bill* was withdrawn and its provisions were broken up into a number of smaller Bills. Eleven Bills were introduced into the Parliament; however, none passed into law due to the opposition of the ALP and the Australian Democrats. Among these Bills were the:

▲ *Workplace Relations Amendment (Prohibition of Compulsory Union Fees) Bill 2001*;

▲ *Workplace Relations Amendment (Secret Ballots for Protected Action) Bill 2001*;

▲ *Workplace Relations Amendment (Termination of Employment) Bill 2001*;

▲ *Workplace Relations Amendment (Transmission of Business) Bill 2001*; and

▲ *Workplace Relations Amendment (Registered Organisations) Bill 2001*.[44]

The Liberal Coalition Government was re-elected in 2001. The industrial relations Bills were resubmitted to Parliament. Essentially, these Bills are identical to those previously submitted, such as:

▲ *Workplace Relations Amendment (Fair Dismissal) Bill 2002*;

▲ *Workplace Relations Amendment (Fair Dismissal) Bill 2002 No: 2*;

▲ *Workplace Relations Amendment (Fair Termination) Bill 2002*;

▲ *Workplace Relations Amendment (Genuine Bargaining) Bill 2002*;

▲ *Workplace Relations Amendment (Prohibition of Compulsory Union Fees) Bill 2002*;

▲ *Workplace Relations Amendment (Secret Ballots for Protected Action) Bill 2002*;

▲ *Workplace Relations Amendment (Improved Remedies for Unprotected Action) Bill 2002*; and the

▲ *Workplace Relations Amendment (Simplifying Agreement Making) Bill 2002*.[45]

Very few of the Bills have passed into legislation, the *Workplace Relations Amendment (Registration and Accountability of Organisations) Bill 2002* and the *Workplace Relations Amendment (Prohibition of Compulsory Union Fees) Bill 2002* being two exceptions. Bills amended by the Senate, where the amendments are not acceptable to the Government, are generally withdrawn by the Government and resubmitted at a later date.

INDUSTRIAL RELATIONS INSTRUMENTS

Agreement-making

The focus of the *Workplace Relations Act 1996* is on facilitating the making and certifying of workplace or enterprise agreements.[46] Employees whose conditions of employment are governed by the Federal jurisdiction may have these conditions regulated by one or more of three ways—awards of the AIRC, certified agreements of the AIRC, or Australian Workplace Agreements (AWAs) which are overseen by the Office of the Employment Advocate (OEA).[47] The Act requires that the parties seeking to make an agreement comply with a number of steps in order to obtain the protections provided by the Act.

The bargaining period

During the term of an agreement, industrial action is prohibited. However, when an agreement is about to expire or when a new agreement is to be negotiated, Section 170M of the Act provides for the initiation of a bargaining period by either an employer, an employee or a union. The purpose of the bargaining period is to give written notice to the other bargaining parties and to the AIRC of an intention to commence bargaining. The bargaining period commences seven days after notice has been given.[48]

During a bargaining period, the parties may engage in protected industrial action, which protects the parties from any civil prosecution arising from industrial activity. In a nursing context, such industrial action may take many forms, including bans on completing paperwork, refusing to wear a uniform, closing beds, and conducting rallies and strikes. Similarly, during the bargaining period, the employer may take protected industrial action, which may include locking employees out of the workplace and replacing them with alternative labour. The industrial action must be lawful in other respects, in that it does not involve injury to persons or damage to property.[49]

The AIRC may suspend or terminate a bargaining period if it is satisfied that a party is not genuinely trying to reach an agreement or is not complying with any directions given, or if any industrial action is threatening to endanger the life, safety, health or welfare of the population or part of it, or causing significant damage to the Australian economy. If a bargaining period is terminated, the AIRC may decide to exercise its conciliation powers under Section 170MX of the Act to resolve the matters in dispute. If this is unsuccessful, a Full Bench of the Commission can exercise arbitral powers.[50]

Certifying an agreement

The Commission must certify a collective agreement if the parties have taken the appropriate steps prior to seeking certification of the agreement and the proposed agreement passes the 'no disadvantage' test. Those steps include:

▲ the employer must have taken reasonable steps to notify all persons who will be covered by the agreement that the agreement is to take effect;

▲ the employer must have explained the terms of the agreement to all of the employees;

▲ the employees must have been given 14 days to view the proposed agreement; and

▲ the majority of the employees to be covered by the agreement must have indicated their support for the agreement.[51]

After a matter is concluded, either by conciliation or arbitration, the Commission may issue a decision, and where required, an order. A decision is a statement of findings and reasons for the determination, which are subsequently reflected in the Commission's order. The order is a legally binding instrument having the force of Federal law.[52]

The 'no disadvantage' test

The Commission must not certify the agreement if, in the view of the Commission, the agreement does not satisfy the 'no disadvantage' test. The 'no disadvantage' test is a global test which ensures that the terms and conditions of employment under the agreement are no less than those currently provided by the relevant State or Federal award. This requires the Commission to examine the content of the agreement and decide whether the employees will be better or worse off.[53]

Australian Workplace Agreements (AWAs)

The *Workplace Relations Act 1996* introduced, among other things, Australian Workplace Agreements (AWAs). The view of the current Federal Government is that, wherever possible, industrial arrangements are the exclusive business of the employer and the employee at the workplace.[54] AWAs are heavily promoted as the preferred industrial instrument.[55] Unlike collective agreements, however, the AIRC does not certify AWAs. Instead, they are filed with the OEA. The main functions of the Employment Advocate are to process AWAs and investigate breaches of the freedom of association provisions of the Act.[56]

AWAs reached between individual employers and individual employees have the same legal status as awards or collective agreements. In contrast to collective agreements, however, AWAs override Federal or State awards, or existing collective agreements. Once the AWA is approved, the link between the agreement and the award is broken.[57] AWAs are not public documents and are not subject to public scrutiny, although employers and employees are not required to keep the contents confidential.[58]

The OEA assesses the AWA against the award, not the agreement that would otherwise cover the employee, using the 'no disadvantage test'. If the AWA meets the 'no disadvantage test', it is approved.[59]

Under the Act, an existing employee cannot be forced or placed under 'duress' to accept an AWA, nor can their employment be terminated for refusing to sign an AWA. However, an offer of employment to a prospective employee may be made conditional on signing an AWA. This is not seen to constitute 'duress', as the person is free to accept the employment with that condition or refuse the employment. The AWA must be given to a prospective employee five days prior to signing, and to an existing employee 14 days prior to signing. An employee can appoint a bargaining agent, which may be a trade union.[60]

When the Act was first introduced, the Australian Nursing Federation (ANF) and other unions argued that a deregulated industrial relations environment would not deliver fair and just wage outcomes. The focus in the Act is on individuals negotiating on their own behalf. In an employment context, the capacity of the individual to achieve a desirable outcome is limited if there is unequal bargaining power between the employee and the employer, particularly when, under the Act, the outcomes are not automatically subject to public scrutiny. This view is supported by the fact that wage outcomes under agreements negotiated between unions and employers deliver more favourable outcomes than agreements negotiated between individuals and employers.[61] The ANF further argued that, in an industry such as nursing, where nurses make up 45.1 per cent of the health workforce in acute public hospitals,[62] the administrative cost of negotiating and maintaining individual agreements would be prohibitive,[63] and, with the potential for infinite variance in outcomes between employees, they would also divide the workforce and give rise to industrial unrest.

Since their introduction in 1996, there has been only a limited uptake of AWAs. For example, at the end of 2002, only 1.63 per cent of the working population were covered by 'live' AWAs.[64]

INDUSTRIAL RELATIONS OUTCOMES FOR NURSES

Nursing awards and agreements

Nursing salaries and employment conditions are in the main regulated by Federal laws, with the exception being nurses employed in New South Wales and some private hospitals in Queensland, who are regulated by State industrial legislation. Nursing awards have traditionally been 'paid rates awards'. Paid rates awards specify the actual rate of pay, rather than the minimum rate. Under the *Workplace Relations Act 1996* no new paid rates awards are to be made by the Commission, and over time, paid rates awards are to become minimum rates awards.[65]

Wages and conditions of employment for the vast majority of nurses in Australia are predominately determined by collective bargaining agreements reached between the Australian Nursing Federation (Federal Office or State or Territory branches) and employers. Collective agreements supplement rather than replace the terms of the award. If there is a conflict between the agreement and the award, the provisions in the agreement prevail.

Although agreements may differ, they typically apply for a two- to three-year period, provide for an annual increase in wage rates and wage related allowances, and seek to address issues that are of particular concern either to nurses at the workplace or to the profession generally.

Most awards or agreements cover a range of workplaces in a common industry. For example, in nursing there are awards and agreements that cover all nursing staff employed in that State's public sector. The cost of negotiating separate enterprise agreements for each health facility where nurses are employed would be both time-consuming and costly, and could also introduce the potentially negative effect of competition between health facilities for nursing staff, particularly in times of labour shortages, resulting in different levels of health care being provided in different facilities.

The manner in which agreements for nurses are negotiated falls within the definition of 'pattern bargaining', which was to be prohibited in the *Workplace Relations Legislation Amendment (More Jobs, Better Pay) Bill 1999* and the *Australian Workplace Amendment (Genuine Bargaining) Bill 2002*. Pattern bargaining is where the same agreement is used to cover a number of employers in an industry. In nursing, for example, agreements in the public sector, which cover all public hospitals and health services, are negotiated with State and Territory health departments, rather than with individual hospitals. Pattern bargaining in such industries as nursing and teaching, it is argued, is in the public interest because it results in lower industrial relations costs for enterprises, it promotes industrial harmony, and maintains similar employment standards across the sector. The effect of the proposed Bill on occupational groups such as teachers and nurses was one of the major reasons for the Australian Democrats' opposition to it.[66] The prohibition of pattern bargaining is back on the Government's industrial agenda following the 2003 release of the report of the Royal Commission into the building industry.

Collective agreements may include any matter that is part of the relationship between the employer and the employee. Consequently, nurses have been able to pursue improvements in their working conditions through their collective bargaining agreements, such as no lifting clauses, workload management clauses, clauses addressing occupational health and safety issues (such as nurses working alone), and clauses that seek to reduce and deal with violence at the workplace.

Awards or agreements are legally binding on both employers and employees and are legally enforceable. They set out the minimum wages and terms and conditions of employment applicable to a particular job.

The conditions of employment usually found in any award or agreement are:[67]

▲ classifications (job titles and definitions) and career structures;

▲ hours of work, including rest breaks, variations to working hours, and shift work;

▲ types of employment, such as full-time, part-time or casual;

▲ rates of pay (such as hourly rates and annual salaries);

▲ loadings for working overtime or for casual or shift work;

▲ penalty rates, e.g. weekend work or public holidays;

▲ allowances, e.g. meal allowances, uniform allowances;

▲ annual leave and leave loadings;

▲ long service leave;

▲ other leave, such as parental leave, carer's leave, sick leave, bereavement or compassionate leave, cultural leave and other like forms of leave;

▲ public holidays;

▲ superannuation;

▲ notice of termination;

▲ redundancy; and

▲ dispute settling procedures.

In addition to an award or agreement, nurses (like other employees) are also subject to a contract of employment, which is usually provided by the employer on appointment. The employment contract is written advice confirming the appointment and stating the position or classification of the appointment, along with details of the wage payable. The contract should also indicate the terms and conditions of employment, and identify the relevant award or agreement that applies at the time. Contracts may include other matters relating to the employment relationship, provided those conditions are not less than the relevant award or agreement.

For nurses not covered by an award or agreement, it is important that the contract specifies the items that would normally be found in an award or agreement, such as those listed above. It is sensible practice, prior to signing, to have all contracts checked by a person or organisation (such as the ANF) with the expertise to do so.

Nursing industrial bodies in Australia

The Australian Nursing Federation is the national union for nurses in Australia. The Federation was established in 1928 and comprises a national office and branches in all States and Territories. Four of the branches are also State-registered unions—New South Wales (the NSW Nurses' Association); Queensland (the Queensland Nurses' Union of Employees); Western Australia (the Industrial Union of Workers Perth); and South Australia (the Australian Nursing Federation South Australia). New South Wales and Queensland State unions did not join the Federation until 1986.

The ANF describes its core business as the industrial and professional representation of nurses and nursing, with a primary focus on providing a high standard of industrial representation and service to members; and sustaining a leadership role in a changing industrial relations environment in relation to nursing education, policy and practice; and health policy, funding and delivery.[68]

Most countries have at least one national nursing body with a responsibility for negotiating nurses' wages and conditions of employment. In some countries, the national nursing body may be part of a comprehensive health union which does the negotiations on their behalf, while in others the national nursing body may have only professional responsibilities, with nurses' industrial needs being met within the broader union movement. The International Council of Nurses, established in 1899, does not have a direct role in wages and conditions negotiations on behalf of member countries; however, within their socio-economic welfare platform, they provide education and training on industrial issues such as occupational health and safety, human resource development, negotiation skills training, and career pathway development.[69]

Nursing unions in Australia have shown positive membership growth and participation when compared with other unions.[70] Nurses see their union as a professional as well as an industrial body, involved in setting practice standards, education and training, policy development, regulation, advocacy, political lobbying, professional representation, providing information, and being a role model on social justice issues.

After a decade of declining numbers, the trade union movement in Australia showed an increase in membership over the two years 2000 and 2001; however, in 2002

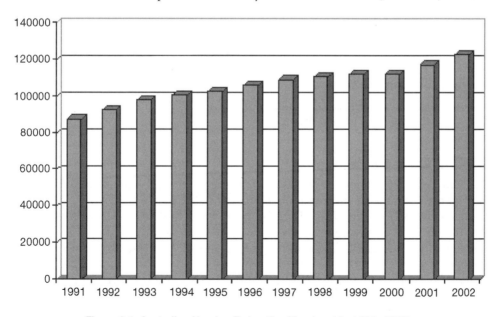

Figure 8.1 Australian Nursing Federation Membership 1991–2002

Source: Branch Declared Membership 31 December each year.

membership decreased by 69 000. Union density continued to decline, from 25.7 per cent in 1999, to 24.7 per cent in 2000, 24.5 per cent in 2001, and 23.1 per cent in 2002. The biggest increase in union membership is in the female workforce. Females now make up 43 per cent of union membership compared to their share of the workforce, which is 46 per cent.[71]

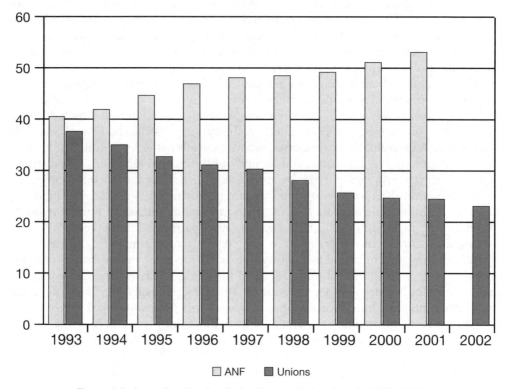

ANF   Unions

Figure 8.2 Australian Nursing Federation and Union Density 1993–2001

Note: Nursing density for 2002 is unable to be calculated as nursing labour force figures are not yet available beyond 2001.

Source: AIHW 2003 *Nursing Labour Force 2001*; ABS 2002 *Australian Social Trends* 4102.0 p.125; ANF Declared Membership 31 December 2002.

Nursing wage outcomes

Generally, wage outcomes for nurses in the acute public and acute private sector have been above average. In the December quarter 2002, the Average Annualised Wage Increases (AAWI) per employee for all current wage agreements in the public sector was 4.0 per cent. In the community services and health sector it was 3.7 per cent.[72] The AAWI for nurses for all current wage agreements in the public sector at the same period was 4.9 per cent.[73]

Workers covered by unions generally also achieve better industrial outcomes than workers not covered by unions. The AAWI per employee in agreements certified in the December quarter 2002 and negotiated by employee organisations (unions) was 4.1 per cent. By comparison, the AAWI per employee for agreements negotiated directly between employers and employees was 3.3 per cent.[74] Figures released by the

Australian Bureau of Statistics in August 2002 put the difference in the unions' favour at $33.38 per week for full-time workers and $168.37 per week for part-time workers. Full-time female union members were $63.38 better off per week, with part-time female union members being $153.62 better off. Full-time male union members were $11.75 better off per week, with part-time male union members being $206.87 per week better off.[75]

Table 8.1 Australian State/Territory public sector nurses' award and agreement outcomes

State	Outcome	Expiry
NSW	22.00% over 4.5 years	30.06.04
Victoria	12.50% over 3.5 years	31.04.04
Northern Territory	11.00% over 2.0 years	09.08.03
Tasmania	12.50% over 3.0 years	01.04.04
Western Australia	13.50% over 2.0 years	01.05.04
South Australia	12.50% over 3.0 years	31.03.04
Queensland	15.40% over 3.0 years	25.10.05
ACT	14.25% over 2.0 years	20.12.03

Note: The NSW Public Sector Nurses' State Award provided for a 16 per cent increase over 4.5 years; however, NSW nurses were granted an additional interim salary increase of 6 per cent on 1 January 2003 as part of the special rates case run by the NSW Nurses' Association (ANF NSW Branch). A final decision in the special rates case is yet to be determined.

Source: Australian Nursing Federation January 2003.

USING INDUSTRIAL INSTRUMENTS TO FACILITATE NURSING CAREER PATHS

Nursing awards and agreements are organised to reflect the career structure currently in place for the nursing profession, to attach appropriate remuneration to each point in the career path, and to maintain appropriate relativities between the different classifications.

Nursing industrial instruments cover all nursing classifications—clinical nurse, nurse manager (including senior nurse managers such as directors of nursing), nurse researcher, nurse educator, enrolled nurse, assistant in nursing, and many others that are specific to particular contexts, such as nurses working in general medical practice, Aboriginal medical services, detention centres, prisons, the Red Cross or the Royal Flying Doctor Service. Nursing industrial instruments also cover nurses working in many different sectors: public hospitals, private hospitals, community health, residential aged care, schools, workplaces, and offshore facilities, to name just a few.

In addition to maintaining currency and relevancy, nursing industrial instruments need to be responsive to new initiatives in nursing practice. For example, the introduction of clinical nurse specialist, clinical nurse consultant and nurse practitioner positions in Australia required not only appropriate remuneration, but also working conditions which supported the nursing practice.

In December 1998, after nearly ten years of consultation, the NSW Parliament passed legislation establishing the position of nurse practitioner in that State. The nursing position was the first in Australia to have legislative support for prescribing medicines and initiating diagnostic investigations. However, before nurses could be appointed to nurse practitioner positions, an appropriate classification needed to be developed and inserted into relevant awards and agreements. Subsequently, a definition of nurse practitioner was inserted into the NSW Public Hospital Nurses' (State) Award and an appropriate salary rate determined. In this way, industrial legislation is used to support new models of nursing practice.[76]

Different models of nursing practice, such as community midwifery, also need to be supported by nursing industrial instruments so that practitioners can be remunerated appropriately and their practice supported by clear and unambiguous conditions of employment. The introduction of community midwifery programs in Western Australia meant that midwives would not be working 'traditional' eight-hour shifts. Without some adjustment to the agreement covering their employment, the overtime rates for shifts that extended beyond eight hours make the cost of the service prohibitive. As a result, a clause was inserted into the Nurses' (ANF WA Public Sector) Award so that certain conditions in the award, such as overtime, shift penalties, recall and on call, would not apply to the community midwives. Instead, a calculation was made of the value of those entitlements, which was then added to their base salary.[77]

USING INDUSTRIAL INSTRUMENTS TO MANAGE NURSING WORKLOADS

Excessive workloads have been identified as a significant factor in the current shortage of nurses in Australia. Between 1995–96 and 1999–2000 in acute public and psychiatric hospitals, there was an 11.7 per cent increase in the number of patient separations per full-time equivalent nurse. Nurses in Australia are increasingly turning to part-time and casual work in an effort to manage their workloads. In 1999, 53.8 per cent of nurses worked part-time (51.7 per cent of the registered nurse workforce and 61.9 per cent of the enrolled nurse workforce). Additionally, the number of hours per week nurses worked decreased.[78]

In 1999, the ANF Victorian Branch commissioned the Australian Centre for Industrial Relations Research and Training University of Sydney to research working conditions for nurses in Victoria. A survey form was sent to a stratified random sample (n = 4000) of the 30 000 members of the ANF Victorian Branch. The return rate was over 50 per cent (n = 2161). The subsequent ACIRRT report, *The Hidden Costs of Understaffing: An analysis of contemporary nurses' working conditions in Victoria,* revealed that 65 per cent of respondents worked overtime, with fewer than one in five paid to do so. The report estimated that through working unpaid overtime, nurses were 'donating' between 209 and 256 full-time equivalent positions per week. Additionally, more than eight out of ten respondents were not regularly receiving their full meal break entitlement. By working through meal breaks, nurses were 'donating' a further 100–200 full-time equivalent positions per week. Work-related stress was reported by 87 per cent of respondents as a result of their working conditions.[79]

The problem of unpaid overtime is not limited to the nursing profession. The 2002 JOB Futures/Saulwick Employee Sentiment Survey of 1000 workers found 37 per cent work an average of 7.3 hours of unpaid overtime each week. The figures for full-time workers showed 47 per cent work an average of 7.9 hours unpaid overtime each week.[80]

Nursing has turned to industrial instruments in an effort to control workloads, achieve safe staffing levels and promote safe practice. Many nurses no longer have confidence that their employer will provide them or their patients with an environment that allows safe care and safe practice, and this clearly has implications for nursing leaders.

In a landmark decision in the Victorian public sector in 2000, the AIRC mandated nurse-to-patient ratios. Hospitals were categorised into different levels—major metropolitan hospital, smaller metropolitan hospital, rural hospital, or aged care facility—and minimum staffing levels established. If the staffing levels cannot be achieved, beds close. This ensures that sufficient numbers of nurses are available to provide appropriate nursing care.[81] The introduction of nurse to patient ratios has resulted in over 3000 nurses returning to Victorian public hospitals.[82]

Table 8.2 Nurses (Victorian Health Services) Award C2000/35605 31.08.00

Category	Ratio
A	1: 4 plus in charge a.m. and p.m.; 1: 8 nights
B	1: 5 plus in charge a.m. and p.m.; 1: 10 nights
C	1: 6 plus in charge a.m.; 1: 7 plus in charge p.m.; 1: 12 plus in charge nights
D	1: 7 plus in charge a.m.; 1: 8 plus in charge p.m.; 1: 15 nights
Emergency	1: 3 plus in charge plus triage all shifts
Labour Ward	1: 1 all shifts
Antenatal	1: 5 plus in charge a.m. and p.m.; 1: 8 nights
Postnatal	1: 5 plus in charge a.m. and p.m.; 1: 8 nights

The AIRC took a slightly different approach in the 2001 Western Australian public sector decision, establishing nursing hours per patient per day. The categorisation is done at a ward or unit level, but the principle and the outcome are much the same. In the WA decision, the AIRC stated that the employer has a duty to prevent sustained and unreasonable workloads.[83]

Table 8.3 Nurses (WA Government Health Services) Exceptional Matters Order C2001/1910 11.02.02

Category	NHPPD	Criteria
A	7.5	High complexity / dependency; tertiary step down ICU; tertiary paediatrics
B	6.0	High complexity; moderate / high intervention; secondary paediatrics; tertiary maternity
C	5.75	High complexity acute; moderate turnover; emergency admissions >50 per cent; psychogeriatric mental health
D	5.0	Moderate complexity / turnover; secondary maternity; acute rehabilitation
E	4.5	Moderate complexity / turnover; sub acute; rural paediatrics
F	4.0	Moderate to low complexity; sub acute; aged care awaiting placement
G	3.0	Ambulatory care; day surgery; renal dialysis

The insertion of measures to manage workloads into nursing awards and agreements is an effective use of industrial relations instruments to respond to nursing practice issues. In addition to Victoria and Western Australia, workload measures have been agreed to in Queensland and Tasmania. A workloads clause also forms part of the NSW claim in their Special Rates case currently before the NSW Industrial Relations Commission.

LEADING AND MANAGING INDUSTRIAL ISSUES

Workplace values and culture

In a survey of public sector organisations in NSW in 2000, the NSW Independent Commission Against Corruption (ICAC) found that the prevailing ethical culture of an organisation has more influence on an individual's behaviour in the workplace than their personal moral beliefs or values.[84] They found that the key elements to promoting a positive culture in the workplace were establishing values (such as honesty, openness, accountability, objectivity, courage), communicating the values (using tools such as codes of conduct, policies and procedures, education and training), and by the organisation's leaders demonstrating the values by example.[85] According to the ICAC, values have two important roles: firstly, to guide individual decision-making and the resolution of ethical dilemmas, and secondly to underpin and enhance an organisation's operations.[86]

The ANF's Strategic Plan contains the following operational values:[87]

▲ to be inclusive and involve people in decision-making;

▲ to be cooperative and work as a team;

▲ to be consistent, congruent and ethical in our decision-making and behaviours;

▲ to be tolerant and accepting of others;

▲ to be open, forthright and have integrity in our dealings with other people and with each other;

▲ to be flexible, innovative and determined in order to achieve our objectives;

▲ to be committed and contribute to the objectives of the organisation;

▲ to be an effective and efficient organisation; and

▲ to be responsible in our use of internal and external resources.

A further key finding by the ICAC was that employees who felt that their work was valued by their organisation were more likely to stay in their job.[88] This is of significant importance to nurse leaders when there is a contracted employment market. There are also cost savings in terms of recruitment, increased productivity with lower staff turnover, and enhanced quality and continuity of care. Establishing or affirming and demonstrating the values of an organisation is a key leadership responsibility, particularly as it has been shown that this enhances an organisation's operations.

Industrial relations negotiating principles

The environment in which nursing agreements are negotiated is characterised by constant change, funding constraints, increasing demands and recruitment difficulties.

Within this environment, the ANF has proposed a set of industrial relations negotiating principles, which have allowed them to achieve above average outcomes for nurses.

Know what you want to achieve

Both sides must be clear about what they want to achieve, in order to be able to clearly articulate their desired outcomes to the other negotiating party, and develop strategies and counter-strategies to achieve their objectives. Writing down what you want to achieve often helps to clarify your thinking. To maintain your 'bottom line', you need to know what your 'bottom line' is.

Establish the ground rules

It is important to establish the ground rules for the negotiation right from the beginning. Ground rules might include the number and length of meetings, consistent attendance at meetings, how points are to be clarified or agreed to, a process for calling 'time out' if discussions indicate a break is needed, and the confidentiality of discussions. The ground rules should be revisited and reconfirmed at the beginning of each meeting.

Expect and accept difference

Negotiation is a matter of give and take. If every person agreed on every issue, there would be no need to negotiate. In an industrial context, negotiating parties are commonly unable to grasp or agree with each other's positions. However, if both parties start from a position of expecting and accepting difference, they can spend their time and energy focusing on finding common ground, rather than trying to convince the other party that the position they hold is incorrect.

Be inclusive, not exclusive

Including all parties with an interest in the negotiations not only saves time but also facilitates acceptance of the outcome and avoids conflict. Excluding those who express an interest gives them little alternative but to become the opposition.

Have meaningful communication

All too often, parties negotiate only because the legislation requires them to do so, and they have no real intention or desire of reaching an agreed position. Both parties have to be committed to meaningful communication for a negotiated outcome to be achieved. In an environment where arbitration is increasingly seen as a measure of last resort, it is wise to go into negotiations committed to achieving an outcome.

Think laterally and be flexible and creative

There is often more than one way to solve a problem. As a nursing leader, it is important to be open to new ideas and to be able to think laterally and be flexible and creative in finding solutions, without compromising your 'bottom line'.

Always keep sight of your ultimate objective

In the heat of negotiations, it is easy to get side-tracked by extraneous issues or by relatively unimportant points. By keeping the ultimate objective in sight, other issues can be measured by how much they contribute to or detract from achieving the ultimate objective.

Keep things in perspective

It is easy to lose your perspective when all your energies are focused on achieving a particular outcome, particularly if you are personally convinced of the rightness or desirability of that outcome. Specific outcomes in time, however, need to be judged against a broader environment—other industries, interstate and international comparisons, world events. The value in maintaining your perspective is that you are more likely to be able to stay calm and reasonable, which in itself will facilitate the achievement of your desired outcome.

Maintain your sense of humour

Maintaining a sense of humour when issues are critical and negotiations are tense is not always easy. A little humour, used sensitively and appropriately, often serves to defuse a tense situation, allowing negotiating parties to relax and re-focus.

Grievance and dispute procedures

All awards and agreements contain grievance and dispute procedures. These procedures establish processes and timeframes for the resolution of an employee grievance or a dispute between employees and the employer at the workplace level. The procedures normally provide that the matters raised as a grievance or dispute, are in the first instance, discussed at the first level of management with the employee(s) and their industrial representative.[89]

In the event that the initial discussions do not resolve the matter, the grievance process provides that further discussions follow with senior management personnel and, where appropriate, more senior industrial representatives. Where matters are unable to be resolved at the enterprise level, the dispute grievance procedures commonly provide for conciliation, and, if necessary, arbitration by the AIRC. Adherence to the procedures is considered significantly important to avoid unnecessary industrial conflict.[90]

Grievances and disputes between employers and nurses can address clinical nursing practice. The line between nurses' responsibility to the employer and nurses' professional responsibility to maintain nursing standards of care can become blurred or in some cases be in conflict. While a matter may be resolved at the workplace level, nurse regulatory authorities and peak nursing bodies may become involved to ensure that professional nursing standards are preserved. Should this occur, it is essential that the nurse obtain legal and professional support and advice from an organisation such as the ANF.

Unfair dismissals

The industrial relations system also provides protection to individual employees from unfair or discriminatory termination of their employment. An employee or their union representative may make application to a tribunal to determine whether their termination was 'harsh, unjust or unreasonable'.[91]

Most claims for unfair dismissal are resolved by conciliation, with the parties reaching agreement. Where an unfair dismissal claim is subject to arbitration, the industrial tribunal is required to determine whether the termination was harsh, unjust or unreasonable, having regard to a number of factors, such as whether the employee was notified of the reason and given an opportunity to respond, or whether warnings had been given if it was in relation to unsatisfactory performance.[92]

If the industrial tribunal finds a termination to be harsh, unjust or unreasonable, it may order either that the employee be reinstated or receive a monetary settlement in lieu of reinstatement. If the employee is reinstated, the industrial tribunal may also order payment for wages lost as a result of the termination.[93]

CONCLUSION

Though industrial relations is a very complex and constantly changing area, nurse leaders require a working understanding of current industrial relations issues to be effective in the workplace. This chapter has provided an outline of some of the issues relevant to nurses in Australia and the manner in which industrial relations can support nurses in their work and enhance the provision of nursing care. Further information can be found in the recommended readings listed below.

Reflective exercise

1 What is the name of the award or agreement that covers your employment? Do you have a copy?

2 Do you know the annual leave, sick leave, long service leave, parental leave, and other leave entitlements specified in the award or agreement that covers your employment?

3 When is it legal in Australia for a nurse to take industrial action?

4 Have you ever had to conduct industrial relations negotiations? How did you or how would you go about it?

RECOMMENDED READINGS

Australian Industrial Relations Commission (1999). *General Information Booklet* at www. airc. gov. au/research/about/about. html.

Dabscheck, B. (2001). The slow and agonising death of the Australian experiment with conciliation and arbitration. *Journal of Industrial Relations, 43*(3), p.282.

Wailes, N., & Lansbury, R. D. (1997). *Flexibility vs collective bargaining: Australia during the 1980s and 1990s.* Working Paper No.49. Australian Centre for Industrial Relations Research and Training University of Sydney.

ENDNOTES

1 Department of Finance and Trade *Australia Now—Workplace Relations in Australia* at http: // www. dfat. gov. au/facts/workplace_relations. html.

2 ibid.

3 http: //www. airc. gov. au General Information Booklet August, 1999, p.1.

4 ibid., p.5.

5 http: //www. airc. gov. au/research/about/about. html Historical Overview Booklet p.2.

6 ibid.

7 ibid.

8 http: //www. airc. gov. au, op. cit., p.5.

9 http: //www. airc. gov. au/research/about/about. html op. cit., p.5.

10 ibid.

11 Dabscheck B. (2001). The slow and agonising death of the Australian experiment with conciliation and arbitration. *Journal of Industrial Relations* Vol: 43 Issue No: 3 p.282.

12 http: //www. airc. gov. au/research/about/about. html op. cit., p.5.

13 ibid., p.6.

14 http: //www. airc. gov. au op. cit., p.3.

15 Wailes, N. & Lansbury, R. D. (1997). *Flexibility vs Collective Bargaining: Australia during the 1980s and 1990s* Working Paper No.49 ACIRRT p.17.

16 http: //www. austilii/edu/au; www. airc. gov. au op. cit., p.11.

17 Wailes & Lansbury (1997). op. cit., pp.17, 18, 48.

18 ibid., p.20.

19 Australian Council of Trade Unions (2002). *A Short History of Australian Unions* at http: // www. actu. asn. au/about/history. html.

20 Wailes & Lansbury (1997). op. cit., p.18.

21 ibid., p.20.

22 ibid., p.75.

23 ibid., pp.20, 32, 39.

24 ibid., pp.21, 75.

25 Dabscheck, B. (2001). op. cit., p.282.

26 ibid., p.283.

27 Wailes & Lansbury (1997). op. cit., pp.21, 75; NSW Department of Industrial Relations *IR in Action: Structural Efficiency Principle and Minimum Rates Adjustment Principle* at http: // www. dir. nsw. gov. au/action/policy/equity/report/wagefix/Page2. html.

28 Wailes & Lansbury (1997) op. cit., p.22.

29 Murray, A. 1999. *Senate Supplementary Report on the Workplace Relations Legislation Amendment (More Jobs, Better Pay) Bill 1999*, November p.389.

30 Wailes & Lansbury (1997) op. cit., p.24.

31 Murray, A. 1999 op. cit., p.391; ACTU *International Body Slams Australia's IR Laws* 24 September 2002 at http: //actu. labor. net. au/public/news/1032847660_15465. html.

32 http: //webfusion. ilo. org.

33 http: //www. dfat. gov. au/facts/workplace_relations. html p.2.

34 ibid; Wailes & Lansbury (1997). op. cit., p.40.

35 Wailes & Lansbury (1997). op. cit., p.25.

36 ibid.

37 http: //www. austlii/edu/au; s.170LJ; s.170LK; s.170 (Part VI D).

38 http: //www. austlii/edu/au; s.170LB(1); s.170LB(3); s.170LC.

39 Dabscheck, B. (2001). op. cit., p.284.

40 http: //www. austlii/edu/au; s.89A; s.88A(b); s.143(1B).

41 Murray, A. (1999). op. cit., p.392.

42 ibid.

43 ibid. p.391.

44 http: //www. aph. gov. au/parlinfo/billsnet/main/htm.

45 ibid.

46 http: //www. dfat. gov. au/facts/workplace_relations. html p.2.

47 Plowman, D. H. (2002). *Awards, Certified Agreements and AWAs: some reflections* Working Paper 75 ACIRRT University of Sydney p.2.

48 http: //www. austlii/edu/au s.170M; Dabscheck, B. (2001). op. cit., p.285; http: //www. cpsu. org/ir_legis/outline. htm ACTU 1996 Outline of the *Workplace Relations Act*, p.4.

49 http: //www. airc. gov. au/research/about/about. html op. cit., p.16; Dabscheck, B. (2001) op. cit., p.285; ACTU 1996 Outline of the Workplace Relations Act, p.5 at www. cpsu. org/ir_legis/outline. htm.

50 http: //www. austlii/edu/au s.90; s.170MW; s.170MX.

51 ACTU 1996 Outline of the *Workplace Relations Act*, p.4 at www. cpsu. org/ir_legis/ outline. htm.

52 http: //www. airc. gov. au/research/about/about. html op. cit., p.10.

53 http: //www. austlii/edu/aus.170LT.

54 http: //www. airc. gov. au/research/about/about. html op. cit., p.2.

55 Wailes & Lansbury (1997). op. cit., p.40.

56 Dabscheck, B. (2001). op. cit., p.284.

57 http: //www. oea. gov. au/AWA AWA Employee Information Statement, p.7; Wailes & Lansbury (1997). op. cit., p.61.

58 Wailes & Lansbury (1997). op. cit., p.50.

59 http: //www. workplace. gov. au/workplace Australia Workplace: Agreement Making in Australia under the *Workplace Relations Act*, p.5.

60 http: //www. oea. gov. au/AWA AWA Employee Information Statement, pp.4–6.

61 Department of Employment and Workplace Relations *Trends in Federal Enterprise Bargaining* December 2002, http: //www. workplace. gov. au/WP/Content/Files/WP/WR/Publications/Trends_S02. pdf.

62 AIHW (2001) *Australian Hospital Statistics 1999–2000.* Canberra. p.37.

63 Plowman, D. H. Working Paper 75 ACIRRT, op. cit., p.9.

64 http: //www. oea. gov. au/graphics AWA Statistics, 1 May 2003.

65 http: //www. airc. gov. au op. cit., p.16.

66 Australian Democrats 2000 *Pattern bargaining bill goes too far* Media Release 00/320, 5 June at http: //www. democrats. org. au/news.

67 Australian Nursing Federation 2002 *PayCheck*, Vol.2, No.1, p.33.

68 Australian Nursing Federation *Strategic Plan 1999–2003* http: //www. anf. org. au.

69 http: //www. icn. ch.

70 Nursing Density Figures—AIHW 2003 *Nursing Labour Force 2001*; Australian Nursing Federation Declared Membership. Union Density Figures—ABS 2002 *Australian Social Trends*, Cat. no. 4102.0, p.125.

71 ACTU Media Releases: 4 April 2001; 28 February 2002 at http: //www. actu. asn. au; http: //www. abs. gov. au/ausstats.

72 Department of Employment and Workplace Relations 2002. *Trends in Federal Enterprise Bargaining* December at http: //www. workplace. gov. au/WP/Content/Files/WP/WR/Publications/Trends_DO2. pdf.

73 Australian Nursing Federation 2002 *PayCheck*, Vol.2, No.1, p.33.

74 Department of Employment and Workplace Relations 2002. *Trends in Federal Enterprise Bargaining* December op. cit.

75 Australian Bureau of Statistics 2002 *Employee Earnings, Benefits and Trade Union Membership* Cat. No: 6310.0.

76 NSW Industrial Relations Commission Decision 2000/2000 23 May 2000.

77 Nurses (ANF WA Public Sector) Award 2002 Appendix 6 Peel Health Service Community Midwifery Special Conditions of Employment.

78 Australian Institute of Health and Welfare 2003. *Nursing Labour Force 2001.* Canberra, pp.31, 101.

79 Considine, G. & Buchanan, J. (1999) *The Hidden Costs of Understaffing: An analysis of contemporary nurses' working conditions in Victoria.* Australian Centre for Industrial Relations Research and Training University of Sydney, pp.2–6.

80 Australian Council of Trade Unions 2002 *Unpaid Overtime Epidemic* at http: //www. actu. labor. net. au/public/news/1032745393_32160. html.

81 AIRC Decision No: C2000/35605, 31 August 2000.

82 Victorian Department of Human Services 2002. *3,300 Extra Nurses in Victorian Public Hospitals* Media Release 30 May 2002, at http: //hnb. dhs. vic. gov. au/web/pubaff/medrel.nsf.

83 AIRC Decision No: C2001/1910, 11 February 2002.

84 NSW Independent Commission Against Corruption 2000 *Organisation integrity: Key areas to consider in building an ethical workplace* September pp.5, 8, 9, 12 and 15 at http: //www. icac. nsw. gov. au.

85 ibid p.2.
86 ibid p.8.
87 Australian Nursing Federation *Strategic Plan 1999–2003* at http: //www. anf. org. au.
88 Independent Commission Against Corruption 2000 *Ethical Culture Survey Results: Benchmarking data* September p.6 www. icac. nsw. gov. au.
89 http: //www. austlii/edu/au s.91 and s.170LW *Workplace Relations Act 1996.*
90 http: //www. austlii/edu/au s.92 *Workplace Relations Act 1996.*
91 http: //www. austlii/edu/au s.170CA *Workplace Relations Act 1996.*
92 http: //www. austlii/edu/au s.170CG(3) *Workplace Relations Act 1996.*
93 http: //www. austlii/edu/au s. 170CH *Workplace Relations Act 1996.*

CHAPTER NINE

Organisation violations: Implications for leadership

Sandra Speedy

LEARNING OBJECTIVES

After reading this chapter, the reader will be able to:

- ▲ understand the nature of organisation violations and the purposes they serve;

- ▲ consider the causes of organisation violations from a range of perspectives;

- ▲ develop a deeper understanding of the consequences of organisation violations;

- ▲ discuss the problem and consequences of trust violation in organisations; and

- ▲ insightfully identify ways of reducing organisation violations in the workplace.

KEY WORDS
Organisation violations, resistance, whistle-blowing, horizontal violence, bullying, sexual harassment

INTRODUCTION

While organisations are created for a diverse range of purposes, they are recognised as having a 'dark side'. This dark side is often identified as behaviours that are unacceptable to management because they disturb the goals of the organisation (generally profit-seeking) and may significantly disrupt its functioning. The range of descriptors given to such 'unacceptable behaviours' include 'oppositional practices' (Collinson 1994), 'organisational retaliatory' or 'anti-citizenship' behaviours, including those labelled 'deviant', 'dysfunctional' and 'antisocial' (Folger & Cropanzano 1998); and 'recalcitrant', demonstrated by sabotage, absenteeism, disobedience and decreased productivity (Ackroyd & Thompson 1999; Robinson & Bennett 1995). Other researchers have used the term 'counterproductive work behaviours' to include aggression, violence and theft (Liu & Perrene 2002); sexual harassment (Sinclair 1998), and incivility (Andersson & Pearson 1999); and horizontal violence, which has specifically been used in the nursing context (Bent 1993; David 2000). Hearn and Parkin (2001) conceptualise the above types of behaviour as 'organisation violations' in order to provide an inclusive framework that takes into account the structure of the organisation, its culture, its enactment of authority and its organisational processes; in other words, the context in which such behaviours occur. They state that the 'ordinary and extraordinary tactics perpetuating oppressions—bullying, isolation, exclusion, harassment, physical violence, emotional assault, demeaning actions, along with cultural ideological and symbolic violences—need to be named as violations' (p.87).

This chapter will consider the contexts of organisation violations and examine a range of violations that can occur. It will then address some of the causes of organisation violation, using a range of examples to demonstrate how workplace abuse is manifest, particularly from the perspective of the employee. Some of the consequences of organisation violations will be examined to see how this knowledge can be used by those in leadership positions to enhance organisational environments. Leaders of organisations need a high level of understanding of organisation violations if they wish to be part of the reform process within such organisations.

CONTEXTS OF ORGANISATION VIOLATIONS

Organisation violations occur in any organisation. Health care organisations are no exception. In fact, there may be more potential for abuse of workers due to the unique characteristics of health care organisations. While all organisations seek efficiencies, productivity and cost containment in order to maximise profits, health care organisations have complexities of function and structures that are not generally characteristic of profit-making organisations. Their goals are often more abstract, authority is more diffuse and there are fewer performance indicators than 'for profit' organisations. Because of their mandate to meet socially recognised public health needs, health care organisations emphasise health rather than organisational issues, making them accountable in a range of ways that do not apply to private sector organisations. Typically, health care organisations are funded by the 'public purse', although increasingly there is a private funding imperative at work.

The major difference between health care organisations and 'for profit' organisations is the division between the 'professional' capacity for control over the 'bureaucratic' function of organisations. Specifically, professionals have the capacity to determine power relationships between the medical, nursing and administrative groups, which results in a political process that is entirely about the control that is exercised. Nevertheless, health care organisations do conform to the generic form of organisations, and hence, organisation violations are likely to occur.

'Unacceptable behaviours' of employees in the workplace, or 'organisation violations' are identified and interpreted by those who have power over those whose behaviour is being judged. Sometimes such behaviours have been labelled 'dysfunctional' or 'pathological'. This label is provided from the perspective of those who are in a position to sanction such behaviours, as their supervisory roles are being made more difficult. Ackroyd and Thompson (1999) insightfully analyse 'organisational *mis*behaviour', suggesting that the 'sociology of opposing interests' (p.9) would be a useful lens with which to examine organisations. Rather than viewing persistent 'troublemakers' as having a personal pathology, they suggest that many misbehaviours are underpinned by informal workgroup norms, and that the organisation has a degree of dependency on them. '[D]esignating misbehaviour is a matter of perspective and definition, and . . . the identification and prosecution of misbehaviour is to be understood in terms of continuing structural imbalances of power' (Ackroyd & Thompson 1999, p.164).

Misbehaviour in this case is defined very broadly to be anything done at work that one is not supposed to do. Ashforth and Mael (1998) also view 'acts of resistance' as attempts to assert power over those who have legitimate authoritative and organisational power. They suggest that the power of resistance is 'partly in its potential to contest *meaning*' (p.92), because employees negotiate their 'work selves' with the organisation.

Romme (1998) asserts that structural explanations of antisocial behaviour in organisations have been neglected in past research, noting that from whose perspective dysfunctionality is assessed is vital, because it can determine whether the behaviour is described as constructive or destructive. What is adaptive and functional for an individual (or a workgroup) may not be adaptive and functional for the organisation, such as whistle-blowing behaviour, which may be negative from a management perspective, but positive from the public's perspective. There are many examples of behaviours that are counterproductive to management, but which assist individuals in adapting to situations that become intolerable (Liu & Perrene 2002). For example, employee theft or aggression may be a response to perceptions of gross injustice, such as being passed over for promotion.

Fox et al. (2001), in reviewing the literature, note that counterproductive work behaviours have been portrayed as 'an emotion-based response to stressful organizational conditions' (p.291), and as a response to organisational injustice. This raises the issue of workplace abuse as a stress agent, to be examined later in this chapter. Folger and Cropanzano (1998) point out that some employees are treated unfairly and may seek justice through the use of retaliatory behaviours, which is not an individually neurotic event.[*] There may be considerable justification for what has been labelled 'dysfunctional, deviant and antisocial' behaviour (p.221).

This chapter takes the focus of employees' organisation violations, rather than violations more likely to be committed by senior management, including, for example, fraud and corporate crime. Management will be examined in so far as they define, interpret and sanction organisation violations of their workforce, and are, in fact, complicit in their management of 'misbehaviour' (Hearn & Parkin 2001; McMillan 1995). This is particularly the case for sexual harassment and bullying, but has also been identified in 'the ordinary enactment of managerial "policy"' (Hearn & Parkin 2001, p.149). Management can, for example, be actively involved in violations, ignore them, or collude with practices that lead to 'cultures of intimidation' (p.150). Additionally, managers may be rewarded for bullying behaviours and thus continue to behave in this way. Observers are likely to emulate such abuses if they are viewed as acceptable in the work setting. Specifically, therefore, they may be the sexual harasser, or treat the harassed individual as 'imagining' the event, or allow the creation of opportunities within the organisation for violation to occur.

CULTURE

The culture of an organisation is significant when examining organisation violations. Graetz et al. (2002) define organisational culture as 'a pattern of beliefs, and expectations that are common to members of a social unit and subsequently set the behavioural standards and norms for all new employees' (p.262).

Liu and Perrene (2002) note that certain organisational values and integrity influence the extent to which employees engage in organisation violations because of the socialisation they receive when they enter it. Other research demonstrates that highly ethical cultural environments encourage and facilitate organisational behaviours that are ethical and honest (Fulop & Linstead 1999). In an organisational culture that is focused on self-interest, employees may lie in order to achieve rewards; conversely, if the lying is to protect a workmate, it may be viewed as justifiable if the culture values relationships (Elangovan & Shapiro 1998).

Senior managements have been known to manipulate the culture of an organisation in order to create a 'strong culture' that will acquire the commitment and dedication of employees. Fulop and Linstead (1999) quote a study in which characteristics were developed for 'good employees', including submissiveness, punctuality, seriousness, malleability and ambition. The formal evaluative criteria for such employees included production per line, per machine, per job, and the number of breakdowns and conflicts they had. However, the danger of strong cultures is that they may have intense attraction, but also the potential for intense resistance (Ashforth & Mael 1998). This can lay the foundation for organisational conflict.

Cultural values reflect the work group's shared understanding and subsequent behaviour, and depending on those values, a trusting or distrusting environment can be created. Whitener et al. (1998) suggest that culture and the structure of organisations may directly influence managerial trustworthy behaviours. Their research proposed that highly centralised, formalised and hierarchical organisations, whose focus is on efficiency, will not generate managerial trustworthiness. Conversely, organisations can encourage trustworthy managerial behaviours when interpersonal values of inclusiveness, open, honest communication, concern and valuing of colleagues are the norm. Managers who engender trust are more likely themselves to be trusting, inviting and to expect reciprocity of trust.

Jordan (2002) also believes that organisational cultures contribute to violations; that bullying, aggressive and coercive behaviours are perpetrated on employees by managers. He notes that cultures that emphasise ends rather than means are more likely to be abusive, and that if short-term gains are valued over means, then the environment is ripe for work abuse. Conflict cannot be managed due to the interpersonal shortcomings of managers, resulting in increased stress levels for those around them. When nursing leaders are appointed on the strength of their clinical knowledge rather than their leadership skills it is conceivable that a contributory factor to organisation violation is that negative managerial practices may be legitimised and rewarded, as previously noted.

Managerial subcultures within organisations are also significant to organisation violations. Sinclair (1998) documents a study suggesting that managerial subcultures are built around masculinities, expressed in a variety of ways. These include traditional authoritarianism, advanced through bullying and fear; protective paternalism (otherwise known as 'the gentleman's club'); entrepreneurialism, expressed as task-focused, excessive commitment to work; and informalism, demonstrated by a boyish, larrikin-like culture. Collinson and Hearn (1994) add 'careerism', which involves valuing expertise and bureaucratic advancement above all else. Such subcultures, Sinclair (1998) asserts, require organisational women to exhibit a higher level of personal sacrifice and greater emotional toughness, and leaves them vulnerable to sexual harassment, aggression and bullying.

THE ROLE OF PERCEPTION AND INTERPRETATION

Individual perception and interpretation of the work situation impacts on whether or not workplace abuse is recognised or acknowledged. Typically, the 'psychological effect of a situation depends on how a person interprets the situation and that such differences in interpretation can vary as a function of significant individual differences' (Skarlicki et al. 1999, p.102).

Furthermore, this study suggested that unfair treatment would not affect everyone subjected to it in the same way. They noted that some individuals had greater sensitivity to environments that had negative effects on them, suggesting that responses to such situations involved personality characteristics, perceptions of fairness, and also the person's perception of common practice. Of course, the relative power of the person abused, and their avenues of support within the organisation, can also impact on how the individual will deal with organisation violation.

The work setting

Lui and Perrene (2002), while acknowledging the role played by situational factors in producing counterproductive work behaviours, do suggest that locus of control and emotional stability are additional individual variables that need to be considered in abusive work settings. Similar findings were reported by Fox and Spector (1999); they explicitly state that employees' perceptions of situational constraints and job characteristics are of greater importance than 'objective constraints and job characteristics' (p.928). They also hypothesised that individual characteristics, such as high trait anxiety (the tendency to perceive stressful situations as threatening), trait anger (perceiving a wide range of situations as anger-provoking), and negative affectivity (the tendency to perceive negative emotions across time and situations in the absence of aversive environmental events) will predetermine an individual's tendency to react more readily to perceived work abuse practices. These reactions will be negative, or '. . .counterproductive, anti-role, antisocial, maladaptive or deviant behaviors' (p.917). Fox et al. (2001) cite a range of studies that indicate perception of unjust practices in the workplace results in a range of negative emotions, including anger, outrage, resentment, theft, vandalism, sabotage, resistance and other general retaliatory behaviours.

Personal perceptions

Ashforth and Mael (1998) reinforce the importance of individual perceptions, asserting that threat is 'in the eye of the beholder' (p.98), and that legitimate resistance can be rationalised 'through the prism of member self-interests' (p.108). They note how versatile people can be in excusing and justifying acts that are 'patently self-serving' (p.108). Nurse leaders can readily think of examples of how their (or nursing's) self-interest can be rationalised against oppressive forces within the organisation. For example, nurses who subject others to horizontal violence may justify such behaviours as being necessary to point out the 'shortcomings' of the target victim. The target victim, on the other hand, may try to resist this by behaving in unprofessional ways (that can be justified) with patients—a psychological mechanism known as displacement.

Morgan (1986) notes the role that individual attributes and emotions can play in organisational behaviour. He suggests, for example, that aggression, greed, hate, fear and sexual desire, while having no official status, often break through, and may be rapidly punished or rationalised. However, any retaliation does not necessarily 'rid the organization of these repressed forces lurking in the shadow of rationality' (p.229). Irrationality is banished, as it is feared as 'dangerous' and needs controlling. Rationality, on the other hand, is designed to enhance our security. However, it will not necessarily result in understanding 'the hidden meaning and significance of the actions that shape organization' (p.229); hence the metaphor Morgan uses to describe the organisation as a 'psychic prison', in which all are imprisoned. This does highlight the importance of recognising the role that emotions and emotionality play in organisational life.

Psychological factors

There is extensive literature taking the perspective that misbehaviour is due to psycho-logical and biological causes. At the individual level, personality has been related to organisational sabotage (Giacalone & Knouse 1990; Kets de Vries & Miller 1984). Psychological causes of misbehaviour have been framed as individuals having 'dark-side traits', which include argumentativeness, interpersonal insensitivity, narcissism, perfectionism, inpulsivity and fear of failure (Hughes et al. 1999). Kets de Vries and Miller (1984) take the view that individuals use their defences to protect themselves against stressful work events, and that in most circumstances such defences are not pathological. Defences become pathological when they are overused or over-developed. However, psychological defenses do tend to restrict the individual's perceptions, range and appropriateness of behavioural responses, 'particularly in emotion-laden situations involving long-standing interpersonal relationships' (p.134).

Thus, organisation violations are complicated by the construction of our own meanings and realities, and the distortions of perceptions that occur. This is particularly so when there are personal threats to our identity. However, there are a range of additional approaches required to understand organisation violations, not the least of which requires an understanding of the role of culture and structure of organisations. This is emphasised by Hearn and Parkin (2001), whose critical approach is sociological and political, but who also warn that 'perceptions and experiences of individuals also need emphasis' (p.48).

Causes of organisation violation

Behaviours that have a direct and visible negative effect on the organisation or members of the organisation can be caused by a range of factors and will, if unchecked, have a corruptive influence on organisational climate (Liu & Perrene 2002). Counter-productive work behaviours are described by Liu and Perrene as

> all employee behaviours, intended or unintended, which are directed at the organization, other organization members, clients and customers or self, and which have the potential to hurt organizational productivity and well being (p.4).

Note that self-destructive behaviours are included in this definition, such as drug or alcohol abuse, suppression of negative emotions, consistently working overtime, the expression of fake positive emotions (known as emotional labour), and even suicide.

As noted above, organisational cultures, structures and processes play a determining role in deeming what is unacceptable workplace behaviour. It is also clear that particular circumstances can be instrumental in encouraging 'misbehaviour'. Ackroyd and Thompson (1999) suggest that 'misbehaviour' can take four directions (pp.25–7). The first direction is disagreement over the *appropriation of work*, with conflict taking the possible form of destructiveness or sabotage. The second is the *appropriation of materials* used in work, and in this case, conflict can result in pilferage, sometimes referred to as 'stock shrinkage' or 'unplanned overheads', also known as 'fiddling' (Fulop & Linstead 1999). The third direction is the *amount of time spent on the work*, and where conflict occurs, employees may engage in a range of behaviours, including time-wasting (often known as 'being absent at work', where toilets are often the place of refuge), or simply leaving the organisation altogether. The final direction is the extent to which employees identify with their work and their employer (known as the *appropriation of identity*), and where this does not occur, the behaviours can range from joking rituals based on horseplay and banter, to subjecting each other to existing subcultural rituals, which may involve initiations that are humiliating to newcomers.

ABUSIVE LEADERS AND ABUSIVE WORK SETTINGS

Wyatt and Hare (1997) perceive that employees who suffer 'work stress' are often operating under abusive work climates that organisations either refuse to acknowledge or take responsibility for. These individuals may then be labelled as 'disgruntled' or 'troublemakers', therefore denying the role that organisations can play in creating an unnecessarily conflictual or unsupportive environment. In nursing, this may take the form of universities poorly preparing the nurse for practice in order to meet the 'realities' of the nursing workplace, including the abuses that lie therein. This is another 'blame the victim' strategy that does not account for the often sanctioned violence that occurs. For example, Bostock (2000) cites the increasing managerialism in universities that has unintended consequences such as restriction of academic autonomy, disempowerment, reduction in intellectual freedom, increased stress for academics and increased psychological violence (and sometimes physical violence when frustration levels are exceeded). He deplores the increase in administrative force which promotes behaviours that are dangerous, citing the case of an academic who was encouraged to commit suicide because he was creating administrative difficulties.

Inequality, oppression and the abuse of power are fundamental to organisation violations (Hearn & Parkin 2001; Itzen & Newman, 1995). Hearn and Parkin (2001) consider that 'gendered, sexualed power provides the material and ideological backcloth' (p.85) to these violations, while Itzen and Newman (1995) view abuse of power as 'damaging and diminishing in humane terms for those who are dominant and those who are subordinate' (p.268). Such oppressiveness effectively silences or excludes employees, resulting in increased denial of violations, since these are not acknowledged. Hearn and Parkin (2001) also note that management takes an explicit and complicit role in violations, particularly those of sexual harassment and bullying, but point out that the ordinary enactment of managerial policy can have the same effect (p.149).

Managers have been found to be sarcastic, verbally abusive, dishonest, intimidatory, harassing and cruel (Sheehan 1996). This unacceptable behaviour is explained in a number of ways. For example, it is hypothesised that the insecure coercive manager abuses the authority relationship because of poor interpersonal skill development, low self-esteem, and inadequate competencies (Sheehan 1996). Wyatt and Hare (1997) suggest that managers who lack personal power may misuse their legitimate role power by becoming abusive. Similarly, Jacques (1995) suggests that a mismatch between organisational roles and the capabilities of those who are assigned to those roles can lead to a manipulative abuse of personal power, 'resulting in an unpleasant environment that resembles a paranoiagenic zoo' (p.343).

Hughes et al. (1999) assert that leaders who have 'dark-side traits', including argumentativeness, interpersonal insensitivity, narcissism, impulsivity, perfectionism and fear of failure, leave a long trail of bruised people in their wake. This emphasis occurs also in the work of Kets de Vries and Balazs (1997), who examine abusive leadership in the context of downsizing, noting its dysfunctionality. They believe that such abusive behaviour derives from severe anxiety and an expectation that they need to 'strike first' before they are attacked. Citing '*lex talionis*', the law of retaliation, commonly described as 'an eye for an eye, a tooth for a tooth', they identify five types of executives who play executioner. These types include: the compulsive/ritualistic; the abrasive; the dissociative; the alexithymic/anhedonic; and the depressive executive. Table 9.1 summarises this theoretical supposition. Adams and Bray (1992) also suggest that abusive people have a past history of aggressively protecting themselves from threat because of their experiences of being attacked for wrongdoing in childhood. In this case, abuse breeds abuse and dysfunctional behaviour patterns are demonstrated.

Table 9.1 Personality characteristics of leaders

Category	Characteristics
Compulsive/ritualistic	Detail-oriented, aloof, emotionally restrained, inflexible, self-controlled, devoted to work/productivity, deferent to authority
Abrasive	Aggressive, hostile, intelligent, impatient, arrogant, quick-witted, poor interpersonal skills, intensely rivalrous
Dissociative	Emotionally detached, lacking sense of reality, anxious, depressive
Alexithymic/Anhedonic	Reality-based cognitive style, lack of emotional connection to others, lack of interest in pleasure activities, frequent somatic complaints, diminished ability to feel
Depressive	Depressed mood, frequent feelings of guilt, gloomy, lacking energy and drive, poor sleeping patterns, lack of interest in food and sexual activities

Source: Adapted from Kets de Vries & Balazs 1997.

The abusive boss has also been identified by researchers as a petty tyrant (Ashforth 1994; Bies & Tripp 1998; Jordon 2002). Variously described as the 'intolerable boss', the 'psycho boss from hell' or the 'brutal boss', the abusive boss primarily seeks to control others, and for various reasons, either personal or organisational, can only do so by creating fear, confusion and intimidation. Bies and Trip (1998) provide a profile of the abusive boss as one who

> acts as a 'micromanager', provides inexplicit direction with decisive delivery, exhibits 'mercurial' mood swings, demonstrates an obsession with loyalty and obedience, derogates the status of employees, is capricious, exercises raw power for personal gain, obsesses on gathering personal information about employees, and at times uses coercion to corrupt employees (p.202).

Such tyrannical behaviour has been described by those exposed to it as a 'social toxin', having a poisonous effect on professional and personal lives (Bies & Tripp 1998; p.210), as it reduces self-esteem, performance, team functioning and leader endorsement (Ashforth 1994). Personal reactions include stress, helplessness and work alienation, particularly where tyrannical behaviours include belittling others, non-contingent punishment and arbitrariness.

Buchanan and Badham (1999) take a wider view of tyrannical behaviour, contextualising it within organisational structures and processes. They suggest that the power and politics of organisations, and the need for managers to achieve a whole range of personal and organisational goals *requires* ruthlessness, authoritarianism, deceptive manipulation, dishonesty and coerciveness because although unpleasant, it is 'a part of 'normal' organizational politics' (p.105). They note that powerless managers tend to be bossy and abusive, indicating the important role that power structures and roles have in organisations. This viewpoint is supported by Bies and Tripp (1998), who ask the question: Why are organisations silent on the abuse of power and tyrannical behaviour? They suggest that tyranny has been 'reframed' in order to acknowledge that while it is cruel and harsh, it is seen as necessary to achieve the best performance from organisations. Or as they state: '. . .the survival of the organization demands tyranny!' (p.216). Their other explanation for the toleration of tyranny is that the focus is shifted from the tyrant to the 'misbehaviour' that occurs when employees resist oppression, which is perceived to damage the best interests of the organisation. When employees feel that they are dangerously out of control, they may seek to regain some semblance of it, and aggressively seek to rectify the situation.

Taking a Foucauldian approach, McCarthy (1996) suggests that there are currents of violence within organisations that are readily channelled into tyrannical behaviour because of 'a brutal struggle for efficiency and profit in turbulent market conditions' (p.48). He emphasises that the misuse of power occurs because of the contextual forces within organisations and markets, rather than as a psychological need in the abusive boss to exert power and control over subordinates. McCarthy contends that naming tyrants civilises the process, by placing them in a 'therapeutic, rehabilitating space' (p.59), and distracts attention from institutionalised, normalised violence. This concurs with Hearn's (1994) view that organisations are sites of violence, and further, that euphemisms for violence are 'power', 'domination', 'control' and 'authority', which are inherent in organisations. O'Leary-Kelly et al. (1996) suggest that aggressive actions and violent outcomes are instigated by factors in the organisation itself. These studies support the view that the organisation context, both internal and external, can be critical in determining the level of abuse that occurs; however, it is also clear that certain individuals are psychologically predisposed to using brutality to achieve their goals.

Another perspective on abusive organisations is provided by Gherardi (1995), who studied a number of public organisations in Britain, finding that authoritarian, highly centralised leadership often set the scene for tyrannical behaviour of managers. He arrived at a conclusion that:

> the structure of organizational dependence reinforced the apparent legitimacy of the relationship, and because the nature itself of the organization, founded on hierarchy and dependence, lays the structural basis for various forms of sexuality, one of which is sado–masochism (p.61),

which could be sustained by the power structures and social legitimation within the organisation. This points to the fact that organisations are gendered, which becomes significant when tyrannical behaviours take on a sexualised form. This will be developed further later in the chapter.

Power inequalities are embedded in organisational structures and contain the antecedents of organisation violations. It cannot be assumed that managers will responsibly wield their power to achieve organisational objectives. As demonstrated in the cited research, they do not, despite attempts to downplay their abuses of power and discredit those who resist or react against it.

A well-recognised form of abuse resulting from power inequities is bullying, a distinct form of aggressive behaviour, which has been the focus of much recent study (e.g. Bies & Tripp 1998; Maslen 2002; Rigby 2002). Bullying has various grades of intensity, ranging from physical actions to slander and individual isolation. Whether a behaviour is bullying or not is dependent on the perception of the individual, but it always involves unwanted behaviour that is intimidating, humiliating, offensive and embarrassing. It is:

> about persistent criticism and personal abuse—both in public and in private— which humiliates and demeans the individual, gradually eroding their sense of self . . . it is designed to undermine a person's ability and convince them that they are no longer good at anything (Adams & Bray, p.49).

Bullying also has a component that is known as 'mobbing' (Jackson 2003). This refers to situations where the bully uses power and influence to incite others to be part of the bullying process, to marginalise and persecute the target, either knowingly or unknowingly, which is common in health care and other organisations. Mobbing can be successful due to a mechanism known as 'identifying with the aggressor' (Sinclair 1998), which involves building alliances with the abuser in order to be in the 'winning camp' (Kets de Vries & Balazs 1997). This serves to legitimise the scapegoating of the 'losers', resulting in the 'victim' developing power over another, while becoming the oppressor.

Rigby (2002) includes a number of elements in bullying: the desire to hurt; the perpetuation of hurtful behaviour by a more powerful person; unjustified and repeated actions enjoyed by the perpetrator, and which the target feels oppressed by. Researchers have identified an extensive range of interpersonal bullying behaviours including scapegoating (Ashforth 1994; Kets de Vries & Balazs 1997; Wyatt & Hare 1997; Yiannis 1998), aggressive teasing and joking at another's expense (Ackroyd & Thompson 1999), trading of insults (Hearn & Parkin 2001), as well as aggressive behaviour directly targeting the organisation, including vandalism, theft and sabotage (Ackroyd & Thompson 1999; LaNuez and Jermier 1994).

Hearn and Parkin (2001) and Jordon (2002) cite a range of studies indicating that bullying is very common by line managers and those in authority over subordinates. Typically, it can last for many years, having a debilitating effect on the individual and the organisation (McMillan 1995; O'Connell et al. 2000). What is more concerning is the finding that an increasing number of managers are witnessing bullying by their subordinates, but condoning it by either ignoring or denying its existence. A doctoral study by Deans (2002), found that 89 per cent of nurses experienced verbal aggression, 77 per cent experienced physical aggression, 47 per cent experienced sexual aggression, and 88 per cent experienced patient aggression. In addition, 71 per cent of nurses experienced aggression from doctors, while 61 per cent reported aggression from nursing colleagues, known as 'horizontal violence'.

McMillan (1995) suggests that nurse managers are identified as being a continual sources of violence and bullying. Jackson et al. (2001) provide further evidence of violence in the nursing workplace, citing a range of international studies which detail such abuses as bullying, assault and harassment, and which are a factor in retaining the nursing workforce. Johnstone's (2002) study of turnover and retention of nurses in the New South Wales' workforce found that frequent reasons given for nurse manager turnover were 'interpersonal conflict including horizontal violence, [and] lack of support from senior management and/or colleagues' (p.24). This conclusion is supported in the literature (see Jackson et al. 2001).

There are enormous organisational costs associated with unchecked bullying, including counter-aggression towards others, withdrawal of services, increased absenteeism, reduction in productivity and 'citizenship' behaviours, increased turnover, incivility (Andersson & Pearson 1999), and a range of stress reactions that can have major physical and psychological impacts on employees. In such situations, an increasingly likely option for employees is ligitation against the organisation. A study by Greenberg and Barling (1999) found that workplace aggression and violence was common when there was job insecurity, unfair justice procedures, and surveillance of employees.

Violation of trust in organisations

A major form of disruption occurs when there is violation of trust in organisations. Systematic research relating to trust in organisations has been carried out for more than 40 years (Darley 1998; Elangovan & Shapiro 1998; Jones & George 1998; Lewicki et al. 1998; Sheppard & Sherman 1998; Whitener et al. 1998). Organisations in which violations are prevalent will not have a trusting climate or culture. Ackroyd and Thompson (1999) postulate that there are low trust and high trust managerial regimes, the former characterised by suspicion of employees, and increased regulation of activities and surveillance, 'bureaucratized, rule bound, introspective and a slave to its history' (p.89). Employees are typically loathe to cooperate with such managements, and may be defined by them as 'recalcitrant'.

Breaches of trust can create vengeful and destructive attitudes among employees, jeopardising organisational processes. Hearn and Parkin (2001), Liu and Perrene (2002), Folger and Cropanzano (1998), and Greenberg and Barling (1999) all note that perceptions of injustice will determine whether employees will indulge in counterproductive work behaviours, such as theft, aggression and withdrawal, while Fox et al. (2001) report that perceptions of justice, and therefore trust, are significantly correlated with job stressors such as interpersonal conflict and organisational constraints. Employees who for any reason feel betrayed by an employer will have little reason to trust in the future, creating a climate of suspicion and vigilance against wrongdoing (Lewicki et al. 1998). Elangovan and Shapiro (1998) note that violations of trust include supervisor behaviours such as coercive or threatening behaviour, withholding of promised support, favouritism, improper dismissal, blaming employees for their own mistakes, misuse of private information, stealing of ideas, lying and sexual harassment. In an argument for acknowledging emotions in organisations, Harlos and Pinder (2000) remind us that 'emotional barrenness of work settings represented mistreatment and misery from systemic injustice' (p.264).

One classic example of trust violations occurs when psychological contracts are not honoured. The psychological contract refers to the tacit understanding between an employer and an employee concerning the mutual and reciprocal obligations of both. Psychological contracts are 'inherently perceptual' (Morrison & Robinson 1997); thus the violation is always from the perspective of the individual. Judgement about, and interpretation of, a breach of contract is subjective and may be perceptually or cognitively biased, having potentially serious implications for the individual and the organisation. When psychological contracts are violated, distrust, anger, betrayal, dissatisfaction, and strong hostile reactions can occur. Thus,

> violations by an employer may affect not only what an employee feels he or she is owed by the employer but also what that employee feels obligated to offer in return (Robinson et al. 1994, p.139).

This may result in a decline in organisational citizenship or extra role behaviours. A study by Turnley and Feldman (1999) found that psychological contract violations resulted in employees neglecting duties and reducing their loyalty in the organisation and in some cases, exiting the organisation altogether. In extreme cases where employees feel violated and betrayed, they may engage in revenge and retaliatory behaviour such as sabotage, theft or aggression, or may initiate expensive legal proceedings.

Fulop and Linstead (1999) suggest that a prerequisite to employee commitment to organisations would be to extend the hand of trust. This would involve particular structures and processes including autonomy, movement away from control and surveillance, and non-abuse of power. Given the context in which organisations are required to perform, it seems most unlikely that trust can ever be anything but tenuous.

Sexual harassment and sexuality in organisations

Nicolson (1996) is concerned to distinguish between sexual harassment and sexual abuse in the workplace. She points out that both 'are about exploitation of (usually) women by (usually) men in a context where the man has power over the woman's work or life' (p.129).

Whether there is a difference or not, the wielding of power in order to have control from whatever source, be it legitimate or driven by personal needs, can be a prime motivator of such behaviours. Sexual harassment is defined as offensive, 'unwelcome sexual advances, requests for sexual favours, and other verbal or physical conduct experienced as negative' (Alvesson & Billing 1997, p.122).

Sexual harassment can have a serious impact on women (and men), ranging from feelings of shame and humiliation, loss of confidence, psychological and/or physical illnesses, absenteeism from work to exiting the workplace. This is particularly the case when the dominant discourse is 'that of the isolated harasser harassing the isolated victim' (Hearn & Parkin 2001, p.51). It is now recognised that such harassment is a problem in workplaces because of gendered power relations. Itzen and Newman

(1995) are convinced that sexual harassment is an abuse of power, which is 'damaging and diminishing in human terms for both those who are dominant and those who are subordinate' (p.268). While it provides gains in power and privilege to the dominant group, and access to prized resources, it 'represents deep personal loss and disconnection from self, self-value and inherent humanness' (p.268).

Sexual harassment demands attention, but this should not be at the expense of sexuality. Sexualisation of the workplace is becoming increasingly recognised as vital to organisational functioning, particularly when sexual behaviour is categorised as misbehaviour, disrupting the social and industrial order, thus posing difficulties for employers. It is obvious that the sexuality of employees is not and cannot be 'parked at the door' for the period of working time, then assumed as one leaves the workplace. This is particularly relevant to a workplace where one gender dominates, such as occurs in nursing, which creates its own vulnerabilities and complexities.

Sinclair (1998) points out that the

> impossibility of eradicating sex from organisations highlights the need to shift focus to understanding more deeply how sexualities manifest themselves in organisations, and how some are accepted and even permeate organisational cultures while others are deeply threatening and rigidly proscribed (p.158).

Sexuality affects social relations, influencing the effectiveness of employee and employer behaviour. It becomes the business of organisations because it impacts on their dynamics and culture. Sexuality is not simply about sexual harassment or sexual affairs (Sinclair 1998) that the organisation seeks to suppress or outlaw, or make marginal. Gutek (1992) suggests that sexual behaviours are considered to be individual, rather than invisible within the organisation because of 'sex role spill-over', that is, the carry-over of gender-based expectations into the workplace. Thus, expectations arising from the female role of subordinate sex object (including the characteristics of passivity, loyalty, emotionality, protection and nurturance) and the male role of dominant aggressor (being rational, analytic, tough, competitive) are carried into the workplace. For Gutek (1992),

> the important point is that the carry-over of sex role stereotypes into the workplace introduces the view of women as sexual beings in the workplace, but it simply reinforces the view of men as organizational beings—'active, work-oriented' (p.60).

Ackroyd and Thompson (1999) note that the 'declining male control of sexuality inside and outside of work' has resulted in increased anger and violence towards women, often manifest in workplaces that are traditionally male dominated (pp. 132–3). This lays the foundation for sexual abuse. The most common forms are joking rituals, sexual banter, pranks, flirting and various forms of 'horseplay', and what Ackroyd and Thompson call 'shop-floor resistance' (p.136). It has been noted that when there is a breakdown in the authority of the employer, one solution to sexual misbehaviour is to ensure that 'women . . . got the bullet' (Ackroyd & Thompson, p.138).

Harlow et al. (1995) note that sexuality may be related to the occurrence of gendered violence in organisations, since the operation of sexuality within organisations (including sexual harassment, sexual dominance and power relations) is now recognised as impacting on organisations. They also postulate that there is a subtle form of workplace abuse, which they identify as silence, which structures relationships between gender, power and the organisation. Silence can be used to include some organisational participants and not others.

Nurses can practise this by targeting their colleagues. Patients may also be a target. Nurses who are not available to patients in the full context of a caring environment may be regarded as 'silent'. This could be interpreted as a form of violating patient rights. Similarly, employees can be silenced by bullying, coercion, 'intimidation, threat, exclusion, marginalisation and put-downs' (Harlow et al. 1995, p.96). When employees fail to be heard, they are effectively silenced. While men can and are silenced, it is more likely to be a problem for women, who are not only silenced by the structure of organisations, but also through interactional processes.

> Men dominate in meetings, interrupt and talk over women, silence women with subtle put-downs, ignore contributions made by women and even attribute them to men. The physical dominance of men through the unwanted touch of harassment and the more subtle social exclusion of women takes place within organizations (Harlow et al. 1995, p.105).

Some support is provided for this notion by the concept of 'organisational voice', which is the opposite to silencing. Sheppard (1992) suggests that

> [v]oice systems provide an opportunity for subordinates to inform their superiors about activities or events that may not be publicly known; unethical or illegal behavior, unfair treatment of some individual or group, or policies and procedures that are not working properly (p.45).

Employees can therefore communicate concerns to employers and conceivably reduce levels of discontent, distress and dissatisfaction. Alternatively, disgruntled employees may choose to voice their issue through what are considered more negative channels, as they have other options denied them. Sheppard argues that healthy organisations need a strong and effective 'voice' system, but also indicates that this is a powerful means of directing dissent into acceptable forms and channels. Such dissent therefore does not escalate and challenge the organisation, but 'preserves and protects the power of those who currently govern the organization' (p.54). In other words, it is a means of managing potential 'misbehaviours' in the workplace that, if left unchecked, might disrupt the organisation.

RESISTANCE TO ORGANISATION VIOLATION

Resistance to organisation violation takes a variety of forms. Ashforth and Mael (1998) define resistance as 'any intentional acts of commission or omission that defy the wishes of others' (p.90), and implies opposition against another's exercise of power. In the organisational context, employee resistance behaviours seek to regain control that employers endeavour to maintain. Thus, 'resistance is very much a *response* to practices of managerial control' (Collinson 1994, p.26), and is a form of power exercised by subordinates in the workplace. Acts of resistance are either positive or negative, depending on the perspective taken. If viewed from an employer's perspective they are negative; from the employee's perspective they may be positive and justifiable.

Researchers propose that resistance serves a range of purposes. For example, Ashforth and Mael (1998) suggest that it seeks to contest meaning, which defines the role and identity of the individual in the workplace. Organisations seeking to colonise the emotionality of its workers, or to define how they should feel about their work, may find resistance from employees who endeavour to assert their 'valued sense of identity independent of—or antagonistic to—the organization's definition' (p.113).

This is defined as 'normative or cultural control' (p.92), and is viewed as insidious because it has the potential to force a workplace identity on employees which is oppositional to that held by employees. Because this impacts on the employee's sense and definition of self, the workplace becomes an invasive and threatening place, to be resisted. Such workplaces have been categorised as 'greedy institutions' because of the excessive demands they make on employees (Flam 1993). Ackroyd and Thompson (1999) suggest that the view of employers, that employees should be willing to identify with the organisation, is not less than 'a startling piece of wishful thinking' (p.27). However, they do recognise the extent to which work experience contributes to the formation of employees' identities, and believe that all 'misbehaviour' derives from processes of identity formation and self-organisation.

A range of resistance behaviours have been identified in the literature. Collinson (1994) proposes that resistance can occur either through distancing or persistence mechanisms. Resistance through distance 'involves a denial of involvement or interest in key organizational processes' (p.50), as employees try to escape or avoid the demands of employers. This strategy, however, reinforces the legitimacy of hierarchical control, fails to challenge management practices, and increases the employees' vulnerability to discipline. An example of resistance through distance is provided by Martin and Myerson (1998), whose study of female executives found that their resistance mechanism to tyrannical and aggressive male behaviour was to not take abuse personally. Further research in this area might consider whether these are gendered responses, or whether they are more generalised.

Resistance through persistence contrasts with this, as employees demand greater involvement in the organisation, seeking 'to render management more accountable by extracting information, monitoring practices and challenging decision-making processes' (Collinson 1994, p.24). It is a more proactive means of behaviour because it involves gaining information and knowledge that will assist employees to critically analyse organisational practices. Nevertheless, current organisational practices of control and discipline derive from a perspective that treats resistance as a form of deviance, aberrant and unjustifiable. Resisters may be called hysterical reactionaries (Ashforth & Mael 1998) by employers, but they can play a valuable role in the organisation. First, they challenge it in various ways to check the validity of arguments for change, and second, they provide an understanding of subversive tactics that can be evaluated for positive value.

As previously noted, organisational cultures are gendered, with corporate cultures in particular being highly masculinised. Foreman (2001) indicates that research addressing

> workplace and occupational subcultures provides insight into the links between culture, resistance and conflict in organization, as well as the ways in which gender forms part of these subcultures (p.228).

Hearn and Parkin (2001) concur, demonstrating that power and resistance questions are central to a gendered analysis of organisations, and the violations occurring therein. However, one of the problems of gendered resistance is that it is rarely organised, thus rendering it less effective. Individual women who endeavour to resist gendered organisational practices and behaviours are 'trying to kill sex discrimination with a thousand pin pricks' (Foreman 2001, p.342). This uncoordinated reaction by women is called 'disorganised coaction', and is relatively futile as a resistance and change mechanism.

There are many forms of resistance, including sabotage, avoiding tasks, withholding labour or 'working to rule', insubordination, violence and whistle-blowing. Sabotage can sometimes be justified as a plausible and practical strategy 'for dealing with an intransigent organization which violates its members' ideals' (LaNuez & Jermier 1994, p.237). Whistle-blowing is an organisational dissenting action that directly challenges managerial authority and power. It is called a 'bottom-up' method by which subordinates can resist organisational abuses (Rothschild & Miethe 1994). Whistle-blowing is 'the disclosure of illegal, unethical or harmful practices in the workplace to parties who might take action' (Rothschild & Miethe 1994, p.254). It is defined as a political act and often receives a political and retaliatory response from management. Whistleblowers usually believe that the organisation's true mission is being undermined or that harm is being done to the public good; their principles are being violated and their position usually has an ethical foundation. For many it is a struggle for dignity and integrity that cannot be suppressed by threats or reprisals from the organisation. This is particularly the case when whistleblowers are nurses who take a patient advocate role (Jackson & Raftos 1997).

The literature shows us that responses to whistleblowers are often swift and vindictive. They have destroyed the tranquillity of the workplace and created problems for management that might have been known but ignored. Whistleblowers are usually discredited in a range of ways: regarded as 'crazy', or accused of being 'malcontents, liars, thieves, or all three' (Messick & Ohme 1998, p.196). A study by De Maria (1996) examined punitive actions taken against whistleblowers in Australia, noting that 71 per cent experienced official reprisals (punishment for speaking out), as opposed to unofficial reprisals, of which 94 per cent were received, such as ostracism in the workplace; 40 per cent received formal reprimands; 14 per cent received punitive transfers, while most were compulsorily referred to a psychiatrist (De Maria 1996). In order to avoid examining the system that may have created the problem, such individuals are regarded as 'sick'—victim blaming is the strategy.

Ashforth and Mael (1998) note that the more dependent the organisation is on the exposed wrongdoing, the greater the retaliation against the whistleblower; the degree of threat to the organisation often determines the fierceness of the response. It is not surprising that the retaliatory action against the whistleblower may have a severe, incapacitating psychological impact. This sometimes leads to the whistleblower exiting the organisation and conceivably the entire industry or profession (Jackson & Raftos 1997). However, as Rothschild and Miethe (1994) point out, these reprisals by management can transform and politicise the whistleblower, galvanising resistance and transforming her or his consciousness. Hearn and Parkin (2001) believe that '[u]ntil whistleblowing is seen as contributing to a violation-free environment, violations will continue to be denied, silenced and confined to the subtext of worker grievances' (p.155).

Wyatt and Hare (1997) suggest that work stress is a euphemism for work abuse. There is no doubt that organisation violations cause stress of varying degrees of intensity (De Maria 1996; Hearn & Parkin 2001; Wilkie 1996). But there has long been a dominant view that stress is an individual problem, to be fixed by the individual. Newton et al. (1995) suggest that this is a managerialist interpretation and a means of obtaining employee consent to advance corporate interest by fostering an image of the well-functioning employee. Stressed employees are urged to seek relaxation training, to keep fit and eat healthily, so that stress levels are not disabling. Newton et al. (1995) offer an analysis regarding stress: '[D]istressful emotions are culturally and discursively constrained, and . . . they are tied to broader power relations, such as capital labour relations, family relations and gender relations' (p.58).

Hearn (1993) and Parkin (1993) both suggest that stress might be a reflection of employer required *containment* of emotion that arises from power relations between employer and employee and between women and men. Both of these authors discuss the way that expression of emotion is gendered, asserting that women may experience greater stress 'because of the way in which emotionality and sexuality in organizations are at the same time both denied and and projected onto women' (Newton et al. 1995, pp.144–5). As a female operating within organisations, Parkin (1993) indicates that her distress is 'not just because of different structures, kinds of work, management styles, public and private, but because of the problematized construction of me as an emotional, sexualized woman' (p.186).

Excessive interpersonal work demands of an emotional kind can result in stress levels of such magnitude that burnout occurs (Brotheridge & Grandey 2002; Kets de Vries & Balazs 1997). This is a common and long-recognised problem within nursing and the health care sector generally. The degree to which organisations require their employees to express emotions they do not feel, or to hide 'unacceptable' emotions (otherwise known as 'emotional labour' in which emotional dissonance can occur), can result in negative physical and psychological symptoms, including exhaustion, detachment, anger and burnout.

One of the difficulties that occurs in organisations is that management sometimes makes concessions towards accepting a certain level of 'misbehaviour'. Turning a blind eye to petty theft, various perks of office, or tyrannical behaviour does implicate management and makes them complicit. In fact, managers themselves may be 'misbehaving' when they are the ones who are expected to be 'responsible for defining and policing the formal and informal rules governing acceptable behaviour' (Ackroyd & Thompson 1999, p.80). Thus, misbehaviour cannot become too visible, and managers must not be seen the bend the rules too far. Hearn and Parkin (2001) note the complicit and explicit role of management in organisation violations, as they are known to be actively involved in harassment, bullying, intimidation and ignoring known perpetrators of violations. Managements who impose unreasonable work demands and policies that disadvantage their workers are included in the violator category. The protection and rewarding of these perpetrators adds significantly to the extent of, and difficulties in resolving, the problem of organisation violations.

CONCLUSION

Organisation violations produce workplace traumas that brutalise their employees. Given our knowledge and understanding of such behaviours, it is important to break the conspiracy of silence (Hase et al. 1999) to address the issues that arise. Given the complexity of organisational cultures, power structures and the idiosyncratic nature of humankind, is it ever going to be possible to eradicate violations, given the purposes these serve?

Ackroyd and Thompson (1999) note that while organisations can attempt to limit 'misbehaviour' such as absenteeism by introducing record-keeping or penalties, employees are innovative in finding alternative and possibly more subtle ways to meet their needs. From the perspective of the employer, misbehaviour is to be dealt with; from the perspective of the employee, misbehaviour is normal, as it is an appropriate reaction to the situation. As previously noted, what might be adaptive for the employee can be maladaptive for the organisation (Liu & Perrene 2002). The workplace thus becomes a contested terrain in which conflict is inevitable because of the competing nature of outcomes in organisations. For Collinson (1992), misbehaviour is an attempt by employees to manage management, rather than remain passive recipients of the work role. As previously indicated, Hearn and Parkin (2001) believe that organisation violations will continue to be rampant until gender and power issues in organisations are addressed.

An examination of organisation violations has exposed complex structures and individual features that require a level of consciousness-raising that is unlikely to occur because of the threat to existing power bases. While it may be claimed that organisational processes are transparent (in some organisations), it is apparent that most organisations have a 'dark side' that is only informally acknowledged (and often only in tea rooms or corridors). This allows for 'manipulation, collusion, blackmail, ambushing' to occur (Hase et al. 1999). Organisations have 'dark sides' because they are composed of individuals who may possess dark side personality traits, which can be counterproductive from all perspectives (Hughes et al. 1999, pp.213–14), as previously described.

Given that 'for profit' organisations need to achieve outcomes that often militate against the best interests of employees, is there anything that can be done to create a more humane workplace? Ackroyd and Thompson (1999) draw attention to some proposals offered by researchers, including the development of a caring, empathetic environment, career-enriching opportunities, job security, enhanced conflict management, interpersonal cooperation and incentives for ethical behaviour. Researchers who have addressed some of these include Mann (1996), who takes an individual psychological approach; Whitener et al. (1998), and Elangovan and Shapiro (1998), who address the issue of trustworthiness in the work environment; Fox et al. (2001), and Liu and Perrene (2002), who recommend the active management of emotionality in organisations to reduce 'counterproductive work behaviours'; Putman and Mumby (1993), who argue that 'bounded emotionality' (the controlled expression of emotions) will enhance working relationships; and Graetz et al. (2002), who put the case for empowerment of employees. Kets de Vries and Miller (1984) suggest the appointment of an organisational ombudsman. Others recommend developing and encouraging a compassionate organisation (Frost 1999); a caring organisation (Kahn 1993), while Palmer and Hardy (2000) discuss the role of power and ethics. But Ackroyd and Thompson (1999) recoil from what they believe are 'motherhood and apple pie' (p.97) formulas, indicating that the theory is most often not the practice, and that attempts to create autonomy, self-management and high trust relations are rare. Their position is clear: the 'deep-rooted conflicts of interest and identity found in the workplace' (p.97) do not lend themselves to simplistic solutions.

Hearn and Parkin (2001), while acknowledging the serious difficulties of creating change to reduce organisation violations, believe that a violation-free organisation is a necessary state to work towards. A first step is to allow violations to be 'voiced and dealt with explicitly' (p.158). Procedures to combat violations would then be developed, allowing continuing challenge to authority and expertise in organisations. Such challenge could result in less hierarchical and centralised structures, which might encourage the identification of 'sites of resistance and struggle' (p.159). Further, they argue that 'a strong focus on how equality and fairness practices can protect workers from violations and create and maintain violation-free organizations and workplaces' (p.160) will assist in the debate, action and consciousness-raising in organisations, and that further, this debate should be taken into the wider society. This is particularly important given the effects of globalisation and increased organisational networks that have been developed. And finally, an important contribution to organisation violation reduction is the focus that has been developed among a body of researchers who explicitly and relentlessly expose, politicise and critique contemporary organisational life.

Reflective exercise

1   Consider your current workplace.

    a   In your experience, do organisation violations occur?

    b   What form do these take?

    c   Can you identify how such abuses impact on the morale, behaviours and motivation of those who are subject to this abuse?

    d   Are you aware of any legitimation or rewarding of abusive behaviours by supervisors of staff?

2   This chapter has addressed organisation violations and suggested ways to reduce abuses. Do any of these suggestions seem valid to you? Or are they well meaning, but unlikely to be successful?

3   If you think they are unlikely to successful, what reasons can you give for this?

4   What are you now going to do about abusive behaviour in your workplace?

RECOMMENDED READINGS

Ackroyd, S., & Thompson, P. (1999). *Organizational misbehaviour.* London: Sage.

Ashforth, B. E. (1994). Petty tyranny in organizations. *Human Relations, 47*(7), 755–78.

Green, L., Parkin, W., & Hearn, J. (2001). Power. In E. Wilson (ed.). *Organizational behaviour reassessed: The impact of gender.* London: Sage.

Hearn, J., & Parkin, W. (2001). *Gender, sexuality and violence in organizations.* London: Sage.

Jackson, D., Clare, J., & Mannix, J. (2001). Who would want to be nurse? Violence in the workplace—a factor in recruitment and retention. *Journal of Nursing Management, 10*(1), 13–20.

ENDNOTE

*   This is a classic victim blaming strategy which places all responsibility on the targeted individual.

PART TWO

Leadership in Clinical Practice

CHAPTER TEN

Leading, motivating and supporting colleagues in nursing practice

Sally Borbasi, Jacqueline Jones & Carol Gaston

LEARNING OBJECTIVES

At the completion of this chapter, the reader will be able to:

▲ understand that nurses are in a powerful position to take a leading position in health care reform;

▲ discuss a number of different approaches to effective leadership;

▲ recognise some of the sociopolitical and economic exigencies impacting on leadership today;

▲ describe the part that mentoring, advocacy, performance management, motivation, organisational culture and change play in effective leadership; and

▲ identify opportunities available to nurses to take up leadership positions in the current climate of health care reform.

KEY WORDS

Leadership, change, mentoring, advocacy, performance management

INTRODUCTION

[Imagine] how things would be if the voice and visibility of nursing were commensurate with the size and importance of nursing in health care (Buresh & Gordon 2000, p.11).

Both the Australian and UK health care systems are increasingly being politically driven and led. Nurses have possibly been slow to realise the important role they have to play in leading health care provision and influencing the future. Perhaps nurses have also found it difficult to influence policy development. Much of this can be attributed to a weakness in nursing leadership at all levels (Pearson & Borbasi 1996). In this chapter we explore the idea of leading, motivating and supporting colleagues in nursing practice in a world of accelerated change. Faced with the current state of affairs in health care—high acuity and throughput, diverse skill mixes, diminishing budgets, limited resources and increasing consumer expectation—one could argue that the need for leading, motivating and supporting colleagues in a nurse's professional life has never been greater. Indeed, it has been stated that 'the activities of the professional nurse . . . have more to do with managing the delivery of care rather than actually providing that care' (Norman 1997, p.4), and that if they are to succeed, twenty-first century registered nurses require unprecedented management and leadership skills (Cherry 2002, p.353; Jones & Cheek 2003).

We know that management is a different concept to leadership. Ideally, however, a good manager should be a good leader and vice versa (Cherry 2002). However, as many have no doubt experienced, this is not always the case. In this chapter we concentrate on the notion of leadership as opposed to management, because it is the leaders who have such a large influence in producing the culture within which management takes place, and it is the workplace environment/culture (the 'system') that so often makes or breaks success. We also explore the concept of constant change, bearing in mind the words of Mann (2002, p.68) who states, '[I]n a previous time drastic upheavals in the health care industry happened once a generation, what is different today is the speed of change'. Such pace then makes for an unstable environment.

Essentially we will explore where we are now and where we are headed in the short term, and look to the longer term future. Through leadership, motivation and support what we hope to achieve is increased voice and visibility for nursing. What do leadership, mentorship and support actually mean in a world of relentless change?

LEADERSHIP

Traditionally, leadership has been construed as the possession of a set of qualities that makes a person a leader, including the notion of providing direction with extreme daring under conditions of duress. It was thought that leaders were born to lead. Such ideas rest on behaviourist assumptions of leadership. Other mental models developed over the years include relationship and activity/task theories and the influence that leaders hold in transforming the actions of others (Ospina & Schall 2001). However, these theories are criticised because they are perceived as inappropriate to a twenty-first century post-industrial society where different attributes in the workplace have become important. Sought-after qualities now include greater collaboration, common good, client orientation, pluralism in structures and participation, consensus-oriented policy-making, among others (Rost 1993). Newer theories on leadership focus on process. Increasingly there has been recognition of the need to develop leaders, and the tools to assist in that development have never been greater. There is an incredible amount of literature on the topic of leadership and, increasingly, mentorship. Numerous individuals and consortiums are putting themselves forward as leadership gurus. Life coaches are emerging. A search of the Internet reveals masses of information and that there is significant money to be made in the field.

There can be no doubt that good leadership skills have become a marketable commodity. Effective and strong leadership is afforded increasing attention because in a number of professional and political arenas, gifted leaders are perceived as a rarity (Nicholson 2002). Perhaps this situation is a result of the age in which we now live. Described as a 'capricious new decade', a newspaper article tells us to 'get ready for a new breed' of leaders and proceeds to describe these individuals as being 'capable of effectively managing strategic and operational challenges in an environment of increased stakeholder scrutiny and dramatic and unpredictable change' (*Advertiser*, 4 January 2003, p.3). However, in the next sentence we are told that the task of producing such leaders is a huge challenge and building leadership capacity does not happen overnight.

Obviously, there is a sense of urgency in producing the talent pool necessary for twenty-first century leadership. Mackay (1999, p.40) points out that when people are experiencing insecurity and uncertainty, as they often do in times of change, they look for 'strength and vision at the top'. He points out that a 'leadership vacuum' (p.132) is potentially a very serious state of affairs for any organisation/community.

Research into finding new ways to understand leadership is also burgeoning. In the United States, for example, academic researchers Ospina and Schall are studying how Americans conceptualise leadership (Louv 2002). In their research, they explore the concept of leadership as both a process and a social construct. Ospina and Schall (2001) take a constructivist view, believing it a useful means of understanding leadership. They see leadership as a process of meaning/sense-making that occurs among groups of people with a common purpose—communities of practice in order to bring about change. It is a collective, shared process that is social, contextual, interactive, sensitive, 'embodied and concrete'. Championing the group's vision may be a shared or rotated activity, or undertaken by one individual or the group as a whole. Seeing leadership as something that is already out there in communities as a collective, social and embedded constituent, takes away from the need for the 'heroic' leadership that society laments to be presently so lacking (Ospina & Schall 2001, p.4).

It seems that the general thrust of 'alternative' visions of leadership (Louv 2002) implies we should be looking for it in places other than those where it has traditionally been found. Indeed, in a previous paper, Gaston (Borbasi & Gaston 2002) suggested the need to look to new avenues for nursing leadership and that more often than not, these would be found in practice-related positions rather than administration or education, as in the past.

It can be seen that collaborative concepts of leadership are emerging as the way forward and leadership through groups, rather than leaders as individuals, is becoming the acceptable model (Louv 2002). Engagement in symbiotic relationships in order to progress change is recognised as something that happens in communities and is to be encouraged and expanded upon (Gardner in Louv 2002). Leadership groups are exhorted to 'find each other' and work together in order to sustain change (Gardner cited in Louv 2002).

Of interest to nurses is the later work of Ospina et al. (2002) that uses the same constructivist framework to examine the ways in which practitioners and academics can work together to generate knowledge on leadership. The researchers perceive the existence of a gap between nursing research literature and the way in which that information can be usefully applied in practice. Their study involves a combination of ethnography, narrative inquiry and cooperative inquiry, which means the co-researchers will be working alongside practitioners, participating in the leadership experience. The data generated will be grounded in practice and therefore useful and relevant in informing practice.

Of course, while Ospina and Schall write from the sphere of public management and policy, much of what anyone has to say about leadership is potentially of use to a practice-based discipline such as nursing. However, whatever the theory, it would appear that the enduring essence of good leadership is embedded in the capacity for articulating a vision and rallying others around it (Champy 2002, p.114). In the late 1990s, Mackay (1999) noted that the leadership traits most desired at the time appeared to be 'passion, enthusiasm' and 'a zest for having a go' (p.142). Both sound remarkably similar. He also observed that society's demand for strong leadership grows in direct proportion to the lack of collective confidence felt by that community. As a result, he states it is an 'unusually difficult time to be a leader in Australia' (1999 p.138). For nursing, the situation is no different.

LEADERSHIP AND NURSING

Change is taking place all of the time. We have all experienced the changes that occur daily in our lives. The biotechnical revolution; biomedical research restructuring as it is, human life, together with an ageing population; economic rationalisation and other key trends have moved us into a new era. In such an era, organisations have had to rethink and reorganise the way in which health care delivery is structured (Fukuyama 2002; Kerfoot 2001; Mann 2002).

Leadership in nursing is about leadership for nursing, as well as leading nurses. As a recent article in *The New England Journal of Medicine* reported, we now have a growing body of evidence that shows nurses make a significant contribution to health outcomes (Needleman et al. 2002). It is important, therefore, to be reminded that the impact of leadership is influenced by the culture of the work environment, the nature of the workforce and the educational background or level of workers (Jones & Cheek 2003). Therefore, just as nurses have the potential to be impacted upon by a leader and their style of leadership, nurses can also make an impact on leadership in their environment and practice domain per se (Firth 2001; Hein 1998; Lett 1999; Mahoney 2001). To ensure that nurses are retained in the workforce, key issues must be examined from within a professional discourse. That is, leadership requires a balance within and between the nexus of industrial and professional concerns to manage and drive change in order to facilitate practice and better health outcomes for communities and individuals.

McMillan et al. (2002) suggests that three major influences have framed how leadership in western nursing has developed. These are the emergence of nursing as a discrete area of professional practice, the influence of feminism on nursing, and the commitment to providing evidence-based practice across the health care sector

(McMillan et al. 2002, p.4). We would add to that, population health as a driving force behind health care reform (Generational Health Review 2002/2003) and the burgeoning impact of violence in the workplace, now argued as a public health issue by the World Health Organisation (2002). The culture of tolerance to violence and negativity within a nursing workplace requires strong leadership, vision and the capacity to step beyond the accepted norm that 'it goes with the job', thus giving credence to the insidious and often latent emotional damage caused to nurses (Turney 2002, p.134–48) (for further detail see Chapter 9). Vision to recognise and then act is imperative for nurse leaders of the twenty-first century, especially in a climate where national reviews (Heath 2002, p.193; Senate Community Affairs Committee 2002) recommend that workplaces should recognise and support the development of future nurse leaders rather than continue with an outdated ethos of tall poppy slaying and neglect. Staff satisfaction is seen as a priority of the organisation because dissatisfaction with work life seems endemic in nursing (McMillan et al. 2002) and has been strongly implicated in the loss of nurses from the workforce.

We know that nursing is being transformed with a different set of expectations to that of even five years ago. Registered nurses are not necessarily going to be hands-on nurses for very long in their careers. With the advent of patient care assistants and their ilk, the move is away from the basic nursing care of activities of daily living, and the registered nurse is carrying out much more higher order work, especially as the role expands to advanced practice. Today's nursing graduates are expected to be change agents, case managers, care brokers. In short, the profession is currently breaking through barriers and pushing boundaries as never before.

To add to the complexity, society is different today. Younger Australians (known as 'Generation Xs') have grown up to 'expect change' and accept the uncertainty of tomorrow. As a result, they are reluctant to commit themselves to aspects of life as readily as the previous generation and often do not place the same value on having work (Mackay 1999, p.117). Attracting talented youth to the job of nursing requires a cultural shift, evident in the frenetic vying that goes on for graduate nurses at a time of severe shortages. The traditional traits of fear and apathy in the workforce as a result of a 'military' model of leadership (Oakley & Krug 1991), common to many organisations not that long ago (some of you may remember the days of hospital training), are rapidly fading. Mackay (1999) points out that 'the rising generation of young Australians are likely to be the sharpest, most assertive, most sceptical and most demanding employees we've ever seen' (p.119). These trends pose enormous challenges to those nurse managers who work in outdated, heavily bureaucratic health care systems that appear to youth as decidedly unattractive places of work. Having multigenerational employees, including Generation Xs, means there is a requirement for 'open discussion of how generational differences influence attitudes towards work and organizations' (Kupperschmidt 2000, p.65). Indeed, it has been shown that health care institutions are the slowest to embrace many of the ideas inherent in contemporary leadership models (Malone 2001).

Gaston recalls her experience of the way nurses traditionally behaved in such an oppressive system:

> They used to say nurses are lions in the tearoom and mice in the corridor. The number of times I was in groups, went yeah, yeah, let's do something. Then you go down to the Director of Nursing's office or the CEO's office and you turn around and they have all gone (Gaston, Dec 2002).

This is a crucial legacy and one she sees as the root of many of today's problems:

That is why we have got the tension and the conflict in the work environment today and where industrial democracy is very difficult. We have got young people who are coming through who have been educated to question, to debate, to take risk in a system full of people who have had it all knocked out of them. That is where you get the violence. It is not about the people, it is the system (Gaston, Dec 2002).

We have all experienced 'the system' to a greater or lesser extent, but essentially what it has meant is that relatively few nurses in the past were considered great leaders, and leadership, even in the current, more enlightened climate, is perceived as wanting (Borbasi & Gaston 2002; Pearson & Borbasi 1996). That is not to say that leadership does not occur—many nurses lead daily within their practice roles. However, given the size of the nursing workforce in relation to other health professions, not many are involved in high-level leadership across multi-disciplinary groups that have political, policy and decision-making powers. Indeed, the issue for nurses has been an entrenched reluctance to accept that leadership is inextricably bound to the use of power and that it involves influencing others in the achievement of certain ends (Malone 2001). The *Report on the Senate Inquiry into Nursing* (2002) notes the problems with nurses' inadequate representation on decision-making boards and calls for their 'appointment to and meaningful participation in management' (Recommendation 57). Additionally, it recommends that nurses be provided with appropriate education and training to support them in leadership roles (Recommendation 58).

At an international level, the World Health Organisation, at its 54th Assembly held in May 2001, also recognised the need to involve nurses in decision-making processes and urged member states to, among other things: '[f]urther the development of their health systems to pursue health sector reform by involving nurses and midwives in the framing, planning and implementation of health policy at all levels.'

So, what does all of this mean for the provision of effective nursing leadership? Basically, at the moment, because of the breakneck speed of change and the fact that much of it is groundbreaking by nature, in some practice areas there are limited numbers of individuals capable of acting as role models or leaders (Clare et al. 2002). Moreover, because the health system is so highly stretched and understaffed, beginning practitioners are expected to 'hit the ground running', yet are provided with very little support or direction in doing so. Consequently, many are burnt out within five years and leave the profession to pursue new avenues of work. Also of note is the movement of those nurses who do hold executive leadership positions but who are lured to take up non-nursing leadership positions. This is an expanding phenomenon and one that Malone (2001) sees has advantages and disadvantages. On the one hand, by giving voice to nursing in other arenas, nurses in non-nursing leadership positions have the potential to further the cause/s of nursing. Yet, on the other hand, there are those who would 'wipe the presence of nursing from their career portfolio' and in doing so, reinforce the stereotypes of 'low status and mobility' attributed to the profession (p.297). Malone (2001, p.295) believes nurses in non-nursing leadership positions function at the 'living edge' of nursing and are to be nurtured, not shunned.

Just as nurses are taking on new roles, so too leadership requires different skills in the 'new world of health care' (Kerfoot 2001, p.292). According to Kerfoot (2001), successful leaders in a rapidly changing health care environment need to be able to access and therefore keep abreast of knowledge relevant to practice and to understand the implications of new found knowledge. They should be capable of entering debate surrounding issues that stem from that knowledge; for example, the human genome project. Leaders need to be consumer savvy, experts at information technology and how to use it in working with patients, have fiscal expertise, know how to manage and model change, be sensitive to diversity, have the ability to empower those with whom they work, coordinate multi-disciplinary teams, and be capable of creating work environments in which employees flourish and where consumers feel physically, socially, mentally and spiritually nurtured (Kerfoot 2001, p.291–2).

That is a tall order and one that might send many a nurse into rapid retreat. In fact, cutting-edge thinking in leadership might criticise such theorising for its lack of application to the complexity of today's practice. For example, Nicholson (2002) states that in many cases, people enmeshed in the real world of practice do not have the capacities to be a leader or, if they do, the organisation determines otherwise. Nicholson (2002) stands against the idea that anyone, given the right set of circumstances (e.g. supportive promotion), can become a leader. Drawing on work stemming from evolutionary psychology, he describes three broad bands of people in the workplace—confident and competent people, who want to be at the top in their profession; the complete opposite, that is, people who might otherwise be good employees but would never be considered leadership material; and finally, those who fall somewhere in between. Given the right circumstances, this third group might just emerge as leaders. He goes on to point out that in many cases, due to the nature of the complex modern environments we have created, organisations often end up with 'ill-suited leaders' (p.34). Nicholson's treatise is that human nature, encoded as it is through evolutionary genetics and equipping us for survival and reproduction, has changed only marginally since we abandoned hunter-gathering as a way of life. He argues that the modern workstyles we are expected to adopt may 'be out of synch with how our brains are wired for leadership' (p.32). Human nature is much more difficult to change than the other things within our environment. He calls for management strategies that work 'with' rather than 'against' the grain of human nature (p.32). For example, many hyper-competitive business cultures reward 'street fighter dominance' and take on a 'slash and burn' mentality, rewarding those leaders with strong power needs who know the business but who have pitiful people skills (p.36). However, ignoring basic human needs and a sense of community in the workplace rarely works. By the same token, bureaucracies where leadership positions tend to be based on seniority or longevity in the workplace or qualifications—and hence, where leadership is predictable—seldom produce inspirational leadership (p.37). Modern psychology suggests that even with drive and vision, unless individuals are rewarded for their efforts, their capacity to achieve is limited. We would question how much of nursing leadership is reward driven rather than penalty-focused?

Nicholson (2002) advocates a new type of leadership for a new age, a move from the traditional 'alpha-male model of leadership' to one of a 'clan-type model' better suited to our ancestral communitarian make-up (p.39). While 'dominance and achievement' remain important characteristics, individuals also need to be able to communicate, innovate and work in a team (pp.39–40). Furthermore, because such characteristics may not be inherent within one individual but may be found in two or more people, the concept of 'multiple power-sharing leadership' is advocated (p.40). Different environments call for different leadership styles. Gender is an influencing factor but so too is the notion that leaders are able to change their behaviour from situation to situation (Vroom & Jago 1998). Thus leadership groups offer greater potential for the diverse environments of health care.

In today's work environment, if organisations are to endure then leadership needs to occur at all levels within it (Ray 1999). Ray, writing about 'organisational change leadership', sees the emergence and subsequent disappearance of various approaches to leadership as evolutionary. Participative management, quality of work life, quality circles, employee involvement, self-directed work teams, and total quality management have all been fashionable approaches to leadership at one stage or other (Ray 1999, p.5). Ray's treatise is 'facilitative leadership', where 'all work is accomplished through relationships' (p.12) and the leader is an 'enabler of change', using influence as opposed to direct power to bring work to fruition (p.25). Relationship-building is therefore important, together with coaching and learning, where information is openly shared. Moreover, the leader adopts a problem-solving approach to work, and action planning and implementation tracking provide clear pictures of how the job at hand is to be accomplished (p.12).

McMillan et al. (2002) suggest that nursing leaders 'are those who cause us to rethink the concepts we have of what it means to be a nurse; to research, to educate and to manage and consider how we enact nursing roles'(p.5). These authors go on to add that all nurses who engage in thinking about nursing have the potential to participate in synergistic leadership in the profession (p.5). Indeed, one could argue that such thinking nurses are also scholars of nursing. Nurses have arrived at a point from which they can engage in scholarly discussion, critique and voice their concerns knowing they have evidence upon which to draw, clinical expertise which they can describe and drive, and the credibility among their peers to do so. Boyer (1990, p.16) provides us with a framework in which to understand the nurse as a professional scholar. A scholar, he describes, is one who is able to step back from his or her practice, look for connections, build bridges between theory, practice and research, and communicate knowledge effectively. A scholar is also one who can respond effectively to critique, who acknowledges the valuable role critique plays in uncovering alternate connections and bridges than was first thought. He or she is also prepared to foster and lead new ideas. However, a scholarly nurse, to be fully effective, cannot 'work continuously in isolation' (p.80). Boyer contends that 'even as individual creativity is recognised and affirmed'; the complex social, economic and political problems of our time require an integrative team approach, a community of scholars with a vision for the future of nursing and health care (p.80). The question arises, who then are such a community of scholars, the leaders in nursing, and by what criteria do they get recognised?

Fundamentally, nursing is a clinical activity. Career pathways in the past have not facilitated keeping nursing expertise and leadership at the clinical interface. There is a need to recognise and value clinical practice and clinical leadership, and to help individuals—that is, all nurses—to develop effective leadership skills (Mahoney 2001, p.269). Collective/shared/relational leadership appears to be the key and certainly sounds promising for nursing. Nevertheless, it should be remembered that no single leadership theory is rated better than any other, and, in many cases, using a combination of approaches is more effective (Cherry 2002). The ability to bring humour into aspects of work, as well as fun and lightheartedness is an advantage (Champy 2002; Ray 1999). What has become clear, however, is that in any modern recipe for creating a sound leadership base, seeking out and establishing mentoring relationships is a key component to success (Malone 2001).

MENTORING AND PRECEPTORSHIP

Mentoring is described by Levinson (1978, cited in Malone 2001, p.295) as 'an intense career building, mutually beneficial relationship between two individuals of unequal power in an organization'. Adults learn effectively through mentoring (Bova 1987). In reviewing the literature, Bova (1987) describes two fundamental roles played by the mentor. The career role involves such activities as sponsorship and teaching, which assist the one being mentored to advance within the organisation through the creation of opportunity. The other role is on a more personal level and involves attributes such as counselling and friendship. In reality, the mentor is someone who passes on useful information and acts as a coach, allowing an individual to learn risk-taking behaviours, communication skills, political skills and specific skills related to the profession (Bova 1987, p.127). The stages in the mentor/protégé relationship are said to be developmental, but not rigid, and subject to degrees of intensity (O'Neil cited in Bova, p.125). The stages include entry, mutual building of trust, risk-taking, teaching of skills, development of professional standards and dissolution (O'Neil cited in Bova 1987, p.127). Bova suggests that mentoring relationships are of critical importance to the 'developing professional' (1987, p.129). Those who want to succeed are advised to actively seek mentors and in turn become mentors themselves. In an era where the performance expectations for novice nurses are high, mentoring is regarded as a useful model for consideration (Norris 2002). Mentorship of future leaders and managers is regarded as so crucial it is seen as the key to the survival of nursing (Cherry 2002).

Mentoring is different to preceptoring, although mentors may be preceptors in the short term (Norris 2002). Nevertheless, the terms are often used interchangeably in the literature (Clare et al. 2002; Heath 2002). Mentoring is more long-term, and we would argue could be considered visionary coaching, while preceptorship is short-term and often used in periods of transition to socialise/orientate an individual to a work setting (Norris 2002) and to share clinical expertise (Clare et al. 2002). Mentoring includes a commitment to teaching and learning on behalf of the mentor/mentee respectively (Chenoweth & Lo 2001, cited in Clare et al. 2002). Preceptors are usually designated, while mentors are chosen (Clare et al. 2002). Mentors may change over the course of an individual's career pathway and may not necessarily be discipline-linked. Preceptors assist the less experienced nurse to 'identify what they do not know and create opportunities' for learning. In addition, the preceptor is responsible for teaching and assessing the novice's performance (Clare et al. 2002, p.202). While preceptors are required to possess certain skills and attributes in order to be successful (see Chenoweth & Lo 2001), they themselves also need skill development in the area (Senate Inquiry into Nursing 2002).

Unless carefully planned, preceptoring often fails in nursing because of the nature of shift work, which means the preceptor may be rostered differently to the student. In view of this, some clinical areas have set up preceptorship teams, where a student may have a number of allocated preceptors and can be assured that at least one of them will be working on the shift. Other contextual issues also constrain the relationship, yet because good preceptoring has proven so important in the field, it is now believed it should be rewarded (Clare et al. 2002).

Recent research by Clare et al. (2002) explored curricula and education issues in Australian nursing. The results of their study generated a profile of a supportive work environment, especially in relation to graduate transition. It was drawn from the opinions of clinicians and employer groups. While employers perceived some of the essential qualities as 'idealistic' in an era of cost containment, the following key elements were generally thought to be essential:

▲ sufficient supportive nurses for the number of graduates—including preceptorship and buddy programs;

▲ quality communication and feedback—including senior staff fostering facilitative interactions between staff, regular staff appraisal, structured orientation;

▲ positive attitudes demonstrated by nurses—a team approach where each member is equally valued, there is solidarity and a positive work environment;

▲ the valuing of professional nursing practice—including an environment where evidence-based practice is encouraged, quality care is provided and graduates are offered appropriate opportunities to extend their knowledge and skills; and

▲ the provision of continuing education—where time is provided for planned learning activities (adapted from Clare et al. 2002, p.209).

All of the qualities listed above relate to the existence of what could be called a caring work culture. As McMillan and Conway (2002) point out, developing a positive culture 'requires effective leadership' (p.5). But as we have seen, leadership does not have to be a lonely pursuit (although in some cases it clearly is). One does not have to be a lone voice at the frontier.

ADVOCACY

Another useful collective strategy with which nurses can support each other is to lead through advocacy. Gaston (2002), in a recent oration to the profession, espoused the nature of advocacy which we now draw on for illustration. The role of nurses and midwives in advocacy is to mobilise all interested parties around an issue that evidence shows will impact positively on health system performance. Nurses and midwives need to build relationships to get messages through to decision-makers at all levels about the need to take action, what actions are possible, and what benefits can be gained from the actions. Some people see advocacy as organising marches and demonstrations; others see it as involvement in political campaigns or lobbying in the corridors of power, while some see it as editorial comment in the mass media. Advocacy may require all these tools.

Advocacy is a combination of individual and social actions designed to gain political and community support for a particular health goal or program. Advocacy by nurses and midwives should involve securing political action that will improve health outcomes and health system performance. A critical starting point for advocacy is knowledge—that is, having a good understanding of the problem and the appropriate responses. So, advocates for nurses and midwives should understand:

▲ how the problem or issue is experienced;

▲ both common and uncommon experiences;

▲ the extent to which cultural, social and economic forces impact on the problem; and

▲ appropriate solutions which are effective given diverse cultural, social and economic conditions.

Advocacy is required at all levels of the health system, whether it be registered nurses or midwives in remote clinics needing to advocate for funding for a particular community development program; nurses or midwives in hospital settings requiring new technology or altered staff mix; directors of nursing in hospital, community or aged care settings requiring additional funding to manage increased demand; or simply advocating for a change of practice amongst colleagues.

Advocacy requires sustained action with multiple players. Advocacy needs to be well planned. Previous advocacy efforts have provided well-worn tracks and it is important to take lessons from earlier endeavours. These include:

▲ being focused and relevant—Being clear about what you are advocating for; establishing common themes and messages; not straying from your message; making it local and keeping it relevant;

▲ working in partnership—Targeting individuals and organisations that can get your message across; recruiting corporate allies; and developing media contacts (including those outside health);

▲ being credible and appealing—Knowing the facts and the numbers; doing your homework and documenting your findings; using prominent individuals who have credibility; and using interesting stories; and

▲ being tactical—Being passionate and persistent; setting realistic goals; planning for small wins; being opportunistic and creative; employing multiple strategies; and being willing to compromise (adapted from World Health Organisation 2002).

PERFORMANCE MANAGEMENT, MOTIVATION AND CHANGE

Coupled with the emergent trends in society already mentioned, is the recent explosion in information available through communication technology, especially the Internet. This has led to an increasing level of knowledge among large numbers of computer savvy consumers, who, as a result, have come to expect much more from service providers. Related to this is the need for competence in the workplace. Knowledgeable consumers are more likely to realise dubious practice, and trends show that litigation for malpractice has risen exponentially. This creates additional pressure in the health care workplace. To safeguard consumers, nurses' and employer's competency outcomes and performance-based evaluation have become requisite (Lenburg 2002), and leaders are encouraged to continually look for ways of improving individual, team and organisational performance (Cherry 2002). Leadership, organisational effectiveness and culture reconfiguration and refinement are thus inextricably interdependent for nursing.

Organisational culture can inhibit leadership and growth of many nurses. The magnet hospital phenomenon provides 'living evidence that the creation of professional nurse practice environments' significantly improves retention of nurses via organisational and workplace reform (Aitken 2002). A nurse leader at the clinical interface is well placed to influence both organisational culture and departmental nuances, thus fostering excellent leadership in individual nurses while having the time, space and legitimacy to lead a vision for nursing beyond the boundaries of the ward to 'a community of leaders' (Boyer 1990). Within the context of constant change that takes place in the field of health service delivery, the successful management of organisational change is a key determinant of health for individual nurses and their ongoing capacity to remain in the nursing workforce. Dollard & Winefield (2002) note that this 'continually changing face and nature of work requires adaptive coping strategies that allow for easier and expected transitions from one type of work to another, in a context of lifelong learning and change' (p.22).

Put these in the context of Maxwell's (1998) laws of leadership. Maxwell argues that in order to build capacity within an organisation the following must be remembered:

▲ personnel determine the potential of the organisation;

▲ relationships determine the morale of the organisation;

▲ structure determines the size of the organisation;

▲ vision determines the direction of the organisation; and

▲ leadership determines the success of the organisation (p.225).

Goleman's (1998, p.282) taking of the organisational pulse (its people) identifies commonly missed opportunities for making an organisation effective. These are:

▲ emotional self-awareness;

▲ achievement;

▲ adaptability;

▲ self-control;

▲ integrity;

▲ optimism;

▲ empathy;

▲ political awareness;

▲ influence; and

▲ building bonds.

People development is recognised as an important component of successful leadership, as it allows the employee to feel valued (Ray 1999). Providing development that takes into account the career directions of the individual and the evolving state of a person's role is the key. Futurists predict an urgent need to stay ahead of change in order to successfully adapt to future shock (Mann 2002). They advocate the need to 'retrain and organise a workforce for the future'. The platform of performance management or evaluation can orientate purpose and vision within an organisation and thus help it stay ahead of change. Challenges within a performance management approach include understanding how to capitalise on 'diversity through cohesion', to 'appreciate humility and teach assertiveness' where 'team, workplace or corporate culture is conceived as negotiation' (Cope & Kalantzis 1997, p.175) to maximise open and flexible relations.

For performance management to succeed in its evaluative and directional intent, performance expectations need to be clearly articulated and situated within the broader organisational context, policies and procedures, and within the life worlds of work and home of the individual. Key questions that inform a coherent vision for leaders, supervisors and nurses (employees) alike include:

▲ What is the health unit/organisation expecting to achieve?

▲ What are the individual and corporate values, beliefs, assumptions, norms, shared meanings?

▲ What is the individual expected to achieve?

▲ What are the personal obligations and responsibilities?

▲ What are the pervading professional standards?

▲ Who are the customers and what is the working relationship with them?

▲ How well is each individual performing?

▲ What needs to be done to achieve personal and organisational goals and outcomes?

Using a framework of negotiation within performance evaluation means acknowledging and taking multiple perspectives on multiple realities. In practical terms, Cope and Kalantzis (1997) suggest that this starts with recognising where people come from; for example, generational difference, such as that experienced by Generation X nurses, who are risk-takers, multi-tasking parallel thinkers, resourceful and independent, yet are resistant to authority (Kupperschmidt 2000, p.68). Negotiating performance evaluation is a process that involves all aspects of performance and is concerned with setting goals in a positive context, where individuals are encouraged and assisted to contribute, to the best of their ability, to achieving the organisation's goals, thereby achieving personal satisfaction and growth, reward and prospects for career development. If the process works well it improves the morale of individuals and their teams, and enhances communication between staff and their supervisors. Poor management, on the other hand, has been linked to nurses' intention to leave (Newman & Maylor 2002). Frustrations can stem from unmet or unrealistic expectations, often within latent competing agendas such as organisational or strategic health policy directions versus professional standards. Psychologists Houkes et al. (2003) argue that work motivation is related to autonomy, job feedback, skill variety and task significance, and is highly influenced by an individual's need for learning and developing themselves. Joint efforts that foster coherent knowledge and understanding by active participation and an agreed plan for a defined time ahead systematically limit the degree to which frustrations and unmet career expectations can arise. Such a joint process requires trust and commitment to exploring and accessing personal growth and development opportunities within and beyond the organisation cognisant of relative workload and social support. Generative dissonance requires active negotiation. Acknowledgement of this can facilitate diverse, creative and productive working communities (p.179) of nurses who are outward looking for the future of nursing, yet are in constant engagement with diverse groups within and between which they work or provide service.

As a joint activity across interfaces of the organisation and personnel, performance management contributes directly to improvement in future management processes and thus leadership capacity building. Indeed, Manley (2000) has demonstrated that clinical leadership brings about performance-enhancing cultural change within an organisation and fosters innovative work practice strategies. However, an ability to 'develop people' requires an understanding of what motivates them to act in certain ways. Motivating workers to self-improve necessitates some understanding of the kinds of things that motivate individuals in their work. Cherry (2002) acknowledges that motivation is a complicated phenomenon involving a mixture of intrinsic and extrinsic rewards, such as job satisfaction brought about by good leadership. People development is a key aspect of performance management. People grow in situations where they have been given responsibility for small tasks. Success in small tasks leads to the sense of being valued, which in turn provides the motivation for behaviour change and progression beyond a comfort zone on to new horizons of practice.

CONCLUSION

Increasingly, nursing leaders will be required to 'maintain a sense of stability in unstable environments . . . the mantra of 21st Century leadership' (Dixon 1999, p.17 cited McMillian 2002, p.5). Having the skills, knowledge and experience to inspire and lead change rather than manage it will prove to be the key to success in health care for nurses, and in retaining nurses within a dynamic health care context (Jones & Cheek 2003). Leaders also need help. Leadership is an isolated position and is highly competitive. Being a leader is not an easy task and not everyone has the requisite skills. While some traits for effective leadership are linked to one's personality, others can be learnt through experience and training. Leadership occurs on differing levels throughout an organisation; some will be at an informal level while the remainder will be formal or designated through position. Increasingly, research is showing the correlation between a professional nursing presence and benefit to the consumer (Fagin 2001). This is something nurses have known all along but have failed to convince in others. This information is now research-based and gives strength to nurses' arguments for more recognition and power. The timing is good; health care systems are under stress and are being redeveloped. The push to reform is ringing in change. To secure a place for nursing in the health care models of the future, and to help shape the direction those models take, will require strong leadership—nurses can and should be at the forefront. Organisations that foster learning networks—allowing for thinking throughout its structures, authentic leadership, empowerment at all levels of staff and promoting communication—are seen as a key to unlocking the potential evident in many nurses practising in today's complex health settings. A nurse leader striving to build a shared vision for nursing practice, modelling commitment to patient-focused care and in partnership with other nurses, invites re-visioning, refining of the purpose, vision and values that reshape practice (Firth 2001; Mahoney 2001; Manley 2000). As Gaston (2003) says,

> [L]eaders across the health system will need to make a commitment to a better way of doing business, have the courage to challenge existing power bases and norms, and be willing to take the initiative to go beyond defined boundaries. This will include taking responsibility for the health of a population and not just the health of a health unit.

RECOMMENDED READINGS

Aiken, L. H. (2002). Superior outcomes for magnet hospitals: The evidence base. In M. L. McClure, & A. S. Hinshaw (eds). *Magnet hospitals revisited: Attraction and retention of professional nurses.* Washington DC: American Nurses Publishing.

Cope, B., & Kalantzis, M. (1997). *Productive diversity. A new Australian model for work and management.* Annandale, NSW: Pluto Press.

Heath, P. (2002) *National review of nursing education. Our duty of care.* Department of Education, Science and Technology, Commonwealth of Australia.

Senate Community Affairs Committee (2002). *The patient profession: Time for action. Report on the inquiry into nursing.* Canberra: Parliament of Australia.

CHAPTER ELEVEN

Leading and managing change in nursing

John Daly, Esther Chang, Karen Hancock & Patrick Crookes

LEARNING OBJECTIVES

At the completion of this chapter, the reader will be able to:

▲ describe and discuss critical leadership attributes in effective change processes;

▲ discuss and explain theories of change;

▲ identify principles that enhance management of change processes;

▲ analyse current issues in facilitating change in nursing; and

▲ implement strategies for facilitating change management processes.

KEY WORDS

Change process, leading change, management principles, planning, transformation

INTRODUCTION

Change may be defined as making or becoming different; substitution of one for another variety (*Concise Oxford Dictionary* 1982, p.154). Change has become a constant part of our lives, and of our professional lives in particular. Porter-O'Grady & Malloch (2002) suggest that we should anticipate change and view it as a journey. While change is always occurring in the health field, it is occurring at a rapidly increasing rate and is becoming increasingly complex (Manion 1994; Menix 2000). This is due to a range of factors such as changing technological, political, economic and social forces, increased consumer participation in evaluation of health services, demographic changes, use of evolving financial and management tools, a shift from centralised bureaucracies to decentralised management systems (Henderson 2000), changing legislative requirements and processes, an emphasis on cost containment and cost efficiency changes in models of care, evidence-based practice, and a focus on health outcomes which have had a substantial impact on the management and delivery of health care (Duffield & Franks 2001; Heath 2002; Henderson 2000; Tappen 2001). These are issues of concern in nursing and health care internationally. Porter-O'Grady and Malloch see the system changes we are confronting in health care and nursing as being related to the fact that we are living in the midst of a major social trans-formation—'a transition to a new way of living and acting' (2002, p.9).

The lack of stability in the health care environment has an impact on the practice of nursing. It means that nurses need to be able to adapt to their changing role and manage both predictable and unpredictable changes. Although nurses may be regarded as 'natural managers' (Mintzberg 1994), they tend to lack a clear identity as leaders considered as a professional body (Commonwealth of Australia 2001; Duffield & Franks 2001). Despite the fact that nurses are the largest group of employees in the health care system, they tend to be excluded from decision and policy-making forums in health care (Borman & Biordi 1992; Duffield & Franks 2001). Nursing lacks senior positions in the wider health care arena where policy and funding decisions are made, which ultimately shapes the practice of the nursing profession (Duffield & Franks 2001). For example, the lack of leadership is evidenced in Australia by a large range of disparate nursing bodies rather than a coherent group that has a voice in developing policy, responding to policy proposals or advising on policy. Lett (1999) describes a similar situation in Britain, where there is a lack of clinical leadership. Grossman and Valiga (2000) argue that nurses need to develop a more positive self-regard, as they have allowed themselves to be exploited and controlled by others with greater prestige. Change can be accomplished by more active involvement on the part of nurses in professional associations and increasing awareness of government policies (Lusky et al. 2002).

The need for health services to move from centralised bureaucracies to devolved management structures has been internationally recognised in the last two decades (Henderson 2000). Tilley & Tilley (1999) found that this is occurring in the United Kingdom in middle-management nursing. They describe how the earlier mode of the classic bureaucratic role (with managerial authority, information and decision-making highly centralised) was increasingly problematic in a rapidly changing environment. Devolving management structures requires adequately skilled managers at all levels, yet there has been a failure to develop managers to meet the new requirements (Henderson 2000). Duffield and Franks (2001) report that in Australia there is little formal preparation for the transition and development of clinical nurses into management positions, with many first-line managers appointed on the basis of their clinical experience rather than managerial potential or educational qualifications. Furthermore, Mackenzie (1993) found that most nursing unit managers surveyed in the United Kingdom believed that their management responsibilities had increased since the start of the National Health Service, but 66 per cent felt inadequately prepared for their managerial role. The United States has also debated about the most appropriate way in which to educate and prepare nurses for leadership and management roles in health care (Cebulski-Alexander 1997).

Professional registered nurses manage change as an inherent and primary responsibility, regardless of the levels of their positions (Boynton & Rothman 1996). That is, all qualified nurses are managers of care (Mulholland 1994) and utilise management skills in the delivery of care. Poggenpoel (1992) suggests that nurses need to understand change as a phenomenon, identify emotional reactions to change and understand change management strategies in order to view change as a challenge that can be effectively managed. This chapter provides an introduction to key ideas regarding leadership of change, change management in the nursing environment, frameworks for analysing and understanding change, planning for change, strategies for leading change, resistance to change and implementation and evaluation of change strategies.

LEADING CHANGE

Leadership of change requires vision, courage, creativity, effective communication and a clear plan. The literature is replete with definitions of leadership. On analysis, the majority of definitions regard leadership as a 'dynamic, interactive process' (Farley 1999, p.458). Three constituents must be considered in any leadership context: the leader, the followers and the situation or environment (Farley 1999). According to Trevelyan (2001, pp.41–2), leaders facilitate change 'by serving as . . . symbols of change . . . creators of cultures of transformation . . . as rewarders and reinforcers of innovation . . . as role models who embody transformation and as givers of meaning to transformation'. She identifies two critical functions in leaders:

> First, leaders construct change by identifying new values, directions and visions. Second, leaders facilitate others to change by leading them into the unknown, providing a sense of security, inspiring and motivating change, and role modelling the new way (2001, p.42).

Leadership styles vary and may be classified as collaborative, consultative, directive or coercive (Stace & Dunphy 1996). Contemporary leadership and management theory emphasises collaboration and consultation over direction and coercion. However, change leadership and management is complex and different change imperatives require the use of specific strategies in particular circumstances. For example, if a rapid change in policy is required, and it is one which the leader determines is critical for an organisation, then directive change may be appropriate (Stace & Dunphy 1996). Leaders and managers of change may use a range of strategies, depending on the context in which they are working to achieve their objectives. It is clear, however, that successful, large-scale change in organisations requires the commitment of the majority of staff. This is best achieved through use of incremental cultural change (Gagliardi 1986), where the leaders and managers seek to win the hearts, minds and commitment of all employees in the organisation (Porter-O'Grady & Malloch 2002).

Leaders of change may be classified as transformational or transactional. The concept of transformation is used in theoretical discussions of change to mean 'organisational change, learning and innovation' (Trevelyan 2001, p.2). A transformational leader 'is one who commits people to action, who coverts followers into leaders, and who may convert leaders into agents of change' (Bennis & Nanus 1985, p.3). They 'do not use power to control and repress but instead empower constituents to have a vision about the organisation and trust the leaders so that they work for goals that benefit the organisation and themselves' (Farley 1999, p.469). Such leaders must live change by example. Porter-O'Grady & Malloch argue that

> the role of today's leaders is to encourage this transformation. Indeed, they must make a commitment to the journey and work hard to incorporate changes in their lives in a very personal way. In other words, rather than simply suggesting that everyone and everything must change, they must lead by example. They must serve as witnesses to the change and show others how to adapt to changes in their own lives (2002; pp.9–10).

Transactional leaders are more focused on achieving short-term results, 'typically by promoting teamwork and working in a practical manner' (Crookes & Knight 2001, p.98). They are able to work within the vision or framework for change provided by transformational leaders. Zaleznik (1981), who has written widely about the differences between leadership and management, believes that leaders and managers are very different kinds of people. He believes that they differ in their own personal goals and their beliefs about the world and in their own personal motivation and their sense of self. Leaders formulate their goals from their passion and beliefs about what needs to be achieved. Managers, by comparison, adopt goals from the organisation. They differ in their orientation toward goals and in their working relationships with others and their view about the world. Managers hold appointee positions in the organisation. They are often appointed for both their technical and leadership experience. Managers have delegated authority, including the power of punishment and reward. A manager is expected to perform functions of directing, planning, organising and controlling. By contrast, leaders may not be part of an organisation or tied to a position of authority. They are not threatened by changes or the views of others.

Grossman & Valiga (2000) provide a number of principles to be considered in leading change, including the following:

- ▲ A change in one part affects other parts and other systems.

- ▲ People affected by the change should participate in making the change.

- ▲ People should be informed of the reasons for the change.

- ▲ Concrete and specific feedback about the process of change will enhance its acceptance.

- ▲ People need assistance in dealing with the effects of the change.

▲ People's suggestions and contributions about the implementation of change should be sought and incorporated (Grossman & Valiga 2000, p.143).

Grossman and Valiga (2000) stress that leaders do not need to be in positions of authority in order to create change. For example, nurses can develop a new patient care form and test it out if they are dissatisfied with the one currently in use.

MODELS OF CHANGE

Our understanding of the dynamics of change processes can be developed by exploring frameworks or models which provide conceptual tools for description, explanation and analysis. In this section a number of models are considered in examining the dynamics of change.

Carney (2000) argues that because nurses utilise management skills in their delivery of care, it is essential that they have insight and knowledge into change models or theories. Models of change in nursing are usually categorised as either linear or nonlinear. While linear planning is appropriate when change is predictable or slow-moving, nonlinear models of change management are necessary in today's health care system (Menix 2001). Nonlinear models are based on the premise that change occurs naturally from self-organising patterns. Begun and White (1995) suggest that nursing is a nonlinear dynamic system, where changes in one aspect of the system affect other parts of the system disproportionately.

Chaos theory was developed by Coppa (1993) as a new model for nursing. Grossman and Valiga define chaos theory as a 'belief that hidden within the seemingly total disorganisation of a situation are patterns of order' (Grossman & Valiga 2000: p.228). This theory encompasses the notion that change environments vary from being stable to being extremely tense, to being chaotic. Manion (1994) states that although unpredictability is a characteristic of change, applying a logical process to managing change can help reduce the chaos.

Menix (2000) conducted a literature review on change management in nursing. She found that undergraduate programs typically teach planned, linear approaches to change. The appropriateness of such a focus is questionable, given that the health care system is so unpredictable and that leaders need to be fluid and flexible in planning and implementing change. Some examples of linear models for planning change that are applied to nursing include Lewin's (1951) three-stage change process, Roger's (1983; 1995) five-step innovation adoption process, Lippitt et al's (1958) seven-phase change process, and Havelock's (1973) six-stage change process. Although it is beyond the scope of this chapter to discuss each theory in detail, one theory that helps understand the process of change is that of Lewin (1951). He identified three phases of change for use to deliberately disturb the equilibrium that exists before change is implemented, following which innovation is supported:

▲ unfreezing, in which people are preparing for change;

▲ moving, in which people have accepted the need for a change and actually engage in the change; and

▲ refreezing, where the new change is integrated into the system and becomes part of the new norm or culture (cited in Grossman & Valiga 2000 p.150).

Unfreezing involves giving the target system a push to get it moving towards change through strategies such as creating disconfirmation (e.g. discussing the inadequacies of the current system), inducing guilt and anxiety, or providing psychological safety (Tappen 2001). Thus, the change process begins with an analysis of the driving forces for and restraining forces against change. The manager then proceeds to work through unfreezing, changing and refreezing phases of change. This approach works best when resistance to change is low to moderate, and when some consensus on the planned change can be reached.

Roger's Diffusion of Innovation Model (Rogers 1995) is the best known of the rational models of change (i.e. those based on the assumption that people/organisations act in a reasonable, objective manner). Three phases make up the diffusion of an innovation:

▲ Invention of the change.

▲ Diffusion (communication) of the information regarding the change.

▲ Consequences (adoption or rejection) of the change.

In nursing, research utilisation involves using research findings to develop innovations in practice and then using the methods of research to implement those innovations and evaluate their impact on patients and staff (Crane 1985). An application of the Diffusion of Innovation Model (Rogers 1995) as a strategy for change is the research conducted by Dufault et al. (1995). In response to the observation that oncology nurses were not consistently applying effective pain management to patients, they assigned 12 nurses to an experimental group and 15 to a control group. Two patient care units were randomly assigned as either the control or experimental groups. The experimental group participated in a series of collaborative research utilisation activities. Fifteen nurses from another oncology ward were assigned to a control group in which they received no intervention. The activities used a diffusion of innovation framework, whereby a sequentially designed set of activities identified for the collaborative model progressed from phase 1 to phase 6 over 28 weeks. Phase 1 involved the investigation of the need for clinical innovation; phase 2 evaluated the relevance of the research; phase 3 designed an innovation meeting the needs of the clinical problem. The innovation was an adaptation of a pain assessment instrument to be used as a baseline assessment of patients. Phase 4 involved testing the innovation on patients and evaluating its utility and applicability; phase 5 involved a decision to adopt, alter or reject the innovation under consideration, and phase 6 was the development of means to extend the innovation to other appropriate nursing settings. Two-thirds of the nurses in the experimental group reported changes in their practice at the end of the experiment, compared with none in the control group. Nurses who participated in the model also improved their competency in research utilisation and their attitudes towards research when compared to a control group who did not participate in the model.

Pearcey and Draper (1996) also used the Diffusion of Innovation Model to influence nursing practice. They used action research (field notes, semi-structured interviews, informal discussions) to identify factors associated with non-utilisation of research findings in a surgical hospital ward. They found that the Diffusion of Innovation Model was a useful tool to enhance research-based change in clinical practice.

Menix (2001) conducted a Delphi study, whereby nurse manager and nurse educator experts validated what linear (planned, step-by-step) and nonlinear (unplanned) change management concepts they believed were relevant in managing change in today's constantly evolving health care environment. The researcher developed a pilot instrument composed of 12 change management concept categories, based on literature analysis of nursing, business and higher education. The nine categories from nursing literature were planned change, change characteristics, change as a process, change agent roles, innovation, responses to change, strategies, principles, and various influences in the change environment. The three categories from business/higher education were nonlinear change (chaos, or change that occurs naturally from self-organising patterns), cybernetic (regulation of systems by managing communication and feedback systems) and learning organisational (the need for organisations to stress continual learning for adequate responses to accelerated change) theories.

Consensus of both groups resulted in the 12 concept categories, indicating that nursing managers are experientially identifying the relevance of chaos, cybernetic and learning organisation concepts, not just planned change models (i.e. change that is expected and deliberately planned for in advance) for managing change effectively. Identifying opportunities in health care situations to apply new concepts is a recommended application of Menix's study.

A range of additional theoretical literature on leading and managing change can be located in the management literature. These perspectives can also be very useful in conceptualising leading and managing change in nursing (see Gagliardi 1986 and Stace & Dunphy 1996 as good examples).

AGENTS OF CHANGE

A change agent is 'the person responsible for moving others who are affected by the change through its stages' (Marquis & Huston 2000, pp.71–2). In nursing, key change agents are often nurse educators who prepare future nurse managers and nurse managers, who then test their educational preparedness in different health care settings (Menix 2001). Supporting professional development, such as in the area of managing change, is an ongoing responsibility of continuing development and staff development (Menix 2001). Wright (1993) argues that achieving change quietly relies heavily on nurses' skills as change agents. He states that change agents need to be assertive and have personal awareness in order to combat managerial repression and conspiracy of colleagues.

Marriner-Tomey (1996, pp.170–1) identifies three set strategies for effecting change by nurse managers:

1 Empirical-rational strategies. These are based on the assumption that people are rational and behave according to rational self-interest . . . Nurse managers who use empirical-rational strategies are likely to want to appropriate persons for specific positions . . . They give considerable attention to recruitment and selection of personnel.

2 Normative re-educative strategies. Based on the assumption that people act according to their commitment to socio-cultural norms . . . The manager fosters the development of staff members through strategies, such as personal counselling, training groups, small groups and experiential learning, because people need to participate in their own re-education.

3 Power coercive strategies. Involves compliance of the less powerful to the leadership, plans and directions of the more powerful . . . These acknowledge

the need to use sources of power to bring about change, e.g. strikes, sit-ins, negotiations, conflict resolution.

Often the change agent uses strategies from each of these three groups (Marquis & Houston 2000, p.12).

PLANNING FOR CHANGE

Planned change is a 'well thought-out and deliberate effort to make something happen' (Marquis & Houston 2000, p.71). Planning is the basis of effective management and 'has its beginning in the mission, philosophy and objectives of the organization' (Cuthbert et al. 1992, p.15). Often change is introduced without considering the realities of particular areas of practice or the needs of individual health care providers (Carney 2000). Furthermore, change agents may disregard the possible consequences of the change on the lives of staff, as seemingly minor changes can have unexpected negative consequences. Thus, change should be managed sensitively, effectively and systematically. It is important to remember that strategic planning alone cannot prepare organisations for the uncertainty of the health care environment, because long-term plans may change according to the environment (Menix 2000).

In planned change, the manager is often the change agent (Marquis & Houston 2000). Some examples of leadership roles in planned change include:

- ▲ being visionary in identifying change needed;

- ▲ risk-taking and flexibility;

- ▲ anticipating, recognising and problem-solving resistance to change; and

- ▲ sensitivity to timing planned change (Marquis & Houston 2000).

They see the following management functions in planned change:

[F]orecasts unit needs with an understanding of the organisation's legal, political, economic, social and legislative climate; recognises the need for planned change and identifies the options and resources available to implement that change; appropriately assesses the driving and restraining forces; identifies and implements appropriate strategies to minimise or overcome resistance; seeks subordinates' input and provides them with adequate information during the change process to give them some feeling of control; supports and reinforces individual staff efforts during change; and identifies and uses appropriate change strategies to modify the behaviour of staff as needed (Marquis & Huston 2000, p.72).

Grossman and Valiga (2000) suggest that in order to be effective change agents, leaders need to know when change is needed, help staff understand the need for change, plan effectively for change to occur, involve those affected by the change in the process, help others realise their role in making change and creating new worlds, maintain a positive attitude through the challenges of change, and know when to maintain the status quo.

RESISTANCE TO CHANGE

Change results in disrupting the balance of a system, so resistance is a natural and expected response (Marquis & Huston 2000). Nurses have been reported as frequently being resistant to change (Clay 1987; Owen 1985; Swan & McVicar 1992). In addition, bureaucracies characteristically have 'built-in resistance to change' (Tappen 1995, p.323). An open system's response to change is influenced by factors such as a group's past experiences, present needs, culture, values, roles and coping abilities. The way in which a change is perceived can be the key to its successful implementation. For example, if an organisation is stable and the change is seen as a threat, there is likely to be resistance to change. However, systems do not always resist change. The level of resistance often depends on the type of change being proposed. Technological changes encounter less resistance than social changes or 'those that are seen as going against established norms' (Marquis & Huston 2000, p.78).

Wilmott (1998) found that there was considerable frustration at the lack of perceived consultation during the development of the new charge nurse role. Wilmott (1998) concluded that more involvement of the charge nurses would have been time-consuming at the initial stages but may have made the process of change less difficult and more effective for all concerned in the long term. This study is an example of how perceived lack of involvement, explanation, education and support for charge nurses resulted in increased resistance to change.

Many theorists recommend involving all members of a multidisciplinary team when considering an alteration in practice in health care (Ford & Walsh 1994; Kieffer 1984; Lewin 1951). This would help overcome peer group pressure, which is the biggest hurdle when considering change involved in a nursing innovation (Balfour & Clarke 2001). Such collaboration is even more important considering that current models of patient care involve working in multidisciplinary teams, with registered nurses coordinating patient care (Lusky et al. 2002).

Barriers to change include factors such as 'decreased resources, lack of support, resistance, poor communication mechanisms, or pressures to get the day-to-day work done' (Grossman & Valiga 2000, p.151). One of the greatest factors contributing to resistance to change is a 'lack of trust between the employee and manager or the employee and the organization' (Marquis & Huston 2001, p.79). Because workers desire predictability in terms of feeling secure and comfortable, and trust is based on predictability and capability, obtaining the trust of workers may be difficult in times of change, which is, paradoxically, the time when it is needed most (Marquis & Huston 2000).

Causes of resistance to change are multifactorial. Examples include anxiety, uncertainty, and feelings of loss of control in relation to how rapid and in what direction change occurs (McPhail 1997). Cutcliffe and Bassett (1997) argue that the most significant reasons for resistance to change are self-interest, a lack of understanding of the proposed change, and the desire to keep the status quo. Staff will 'generally focus on how a specific change will affect their personal lives and status rather than how it will affect the organization' (Marquis & Huston 2000, p.77).

It may take repeated attempts and errors, and a variety of attempts over time, before staff accept that a change needs to occur (Davidhizar et al. 1999). By anticipating negative responses, managers can develop systems to help nurses move through the difficult stages of letting go of the old and accepting the new (Edman 1996).

Thus, resistance is a normal part of the change process, and can be the most difficult response to deal with. The level of resistance can be influenced by factors such as staff values, educational levels, and previous experiences with change. Although resistance to change is not always inevitable, it takes more than seeing the positive value of a proposed change to avoid resistance. Other factors are discussed in the following section. When change agents anticipate resistance, they can put plans into action that help staff move on and accept the change.

STRATEGIES FOR LEADING CHANGE

Nurse managers need the ability to predict, plan and manage both predictable and unpredictable changes, which may be multiple and simultaneous (Menix 2000). Effective change requires leadership skills of interpersonal communication, group management, and problem-solving skills. The leaders and the followers must be motivated to put the changes in place and cope with the constant changes in the health care environment. Individuals who are not motivated to change will 'most likely remain at status quo and be unable to lead or facilitate others' growth' (Grossman & Valiga 2000, p.75). Leaders need to 'help others see the need for change, work with others to implement the change, evaluate the effect of change, and participate in each stage of the change process' (Grossman & Valiga 2000, p.149). Factors that influence an organisation's response to change include the 'perceived value of the change, the rate of change, and the needs, experiences, culture, values, and coping abilities of the system within a given environment' (Tappen 2001, pp.215–16). There has been much debate about what factors are related to implementing change successfully, but there are differing perceptions on how this might be achieved (Carney 2000).

Although change can be exciting and challenging, it can also result in staff feeling powerless, ambivalent, frustrated and stressed (Davidhizar et al. 1999). Thus, nurse managers must not only be able to plan and adjust to change in the workplace, but also help staff work through these feelings. Instead of focusing on eliminating opposition, modern approaches to managing resistance are to identify and implement strategies to minimise or manage resistance to change. One such strategy is to encourage staff to 'speak openly so options can be identified to overcome objections' (Marquis & Huston 2000, p.76). Willmott (1998) conducted a study to explore the experiences of one National Health Service Trust in the United Kingdom in implementing change in the charge nurse's role. Nurses were interviewed and sent a questionnaire to determine whether they were in favour of the changes, satisfied with the way changes were introduced, and if they had sufficient time, knowledge, resources, preparation and support to enable them to undertake their new role. Willmott (1998) concluded that nurse managers did not take full account of the impact the change was having on the charge nurses, nor were appropriate steps taken to alleviate their anxieties. When the results of Willmott's study were presented to the Trust, the charge nurses' concerns were blamed on their 'inability to cope with the change' rather than on the Trust's own failure to prepare and support them through the process. Thus ineffective change management may have led to inadequately performing ward managers who were unable to make the most of this demanding role. They were unable to achieve all that the decentralisation of management responsibility was intended to achieve. Despite the change agents being presented with an enthusiastic, motivated group of people who believed in the need for change, the opportunity to build on this enthusiasm was missed due to a failure by nurse managers to make full use of effective change management techniques. This study demonstrates how enthusiasm is only one ingredient for successful change, and that effective sensitivity and management of staff's feelings cannot be overstated.

Because overcoming peer group resistance is one of the biggest hurdles to consider when considering change, many theorists recommend involving all members of the multidisciplinary team when considering an alteration in practice (Ford & Walsh 1994; Kieffer 1984; Lewin 1951). Staring and Taylor (1997) describe how theory and philosophy were combined to manage a workforce transition on a 31-bed medical/surgical unit. Three key strategies were identified: emotional management, professional empowerment and empowerment by values. Emotional management began by validating the emotions of both the unit's staff and the unit manager. Staff were encouraged to express their emotions. Over time, negative emotions gave way to more positive energy. Staff meetings were redesigned into staff dialogues, with a different staff member facilitating the meeting each month. Professional empowerment occurred by providing an environment that promoted motivation, respect, support and strong communication skills. There was a strong focus on encouraging unit membership and maintaining stability. Staff were encouraged to try new strategies, given permission to make mistakes and use them as a learning experience.

A study by Knox and Irving (1997) demonstrates the importance of communication, recognition of staff welfare and empowerment of staff. They studied nurse managers' perceptions of the behaviour of health care executives during organisational change, and rank-ordered those perceptions. The highest ranks were for frequent communication of plans and progress during the transition, high visibility on work units during the organisational change, verbalisation of commitment to quality patient care and staff welfare during the transition, and empowerment of staff to accomplish changes for which they were responsible.

IMPLEMENTATION AND EVALUATION OF CHANGE

In the implementation phase of the change process, unfreezing has occurred and the environment is moving towards change (Tappen 2001). The leader can start to put into place the planned changes. Tappen (2001) lists the following activities that the leader will perform in the implementation phase:

- ▲ Introduce any new information that is needed to implement the change.

- ▲ Encourage the new behaviour so that it becomes part of the system's regular patterns of behaviour. Allow for practice and experimentation with the change behaviour in such a way that people can make mistakes without punishment.

- ▲ Continue to provide a supportive environment to minimise resistance to change and negative behaviours.

- ▲ Provide opportunities for workers to express feelings of anxiety or other emotions aroused by the change process.

- ▲ Provide feedback on progress and clarify the goals in order to keep people on track for change.

- ▲ Present self as trustworthy to keep open lines of communication.

▲ Act as an energiser to keep interest high and move the change process in a positive direction.

▲ Overcome resistance by using unfreezing methods (Tappen 2001, p.208).

While the leader acts as an energiser, gradually responsibility for the change behaviour/s is delegated to others in the environment, with the leader reducing participation as others become more involved. Tappen (1995) argues that to implement change effectively, the leader should choose a specific person to implement the action required, and provide coaching. The change agent should coordinate efforts of each staff member so that each task is performed in a timely manner. Davidhizar and Shearer (1995) also suggest that the nurse manager should not become too involved with job responsibilities involved in change because if the work regularly involves excessive hours with feelings of exhaustion, the nurse manager is over-involved.

The evaluation process is the final component of the process of change. In order for change to be sustained, it must be continuous and cyclical, allowing evaluation and review (Balfour & Clarke 2001). When the change process has occurred, the overall results of the change should be evaluated. It is important that the leader evaluates the success of the whole change process rather than focusing on its parts (Porter-O'Grady 1998). Part of the evaluation process involves making adjustments as necessary. A decision may be taken to retain, alter, discard aspects, or discontinue the whole change process (Douglass 1996). Gillies (1994, p.477) argues that the most accurate evaluation of change evaluates 'both the change process and the altered reality state resulting from that process'. The change process involves the input from others and the actual process, while the altered state of reality is the output that has occurred as a result of the change process. Gillies (1994) suggests the following criteria should be used to evaluate change: whether the output as a result of change effectively supports the environment's goals; how efficiently the change plan and process achieves the desired outcome(s); and satisfaction of administrators, managers, change agents and change targets with the interactions that were required in order to see the change occur.

Tools to evaluate the process should also be chosen carefully. If a survey is chosen, an instrument that is validated and reliable that would suit the purposes of the evaluation would be preferable to one that has been uniquely developed and not tested for validity. Douglass (1996) argues that group discussions are preferable to anonymous comments, as the latter may reinforce passive-aggressive behaviour. He also recommends that evaluation sessions be held with those affected by the change as changes are in progress. Thus a nurse manager may meet periodically with staff to gain their feedback. By evaluating the change at each step, it is easier to deal with problems in the earlier stages than waiting until it builds up to something that may be extremely difficult to manage. Carney (2000) also concurs that the change process should be evaluated at various stages, and necessary action taken. It is here that feedback should be provided to staff and recognition and acknowledgement of the contribution of staff should be made (Carney 2000).

Warden and McKenna (1998) reported an example of implementation and evaluation of change in terms of introducing team primary nursing in an intensive care unit. They used both objective and subjective assessments. They used Mead's characteristics which identify primary nursing (1991) as a yardstick to measure the effectiveness of the change, as Mead's characteristics were reflective of the goals of the change. The authors were planning an action research study to further evaluate the impact of the change towards team/primary nursing on quality of care, and patient and staff satisfaction. By following a structured change model, such a study helps advance evidence-based nursing practice. Carney (2000) developed and used the 'Change Management Model' to provide nurse managers or change agents with a structured and measurable model for evaluating and managing the change process. The Change Model was developed through reflection on critical incidents related to change by university students using a focus group methodology. The study also developed the 'Measurement Construct Tool' as an instrument to evaluate change. Students agreed that the Change Model was highly effective in describing how change was managed, and that the assessment tool was an objective measure facilitating the evaluation of a change process. This model and the assessment tool both require further testing for reliability and validity, but provide an innovative way of assisting change agents and managers to evaluate change systematically.

CONCLUSION

Change can be exciting and challenging, but also can provoke feelings of uncertainty, anxiety, anger and powerlessness. The nursing profession faces many challenges in its efforts to keep up with the constantly changing environment of the health care system. Such changes are being compressed into shorter and shorter periods. Nurses require an extensive knowledge base, highly sophisticated technological skills, decision-making and critical thinking skills, and the capacity to manage multiple problems simultaneously in order to successfully perform their role. Given that they use management skills in performing their role, knowledge of the change management process and theories can assist them to be more effective. Nurses need to be encouraged to move away from being task-oriented to a more scientific approach to managing change. Adapting the new science of leadership with its focus on empowering others and moving away from a bureaucratic type of leadership will lead to development of new ways of working, and provide a more collaborative and holistic approach to nursing practice. A person does not have to be in a position of authority to be a leader. Assisting nurses to identify their strengths and increase their self-confidence will help to reduce the fear associated with the inevitable changes in the health care environment, and encourage leadership. By understanding change as a phenomenon, how to implement it and overcome barriers to change, nurses can take a more proactive role in the change process that will inevitably continue to occur in the health system.

Reflective exercise

1 What are the key considerations that need to be addressed in planning change?

2 What strategies would you use in your workplace to maximise transformation efforts in leading change?

3 Think of a successful leader you have observed in managing a change process. How did that leader inspire followers to participate positively in the change process?

RECOMMENDED READINGS

Balfour, M., & Clarke, C. (2001). Searching for sustainable change. *Journal of Clinical Nursing,*
10(1), 44–50.

Crookes, P., & Knight, S. (2001). Processes of change in bureaucratic environments. In E.
Chang, & J. Daly (eds), *Transitions in nursing: Preparing for professional practice* (pp.91–106).
Sydney: MacLennan & Petty.

Gagliardi, P. (1986). The creation and change of organizational cultures: A conceptual
framework. *Organization Studies,* 7(2), 117–34.

Porter-O'Grady, T., & Malloch, K. (2002). *Quantum leadership: A textbook of new leadership.*
Aspen: Gatersburgh.

Stace, D., & Dunphy, D. (eds) (1996). *Beyond the boundaries: Leading and creating the successful*
enterprise. Sydney: McGraw-Hill.

CHAPTER TWELVE

Leading research to enhance nursing practice

David R Thompson

LEARNING OBJECTIVES

At the completion of this chapter, the reader will be able to:

- ▲ understand of the role of research in nursing practice;

- ▲ appreciate the need for good leadership in developing a research culture;

- ▲ describe the steps to be followed in establishing a research culture;

- ▲ discuss the factors that impede research utilisation; and

- ▲ explain the principles of evidence-based practice.

KEY WORDS
Vision, evidence-based practice, research culture, research utilisation, consumers

INTRODUCTION

Too often, research is perceived to be a rather esoteric activity somewhat removed from the real world of nursing practice. It is often something that others or outsiders (i.e. researchers) do. Hence, researchers are often described as 'coming in' and 'carrying out' research. While this view is to some extent understandable, it is often forgotten that research has been an important factor in the development and professionalisation of modern nursing. Florence Nightingale systematically collected data in the clinical setting to inform the organisation and delivery of nursing, and was a great believer in the power of statistics, as well as an early pioneer of their use.

For a while after this time there was a dearth of research in nursing and it has only been over the past 40 years that there has been a resurgence of interest in research, although much of the early period focused more on education and management rather than practice.

A major development in the history of nursing research was the establishment in 1986 of a National Center for Nursing Research within the National Institutes of Health in the United States. In 1993 the Center was redesignated the National Institute of Nursing Research; its mission to facilitate national programs of nursing research and promote excellence in the knowledge base for the profession (Hinshaw 1999). No such initiative exists elsewhere in the world and there are arguments as to whether nursing should adopt such a model or take a broader health perspective.

Whatever approach is used, there are a number of issues that need to be addressed including the development of thematic programs (ideally, multi-centred) of nursing research as opposed to small-scale, short-term projects that are unreplicated and ungeneralisable; the identification and securing of research funding; and the building and strengthening of research capacity (Thompson 2000a). In addition, there is a real need for economic evaluations in nursing practice (Jenkins-Clarke 1999).

RESEARCH AND PRACTICE

Practice, the *raison d'etre* of nursing, is, or should be, the hotbed for generating good research questions. However, although research is being used increasingly by practitioners and more of them are engaging in research, there is little evidence that this is closing the theory–practice gap. If the theory base of practice and the practice base of research are to be strengthened, it is vital that clinical nurses undertake research and nurse-researchers investigate areas that are perceived to be relevant to practice (Thompson 2000b).

While nursing knowledge and research have expanded rapidly over the past few decades, much of it driven by the development of systematically generated knowledge to inform and guide nursing practice, research is not always recognised, even by nurses (including nurse academics), as a legitimate area of science and health care. Nurse researchers often lack the confidence and political acumen to persuade others of the potential important contribution that they can make. Although nursing needs to generate and extend its own body of knowledge through research, it is important that nursing research is seen as part of the broader scientific community. However, there are tensions that relate to what is considered to be quality research in nursing and what is considered to be the role of nurses in a multidisciplinary research agenda (Luker 1999). Nurses rarely participate in research collaborations as equal partners, nor do they participate as equals in identifying worthwhile research questions.

LEADERSHIP

As with any other activity, research requires leadership. The aim is to cultivate and nurture nurses to accept research as a normal and integral aspect of their everyday work, to read and understand research reports, to be able to apply research findings to their sphere of practice and, where appropriate and possible, to engage in designing and conducting research. Leadership should thus be supportive of innovation and provide direction, purpose and motivation. Effective leaders have visionary capacity and are good at team building and team playing. Leading research to enhance nursing practice requires a mixture of four things: thinking big and in new ways (vision); being pragmatic, thinking rather than feeling, and being connected (reality); having morality and integrity (ethics); and a willingness to take risks (courage). To borrow terminology from management, good researchers have a clear vision, a competitive edge, a unique selling point and a niche market.

ESTABLISHING A RESEARCH CULTURE IN THE CLINICAL AREA

It is important to develop and sustain an active and vital culture conducive to research in the clinical area, which encourages imaginative and critical thinking. Staff and the environment in which they operate, including support, facilities and supervisory arrangements, will influence culture. It needs to be supportive and enabling, and an environment in which learning, supported by communication and training, is fostered.

Research is a human activity and invariably a team effort. The ideal is to be able to assemble a team of individuals sufficiently different to complement each other. The hallmark of a good research team is that it has an ethos of openness, creativity, flexibility, healthy scepticism and a willingness to question the status quo or accepted conventions (Thompson 1998a). As well as an air of trust and collegiality, a sense of fun is also helpful, even if only to counteract the frequent frustrations and disappointments that most researchers encounter.

The practice of research depends upon the acceptance of certain moral values and the operation of ethical codes. These include honesty in reporting the findings, acknowledgement of the contribution of others and openness in making methods and results available to others for scrutiny. Thus, research can be perceived as threatening, challenging cherished assumptions and beliefs, and there can be difficult issues such as clashes of personality, vested interests and some degree of rivalry.

A clear research focus (strategy) is required, together with research capacity building, training, supervision and mentorship, peer review, and the attraction and retention of staff. A strategic plan may be helpful to guide research by setting out the main objectives and plan. The relevance of research to potential users in practice, policy, education and management and the involvement of users in the development of research need to be made explicit. The research structure and environment will depend on whether the research activity is built around individuals and/or coherent groups.

In order to maximise expertise to improve patient care, a sensible and pragmatic approach is to develop a collaborative partnership between clinicians and researchers. This also has the added advantage of bringing together health care settings and universities. Kitson et al. (1996) identify an organisational framework for promoting research-based practice that includes:

▲ acknowledgement of the importance and inter-relationship of the research implementation and practice development models;

▲ encouragement of staff to use each other's skills in developing and delivering research;

▲ recognition of the skills needed to complete the cycle of getting research and practice combined; and

▲ recognition of the importance of academic and service partnerships for generating and implementing knowledge, and in undertaking rigorous evaluations.

These principles have been used in formulating a strategy for developing research in practice in local settings (Knight et al. 1997). The aim has been to further develop the spirit of inquiry and inculcate a culture of research-based practice, to provide opportunities for nurses to develop their understanding of research, to actively promote the utilisation of research and to contribute, where possible, to the design and conduct of research. Achievements from such an initiative include not only heightened research awareness and research involvement but tangible outputs such as research publications (Martin et al. 1998).

It should be recognised that such strategies are long-term and require investment, commitment and evaluation. They will also need to be flexible, responsive and proactive in order to be relevant in a rapidly changing world. Local considerations are important, but there is also a need to consider the wider context.

In order to lead and manage research and to foster a climate of intellectual curiosity and creativity, there is a need for regular briefings and intellectual stimulation and interaction, as well as to formulate strategy and project management. There is a need to respect epistemiological and methodological diversity, and through this understanding, ensure that the research methods chosen are appropriate, rigorous and sensitive to the problem. In essence, there is a need to value diversity and plurality in nursing philosophy, science, research methods and practice (Jacox et al. 1999).

Staff education and training

Staff members are the greatest assets of any organisation. Their motivation, job satisfaction and commitment are essential for the success of the enterprise. Continuing education, training and professional development are vital and are needed at all levels, including post-doctoral. This will not only improve the quality of research, and thus patient care, but also provide incentives for attracting and retaining staff.

Consideration should be given to the development of innovative and flexible research training schemes, for example, to develop and refine research appreciation and critical appraisal skills before embarking on a specific project. The latter will include areas such as understanding research theory, the ability to design successful proposals, and skills in analysis and dissemination.

Short courses can play a very important part in enabling continuing education for those employed in research. These can often include specific research methods (such as qualitative interviewing, the design of a longitudinal survey or the management and conduct of a clinical trial), methods of analysis, computing and statistics, writing proposals and presentation skills.

Consideration will need to be given to formal training opportunities at postgraduate level in research skills and methods. Training needs should be identified in personal development plans, where this is considered appropriate. It may be the case that there is a mix of multidisciplinary training and some specialist training within the discipline. A wide range of courses is now available, and in the era of the Internet, there is a need to look more creatively and imaginatively at their provision. Regardless of the formal education and training approach adopted, all staff should be encouraged to attend research meetings, seminars and conferences. This will bolster confidence, as well as improve knowledge and skills.

There has been a move towards increasing the role of patients and carers in health care decision-making and policy. Consumer involvement is important because there is a clear mismatch between the interventions that are researched, and those regularly used and prioritised by patients (Tallon et al. 2000). Consumer involvement is likely to improve the way in which research is commissioned, conducted and disseminated. Thus, there is the notion of training and supporting consumers to become involved in research. Consumers can help to ensure that issues important to them, and therefore to the health system as a whole, are identified and prioritised. They can also help to ensure that research does not just measure outcomes that are identified and considered important by health care professionals. They should be involved in all stages of the research process and there should be recognition that there are education and training needs associated with the implementation of this principle.

The importance of learning opportunities presented by being a member of a research team should not be underestimated. An environment where less experienced researchers can learn from senior colleagues, and where they are encouraged to seek advice outside the research team, can be very valuable.

Nurses need to have adequate time, space, resources and intellectual support, with strong mentorship and supervision. However, they also have to work with many other community members. Increasing emphasis is being placed on multidisciplinary proposals and collaboration. There is a danger that, either through ignorance, naivety or nursing imperialism, nurses may alienate themselves from their closest clinical colleagues. This may result not only in nurses being excluded from collaborative ventures, but also in a possible lack of recognition being given to their own unique and valuable contribution (Thompson 1998b). Thus, there is good reason to offer research training and support programs for a variety of staff, representing a range of disciplines and which teach students not only about the relative merits of the different research methods and approaches but to constantly develop the theoretical framework within which nursing and other research is carried out. This is likely to generate more mutually respectful and harmonious working relationships.

Novice researchers must not only immerse themselves in the literature but must begin to serve an apprenticeship to learn the ways in which research is done. This involves much more than acquiring necessary techniques, whether they be observational or experimental; it also requires the attitudes of commitment and relentless curiosity. These come from seeing how other, more experienced and wiser researchers pursue their investigations. Helping and supervising the novice researcher requires careful judgement, sensitivity and tact (Thompson 1998a). Research degrees (i.e. MSc(Hons), MPhil/PhD) are, of course, important, as is the need for nurse leaders to create opportunities for nurses to be supported to undertake these research training opportunities.

DETERMINING RESEARCH PRIORITIES

Establishing and setting priorities will help focus clinical nursing research, and target the growing but still limited funding resources available to support nursing research. National initiatives to set nursing research priorities in nursing have been undertaken in the United States (Hinshaw et al. 1988) and the United Kingdom (Kitson et al. 1997). This can also be done at local level.

There needs to be a well-informed nursing contribution and appropriate representation, and the priority setting exercise should take account of a number of factors with regards to the research:

▲ quality (methods);

▲ relevance;

▲ feasibility;

▲ impact;

▲ importance;

▲ management (including monitoring);

▲ dissemination (strategy); and

▲ implementation.

Other issues that need to be taken into account include:

▲ health gain (actual, potential);

▲ partnership (professional, consumer);

▲ funding (competitive, limited);

▲ resources (staff, equipment, facilities); and

▲ ethics.

RESEARCH UTILISATION

Most of the focus on nursing research has been concerned with designing and conducting studies rather than using the findings. Although not all nurses need to be able to conduct research, they do need to be able to use and apply it in order to practise in a professional manner and in accordance with the best available evidence. Research utilisation skills involve being able to access the literature, being aware of research relevant to their practice, having an appreciation of the study findings and being able to apply the findings in relation to their own practice setting (Thompson et al. 2002).

The apparent chasm between theory and practice is attributed to the separation of researchers (the generators of knowledge) and educators (the transmitters of knowledge) from practitioners (the users of knowledge). There is a need to maximise the impact of research and development to ensure that this knowledge is transferred to practice and education. Greater emphasis is needed on the dissemination and application of research findings in practice, which should include a review of the barriers to, and incentives for, nursing research.

The production and dissemination of quality research information is of no use to nurses if they do not, or cannot, gain access to it. Improving access to current best knowledge is crucial, including journals that scan and distill information into structured abstracts and commentaries by clinicians about implications for practice, and access to electronic sources. The time needed to access is also important (Department of Health 2000).

Specific strategies need to be adopted to encourage implementation of research findings. The strategy chosen will depend on the characteristics of the message, the recognition of external barriers and the preparedness of clinicians to change. Access and uptake also depend on organisational culture and local commitment.

Relationships between researchers, educators and practitioners need to be improved as the basis for strategic alliances between individuals and groups from the health service and university sectors. It is only through collaborative effort that the research to practice gap can be closed. There are strategies that may help diminish the perceived gap between theory and practice and researchers and practitioners (Kitson et al. 1996; Tierney & Taylor 1991).

Though the theory–practice gap is an important issue to be grappled with, we need to recognise that it is not unique to nursing. Medicine, social work and clinical psychology, for example, have all found it problematic. There is a great deal of disparity between knowledge production by researchers and knowledge assimilation by practitioners. Thus, there is a need to examine how knowledge is assimilated and used in practice and to determine what kinds of knowledge for what purposes should be developed.

Many different approaches to encourage the use of research have been developed. For example, in the 1970s the Conduct and Utilization of Research in Nursing (CURN) project was implemented (Horsley et al. 1983). This looked at research utilisation as an organisational process rather than it being just the responsibility of individual nurses (Horsley et al. 1978). Project staff developed research-based protocols for use in general hospital settings. Innovation teams then participated in a series of collaborative workshops, including researchers and clinicians, to implement the protocols in practice with some success.

It is recognised that greater emphasis is needed on the dissemination and application of research findings to practice, and specific strategies need to be adopted to encourage implementation. The strategy chosen will depend on the characteristics of the message, the recognition of external barriers and the preparedness of nurses to change. The choice of dissemination and implementation interventions should be guided by a 'diagnostic analysis' and informed by knowledge of relevant research (NHS Centre for Reviews and Dissemination 1999), although multifaceted interventions targeting different barriers to change are more likely to be effective than single ones, and passive dissemination, such as distributing clinical practice guidelines and didactic educational meetings, such as lectures, appears generally ineffective (Bero et al. 1998).

In an attempt to undertake a 'diagnostic analysis', the BARRIERS to research utilisation scale has been developed (Funk et al. 1989; 1991a, 1991b). The scale has as its theoretical base the model of diffusion of innovation developed by Rogers (1983). This model identified four concepts of factors, which are important to the adoption of change:

▲ the characteristics of the adopter (the nurse);

▲ the characteristics of the organisation (the setting);

▲ the characteristics of the innovation (the research);

▲ the characteristics of the communication (the presentation and accessibility of the research).

The BARRIERS scale was developed from the literature, from the CURN project (Horsley et al. 1983), and from informal data collection. It consists of 29 items and respondents are asked to rate each in relation to the extent to which they perceive the item to be a barrier to research utilisation. Items concern things such as time, cooperation, authority and accessibility to research sources. Thus, for example, a recent study reporting its use (Bryar et al. 2003) found that nurses need time to read and apply research, authority to change practice, critical appraisal skills, an understanding of statistics, and support from managers and doctors to achieve successful practice change.

A different approach, using a mix of observation, interview and Q methological modelling (McCaughan et al. 2002; Thompson et al. 2001a; 2001b) has shown that in clinical settings, human sources, such as clinical nurse specialists and link nurses, are often more accessible than text-based and electronic sources. These roles could act as conduits through which research-based messages for practice, and information for clinical decision-making, could flow (Thompson et al. 2001a; 2002b).

Nurses have been found (McCaughan et al. 2002) to cluster around four main perspectives on the barriers to research use:

▲ problems in interpreting and using research products, which were seen as too complex;

▲ nurses who felt confident with research-based information perceived a lack of organisational support as a major block;

▲ many nurses felt that researchers and research products lacked clinical credibility and that they failed to offer sufficient clinical direction; and

▲ some nurses lacked the skill and, to a lesser degree, the motivation to use research themselves.

Thus, the presentation and management of research knowledge in the clinical setting represents significant challenges for clinicians, researchers and policy-makers.

EVIDENCE-BASED PRACTICE

In the current health service culture, the emphasis is placed firmly upon evidence-based health care (Guyatt & Rennie 2002), and the rhetoric is replete with terms such as evidence, effectiveness and efficiency. This has resulted in nurses increasingly being expected to justify and account for their actions in such terms. This is especially true for those nurses working in clinical practice who make many, often rapid and complex decisions that, directly or indirectly, determine the use of often expensive and scarce resources and the outcomes of patient care.

Evidence-based practice is an attempt to improve clinical practice and thus patient care. It is about solving clinical problems and it acknowledges that intuition and unsystematic clinical experience, for example, are insufficient as a basis for clinical decision-making. Proponents of evidence-based practice also acknowledge that evidence alone is never sufficient to make clinical decisions; values and preferences play an important role. Evidence-based practice is about weighing up the benefits and risks for individual patients.

Evidence-based practice in nursing is not without its critics (Rolfe 2002). A major point of contention is what counts as evidence and the nature of evidence that is valued or devalued. However, while evidence-based practice is not a panacea for nursing, its critics offer no better alternative to improve patient care.

CONCLUSION

Nursing is in essence an applied discipline with unclear boundaries, broad and loosely defined problems, a vague theoretical structure and numerous overlaps with other disciplines. Research has an important and distinct contribution to make, both to the profession and to the health service, but to be successful it needs to develop and promote a wide range of methods and approaches.

Leading research to enhance nursing practice requires that the highest intellectual, technical and ethical standards be maintained, that effectiveness is maximised, and that capacity, reputation and prestige are raised. Leadership needs to take account of the diverse interests, skills and ambitions of staff, their strengths and weaknesses and the opportunities and threats to the research endeavour. It is important that there is a sense of satisfaction and fulfilment, and that talents and potential are tapped.

Reflective exercise

1　How can good leadership facilitate a culture of research?

2　What factors are important in establishing a research culture in a clinical setting?

3　What strategies could you use in your workplace to raise the profile of nursing research?

RECOMMENDED READINGS

Crookes, P. A., & Davies, S. (eds). (1998). *Research into practice.* Edinburgh: Baillière Tindall.

Guyatt, G., & Rennie, D. (eds). (2002). *Users' guide to the medical literature: A manual for evidence-based clinical practice.* Chicago: AMA Press.

Hinshaw, A. S., Feetham, S. L., & Shaver, J. L. F. (eds). (1999). *Handbook of clinical nursing research.* Thousand Oaks, CA: Sage.

Martin, C. R., & Thompson, D. R. (2000). *Design and analysis of clinical nursing research studies.* London: Routledge.

CHAPTER THIRTEEN

Nursing leadership and management in the community: A case study

Tina Koch, Julie Black, Maree Rogers & Judy Smith

LEARNING OBJECTIVES

At the completion of this chapter, the reader will be able to:

▲ differentiate between leadership and management;

▲ describe some of the leadership styles that might be found in one community organisation;

▲ appreciate that it is possible to have several leadership/management styles successfully operating in one organisation;

▲ discuss the role of the Ottawa Charter in shaping an organisation's vision.

KEY WORDS

Primary health care, lifelong learning, transformational leadership, situational leadership, charismatic leadership

INTRODUCTION

Although it is recognised that diversity exists in nursing service delivery in the community, we have selected one nursing organisation as a case study for this chapter. In the section to follow we will give the leadership perspectives used for managing health services in the community. The content of this chapter is informed by the practice of four people working in a community health service. Together they comprise the fields of research, nursing executive (clinical leadership), education and human resource management. The organisation for the case study is Royal District Nursing Service (RDNS, SA Inc). RDNS is a service health care service organisation that seeks to offer a quality nursing service, primarily to the population of Adelaide, South Australia, and the greater Adelaide suburban area.

LEADERSHIP AND MANAGEMENT

Early leadership research focused on personal traits such as intelligence, appearance and energy, closely followed by research that tends to favour functionalist, that is, behavioural approaches. Influenced by research in North America, attention then shifted to contingency approaches such as Hersey and Blanchard's situational theory (Daft 1997). Leadership concepts have shifted to include charismatic, interactive, transactional and transformational styles. Debates in the current literature reflect the debates surrounding leadership and management (Collins & McLaughlin 1996; Daft 1997; Ellyard 1998; McKenna 1999), and the debatable point is whether they are the same or different. It is clear that managing and managers can be viewed from several perspectives. We take the position that it is paramount to understand and respect that there are many ways to lead and manage.

The awareness of differences in leadership styles and preferences is crucial in the establishment of organisational relationships. Each of the four authors will offer their perspective on nursing leadership and management, and while they hold a diversity of theoretical views on this topic, their work is shaped by the Ottawa Charter principles. Translation of the principles to guide leadership and management are as follows:

▲ The ability to advocate a clear political commitment to health and equity in all sectors will assist in **building healthy public policy**. One strategy derived from this statement is that service delivery is based on the identified needs of the community.

▲ The ability to speak to the health of the workforce in the awareness that working conditions are safe, stimulating, satisfying and enjoyable. This results in **creating a supportive environment** for all staff in the organisation. Situational management is one such strategy.

▲ Being able to generate empowering ideals through developing ownership and control over nursing practice. Professional autonomy is recognised as self-directed, self-regulated, competent, and strives for evidenced-based nursing practice. Professional autonomy **strengthens the action of a community workforce**. Transformational leadership is participative and congruent with this principle.

▲ Being able to support personal and social development through the provision of human resources and education. **Developing personal skills** assists with the development of lifelong learning strategies.

▲ The ability to see the broader pictures in health so that the service is sensitive and respects diverse cultural needs. It may be necessary to **reorient or expand the health service mandate** to meet identified population diversity.

It is argued here that the Ottawa Charter principles are useful for guiding leadership and management in a community organisation. In the preparation, maintenance and further development of a community nursing service, these principles can underpin action.

SHARED COMMON VISION

Although health services differ in community settings, there are certain common factors that are beginning to influence their evolution. As argued, one of the influences is the philosophical framework of the Ottawa Charter for Health Promotion (1986). Leaders in the community can lead through articulating a vision, guided by primary care principles from the Ottawa Charter. Central to this community service organisation is the delivery of primary health care. Primary health care can be two things: a level of service provision or a philosophical approach to health care. We argue that it is both. Although this chapter deals specifically with a nursing service, it is understood that the way primary health care is ideally organised is within an integrated team and supported by a community network that includes not only the health care workers and service providers but also the community as partner. The principles of primary health care are health education and promotion, early identification of disease, working with entire families rather than the individual. These activities closely reflect community nursing practice. However, primary health care also incorporates a wider definition of health to include social health. It corresponds with a move from a biomedical model to a social model for health, and includes wider social and political reform. The way in which a community service can transform itself to include the wider primary health care definition is through its leadership. Preparation of nurses to lead health reforms is one of the tasks of managers and leaders in the community.

INTERACTIVE LEADERSHIP: A RESEARCHER'S PERSPECTIVE

RDNS has a dedicated research unit with team members who are doctorally prepared nurses. The aims of the research unit are to respond to research questions arising from practice, the organisation or the community; to enhance RDNS research capability; to develop a focused, well-recognised research program; and to make a difference to practice and in the wider community. The research strategies we utilise are interactive; that is, we rely on working with clients and community nurses to foster the research agenda. We use collaborative approaches such as participatory action research and fourth-generation evaluation. Research activity is driven by the belief that the nursing service exists so that it can provide quality nursing care to clients and the wider community. On a practical level, the professional code guiding an individual nurse's practice means that the nurse is accountable for her or his practice. This requires the use of the latest available knowledge or 'evidence-based practice'. Is quality providing the best evidence on which to base practice? What is best practice for leg ulcer wound management? What is the best way to facilitate diabetes self-care management? Driven by such questions, research-finding utilisation completes the 360-degree circle. However, the organisation must have a structure for the dissemination of research findings and their incorporation into daily practice.

Clients and the wider community need to know that nursing practice is ideally based on evidence. Indeed evidence-based practice is a precursor to another concept relevant to nursing—clinical governance. There is no doubt nursing leaders and managers would agree that the clinical needs of patients/clients and services based on identified community needs should shape the administrative framework for their delivery. Their role is to create an environment that supports services driven by need. Not only should evidence-based clinical practice be good management practice, but also every decision managers make should be based on the best evidence available. Accomplishing this means finding the best available evidence relating to a particular decision. To successfully complete this task the decision-maker requires a number of research skills. These are:

▲ to define criteria such as effectiveness, safety and acceptability that relates not only to service delivery but the larger social health agenda, e.g. health promotion;

▲ to find key resources, e.g. current articles on the effectiveness, safety and acceptability of new nursing practices/service delivery;

▲ to assess the quality of the evidence; and

▲ to assess whether results of research papers are applicable to the local context.

Research activity

In trying to enhance the research capabilities of staff, researchers respond not only to questions from practice but need to involve staff in the actual research process. We cannot underestimate that critical, systematic reading of research papers requires some research knowledge and understanding. Participation in research endeavours is the key ingredient, followed closely by further educational preparation. Such preparation will indirectly lead to better prepared staff who are able to discern what constitutes best possible evidence. The role for community leaders is to provide an educative and supportive framework in the quest for evidence and to assist in the preparation of its practitioners.

One important research activity is establishing community need. Here it is argued that delivery should be based on the identified needs of the community. It is necessary for the RDNS to formally identify, on a regular basis, the gaps in its service—and to subsequently adjust service delivery based upon the needs identified that pertain to the service gap. Synonymous with this aim is the identification of what groups of persons are accessing RDNS services in proportion to their representation within the general population of the community served—and to ascertain the reasons for any disparity. The community can be viewed as (a) a structure or locale; (b) the people; and (c) the social systems. A complete assessment involves a careful look at each component to begin to identify needs for health policy, health program development, health issues and service provision. These data provide evidence for decision-makers within organisations, in the wider political arena and towards healthy public policy.

Evaluation of service is the third research activity. As congruent with the RDNS ethos, vision, mission and strategic plan, and as expected by pertinent accrediting and funding organisations, this service is required to regularly evaluate not only the effectiveness of the service it provides, but also to what extent community needs are met.

So, who are the clients of this community service? The majority (75 per cent) of the clientele are people living with a chronic illness. In 1997 nurse clinicians, together with researchers, commenced a series of collaborative group research projects with people who live with chronic illness. The research questions arose from the practice of nurses who recognised that most of their clients lived with chronic illness but had varied self-management approaches that ranged from effective to deficient. Our research interest has focused on how community nurses can assist people living with chronic conditions to live well. We have applied the principles of participatory action research (Stringer 1996). We envisaged a community-based action research program that sought to change the social and personal dynamics of the research situation and enhance the lives of all those who participated. One other important justification for us to use a participatory action research approach is that the principles are closely aligned to the primary health care concepts of collaboration and empowerment. Primary health care emphasises the participation of people in the planning and development of their own health care—an important foundation for evidence-based community nursing practice.

How can community action be strengthened?

Managing and leadership in the context of the emerging research agenda is *interactive*, concerned with consensus building, inclusiveness and participation (Hill 1994; Rosener 1990). Although this may reflect a personal style, its success is contingent on others in the organisation and their willingness to appreciate cultural diversity in management.

TOWARDS TRANSFORMATIONAL LEADERSHIP: A CLINICAL NURSE'S PERSPECTIVE

The style of leadership that is most appealing to my case is *transformational,* as it most closely resembles the participatory ideals of the Ottawa Charter (Alexander 1998; Howell 2000; Trofino 2000; Trott & Windsor 1999). Traditional management functions are described as planning, organising, leading and controlling (McKenna 1999). The point raised here is that while transformation is an appealing notion in terms of bringing about innovation and change, it means a slow transition from traditional management functions towards collaborative management. One of the reasons for its appeal is that research demonstrates that increased participation in management leads to increased job satisfaction and increased retention of nurses (Trott & Windsor 1999). The development towards a participative model is a slow, methodical process. However, if we are to achieve a health system that strengthens the action of a community (nursing workforce), participation is central.

As the clinical director of the service, the application of the Ottawa Charter referring to strengthening community action means creating a safe and stimulating organisational context for nurses to practise autonomously in the 'field'. In this sense, the term community is applied to a community of district nurses. It means striving together for a vision fostering the belief that the profession is self-directed, self-regulated, competent and aims to base its practice on the best possible evidence.

While the generic RDNS consists of 400 employees, the 'field' workforce consists predominantly of 350 registered nurses, who visit people at home or at clinics. The services comprise nursing specialty areas such as wound management, diabetes, continence, HIV AIDS and disability, and includes health programs for homeless people. Contrasting acute care heath systems, nursing services are mobile (each nurse has a vehicle) and the environment (people's homes) is uncontrolled.

The transformational style of leadership is defined by four key behaviours. It is based on the work of Howell (2000):

▲ Visioning—Creating a shared vision.

▲ Inspiring—Communicating the vision in convincing and compelling ways.

▲ Stimulating—Encouraging the rethinking of ideas or problems: questioning tried and true ways of doing things.

▲ Coaching—Coaching people to take on greater responsibility for developing and improving performance.

Crucial to the role is supporting staff and ensuring that all policies, systems and resources are in place to enable staff to undertake their autonomous professional practice, encouraging nurses to search for evidence to underpin practice, to be risk-takers and to try new ideas is part of stimulating staff. It is assumed that nothing is set in concrete and that failure of a new idea to come to fruition is not a failure in itself but merely a failure of that idea.

A deeper examination of a healthy community culture would show extensive evidence that a leader in service delivery:

▲ is driven by a primary health care philosophy;

▲ displays commitment to the goals of transformational leadership;

▲ welcomes diversity in its broadest sense;

▲ ensures the safety of workers through the organisation's occupational health and safety structures;

▲ focuses on continuous quality improvement;

▲ drives policy, structures, processes and portfolios that support staff within their practice environment;

▲ articulates competencies (based on the ANCI competencies) and processes that ensure staff are competent to deliver both clinical and management services;

▲ provides innovation towards creating a suite of community-based clinical pathways and clinical guidelines, embedded in evidence that guides nurse practice;

▲ provides incentives for staff to enhance research capabilities;

▲ organises a suite of performance measurement tools that lead clinical governance, such as key performance indicators and clinical indicators;

▲ is committed to self-development, lifelong learning and continuing education;

▲ privileges a risk-management process across all facets of the organisation, including financial risk management, clinical risk management and occupational health and safety risk management;

▲ networks with professional agencies such as the Australian Council of

Community Nursing Services (ACCNS) and the Royal College of Nursing (RNCA); and

▲ advances an evidence-based culture.

The practice of evidence-based health care enables those managing health services to determine the mix of services that will give the greatest benefit to the population served by the health service. Ensuring that a population receives the maximum health benefit at the lowest possible risk and cost from the resources available is also determined by the quality of management.

The success of a leader lies in his or her ability to make the necessary changes that lead to a more participative style. The leader articulates a common vision that drives the commitment and passion of staff for the mission and values of the organisation, and in so doing, identifies the future of the organisation.

CHARISMATIC LEADERSHIP: AN EDUCATOR'S PERSPECTIVE

The theory that most closely resembles my position as educator is *charismatic* leadership. Education is viewed as a lifelong journey and the impetus for learning must come from the individual; however, a catalyst is often needed. As a catalyst, a leader must have the ability to motivate people to transcend their expected performance (Daft 1997). My perspective as an educator is that managing in education is about selling and managing learning. So what needs to be marketed? It is formal preparation for nurse education, alongside identifying learning needs, preparing people for lifelong learning, continuing education and paying particular attention to the learning environment. Charismatic leadership relies on persuading others to take action.

Preparing nurses to work in the community

Nurse education has undergone dramatic changes in the last decade, corresponding to the transition of education to the tertiary sector and developments in health care provision. Although education of undergraduates at tertiary level is very broad, it does not prepare nurses for work in the community. It is important that novice nurses have two to three years of nursing experience before they embark on work in the community. This is because community nursing requires an extensive knowledge of all areas of the health management spectrum. It is therefore recommended that nurses wishing to take up community nursing are not newly graduated registered nurses. With early discharges from hospital and the trend of managing complex clients, including palliative care patients in their home, the district nurse's understanding of the wide range of equipment and care required is forever growing and often needs to be taught face to face. Advancing the practice of district nurses is contingent on a well-prepared workforce.

Preparation of district nurses involves providing resources and education to prepare for:

▲ assessing and meeting nursing needs of clients in the community;

▲ imparting skills and knowledge to clients and their families;

▲ basing practice on the best possible evidence;

▲ communicating, establishing and maintaining relationships;

▲ coordinating appropriate services;

▲ understanding management and organisational principles;

▲ analysing the needs of their community and planning action; and

▲ contributing towards future development of the service and the community.

Educational preparation not only relates to the delivery of nursing care to clients in the community, but should also address issues such as the importance of safety for nurses. Much of district nurse care is delivered in people's homes, and efforts to create a safe environment are paramount.

It can take many years of work and experience to achieve the clinical and survival skills necessary for a novice registered nurse to become an advanced practitioner. Although we accept the role of formal education and staff development as essential, many role aspects described above can only be learnt through experience and close association with expert practitioners (Grealish 2000).

New roles for district nurses have emerged as the public health agenda of social inclusion and the addressing of health inequalities are 'discovered' and acted upon. In the effort to meet community needs, the nursing profession continues to change. The changing community includes the ageing population, early discharge from hospital, the increase in chronic illness/disease, and management of mental illness in the community (Nay & Pearson 2001). These changes have implications for educational preparation of district nurses and need to be identified.

Identifying learning needs

Nurses work in an isolated and autonomous environment, where the focus on client needs is often at the expense of self-development. It is therefore essential that nurses are encouraged to remain in charge of their learning environment and identify what they require. Formal processes need to be in place so that these learning needs are identified through appraisal systems. Clinical practice and education should be closely linked into the nurse's annual appraisal. This is often a time when past objectives can be reviewed and new learning opportunities identified.

Arguing for lifelong learning

One of the problems with the word 'learning' is that its meaning has been contaminated. In common usage it is associated with teaching as the transmission of knowledge, usually facts. Hence there is talk about giving education to someone. However, we cannot be sure this means that the person receiving the education has learnt. A less common conception of learning attempts to understand the way people actually learn or the way they interpret the world. Here is it argued that the concept of learning must include knowing how to learn. Once a person knows how to learn, a lifelong learning process can begin.

The information explosion and continual changes in the means of accessing information have reinforced the importance of preparing nurses to direct their own learning throughout their careers (Lewis 1998; Miflin et al. 2000). Lifelong learning is based on the self-assessment of clinical knowledge and competence (Gopee 2000). The focus is on how people learn and are motivated to continue their growth and development independently. It is in the ambit of the manager/leader in education to provide a supportive and challenging environment for growth to continue. Mastery of computer technology and the resources it brings to nurses will be essential for future practice. The Internet, probably the most valuable resource brought to clinical practice by computers, is a potential tool to fulfil goals of lifelong learning (McCarthy 2000). Here the library and access to electronic resources are central.

The importance of continuing education

Continuing education is an essential element in the development of the comprehensive systems of personnel development (McFarlane 1999). Competency-based training and education has re-emerged over the past decade as the panacea to develop a flexible and skilled Australian workforce (Winskill 2000). Advanced practitioners such as clinical nurse consultants specialising in wound management, continence or diabetes develop not only core competencies but also clinical pathways. Clinical pathways are seen as one way to orchestrate this professional mandate.

The educator in this field establishes and maintains the processes and structures for competency and clinical pathway development. It is believed that competency-based learning allows nurses to utilise self-assessment resources and assists them to identify gaps in their educational requirements. It is up to the nurse to take the necessary steps to address the identified areas. Crucial to this development is the support of the organisation. Structures and resources need to be in place to facilitate this process. In the RDNS, competency-based learning objectives are useful methods for demonstrating skill, for attaining best practice management and for gaining information for appraisals. This supplies evidence for the nurses' registration body (The Nurses Board of SA) for annual renewal of registration.

Creating a learning environment

Nursing education literature from the 1990s advocated problem-based learning as an approach that promotes conceptual understanding, the development of clinical reasoning skills, and self-directed learning strategies (Magnussen 2001). Although we are advocates of problem-based learning, the logistics of coordinating learning experiences outside the classroom for a mobile workforce based in the community are a challenge. A major impact on education is the issue of travel, with nurses based over a wide area. To address this, the concept of self-directed learning packages and online learning have been effective in many areas. In the health professions, online information supply is beginning to transform education and nursing practice (Gillham 2001). It should be remembered that while learning through distance education is an important resource for nurses working in the community, face-to-face education still plays an important part.

In summary, nurses working in the community need to identify their own learning needs and set clear goals and objectives to achieve these. They need to work closely with their organisation to achieve their educational requirements. Their workplace should also have clear guidelines of the knowledge the nurse is required to have as part of their practice. It is the role of the education department in this organisation to provide a supportive learning environment. Ultimately, education remains the responsibility of each individual nurse.

SITUATIONAL LEADERSHIP: A HUMAN RESOURCE MANAGER'S PERSPECTIVE

From this point of view, Hersey et al.'s (2000) *situational leadership model* is appealing. These theorists argue that effective leaders match their approaches to the maturity levels of their subordinates (Daft 1997). According to this contingency model, there is no one best way to influence people. The choice of which leadership style to use with individuals or groups depends on their readiness and willingness to learn (Hersey et al. 2000, p.173).

The basic concept of the model is firstly the classification of two leader behaviours, namely *task behaviour*, defined as 'telling people what to do, how to do it, when to do it, where to do it and who is to do it' and *relationship behaviour,* defined as 'listening, facilitating and supporting' (Hersey et al. 2000, p.173). The second part of the model is to match the appropriate leadership style to the competence level and willingness, that is, 'follower readiness' of the employee being managed to achieve the best outcome. If managers do not understand the concept or how to apply this theory to managing it can result in their employees being left to complete new or complex tasks without the appropriate level of delegating, supporting, coaching or directing. Conversely, it can be seen as highly intrusive if a manager is continually checking on the work of an employee who does possess the appropriate level of competency for the task. In addition, the employee may perceive the manager's interference as being a lack of confidence in their ability, which can adversely affect the working relationship.

Critics of the situational leadership model may question why the same management style cannot be used for all people in all situations. Consistency is important and, in fact, the model promotes consistency by suggesting the same approach is used for all *similar* situations (Hersey et al. 2000). However, situational leadership principles clearly do not suggest using one management style for every situation. It is important to consider the competency of the person doing the task, as well as their willingness to perform it well.

Choosing to manage

Although managing people well is one of the most difficult tasks in the workplace, it is a function that many assume comes easily to all, particularly those people who have demonstrated that they are high achievers in their chosen professional field. Organisations have promoted people into senior management positions on the basis of their competence in 'technical/professional' work, failing to recognise that the skills required to manage people are vastly different from those previously used.

Paradoxically, individuals are often promoted to first-level management because of good technical skills, without sufficient consideration of the adequacy of their human resources skills. Individuals lacking sufficient human resources skills usually have difficulties in dealing with people inside and outside their work units (Bartol et al. 1995, p.29). We believe it is essential to the effective operation of the organisation to have in place managers who are skilled specialists in managing people.

Nurses seeking to move into a management position or a combined clinical/management position need to be aware of the different challenges these types of roles present compared with clinical roles. What are these challenges? The most significant of these is to recognise that a manager is not only responsible for performing their own work in a competent manner, but is responsible for achieving results through the work of others.

It is highly recommended that any nurse working in the community who is contemplating progressing into the management stream do so only after researching organisational management. There is literature available on the theories and practical application of this type of management (Bartol et al. 1995; Daft 1997; Hersey et al. 2000; Senge 1995). In addition, forming a relationship with a mentor who is currently operating at management level would be an asset in developing a comprehensive evaluation (that is, a reality check) of the requirements of a management role (Henricks et al. 1996).

The significance of a career decision to move into management cannot be underestimated, particularly for nurses. A well-considered commitment to move away from clinical work is required by any nurse wishing to progress into management. It needs to be recognised that a future in management will provide little opportunity to perform hands–on nursing care to patients/clients. Education in leadership principles is included in Master degree programs for nurse practitioners (Joyce 2001).

Key aspects of managing human resources in the community

Managers working in the community have similar position responsibilities to those working in the institutional/acute sector. Depending on the specification of the management role, these can include responsibilities for rostering staff, motor vehicle coordination, budget/financial management, staff performance, counselling and formal disciplinary action. Specific aspects of managing people in a community organisation have been selected for particular focus. These are some of the most critical aspects to achieving success in the management role, but often fall into the category of those that are managed poorly in organisations.

Positive performance management

From a manager's perspective, the essential ingredient to achieving a harmonious and productive workplace is developing a relationship with each individual employee. A good manager/employee relationship is founded on mutual respect and the giving and receiving of regular feedback about performance. The objective of the manager is to develop a working relationship where the employee is motivated to consistently perform well. White (1995, p.168) defines motivation as 'getting someone to do what *they* want', establishing an environment where the employee not only demonstrates that they are motivated but believes the manager values their personal contribution is an important ingredient in successful management. Bartol et al. (1995) confirm the importance of this through the management competency defined as 'positive regard':

> They use verbal and non-verbal behaviour which cause their peers and subordinates to feel that they are valued ... It translates to people as having respect for them and acknowledges their skills and worth. Subordinates will invest much more effort for a manager who makes them feel valued ... (p.441).

On any occasion when the employee does not perform well, it should be managed in the same way—by honest and open discussion (in private) about how the deviation from practice occurred, without denigrating or demoralising the employee. In a participative mode, both manager and employee should agree on how the problem can be resolved, which must include preventative strategies to avoid a reoccurrence. The majority of deviations from good performance can be traced back to insufficient preparation and/or education in the task, incomplete instruction about the work to be done, role ambiguity, poorly designed systems or procedures, rather than the employee blatantly choosing to perform badly. A 'poor performance' incident is an opportunity to question not only the individual but the systems relevant to the incident.

Formal review mechanisms used in organisations, such as probationary reviews or performance appraisal systems, are not used in isolation. Many managers regard handling disciplinary problems and criticising an employee's performance as the most stressful aspects of their job. If positive performance strategies are used regularly and the relationship is developed effectively by the manager, the formal reviews should simply confirm the regular healthy interaction that occurs between the manager and the employee about achieving predetermined job goals.

Managing safety in the community

The differences evident in community services management centre around the volatile environment in which the nursing practice takes place. Community nurses have a diverse range of 'workplaces' that can vary daily. These include:

▲ *people's homes*—some of which are comfortable, hygienically clean and well set up to perform the care safely; others can be found to be very much the opposite;

▲ *motor vehicles* used by the nurse to travel to the patient/client;

▲ *schools* that are attended by children who require nursing care (many do not provide an ideal care setting);

▲ *the office setting*, where nurses will perform care planning, computer work, telephone and clerical tasks, replenishing nursing supplies etc.; and

▲ *nursing centres* in various locations. Ambulant patients/clients are encouraged to attend these centres as this can be a more cost effective method of providing the care.

The 'uncontrolled' environment in which community nurses are required to work has the propensity to expose them to sometimes unique hazards in their daily working environment that are volatile and not common to the more controlled institutional setting. It is clear that specialised safety management is required to meet the challenges surrounding the level of risk to which nurses may be exposed by working in these diverse environments.

Most medium- to large-size community organisations employ a safety advisor to provide advice to management in developing, implementing and reviewing for continuous improvement a safety management system. Other smaller community-based organisations may have access to safety specialists in the government department that provides their funding. Alternatively, most State governments have statutory authorities such as WorkCover (SA), WorkSafe (Vic & WA) and ComCare (Federal), which provide an excellent safety prevention advisory service including library facilities. Managers in the community therefore have extensive resources and access to practical advice on ensuring that their employees operate safely. An initiative of WorkCover SA is the publication of a *Guideline for Managing Occupational Health & Safety in the Community*. This practical safety manual provides managers working in the community with a comprehensive guide for safety prevention, including sample policies, work instructions and forms, and incorporates case studies from the community in effectively managing safety.

Guided by the principles of the Ottawa Charter, the human resources manager creates a supportive environment and ensures that working conditions are safe, stimulating, satisfying and enjoyable. Management work can be defined as being responsible for achieving job-related goals and organisational strategic objectives by leading, coaching and supporting people for whom the manager is professionally accountable.

WHAT IS A SITUATIONAL LEADERSHIP MODEL?
AN ORGANISATIONAL RESPONSE

The responsibilities for primary health care-directed health services are shared among individuals, community groups, health professionals, health service institutions and governments. This means working together towards a health care system that contributes to the pursuit of health. Reorienting health services also requires stronger attention to health research, as well as changes in professional education and training.

Central to the Ottawa Charter is collaboration. It may be observed that the particular leadership approaches selected by each author as guiding their practice involve staff in processes that affect them on a daily basis; that is, they invite participation and enhance the positive aspects of persons. The outcome of a united vision focuses our attention to health in the wider community and the social reform envisaged by the Charter towards community wellbeing (Ellyard 1998).

CONCLUSION

In the last few years much has been written about the differences between leadership and management. We argue that both are important to an organisation; managers may be more involved in operational issues, whereas leaders may drive an organisation through their creativity and the promotion of its future. Appreciation of diversity in management approaches is vital. We suggest that leadership and management are interchangeable but only if the organisation shares a common vision and invites collaboration in shaping the direction of change, given that change in health service delivery is inevitable.

It is now an opportune time to reflect on the style of leadership/management you can identify with and/or explore for your future development. Understanding leadership styles of people with whom you work (peers, associates and /or your 'boss') can be useful in determining not only your situation and your response to their style, but also crucial to establishing organisational relationships. If we have convinced you that lifelong learning strategies are important, what strategies for lifelong learning (in the area of research, human resource management, clinical practice and/or education) have you decided upon? Take time now to develop an action list and take note of the ways in which you can address these issues and evaluate your own progress in the future. Can the Health Promotion Charter developed in Ottawa (1976) shape your organisation's vision?

Reflective exercise

1 How can we prepare community nurses to take their role in health reform seriously?

2 Do you agree that the role of leaders/managers is to create an environment where services driven by need are supported?

3 Making a shift in one's management/leadership skill from traditional styles of the twentieth century toward new 'participative' leadership styles of the twenty-first century takes . . .?

4 What is lifelong learning and how does it apply in your setting?

5 How can individual learning needs be identified?

6 What constitutes a supportive learning environment?

RECOMMENDED READINGS

Bartol, K., Martin, D., Tein, M., & Matthews, G. (1995). *Management: A Pacific Rim focus.* Sydney, Australia: McGraw-Hill Book Company.

Collins, R., & McLaughlin, Y. (1996). *Effective management.* (2nd edn). CCH Australia Limited.

Ellyard, P. (1998). *Ideas for the new millennium.* Australia: Melbourne University Press.

Trofino (2000). Transformational leadership: Moving total quality management to world-class organisations. *International Nursing Review, 47*(4), 232–42.

Trott, M., & Windsor, K. (1999). Leadership effectiveness: How do you measure up? *Nursing Economics, 17*(3), 127–30.

CHAPTER FOURTEEN

Managing finances in the nursing practice setting

Jane Gordon

LEARNING OBJECTIVES

At the completion of this chapter, the reader will be able to:

- ▲ discuss the principles of financial management for middle managers of nursing;

- ▲ develop measurable objectives for their organisation or unit;

- ▲ understand the processes for managing finances in health;

- ▲ prepare and implement budgets and strategies to ensure budget parity; and

- ▲ understand reports that track and evaluate current financial positions.

KEY WORDS
Planning, financial goals, budgets, activity, expenditure

INTRODUCTION

Increasingly, nurses are required to be responsible and accountable for fiscal management. Sound economic decision-making is a hallmark of effective leadership and management. This chapter will outline the responsibility that leaders and managers have in planning, implementing and evaluating both the activity and finances required for the provision of effective health care. In health there is now an expectation that managers, particularly nurses, will have the skills to perform financially by assessing the budget available against the actual expenditure that occurs in wards and units or services. An important aspect of management expertise includes the ability to manage financially. Nurses are in an ideal situation to ensure the effective financial management of a health care facility.

The most appropriate level to identify and manage costs is at point of expenditure. It is at the ward or facility level that this expenditure occurs. Nurses incur most clinical expenses as they care for their patients/clients. An administrative requirement for managers is the ability to prioritise expenditure according to available money. The financial practices at work are no different from the financial management expertise required in your personal life. For example, matching the money you are paid each week with the expenses you incur means that if you are paid $500 per week and your rent is $250 per week, there is $250 to spend on food or other items. This simplistic example is mirrored in Table 14.1 below. The first two columns identify the budget and the actual expenses incurred. The third column provides details of the variance between the money allocated and expended. This example highlights that Ward One had a negative variance while the expenditure of Ward Two was less than budgeted.

Table 14.1 Summary of costs—year to date

Directorate	Budget	Actual	Variance unfavorable ( )
Ward One	1 402 297	1 650 353	(248 056)
Ward Two	1 663 445	1 617 904	45 541

Source: Wentworth Area Health Service (WAHS) Finance Department Template 2002.

The most effective management of resources occurs when knowledge of budgeting principles is in place. As the demands for services increase, there is an increasing emphasis on quality and outcomes but no increase in funding. Therefore, an ability to use budgeting as a planning tool to manage finances within the health care setting is essential.

It is necessary to ensure that management objectives (that is, the organisation's strategic plan) form the basis of financial planning at the ward/unit level. If the nurse manager's perception of what the ward's or unit's objectives, throughput and outcomes are, does not align with the organisation's goals and objectives, it becomes impossible to achieve financial balance and harmony. This can be quite complicated because in a way, the nurse manager is expected to predict the future. And of course, this can be difficult to do with any degree of accuracy (Jopling et al. 1998).

PRINCIPLES OF FINANCIAL MANAGEMENT

The principles associated with financial management are based on accounting and budgeting. These are the financial or monetary quantification of the goals and objectives of the organisation. Budgeting is the management tool used to plan and control the expending of finances, while accounting is the process of recording, classifying, interpreting and reporting financial data to provide a source of financial information (Levy 1985).

Budgeting

Budgeting is a tool for planning, monitoring and controlling costs. It is part of a suite of management tools used in association with other management functions such as planning and controlling. Once the goals of the organisation have been identified, budgeting ensures that they are met by allocating money to them (Rowland & Rowland 1985). The stages of budgeting include:

▲ quantifying objectives, policies and plans;

▲ evaluation of financial performance;

▲ controlling costs; and

▲ creating cost awareness across the organisation (Rowland & Rowland 1985, p.224).

Budgeting is an important skill for managers. One of the principal responsibilities of a nurse manager is to plan and implement the objectives of their unit/ward/department. This is undertaken by identifying the casemix of the patients/clients and determining the predicted throughput, either by calculating the number of patients utilising a predetermined number of beds, or by counting the number of clients attending a community or outpatient-based clinic/service. Once the plan of activity has been articulated, it is time to attach a dollar figure to it. If it costs $2000 to treat one patient and it has been determined that the service will treat 200 patients per year, then the total costs associated with providing the service would be $400 000. This is the planning phase of budgeting. The major issue in providing public health care is not so much identifying the cost of care provision but prioritising the expenditure against the funds available.

The next stage of budgeting is the comparison of the budgeted costs with the actual expenditure. Table 14.1 demonstrates this comparison.

The differences between the two results—those planned and the actual results—need to be examined closely. There is a natural tendency not to worry about a favourable result and to only be concerned about an unfavourable one. However, any deviation from the expected outcome warrants assessment. This review is necessary because if the budget plan reflects the actual activity and costs, then the result should not be favourable and may reflect a problem with the accounting process, for example, an invoice that may not have been paid. Reasons for unfavourable results also require examination and may include an increase in patient activity (e.g. more patients than planned), an increase in costs (e.g. disposable goods such as gauze squares significantly rise in price once the budget has been set), or there is a change in casemix (e.g. the acuity or complexity of care required for patients increases or the ward commences treating medical patients and changes its role to an oncology ward).

Accounting

As explained previously, accounting is the process of recording, classifying, interpreting and reporting financial data to provide a source of financial information. This information informs managers of their performance in comparison to the set budget. The various elements associated with accounting practices include assets (buildings, land), expenses (salaries), liabilities (accrued annual leave) and revenue (private patients, car-parking fees). Accounting practices commence with an analysis of 'source documents' (Jopling et al. 1998, p.19), including invoices, receipts and purchase orders. This information is summarised and entered into journals and then into the general ledger. If a manager needs to question the actual financial result at the end of a specific financial period it is the general ledger that provides the detail of expenditure by item. This is one of the reporting tools that managers need to be competent in using to ensure their appropriate understanding of the financial management required within their department/ward.

There are two methods of accounting used in health care. The first method is cash accounting, which identifies revenue when cash is received and expenditure when goods have been delivered. The disadvantages of this method are that the true value of the organisation is not recognised (buildings and other non-cash assets are not identified or represented) and there is the temptation to defer costs until the next financial year. The other method used within health is accrual accounting. In this system, revenue is recognised in the financial period in which it has been earned, while expenditure is realised when the order is placed or the shifts are actually worked. This way, revenue and expenditure are matched. All the assets of an organisation are taken into account when its financial position is reported.

PROCESSES FOR MANAGING FINANCES

When building a budget it is necessary to identify what is included within it and what services the budget actually encompasses. Historically, organisations were managed centrally with finance departments controlling the allocation and approval functions. Budgets were not devolved to ward or unit levels. However, as hospitals and other health care institutions have become more complex and clinicians have demanded greater control over health care finance, devolution of financial responsibility has occurred in many clinical settings. With this transfer, other models of health funding and budgeting have evolved, including output-based, which allows for more accurate assessment of costs associated with individual patients for a specific episode of care (Gordon & Clout 2002).

Dividing the organisation into groupings of same or similar services together may be referred to as a cost centre. This allocation is a business decision allowing specific costs associated with the service to be identified. In health, cost centres are generally determined by either departments, such as individual wards (e.g. intensive care), or services such as radiology and pathology. They may also be service units, for example, catering or linen services.

Types of costs

Costs associated with the delivery of care provided in health fall under four main cost concepts of:

▲ direct;

▲ indirect;

▲ fixed; and

▲ variable.

Direct costs are those costs that can be directly associated with a particular cost centre. The nursing salaries and wages for a particular ward are direct costs, as are the disposable medical and surgical supplies, such as cotton wool balls. Indirect costs arc the costs associated with services supplied indirectly to the cost centre or which cannot be billed directly. For example, the hospital may only receive one electricity account for the whole facility that cannot be broken down into individual ward accounts. In this instance, the cost centre would be billed for a proportion of the total account. Other examples include a division of the costs of a support service, such as medical records, where once more the costs would be distributed across the clinical cost centres.

Fixed and variable costs relate to the activity of the organisation. The activity may be measured in patient days, level of acuity, number of presentations, number of operations or number of meals. Fixed costs remain the same regardless of the level of activity within the cost centre. Examples of fixed costs include contracts for servicing equipment that may be in place for a specific period of time, such as five years, and lease arrangements for equipment. Variable costs are directly linked with the activity of the organisation. The individual cost per unit may not change but the costs will rise as more is undertaken. For example, if the hourly rate of a nurse is $20 and each nurse cares for five patients, the hourly nursing costs for ten patients would be $40, and for 20 patients the cost would be $80 (Courtney 1998).

This is the reason why there is such heated debate over staffing allocations in nursing. If the number of patients/clients and their acuity or clinical care requirements all remained the same, nursing would be a fixed cost. However, in health care today the increasing demand and increasing age and infirmity of the patients means that there is a need to constantly re-calculate the staffing requirements. How this is done is the basis of debate in both nursing and health care settings today. Across Australia there are many formulas that can be applied. Some are government regulated, such as in Victoria where there has been a patient number assigned to nurses. In other States, acuity systems are in use, such as nursing cost weights for individual diagnostic related group (DRG), nursing hours per patient day or the recommendation of an experienced nurse manager to identify the number and skill mix of the staff required on each shift. There is a requirement for an agreed methodology to determine adequate nursing numbers before a budget can be set. As the casemix and patient numbers vary, so does the need to vary the budget, and for this reason both management and clinicians must understand and agree to the financial implications of increased throughput, even though there are recognised economies of scale as patient numbers increase.

When identifying budgets it is important to understand some basic economic terms. Opportunity cost in economic terms is seen as the cost of the best alternative foregone (McTaggart et al. 1996). When developing a budget it is necessary for nurse managers to use their management skills to consider opportunity costs in their decision-making. This is useful in a workplace where there are limited resources and managers need to make choices between purchasing different consumables and using more creative staffing methods. Another way to consider this issue is to ask the question, 'With my known fixed budget, is it more important to purchase item X or item Y?'

Nurse managers make these types of decisions on a regular basis with money that has been donated—should a new piece of equipment be purchased or the donation used to provide extra training for staff? Or should a replacement monitor be purchased with the knowledge that the existing one has passed its expected economic life span but is still functioning, or should this money be used to purchase the ward's first computer, which could be used by staff and for patient education, as well as statistical collection. In each of these examples there is no clear answer. The actual decision made will depend upon the local circumstances, including the origin or source of the funds, the delegated authority of the manager and the relative importance of the choices in the local environment (Gordon & Clout 2002, p.4).

Types of budgets

There are a number of different types of budgets that can be used, depending on the focus of the nurse manager's ward/unit or facility. The purpose of a budget is to set the financial goals and objectives against which the nurse manager's service can benchmark results. This means that comparisons can be made against the figures originally identified, as well as with other similar/like services to ensure that the service is both competitive and striving for better practice. The required outcome may differ depending on the organisation. If the facility is a private organisation then a profit-driven outcome will be required, while if it is a public organisation, higher throughput and shorter length of stay may be the imperative. To achieve realistic financial outcomes it is essential to devolve the developments of budgets to relevant staff (Courtney 1998).

Historical budgets

Historical budgets are based on financial information from previous years being utilised to develop subsequent budgets. While allowances are made for inflation or efficiency savings, the process is based on a couple of assumptions. These assumptions presume that the information from the previous year is correct. This includes data on activity, acuity staffing levels and skill mix. It presumes that this data will be the same for the coming year. It also assumes that the allocated budget has met the needs and demands for that year. The process of developing a historical budget is relatively simple and quick (Courtney 1998).

Fixed and flexible budgets

Fixed and flexible budgets are based on activity. Fixed budgets are usually set for a predetermined level of activity and may include revenue or expense budgets. The recent increase in emergency department throughput has adversely affected the public hospital's revenue budget, as an increased number of patients identified as privately insured have been transferred to private hospitals to free up public beds for acute presentations. This has obviously affected the revenue budget so this financial plan is now of limited use to a public organisation.

Flexible budgets involve the determination of the fixed budget, together with a calculation of the relationship between variable costs and throughput to identify the actual costs and utilisation (Courtney 1998).

Program budgeting

Program budgeting focuses on the costs and benefits associated with a specific program, which may be defined as a collection of activities for a particular group or service. Program budgets differ from other budgets as they are more detailed and contain long-range planning information, although for a specific program (Courtney 1998). Examples may include drug and alcohol services that contain more than one cost centre and that may be a subset of a larger service such as a division of medicine.

Capital budgets

Capital budgets focus on the capital nature of planning and expenditure. Organisations have developed protocols and procedures for requesting, selecting and evaluating equipment alternatives that are deemed to be of a capital nature. Processes specifically involved in developing a capital budget include cost effectiveness analysis, cost benefit analysis and identifying opportunity costs. This is to ensure that the probity issues surrounding capital expenditure are met. Examples include reviewing the cost of refurbishing a building and comparing those costs with the expense of building a new facility (Courtney 1998).

Global budgeting

Global budgeting is usually utilised for block grants or facility-wide allocation of funding. Once this amount of money is allocated it is the management's responsibility to allocate the funds to the various cost centres and identify how the funds will be allocated (Courtney 1998). This focus of global budgeting is often used in conjunction with historical funding.

Zero-based budgets

Zero-based budgets are quite different from those already described. One of main reasons for choosing a zero-based approach is to ensure that the continuously perpetrated errors of historical budgets do not continue. To develop a zero-based budget, the existing budget must be ignored and the current budget developed from scratch. Each item of likely expenditure is examined and appraised, based on the planned throughput and acuity or casemix. This methodology is very labour intensive and requires careful review (Courtney 1998). One instance where a zero-based budget is used is when a new service is being developed, such as renal dialysis. The number of patients requiring dialysis is determined, the capital equipment required for this number of patients is identified and costed. Then average costs are compared with peer hospitals of a similar size and casemix throughput. A zero-based budget is then developed.

Clinical budgeting

Clinical budgeting is a relatively new form of budgeting in Australia. It is further advanced in some States than in others. Victoria and South Australia have utilised clinical budgets for a number of years, while New South Wales has focused on other financial strategies. Most of the other budgets discussed above have concentrated on inputs to the ward/unit, such as patients, clients, meals and linen. Clinical budgets centre on budgets formulated on the agreed outputs of hospitals. These are patient treatments which have been predetermined for each DRG. In a clinical budget the number and cost of patient treatments is forecast. Therefore, the income to be provided is determined by historic casemix costs, together with comparisons with peer hospitals of similar size and casemix. This means that the ward/unit would identify that a cholecystectomy in hospital X would cost $5000 and that ward/unit would undertake 100 cholecystectomies per year; therefore their clinical budget would be $500 000.

Operating budgets

Operating budgets are the process by which most nurse managers become involved within their wards/units. Basically, it is a forecasted expense statement for the year divided into months. It is an estimate of undertaking business by maintaining the routine activity of that ward/unit. This type of budget should include projected income in order to allow comparisons between income versus expenditure. For nurse managers to be able to perform financially it is essential they have access to timely, accurate financial reports that include these comparisons. An example is outlined in Table 14.2.

Table 14.2 Summary of controllable costs—year to date

Directorate	Expense budget	Expense actual	Expense variance Unfavourable ()	Revenue budget	Revenue actual	Revenue variance Unfavorable ()
Ward One	1 402 297	1 650 353	(248 056)	48 789	70 800	22 011
Ward Two	1 663 445	1 617 904	45 541	40 401	20 000	(20 401)
Total	3 065 742	3 268 257	(202 515)	89 190	90 800	1610

Source: Wentworth Area Health Service (WAHS) Finance Department Template 2002.

PREPARING AND IMPLEMENTING A BUDGET

When developing a budget plan, the allocation of funding or identification of expenses is undertaken under a number of headings. These are called line items. Within a cost centre report, the line items are the sections or categories that group like areas together to display planned and actual budgets and expenditure. There are a number of different line items that include visiting medical officer's (VMO's) payments and super-annuation, but there are three major line items that contain most of the funding in most budgets, in most organisations. These are:

▲ salaries and wages (S&W);

▲ goods and services (G&S); and

▲ repairs, maintenance and replacement (RMR).

Salaries and wages

Salaries and wages account for the largest expenditure items of any health organisation and in most facilities the nursing salaries and wages can often account for up to 50 per cent of the total salary and wages budget. When formulating the salaries and wages component of the budget, it is necessary to identify the number of staff required to fulfil the planned outputs or anticipated activity level of the ward/unit. This may be undertaken by utilising accepted formulas for specific clinical areas (e.g. intensive care, community mental health nursing, etc) or by some scientific method of calculating patient acuity (time and motion studies, patient dependency systems, etc). The grading or skill mix for each position, together with the costs associated with the base salaries of each position (i.e. check Award entitlement) need to be identified. Oncosts and superannuation must also be calculated.

Oncosts associated with salaries and wages are the additional costs that staff are entitled to, on top of their base salary, in accordance with award conditions or legislative requirements. It is essential that these costs are included in any salary calculations or the ward/unit may be grossly under-funded.

It is necessary to calculate the oncosts for each individual as entitlements may vary from individual to individual. However, following examination of end-of-year financial results, the human resources (or equivalent) department should have the average additional percentage of the base wage, which is then identified as the oncost for specific wards/units. This may be as low as 5 to 10 per cent if the ward/unit functions from 8.00 a. m. to 5.00 p. m., Monday to Friday, to as much as 30 to 40 per cent if the ward/unit functions 24 hours per day, seven days per week, with additional 'call backs' or overtime. It is clear that the financial impact of non-inclusion of oncosts in the budget build-up can result in under-funding by more than 40 per cent. If your budget is $100 000, then you will be under-funded by $40 000, or about one full-time equivalent (FTE) registered nurse position.

Other issues may be handled as oncosts in some organisations or costed separately depending upon local traditions. When calculating oncosts, the following items need to be identified and included in your salary estimates:

▲ annual leave loading (currently 17.5 per cent or the equivalent of normal shift penalties for a period of four weeks—whichever is greater);

▲ shift penalties;

▲ overtime;

▲ public holiday loading;

▲ allowances—including uniform, laundry, stockings and shoes, etc;

▲ allowances—including higher grade duties, in charge shift, on call;

▲ casual loadings;

▲ extra leave;

▲ workers' compensation; and

▲ FACs leave—family and community leave (in NSW this replaces compassionate leave, fire and flood leave and crisis leave).

Other areas that need to be identified when calculating what to include as oncosts, or that may be dealt with and funded separately depending on your finance department, include:

▲ maternity leave (the paid component);

▲ long service leave (long service leave taken as part of an individual's employment is usually calculated as an oncost, but long service leave taken on termination may be funded from a central pool of funding);

▲ Workers' compensation (the backfilling costs are usually managed as an oncost but the premium, etc, may be managed centrally); and

▲ Agency fees (nurses employed casually through an agency may have the fees to the agency funded centrally or included in each cost centre as part of the oncosts) (Gordon & Clout 2002, p.10–11).

Goods and services

The elements included in the G&S line item will vary from organisation to organisation, therefore it is essential to check the composition of this line item at your own organisation. Goods and services may include food supplies, drugs, medical and surgical supplies, domestic and administrative charges, linen, telephone charges, ambulance accounts and cleaning. Unfortunately, the tendency of most staff is to utilise historical data to calculate the goods and services budget with the inclusion of additional money for inflation and a slight reduction for productivity or efficiency savings. This approach perpetuates inefficiencies and ensures waste is embedded in the system.

To identify the costs in your ward/unit, list the major items utilised in it, then monitor consumption of these items. G&S are usually divided into stock and non-stock items. Stock items are usually high-use goods while non-stock goods are usually either items that are used infrequently or those that are expensive. When developing the G&S budget, a risk management approach can be effective. By identifying high use and high cost goods inappropriate use of items can be noted, and significant savings made. Identification of the costs for individual items, together with the information on their consumption will provide an approximate G&S expenditure (Gordon & Clout 2002).

Repairs, maintenance and replacement

The line item for RMR will be managed differently from organisation to organisation, as it is the least predictable of all line items. It includes the costs associated with the repairs, maintenance and replacement of equipment, the ongoing maintenance of buildings and the service contracts associated with both plant and equipment. In some organisations this expenditure and the budget may be devolved to the unit level or it may be maintained centrally by the maintenance or engineering departments, as the high costs associated with major equipment and plant repairs may require pooling of RMR budgets (Rigby 1993, pp.93–6). This is the reason it is the least predictable. The unplanned collapse of water tower or the failure of an elevator can have devastating effects on the RMR budget (Gordon & Clout 2002, p.11).

CONTROLLING COSTS AND EVALUATING FINANCIAL PERFORMANCE

As stated previously, it is essential for nurse managers to understand how to develop, interpret and understand financial reports. In order to perform financially, nurse managers need to have access to accurate, timely financial information. This information must provide reports that compare monthly expenditure to monthly income by the line items of S&W, G&S and RMR. This needs to be rolled up to a year-to-date figure that allows tracking of the current monthly financial position to a year-to-date position. Together with this report, nurse managers must have access to the data that will inform them of variations to the expected financial situation.

There are a number of strategies nurse managers can use to control costs. Areas that require closer examination include:

▲ staff allocation and rostering practices—staff need to be rostered according to the needs of the ward/unit rather than historic practices. Reviewing the use of Monday–Friday staff or part-timers may increase the number of staff available;

▲ linen usage—more effective use of linen is always a cost saver. By not using towels etc to clean up spills, not using bedspreads and using linen skips appropriately, less linen is thrown out;

▲ food wastage—ensuring liaison between food services and any nursing unit so that they are informed of the needs of patients/clients in your ward/unit. When patients/clients are from a non-Australian background, cultural requirements need to be reviewed to reduce food wastage;

▲ drug usage—use of generic drugs and 'drug and therapeutics' committees to more rigorously control use of expensive drugs;

▲ operating theatre (OT) utilisation—effective data collection of OT times can ensure this very expensive department can be optimally utilised;

▲ imprest stock (list of regularly accessed items held as stock within the organisation) —ensure specific records are available on usage of stock items. This allows for early identification of overuse or wastage; and

▲ motor vehicles—careful maintenance and record keeping ensures trade-in value on vehicles is maintained (Gordon & Newman 2001, p.7).

The benefits of implementing effective financial strategies allow funding to be more efficiently used for reducing the length of stay in hospitals, thus increasing throughput and reducing waiting lists for elective procedures and waiting times for emergency patients.

CONCLUSION

In health care today, greater and greater demands are being placed upon nurse managers to be responsible for financial planning and preparing comprehensive budgets that accurately reflect the needs of their departments. As the budget restrictions continue, there are greater demands for health care from the community and increased expectations of the quality of the service being provided. It is essential for nurse leaders and managers to have access to accurate and timely financial reports, and to have the ability and skills to quantify the ward's or unit's goals and objectives in order to prepare and manage the budget.

Reflective exercise

Within your ward or clinical unit identify five items that may be classified within the following categories:

- direct costs

- indirect costs

- fixed costs

- variable costs.

RECOMMENDED READINGS

Eastaugh, S. R. (2002). Hospital nurse productivity. *Journal of Health Care Finance, 29*(1) 14–22.

Ellis, J. & Hartley, C. (2000). Health care finance and control. In J. Ellis, & C. Hartley (eds). *Nursing in today's world: Challenges, issues and trends.* (7th edn). Philadelphia: Lippincott.

Finkler, S. & Kovner, C. (2000). *Financial management for nurse managers and executives.* Philadelphia: W. B. Saunders.

Summer, J. & Nowicki, M. (2002). Managing organisational improvement in a resource-challenged environment. *Healthcare Financial Management 56*(7) 60–2.

Swansburg, R. (1997). *Budgeting and financial management for nurse managers.* Sudbury: Jones & Bartlett.

CHAPTER FIFTEEN

Leading and enhancing quality in nursing care

Rhonda Griffiths & Jill Wiese

LEARNING OBJECTIVES

At the completion of this chapter, the reader will be able to:

- ▲ describe the key components of a quality improvement program;
- ▲ identify approaches to measuring quality in health from an individual and system-wide perspective;
- ▲ describe a model of leadership that nurse managers can use to guide implementation of quality improvement;
- ▲ describe the activities implemented by nurses to measure and enhance quality and promote professional development;
- ▲ integrate the consumer perspective into the measurement and improvement of the quality of nursing care;
- ▲ reflect upon practice, considering concepts of quality; and
- ▲ design a process to evaluate a quality improvement strategy in the clinical area.

KEY WORDS

Nursing, total quality management (TQM), quality culture, clinical indicators, evidence-based practice, organisational change, evaluation, monitoring.

INTRODUCTION

> Everybody is talking about quality ... If everybody knows how important quality is, why are we still having problems with it? (Bernstein 1995, p.265).

In its simplest form, quality management has two aims: the first is to achieve agreement about the characteristics of quality goods and services, and the second is to develop processes to ensure that quality is achieved in an efficient manner (Geboers et al. 1999). According to Berwick (1989), there are two principal approaches to quality improvement: one is to search for the 'bad apples' and remove them from the system; the other is to prevent problems before they arise. The 'bad apples' approach to quality assessment, also known as 'quality by inspection', aims to identify areas of low quality, using methods that are highly sensitive and specific for identifying opportunities to improve quality (Buetow & Rowland 1999). The resulting data describes *what* is at fault, and *who* is at fault, but it provides little information about *why* a lapse in quality has occurred. This is the principle driving many of the quality assurance programs that have been implemented successfully by the manufacturing industry to guarantee the quality of products.

As leaders and managers became more familiar with the principles of the quality movement, they recognised that simple identification of faults with particular parts of the system after a problem occurred did little to improve performance and outcomes. They recognised that preventing problems was a more sensible approach to quality than reacting to problems where and as they arose. The second approach, total quality management (TQM), has evolved as a philosophy and a management approach that can be used across an organisation to promote technical quality and satisfaction in all aspects of performance (Baird et al. 1993; Shalala 1995).

Berwick (1989, p.54) proposed that in order for an individual to value quality and strive for excellence, the organisation must be committed to ongoing improvements because 'quality fails when systems fail.' This applies equally to health care as to manufacturing.

This chapter focuses on quality as both an organisational responsibility and a clinical goal. The aims of the quality movement are introduced and the implications and responsibilities for organisations and individuals committed to ensuring quality are discussed. There is a particular emphasis on implementing and monitoring quality initiatives in the clinical setting. The case is put that all health professionals have a role and responsibility to ensure quality care and services.

WHAT IS QUALITY?

Quality is a widely held and strongly embraced principle; however, there is no standard understanding or set of common principles or stated goals that are universally adopted and used to describe quality (Leatherman & Sutherland 1998). One definition of quality used in health is 'the degree to which health services for individuals and populations increase the likelihood of desired health outcomes and are consistent with current professional knowledge'(Lohr et al. 1992, p.120). The impetus for quality in business began in earnest in the 1940s and 1950s, with the focus being to ensure that a product fulfilled its intended purpose (Katz & Green 1992). That definition was subsequently broadened to include compliance with defined standards or specifications. Health services are also committed to providing quality care and the concepts developed by industry have been adapted to measure the performance and outcomes of individuals and organisations.

LEADERSHIP IN QUALITY MANAGEMENT

The provision of safe, effective, appropriate and accessible health care requires continuous quality improvement. While managing some quality problems is straightforward, in the presence of clinicians who may be skeptical about the motives and unconvinced by the evidence and/or the benefits to patients, a systematic sequence of inquiry and action may assist nurse managers to address complex quality problems (Ovretveit 1999).

Porter-O'Grady (1998) has described seven basic rules to assist managers to provide leadership in implementing change. These principles can be adopted, or adapted, by nurse managers for use in a variety of situations that require a review of service provision. First, no individual working in the area is exempt from the requirements to follow best practice and the manager must not sanction through silence the practice of those who disregard the policy. Second, the manager is unlikely to be able to predetermine or predict the path to implementation, rather they will need to call on experience to identify indicators. The effective manager is skilled at anticipating the challenges, identifying the risks, and moving carefully but confidently ahead. Openly engaging the processes of change assists a smooth transition from concept to reality. Third, emphasising patient outcomes rather than the process of providing care may assist clinicians to shift their focus from the tasks and functions that are familiar to them, to develop a 'vision' of how care could be delivered. Presenting a clear vision will assist clinicians to commit to achieving the outcomes against which they can measure the quality of care. Fourth, empowering clinicians to recognise their potential, and indeed their responsibility, to contribute to point-of-care decision-making recognises the increasing dependence of organisations on the knowledge of workers. Hierarchical structures work against empowered decision-making, a point that many organisations have recognised and are attempting to redress. However, clinicians are unlikely to be empowered unless managers create opportunities to participate in critical decision-making. Fifth, the manager needs to ensure that organisational structures at ward and unit level promote empowerment of clinicians. Staff must understand that the structure, and the role of the manager, is to support rather than parent members of the team. The seventh principle is to evaluate, adjust and evaluate again. It is difficult for clinicians working with nursing staff shortages and demands for decreased length of stay and other efficiency measures to stay focused on the reasons for the change, and the outcomes of value. Nevertheless, the manager needs to stay focused on the desired outcomes, and continue to see the whole rather than its parts.

The principles described by Porter-O'Grady (1998) are neither complex nor demanding, and they present a framework that managers can apply to the planning, implementation and evaluation of quality initiatives.

MEASURING QUALITY IN HEALTH

> Contemporary measures of quality in health represent a fundamental shift from the way quality was traditionally defined when health professionals judged the quality of care (Brook et al. 1996, p.966).

Discussions about quality in health have tended to focus on two aspects of technical excellence: the appropriateness of the services provided and the skill of the provider. Quality is context based, and the expectations differ between people and groups. There are three constituent groups in health: individual patients, patient groups (for example, people with diabetes, the elderly), and the system as a whole. Each group has its goals, priorities and ideas about quality and the standards they expect and accept (Leatherman & Sutherland 1998). Quality in health is also underpinned by the ethos derived from the values and cultures of the health service, the sense of service to all members of the community, and the motivation to improve (Wilson & Goldschmidt 1995). Priorities for quality improvement may vary according to the nature of the service, the organisation's priorities, and the individuals involved, and at times there may be conflict (Buetow & Roland 1999). For example, ensuring efficiency and effectiveness from the perspective of the health service for a transplant unit, may mean that access and acceptability are compromised from the perspective of patients.

Six concepts have been described against which services or products can be measured: effectiveness, efficiency, equity, access, acceptability and appropriateness (Buetow & Roland 1999). In reality, the components of quality are weighted, and it cannot be taken for granted that there is concurrence between professional and public perceptions of and priorities for quality. According to Klein (1998), equity and access are predominantly about resource allocation, while effectiveness and appropriateness are mainly about clinical practice. The quality of services at the point of delivery to patients depends crucially on the values and processes which direct the organisation. In health, most of the dimensions of quality link clinical and organisational issues, therefore the focus on clinical governance is paramount to those committed to ensuring quality clinical services. One of the problems associated with health services is that policy-makers may have little understanding or appreciation of the inter-dependency between organisational processes and patient outcomes. The involvement of clinicians in management, as well as clinical policy development, reduces the perception that quality improvement activities are 'owned' by management.

A perspective on quality that has recently come to the fore is the degree to which services meet the expectations of patients and other users of health care (Blumenthal 1996a). Consumers of health care expect that health professionals have the technical skills and knowledge to provide appropriate and safe care, and the interpersonal skills to communicate effectively to establish a level of trust, recognise the patient's concerns and demonstrate tact and sensitivity.

Health professionals have expressed skepticism that the emphasis on quality care will result in improved patient outcomes. The inability of programs to focus on issues considered important to patient care, the absence of evidence that past quality programs have resulted in improvement (Chassin 1996), and the belief that quality improvement is a tool for cost containment or marketing (Blumental 1996b; Chassin 1996; Wilson & Goldschmidt 1995) have been cited as reasons.

Clinicians have also expressed the view that quality programs focus on identifying errors in practice and imposing punitive sanctions rather than addressing the cause of the problem, which is often attributed to the system (Buetow & Roland 1999). Organisational performance is rarely measured as an indicator of quality, when, in fact, indicators such as staff turnover and dissatisfaction (McKee et al. 1998) and customer satisfaction (Miller 1995) are strong predictors of process measures of quality of care.

It is relatively easy to identify what an organisation does well; however, obtaining an understanding of the gaps and deficiencies is not straightforward. Nevertheless, that was the approach taken by the National Health Service (NHS) the United Kingdom to obtain some understanding of the problems that were common across the system. A list of consumer and health provider concerns was developed into a set of aims that could be used by health facilities and units to evaluate the outcomes of quality initiatives (Leatherman & Sutherland 1998). Developing a rationale for quality initiatives, explicit objectives and minimum levels of performance and improvement in the organisation, contributes to a shared understanding and set of common standards.

ORGANISATIONAL CHANGE AND QUALITY

[A] company that seeks merely to meet standards cannot achieve excellence (Berwick 1989, p.56).

When an organisation identifies improvement as an aim, the work practices of every person in the organisation will change in some way. The structure of the organisation and the type of services it provides, the roles and functions of staff, staff mix, relationship with other facilities, and efficiency through redesign, rationalisation and scheduling of services will all be scrutinised in the process of searching for opportunities to improve outcomes (McKee et al. 1998).

Health reform is on the agenda of governments in the majority of industrialised countries, and the inevitable change to the roles and functions of facilities and individuals is a major issue for health systems (Garside 1998; McKee et al. 1998). Health professionals, government and consumers have implemented strategies to advance the quality culture in health using the premise that quality:

▲ can be defined and measured;

▲ develops from continual improvement;

▲ involves a competitive edge;

▲ is related to outcome; and

▲ is everyone's responsibility (Katz & Green 1992).

This applies whether the quality initiative is relevant for the entire organisation or to a single clinic. The focus has been a greater emphasis on the role of primary care-givers to prevent hospitalisations, changing methods of working in hospitals, rationalising facilities and selective targeting of staff, particularly nursing staff (Aiken et al. 1998; McKee et al. 1998).

Much of the organisational restructuring has been effected under the banner of TQM and continuous quality improvement. However, one weakness of the initiative, limiting the potential for improvement, is that few projects are evaluated, and as a result clinicians and other non-management staff have become skeptical about the function of the reform (Aiken et al. 1998). The concern for many commentators is that cost containment is being pursued at the expense of quality (McKee et al. 1998).

The health reforms have brought major change to the health workforce, which is the largest single cost to health facilities, and is reflected in both staff mix and numbers. While physicians appear to have been relatively unaffected by restructures and mergers, nurses and administrators were adversely affected (Aiken et al. 1998). The research suggests that patient outcomes are influenced by organisational features that affect what nurses do (McKee et al. 1998). Changes in the nursing workforce have been linked to job satisfaction, which have in turn been linked to patient outcomes.

Garside (1998) proposes that change management is the link between the vision of the organisation and its workings; the process by which strategy is actually implemented, and by which changes are actually made to happen. The involvement of clinicians at the administration level of organisations is one means by which change and quality initiatives can be driven from the top and with the knowledge of clinical imperatives. However, to achieve this does require a change in the traditional role clinicians assume within the organisation, and to that end clinicians are being appointed to senior management positions in health services (Buetow & Roland 1999).

The sociological literature identifies causal relationships between the environment in which organisations operate, organisational structures, the level of skill, technology and knowledge associated with tasks, and the processes including the informal organisation, power and learning (West 2000). Health care involves the division of labour, structural and social barriers to communication, diffusion of responsibility and organisational pressures, and each of these increases the risk of error. The division of labour also means that it can be extremely difficult to determine an individual's contribution to patient care, therefore it is as difficult to identify those who provide quality care as it is to identify those who do not. Health care facilities are an example of organisations that were established for one purpose, that have since striven for very different goals and have had the attention diverted to activities other than patient care (West 2000).

DEVELOPING A CULTURE OF QUALITY IN AN ORGANISATION

> Organisational culture is a crucial variable in the management of organisational performance (Davies et al. 2000, p.111).

While there is much discussion about organisational culture in the management literature, the definition of organisational culture remains a personal construct in the absence of a consensual definition. In essence, the culture emerges from what is shared between colleagues in an organisation, including shared beliefs, attitudes, values and norms of behaviour—'the way things are done here', as well as understood, judged and valued (Davies et al. 2000). Unfortunately, the literature provides little insight into how organisational culture impacts on performance and there is limited empirical exploration of the association (Davies et al. 2000). Nevertheless, organisational culture does appear to be a crucial factor in understanding the ability of any organisation to perform and compete.

How can an organisation's culture be changed? New and old features, attitudes of existing and new staff and structures shape the culture of an organisation. In health, professional ethics, media reporting, regulatory frameworks and public opinion also influence the culture.

Davies et al. (2000) have identified four factors relating to organisational culture that need to be verified as part of the change to health systems across the developed world. These have as their basis improvement of quality and cost containment. First, the values of the organisation need to be articulated and agreed upon. Second, those aspects of the culture that facilitate and hinder performance need to be identified. Third, the interventions and management strategies need to take into account the desires, fears and motivations of staff at all levels. Fourth, organisational culture can be influenced by factors outside of the organisation. Therefore, consultation with professional bodies, specialist groups and the media is as important as coherence within the organisation for substantial change to be achieved and maintained.

Nicklin (1996) suggests that organisations most likely to demonstrate a culture that promotes quality, are those that exhibit:

▲ staff with the skills, knowledge and attitude for the job;

▲ staff who work in an environment of trust, where the culture is not to apportion blame; and

▲ empowered individuals who are clear about the organisation's core values and their personal contribution to their achievement.

IMPLEMENTING QUALITY IMPROVEMENT IN THE CLINICAL SETTING

Geboers (1999) has identified the principles upon which a successful continuous quality improvement program is developed, and suggests that quality improvement is most likely to be successful when:

▲ all staff are involved;

▲ targets for improvement are set and agreed upon;

▲ areas for quality improvement identified and prioritised;

▲ easy-to-use tools and techniques are applied; and

▲ the process follows a quality cycle (a systematic plan).

These authors were describing a model of continuous improvement that was established in a group of small, general practices, and they made the point that a series of small and easy-to-handle projects can make a significant contribution to improving the overall quality of the organisation. This point has particular relevance to the nurse unit manager, because outcomes of decisions, practices and policy at the ward level may be reported at an organisational level, but without a depth of analysis that enables deficits within the system to be identified.

At the ward level, nurses are frequently required to adopt the quality framework of the organisation, and to demonstrate the quality of their practice, in terms of its effect on consumer outcome, and organisational benchmarking (Harris & Warren 1995; Irvine et al. 1998). The literature describes a range of quality improvement strategies that are well suited to quality activities in clinical areas.

Quality teams

Quality teams (also known as quality circles and self-directed work teams) are established in response to an identified problem, for example, an increase in the frequency of reported medication errors from a ward. The teams are frequently multidisciplinary, terms of reference relate to the identified problem, and a range of problem-solving activities are undertaken to identify a causal link or association between the problem and the steps within the procedure (Ovretveit 1999). A variety of data collection tools might be used, for example, cause and effect diagrams, audits, and review of incident/accident forms (Merry 1993). The function of the team is to oversee collection of data from various sources, which will be analysed to determine the extent of the problem, the nature of the problem and the presence/nature of precipitating events. The findings need to be presented in a format that is meaningful and useful at the ward level (Ovretveit 1999).

Finding a solution frequently requires the team to engage in a series of problem-solving activities such as brainstorming, that may or may not involve further research and consultation with appropriate committees within the organisation. Recommendations arising from this process of consultation and problem-solving may require changes at different levels; for example, the problem may be linked to informal practices that have developed, to the nature of the procedure, or to the effect of an organisational policy on clinical areas.

An important component of the quality team is ongoing monitoring, evaluation and reporting which might be at a ward level or integrated into routine quality assessment of the organisation.

Audit

An audit is a systematic critical analysis of care (Cheater & Keane 1998) that is now an expected part of the work of all health professionals. Procedures for medical audits have been in place for many years, and more recently audits have been revised to include nurses and other professional groups.

Audits can take various forms. For example, an audit of nursing care might focus on medication errors in a ward, while a process audit tracks a patient during their hospital stay from admission to discharge, monitoring the care across disciplines and departments. The design of the data collection tool and the process of the data collection are critical factors in the design and execution of an audit. Without a well-designed tool to extract data from documents in a systematic and objective way, the results and therefore the value of the report, may be compromised. Audits are viewed as key components of clinical effectiveness to determine the extent to which policy and protocols are reflected in patient care (Cheater & Keane 1998).

The literature identifies pertinent findings relating to nurses' involvement in audit teams at an organisational level. Although most audit groups are multidisciplinary to some degree, medical leadership is regarded as a key factor in determining whether the audit has credibility with doctors (Chassin 1996). The extent to which non-medical disciplines contribute to the work of audit groups has been reported to vary considerably. A variety of factors have been attributed as barriers to nurses participating in audits. The hierarchical nature of the nurse–doctor relationship, poor organisational links with other groups (Chassin 1996), lack of support from senior nurses to support nursing audit, workload pressures, lack of logistical support to undertake an audit, lack of knowledge and skills of the audit process, and low priority for training, are proposed as reasons for the situation which is not unfamiliar to nurses (Berwick 1989).

Consumer satisfaction

The experiences and judgements of patients provide important information for service development and quality review in health. Consumer satisfaction is frequently used as a benchmark by clinicians, facilities and government (Draper & Hill 1996); however, little has been done to clearly articulate the values and preferences of consumers into a set of quality measures (Cleary & Edgman-Levitan 1997; Larrabee et al. 1995).

Recent research has shown a distinct difference between the traditional method of gaining consumer perspectives—the consumer satisfaction survey—and the establishment of consumer-driven quality criteria (Larrabee et al. 1995). There is a tendency to base quality assessment on implicit assumptions about how people define quality and what information they value (Cleary & Edgman-Levitan 1997) and on outcomes focusing on non-clinical aspects such as hotel services, as a measure of overall satisfaction (Draper & Hill 1996).

Cleary and Edgman-Levitan (1997) have identified ways of using consumer information to improve the quality of care. Providing feedback to consumers to facilitate choice, providing feedback to planners and clinicians for internal quality improvement, providing feedback to purchasers to influence choice, using information from consumers to set standards for services and marketing, and establishing rules and regulations based on consumers' values are actions that link consumer data to quality improvement initiatives. Consumers do need to be heard, and mechanisms should be in place to ensure that their suggestions can be considered for action. Inclusion of consumer representation on boards and committees (including research ethics committees), at organisational and government level is now common practice.

PROMOTING QUALITY NURSING PRACTICE: THE USE OF EVIDENCE

McKenna and Hsu (1998, p.17) suggest that that only 10 per cent of all clinical care is based on evidence, and of that 10 per cent, only about half is based on the best available research.

Research has made a major contribution to health care, particularly in technology-led areas, for example, pharmacology, diagnostics and surgery. However at the bedside, clinical decision-making continues to reflect convention and tradition (Buetow & Roland 1999; McKenna & Hsu 1998).

Evidence for clinical practice is a combination of results from research, clinical expertise and patient choice (Kitson et al. 1998). Evidence is most effectively used when it provides information about practice, and does not presume to dictate practice (McKenna & Hsu 1998). Nurse researchers have proposed ways they can involve nurse clinicians in the generation of evidence-based practice with encouraging results. Johnson and Griffiths (2001) have described ways to support clinicians as members of research teams undertaking systematic reviews and to assist clinicians to apply models of research utilisation to answer their clinical questions. Kitson et al. (1998) have developed a conceptual framework that can be used by nurses to guide their endeavours to implement research into practice, to analyse outcomes, and plan more effective strategies.

The involvement of clinicians in the generation of research evidence may challenge the traditionally defined and accustomed roles of researcher and clinicians. However, evidence-based practice is unlikely to be adopted at the point of patient care unless evidence-based clinicians can evolve from within the health service. Evidence-based clinicians are the future leaders of clinical practice change, and should therefore remain at the forefront of clinical review, with the support of their organisations.

Learning from errors

The cost of 12 preventable iatrogenic injuries accounts for 2–3 per cent of the annual budget of an Australian hospital of 120 beds (Rigby & Litt 2000, p.218).

One of the issues health facilities must address in the context of quality is reducing the incidence of adverse events and iatrogenic injuries (Rigby & Litt 2000; West 2000). Research in one Australian State demonstrated that around 5 per cent of separations from public and private hospitals are complicated by adverse events (O'Hara & Carson 1997).

While some adverse events may be unavoidable, for example, an adverse reaction to a drug, the 'blame culture' continues to be located in the behaviour of individual staff members, rather than in the social organisation of work (West 2000). It is suggested that errors are found usually to be multifactorial, often linked to stressful work environments, inexperienced staff, inadequate supervision and support, and a lack of knowledge (Meurier & Vincent 1997; Rigby & Litt 2000; West 2000). It is a challenge for health care organisations to encourage analysis of systematic sources of error (Meurier & Vincent 1997; West 2000).

While nurses are reluctant to discuss or publicise errors, they do report making changes to their practice as a result of an error (West 2000). However, the culture of health care organisations, which tend to focus blame on the individual, militates against using adverse events as a source of information. As a result, opportunities for improvement which will have advantages for the patient, employees and the organisation are lost (Buetow & Roland 1999).

Meurier and Vincent (1997) suggest ways to reduce the incidence of errors in nursing practice. The development of supervisory frameworks at ward level, although still a relatively new concept, is becoming a fundamental component of quality management that will assist managers in the current health service environment where insufficient staff, high staff turnover and an increasing reliance on inexperienced, temporary and agency staff is common. Increasingly, performance management has moved from an ad hoc and largely punitive process to being integrated into the role of the nurse manager, standardised within the human resource practices through mechanisms such as position descriptions, and underpinned by a commitment to professional development according to needs of the individual and the organisation. A well-structured system of supervision facilitates and encourages opportunities to learn from one's peers, and in doing so, provides a means for nurses to seek advice in a supportive environment.

MONITORING AND EVALUATION OF QUALITY IN HEALTH

[M]easuring quality can help clinicians and institutions improve the quality of the medical care they provide (Brook et al. 1996, p.966).

Two questions are vital when evaluating quality improvement processes: how did this improve organisational performance? and how did this improve the quality of care? (Baird et al. 1993). When considering what to measure there is agreement that the structure (resources), process (the activities) and the outcomes (results) need to be considered (Baird et al. 1993; Batalden 1993; Brook et al. 1996), with the quality of care being assessed on several levels: the individual, the health care professional, and the system (Baird et al. 1993; Brook et al. 1996). Quality improvement is, in essence, about implementing a change, evaluating its effectiveness, incorporating it into policy, procedures and /or practices, then monitoring and measuring the change. Baird et al. (1993, p.100) refers to this 'as holding the gains'.

Structure evaluation focuses on the infrastructure that has been established to support quality initiatives, and takes into account the systems that have been put into place at each level of the organisation to promote a quality culture. Structure evaluation assesses, for example, characteristics of the health professionals involved, the nature of staff support (which includes education), resources (which includes staff dedicated to promoting quality activities in the organisation), and dedicated time for quality initiatives (Brook et al. 1996).

Process evaluation focuses on the quality improvement activities within the organisation (Batalden 1993), and the differences the activities make in outcomes (Brook et al. 1996). Formal audits of adverse events, monitoring of diagnostic tests, analysis of morbidity and mortality data and complaints handling are examples of process evaluation. Organisational structures and processes are linked, and that association needs to be reflected in the evaluation (Batalden 1993).

Outcome evaluation focuses on the results, measuring the benefits to the patient (which includes subjective judgements) and benefits to the organisation (which are usually the technical outcomes of the process) (Batalden 1993). Collecting relevant data and accurately measuring the outcomes may not be straightforward because the priorities of the organisation and customer may differ (Leatherman & Sutherland 1998). For example, a young man was involved in a motor vehicle accident which resulted in the amputation of his leg. From a clinician's perspective the life of the man was preserved, the operation was successful and there were no adverse events; the episode of care was technically successful. From the patient's perspective, the loss of his leg was an unsatisfactory outcome which could result in adverse social, psychological and economic consequences.

One approach to measuring outcomes is to identify the variable of interest—for example, length of stay—identify individual or organisational outliers and their cause, and determine corrective action (Batalden et al. 1994). However, measuring these factors independently, while useful, might not provide the most robust data. Merging these components of quality activity gives a more powerful predictor of the quality of the system. Batalden et al. (1994) have developed the 'Serial V' concept to provide an integrated approach to measuring clinical improvement.

The 'Serial V' is the progressive linking of measurements, process knowledge and pilot testing of improvement cycles that are connected to the outcome of interest.

Seven steps are described:

▲ Measuring outcomes (health/satisfaction/costs).

▲ Developing a flowchart of basic processes.

▲ Measuring basic processes (performance measures).

▲ Developing a flowchart of high leverage processes.

▲ Measuring the high level processes.

▲ Pilot testing the solution.

▲ Measuring the impact on original outcomes.

Imbedded in this model is the Plan–Do–Check–Act (PDCA). The Hospital Corporation of America Quality Resource Group has further developed this model to include a feedback loop (Batalden 1993). The FOCUS PDCA framework is a systematic process for improvement that moves through the following steps:

▲ Identify the process to be improved.

▲ Organise a team familiar with the process.

▲ Clarify current knowledge of the process.

▲ Understand sources of variation.

▲ Select the improvement.

▲ Plan the improvement and continued data collection.

▲ Do the improvement, data collection, and data analysis.

▲ Check and study the results.

▲ Act to hold gain and continue improving (Batalden 1993).

CONCLUSION

Quality in health is no longer discretionary (Berwick 1989, p.53) . . . or a luxury (Blumenthal 1996a, p.891).

Some quality problems can be solved in the course of everyday management, while others require a more complex approach that may include coordination and communication between professions and across services. Experience has shown that implementing quality is not easy or straightforward; particularly in a situation as complex as health. Health services are highly regulated, multicultural organisations that are subjected to cultural influences from outside that may be at odds with the internal culture.

Each manager and clinician working in a health care facility is required to demonstrate how he or she is contributing to organisational quality whether it be measured by patient satisfaction, resource use, or the cost of care. If a change in the culture and management of quality is to occur at the ward level, then the promotion of self-analysis and open discussion of errors, as opposed to a punitive approach, needs to be encouraged.

Nurses are required to be vigilant in their pursuit to demonstrate quality, and diligent in their efforts to develop and implement reliable and valid measures. It is a challenge that clinicians, educators and researchers in nursing must embrace to further promote the professionalism of nurses and the clinical value of nursing care.

Reflective exercise

1 How does your organisation measure against the following quality tests? Answer 'yes' or 'no' to each of the following statements:

a The services (diagnostic and treatment) are developed with individual patients in mind.

b The outcomes of care are evaluated.

c The health of groups is promoted through provision of appropriate resources and interventions.

d The health status of the community is evaluated and considered in planning and policy development.

e The public is engaged in planning as informed consumers and active patient participants.

f Quality initiatives reflect macro-health policies.

g Quality initiatives are designed to enhance the programs and the organisation as a whole.

h Relevant health-related data is accessible to people within the organisation.

Now repeat the exercise, substituting your clinical area for the organisation. Does your clinical area meet the quality tests?

2 Does your organisation have clearly defined policies and procedures to measure quality? Answer 'yes' or 'no' to each of the following statements:

a There are procedures to review clinical practice and services.

b There are formal procedures for the review of quality initiatives that have as a priority the requirement to demonstrate conceptual coherency and operational integration. For example, is there a process in place to monitor whether clinical initiatives reflect practice guidelines, and inform selection of audit topics and performance monitoring?

c There are clear lines of authority and accountability.

d Indicators of quality take into account clinical care and efficiency.

e There are procedures to recognise high performance, and procedures to address poor performance.

f There is sufficient data capacity to facilitate collection, analysis and reporting of data using appropriate and valid instruments.

(cont.)

Reflective exercise *(cont.)*

g   The program of quality is clearly described and the processes link to the outcomes in a logical manner. (Adapted from Leatherman & Sutherland 1998).

3   An elderly patient is admitted to a clinical unit for a knee replacement. The procedure has an average length of stay of six days. Throughout this episode of care there are numerous activities that may impact on length of stay—a clinical indicator of significance to the organisation.

Assuming surgery and recovery are without complications, what events (nursing and non-nursing) in the preoperative, perioperative and post-operative stages could lead to a delay in discharge?

RECOMMENDED READINGS

Blancett, S. S. (1995). *Re-engineering nursing and health care: The handbook for organisational transformation*. Meryland: Aspen Publishers.

Cabban, P. T., & Caswell, J. R. (1997). *Hospital quality control: A user's manual*. (3rd edn). Sydney: Community Systems Foundation.

Gray, J. A. M. (2001). *Evidence-based healthcare*. (2nd edn). Edinburgh: Churchill Livingstone.

Kirk, R. (1997). *Managing outcomes, process and cost in a managed care environment*. Aspen: Gaithersburg Md.

Wilson, L. L., & Goldschmidt, P. (1995). *Quality management in health care*. Sydney: McGraw–Hill.

CHAPTER SIXTEEN

Leadership to enhance quality of work life

Reta Creegan & Christine Duffield

LEARNING OBJECTIVES

At the completion of this chapter, the reader will be able to:

- ▲ understand the concept and components of a quality work life;

- ▲ understand those internal and external environmental factors that impact on work life quality;

- ▲ assess their own work setting against those identified internal and external factors;

- ▲ apply the knowledge gained to develop strategies for implementation in their own work setting; and

- ▲ discuss leadership strategies to enhance quality of work life.

KEY WORDS

Occupational, social capital, health and safety, workforce, casualisation, organisational culture

INTRODUCTION

Quality of work life is a concept that is gaining currency in the international nursing literature. In the context of a worldwide crisis in nursing workforce supply, the concept is increasingly becoming the subject of intense discussion and analysis as health service managers endeavour to find a solution to this rapidly deteriorating situation. There are many definitions but the most comprehensive refers to an array of concerns that include 'adequate and fair compensation, safe and healthy working conditions, opportunities for continued growth and security and for the use and development of human capacities, social integration into the workplace, the social relevance of work and the rest of one's life' (Attridge & Callahan 1990).

Legislation and industrial agreements mandate the levels of compensation and safety standards within the work environment, which bind health care organisations to act within those frameworks. The other aspects of the workplace—to do with human development and the social congruence between the individual's work and personal life—are linked to the philosophy of leadership, human resource management policies and practices, and the wider social, political and economic environment. The culture within the organisation will be reflected in the attitudes and values underpinning employee–employer and employee–client relationships. Over the past decade, the term culture is:

> increasingly used to refer to work itself—the culture of the organization, corporate culture, the cultural image an organization presents to its clients, the culture of a work team, the learning culture of an organization. Culture is now used to describe human bonds, the shared goals and aspirations that drive people at work—the things that make people want to work (Cope & Kalantzis 1997, p.2).

The qualities and attributes of the leader are critical determinants of the organisation's culture and how employees perceive it. In this context, the culture of the organisation will be reflected in the work environment, which has physical and psychosocial dimensions, manifested in the employee's sense of belonging, job satisfaction, commitment to the organisation and productivity (Lowe & Schellenberg 2001).

There are many interacting factors at an individual, organisational and systems-wide level that can impact on work-life quality for nurses. This chapter discusses these factors as, first, the physical aspects of the work environment (workload issues, control in the workplace, occupational health and safety and staff management practices); and second, the psychosocial aspects of work (trust, commitment, collegial relationships, job satisfaction, personal growth and development). There is a growing body of evidence suggesting that the quality of the work environment is a critical factor in influencing nurses' decisions to either work casually, work reduced hours or to leave the profession altogether (Duffield & O'Brien-Pallas, 2003). Rapid changes to the health care environment over the past decade or more have created a work environment for nurses that is characterised by excessive workloads, feelings of disempowerment and not being valued as professionals (Department of Education Science and Training [DEST] 2002; Duffield & O'Brien-Pallas, 2003).

Organisational restructuring and downsizing in response to financial constraints have also been part of the past decade of change where nurses' work-life concerns, the quality of their work-life experience and their career aspirations have often been overlooked (Duffield & O'Brien-Pallas 2002). In addition, there has been a dramatic increase in the casualisation of the workforce, changing the nature of employee–employer relationships. While in most industries casualisation has been employer driven, this is not so in nursing, where much of it is employee driven. It may be a manifestation of a work life that is no longer meeting nurses' needs personally or professionally (Creegan et al., 2003; Duffield & O'Brien-Pallas 2002; Fagin 2001).

THE CHANGING WORKFORCE PROFILE

Changing attitudes in society, where individuals are now seeking more balance between work and lifestyle, is a driving force for change in employment patterns, and as a consequence, the profile of the nursing workforce has changed considerably. During the past decade there has been a shift away from standard full-time employment to non-standard forms such as part-time, temporary, casual and contract-based employment (Mangan & Williams 1999). Campbell and Burgess (1997) estimate that 25 per cent of all employed persons in Australia work on a casual basis. Compared to other OECD countries, Australia has one of the highest levels of non-standard employment, and the growth in casual employment has doubled over the past decade. Nurses also follow this employment pattern. For the period 1994–97 the proportion of nurses working part-time increased from 48.6 per cent to 51.8 per cent, resulting in a fall in the average weekly hours worked from 32.5 to 31.8 hours, while the national average number of hours worked weekly by agency nurses (excluding NSW) was 25.6 hours (Australian Institute of Health and Welfare [AIHW] 1999). Correspondingly, there is an increasing nurse vacancy rate and an increasing utilisation of hospital pool and agency nurses to enable service demands to be met (DEST 2002).

Casualisation of the nursing workforce has had a considerable impact on nurse managers, who are faced with a larger population of nursing staff (by head count) to manage. The transient nature of the employment contract in many instances adds to the complexity of maintaining a work environment that meets the needs of the total staff complement. Compounding this emerging difficulty are other changes to the nursing workforce profile. The workforce is ageing and nurses are potentially retiring faster than they can be replaced (AIHW 1999; Buchan 1999; O'Brien-Pallas et al. 1998). The high recognition given to Australian nurses, their educational preparation and experience (DEST 2001) means that many are being offered positions outside nursing (Duffield & Franks 2002). Nurses are becoming better qualified, with many clinicians and nurse managers now holding higher degrees (Duffield & O'Brien-Pallas 2002; DEST 2001; Duffield & Franks 2001; Pelletier et al. 1999). There are also indications that more nurses will be required, with the introduction of new roles relating to specialty practice and clinical case coordination. These specialty roles are likely to be more flexible in terms of work hours and conditions, which may act as an additional incentive for nurses to leave the more restrictive hospital environment where the imperative for care 24 hours a day, seven days a week will remain constant.

Intergenerational differences in attitude to work and lifestyle has also been identified as a potential source of work-life conflict. Baby Boomers (born 1946–64) in management are grappling with the population of Generation Xers (born 1961–81), who value flexibility and work-life balance and see themselves as individual contributors rather than team members (O'Bannon 2001). This author also states that they tend not to have aspirations for lifelong employment with a single company.

Green (2000) describes the Net generation, who were born between 1977 and 1997, as people who have grown up on technology, and with that knowledge and experience they are provided with an understanding of its potential to change the environment in which they work. The life experiences of the Net generation have provided them with an inquisitive spirit and willingness to think independently (Green 2000). The challenge for the Boomers in management will be to reconcile the different work-life views and expectations of each generation to successfully retain nurses in the health service.

FACTORS INFLUENCING WORK-LIFE QUALITY

Effective leadership

Effective leadership is pivotal to the creation of a work environment that allows nurses, the largest employee group in the health service, to grow and expand their individual capacities. Leadership in contemporary times is not the sole province of the top echelons of management. Contemporary organisations require leadership at all levels of the organisation, with an understanding that the essential element of success is in being able to access the intelligence, commitment and caring of staff (Mintzberg 2002). Organisational loyalty comes from employees who feel a sense of belonging and connectedness (Arbuthnot 2002).

Nurse leaders are well positioned to play a key role in transforming existing relationships using partnership and stewardship as the guiding principles. Good leaders have the ability to create and articulate a vision, develop a strong sense of teamwork through partnership with others and create an environment that nurtures growth and development of staff. Good leaders understand the importance of mentoring and succession planning.

Kotter (2001) argues that leaders press for change, which is about aligning, motivating and inspiring people to cope with the change, while management promotes stability, coping with complexity using planning, organising, controlling and problem–solving functions. Good leaders understand that working relationships that empower individuals and teams will achieve more effective and better outcomes than those that are tied to rigid chains of command. Leadership is about harnessing the collective strength, developing the membership and sharing the successes.

Occupational health and safety factors

Over the past decade, occupational health and safety factors in the workplace have increasingly become major issues of concern for health service personnel. Unsafe working conditions that interfere with the delivery of quality care were identified by 75.8 per cent of the 4826 nurses surveyed by the American Nurses Association. This concern also extended to an acknowledgement by 87.9 per cent of respondents that their health and safety concerns influenced their career choices, including the nature of the nursing work they undertook, and, whether or not to remain in nursing (Nursing World. org Health and Safety Survey 2001).

Safe working conditions includes work practices, systems of work, the physical and psychological work environment, and the education and training of staff in hazard prevention. It is widely accepted that employers have a responsibility to identify, assess and control all workplace risks, including workplace aggression and violence instigated by patients or clients towards staff, as well as staff to staff aggression. In many instances, the rights and responsibilities of insurers, employers and employees with respect to workers' compensation and injury management are specified in accompanying legislation and supporting government regulation. A compensatable injury must be work-related and it can be either physical or psychological (*NSW Occupational Health & Safety Act 2000*).

Other aspects that are relevant to the provision of a safe and healthy work environment include a requirement for non-discriminatory behaviour and the protection of personal information relating to clients and staff. In this situation, it means behaviour that is non-judgemental of the person's race, sexual preference, transgender status, marital status or disability. The protection of information relates to the collection, use, storage and disclosure of personal information. Penalties for non-compliance may be specified in the related Acts and supporting regulations where they exist (*Anti-Discrimination Act 1997, NSW Privacy and Personal Information Protection Act 1998*).

It could be argued that in the past, prevention of physical injury in the workplace was the main emphasis for most organisations. However, in more recent times the potential for psychosocial injury has gained momentum and specific policies and procedures are being developed to manage the increasing incidence of verbal and other forms of intimidating behaviour. Unsafe work environments, characterised by safety issues such as bullying and harassment, impact negatively on staff retention (Duffield & O'Brien-Pallas 2002; O'Brien-Pallas & Baumann 2000). This form of occupational hazard is gaining widespread importance, to the extent that in some places legislation covers 'at risk' occupational groups such as doctors, nurses and police to provide specific penalties for the perpetrators who injure them in the course of their work.

Leading to promote effective employee–employer relations

One of the most significant factors impacting on the quality of work life is the quality of the relationship between the employer and the employee. Industrial factors, increasing casualisation, the ageing of the workforce, and intergenerational differences add to the complexity of that developing relationship. However, as Lowe and Schellenberg (2001, p.14) argue:

> Strong employment relationships are the key determinant of job satisfaction among paid employees and self-employed individuals. Not only does job satisfaction reflect a person's overall quality of working life, it also has been linked to a range of outcomes important for employers—including productivity.

These authors examined the impact of trust, commitment, influence and communication on the quality of the employment relationship and found a healthy and supportive environment to be a critical factor (Lowe & Schellenberg 2001). A healthy and supportive environment includes a spirit of collegiality, interesting work, a safe and healthy workplace, reasonable work demands and an environment that supports staff to achieve a balance between their work and personal lives. Having sufficient resources to do the job, including training, equipment and information, is the second most important factor. High levels of job satisfaction are also linked to skill development and use, high workplace morale and lower levels of absenteeism (Lowe & Schellenberg 2001).

Shapiro (1998) argues that universal markers of job satisfaction for nursing are difficult to identify due to nurses having different priorities at different stages of their lives. For example, nurses in the early stages of their career want recognition and flexible rostering, whereas nurses in the mid- to later career stages want autonomy, opportunities for career pathways and financial rewards associated with childcare needs (Shapiro 1998). Job satisfaction reflects not only the overall quality of the individual's working life but has also been linked to a range of positive outcomes for employers, such as increased productivity (Lowe & Schellenberg 2001).

FACTORS IMPACTING ON CONTROL IN THE WORKPLACE

The work environment today is characterised by higher patient acuity, increasing workloads, a diminishing supply of nursing staff and an accompanying decrease in the level of control nurses are able to exert in the work setting (Duffield & O'Brien-Pallas, 2003). As a consequence, the demands on nurses to deliver quality holistic care that meets community expectations are becoming increasingly complex. While this may reflect the situation in many hospitals, there are others, known as magnet hospitals, which, by virtue of the professional practice environment provided, can attract and retain nursing staff despite shortages elsewhere (Kramer & Schmalenberg 1988). The unique characteristics of these hospitals are identified as autonomy in clinical decision-making, control of the practice environment and good communication with the medical staff (Ritter-Teitel 2002).

The extent to which nursing is constrained by decision-making in matters that relate to standards of patient care delivery is dependent upon the strength of belief each nurse has in their personal capacity to influence organisational events. The strength of that belief will determine the level of confidence and assertiveness exercised by the individual to control work-life events. Erbin-Rosemann and Simms (1997) found that feelings of work excitement in nursing were influenced by their beliefs about the 'role of internal and external forces in the distribution of rewards at work, feelings that powerful others have control over their work lives, and feelings they have no influence in the work arena' (p.7). Nurses' loss of decision-making control over the work they do and the setting in which the work is done has been widely reported (Buchanan & Considine 2002; Department of Human Services Victoria 2001). The lack of respect for nurses' work by institutional administrators, coupled with the lack of influence over how work is to be undertaken, are significant factors in nurses' decisions to remain in or leave the workforce (Aiken et al. 2001; Duffield & O'Brien-Pallas 2002; Fagin 2001). Control over practice and work life have been identified internationally as key work environment issues for nurses and are critical in staff retention (Aiken et al. 2001; Baumann et al. 2001).

The opportunity for nurses to be active partners in clinical care delivery and the management of the work setting is unlikely to occur without them first addressing their internal feelings of powerlessness. Equal status in the partnership of care delivery, control over workload expectations and the opportunity to think independently are essential ingredients for the growth and development of the nursing profession. A critical first step in any strategy that seeks to deal effectively with the poor retention rates of nurses in the workforce is to balance workload expectations with staff availability in collaboration with the nursing staff.

LEADERSHIP IN A TIME OF ORGANISATIONAL RESTRUCTURING

For the past two decades, health service organisations have been subjected to reorganisation, consolidation, downsizing or closure. For example, since 1982 in Australia, there has been a 40 per cent decline in the number of beds available in the public sector and a 5 per cent drop in the private sector (Duckett 2002). Correspondingly, there has been a 40 per cent increase in separations per capita and a 40 per cent decline in inpatient lengths of stay (Duckett 2002). This is a global phenomenon and one in which the impact on personnel is negatively linked to the quality of the work-life experience of employees. Downsizing and restructuring are associated with reduced levels of trust, commitment, communication and worker influence (Lowe & Schellenberg 2001), low staff morale and diminished loyalty to organisations, thus potentially increasing turnover (Baumann et al. 2001; Beyers 2001; Greene & Nordhause-Bike 1998). Perhaps more importantly, Aiken et al. (2000) found a significant deterioration in hospital practice environments, patient satisfaction and patient outcomes.

In Australia, work by Buchanan and Considine (2002) found that changes in hospital management increased the stress of nursing work and decreased the level of work satisfaction for nurses, resulting in many nurses leaving or considering leaving the profession. Participants felt their capacity to provide quality patient care and to develop mutually supportive working relationships with nursing colleagues was diminished, and this impacted negatively on their level of work satisfaction (Buchanan & Considine 2002). Aiken et al. (2001) found that burnout, job dissatisfaction and the intention to leave the present job were highly correlated. The perception of high quality care on the unit was found to be associated with higher job satisfaction and high rates of staff retention (McGillis Hall et al. 2001; Newman et al. 2001).

There are, and there will continue to be, reasons for the restructure of institutions. The extent to which they restructure successfully will be dependent upon decision-makers being sensitive to the potential consequences on the work life of all staff. The quality of the change process and the quality of the outcome will be subjectively measured by those who work in the environment, and objectively measureable through the level of workplace morale, job satisfaction, retention rates, absenteeism, loyalty and commitment to the goals of the organisation (Buchanan & Considine 2002).

CONSEQUENCES OF A POOR WORK ENVIRONMENT: WHAT LEADERS NEED TO KNOW

Work-life conflict

The past decade has been characterised by a marked increase in work-life conflict as more employees attempt to balance competing roles as employee, parent, spouse and elder caregiver. The main sources of conflict that are increasingly challenging employees and employers as they seek to meet personal, professional and organisational goals include work to family conflict, family to work conflict and role overload. Work to family conflict occurs where the demands of work interfere with the employee's family life and family responsibilities. Family to work conflicts occur in circumstances where family conflicts, roles and responsibilities interfere with the individual's capacity to fulfil work-related expectations (Duxbury & Higgins 2001). In a comparative study between 1991 and 2001 of the Canadian workforce, the authors found that there was a substantially higher increase in role overload from 47 per cent to 59 per cent among respondents (Duxbury & Higgins 2001). They also found that the source of work-life conflict was more likely to be a high work to family conflict rather than a family to work conflict. Despite an increase in high and medium family to work conflict (5 per cent and 4 per cent respectively), the amount of personal time employees spent on family-related responsibilities decreased from 16 hours each week to 11 hours over the duration of the study. The authors concluded that the increase in role overload was attributable to the increasing demands of work rather than the increasing demands of family-related factors. Not surprisingly, women with young children were found to have higher levels of stress and depression (Duxbury & Higgins 2001). These findings are particularly relevant in nursing where there is a predominance of women, and where many are primary caregivers. Such a workforce composition provides an imperative for health services to develop human resource management policies that are not only gender sensitive but also sensitive to the requirements of employees, who have multiple roles in society.

Patient and nurse safety outcomes

The link between nurse retention and a poor work environment is well established in studies undertaken overseas (Aiken et al. 2001; O'Brien-Pallas & Baumann 2000). Newman et al. (2001) highlight the ethical dilemmas faced by nurses as they struggle to provide a standard of care that meets the code of professional practice.

Health service organisations and the performance of their managers are measured against workload targets and budget performance. Consequently, nurses as caregivers over the 24-hour period largely carry the responsibility for meeting the performance measures of others, including workload targets. When there is an absence of nursing input into those decisions a negative perception of the values and principles underpinning the organisation is created. The standard of organisational ethics is questionable in situations where nurses are increasingly being asked to carry heavier workloads without regard to the consequences of that business decision. It is also an issue that attracts very little internal (to the profession) or external (politically or organisationally) debate, despite ample evidence to link work overload to nurse retention and workplace-induced stress (Baumann et al. 2001; McGillis-Hall et al. 2001).

There is a potential for the quality of patient care to be compromised as a consequence of the trend towards a transient nursing workforce, which increases the risk exponentially as the proportion of agency nurses increases (Auditor General Western Australia 2002). In part, this relates to situations where there is limited orientation available, particularly for agency nurses, and where the service sector has little control over the skills and attributes of the agency nurse who presents for work. As agency use increases, so do costs of discharge by 36 per cent, and mortality rates (Joint Commission on Accreditation of Healthcare Organisations 2002).

In intensive care units, variation in mortality rates may be partly explained by excessive workloads (Tarnow-Mordi et al. 2000). Lower nurse to patient ratios were found to result in more complications and poorer patient outcomes (Aiken et al. 1996; American Nurses' Association 1997; Blegen et al. 1998; Kovner & Gergen 1998; Needleman et al. 2002). It has also been found that increases in the number of adverse events mean an increase in the number of nursing hours required (Cohen et al. 1999).

A perception of a high nursing workload increases the incidence of musculo-skeletal symptoms in the nursing staff (Bongers et al. 1993). Similarly, when nurses have better relationships with medical colleagues there is a decrease in the number of musculo-skeletal claims and time off work (Shamian et al. 2001). Staffing strategies that fail to take into account the work-life requirements of nurses were found to have a negative impact on nurse job satisfaction (Blegen et al. 1998; Kramer & Schmalenberg 1988; McGillis Hall et al. 2001) and on patient satisfaction with nursing care (McGillis Hall et al. 2001). Job dissatisfaction and burnout increase as the ability of nurses to provide basic nursing care decreases. This has a correspondingly negative effect on nurse retention (Aiken et al. 2001; Gray et al. 1996). A manageable workload improves staff and patient satisfaction; a critical factor in nurses' beliefs about the quality of their work life (Baumann et al. 2001).

Workplace bullying

Workplace bullying, commonly featured in today's popular press, is of growing importance as an issue for individuals, employers and governments. Workplace bullying includes a broad range of overt and covert behaviours and it may be characterised as 'offensive, intimidating, malicious or insulting behaviour, an abuse or misuse of power through means intended to undermine, humiliate, denigrate or injure the recipient' (Queensland Department of Industrial Relations 2001, p.10).

Workplace bullying is a factor that can impinge on quality of work life. The consequences of not addressing adverse communication styles and behaviours may be manifested in poor staff retention rates and an escalation of conflicts and costs associated with litigation. This topic is addressed in more depth in Chapter 9.

Staff absenteeism

Absenteeism in the workplace can be a signal that an individual is struggling with a personal situation or a statement about a range of negative work environment factors, including low morale, work-related stress and work overload (Aiken et al. 2001). There is a high correlation between absenteeism and turnover as stress on the remaining staff increases (Lowe 2002). In Canada, nurse absenteeism is reported to be 8.1 per cent compared to 4.5 per cent among other occupational groups (Canadian Nursing Advisory Committee 2002). This means 16 million hours of registered nurse time (equating to 9000 full-time equivalent staff) is lost due to illness and injury over the course of a year. The social and economic consequences are considerable for the employing organisation (Canadian Nursing Advisory Committee 2002). As nursing shortages deepen, rather than closing beds to match nursing hours available, some organisations are using overtime as a staffing solution (Baumann et al. 2001; Fagin 2001). The cumulative impact of this as a management strategy was found to have a negative effect on the health of nursing staff. An almost perfect correlation has been noted between sick time and overtime ($r = .93$, $p < .0001$) (O'Brien-Pallas et al. 2001).

Staff turnover

One of the obvious manifestations of a poor work life is an increase in staff turnover (Aiken et al. 1996). In the health industry, staff turnover now exceeds the annual turnover rates in all other industries (Martin 2002). Turnover is usually defined as the percentage of nursing staff who leave an organisation in a year. A range of factors are linked to staff turnover, including human resource management policies and practices, managerial style, lack of adequate recognition, lack of competitive remuneration and a 'toxic' workplace environment. A toxic workplace environment is described as one where the organisation makes it difficult for people to satisfactorily manage a personal life and a career, and where people are seen as costs and factors of production rather than as assets (Abbasi & Hollman 2000). When the work environment has become toxic to employees it may be reflected in increased turnover rates, vacancy and absenteeism rates, work-related illness and injury, and a diminishing number of people choosing careers in the health industry.

In Australia, the rate of turnover and the factors influencing voluntary turnover are not well established, which may indicate a low investment in nursing labour force research and development by both State and Commonwealth governments. Without accurate and adequate information it is difficult for an organisation to develop strategies that will adequately stem the human and financial costs of turnover. The full costs and consequences of turnover are often underestimated, with attention mainly focused on visible expenditure (advertising, recruitment, orientation to the job and administration), which is more easily quantified than the hidden costs (disruption to workflow, temporary staff replacement and the erosion of staff morale and stability) (Abbasi & Hollman 2000). However, recently a hospital in Alice Springs (Australia) reported that their annual cost of nurse turnover was $300 000 (DEST 2002), and in the United States it has been estimated that there is a 30 per cent efficiency loss in the first month following a vacancy (Gray et al. 1996).

Casualisation of the workforce

While increased casualisation is a feature of today's employment patterns, it can also be a consequence of a deteriorating work environment. The decision by an increasing number of nurses to work casually or leave nursing altogether has the potential to increase turnover by increasing the work burden on those who remain in nursing (Baumann et al. 2001; Fagin 2001; O'Brien-Pallas et al. 2001). Increased workloads associated with the commencement of new staff, or agency and casual staff who are unfamiliar with the unit, also increase the remaining nurses' distress (DEST 2001). Rostering staff becomes more difficult as full-time members are often faced with working around those on casual and fixed part-time shifts, significantly impacting on their work life quality (Creegan et al. 2003). However, there are also consequences for nurses who work through a hospital casual pool or agency. Potentially they have unequal access to training and development opportunities by virtue of their transient employment contracts. In the absence of an agreement with the employing body that mandatory and other skills development education will be provided as paid time, the likelihood that both hospital pool and agency nurses are up-to-date is greatly diminished. In the United Kingdom, only 23 per cent of registered nurses working solely with a hospital pool attended any training sessions in the previous year. Registered nurses with agency-only arrangements were reported to have a higher uptake (57 per cent) of training over the same period, reflecting the agencies' investment in staff development (Audit Commission 2001).

LEADERSHIP STRATEGIES FOR IMPROVING QUALITY OF WORK LIFE

The decreasing supply of nurses, brought about in part through ageing, retirement and the apparent inability of health services to influence the career choices of the young, provides the imperative for urgent action to address the workplace-related reasons that have contributed to this situation. Responsibility for addressing these issues does not lie with any one individual or organisation. The creation of a high-quality work environment will require a whole-of-government approach that is committed to changing workplace cultures through the development of policies and strategies that promote a comprehensive and collaborative approach. Health care professionals, as members of their respective professional associations, have a responsibility to be active participants in any process led by the government to bring about the required changes. Equally at a local level, individuals have a responsibility to actively participate in shaping their work environment to produce an outcome that matches their aspirations. To improve the quality of the workplace the focus of strategy development needs to encapsulate those things that have been found to have the most significant impact on work-life quality including occupational health and safety in the workplace, collegial inter-disciplinary relationships, management support and decision-making influence.

Leadership fostering collegial inter-disciplinary relationships

Collegiality is based on the principles of equality in a working relationship, where functional relationships are not constrained by rigid organisational structures that specify superior–subordinate status. Multidisciplinary work teams are commonplace, and they are likely to continue into the future. There is merit in teams meeting to discuss and resolve issues, particularly those that relate to their own team functioning. All too frequently, hospital management structures act as a barrier to the free flow of information and networking on issues of mutual concern. This may have the effect of leaving issues unresolved, including patient care issues, to escalate in magnitude and significance.

At a systems level, Koehoorn et al. (2002) propose a multidisciplinary approach that involves employers, employees, unions, professional associations and the community as key stakeholders. The model highlights the interaction between those factors that create or constrain the achievement of positive outcomes for all parties. The interacting factors include the work environment (human resources policies and practices), the structural elements (job design and organisational structure), the functional elements (inter- and intra-collegial and employee–employer relationships) and industrial and professional relations. They argue that a less adversarial relationship between employers and the professional and industrial organisations could benefit employees by addressing some of the less tangible aspects of the employment environment, such as advancement opportunities, work scheduling flexibility, childcare provision and more effective communication mechanisms (Koehoorn et al. 2002). Some health-related professional associations—for example, the medical associations—have been stronger in their advocacy for their members, due to a well-developed understanding of the political processes of government. Traditionally, other groups have not utilised their lobbying potential to the same extent, which has limited their power to influence (Koehoorn et al. 2002). The link between nurses' health, patient mortality and the quality of working relationships between medical and nursing staff provides the imperative for doing so.

Leading establishment of a supportive culture

Social capital is a term used to describe the relationships that make organisations work more effectively. It refers to the investment by management in developing networks and collaborative activities that bind people together as part of a strategy to improve organisational performance (Prusak & Cohen 2001). Unfortunately, the changes in hospital management systems and the flow-on impact of those changes (increased intensity of care delivered, increased level of responsibility, increased levels of accountability) is perceived to have eroded working relationships rather than gained any new momentum (Buchanan & Considine 2002). In this context, the skills and attributes of the nurse leader or manager will be critical to any strategy that seeks to retain the loyalty and commitment of the staff to the organisation.

The nurse leader or manager will need to develop mechanisms and strategies that strengthen the staff's sense of belonging and ownership of the work setting. This will require the manager to understand the benefits of power sharing and to develop a collaborative communication style based on professional respect. In addition, the manager will need to be visible and accessible to the staff he or she leads, and knowledgeable about the work–life aspirations of each staff member. Strategies that empower staff include participative staff scheduling, fair and equitable access to learning and development, information sharing, performance management based on agreed objective measures, setting of workload targets, workload distribution, monitoring and evaluation of throughput against benchmarks and sharing the results with staff. Shared governance at a unit level will need to be supported by a communication system that is inclusive of all staff and based on openness and transparency if it is to be effective. It is likely that through this harnessing of the collective talent, the nurse leader will feel supported and gain strength and courage as a consequence.

Decision-making influence of nurse leaders

The health industry invests considerable resources in the ongoing education and skill enhancement of its staff. Increasingly, nurses are maximising their opportunities for further learning and they have the capacity and knowledge to support independent thinking and decision-making (Duffield & Franks 2002). Indeed, it has been shown that one of the most significant factors influencing nurse retention is the opportunity and authority to make patient care decisions and decisions relating to the setting in which nursing care is delivered (Aiken et al. 2001). In many instances, health care organisations make the situation worse by failing to capitalise on the knowledge, expertise and enthusiasm of the staff to improve the organisation's performance (Hansen & von Oetinger 2001).

Devolved organisational structures purport to mean devolution of responsibility, authority and accountability; however, in many instances the level of delegated authority does not match the level of delegated responsibility and accountability, and this can be a source of staff dissatisfaction (Buchanan & Considine 2002).

Nursing staff—in particular, nurse managers—may not be able to fully satisfy all their requirements for greater control over their work environment, but critical to their pursuit is an understanding of the decision-making structure and processes within the organisation. Other factors that influence the quality of the outcome for nurses rest in their ability to establish common professional goals and to be unified in purpose. This will require nurses to network, work collaboratively and be unified in the development of a new professional reality based on mutual respect.

At a unit level, the model of patient care delivery needs to be explicit in its delineation of roles, responsibilities and authority. Performance measures of accountability need to be sensitive to those workplace environment factors that are within the control of the individual whose performance is being assessed. Any barriers to free-flowing cross-discipline dialogue should be removed in the interests of good patient care and enhanced work environment quality for the various professional disciplines. The trend towards clinical teams and clinical streaming across geographical boundaries requires nurses to be free to function in a context that extends beyond the walls of a single unit. Management has a responsibility to ensure that nurses are educationally and professionally equipped to do so.

Management is accountable for the provision of adequate resources (human, capital and material) to meet patient care demand. Recently in the United States it was reported that 24 per cent of sentinel events (events leading to mortality or morbidity) related to nurse staffing decisions where demand exceeded the capacity of available staff (Joint Commission on Accedition of Healthcare Organisations 2002). Nurses in leadership positions are ideally placed to support first line managers in their advocacy for staff and patients in situations where more resources are required or the workload needs to be contained. The capacity of those nurses in leadership positions to influence the work lives of the nursing constituency is dependent upon the level of authority vested in the position held. Fagin (2001) argues that the loss of nursing leadership or a nursing voice has contributed enormously to nursing shortages and it is an issue that the nursing profession is slow to address professionally or industrially. It could be argued that the by-product of a silent nursing leadership will be to diminish the capacity of future generations of nurses to be active and equal partners in the health care delivery business and it could impact on the health system's effectiveness to achieve the best quality patient care outcomes.

CONCLUSION

The factors identified in this chapter impact positively and negatively on the creation of a work environment that meets the needs of employees, employers and the community. The provision of a quality work environment in the health care sector that is attractive to the current and future health service workforce is the major challenge confronting health services today. The amelioration of the signs and symptoms of the problems will require leadership by governments and their agencies, key stakeholder organisations, individuals and the community, if the long-term viability of the health service is to be secured. The approach, therefore, will need to be multi-dimensional and multidisciplinary.

The challenge for governments, professional and industrial bodies and health service organisations will be to re-examine many of the environmental and job-related aspects that influence the career and employment choices of the population. The predictions for health services worldwide to meet their workforce requirements in the next decade, particularly nursing staff, are pessimistic at best. There is a need for a new way of thinking and managing the health service workforce if these predictions are to be avoided. The starting point will require recognition that the best organisational performance will only occur in an environment that values motivated, knowledgeable and adequately resourced employees; that is free from preventable occupational hazard, and that supports personal and professional growth and development. Commitment to the work they do and to the organisation in which they work will be the positive consequence of this level of employee care. In this, the ingredients of a well-functioning or healthy organisation are indistinguishable from those ingredients that produce a healthy work environment (Koehoorn et al. 2002; Kotter 2001).

Reflective exercise

1 What are the main hazards that impact on the quality of your workplace life? How are these managed by your organisation?

2 Do the nurse leaders in your organisation promote an environment that is employee friendly? Do you see room for improvement? How would you improve it?

3 Some conflict is a feature of the workplace. What strategies can leaders use to assist staff to manage conflict?

RECOMMENDED READINGS

Abbasi, S. M., & Hollman, K. W. (2000). Hanging on or fading out? Job satisfaction and the long-term worker. *Public Personnel Management, 29*(3), 333–43.

Attridge, C., & Callahan, M. (1990). Nurses' perspective of quality work environments. *Canadian Journal of Nursing Administration, 13*(3), 19.

Baumann, A., Giovanetti, P., O'Brien-Pallas, L., Mallette, C., Deber, R., Blythe, J., Hibberd, J., & DiCenso, A. (2001). Health care restructuring: the impact of job change. *Canadian Journal of Nursing Leadership, 14*(1), 14–20.

Creegan, R., Duffield, C., & Forrester, K. (2003). Casualisation of the nursing workforce in Australia: Driving forces and implications. *Australian Health Review* 26(1), 201–8.

Lowe, G. (2002). High-quality healthcare workplaces: A vision and action plan. *Hospital Quarterly.* http: //www. longwoods. com/hq/summer02/index. html

CHAPTER SEVENTEEN

Leadership in health informatics: Roles and responsibilites

Jennifer Hardy

LEARNING OBJECTIVES

At the completion of this chapter, the reader will be able to:

▲ define health informatics in relation to:

- use of information and communication technologies;
- roles and responsibilities of nurse leaders in the adoption of information technology (IT);
- exemplars of systems currently in use; and
- nursing informatics;

▲ recognise the challenges of introducing change and 'skilling' clinicians in the use of IT;

▲ relate the changes in health care delivery systems to IT advancement;

▲ discuss the expected benefits of IT from a health outcomes information and education culture perspective; and

▲ recognise the importance of evaluation in IT implementation.

KEY WORDS

Health information management, health informatics, nursing informatics, information technology (IT)

INTRODUCTION

This chapter attempts to highlight the impact of information and communication technologies on health care delivery and the changing roles and responsibilities of nurse leaders. Nurse leaders are challenged by health services that are in a state of constant change, increased accountability and the need to share and track more and more information on patients, services, costs and quality. They are responsible for providing high-quality cost-effective nursing care, and maintaining currency on best practices for shaping future health care delivery (Hovenga & Hay 2000). Other challenges facing nurse leaders include the effects of care delivery models, clinical interventions, technologies and workforce changes on patients and staff (Goode 2001). Information and communication technologies provide tools to assist nurse leaders in dealing with these challenges. This chapter presents the reader with an overview of issues related to the adoption of IT within a nursing context. The overview commences by setting the health informatics scene, followed by a discussion of current issues, making the case for change, exploring expected benefits, and finally the question is posed—how do we know it works?

SETTING THE SCENE
What is health informatics?

The increasing reliance on information in all areas of health care is well documented (Bowles & Teale 1994; Coiera 1998; Matthews & Newell 1999; Smaltz 2001). Information is a key resource, its availability and relevance is directly related to the quality of health care. The term 'informatics' has its foundations in the French word 'informatique' (Strachan 2002). Health informatics is broadly defined as the use of IT, telecommunications and computers in health care to improve patient care, communication, research and education. Further, it encompasses processing of data and information and knowledge management for use in health care delivery. Terminology is used to describe the different types and functions of the technology. The delivery of health care information, products and services over the Internet is defined as Web-based health, or e-health. The data is digital and is transmitted, stored, accessed and retrieved electronically for clinical, educational and administrative purposes, both locally and at a distance. Other terms, such as telemedicine or telehealth, are used to refer to the remote provision of consumer care, education and public health.

As the cost of the technology and its more 'user friendly' approach have evolved, its adoption in health has accelerated. The implications for health care workers are considerable. To use information systems appropriately there needs to be fairly radical changes to the implementation standards for both data access and data manipulation. Information skills are basic for all health care workers. They need to be educated to use information tools to manage information and create knowledge, as well as trained in the use of information systems and data analysis. Clinicians, in particular, need both computer and information literacy skills to understand the principles of data interpretation and the management of clinical knowledge (Coiera 1995).

Defining nursing informatics

The term 'health informatics' has been used to include all health care professionals; however, both medical and nursing informatics are used extensively in the literature.

Nursing informatics has been defined by a number of experts in the field. Earlier definitions included:

▲ Hannah: 'nursing informatics is the use of information technologies in relation to any function which are within the purview of nursing and which are carried out by nurses in the performance of their duties' (1985, p.181);

▲ Grobe: 'the application of the principles of information science and theory to the study, scientific analysis, and management of nursing information for the purposes of establishing a body of nursing knowledge' (1988, p.29); and

▲ Graves and Corcoran: 'a combination of computer science, information science and nursing science designed to assist in the management and processing of nursing data, information and knowledge to support the practice and delivery of nursing care' (1989, p.227).

More recent definitions include:

▲ Goossen: 'the multidisciplinary scientific endeavor of analysing, formalising and modeling how nurses collect and manage data, process data into information and knowledge, make knowledge-based decisions and inferences for patient care, and use this empirical and experiential knowledge in order to broaden the scope and enhance the quality of their professional practice' (1996, p.187); and

▲ American Nurses Association: 'a specialty that integrates nursing science, computer science to manage and communicate data, information, and knowledge in nursing practice. Nursing informatics facilitates the integration of data, information and knowledge support patients, nurses and other providers in their decision-making in all roles and settings. This support is accomplished through the use of information structures, information processes, and information technology' (2001, p. vii).

Who leads the charge?

Throughout its history the nursing profession has been responding to changing educational, social and technological forces. The current wave of technological changes present additional challenges to the profession, particularly to nurse leaders. Currently available technology is capable of meeting the information, knowledge and communication needs of all health care stakeholders.

Nurse leaders need to set goals and champion the cause. Goals can relate to:

▲ organisational readiness;

▲ advancement of a service learning culture;

▲ change; and

▲ benefits.

Information management can be defined as 'the art and science of using standard health care data to answer clinical and managerial questions' (Diers & Pelletier 2001 p.74). Development of information literacy skills supports evidenced-based practice.

Such skills include the recognition of the requirement for information, critical appraisal of information and applying information to a given clinical problem.

Scope of the challenges

The challenges facing the health care system includes clinicians not only mastering the technology, but accepting those technological advances that can improve the quality of patient care. The National Health Service in the United Kingdom recommends health informatics training for all clinicians. The recommendations highlight common elements of clinical practice relevant to all health care workers, including communication, knowledge management, data quality and management, confidentiality and security, clinical and service audit and telehealth. Research is fundamental to all stages of information and technology uptake, both for assessing the needs and evaluating the outcomes. Therefore, research pays an essential role in the adaptation and implementation of technological changes. The American Organisation of Nurse Executives (AONE) believes that nurse leaders guide such adaptation and implementation of technology changes. They have proposed the following categories for technology research priorities:

▲ technology adaptation (patient and staff outcomes from use of technology);

▲ systems improvement (infrastructure changes to accommodate new technology);

▲ utilisation of information technology to promote continuous learning (for health professionals and consumers);

▲ designing, implementing, and evaluating electronic patient information systems and an electronic patient record (attention to nursing practice and outcomes utilisation of a standardised nursing language, assuring nursing interventions, and outcomes are included in the electronic patient record); and

▲ the impact of the Internet (on consumers and professionals)(Goode 2001).

CURRENT ISSUES

Health care environment

In the changing health care environment, nurse leaders are constantly challenged to decrease costs and measure quality outcomes. In the United Kingdom, the United States and Australia the response has been to restructure traditional care delivery systems and practice patterns at all levels of primary and tertiary care. Each country has approached this from a different perspective. Managed care has been a fundamental constituent in all approaches. The managed care concept embraces systems of health care delivery that manage three things: resources, quality of care and access to health care. Key elements of any form of managed care include capitation, clinical pathways, measuring outcomes and coordinated care. The coordination of care can be either by an individual or group of individuals, termed case managers.

Models of care and technology

Nurse case managers are required to have knowledge of, and influence over, the application of technology and information systems (Coile 1999). Areas that need improvement to support communication, documentation and outcomes reporting include information management and software support (Zerull 1999). The evidence from long-term management of chronic illness and prevention or early identification of disease among high-risk populations indicates a major role for information technology applications. Coile (1999, p.244) contends that communication and information technologies connect case managers with high-risk and chronically ill patients, enabling them to harness optimal software, such as care management software, expert systems and remote monitoring. Case managers deal with multiple and diverse information sources, and an increasing demand on them to be competent in managing data, data exchange, use of area networks and the Net/Web (Ball 2000).

Maehling and Badger (1996) raise the question of whether emerging clinical systems and software meet the various needs of a case manager. Functions integral to the role that require computer systems support include the five categories: patient profile; history of encounters; current and past diagnosis—problem list; plan of care; and expected outcomes. The increasing use of clinical pathways as a means of documenting and managing delivery of care, presents a challenge to most vendors. Maehling and Badger contest that software vendors struggle with co-morbidities and the merging of clinical pathway elements to meet unique patient-specific conditions. They suggest the most important clinical pathway application functions are automation of both standardised and customised multidisciplinary clinical paths (individualised modifications), ability to handle co-morbidity and/or combine carepaths, ability to track and analyse path variance, decision support capabilities and integration with clinical documentation (Maehling & Badger 1996).

Clinical documentation in itself poses another problem. Several methods of documentation are currently in use by different health care professionals. These range from narrative documentation to a system called Problem-Oriented Medical Record, a way of organising the description of patient care according to an acronym—for example, SOAP—Subjective, Objective data, the Assessment, and Plan (Williams 1998). Physiotherapists (physical therapists) often use SOAP and other health care professionals use a variation of the PIE system (Problem, Intervention and Evaluation). Williams outlines some of the requirements for computerised documentation systems for case managers, such as: keeping information in more than one format (both forms and narrative capabilities); allowing adequate computer memory for copious amounts of data; having the capacity to document, archive and retrieve information, and readily provide cost-related information.

Information technology solutions that can improve clinical processes have existed for some time. Few organisations have had the resources to explore the potential that such technologies provide at the clinical level. Such patient safety technologies include:

▲ risk management—records and analyses adverse events;

▲ clinical alerting systems—warns clinicians of potential medication problems; and

▲ medication administration—addresses the five rights (right patient, right drug, right dose, right time and right route of administration) by improving the legibility of medical officers orders (Lanser 2001).

Information and operational management

There are vast amounts of administrative data that are regularly reported and stored in hospital information systems. Such data 'can also speak to clinical and managerial issues' (Diers & Pelletier 2001 p.74). According to Diers and Pelletier, information management can find practice variance analysis of clinical pathways and data mining by using the tools of epidemiology and an IT platform. In this context, information management is also related to casemix management.

Diers and Pelletier use the term operational management, whereby analysis of data is based on aggregates of patients (usually) defined by diagnosis related group (DRG). Issues emerging from analysis include cost and quality; systems problems in delivery of care to defined population groups; evaluation of the need for and results of changes in care delivery systems and 'medical errors' as systems problems (Diers & Pelletier 2001, p.74). Implications for case managers responsible for collecting the information include:

▲ continuing education in the management and measurement of patient outcomes data;

▲ hands–on instruction in the use of relational databases, spreadsheets and statistical analysis programs (Nolan et al. 2000); and

▲ development of data competence, and advanced skills in the measurement, analysis and graphic presentation of patient outcomes data (Nolan 2000).

Outcomes measurement

The accurate measurement of patient outcomes is fundamental to the evaluation of case management as a process to manage cost and quality of care. At present many organisations are on the verge of developing fully integrated patient data systems. Being on the 'verge', however, could still mean that change is years away. In the meantime, health managers have to decide on what intermediate systems can be used. Factors to be considered are cost, personnel and time associated with the systems. There are a number of different technologies available which support performance improvement, case management and research (Nolan et al. 2000). Three such examples are traditional data entry, auto data scanning and handheld computing devices (Johnson & Nolan 2000).

However, it is important to recognise that the technologies are only one part of the solution. Technology is about more than automating processes. Technology will drive the course of change in the way in which health care is delivered. Importantly, it should not be viewed as a panacea, otherwise the cultural change and potential resistance that is part of organisational re-engineering and innovation will overwhelm and inhibit the realisation of the promise that technology offers (Lanser 2001).

Some exemplars

Health care organisations have, are and will be entering into partnerships with companies that can provide reliable, efficient and effective e-health solutions. An example of a company that operates worldwide is Cerner. Cerner believes there are four key pillars to e-health.

Reduction of error

A major challenge has been to automate routine manual transactions—such as switching from handwritten prescriptions that give rise to mistakes and medical errors to a process called e-prescribing. Another example has been the integrated electronic care pathways based on best practice to reduce variations in the quality of care given.

The Wesley Private Hospital, Brisbane, Australia, is undertaking a three-part project that incorporates a patient information system, clinical paths and integration operations. On completion, the project will span five hospitals and at least two other facilities.

Empowering clinical staff and optimising resource use

The use of electronic records, integrated with knowledge management and clinical decision support tools, assists staff in gaining access to up-to-date clinical evidence, guidelines and protocols.

The Alfred I. duPont Hospital for Children, Wilmington, Delaware, USA, utilises an order management and electronic medical record. Staff are able to place orders, retrieve results and chart medications. Immediate access to medication history and orders is also available.

Care across the community

Acute, primary and community care is delivered now by many different health and social care professionals working for a variety of different public, private and voluntary organisations. The need to integrate care and enable information to be effectively shared across these new care networks is immediate.

Eastern Maine Health Care, Bangor, USA, use *PowerChart*, an electronic medical record system, within a remote access infrastructure. *PowerChart* is capable of capturing clinical information about a patient, including inpatient and outpatient records, physician's notes, medications, diagnostic tests and electronic messages (Cerner 2003).

Lusky (2000) reported on a project involving Korean nurses and physicians, where a mobile nursing information system was implemented using PDAs (handheld computers, or Personal Digital Assistant) at the Clinical Trial Center, Seoul National University Hospital. Using their PDAs, nurses could retrieve physician orders and lab tests anywhere, anytime. The system also included an automated vital sign graph, a pain assessment tool, and a fluid intake and output calculator.

Transformation of process

The real challenge for the health care sector and nurse leaders in particular, is to re-engineer care processes and support the new processes with IT to deliver more efficient, safer and higher quality care.

THE NEED FOR CHANGE

The environment

Organisational health environments are increasingly complex and uncertain. Health care leaders, and nurses in particular, need to be involved in the promotion of creating environments that have capabilities for anticipating, reacting and responding to change, complexity and uncertainty. Dawson (1986) believes that staff perceptions are an important factor in the change process in any organisation. Change can be precipitated by perceived or anticipated changes in any of five features within an organisation, these include: stimulating factors; the need for change felt by staff; decisions or plans for change; means of implementation; and intended and unintended outcomes (Wells 1995).

Hospitals are under pressure to achieve a balance between decreasing revenue generation and an increase in demand for services. Nursing management requires timely and accurate information for nurse managers to adjust resource utilisation within shorter and shorter time frames (Diers et al. 2000). Information management technologies can provide the means (tools) to collect and interpret the data, but nurse leaders must also educate nursing staff members about the technological tools (decision support systems). Decision support systems for nurse managers need to evolve in context; that is, within the model of care employed by the particular agency. Nurse leaders also need to have an adequate conceptual model of the clinical care delivery process; an understanding of what data emerges and is communicated; how data becomes information; how knowledge is applied; what decisions are made; what care is given and with what result. Furthermore, implementation of any system will only be successful if the organisational climate and individual practitioners are receptive to change or there is an 'organisational readiness' (Barr 2002 p.1090).

The process of change

> [T]here is nothing more difficult to take in hand, more perilous to conduct, or more uncertain in its success, than to take the lead in the introduction of a new order of things. Because the innovator has for enemies all those who have done well under the old conditions, and lukewarm (indifferent, uninterested) defenders in those who may do well under the new (Machiavelli's analysis of the acceptance or acknowledgement of change within a traditional system 1513, chapter 6).

In an article on the development of a nurse executive decision support database, Linda Urden (1996) stated that trying to maintain momentum and enthusiasm in a rapidly changing environment is difficult. However, the challenge can be met by clearly identifying what needs to be measured and for what purposes, and designing a system for monitoring and evaluating the impact of the changes that take place. Perhaps little has changed. Coiera (2000; 2001) suggests an emphasis in the first instance on exploring and defining the information and communication needs of the stakeholders, and developing interventions that best meet these identified needs.

There are a number of approaches to change management and the adoption of technological innovations. One is based on innovation–diffusion theory, which involves using social channels within a group or organisation to examine the process by which innovation is communicated (Barr 2002). Another approach, 'soft systems' methodology (SSM), is used comprehensively in information systems and management science (Ledington & Donaldson 1997). SSM is derived from the work of Peter Checkland at the Department of Management Science, University of Lancaster, UK. This methodology uses the concepts derived from systems theory of hierarchy, survival, communication and control as the properties of an adaptive whole (Checkland & Scholes 1999). The method can be utilised to analyse an organisation of any size, focusing on organisational systems within the context of planned human activity. Underpinning the method is a belief that in a problem situation there is often a sense of discontent without focus (Checkland 1981). SSM consists of a logical stream of seven stages:

▲ problem identification;

▲ descriptions from different viewpoints;

▲ definition of the ideal system;

▲ conceptual model of the ideal system;

▲ comparison with the real world;

▲ discussion; and

▲ implementation of solutions.

Additional approaches can be included concerning the problem–solving itself, the social system, and the political systems. The process is not linear and it is possible to commence it at any of the stages and apply it in a cyclical and recurrent manner.

Hence the key to successful implementation is to adopt a participative change strategy. Therefore, the essential ingredients for successful change management are teamwork, consultation, collaboration, and education and training.

Education, training and development issues

Because health organisations are in an increasingly complex and uncertain climate, nurse leaders will need to contribute to developing and fostering a learning organisation with the capabilities for anticipating, reacting and responding to change, complexity and uncertainty. In developing the capabilities to respond to change, information management and technology, learning is considered an essential component for fostering innovation, knowledge management, and lifelong learning (NSW Health 2002, p.20). Leading and managing change are discussed in depth in Chapter 11.

Models of education, training and development (ET &D) assist in the articulation of an organisation's priorities and expected outcomes. An example of a model is illustrated in Figure 17.1. NSW Health developed the model to identify the most important aspects toward achieving a successful implementation of health information systems.

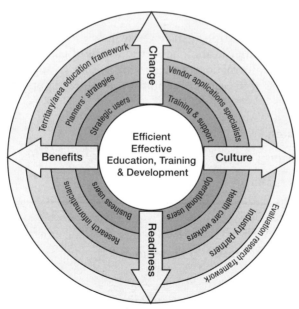

Figure 17.1 Education, training and development model

Source: Adapted from NSW Health Department, Information Management and Technology Education, Training and Development Strategy—A strategy for NSW Healthcare Workers. NSW Government Action Plan, Sydney 2002 p.37.

The core goal is to provide targeted, accessible education, training and development and ongoing support to all levels of health care workers using or affected by the systems. The model puts into context a collaborative strategy, whereby sections of the health care industry can operate strategically. The operation is in line with their core business of health, requiring involvement of managers, clinicians, information and technology specialists, analysts, planners, vendors, trainers and educators from the health, education and research sectors (NSW Health 2002 p.37).

The arrows signify key result areas which traverse the four levels (rings) of the model. The areas within the rings are:

▲ organisational *readiness* to embark on the implementation of technology to enhance its core business;

▲ fostering a service learning *culture* that is supported by quality education, training and development, thus enabling the development of a more flexible and skilled workforce;

▲ *change* brought about by competency/standards development; practice and process changes; enhanced knowledge application and maximising organisation performance, resource management outputs and service outcomes; and

▲ *benefits* achieved, which range from research links between business outcomes, investment in staff education, training and development and improved health services and community outputs and outcomes (NSW Health 2002, p.37).

EXPECTED BENEFITS

Health outcomes information

The value of effective information management in health can have a direct impact on quality outcomes for patient care. The introduction of technological innovations to bring about effective information management, within an appropriate framework (structure and process), can inform and monitor the following outcomes:

▲ clinical practice change;

▲ prevention programs;

▲ quality improvements;

▲ local initiatives in health;

▲ funding decisions;

▲ well-informed consumers; and

▲ areas for research (NSW Health, in Hovenga 1994).

Educational culture

By incorporating an effective education, training and development strategy into a technological adoption model, benefits at the levels of health care worker, organisational and consumer can be predicted. The attainment of higher work competencies, better analytical and decision-making skills leading to enhanced staff satisfaction with their job, and improved work practices, would in turn lead ultimately to better health outcomes for the serviced communities (NSW Health 2002).

Knowing it worked

> Evaluation is central to establishing the way forward—or to finding that one has started from the wrong place (Wyatt 1995, p.179).

Evaluation is not easy and should address structure and function of information resources and the impact on care providers (users) and patient outcomes. Wyatt suggests a list of questions to help in determining evaluation methods. He suggests two types of questions, one set of questions about the resource and one set about the impact of the resource. For example, about the resource, is there a clinical need for it? and is it reliable? About the impact, does it improve users' efficiency? and does it help patients? (Friedman & Wyatt 1997). Wyatt (1995) contends that a variety of methods need to be applied, from ethnographic approaches, user–centred design workshops to full-scale randomised trials.

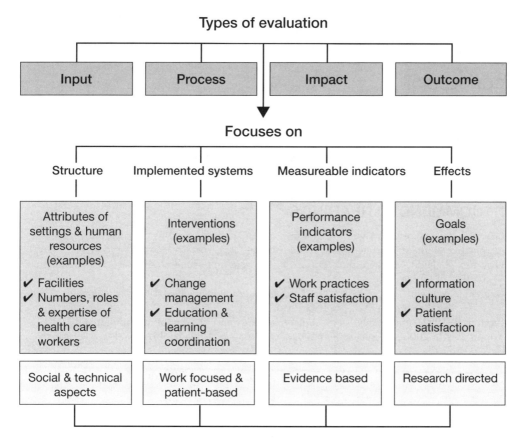

Figure 17.2 An outline of a evaluation model organised within a structure, process impact and outcomes framework. It also highlights a technical, social and human systems approach. A similar approach has been proposed for the NSW Health Information Management and Technology Education, Training and Development Strategy (2002, p.47).

Southon (1997; 1999) believes that effective evaluation is important for the deployment of information and communication technologies. Further, challenges to traditional approaches to evaluation arise because of the board range of roles and environments in which technology is used. He explains that health information is identified in terms of three basic dimensions of information associated with managers, health care workers and patients, and therefore focuses on different objectives. Likewise, the structure and function of the information is different, different social processes control the information, and the information is complex and diverse within the dimensions.

Another perspective is based on Donabedian's quality of care assessment (structure, process and outcomes) approach. Such an approach (theoretical basis) aims to link social systems theory to developments in organisational sociology, organisational behaviour, management studies and soft systems methodology (Rose 1999). A suggested model structure is outlined in Figure 17.2.

Fundamentally, the model illustrates the potential to integrate policy along with social theories and science and determine which interventions are best suited to different outcomes.

CONCLUSION

Nurse leaders have a crucial role to play in all aspects of the development, implementation and evaluation of health and nursing informatics. In addition, nurse leaders have the responsibility of ensuring that nursing has a strong and powerful voice in the development and application of technology to enhance patient care and outcomes.

RECOMMENDED READINGS

Graves, J. R., & Corcoran, S. (1988). Design of nursing information systems: conceptual and practice elements. *Journal of Professional Nursing*, 4(3), 168–177.

Hovenga, E., Kidd, M., &Cesnick, B. (eds) (1998). *Health informatics: An overview*. Melbourne: Churchill Livingstone.

Mantas, J., & Hasman, A. (eds) (2002). *Textbook in health informatics: A nursing informatics perspective*. Amsterdam: Vol. 65, IOS Press.

Procter, P. (1992). *Nurses, computers and information technology*. London: Chapman and Hall.

Young, K. M. (2000). *Informatics for healthcare professionals*. Philadelphia: F. A. Davis Company.

CHAPTER EIGHTEEN

Leadership, management and reflective practice

Genevieve Gray & Jennifer Greenwood

LEARNING OBJECTIVES

At the completion of this chapter, the reader will be able to:

- ▲ define inside-out and outside-in strategic thinking;
- ▲ compare the defining features of traditional and generative leadership;
- ▲ discuss the role of reflection at three different levels in the development of generative leadership;
- ▲ undertake a situational analysis of their own unit; and
- ▲ discuss the three main purposes of planning.

KEY WORDS

Traditional leadership, generative leadership, planning strategic management, reflection

INTRODUCTION

> There are three kinds of people in the world –
> those who make things happen
> those who watch things happen, and
> those who wonder what happened!
>
> (Anonymous)

This memorable quotation reflects the two types of thinking generally engaged in by nurse managers and leaders; that is, inside-out strategic thinking and outside-in strategic thinking (Thompson & Strickland 1995). This chapter has been written to assist those readers who wish to be among those who make things happen and who will, in order to do this, engage increasingly in outside-in strategic thinking.

The chapter begins by typologising these two distinct ways of thinking and then demonstrates why, in the face of turbulent and continual organisational change, outside-in thinkers will be increasingly required. The centrality of short and long-term planning to organisational or unit effectiveness will be emphasised. The chapter will then focus on leadership, the traditional view, that of the warrior-hero, and a more contemporary view, that of generative leadership, and link the latter explicitly to outside-in thinking. Then, and as the chapter title suggests, the nature and role of reflection in the development of generative leadership will be discussed. Some guidelines to assist nurse leaders and managers and those who aspire to such roles to become reflective, generative leaders will also be provided.

Readers should note that no distinction is made between the roles and qualities of leaders and managers, as is typically the case in leadership texts. This accords with the views of Grove (1986) and Gardner (1986), who distinguish only between leader–managers and routine managers. Leader–managers think long term, are visionary, inspirational and think outside-in. Routine managers, in contrast, think short term and inside-out, and are concerned with coordination and supervision.

INSIDE-OUT AND OUTSIDE-IN STRATEGIC THINKING

Inside-out strategic thinking

Inside-out strategic thinking is governed by a range of conservative/reactionary factors. These include the organisation's traditional approaches to innovation and threat; what is acceptable to various internal political coalitions; what is philosophically comfortable with anyone likely to be affected and, what is safe, organisationally and professionally (Thompson & Strickland 1995). Nurse (and other) managers who are inside-out thinkers tend, unremarkably, to be risk averse, to undertake little in the way of environmental scanning (because they are uninterested in external events and influences), and they generally see new developments as unimportant (Thompson & Strickland 1995). Typically, inside-out leaders respond to new developments in one of two ways. Firstly, they claim the new developments will not affect their unit or team. Secondly, they study the new development ad nauseam before initiating any action. These leaders and managers typically focus their energies and attention on internal problem-solving, processes, procedures, politics, reports and the administrative responsibilities of their jobs. If any strategic thinking takes place at all in their units, it is at their behest and is incremental and extremely slow.

Outside-in strategic thinking

Outside-in strategic thinking involves precisely what its title suggests; that is, keeping the closest eye on the unit's operating environment for early signs of change. This 'change spotting' allows outside-in thinkers to consider how their unit could be affected by the possible changes they spot, and plan to maximise any potential advantages and minimise potential disadvantages. Such leaders tend to be the ones who initiate change first in an organisation and their moves are often bold and sweeping. Of course, however, serious environmental scanning takes time; outside-in thinkers make the necessary time available by allowing their teams to make the day-to-day operational decisions (Thompson & Strickland 1995).

THE NECESSITY FOR OUTSIDE-IN STRATEGIC THINKING

Scholars at the Massachusetts Institute of Technology currently estimate that the world's total stock of knowledge (i.e. all disciplines) doubles every ten years; by 2010, however, they estimate that it will double every two years (Aitken 1997). This has enormous implications for everyone, including those working in health (Sullivan 1998). Technological and social advances, which are the result of the knowledge explosion, allow or require the treatment of people who previously were considered (relatively) untreatable; this includes the very young and the fragile elderly, those with chronic and degenerative disorders, and those with life-threatening infectious diseases, e.g. HIV/AIDS. This puts increasing pressure on health service managers to provide more cost-effective services (Beardwood et al. 1999; Cullen 1998). Cost-effective measures have resulted in massive and repeated health service restructurings, workforce redesign, deinstitutionalisation of people with disability and chronic mental health problems, the movement towards evidence-based and interdisciplinary health care, and the promotion of preventative and primary care in all developed countries (Reid 1994).

All these general trends have implications for nurse leaders: outside-in leaders will consider what these implications are and, as noted previously, plan to take advantage/ avoid disadvantage if and when they eventuate. Only in this way, by being deliberately strategic, will they provide leadership in their working environments. Environmental scanning and planning in the light of it are absolutely essential to unit wellbeing. This is especially true in times of turbulent and seemingly continuous change.

THE IMPORTANCE OF PLANNING STRATEGICALLY

According to the *New Shorter Oxford Dictionary* (1993), a strategy is the action to be taken, as a result of careful planning, towards a desired end. Strategic planning, therefore, is concerned with the setting of objectives (desired ends), the development of procedures for implementing the objectives (actions to be taken), and monitoring the extent to which they are achieved. It always takes account of the organisation's operating environment and should be developed consultatively with those who will implement it and be affected by it.

THE PURPOSES OF PLANNING

There are three main purposes of planning; these are to enhance decision-making, to facilitate audit and, importantly, because the process is intrinsically valuable.

(a) *Planning is intrinsically valuable*

▲ It enhances loyalty and commitment.

▲ It provides opportunities for individuals to develop personal and professional potential (in line with the unit's strategic direction).

▲ It creates an effective rationale for the devolution of responsibility and accountability (who is to do what, within what timeframe and with what resources).

▲ It builds morale and *esprit de corps.*

(b) *Planning enhances decision-making*

▲ It reflects on fundamental strengths and weaknesses and the long-term directions the unit team wishes to take.

▲ It imposes systematic, informed deliberation on all major decisions (this is critically important).

▲ It invests futurity into current decisions.

(c) *Planning facilitates audit*

▲ Are goals being achieved?

▲ Are strategies achieving objectives on time?

THE TASKS OF STRATEGIC MANAGEMENT

The first task is to collaboratively form a strategic vision with the unit team; that is, a succinct statement of what the unit wishes to become (for example, 'To become one of the top 10 per cent of units in terms of cost effectiveness of care through the systematic development of reflective and evidence-based practice'), in order to infuse a sense of purpose and provide long-term direction to the team. The second task is to convert the strategic vision into measurable objectives, both short-term (one to three years) and long-term (five to ten years) and performance indicators. The third is to craft strategies to achieve the objectives; the fourth is to implement the strategies and, the fifth, to evaluate performance against objectives. This last task involves reviewing new developments, adjusting long-term direction, strategies and objectives in light of experience, changing conditions, new ideas and new opportunities (Thompson & Strickland 1995). There is, however, another vital task to be undertaken between formulating the vision and setting objectives; that is, undertaking a situational analysis.

Situational analysis

A situation analysis has both exploratory and decision-making components. In the exploratory component the context in which the unit operates, the likely trends in health and nursing services and the other internal and external influences which could influence the development of the unit are all identified.

Identification of internal and external influences is known as a SWOT analysis (strengths, weaknesses, opportunities, threats). Strengths and weaknesses arise from an examination of the internal influences which are under the control of the unit; see Table 18.1 for some common internal influences.

Table 18.1 Some common internal influences on unit development

▲ Unit leadership/management style (e.g. traditional, generative).
▲ Numbers, qualifications, age, gender and ethnicity of unit nurses.
▲ Nursing service delivery system (e.g. primary nursing, patient assignment, task assignment).
▲ Staff development programs.
▲ Relationship with management, medicine, allied health, etc.

Opportunities and threats arise from external factors and issues which are beyond the unit's immediate control; see Table 18.2 for some probable external influences.

Table 18.2 Some probable external influences on unit development

▲ Changes in community values in relation to health and nursing services.
▲ Changes in government policies relating to both health services and health professionals' education (e.g. interdisciplinary services; evidence-based practice; nursing shortages).
▲ Economic trends and pressures (e.g. outcomes focused funding; privatisation of health services).
▲ Hospital/health agency mission and policies.
▲ Demographic trends (e.g. ageing population; multicultural populations).
▲ Epidemiological trends (e.g. increased evidence of 'lifestyle' diseases – heart disease, diabetes, cancers; increased infectious diseases – HIV/AIDS, tuberculosis).
▲ Technological trends (e.g. diagnostic, therapeutic).

In the decision-making component, the unit team answers the following questions:

▲ Which of these factors are really important to this unit?

▲ What strategic advantages can be achieved for this unit by capitalising on its strengths?

▲ What major blocks/impediments are likely to prevent the unit from operating successfully?

▲ What priorities for development are appropriate? (Thompson & Strickland 1995).

The unit team is now ready to consider the objectives it would be appropriate to pursue.

GENERATIVE LEADERSHIP

The rapidly expanding and exploding socio-technical knowledge, the massive and instant global communications, and international and seemingly boundary-free markets (Covey 1996; Sullivan 1998) require an appropriate response from health agencies. That response is generally considered to be adaptive (Bass 1990a; Senge 1992). Such an approach, however, is inadequate because it focuses on practical exigency

(Greenwood 1999a), that is, problem solving, dealing with aspects of the current reality that are undesirable. (Note that outside-in managers would have probably foreseen potential problems and initiated pre-emptive action.) Healthy, 'change agile' units do not focus solely or even mainly on adapting to practical exigency; rather, they focus mainly on what sort of unit they wish to become and/or what vision or purpose they wish to pursue.

Both orientations generate energy. A problem-orientation generates the energy to put right what is perceived to be wrong, but the energy generated dissipates as soon as the problem is resolved. A vision or mission orientation is quite different; it generates energy through the creative tension produced by the recognition of the difference between the unit's vision for itself and current reality. It is, therefore, much longer term. Visions typically take much longer to actualise than problems do to solve, and the strategies implemented to achieve the vision are continuously revised and improved, as they must be in an ever-changing operating environment.

Problem-oriented units tend to focus on the superficial symptoms of problems. Consideration of the causes of the problem at system or structural level is seldom undertaken and this seriously limits the unit's potential to shape its own future. At best it is an adaptive unit as it attempts to adapt to the changing superficial features of the environment. A unit that focuses on the systematic and structural causes of behaviour, however, gathers causal intelligence; it should be well-equipped, therefore, to create the realities it envisions for itself. Such units are generative units (Senge 1992) because causal intelligence permits a creativity and productivity in planning and response that superficial problem-situational analyses typically do not.

Healthy, 'change agile' units of the future will incorporate both orientations; an adaptive orientation to deal with everyday practical exigency and more importantly, generative orientation through which to realise its vision.

It should be noted that the development of generative units is imperative, given the knowledge explosion. No one person could ever hope to acquire all or even a substantial amount of the knowledge required for decision-making in our awesomely complex and continuously changing health care systems. Generative units require enabling or transformational leadership (Bass 1990a; Cottingham 1994; Parry 1996; Sullivan 1998); leadership which is informed and energised by vision but which ensures that everyone in the unit acquires the skills to fulfil the vision.

Generative leaders differ substantially from the traditional model of leadership, that is, of the warrior-hero leading the charge (Bass 1990b); generative leaders are not usually warrior-heroes, they are designers, stewards and teachers (Senge 1992). They are designers of enabling environments where their designs find expression in participatively and transparently created policies and structures (De Pree 1989). They are stewards of the unit's vision for itself where vision inspires and gives meaning (Bass 1990b; Javidan 1995); and, they are teachers to the extent that they role-model the values they claim to espouse, they model the behaviour they expect of others (Covey 1998; Parry 1996), and they make available the resources required for ongoing staff development.

Nurse leaders will be able to assess their effectiveness in designing generative units to the extent that they prevent crises (and have less need of warrior-heroes to manage them), and they are required to operate less frequently in an essentially reactive manner. The warrior-hero model of leadership is now embarrassingly inadequate; decision-making in a generative unit should involve everyone who has a meaningful contribution to make.

GENERATIVE LEADERSHIP AND OUTSIDE-IN THINKING

It was noted above that outside-in leaders consider it vitally important to scan their units' operating environments to identify, at a very early stage, potential changes which could affect their units. Clearly, serious environmental scanning is important for generative leaders; generative leaders are stewards of the unit's vision and, in order to ensure that it is fulfilled as expeditiously as possible, they need to identify potential impediments early on and ensure that the appropriate pre-emptive action is taken. The taking of appropriate pre-emptive action, in turn, hinges critically on causal intelligence.

It was also noted above that serious environmental scanning takes time and that outside-in leaders made the requisite time available by delegating to their team members and giving them the authority to make decisions. Generative leaders do this, too. It should be borne in mind, however, that health services remain largely autocratic and controlling in management orientation (Greenwood 1999b) and team members in generative units will need to acquire both the skills of informed decision-making and participatory governance and the confidence to use them. Resourcing this kind of staff development will be critical to the generative development of a unit.

Rather obviously, too, the development of unit leader's generative leadership skills and outside-in thinking is critical to the development of generative units. Fortunately, both of these may be developed through structured, systematic reflection.

THE NATURE AND ROLE OF REFLECTION

[Reflection is] . . . the process of creating and clarifying the meaning of experience (present or past) . . . The outcome of the process is *changed conceptual perspective* (Boyd & Fales 1983, p.101, emphasis added).

By 'changed conceptual perspective', Boyd and Fales simply mean coming to see things differently. Reflective (rather than merely thoughtful) practice requires that nurses learn from their reflections, revise their conceptual perspectives appropriately and act differently in the future as a result (Jarvis 1992; Andrews 1996).

Reflection has three components, namely, anticipatory reflection or reflection before action, reflection-in-action and reflection-on-action (Schon 1983; 1987). Anticipatory reflection entails the careful consideration of what to do and why to do it, prior to engaging in action, in any novel or problematic situation. Reflection before action, therefore, should reduce human error. Reflection-in-action means to think what one is doing while one is doing it. It is usually stimulated by surprise, by something that puzzles the practitioner concerned. As the practitioner tries to make sense of the immediately problematic situation, they ask themselves why they decided to act as they did, what made them adopt the course of action chosen and how they initially formulated the problem. They surface all this, criticise it, restructure their problem solution and express it in further action. Thus, reflection-in-action allows practitioners to reshape what they are doing while they are doing it. Reflection-on-action, as its name implies, involves a cognitive post-mortem (Greenwood 1993). The practitioner looks back on their experiences to explore again the understandings she or he brought to them in light of the outcomes.

Two kinds of knowledge inform professional practice (Schon 1983): that derived from science, and typically learned deliberately and consciously (what nurses construe as 'theory'); and that derived from experience. Knowledge gained through practical experience is notoriously difficult to articulate because it is learned largely unconsciously as nurses go about their everyday nursing activities (Berry & Dienes 1993; Garnham & Oakhill 1994).

This knowledge is learned (or, more accurately, constructed) by working with or alongside other nurses who already possess it. The gradual acquisition of this type of knowledge constitutes an individual's professional socialisation. It includes all the implicit beliefs, values and norms which characterise nursing (and, nursing leadership and management). Thus, largely unconsciously, simply through engaging in repeated, everyday activities, nurses (and nurse leaders) learn what to do, to whom, when, where, how, with what resources and with what end in view (Greenwood 2001). Such knowledge is learned in practice and expressed in practice.

There can be, however, very important limitations to experiential knowledge. It is best subjected to expression interrogation critique, to enable judgements to be made about its ethical and technical veracity. This is important in terms of leadership and management because everyday practice knowledge is, as its name indicates, used *every day*. In terms of quality leadership, therefore, it is very important. It is for this reason that nurse leaders and managers should ensure that their everyday leadership activities are generative, that is, appropriate both ethically and technically. Reflective practice enables nurses to do this.

Reflective practice also enables nurse leaders to explore their leadership practice at three levels (Van Manen 1977). It allows them to:

▲ improve the technical aspects of leadership, for example, involve others in decision-making;

▲ appreciate the theoretical/scientific basis of their leadership practices, for example, that participatory governance is empowering (generative); and

▲ identify the sociopolitical and economic influences including the cultural norms, beliefs, values and the systems and structures in which they are institutionalised in health care.

Reflective practice, therefore, certainly at the third level, allows the gathering of the causal intelligence upon which generative leadership depends.

These cultural norms and sociopolitical and economic influences are expressed in the language nurses use, the activities they engage in and the social relationships they establish and maintain (Kemmis & McTaggart 1988). That is why it is important for nurses to reflect on precisely what was said by whom to whom in a particular situation, precisely what was done by whom and with what results and then, of course, why it was said and done.

SOME BENEFITS OF REFLECTIVE PRACTICE

Reflection at these three progressively more sophisticated levels results in important benefits for nurses and nurse leaders. These include improved analytic thinking skills (Durgahee 1996; Kobert 1995); exploration of the leader's own role and boundaries and those of other managers and health professionals (Johns 1994); an understanding of the conditions under which practitioners and leaders work, and, in particular, the impediments to their autonomy (Emden 1991; Johns 1994); and, the monitoring of increased leadership effectiveness over time (Johns 1995; Landeen et al. 1995).

LEARNING TO REFLECT

Despite a commonsense view to the contrary (Reid 1993), nurses and leaders must *learn* to reflect (Mallick 1998). As much of the above implies, reflection is a highly sophisticated intellectual skill, which, like all such skills, requires learning through repeated cycles of feedback—governed practice (Greenwood 1990). The novice reflective leader, therefore, requires someone with whom they can share and explore their reflections and who can provide them with constructive but thoughtful feedback (Cox et al. 1991). Ideally, this person will focus progressively on the causal systemic and structural influences on behaviour.

Reflection is facilitated by the use of a reflective framework, which, typically, is constructed of a series of questions meant to probe the three levels attainable through reflection and, rather obviously, something of substance to reflect on. There are a number of frameworks currently available in the literature, for example, Smyth (1989), Smith and Russell (1991), Burrows (1995), Johns (1995), and Greenwood (2001). Readers are recommended to sample these for 'best fit' and, if necessary, construct their own framework from the integration of aspects from some/all of them.

It is surprising how often nurses and nurse leaders claim to have no experiences worthy of reflection (Bond & Holland 1998). So much of what they do every day is done almost on 'automatic pilot' that they notice relatively little that appears novel or interesting. (You will recall that it is precisely these 'everyday' experience beliefs and values that reflective practice aims to uncover and interrogate.)

For nurse leaders seeking to become generative, their reflections should focus on the extent to which their activities are or are becoming generative. For example, in terms of designing generative and enabling environments, how seriously participatory are their decision-making practices? What policies and procedures are being designed to enable the team to develop and contribute? And, of course, what particular influences are instrumental in facilitating/impeding these? In terms of stewardship of vision, how frequently is the team reminded of the vision? How often is it used to inspire, to motivate? What factors influence this? And, in terms of teaching, does the leader's behaviour genuinely reflect the beliefs and values they and their team espouse? What socio-cultural and political factors operate to impede such behaviours?

One last point on reflection: novice reflectors who wish to use reflection to develop their generative leadership skills should ensure that the person they select to reflect with understands both the nature and purposes of reflection and the nature of generative leadership. If the nurse is unfamiliar with either of these, the utility of the reflective sessions will be seriously limited.

CONCLUSION

Outside-in strategic thinking and generative leadership will be increasingly required to manage 'change agile' units of the future. Both outside-in thinking and generative leadership seek causal intelligence with respect to actual and potential operating problems; causal intelligence, in turn, allows more meaningful control of a unit's operating environment. Causal intelligence should inform a unit's situational analysis and development planning. Situational analyses involve both an exploratory component (that is, a SWOT analysis) and a decision-making component (what priorities/objectives to pursue in light of the SWOT analysis).

Reflection allows nurse leaders and managers to probe their practices at three causal levels, that is, the practical level (what they actually do), the theoretical/scientific level (the theoretical/scientific basis of their practices) and at the systemic/structural level (the sociopolitical and economic influences on their practices).

Reflective exercise

Consider a critical incident that you have been involved in. Ask yourself the following questions:

1 What was your role in the incident?

2 What actions did you take?

3 Why did you choose this course of action?

4 How did you initially frame the problem?

5 Are there any other ways that the situation could be framed?

6 What actions could have resulted in a different outcome?

7 What knowledge have you gained through this experience?

8 How will this knowledge shape your future practice?

RECOMMENDED READINGS

Burns, J. M. (1978). *Leadership*. New York: Harper & Row.

Greenwood, J. (2001). Writing nursing, writing ourselves. In E. Chang, & J. Daly (eds), *Preparing for professional nursing practice: An introduction*. Sydney, Australia: MacLennan & Petty.

Holly, M. (1984). *Keeping a personal-professional journal*. Victoria, Australia: Deakin University Press.

Sullivan, T. J. (1998). Transformational leadership. In T. J. Sullivan (ed) *Collaboration: A health care imperative* (pp. 467–98). New York: McGraw-Hill.

Thompson, A. A. Jr., & Strickland, A. J. III (1995). *Strategic management: Concepts and cases*. 8th edn. Chicago: Irwin.

PART THREE

Leadership in Action

CHAPTER NINETEEN

Leading contemporary approaches to nursing practice

Patricia M Davidson, Doug Elliott & Kathy Daffurn

LEARNING OBJECTIVES

At the completion of this chapter, the reader will be able to:

▲ appreciate the social, economic and political influences that impact upon nursing practice;

▲ understand the discrete differences between leadership and management in relation to nursing practice;

▲ recognise the impact of leadership and management upon clinical practice and patient outcomes;

▲ appreciate the importance of visionary leaders in facilitating change management in a clinical environment; and

▲ identify professional and organisational factors that facilitate effective leadership and strategic management.

KEY WORDS

Advanced practice, clinical development units, clinical leadership, clinical management, nurse practitioner, transformational leadership

INTRODUCTION

Excellence in clinical practice is the key to legitimising nursing leadership. This chapter seeks to analyse contemporary trends influencing clinical practice and models of care delivery. Characteristics and attributes of leaders in the clinical workplace are identified and the importance of expert clinical practice in shaping the destiny and future of nursing practice is justified. The chapter also provides insights into the way expert practitioners, functioning as leaders in the clinical setting, can face challenges, and successfully implement strategies to improve patient care and advance nursing practice.

Internationally, contemporary clinical, administrative and policy environments of health care render unique challenges to both health care professionals and consumers (Heath 2002; Hinshaw 2000; Williams et al. 2000). Despite significant impediments, such as fiscal constraints and the widespread shortage of nurses, the health care environment has never been so welcoming for dynamic nurse leaders and managers. This is because contemporary health care systems are no longer based upon hierarchical medical leadership but are more inclusive and interdisciplinary (Aiken et al. 2000). In order for nurses to function effectively in such environments, and, importantly, exert influence to optimise patient care, they need to appreciate the multiple factors that impact upon nursing practice and health care delivery. These factors are as diverse as the nature of nursing practice itself. In this chapter we explore the notion of clinical leadership within the current health care environment, and consider how individual nurses have engaged the system to develop nursing practice, improve quality of care and optimise patient outcomes.

HEALTH CARE IN CONTEXT

Contemporary health care systems are often portrayed as a system in crisis. Currently, the worldwide nurse staffing shortage continues to attract government and public comment (Buerhaus et al. 2000; Duffield & O'Brien-Pallas 2002; Jackson et al. 2001; McElmurry et al. 2000). Nursing as a predominantly female profession has experienced chronic staff retention issues over many years, and there is evidence of an ageing workforce (American Association of Colleges of Nursing Task Force 2002; Australian Institute of Health and Welfare [AIHW] 2001), with the current average age of nurses in Australia being over 40 (Heath 2002). Governments continue various initiatives to entice ex-nurses back to the workforce, but a skills-set that includes applied problem-solving, flexibility, communication and management skills, is transferable to other work contexts and attractive to prospective employers. For example, ex-nurses work in the legal, government, commercial and academic sectors in roles that often have a health focus but are not directly related to nursing. Others thrive in non-health sector roles.

In Australia, two recent government inquiries into nursing and nursing education (Heath 2002; Senate Community Affairs Committee 2002) have recommended many initiatives to improve the critical status of nursing. Included in their recommendations were the establishment of a national nursing council to promote nursing leadership and build capacity through quality education and sustainable workforce initiatives, and increased collaborative partnerships, including additional clinical education funding and re-building of clinical education systems and infrastructure in hospitals and health services. Of particular relevance to the topic of managing nursing care delivery were identification of a national approach to the scope of practice, including nurse practitioners; examining whole-of health perspectives on health service planning; and examining work organisation and culture in health services (Heath 2002).

In 2001, a New Zealand review identified similar challenges facing nursing and the health care system there (Nursing Council of New Zealand 2001), including retention and recruitment issues (Grant-Mackie 2002; Prebble 2001). In response, the Ministry of Health and the Nursing Council launched the nurse practitioner (NP) career path to create highly skilled nurses and to encourage expert clinicians to stay and practise in New Zealand. This is a trend also seen in Australia, mainly to address the shortage of doctors in rural and remote areas, but also to meet the demands of nurses for recognition of advanced practice roles. More recently, a roll-out of NP positions has been occurring in metropolitan health services.

OPPORTUNITIES FOR CLINICAL NURSING LEADERS

Despite the difficulties outlined above, the Australian health system is relatively efficient and effective in operation, and continues to deliver care that has significantly improved patient outcomes and demonstrated examples of clinical excellence. One example is the decrease in mortality from coronary heart disease (Australian Bureau of Statistics 2002; Tonkin et al. 1999). While similar trends are demonstrated in other industrialised countries, internationally health care professionals are increasingly challenged to deliver health care in an equitable and accessible manner while dealing with issues of quality and safety (Institute of Medicine, Committee on Quality Health Care in America 1999; Meleis et al. 1995; Wilson et al. 1999). Further, the increasing trend towards globalisation means that we have to consider issues beyond our local environment in health care policy and delivery (Messias 2001).

Within this context, nurses now also have increasing opportunities to influence health care policy and practice. This new position of power is evidenced by representation on various state multidisciplinary committees and changes in practice following credible scientific research. Undeniably, significant barriers continue to exist, but these are not insurmountable (Heath 2002). Recognition that the greatest power base for nurses exists within the practice domain, with demonstration of clinical excellence and innovation are important factors in overcoming these barriers. For example, nurses in the management of chronic heart failure have demonstrated their ability to influence patient outcomes and policies through nurse-coordinated programs (Blue et al. 2001; McAlister et al. 2001).

As a consequence, leadership in the clinical domain is an important tool, and strategies to achieve this are discussed below. A clinical leader is a nurse who demonstrates the ability to influence and direct clinical practice (Lett 2002). This clinical leader also has a vision for the direction of nursing practice. This vision is informed by expert knowledge and analysis of the social, political and economic trends influencing health care. Fedoruk and Pincombe (2000) suggest that current and future nurse leaders need to let go of traditional managerial practices and behaviours to focus on achieving change management and process re-engineering. To achieve this goal, contemporary nursing leaders have to adopt a flexible, innovative and collaborative practice model. Pressures on the health care system—for example, financial pressures and increasing chronic disease burden—represent significant challenges for nurses. However, innovative models of care, increasing emphasis on independent nursing practice, and institution of clinical governance structures will likely serve nurses in addressing these challenges.

POLICY FRAMEWORKS FOR NURSING PRACTICE

In order to engage a system, direct change and assert leadership, it is important to appreciate what 'drives' this process. This observation is relevant at both a macro and a micro level of operation. Politics can be just as intriguing and complex within a hospital ward as at the bureaucratic or parliamentary levels. However, at all levels it is important to be aware of social, political and economic factors that direct health care systems (Borthwick & Galbally 2001). As members of society we have to remember that our part of the world is influenced by external factors and we need to be cognisant of these to understand the workings of our local environment.

The working environment of nurses is influenced by the social, economic and political systems of the health care system. Table 19.1 compares the policy environments and roles of nurses in Australia, New Zealand, United Kingdom, Taiwan and the United States. In some instances, policy can be either a barrier or facilitator to clinical leadership. For example, policy environments in Australia do not favour independent nursing practice, whereas in the United States nurses can function as independent nursing practitioners (American Association of Colleges of Nursing Task Force 2002; Whitecross 1999). Internationally, health care professionals strive to ensure the delivery of safe and effective evidence-based care. Frameworks such as clinical and shared governance serve as a structure to achieve this goal. Clinical governance is a mechanism through which health care organisations are held accountable for continuously improving the quality of their services and ensuring high standards of care (O'May & Buchan 1999; Porter-O'Grady 1995, 2001; Prince 1997; Swage 2000). These concepts are discussed in greater depth in Chapter 22.

Table 19.1 Policy environments and nurses roles in Australia, New Zealand, United Kingdom, Taiwan and the United States

	Australia	New Zealand	United Kingdom	Taiwan	United States
Health care system	Universal coverage	Universal coverage	Universal coverage	National health insurance program	Fragmented user pays system
Role of nurses within the health care system	Collaborative Interdisciplinary practice	Collaborative Interdisciplinary practice	Collaborative Interdisciplinary practice	Collaborative Interdisciplinary practice	Collaborative Independent nursing practice
Nurse practitioner role	Newly established	Newly established	Established	Established	Well established
Key health issues	Increasing burden of chronic illness Diversity health Adverse outcomes for ATSI	Increasing burden of chronic illness Striving for cultural competence	Increasing burden of chronic illness	Cancer leading cause of death High rates of hepatitis	Increasing burden of chronic illness Inequity of access

cont.

Table 19.1 cont.

	Australia	New Zealand	United Kingdom	Taiwan	United States
Key health issues	Rural health Control of escalating health costs	Control of escalating health costs	Control of escalating health costs	Control of escalating health costs Integrating traditional Chinese and western medicine	Control of escalating health costs
Impact on clinical leadership	Striving to nurture a clinical progression strand Retention and recruitment issues	Striving to nurture a clinical progression strand Retention and recruitment issues Midwifery-specific programs	Striving to nurture a clinical progression strand Retention and recruitment issues Shared governance	Promoting nurses' welfare Providing continuing education Development of nurse specialist programs establishing clinical career ladders	Striving to nurture a clinical progression strand Retention and recruitment issues Shared governance
Nursing workforce	National nursing shortages Ageing workforce Pressure to deregulate health care workers	National nursing shortages Ageing workforce	National nursing shortages Ageing workforce	Low nursing wages Professional issues Integrating traditional and western medicine	National nursing shortages Ageing workforce
Nursing education	Technical and further education programs (EN) University UG degree (RN) programs Postgraduate programs	University UG degree programs Postgraduate programs	Vocational entry Diploma programs University UG degree programs Postgraduate programs	Vocational schools Junior college UG university, masters and doctoral programs	UG Diploma, Associate & Baccalaureate programs Postgraduate programs
Levels of nursing care provision	Nursing assistant Enrolled nurse Registered nurse Nurse practitioner	Enrolled nurse Registered nurse	Nursing assistants Practice nurses Registered nurse Level 1 & Level 2 Nurses (Part 1–15)	Physician assistant	Practical nurse Registered nurse Nurse practitioner Clinical nurse specialist Physician assistant

Sources: Australia: AIHW 2001; Heath 2002; Victorian Health Department 2002; Whitecross 1999. New Zealand: Grant-Mackie 2002; Nursing Council of New Zealand 2001; Prebble 2001. United Kingdom: Nursing and Midwifery Council 2002. Taiwan: Chen 2001; Chui 1999, Yin et al. 1997, 2000. United States: Institute of Medicine 1999; Needleman et al. 2002.

CHANGING MODELS OF CARE DELIVERY

A variety of care delivery models are used in health care—some relate to nursing only and are historic (Nelson 2000), while others are interdisciplinary and contemporary in focus (see Table 19.2). The changing health care environment—characterised by increasing short-stay surgery, decreasing lengths of stay and numbers of acute beds, combined with increasing patient acuity related to co-morbidities—requires vastly different models of care delivery from even a decade ago. Novel models of care are commonly developed in response to actual or perceived deficits in existing care delivery (Davidson & Elliott 2001).

Table 19.2 Common care delivery models

Care delivery model	Characteristics
Functional nursing	Ward-based care with allocation of specific clinical tasks to nursing staff (perhaps with different educational preparation) (e.g. physical care; medication administration)
Team nursing	Ward-based care where a small team of nurses (perhaps with different educational preparation) provide all care to a patient group Includes 'care-pairs' (RN plus EN/AIN) (Kenney 2001)
Patient allocation/total patient care	Ward-based care provided by an RN on a shift by shift basis to a number of patients (e.g. 1: 6 or 1: 8)
Primary nursing	Ward-based care with an RN assigned to patients for their entire admission period Plan of care is developed, implemented and evaluated by the 'primary' nurse, with 'associate' nurses continuing the plan in the absence of the 'primary' nurse
Care management / clinical pathways	Ward or hospital-based multidisciplinary co-ordinated patient care for a specific case type (e.g. patients with total hip replacement) Incorporated a 'critical' or 'clinical path' tool to 'map' and document care, including the sequence and timing of interventions
Case management	Hospital, outreach and / or community-based multi-disciplinary care that provides continuity of care for a specific case-type of patients (e.g. patients with heart failure) across the entire episode of care (beyond hospital admission)

Sources: Crisp and Taylor 2001; Reiter-Tetel 2002; Urden and Walston 2001

Patients are admitted to acute care hospitals primarily for collaborative or independent nursing care, as many medical diagnostic and therapeutic procedures can now be conducted in ambulatory care settings, except in critical or emergent circumstances. However, efficient and effective care also requires continuity of patient management beyond the traditional hospital admission period to encompass the entire episode of care, particularly for those with continuing chronic disease. Coordinated care trials for patients with chronic and complex care needs, including integrated hospital and community care approaches (e.g. hospital in the home) are now being implemented and evaluated (Esterman & Ben-Tovim 2002).

The Commonwealth Government in Australia is currently funding Enhanced Primary Care Options—in particular, the development of collaborative health plans and review of patient outcomes through case conferencing—to enhance the management of chronic disease (Davis & Thurect 2001; NSW Health 2001; Whitecross 1999). In addition, issues of skill mix and different levels of nursing roles (registered nurse (RN), enrolled nurse, assistants in nursing) continue to be discussed because of budget constraints and staff shortages. However, one large US study using retrospective administrative data demonstrated a link between higher levels of RN care and shorter lengths of stay and a lower incidence of adverse events for patients (Needleman et al. 2002). Some health authorities are now mandating a specific nurse: patient ratio for acute ward areas in an attempt to maintain quality care (Steinbrook 2002; Victorian Health Department 2002), although any potential benefits are continuing to be debated professionally.

WHAT IS LEADERSHIP?

Rafferty (1991) defined leadership as 'the ability to identify a goal, come up with a strategy for achieving that goal and inspire your team to join you to put that strategy into action'(cited in Davenport et al. 1998, p.107). The dynamic and changing health care systems place change as a focus in contemporary health environments (Borbasi & Gaston 2002). Unless nurses choose to be swept along by change, they need to actively engage the process on both a personal and political level (Wright 1998). A primary function of a leader is to negotiate the change process and pave the way for their team (Lett 2002). Leadership in nursing is an under-researched phenomenon and much of the literature base to inform our knowledge is founded in models of private enterprise. Concepts that make nursing leadership unique include responsibility for the care and safety of patients and a need for clinical governance (see Chapter 22). Atsalos and Greenwood (2001) believe that contemporary nursing leaders need to form symbiotic professional relationships in order to inspire and influence changes in groups and organisations.

Leadership has long been an important part of the function of any organisation. Leadership styles vary along a continuum from authoritative to participatory, although common characteristics for leaders include being a visionary and having a plan to take individuals and services to the future (Mahoney 2001). O'Rourke (2001) defines a visionary leader as one who can simultaneously have a vigilant focus on promoting health; the capacity to build teams, articulate and demonstrate what others cannot see, and address immediate challenges as well as leading their team into the future of often unchartered waters. Leadership is influenced by the values of individuals and organisations, as well as society. Values are a set of beliefs and concepts derived from knowledge, experience and aspiration. In order to function effectively and avoid role conflict there needs to be a congruency between the values and beliefs of the individual and the organisation in which they work (Cameron & Wren 1999).

Figure 19.1 describes the relationship between personal, professional and organisational values and leadership styles. It is generally considered that for leaders to be effective they need to demonstrate honesty, integrity and inspiration (Heller 1999). Figure 19.2 demonstrates the influence of vision and direction on clinical leaders. This leadership is inextricably linked to the cultural values of the systems, resources and support available. Policy and practice environments, as described in Tables 19.1 and 19.2, also have significant influence on leadership direction.

One delineation of leadership characteristics and behaviour is that of transactional versus transformational leaders. Transactional leadership focuses on transactions or exchanges between leaders and others, with self-interest the key motivator. In contrast, transformational leaders create a culture of leadership for all stakeholders, generating empowerment, open dialogue and inclusive decision-making (Bowles & Bowles 2000; Cook 2001; McCormack et al. 2002). An additional concept, 'breakthrough leadership', incorporates role-modelling, clarification of own values, and respects others' views (Lett 2002). Explicit role-modelling, mentoring and succession planning are vital aspects in preparing current and future nursing leaders (Benton 1999; Borbasi & Gaston 2002; Borthwick & Galbally 2001; McCormack & Hopkins 1995; McCormack et al. 2002).

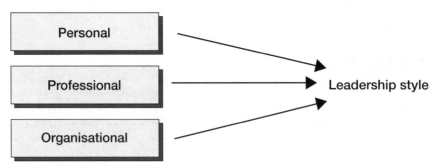

Figure 19.1 Value systems contributing to leadership style

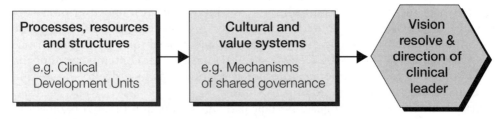

Figure 19.2 Relationship between organisational resources, values and culture and the vision, resolve and direction of the clinical leader

WHAT MAKES A CLINICAL LEADER?

In organisations such as hospitals, there are different nursing leaders functioning at all levels of the organisation. The individuals that readily come to mind are often those who are very visible in organisations, such as directors of nursing. However, it is important to differentiate between management and leadership (Fedoruk & Pincombe 2000). Management refers to the planning and organisation of services. The term leadership infers that an individual is visionary and pivotal in directing and shaping clinical practice. Implicit in functioning as a clinical leader is a significant mentoring role. Table 19.3 describes the attributes of a clinical leader (Borbasi & Gaston 2002; Lett 2002; Mahoney 2001). Cook (2001) states that we must question the assumption that the leader making the difference to care is at the hierarchical apex of the organisation. He believes that the most influential individuals, in terms of improving direct care provision, are those who directly deliver nursing care. Therefore, clinical leaders are involved in the provision of patient care and are implicitly clinical experts in their field.

Table 19.3 Attributes of a clinical leader

Expert clinician	Patient focused
Vision	Stamina
Innovation	Dynamism
Confidence	Selflessness
Assertiveness	Collaboration

Cook (2001) compared nursing practice in two clinical practice settings, and noted that the factor differentiating a vibrant research-based, evidence-based practice culture and one based upon routine and ritual was the nursing leader. In the section below we describe the experiences of one clinical nursing leader and her opinions and strategies for achieving change.

Nurses can make a difference to patient outcomes by demonstrating leadership and innovative clinical practice. Margaret Fry, a clinical nurse consultant (CNC) in Emergency at St George Hospital in Sydney Australia, has achieved recognition and awards for her work in Emergency Nursing, in the professional, academic and clinical domains. In her role, Margaret has demonstrated her leadership abilities in advancing nursing practice. The CNC role has four discrete foci: clinical, research, education and professional domains. To be a clinical nurse consultant, nurses must be clinical experts in their field, but also possess the skills and demonstrate leadership to explore and evaluate new models to improve nursing care.

Two of the advanced practices piloted and evaluated by Margaret include 'Nurse-initiated administration of narcotics' and 'Nurse-initiated ordering of X-rays' policies (Fry 2001). These strategies have not only served to increase the professional standing and autonomy of nurses but also have expedited the treatment process and increased the quality of nursing care. Instituting these practices involved demonstration of leadership skills by engaging key stakeholders, developing and implementing research, compiling evidence to justify the approach, and undertaking systematic evaluation and assessment. Margaret's experience demonstrates that changing practice is based upon a systematic change management process not charismatic leadership (Evans & Haines 2000; Valentine 2001). Of note, Berwick (1998) emphasised that leadership of change is the key to improving health care outcomes.

DEMONSTRATING NURSING LEADERSHIP IN INTERDISCIPLINARY TEAMS

It is clear that patients with complex disorders, particularly in the context of psychosocial implications, require the professional services of different occupational groups. Nurses have demonstrated their ability to work as part of a team and be collaborative and participatory in their actions and decision-making (Blue et al. 2001; Stewart et al. 1999). Hall and Weaver (2001) identify two emerging issues in health care as clinicians face the complexities of current patient care: the need for specialised clinical experts and the need for these professionals to collaborate. Interdisciplinary health care teams with members from many disciplines increasingly work together to optimise patient care. Examples of these teams are found in trauma, neonatal retrieval, geriatric assessment, and drug and alcohol areas of clinical practice.

LEADING CONTEMPORARY APPROACHES TO NURSING PRACTICE

This section discusses a number of contemporary initiatives that facilitate the development of nursing practice and professional growth—clinical chairs (i.e. clinical professors of nursing), professional organisations and nursing development units.

The clinical chair as a vehicle for clinical leadership

The establishment of clinical professors in nursing in Australia has also provided the opportunity to lead and support clinical practice development, as well as research and education, across the health care and education sectors (Dunn & Yates 2000). The introduction of clinical professorial positions followed a period where joint appointments at lower levels were trialled in the United States, United Kingdom and Australia (Elliott 1997). Despite the high status, appointees to these positions continue to suffer role ambiguity and role strain in working across both health care and education sectors, with local politics forming a substantial domain of work (Dunn & Yates 2000). Nevertheless, nurses in clinical chairs have the ability to provide leadership and direction for clinical nurses and to facilitate dialogue between the academic and practice domains. These developing linkages are important, as the increasing presence of nurses in decision-making roles has occurred because of the professional confidence and credibility associated with the introduction of the full range of formal academic preparation and qualifications for nurses (Crookes & Bradshaw 2002).

Professional societies and organisations to promote clinical leadership

Professional societies play an important role in terms of not only providing an environment of collegiality but also leadership, mentorship and promotion of clinical excellence. These aims are achieved through development of policy documents, publication of professional journals, conduct of scientific meetings, and sponsorship of research and attendance at professional meetings. Some organisations serve the nursing profession broadly, focusing on an array of nursing issues, while others maintain a specialty focus. Examples of this in Australia are specialty groups such as the Australian College of Critical Care Nurses Ltd [ACCCN] (Wiles & Daffurn 2002), more generic organisations such as the College of Nursing (incorporating the NSW College of Nursing), the Royal College of Nursing Australia and internationally, Sigma Theta Tau International and the International Council of Nursing.

ACCCN has a discrete focus on the specialty of critical care and represents over 2500 critical care nurses. Its members work across the critical care clinical spectrum including emergency, coronary care, high dependency, cardiothoracic and general intensive care units, as well as academic and educational settings. The activities of ACCCN focus on the care of both adult and paediatric critically ill patients, strong professional relationships with other national and international peak nursing bodies and government agencies and individuals (ACCCN 2002; Wiles & Daffurn 2002). These activities provide a forum and structure for professional, clinical practice and related policy developments.

Sigma Theta Tau International, on the other hand, has a particular emphasis on promotion of leadership with the mission to create a global community of nurses who lead in using scholarship, knowledge and technology to improve the health of the world's people. There are over 420 chapters of Sigma Theta Tau throughout the world.

The Sigma Theta Tau International Leadership Institute (ILI) focuses on the development and advancement of nurses as exceptional health care leaders. The ILI assists nurses internationally to develop leadership skills by creating and sharing knowledge (Sigma Theta Tau 2002).

Increasingly, professional nursing organisations are playing a role in terms of social advocacy and also mentoring and supporting nursing colleagues in developing countries. Particularly in situations of social disadvantage, nurses can play an important role in advocacy. What is increasingly apparent in a variety of settings is that a united nursing voice can be a powerful force (Sigma Theta Tau 2002).

Nursing development units/professional practice units

Nursing development units (NDUs) were first established in the early 1980s in the United Kingdom (Redfern & Stevens 1998) as centres of nursing excellence, innovation and leadership development (Bowles & Bowles 2000). In a comparative study of the leadership provided by nurse managers and leaders in NDUs and conventional clinical settings in the UK, Bowles and Bowles (2000) demonstrated that NDU leaders provide leadership of a more transformational nature than colleagues working in conventional models.

In the Western Sydney Area Health Service, Australia, in 1997, a network of nine clinical development units (nursing) (CDU(N)) was established. These units were designed to develop patient-focused nursing practice through action research, informed by the principles of transformational leadership. Atsalos and Greenwood (2001) undertook a qualitative review of the evolution of these units, and an emergent theme from this inquiry was the CDU leaders' own need for leadership in order to sustain momentum and motivation. These findings underscore that breaking new ground, particularly within complex clinical environments, is not an easy road. Similarly, McCormack and Hopkins (1995) identified the inherent difficulties of operationalising the notions of nursing leadership. A model of clinical leadership through a collegiate model using reflective practice was advocated, along with the need for both clinical leaders and practitioners to have a supportive organisational culture to achieve their aims.

LEADERSHIP AND MANAGEMENT IN EVIDENCE-BASED PRACTICE

The measurement of nursing interventions and patient outcomes is becoming increasingly important. Increasing emphasis on an evidence-based approach to clinical management, and the increased professionalisation of nursing mandates a patient-centred, continuous quality improvement focus. These approaches also require a degree of innovation (Davidson & Elliott 2001; Mitchell et al. 1998). Outcome evaluation continues to be an important but often elusive component of health care delivery, but is an important way in which nurses demonstrate their influence, not only to others but also each other (Bond & Thomas 1991; Davidson & Elliott 2001; Middleton & Lumby 1998). In spite of this, few studies exist that have compared models of care, or provided an evidence base on the benefits of nursing within the health care system (Heath 2002; Nelson 2000). Similar findings were evident in a review of continuity of care research where designs and measurement were limited and hence provided little generalisability and evidence (Sparbel & Anderson 2000). Even when studies provide the necessary 'evidence' for a change in practice, there is resistance to modifying policy and practice (Greenwood & Gray 1998; Harrow et al. 2001)—often because of local politics or ritual. For example, while current research indicates that ingestion of clear fluids is safe two to four hours pre-operatively, the continued practice of 12 hours of fasting is pervasive. Harrow and colleagues provided an example of patients fasting pre-operatively and describe the process of a clinical leader facilitating practice change in their local environment (Harrow et al. 2001). This experience underscores the fact that to be an effective clinical leader, beyond the charismatic attributes, nurses need to not only interpret and implement clinical evidence but also evaluate the efficacy of nursing interventions.

Significance of expert clinical practice

Expert clinical practice remains the foundation of nursing professionally and philosophically, and is the currency nurses use to negotiate and engage with other health professionals, express the theoretical foundations of nursing science, and deliver care to our communities. Clinical practice, informed by nursing science, is what makes nursing exceptional and unique, and is the key to our autonomous, professional practice. This underscores the importance of emphasising expert nursing within models of professional practice, education and research (O'Rourke 2001). Some of the roles that are the vehicles for this purpose have been discussed in this chapter: clinical nurse consultants, nurse practitioners, clinical nursing chairs, and practice development units. Internationally and even nationally, the names for these roles may differ, but the fundamental attributes are similar. Nurses who function as leaders in these roles carry not only the privilege but the professional responsibility to direct health care practices so as to optimise the health of the populations they serve.

CONCLUSION

In this chapter we have discussed the challenges, strategies and progress for clinical leadership. Excellence in clinical practice is pivotal to legitimising nursing leadership (O'Rourke 2001). The challenge remains to inextricably link leadership and management with nursing practice, and develop innovative strategies to deal with a dynamic and evolving health care environment. In order to achieve this, a system of mentoring, career progression and succession planning in the clinical arena needs to be created and nurtured. Clinical and academic environments require a culture that develops innovation and fosters leadership potential. It is important to realise that at every level of an organisation, and regardless of whether nurses are in clinical, education and management streams, they have the potential to influence and direct patient care by exemplary leadership and excellence in clinical practice. The importance of clinical practice empowers clinical nurses to improve clinical care and lead clinical practice into the future in order to optimise health-related outcomes for all members of our society.

Reflective exercise

1 What is visionary clinical practice?

2 Consider two or three individuals who you believe are 'clinical leaders'. What are their leadership characteristics or behaviours? List them and compare to a colleague's list. Now compare the traits to those listed in Table 19.3 of this chapter. What are the common elements? What are the unique elements identified?

3 Identify a professional nursing organisation, and review their activities relating to leadership. This exercise may require review of journals, websites or other publications. What are the important elements?

RECOMMENDED READING

Aiken, L., Havens, D. S., & Sloane, D. M. (2000). The magnet nursing service recognition program: A comparison or two groups of magnet groups. *American Journal of Nursing, 100*(3), 26–36.

Beech, M. (2002). Leaders or managers: The drive for effective leadership. *Nursing Standard, 16*(30), 35–6.

Cook, M. J. (2001). The renaissance of clinical leadership. *International Nursing Review, 48*(1), 38–46.

Fry, M., Borg, A., Jackson, S., & McAlpine, A. (1999). The advanced clinical nurse—a new model of practice: Meeting the challenge of peak activity periods. *Australian Emergency Nursing Journal, 2*(3), 26–8.

Gould, D., Kelly, D., Goldstone, L., & Maidwell, A. (2001). The changing training needs of clinical nurse managers: Exploring issues for continuing professional development. *Journal of Advanced Nursing, 34*(1), 7–17.

CHAPTER TWENTY

Leading and enhancing patient-focused care: The human becoming theory in action

Gail J Mitchell

LEARNING OBJECTIVES

At the completion of this chapter, the reader will be able to:

- ▲ gain personal insight into the values that guide nursing actions and nursing leadership;

- ▲ better understand and articulate how nursing theory can direct a nursing leader;

- ▲ identify processes of a major change project in a large teaching hospital; and

- ▲ explore and specify the assumptions and values of patient-focused care and human becoming theory.

KEY WORDS

Patient-focused care, servant leadership, philosophy, values, standards of care

INTRODUCTION

This chapter is about leading and facilitating the transformation of a culture of health care in a large hospital that professed to be moving from a provider-driven system to one that truly manifests the values of patient-focused care. It is also an examination of nursing leadership and the impact that nursing theory can have on the quality of care and quality of work life for nurses. I have the privilege of being in a leadership role with approximately 2700 nurses and also of belonging to a senior team that is courageous and committed to values and principles, as well as clinical excellence. Sunnybrook and Women's (S&W's) College Health Sciences Centre is a three-campus teaching hospital with more than 7000 employees and with services that include clinical specialties such as oncology, perinatal care, critical care, ambulatory care, trauma, and gerontology—to name several.

S&W's staff have a unique and innovative commitment to promote and integrate four corporate themes or directives throughout the entire organisation. The four themes are ageing, strategic alliances/partnerships, women's health, and patient-focused care. A corporate focus on patient-focused care means that program and discipline leaders, as well as practitioners and providers of care are expected to and held accountable for advancing the organisational commitment to a specific patient-focused philosophy and set of standards. Nurses at S&W have provided leadership in the integration of patient-focused care and the chief nursing officer (CNO) role has been supported as pivotal to the change process (Bournes & DasGupta 1997; Linscott et al. 1999; Mitchell et al. 2000; Saltmarche et al. 1998). Almost a decade of leadership has provided learning, joy, excitement and struggle. Becoming a leader has been a journey that for me began with opportunities to develop a view of nursing as a discipline, a basic science and an art.

DEVELOPING A VIEW OF NURSING

An essential requirement of nursing leaders is that they can articulate and promote the art and science of nursing. Prior to leading others, most nursing leaders have examined and clarified their own beliefs about the nature of nursing and the ultimate purpose of nursing work. Clarifying one's personal beliefs requires exploration, contemplation, interrogation and confident articulation (Mitchell 1990, 1991, 1994, 1999, 2001; Mitchell & Cody 2002). It is not possible to be a strong leader or a strong nurse until clarity of intent and consistency of action emerge in one's thoughts and expressions about nursing.

I believe that nursing is a discipline, meaning that the discipline of nursing consists of particular knowledge essential to nursing practice and research (Barrett 2002; Cody 2001; Daly & Jackson 1999; Daly et al. 1996; Major et al. 2001; Mitchell 1994, 1999, 2001; Mitchell & Pilkington 2000; Parse 1993, 2001a, 2001b). Nursing knowledge is housed in extant nursing theories that provide different views about the nature of reality and the intent of nursing practice. Theories define context and direct nurses to attend to specific purposes and goals in the nurse–person process. Nursing knowledge is expanded through research projects that examine human experiences of health and quality of life through the lens of a specific nursing theory (see for example, Bournes & Mitchell 2002; Carson & Mitchell 1998; Cody 1991, 1995; Mitchell & Lawton 2000; Parse 2001c; Pilkington 1993).

Not all nurse leaders agree with the idea that nursing is a discipline in its own right. Fralic (2000), for example, considers nursing knowledge to be based in physiology, pharmacology, chemistry, anatomy, psychology, technology and physics. In contrast, I would suggest that although nurses have a broad base of knowledge in all these areas, as do physicians, physiotherapists and dentists, this generic knowledge does not make a nurse. Nurses require a unique focus or area of concern that provides unity and community towards a common vision and purpose. Fralic (2000) contends that if it cannot be measured, nursing should not be doing it. Her statement limits nursing phenomena to sensory data that can be measured. In contrast to Fralic's views are others, including myself, who suggest that although nurses do indeed perform critically important activities based on sensory data, primarily for persons in hospital settings, the phenomena of concern for nurses, as a group of professionals and scholars, requires foundations in human lived experiences of health, illness, dying, healing and quality of life (Barrett 2002; Cody 2001; Cody et al. 2000; Cody & Mitchell 1992, 2002; Daly & Jackson 1999; Daly et al. 1996; Mitchell & Cody 1999). The point of this discussion is that there are very different views about nursing and that is why a nurse leader requires clarity about personal beliefs and professional theories that guide practice and research.

I also believe that nursing is a basic science and a human science (Cody & Mitchell 2002; Fawcett 2002; Mitchell & Cody 1999; Malinski 2002; Parse 1987, 1998). This means that nursing knowledge, as developed in nursing theories, is extended through research that expands understanding of nursing phenomena—such as the lived experiences of health—as opposed to an applied science that expands the knowledge base of other disciplines. There are different views about the meaning of human science (Fawcett 2002; Malinski 2002), but the most critical view to contemplate is whether nursing knowledge needs to be different from medical, social or psychological knowledge (Mitchell & Cody 1999). From my perspective, the knowledge nurses require to care for human beings is different from what other disciplines generate and it is also different from the technical and clinical expertise that nurses develop on the job. In addition to the medical, clinical and technical knowledge nurses use on the job, there is a critical need for knowledge that helps nurses to be with people in ways that make a difference to the person's health and quality of life (for example, see Cody & Mitchell 1992; Daly et al. 1996; Fisher & Mitchell 1998; Jonas-Simpson 2001).

Nursing theories help nurses to articulate an intent that informs the nursing process and thus the nurse–person relationship. I think it would be very helpful if nurses could clearly state the purpose of their practices and the contributions they make to human health and quality of life. Nurses may identify self-care, quality of life or expanding consciousness when they address the contribution of their unique and autonomous practice. Nursing theories help to make the work of nursing understandable to the discipline and to the public at large. It is important to note that the knowledge of nursing theory co-exists with other knowledge about how to complete clinical skills and how to promote patient safety. All disciplines need knowledge about clinical skill and patient safety, but in addition to this general biomedical expertise, nurses require a purpose for being in a relationship with patients and for being a unique player on the health care team.

I had many opportunities during my career and during my scholarly pursuits to question my own beliefs and values. After years of exploring and clarifying, I choose the human becoming theory (Parse 1981, 1987, 1992, 1995, 1997, 1998), because it best aligns with my personal beliefs and vision of how nursing practice can happen with others. I have remained committed to the human becoming theory because it is a source of understanding and discovery, and because it supports a philosophy of health care delivery called patient-focused care (Linscott et al. 1999; Mitchell et al. 2000). I explored many other theories and models along the way but the human becoming theory provided the best fit with the kind of nurse I want to be, as well as the kind of nursing I want to experience. Perhaps you might think about the kind of nursing you want to experience as you consider the questions in the reflective exercise at the end of the chapter, regarding your beliefs about nursing theory.

Nursing practices underpinned by human science beliefs provide a unique service to humankind and one that is closest to the primary responsibility nurses bear—to be helpful to people during their life experiences. Nurses change, for better or for worse, what people experience and that change can enhance or diminish quality of life in important and lasting ways. The human becoming theory helps health care professionals to create a reality or a culture where persons who engage health services are met with a genuine regard for their humanity and for the wisdom people possess about their own quality of life and potential for change. Helping to create a reality where specific values are lived in relationships with others provides for leadership opportunities and challenges.

LEADERSHIP OPPORTUNITIES: A CHALLENGING JOURNEY

The pathway to becoming a nursing leader began when I started to question my practice, about six years after graduating from a hospital diploma program. I began to see my practice as limited and unsatisfying. I am not sure why I became dissatisfied, but I recall feeling disappointed and even ashamed of some of the things I was participating in. I loved nursing but I found the culture of nursing and the focus on tasks was not always helpful for the people we were supposed to be caring for.

After considering alternatives, I recommitted myself to nursing and returned to school with the hope that I might find ways to become the kind of nurse I wanted to be, and so that I could contribute to the discipline of nursing in ways that might benefit others. The discomfort and shame I experienced early in my career helped me to clarify what I was not willing to sacrifice in my work as a nurse. I think that professional integrity is critical for nurses and I sometimes wonder how many other nurses experience this kind of dissonance and disappointment in their careers. It became clear to me over time that at least part of my disappointment was with the knowledge and skill that I lacked to inform the kind of care I wanted to provide.

It was through my own growth as a practitioner of nursing that I learnt about being a leader for others who struggled as I did in the modern world of health care. I believe that people (patients, families, clients) experience unnecessary suffering because of nurses' insufficient understanding and knowledge about human beings and their meanings, relationships, and experiences of health and quality of life. Like others, I believe that the choice of one's nursing approach and theoretical guide is a moral matter with important ethical implications (Gadow 1990; Milton 1999; White 2001; Young-Mason 2001), and that the quality of nursing influences health outcomes and quality of life for clients.

During my years of learning about nursing as a field of study, I thought about the times I had walked away from difficult situations because I did not know how to be with people or how to be helpful. I had seen too many people hang their heads in shame when lectured by a health care professional about how they should have known better. I learned along the way that I did not want to be a nurse who punished, lectured, ignored or pressured people. I saw that life and lived experiences were far more complex than I could possibly understand. I realised that what I wanted was knowledge that would help me to be with the realities that people were experiencing—and to be there in ways that showed the compassion and caring I felt for others.

I will never forget the day a doctor asked me to go and talk with a young girl who was considered obese by physicians, to see if she realised she should lose weight. I recall looking at him and trying to understand the abyss that separated professionals from the people they were there to serve. Or other times when patients were punished for not complying with what professionals thought was best for them, even when people were not involved in decisions about their care. Still today I observe or hear about how some health care providers show hurtful and judgemental attitudes and actions toward patients and families, and it both angers me and strengthens my resolve to keep trying to contribute to systems that truly demonstrate a genuine regard for patients.

Study and contemplation, analysis and reflection, helped me to make the choice to align my nursing practice and research with the theory of human becoming (Parse 1981, 1987, 1992, 1995, 1997, 1998). It has been 15 years since I first began to learn what the human becoming school of thought could offer me as a nurse searching for meaningful practice. Learning the theory is not a swift or easy matter because it requires openness and a persistence to question predominant views and the status quo (Linscott et al 1999; Mitchell 1990; Saltmarche et al. 1998). It takes time to unlearn and repattern understanding and intentions in practice. Personally, the theory of human becoming has been a source of discovery and has provided alternative views helpful to me in practice (Cody et al. 2000; Cody & Mitchell 1992; Mitchell 1988, 1990, 1991, 1999, 2001; Mitchell & Bournes 2000; Mitchell et al. 2000; Mitchell & Cody 1999; Mitchell & Pilkington 2000) and research (Bournes & Mitchell 2002; Carson & Mitchell 1998; Mitchell & Lawton 2000; Fisher & Mitchell 1998; Mitchell 1998). Leadership in nursing requires passionate beliefs and a breadth of knowledge that includes knowledge of nursing theory. It is with this history and the personal commitment to human becoming that I embraced the opportunity to become a leader of nursing at a large teaching hospital in Canada.

Becoming a leader of nursing

The opportunity to become a nursing leader happened at a hospital that was implementing the operational model called patient-focused care. Senior administrators knew they had successfully changed the structure of the hospital from centralised departments to decentralised programs, and some processes of care delivery had changed, but they were struggling with how to change the philosophy of care from a provider-driven to a patient-focused model. At the time of questioning about how to change practice approaches, including the values and beliefs of professional staff, I had the opportunity to articulate a vision of patient-focused care that was informed and shaped by the assumptions and values of the human becoming theory (Parse 1981, 1987, 1992, 1995, 1997, 1998, 2001c). Articulation of the vision opened the door to what has been an eight-year odyssey into change and values clarification, conflict and opportunity, innovation and risk, joy and sorrow, satisfaction and growth.

Leadership theory has also helped me to become the kind of nursing leader that I have always hoped to be. There are many good articles that describe the qualities and skills that make a leader inspiring and transformative (see for example, Campbell & Rudisill 1999; Dixon 1999; Porter-O'Grady 1999; Warden 1999). The philosophy of leadership called servant leadership has provided meaningful and consistent beliefs in my role as chief nursing officer (Hunter 1998). This philosophy elevates notions of meaning, relationship, humility, partnership and empowerment so that service is the focus of the leader and staff cultivate a strong sense of ownership and responsibility.

Establishing vision and direction

Articulating a vision for change with more than 2000 nurses in a large university hospital that has itself experienced major change, including an amalgamation and financial crisis, can be very challenging. I have found that change theories directing leaders to advance people through various stages and phases before executing desired change—are not helpful or consistent with my experience. Real change is about personal choice, and like every personal choice, change happens differently with every person and at a different speed and with different questions amid different thoughts and feelings. Human change is a dynamic process that can be engaged and inspired but not controlled or manipulated by a leader. I would suggest that real change requires mutual respect and quality of relationship, meaningfulness and clarity of intent, fortitude and vulnerability.

Getting ideas into the public discourse was the first hurdle on the road from provider to patient-focused care. I decided to publish a newsletter that acted as the vehicle to introduce ideas to the community of professionals at S&W. Ideas covered in the newsletter included notions of different paradigms of science, how values get translated in practice, the limitations of the *fix-it* model of health care, and the meaning of patient-focused care. The newsletter sparked debate and, in keeping with real change, much of the debate for the first year was particularly challenging and negative. The predominant message from staff early in the change was pretty much 'no thank you'—not always said so politely. The predominant message from my supervisor, the CEO and president of the hospital was: if you are not upsetting somebody you are not doing your job. Thank heavens for his insight. I needed his understanding and public support, especially during the first years.

The newsletter became the vehicle for extending the debates and the community dialogue. For example, one issue of the newsletter focused on the most common reasons given by staff for why patient-focused care could not be practised. Common reasons offered by staff for why patient-focused care could not or need not be practised included the following:

▲ There is no time to practise patient-focused care.

▲ It is impossible to let people lead their own care because people do not know what they do not know.

▲ Patient-focused care will lead to chaos and anarchy.

▲ Health care systems do not have the resources to be able to give people what they want.

▲ Staff are already focusing on patients, so the suggested patient-focused care model is unnecessary.

▲ Social workers and psychologists are the professionals who attend to what patients want, so there is no need for other professionals to practise in a patient-focused way.

These statements show how new ideas can be viewed and sometimes misunderstood. Patient-focused care is not about people getting what they want at others' expense, and the philosophy does not lead to mayhem, as feared by some. Patient-focused care can actually save time and help professionals focus on what is most important to patients and families. In my 30 years of experience I have seen more upset and clashes of will when practice models do not respect patients as knowledgeable partners in their care. Along with those staff who offered reasons for why they could not change were those who indicated a willingness to engage the ideas and a desire to become a practitioner who lived the values of the patient-focused model.

Daring to dream

There are always people who dare to dream and who are able to picture an alternative reality that is worth pursuing. This group of dreamers stepped forward and many chose to clarify and articulate their personal alignment with patient-focused care and the human becoming theory (Parse 1981, 1987, 1992, 1995, 1997, 1998). Nurses and other professionals connected through dialogue in order to advance the change in culture from provider to patient-focused care. Professional leaders developed a course to create opportunities for staff to come together to reflect on their personal values and beliefs and to begin the process of introducing alternative beliefs and alternative practice approaches (Bournes & DasGupta 1997; Linscott et al. 1999). Over time, practice leaders were integrated in clinical programs and their responsibilities to help transform the organisation became more formalised and more visible in the organisation. Along the journey, staff looked to symbols of leadership for inspiration and encouragement.

Figure 20.1 The Inukshuk: A symbol of leadership

There are many symbols of leadership. At S&W's, leaders identified with the Inukshuk. The Inukshuk is a structure of human form that has been providing direction to humans in Northern Canada since the last Ice Age. Inukshuks show the way so that others can keep moving to distant horizons. It is important to realise that the Inukshuk can show the way but the traveller must choose to go there. The Inukshuk stands for knowledge and the wisdom of those who have gone that way before. It is a symbol that depends on community and vision for meaning. At S&W's the Inukshuk stands for transformation, community and hope.

Establishing organisational support

Leaders are able to influence and inspire others. They can present opportunities and invitations to learn and change. But one thing that has been shown is that leaders need organisational support in order to help staff sustain change.

Organisational change of the magnitude happening at S&W requires strong and ongoing support from senior leaders, including Board members. Resistance to real change is intense and if people do not believe there is a strong organisational commitment, sustained change may be thwarted. Senior management at S&W not only verbally supported the change to patient-focused care, they also trusted the instincts of the CNO and other leaders to create a new, advanced practice nursing role called the professional practice leader (PPL). It was the PPL who became the primary change agent within clinical programs and services (Bournes & Das Gupta 1997; Linscott et al. 1999; Mitchell et al. 2000).

The PPL at S&W is a Master's prepared nurse who has the knowledge and the commitment to lead the change to patient-focused care. This means a knowledge base consistent with human science nursing theories like human becoming and the commitment to a culture of care where patients are truly respected as partners and as experts about their own health and quality of life. The professional leaders accepted the challenge of being the direct change agents on units with teams of their colleagues. I know that many professional leaders encountered pressure, ridicule, sabotage, critique and rejection while advancing the philosophy of patient-focused care. It can be a real test of conviction to engage conflict and rejection day after day. The idea of facing conflict and rejection was a common topic of discussion among staff nurses, who were also challenged by their colleagues for being the first ones to change. Professional leaders and staff also experienced a renewed sense of joy and satisfaction with their practice. A sense of growth and professional development reported by staff nurses inspired others and helped to create and sustain a grass roots movement to patient-focused care.

The PPLs and the CNO met regularly to discuss how change was progressing and to strategise about how to keep pushing and resisting with the staff and the realities of trying to do things differently. The PPL group used metaphors to describe their realities. Discussion would flow from talk of swimming with the sharks, and scaling steep cliffs, to watching a butterfly emerge from a cocoon. Most days the metaphors were a mixture of dark and light, fear and uncertainty, commitment and despair. Fortunately the leaders were at different places with change and so they were able to support each other, as one by one they moved with times of great challenge, as well as times of great joy and success. When the change started to happen for staff nurses, they too had times of fear and uncertainty, excitement and upset. During these times of uncertainty and fear, the professional leaders would be there to support staff and to help them think of strategies for keeping on.

One strategy staff nurses relied on was to imagine themselves in a situation with colleagues when they had to rely on moral courage to stick to their convictions. Nurses viewed the movie *Babe*, for example, to review the scene where the farmer—breaking with all tradition—took the pig, Babe, instead of the sheep dog, onto the field to herd the sheep. The crowds jeered and slung caustic comments at the farmer for daring to be different. However, once the crowd saw that the pig could successfully herd the sheep, the crowd shifted to celebrate the farmer's ingenuity. So too, nurses had to be courageous enough to withstand the jeers and pressures of colleagues who wanted them to get back in line and stop rocking the boat. Fortunately, the philosophy and standards of patient-focused care, as well as the human becoming theory, for those who choose to live it, make a favourable and meaningful difference in practice, and this difference sustains the grass roots change. Patient-focused care philosophy helps nurses to be more like the nurses they want to be, and this professional integrity makes all the difference.

Strategies for engaging discomfort and enhancing dialogue

One of the most important strategies for nurturing change at S&W was the creation of a course for staff (Linscott et al. 1999; Mitchell & Bournes 1998). More than 1500 multi-professional staff have attended the patient-focused course which was held several hours a week for eight consecutive weeks. Evaluations from the course consistently indicate that staff listen more to patients, involve patients and families in decisions, and act on patient concerns and issues more frequently after taking the course. Staff are given a certificate and celebratory luncheon upon completion of the course and many invite their managers and other leaders to witness their success and to hear staff testimonies about how they have changed with new knowledge and understanding of patient-focused care. Staff on units with managers who support the patient-focused philosophy report greater success with integrating standards of care and with teamwork.

Creating standards of care

The purpose of the patient-focused care course, which happens in small groups for several hours a week over eight weeks, was to create a safe space for questioning and challenging traditional beliefs and for considering alternative views and options about how to be with persons and families (Linscott et al. 1999; Mitchell & Bournes 1998). The course provides leaders with opportunities to introduce alternative frameworks for thinking about familiar situations. It has become clear that to think differently, nurses need different knowledge. Nurses need to be given opportunities to engage alternative ways of thinking so that they can choose whether or not they want to change their practice based on what they have just learned (Bournes & Das Gupta 1997; Linscott et al. 1999).

The course was also the primary way that practice leaders and staff discussed and explored the patient-focused standards that were written by nurses on Council with the Chief Nursing Officer (Mitchell 1998). The standards developed during the early years of patient-focused care were linked to the following core processes:

1 *Identifying concerns*—Staff approach individuals (patients, families, groups) with the intent to identify concerns and issues. Staff listen to individuals and their meanings, needs and hopes.

2 *Decision-making*—Staff and individuals clarify and discuss priorities and explore options and plans for care and service.

3   *Care and service*—Staff document individuals' concerns and needs and the professional actions taken to address priorities.

4   *Evaluating outcomes*—Individuals (persons, families, groups) evaluate change and progress towards desired goals. Staff record individuals' evaluations.

Nurses developed self-learning guides, a video and a course outline in order to advance learning about patient-focused care. Staff began to embrace the changes being witnessed and experienced when they followed the patient-focused standards. The human becoming nursing theory (Parse 1981, 1987, 1992, 1995, 1997, 1998) inspired the way patient-focused care was translated and practised. It is the nursing theory that provides a continuous source of understanding human beings differently. The human becoming theory inspires a kind of practice that is different from and complementary to clinical nursing (Mitchell & Cody 1999). Indeed, clinical indicators of quality and outcomes related to patient safety may be improved significantly when nurses follow a philosophy and standards based on human becoming (Mitchell & Pilkington 2000; Whittemore 2000). Additional research is required to increase understanding about how the human becoming theory favourably impacts quality of care (Parse 1995).

The theory of human becoming (Parse 1981, 1987, 1992, 1995, 1997, 1998) also inspires resistance and rejection among some nurses who are uncomfortable with the basic beliefs and tenets of the framework. And so it continues today. Some nurses articulate a clear link with the human becoming theory (see for example, Jonas-Simpson 2001; Ross 1997). Other nurses identify with the basic values and beliefs of patient-focused care but not with the human becoming theory. And still others are aligned with the more traditional belief system of clinical nursing. Diverse values are reality and they coexist and co-mingle with nursing leaders who inspire and support patient-focused care. What is most important is articulation of the intent and actions of nurses and the awareness that nursing is a knowledge-based discipline whose members require theory in order to practise in a reflective and deliberate way.

Nurses require opportunities to think and speak about their practices, the change to patient-focused care, and the knowledge that helps them to be the nurses they want to be and become. Nurse leaders are responsible for facilitating the dialogue and the transformation to different ways. Some of the topics discussed by groups included the *what* and *how* of the following desired changes.

Table 20.1 Desired changes for staff learning to practise patient-focused care

Changing from	Changing to
Focusing on persons as problems who need to be diagnosed and fixed	Focusing on persons as complex beings who, as partners in care, know best about their own quality of life
Thinking of persons in terms of data and generalisations	Respecting individual realities and personalising care and service according to client values and priorities
Teaching and telling people	Listening and believing people
Dispensing standardised information	Providing meaningful dialogue and relevant information
Expecting compliance	Enabling choice

Nurses also discussed the language that was used when speaking about patients and families, and a new way of talking with and about people was developed. Staff proposed words that were commonly used when caring for people and then they explored origins of the words and what it might be like to have such words used on oneself or with a loved one. New words were also discussed in order to explore their consistency with the patient-focused philosophy. Dialogue helps nurses to make choices about what words they want in their nursing vocabulary.

Table 20.2 Words to speak and think about

Difficult	Experience	Unrealistic
Dysfunctional	Presence	Perspective
Uncooperative	Choice	Values
Inadequate	Multidimensional	Mystery
Noncompliant	Discovery	Demanding
Emotional	Uniqueness	Data
Being with	Opportunities	Objectivity
Mutual Process	Situated Freedom	Determinism
Prescription	Participation	Meaning
Generalisation	Intentionality	Causal

ACCOUNTABILITY AND NURSING PRACTICE: IMPLICATIONS FOR LEADERS

Leaders are responsible for enabling processes of care that support professional nursing practice and for modelling the very beliefs and values that they want to nurture in staff. Most recently, nurse leaders, in collaboration with staff nurses, have developed indicators that will help to evaluate progress towards excellent care and service. The group linked indicators from patient surveys and chart audits. For example, in a provincial patient survey, patients are asked to indicate how comfortable they feel when discussing concerns with nursing staff. Patients are also asked how much respect they experience. Nurses have three years of survey findings that provide a way to see if specific standards and systems of accountability can help nurses to improve patient experiences as captured by the survey.

Indicators also help nurses decide how they want to focus in particular ways to work on improving quality of care across the organisation. For example, nurses across the three campuses of S&W may select pain management as one area to improve over the next year. Such a commitment requires the involvement and support of other disciplines as well as managers. This nursing quality improvement initiative requires leaders across the organisation to inspire, teach and monitor progress towards desired change.

Another area that is favourably influenced by S&W's commitment to patient-focused care is nursing morale and the meaningfulness of nursing work. Nurses have three years of survey findings that indicate both morale and meaningfulness are increasing for nurses at S&W. Findings show that despite high acuity and workload, nurses believe their work is very meaningful. On a scale of one to seven, 640 nurses scored 5.5 on the question of how meaningful they thought their work was.

It is important to strive to meet performance indicators for quality of care. And it is important to note the things that are not measured or tracked. There is not currently, to my knowledge, any way of examining acts of omission—all the things that do not happen, that should or could happen. How do we capture times when nurses do not listen, do not attend to patients' pain and suffering, do not address the concerns, fears, and needs of persons? What are your thoughts about acts of omission? Are you aware of any acts of omission in your workplace?

Teaching—learning about values

One thing that has become clear to me over the past eight years as CNO is that organisational change happens through individual discovery and commitment to live a certain set of values and beliefs. Teaching–learning opportunities happen through dialogue as nurses think about and express their stories about what happens in their relationships with patients and families. Nursing leaders are skilled at helping nurses explore their beliefs and to consider alternative views of reality. We have learned that it is not enough to ask people to be different. Along with that request must come an alternative way to think and act and a rationale for change that is value-based.

The patient-focused course is changing as S&W continues to evolve as a new and dynamic teaching centre. The new course will integrate universal lived experiences that have been identified as important to women, older persons, and others engaging health care systems. Each teaching–learning session will include a discussion about how the staff think about the experience—how they have lived it, what the literature says about the lived experience, and how practice might be changed in light of the knowledge and understanding about the theme. For example, one theme identified is being listened to. Others include caring for another, deliberately choosing to move on, feeling vulnerable, feeling respected, and living with loss.

The standards and teaching–learning strategies for patient-focused care were originally inspired by the human becoming theory and the theory continues to be helpful to nurses and other disciplines for thinking about practice and for designing research programs that will inform understanding about lived experiences of health and quality of life. The patient-focused standards and teaching–learning format have been useful for leaders and nurses in many other health care settings. The Registered Nurses Association of Ontario (RNAO) has published Best Practice Guidelines on Client Centred Care that were informed by the S&W standards (for information go to: www. rnao. org). Nurses are encouraged and supported by leaders in the organisa-tion to practise patient-focused care, and to demonstrate the principles of women's health and ageing when organising and providing care and service. Indeed, actions and attitudes consistent with patient-focused care, women's health and ageing have been identified and incorporated into corporate goals and performance reviews for all staff, and for guiding clinical programs as strategic plans and goals are developed.

STRATEGIES FOR ENHANCING QUALITY, HUMANITY AND CARING IN NURSING PRACTICE

My advice to any nursing leader or any nurse who wants to be a leader is to keep focused on the kind of nurse and the kind of leader you want to be and find what you believe in so you can inspire others with the passion of your convictions. There are many barriers to change and many obstacles to halt creative thinking and acting. When I have moments of discouragement, I often ask myself: What is the alternative to staying and sticking things out? You can always walk away from difficult situations. But I figure at the end of the day I want to be able to say that I lived what I believed, and lived with the consequences of my choices, even when they were challenging. Find mentors and authors who are meaningful to you and engage their work for inspiration.

CONCLUSION

Nursing is the most wonderful work. Being present with others in service and with the knowledge and skill to be helpful, is very honourable work. Nurses have been encouraged to obey the rules, follow the procedures, consult the authorities, refrain from upsetting others, avoid loving patients, provide the data and facts, believe in certainty, and compete to be the expert. Patient-focused care asks nurses to let go of these rules and trust that patients and families know the way and if they are respected as leaders of their care, they will show the way for professionals to make the greatest difference to their health and quality of life.

Professional nursing requires courage—to step outside the rules and to risk the security of mediocrity. Nurses will have more opportunities to be helpful when they develop comfort with the ambiguity and uncertainty of genuine relationships. There is an old Chinese proverb I like: 'To be uncertain is uncomfortable, but to be certain is ridiculous' (Ash 1996, p.107).

Leadership is about challenge, opportunity, and choice. Opportunity brought me face to face with the knowledge and language of human science and the human becoming theory (Parse 1981, 1987, 1992, 1995, 1997, 1998, 2001c). The opportunities with human becoming theory have helped me to develop a deep and sustaining knowledge base of lived experience and human quality of life. Challenge has primarily taken the form of exclusion; meaning being ignored and excluded from some groups and activities. And choice has led to integrity and trust. I consider leadership an honour and a privilege, and if I have made any difference it is because of the wonderful nurses, colleagues and mentors who have lifted me on their wings.

Reflective exercise

1 Consider the following questions about your beliefs about nursing.

   a What are your personal beliefs about nursing theory?

   b Which nursing theories best fit with your personal beliefs about how people experience and live health and quality of life?

   c How do you want to practise with clients?

   d What is most important for you as a nurse?

   e What do you want others to remember about you as a nurse?

2 Think of a symbol from your life that might stand for leadership. What is it about the image that links with leadership? What qualities of a leader are most important from your perspective? What kind of a leader do you want to become? Which leader in nursing would you like to interview? What would you ask that leader?

3 Imagine a time at work when you want to say or do something that goes against the customary or the status quo. Picture how you might act when your colleagues tease and pressure you to get back in line. You may be teased and even denied help. How will you be with that situation? What beliefs do you have that could withstand such an attack? What might help you to have moral courage? With whom can you discuss your values and beliefs?

4 Think about the meaning of the words in Table 20.2. Look up some definitions. Discuss how health care professionals use the word. What does the word mean to you? What messages accompany the word? How do you feel about using the word with others?

RECOMMENDED READINGS

Bournes, D. A., & DasGupta, T. L. (1997). Professional practice leader: A transformational role that addresses human diversity. *Nursing Administration Quarterly, 21*(4), 61–86.

Cody, W. K., Bunkers, S. S., & Mitchell, G. J. (2000). The human becoming theory in practice, research, administration, and education. In M. Parker (ed.), *Nursing theories and nursing practice* (pp.238–62). Philadelphia, PA: F. A. Davis.

Hunter, J. C. (1998). *The servant: A simple story about the true essence of leadership.* Rocklin, CA: Prima.

Linscott, J., Spee, R., Flint, F., & Fisher, A. (1999). Creating a culture of patient focused care through a learner-centered philosophy. *Canadian Journal of Nursing Leadership, 12*(4), 5–10.

Mitchell, G. J., Closson, T., Coulis, N., Flint, F., & Gray, B. (2000). Patient focused care and human becoming thought: Connecting the right stuff. *Nursing Science Quarterly, 13,* 216–24.

Mitchell, G. J., & Cody, W. K. (1999). Human becoming theory: A complement to medical science. *Nursing Science Quarterly, 12,* 304–10.

Parse, R. R. (1998). *The human becoming school of thought: A perspective for nurses and other health professionals.* Thousand Oaks, CA: Sage.

CHAPTER TWENTY-ONE

Clinical leadership in action: Developing the health care management team

Robert Anders & James A Hawking

LEARNING OBJECTIVES

At the completion of this chapter, the reader will be able to:

- ▲ identify exactly where the process of leadership begins;
- ▲ identify a number of qualities of leadership, their definitions and potential impact on the nursing unit;
- ▲ identify why a nursing unit should depend on the team and how the team can benefit the quality of patient care and the management of risk within the organisation;
- ▲ identify the steps that a nurse leader should follow in building a winning team within the nursing unit;
- ▲ identify general rules that the nurse leaders should follow when working with senior managers;
- ▲ identify steps and recommendations to follow for presenting problems to a member of senior management; and
- ▲ identify the historical reasons for the tensions between doctors and nurses.

KEY WORDS

Teamwork, diversity, delegation, team building

INTRODUCTION[1]

The concept of leadership that relies on teamwork and building success through consensus management is substantially different from the concept of leadership that was taught to health care managers just a single generation ago. In today's demanding health care environment, the effective nurse leader knows that success depends on the ability to get others to *want* to do the things that need to be done, rather than simply ordering people to perform. Ability to do this begins with placing the needs of those individuals that she leads ahead of her own. This means that her mission, from its creation through its realisation, needs to include staff every step of the way. A mission that is simply goal driven, with no concern for the individual staff member, is a recipe for failure.

Obviously, the most expeditious method of accomplishing anything in the nursing unit is to simply order someone to perform what is necessary to get it accomplished. But that procedure is seldom truly effective and is not representative of what leadership in health care requires today. Today, the nurse leader will have difficulty finding anyone who will tell her that leading her unit will be an easy process to accomplish, or that dictatorial direction is the most proficient method of management, because those things simply are not true. In fact, developing and leading a team of professionals in today's health care organisation is far more difficult than simply giving orders to the staff. But the extra effort required to accomplish the process is worth the price because the effect that a well-organised and motivated team can have on the success of a nursing unit is readily apparent. In virtually every performance area known, team performance has proven itself to be far superior to individual accomplishment. The hard work and effort that the nurse manager puts into developing and managing her team will pay off in increased production, higher quality patient care, lower turnover and absenteeism, lower risk, and improved staff loyalty (Blanchard 1999).

The effort required to build a team of professionals, regardless of the specific environment in which it is developed, starts with the leader, but must be participated in by every member of the staff. In fact, there can be no team if the person in charge decides that she will assume the responsibility for everything accomplished by the group. Performance must be a team event, with both the leader and the followers accepting responsibility for their individual actions and the accountability that goes with it.

There is no quick or simple way to develop nursing leaders or the teams of performers that will follow them. It is a process of learning, trusting, supporting, and, above all, caring. It requires managers and individual members of the staff to continually extend themselves towards improvement and never allow themselves or any member of their team to be above gaining new insights or studying innovative procedures and methods (Loeb & Kindel 1999).

CREATING A WINNING TEAM

The sensations experienced through winning and success are extraordinary. These sensations alone should provide a natural incentive for leaders to create the best possible teams, but that is not always the way things occur. In fact, it takes a tremendous amount of effort, perseverance and insight to create a winning team. The leader must employ an understanding of human nature, as well as demonstrate an ability to carefully align skills and personalities. It is the effort put into the creation of the team by the leader that ultimately signals the team's ability to succeed.

While most people in leadership roles will be quick to acknowledge the importance of the team, few really understand what needs to be done to create, nurture and guide such a unit (Belasco & Stayer 1994). As the complexity of health care continues to grow, the practice of effective team creation will become more and more critical to future success; therefore, it is important that every nurse manager understands what team building is about. If the individual nurse manager implements and follows the procedures outlined below, she should be able to develop effective teams that will satisfy the growing demands of her unit (Melohn 1994).

Step 1—Hire the right people

If you have ever watched children pick teams for a game of baseball, you can understand the fundamentals necessary in selecting the right people for a team. The leaders will carefully pick the most capable, the most proficient, the fastest, and the smartest from the available group. Gradually, the group will be teamed off, until only the perceived poor performers are left.

In the business of health care, it's the individual unit leader who is responsible for choosing the members of her team. Even when a new leader inherits a pre-established team, there is usually an opportunity to reshuffle and realign until the leader feels the maximum potential has been developed out of the raw material she inherited.

A successful team, regardless of its size or complexity, is realised through the combined efforts of the people that comprise it (Belasco & Stayer 1994). The individual staff members are joined to form a performance team that ultimately becomes the foundation of the nursing unit. It is through the individual staff members that the patient *perceives* the quality of care provided. Because it is the perception of the patient that governs the quality of the unit, the process of obtaining the proper people to make up the nursing team becomes one of the most critical parts of running the nursing unit. Or, in very simple terms, the best way to avoid problems in patient care is to hire only the very best of the available high quality personnel (people who meet or exceed the standards of the unit) (Hawkins 1997).

As the leader of the nursing unit, the nurse manager must keep herself, and the members of her team, extremely concerned with exactly whom they *allow* to become new members of the team. The reason for being extremely careful is easy to understand; the people that they *allow* to join will eventually become the exact individuals who help shape the unit's and, ultimately, every individual team member's continued success. The people that the nurse manager hires become part of the only real tool she has to perform the mission she has been given. With this thought in mind, it becomes very easy to see just how critical it is for the manager to put the right person, at the right time, in the right position. Failure to accomplish this fundamental process correctly is more than simply wrong; in fact, such an error can have wide-ranging ramifications. One of the truisms of management is that it is better to keep the position open than hire the wrong person. The nurse manager should resist the natural impulse to allow the availability of qualified personnel, or lack thereof, to influence her determination to find a quality employee.

Step 2—Make your team diverse

Diversity is one of those words that mean different things to different people. Mostly, 'diversity' in today's business language means the process of incorporating people who are culturally different from the traditional Caucasian who has dominated the business scene for most of the twentieth century. However, for the purposes of this chapter, let's focus on a narrower meaning of the word.

When you are building your team, it is important that you do not create it in your own image (Nanus & Bennis 1997). A team should not be a reflection of the leader. The team should perhaps complement the leader's style and beliefs, but in large part should present a means for providing:

▲ An offset for the shortcomings of the leader—No one can do everything well, or has the ability to do all of the things that a team will have to perform. Therefore, the leader should look for people who have skills that the leader does not have. The truly professional manager understands that she needs expertise that both complements her talents and offsets her shortcomings. To not select personnel who are capable of providing this necessity is unprofessional. (Some managers actually hire people they feel comfortable with, and that they do not feel will offer a challenge to them. If you are one of these managers, you are doing yourself, your unit, and your organisation a severe disservice.)

▲ A wide range of views—You will want people who perceive things differently than you do. While it is certainly more difficult to manage people who view things differently, it is also an invaluable asset to have different outlooks available to you. These different views can provide you with at-hand information about market diversity, the potential impact of actions, and different opinions. All of these are invaluable to the leadership of a growing company.

▲ Different skills—When hiring different members of the group, look for people who possess varying skills. Some might be technically oriented, others good administrators, and still others have excellent sales and service skills. The mix will provide the growing business with resident expertise and the ability to cross-train individual members of the team.

While it is generally preferred to lead a team comprised of seasoned veterans, it is most often far more productive to have a good mix of experience and youth. The rookies will force you to sacrifice a little in the professional categories, but they will bring you a fresh perspective and significantly different attitudes. Part of the problem with hiring elite professionals is that they have *been there and done that*—some of them many times before—and others will think that they have. While experience provides benefits, a growing organisation needs to have enthusiasm, energy and a willingness to try new approaches and concepts. If you load your team down with too much experience, you may be creating a situation where the flexibility you need most will be sacrificed to those who are unwilling to deviate from traditional roles and approaches (Mackay & Blanchard 1999).

We have said that diversity is what you want to strive for in establishing your team. Now, let's throw in a word of caution: Do not try to make your team too diverse. Diversity can also work against you. For example, if you look into the talent pool and select nothing but newcomers with new, untested ideas, you will run the risk of having to spend your time acting like a firefighter, running from place to place putting out fires. A classic example of bringing in too many young, talented and creative people and not enough seasoned veterans can be seen by reviewing the performance of the Clinton White House in its first 90 days. President Clinton brought a tremendous pool of talented, excited and energetic individuals with him to staff the White House; the problem was that very few, including the President and First Lady, had previous experience in government at that level and together they made some colossal errors. Seemingly insignificant decisions, such as how the White House travel office would be run, ended in a powerful backlash and embarrassing situations for the new president and his government. The lesson learned from the early Clinton days was that intelligence, desire and imagination are not all that is needed to run an organisation. These things need to be tempered with experience and commonsense. Too many inexperienced people will force the leader to spend a disproportionate amount of time solving their problems, instead of working on the team's goals.

Step 3—Limit team size

The successful team is begun a long time before the first team member is placed. Quality nurse managers will begin developing their team on paper by building a perfect model: i.e. what would the team look like if the organisation could provide the nursing unit with unlimited resources (money, material and people)? After the perfect 'dream' team is constructed, the quality leader will immediately start to restructure it so that it fits into the reality of the current nursing unit environment. To do this, the nurse manager asks herself questions such as: 'Who or what can I do without?' and 'Who or what can be eliminated without degrading the potential performance of the team?'

Believe it or not, having a team that is 'traditional in size' means very little in establishing its effectiveness or ability to contribute effectively. For example, a 'traditionally-sized' professional softball team has nine starting players and a roster of approximately 25 support players. People throughout the sport use the number 34 as the 'required' size of a ball team, the belief being that less would not provide sufficient depth to get the team through the season. However, during much of the first half of the twentieth century, a softball team comprising of just five players, and no reserves, toured the country playing other professional ball teams. There was a pitcher of incredible talent, a first baseman, an infielder, outfielder and a catcher. These five players studied softball as a science.

While the nursing unit is a far cry from a baseball field, good ones are developed around a team concept that involves very similar concepts, and, if developed correctly, a small, well-honed team can and will always outperform a large, unprepared one (Bridges 1998). It is not the size that matters in softball, or in nursing—it is the quality. As the developer of the nursing unit's team, the nurse manager should always be looking to 'right-size' her team. In fact, it is a primary responsibility of management to continually look for means to reduce costs and overhead expenses, and if you are not taking hard looks at the size of your unit and developing methods of getting the work done more efficiently and with fewer personnel, you are not doing the complete job. If, however, you are doing these things, your efforts should be governed by the following two basic concepts of team management:

▲ Do not overwork the team—reducing the size of the team, and then forcing the remaining members to pick up the workload of the departed team members can only work if there is a balance between workload and team members. This means that the workforce should not be reduced out of a whim, or because it is fashionable, or even if your immediate senior wishes you to do so (you may have to in this circumstance, but it would then be necessary to advise your senior of the potential ramifications of such an action). While it is important to keep team members challenged by ensuring that each has a full requirement of responsibility, loading them up to a point where they are so burdened that they cannot perform well, or have little or no time for creativity, or they make mistakes, is foolhardy. If you cause the team to become burdened in this regard, what you will be creating is an environment that no one wants to work in, and one in which absenteeism and turnover rates will exceed acceptable norms.

▲ Do not put the team in danger—increasing workload can have severe mental and physical ramifications for the individual members of the team, and this includes the nurse manager. Overworked and highly stressed performers who do not have the time to offset their responsibilities with relaxation and diversity soon see their health failing. Unhealthy people do not make quality decisions, maintain enthusiasm, or continue to work in the same job. The end result of this is that the patient quality provided by the unit will decrease, and absenteeism and turnover will skyrocket totally off the chart. Team members will take the time to care for themselves, and increased sick time will make the nurse manager's job exceptionally difficult. Do not put your team or any of its members at risk.

Step 4—Establish an agenda

As the team leader, it is the nurse manager's responsibility to determine the team's agenda. An agenda is a step-by-step process by which work flows through the group. The leader is tasked with the responsibility of deciding what the individual priority is, where resources and effort should be concentrated, where the opportunities are, what is worth taking advantage of and what is worth passing on.

As the team leader of a dynamic nursing unit, the nurse manager's job is not as clear-cut as it would be if she were managing a baseball team or if she were a military commander. Those leaders live and work in very structured environments and individual team members perform very well-defined roles. In nursing, it is not that easy. Staff nurses are well-educated and individually capable professionals who look to perform their job with little or no supervision, and who, on their own, frequently handle difficult assignments that do not fall in the realm of what is considered normal. Therefore, setting the nursing unit's agenda is not a clear-cut process. For one thing, the day-to-day operation of the nursing unit has no cast-in-concrete standard body of rules; for another, what constitutes winning and losing is not always clearly defined; and still another is that individual performer's roles can actually change as the circumstances demand it. Therefore, an astute nurse manager needs to identify a different method of establishing her team's agenda than what would be used by a baseball coach or military officer. The following approach is offered for consideration; however, if it is used, its contents should be modified to fit your unit's specific circumstances.

Have regular team meetings

Meetings often present an inexpensive method of keeping the team's agenda in front of all of the members. It is the role of the leader to maintain a sense of consistency in these meetings, a job that can easily be done if she establishes and follows a standard format each time the team gets together. There are a variety of methods that can be used, but whatever you decide, stick to it and keep the meetings germane to team business.

CAUTION: Meetings have a way of becoming perceived as social gatherings and periods of time off unless they are kept short and to the point. High quality leaders will ensure that their meetings are not held unless: (a) there is no other way to disseminate the intended information; (b) there is a specific agenda of topics to be discussed; and (c) a definite time period is established for the meeting.

It is also not a good idea to convene a meeting just to get the individual members together. Only under rare circumstances should a 'get-together' be accomplished in the guise of a business meeting. The difference between a meeting and a get-together is simple; i.e. business meetings have agendas, get-togethers do not. Even the smallest meetings should have an agenda available before the meeting is convened and minutes taken during its process, or it does not need to be held. There is no sense in having a meeting if it is not planned or if the information discussed is not recorded.

Review your goal and mission

Agenda-setting goes beyond controlling meetings. An agenda is also the combination of mission and goals, as well as the day-to-day challenges faced by your team, which you must talk over with the team and then take action to overcome. It is the job of the leader to keep the unit's vision, goals and objectives at the forefront of each team member's mind. The use of an agenda can be an effective tool for doing this. Simply make sure that each line item of the agenda is directly linked to a specific goal or objective, and that the vision is clearly printed on the paper. Go over the vision quickly, and when each agenda item is discussed, make sure that the goal it is linked to is identified. This is referred to as communicating the vision.

Review progress

The establishment of an agenda provides the nurse manager with an effective means of bringing the team's behaviour in line with the vision. It is imperative that the nurse manager continually reinforces the concept that the team's purpose is not simply to perform day-to-day functions, but to achieve higher goals. Team progress should always be measured against the unit's established goals, and the progress toward those goals is what the leader uses to motivate and reward the performance of the team.

Teams, no matter how well developed, often get to a point where they are content to continue their performance in a mode that is both comfortable and not very challenging. This behaviour (complacency), while certainly common enough, is a death knell for the dynamic nursing unit. As the leader of the unit, the nurse manager must keep the team motivated and excited. It is extremely important that she keeps every team member reaching toward a new goal, and is never willing to accept the mediocrity that complacency presents.

The nurse manager can keep the tempo exciting and the individual team members motivated if she rewards performance by recognising excellence and never tolerating mediocrity. When team members understand that they will excel only if the team does, then the team will move forward.

Step 5—Create a learning environment

It is imperative that everyone on the team learns from one another. The sharing of experiences, talent, opinions, creativity, attitudes and concepts is the biggest advantage of working with the challenges presented by the team concept (Dettmer 1998).

Teams learn as they perform, and keeping a record of successes and failures is important. The team leader should ensure that an accurate record of team accomplishments is kept, and that it is continually updated. Membership is rarely a permanent quality of the team, and the collective learning that can be developed through the team concept will need to be passed on to new members as they come on board, or even to a new team leader, for that matter. Suppose that the administrative demands of the nursing unit grow to a point where it is physically impossible for the nurse manager to take an active daily leadership role in the operation of the team, and an assistant is appointed to assist. The nurse manager spends more and more time in her office performing other duties and has direct contact with the team on a less frequent basis, and the assistant spends most of her time interacting with the team. What must not occur is the team arguing with the new assistant that they have already done what the leader wants to accomplish and failed. You will want to prepare your assistant to assume the clinical side of the nurse manager's role, and one of the best ways to do that is to provide a record of what you have done, and why it failed, or succeeded.

Keep a record for the team

The great United States explorer team of Louis and Clark kept a diary as they explored the West. Many professional researchers keep journals when they are working to solve a problem. If the nurse manager maintains a file that contains a copy of reports, analysis, observations of team behaviour, discipline concerns, morale issues, personal notes and opinions, internal correspondence, and hard copies of all email that is generated in respect to specific work issues, she will have a comprehensive turnover portfolio to hand to a new leader, or an assistant, as described above. This can also serve as a means to bring new members up to speed on team history if the nurse manager separates personal information from team issues.

Require the team to share information

If the team develops anything, whether as a result of group or individual activity, the developed entity belongs to the entire group. Failure to share should be considered detrimental to the best interests of the team, and the offender should be subject to an appropriate level of discipline.

It should be expected of the team that every member share information with the rest of the team. This means that individual and team skills should be shared to the greatest extent possible. The actual form that teaching takes can vary to fit the specific circumstances of the nursing unit and the material that is to be shared. Some teaching venues can be informal, such as in a team meeting (if appropriate notes of the meeting are taken), and others conducted in a formal training session.

Strive for best practice

If a member of the team develops a better way to do something, competent authority should review it and, if approved, it should be shared with the entire team, thereafter becoming part of its day-to-day practice. Write the procedure down, and make sure that each member sees it, then follow up to ensure that all members of the team are using it. When you see the new procedure in practice, offer congratulations and recognition; when you do not, ask why and correct the situation immediately.

Every nursing unit can take team learning and embed it into its operational procedures. Your organisation should keep a listing of best practices and update it frequently. When a new, better method is discovered, it should supersede the old. The nurse manager should include her performance tools, analytical reasoning processes, reporting requirements, performance methodologies, and processes for measurement and qualification in such a format that everyone can be made aware of them, they can be easily updated, and changed as necessary.

Step 6—Fix the problem, not the blame

There are two important parts of team building that are absolutely critical to the success of a team; they are:

▲ acceptance; and

▲ forgiveness.

The team needs to keep its focus on moving forward towards the accomplishment of the goals and mission of the company. Nothing can interrupt this focus more than an overzealous pursuit of placing blame; i.e. the witch-hunt (Hawkins 1999).

Things will go wrong. That is a part of nursing that is as predictable as change. Great organisations use these unfortunate occurrences as learning opportunities and not as persecution processes; the nursing unit should not be an exception. This process, or one very close to it, is used throughout the health care industry to examine why certain medical procedures turn out the way they do, and the knowledge gained is shared freely. Why should the day-to-day functions of the individual nursing unit be any different? After all, the goals of both are identical—improvement of patient care.

Building into the team a system of checks and balances eliminates problems. These checks are part of a monitoring system that the leader can use to measure performance on a continual, or at least a regular or ongoing basis. If a leader does not incorporate a system to monitor the performance of the team as part of normal business practice, then what goes wrong is the leader's fault, and no one else's. The team leader's job is to find ways to anticipate problems and to avoid them. If the efforts of the team are brought to a halt by a problem, and the individual members are busy pointing fingers and accusing each other, then the blame is always the leader's—and never any one else's. Therefore, there is never a need for a witch-hunt.

Those teams that have achieved significant notoriety in their fields often have been found to practise a technique for fixing problems instead of blame, that has been dubbed the loose constructional method. This term refers to a loose interpretation of the Constitution of the United States of America, and it says, '*Anything that is not expressly forbidden is permitted.*' For example, in the United States, the nurse manager can apply this procedure to her unit by letting it be known that any team member is free to complete assignments any way they wish, as long as nothing is done that has been expressly forbidden. How the team actually cares for the specific patient, as long as best practice is followed, is the responsibility of the whole team. By not handicapping the team's performance with a myriad of specific procedures that must be followed, the intelligent nurse manager is actually encouraging them to develop, on their own, solutions to problems that occur.

Of course, there is an opposite approach, known as '*strict constructionism*', and sometimes the application of this '*strict constructionism*', is just the thing that helps a team to move forward. Strict constructionism is also another constitutional law term. It says, '*Only that which is expressly permitted can be done*'. This process forces the team to follow a rigid approach to performance, and if your team's goals require tight adherence to tolerances, rules, and even appearances, this is the way to operate the team. You will find this type of leadership applied within many nursing units where little tolerance is allowed from established rules and regulations (McCormack 1988).

Step 7—Delegate

One of the most effective methods of developing the individual performer, and consequently the team, is to pursue an aggressive program of delegation and cross-training. While it is realistic not to expect everyone to perform proficiently at all levels of the organisation, each team member should be flexible enough to lend a hand in at least one performance area that is different from their primary focus. To facilitate this learning, the nurse manager must provide the opportunity and the motivation to learn. All too often, team members will be reluctant to share specific skills, and many times other team members will be reluctant to take on additional responsibilities. Providing the motivation for this exchange of knowledge is the team leader's responsibility. One of the best ways to accomplish this, without creating dissension, is to delegate.

Delegation is one of the most frequently overlooked responsibilities of the team leader (Muihead & Simon 1999). While it is important to allow your individual team members to perform their individual work, it will enhance the unit's growth if each staff member can take on a larger portion of the overall performance requirements, or act as a backup to another team member. The nurse manager, as the team leader, cannot, regardless of her personal skill and dedication, do everything. If she should try, experience says that her overall proficiency will be significantly reduced, and that will have a detrimental effect on the nursing unit's future success (Muihead & Simon 1999).

Many leaders resist delegation. These non–delegators delude themselves into thinking that they can perform most tasks better and faster than other people can. Senior administrators and highly experienced managers come by this belief honestly, through past experience, and should not be held up for ridicule for entertaining it. Most successful health care organisations got that way because their administrative leaders have had a history of being great performers.

It is natural that highly motivated leaders suffer frustration when work is done slower than when they themselves are used to doing it. Some even get irritated when there are errors that need correcting. Finally, almost every person who has built a successful career as a high quality performer will be amazed when someone new uses a different approach to perform a specific task. In short, it is difficult to give up what you really enjoy accomplishing.

However, the process of delegation is critical to continued growth of every organisation, and those people who do not, cannot or will not delegate create real problems within their organisations. When leaders continue to insist on either conducting the performance themselves, or micro-managing the performance of others, they run the risk of infuriating and demoralising their subordinates (Kriegel & Brandt 1997).

What then is delegation? And what is the leader's role in the process?

Delegation is the simple act of providing both the authority and responsibility for performance. Another member of the team must be given the authority to conduct the performance, and the responsibility to ensure that it is done correctly. This means the team member who is doing the work has the right to make choices, make decisions, use discretion and personal methods.

Additionally, team members must be held accountable for the actions used to complete the work and for the quality of their performance. While the team should be free to decide how they will accomplish the task, they must ensure that the method used allows for completion, accuracy and timeliness is approved, of high quality, and centred on providing quality patient care at low risk to the unit.

What is the team leader's role? The team leader's role starts with the actual delegation. The high quality leader makes sure that she delegates both elementary jobs and difficult ones—work that brings high return, and work that provides no return at all. The process of providing the team with all of the difficult or thankless work is commonly referred to as *dumping*. When a leader '*dumps*' assignments on junior personnel, the process of delegation will do little to enhance team performance. To the contrary, this type of action will only serve to reduce overall team performance.

The simple act of delegating the work, and the authority and responsibility for performance, does not reduce the leader's responsibility or overall authority for the success of the team. The team leader always retains the authority to ensure accurate and timely completion of the delegated task. The difference is how a leader applies this authority when working with subordinate personnel. High quality leaders administer this authority through a monitoring process that allows the leader to observe progress, offer suggestions for improvement, make recommendations for change, and assign more help to the project without interfering with the direction or actual performance itself.

Quality leaders are careful to channel their leadership through the person who has been delegated the authority for the project. What this means is that the team leader should not go to anyone other than the person who has received the authority and responsibility for the job to monitor the progress of the work. The job has been delegated; therefore, the team leader should offer suggestions for change and any alternative suggestions she might have only to the person who has the delegated authority. Additionally, the reward and recognition of success should also come through the delegated junior or, if the leader wishes, at least in the delegated junior's physical presence.

The team leader's role in the delegation process is one of a patient facilitator or coach. The team leader gives out the assignments, guides the performance and ensures accurate compliance. Throughout the process of completing the delegated task, the team leader reviews the work for accuracy and timely progression. It is critical that the leader performs this follow-up because it is she who is ultimately responsible for the completion of the task. Failure to follow up may mean that the project will be done wrong, or not meet the necessary deadline. If the team leader has not periodically checked on the project while it is in progress, she is responsible for any failure that may occur, and no part of this responsibility can be laid at the foot of the performer. (This goes beyond the normal fact that the leader always retains ultimate responsibility.)

Team leaders can realise the benefits of delegation if they: (1) exercise discretion when they delegate; (2) ensure clarity when they outline the project; (3) exercise patience when they guide performance; (4) use sensitivity when they offer suggestions and corrections; (5) be enthusiastic when they recognise excellence; and finally (6) reward noteworthy performance.

Reluctance to delegate is evident when a team leader asks the question, '*Do I just give 'em the ball?*' The answer is, of course, *probably not*. If the team leader exercises sensible management practices, she will be careful when passing the ball. That is, the team leader will not give out the work and disappear. Instead, she will be available to the group for assistance when requested, and periodically check on progress. This practice is called *follow-up*. Applied correctly, the team, and its individual performers, will truly believe they are controlling the project and the team leader will be comfortable with how the work is progressing. Delegation provides an excellent arena for the team leader to practise Management by Wandering Around (MBWA).[2] The mere act of the *wandering* around will put the team leader into contact with the team to ask gentle, persuasive questions that will gently steer the team onto the desired course, without providing the perception of micro-management.

One last word about delegation. The team must perceive that the leader is delegating work that will enhance the team's capability, or that is for the good of the unit or organisation. It is critical that the team leader is never perceived as delegating work that she simply does not want to do. Dumping unwanted, or undesirable, work is *not* delegation, and the practice can be disastrous to the team. Team leaders need to make sure that they delegate most of the good jobs and keep the undesirable work for themselves.

CONCLUSION

In this chapter we have provided you with some suggestions in how to build and maintain an effective health care team. The concepts, while seeming uncomplicated, are challenging for many managers to actually implement. The development of a productive team takes time and commitment from the manager. Today's nursing and health care environment demands efficient and productive work teams. The combined resources of many talented individuals are needed to plan, organise, implement and monitor the many changes required. Following the simple concepts described in this chapter will give the enlightened manager a distinct advantage in developing such a team.

Reflective exercise

Think about your area of practice. What key qualities would facilitate best practice in your area?

RECOMMENDED READINGS

Dettmer, H. (1998). *Breaking the constraints to world class performance.* Milwaukee, WI: ASQ Quality Press.

Kriegel, R., & Brandt, D. (1997). *Sacred cows make the best burgers: Developing change-ready people and organizations.* New York: Warner Brothers.

Melohn, T. (1994). *The new partnership.* Philadelphia: John Wiley & Sons.

Namus, B. & Bennis, W. (1997). *Leaders' strategies for taking change.* (2nd edn). New York, N.Y.: Harper Business.

ENDNOTES

1 This chapter is adapted from an electronic textbook Anders, R. and Hawkins, J. (2002) *Exceptional nursing management*. Directions, Inc.: Honolulu, Hawaii.

2 MBWA, or Management By Wandering Around is a process of leadership that causes the leader to turn her casual movements through the business environment into leadership opportunity. As the leader passes through the unit, she will talk to one person, thank another, remind someone of an upcoming event, let drop important information, casually follow up on a project, etc. By keeping the contact informal and low-keyed, the leader can verify, affirm, motivate, and encourage others without providing the perception of micro-management.

CHAPTER TWENTY-TWO

Governance of practice and leadership: Implications for nursing practice

Maria O'Rourke & Patricia M Davidson

At the completion of this chapter, the reader will be able to:

- ▲ demonstrate an understanding of the conceptual link between models of professional practice and governance of practice;

- ▲ appreciate the importance of the evaluation of professional practice;

- ▲ describe methods of evaluation of shared health outcomes; and

- ▲ identify an area of concern in their own workplace and develop a hypothetical model of shared governance and outcome evaluation

KEY WORDS

Governance, leadership, interdisciplinary practice, theory-based practice, sentinel events, visionary leadership

INTRODUCTION

This chapter aims to provide a rationale for the concept of governance of practice and describes the importance of this concept in contemporary clinical practice. The importance of a framework of governance for professional nursing practice is discussed and the utility of this framework for the achievement of optimal patient outcomes is explored. Of significance in this discussion is the nursing role in interdisciplinary teams. Models of governance also have important implications for existing nurse leaders and those of the future. Within this chapter the importance of evaluation of practice and its impact on patient outcomes is discussed and strategies to achieve this goal are proposed.

MODELS OF GOVERNANCE AND CONTROL OF PRACTICE

The concept of governance of practice has long been associated with the professions and the professional role (Bixler & Bixler 1966). This obligation carries with it the need for health professionals to be responsible for controlling the quality of their practice through oversight and monitoring, so as to ensure high quality care (Alfano 1971; Larson 1977; O'Rourke 1976). A variety of models of governance have emerged to assist professionals meet this obligation and play an important role in health care planning, improving care delivery and ensuring quality care. In the United States, shared governance is a common term, whereas in the United Kingdom the key concepts of shared governance are subsumed under the term clinical governance. In Australia, the term clinical governance is more prevalent. It is important, however, to distinguish between the different models of governance as each has its own variation and individual characteristics. In the United States, the term 'shared governance' is sometimes viewed with skepticism by some levels of management, which see it as a possible intrusion into operations and corporate authority.

Shared governance is defined as a decentralised approach to organisation and management that gives nurses a greater autonomy over their practice and workplace (O'May & Buchan 1999; Porter-O'Grady 1995; 2001; Prince 1997). This approach serves as a framework to support empowerment processes in clinical decision-making for nurses, and represents an excellent opportunity for nurses to play a leading role in health care planning, delivery and evaluation. This framework establishes processes by which professional staff in the workplace can participate in decisions that affect their practice, professional development and work environment. The trend towards governance mechanisms has emerged in response to a need for health professionals to take responsibility for their practice, monitor outcomes and to work together to achieve optimal outcomes. This is also in response to a perception of the failure of traditional, hierarchical models and the seduction of charismatic leadership. The importance of interdisciplinary collaboration and communication is underscored in models of clinical governance (Swage 2000).

To implement a mechanism of governance, organisational changes and mechanisms for participation in the decision-making process need to be established. In a hospital that implements shared governance, nurses are able to share information and opinions, increase responsibilities and improve their education, thereby increasing the opportunity to provide better patient care. Porter-O'Grady (2001) challenges health care systems to more effectively create their own destinies, and challenges leaders to develop new ways of thinking, knowing and doing, because he asserts this change of focus will improve health outcomes. It is important to remember that the underlying principle related to governance is ensuring that standards of professional practice are upheld.

Another model, termed clinical governance, has achieved considerable momentum with many nurses playing key roles in the decision-making of the health care system. Clinical governance means that there is organisational accountability for clinical performance, health outcomes and effective use of resources, including systems that regulate clinical activity, ensure patient safety and promote the highest standards of patient care (Swage 2000). In this approach, through an organised structure clinicians can be held accountable to make cost-effective choices that do not undermine the standard of practice or care. Clinical governance allows clinicians to work closely with management to identify and manage resources. In this chapter the discussion of clinical governance focuses upon the clinical practice setting.

WHY CLINICAL GOVERNANCE?

Increased autonomy and power for the professional role brings with it an increased measure of professional responsibility and accountability. Licensure and professional standards, as well as increasing expectations at government and local institutional level, regulate this accountability. As a result, professional practice is moderated and controlled on a range of levels from registration or licensure at a government level, development of professional standards of practice by professional and specialty organisations, and the individual's commitment to their goals of practice. By these mechanisms, professions such as nursing can exercise their power and authority to provide care through their knowledge and practice expertise. Implicit in accepting this power is a commitment to accountability for standards and evidence-based practice and participation in decision-making structures within the organisation. This acceptance of this power can be an empowering event in itself.

A recent report (Aiken et al. 2000) documents widespread nurse dissatisfaction with management. These authors report nurses feeling undervalued by management and not provided with adequate professional opportunities. Mechanisms of governance can likely overcome these concerns and become an impetus for recruitment and retention of nurses.

The professional work that nurses are authorised to do can be accomplished through governance structures (O'Rourke 1976, 1979, 1985, 1989, 2001). Professional practice is authorised and controlled on a range of levels from licensure at a government level to development of professional standards of practice by professional and specialty organisations, as well as through individual practitioner commitment to a code of ethics (ICN 2002). In order to implement an accountability-based practice model, management must institute structures that support the core business of patient care delivery (O'Rourke 2001). Further, management must nurture work environments that empower individuals to deliver patient care in an effective and efficient manner. In health care the professional disciplines, such as medicine and nursing, assume the important role of leader and decision-maker on the care team. These professionals require an environment that supports this professional work. Professional disciplines exercise powerful authority over the course of action to be taken and the impact on patient outcomes. Thus, it is important when discussing professional work to understand the essential elements of the professional role and its primary obligation to use standards to govern practice. Implicit in this role, professional work carries with it the requirement for monitoring and evaluating clinical practice to ensure the highest levels of quality (O'Rourke 1985, 1989).

The genesis for these role obligations is the definition of a profession which is defined as an occupation with special power and prestige granted by society because of the occupation's competence in esoteric bodies of knowledge that are linked to the central needs and values of the social system (Larson 1977). The three key dimensions of a profession derived from this definition include:

▲ the normative dimension, which includes the service orientation and ethics that justify the privilege of self-regulation. The profession regulates itself through professional standards of practice as well as statutory and regulatory bodies;

▲ the evaluative dimension, which includes autonomy and control of professional activity and monitoring of standards of practice. It is here that the governance structure of an organisation assists professionals to meet their role obligations and carry out their work; and

▲ the cognitive dimension, which includes the body of knowledge and techniques that are applied in practice, with necessary training and skill to master such knowledge.

Health professionals are bound by obligations, and governance structures help them keep their commitment to the public to deliver high quality care (Curtain 2000). Adherence to professional obligations provides the role authority for nurses and other professional disciplines to act on behalf of the patient. The professional role and role expectations, depicted in Figure 22.1, illustrate the rationale for governance of practice (O'Rourke 2001).

O'Rourke's model is based on three professional role components: scientist, leader and practitioner. These factors function to form a dynamically integrated set of expectations and competencies. From these three components are derived the expected role capacities of self-direction, theory-based practice, transfer of knowledge and provision of care (Alfano 1971; O'Rourke 1980, 1989, 2003). The three role elements are performed in concert so as to act synergistically with one another within one role and one person. These components cannot be separated.

This integrated set of expectations constitutes the professional role and expectations that are to be upheld, irrespective of the functional role held, such as staff nurse or educator. O'Rourke (2001) cautions not to turn these three role components into discrete, functional roles and assign them a job title. For example, one does not have to be hired as a nurse researcher to identify with the characteristics of a scientist and to demonstrate scientific accountability. Further, a registered nurse (RN) does not have to be in charge of the unit to demonstrate leadership in practice. Influencing care decisions through clinical leadership is an inherent part of the professional role, irrespective of the location or level practised by the RN.

Using these three components in dynamic interaction is a key competency of the professional role, irrespective of the discipline, particular role or specific job title. Nurses must be educated and socialised to see themselves in the role of scientist–practitioner–leader, a role that is prescribed for members of a profession. These considerations have significant implications for the education and preparation of nurses.

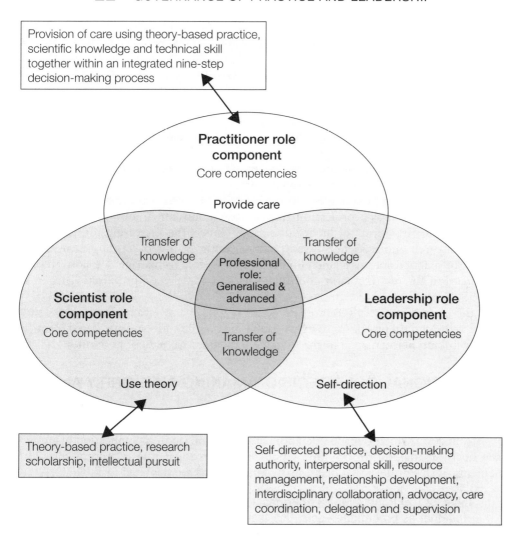

Figure 22.1 Professional role – A framework for role and competency clarification

PROFESSIONAL ROLE AUTHORITY AND ACCOUNTABILITY

An understanding of this model is particularly important because currently in health care a narrow view of the professional nursing role is being portrayed. This view describes a nurse as a practitioner who plans and supervises the implementation of tasks, generating an incomplete picture. When described in this way, nursing is not viewed as an intellectually-based practice discipline. This view de-emphasises the important value of our role to advance the cause of health and limits the consumer's understanding of our practice. The International Council of Nurses' (2002) definition of nursing includes promotion of health, prevention of illness and care of ill, disabled and dying patients. It is these goals and not the tasks that frame our thinking about what to do and how to do it.

Engaging in scholarly activity is essential for nurses, so that as key members of the team they can generate the science that helps determine whether their actions are helping people cope and manage their health and illness problems. Using nursing science within the team helps us to be better clinical leaders in directing and coordinating care and care delivery. The current overemphasis on the 'how to' and 'practical' thinking side of our practice obscures our larger social value as a profession. The 'how to' tasks must be performed in support of the goal of nursing, which is our independent function, and in support of the medical goal, which is our dependent function. Moreover, this incomplete and narrow view undermines the complexity of our professional role that stems from the interaction of the three professional role components; in this case the sum of the integration of practitioner, scientist and leader is more complex than each of the parts individually. Our practice authority stems from our public assertion as a profession that we use a substantial amount of scientific knowledge, not tradition, to direct our action. Hence, the increasing importance of nursing research and evidence-based practice. Without this overriding professional image, our practice authority and clinical leadership role to manage decisions that set the direction for recovery and coordinate patient care is compromised (Blegen et al. 1998).

In the United States, O'Rourke (1994, 2001, 2003) has used a professional practice model as the clinical practice system for establishing a role and standards-based practice, and for linking performance to the practice standard with patient outcomes.

PROFESSIONAL ROLE DECISION-MAKING AUTHORITY AND PROCESS

The professional role and its leadership position on the team is founded on the concept of self-direction which is made operational through the rigorous application of a nine-step decision-making process for which the professional role is accountable. The elements of this professional decision-making process are depicted in Table 22.1.

Table 22.1 O'Rourke Model of Professional Role Competence: Putting it all together as practitioner–scientist–leader. Professional practice requires nine core competencies

Professional Practice Process		
Six competencies	1	Data collection and data assessment
	2	Comprehensive assessment of the patient condition with diagnosis
	3	Planning
	4	Implementation
	5	Evaluation
	6	Teaching
Seventh competency	7	Dynamic integration of six steps using critical thinking
Eighth competency	8	Determination of stability of the patient condition
		• Breadth and depth of clinical knowledge and experience with the patient condition and patient population

cont.

Table 22.1 cont.

Professional Practice Process

Ninth competency	9 Dynamic integration of previous eight steps using
	• Critical thinking
	• Substantial scientific knowledge
	• Theory (general and discipline specific)
	• Use of research findings
	• Delegation and supervision
	• Care coordination

Source: Copyright 2002, Maria Williams O'Rourke.

Given this powerful decision-making authority, it is important that organisations set up structures that allow practice to be monitored to ensure quality, as well as linking that practice with patient outcomes. O'Rourke (2001, 2003) believes that in planning clinical care, intended outcomes must be considered and the health care member must be able to deliver this outcome in the most effective and efficient manner. Through governance structures organisations can assist the nursing profession to meet its professional duty to monitor and evaluate practice and support this important work in real time.

BUILDING A PATIENT CARE MODEL TO SUPPORT PROFESSIONAL ROLE ACCOUNTABILITY AND PRACTICE

An understanding of the professional role and its obligations is not enough to ensure that evidence-based practice is being implemented. Clinicians require a practice setting to implement their role, and therefore the organisational model for care delivery has major significance for the practitioner's ability to be empowered to do their professional work. Clinical practice is influenced by the organisation's structure, in that the structure serves to promote or control practice behaviour within the organisation (O'Rourke 2001). This control of practice is made operational through policies and procedures, which funnel and direct activity and resource allocation. For example, a tool as simple as a form can direct and reinforce practice behaviour. Professional, best practice goals can best be achieved through a well-designed and explicit patient care model. The patient care model of an organisation is the structure that guides and controls organisational behaviour related to the provision of care. A defined model ensures a consistent and systematic approach to care and care delivery. An example of a patient care model developed by O'Rourke is depicted in Figure 22.2. This model is composed of three components and supports the belief that the core operating system in the organisation is professional clinical practice and therefore the organisation must provide the environment for that practice to flourish. This can be accomplished through the development of governance structures within the organisation and is part of the organisational competence component of the O'Rourke model.

Establishing an environment conducive to maximising the knowledge and skill of the professional role enhances the effectiveness and efficiency of the organisation to produce high quality patient care. The structure of the clinical practice model

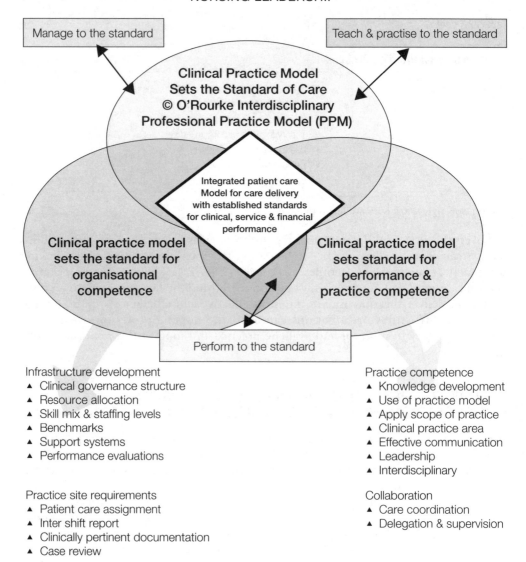

Figure 22.2 Patient care model—an integrated clinical practice system for improving the quality of care

determines the type and level of resources required. For example, in a professional practice model of care delivery, the number of RNs must be determined so as to uphold role obligations and professional standards. A governance structure helps to clarify and determine the nature of the model of care needed for a particular patient population and helps management better understand the need for obtaining appropriate resources. Moreover, the patient care model determines what roles are needed, who has decision authority and what kind, and establishes role relationships within the team.

STRUCTURES FOR MONITORING OF PRACTICE BY PROFESSIONAL ROLE

O'Rourke (2003) has implemented a clinical governance structure in the United States that ties professional role authority, standards and the monitoring and evaluation of practice to the core of the organisation's quality improvement program. As mentioned earlier, she has intentionally not termed her model 'shared governance', because in the United States there is some concern within management that it implies an infringement on management authority and control of operational and corporate activity rather than the monitoring and control of standard and role-based practice by the professional staff. An example of this clinical governance structure using a council concept is depicted in Figure 22.3.

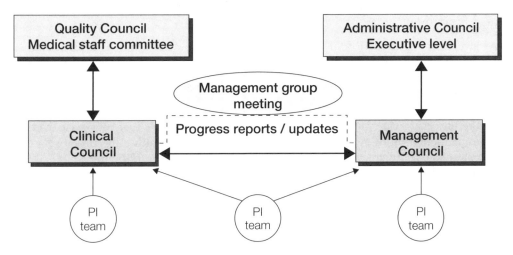

Figure 22.3 Clinical governance structure

Note: PI = Performance Improvement

The purpose of a clinical council is to ensure that there is organisational accountability for clinical performance. This accountability involves:

▲ clarifying the clinical standard monitoring and evaluating performance to the agreed-upon clinical standard;

▲ developing strategies to support practising to the clinical standard and financial outcomes;

▲ developing strong clinical leadership capable of managing to the clinical standards;

▲ functioning as a clearinghouse for clinical issues; and

▲ aligning with other structures within the organisation to assure that the standard is met.

By setting in place a structure for governing practice, such as a clinical council, and monitoring and evaluating outcomes, the organisation is better able to ensure quality practice. Mechanisms by which the clinical council achieves its goal include:

▲ clarifying the clinical standard;

▲ supporting evidence-based practice;

▲ instituting best practice; and

▲ developing role-based collaborative relationships within the team.

In addition, the council must ensure compliance to the standard which would include development of job descriptions that are aligned with clinical standards, developing competence related to critical thinking and interpersonal skills, and becoming partners with physicians in managing and coordinating care. The council would be responsible for working with the quality improvement staff to set up ways to measure the impact of practice on outcomes.

Within models of practice, governance outcome and process measures are frequently used to monitor and evaluate performance. Some examples of commonly used measures include:

▲ level of implementation of clinical interventions for which there is evidence of effectiveness;

▲ the extent of organisations developing evidence-based standards and guidelines for practice, and successfully implementing these;

▲ the process of care indicators where there is good evidence that they relate to the implementation of evidence-based practice and better health outcomes for patients (e.g. aspirin prescription and cardiac rehabilitation following acute myocardial infarction);

▲ patient outcome as measured by traditional means such as morbidity (e.g. infection rates) and mortality;

▲ patient recorded outcomes measurements, such as quality of life;

▲ health care resource utilisation including procedural rates, admission rates and lengths of stay; and

▲ direct and indirect costs of development and implementation of organisational interventions.

LEVELS OF PATIENT AND STAFF SATISFACTION

As noted above, in contemporary clinical practice there is an increasing emphasis on interdisciplinary practice, role-based accountability and collaboration within the clinical team. When looking at systems of governance, nursing practice includes independent, dependent and interdependent role relationships. Nurses frequently practise in collaboration with other disciplines. Confusion often exists as to the difference between multidisciplinary and interdisciplinary practice, and often these terms are used interchangeably. However, multidisciplinary practice often means that individual disciplines or specialties contribute discrete elements to the patient's care. Interdisciplinary practice better describes that nurses work collaboratively, while taking responsibility for their individual practice. Although there may be shared tasks among members of the team, the sharing of the task does not necessarily change the fundamental role authority of the clinician performing the task. For example, nurses, doctors, dietitians and pharmacists may counsel patients on dietary considerations. Each retains their unique role while sharing their knowledge with each other to enhance each role. This kind of interdisciplinary, collaborative practice occurs when general practitioners and nurse practitioners work together to achieve a mutual goal (McCloskey & Maas 2001). The likely benefits of this collaboration include better primary care for under-serviced and remote areas, and reduced general practitioner workload (Davis & Thurect 2001). In Australia, the medico-legal and funding frameworks need to be developed if nurse practitioners are to work in general practice.

EMPOWERMENT THROUGH PROFESSIONAL ROLE AUTHORITY

With increasing emphasis on interdisciplinary, collaborative practice it is imperative that nurses continue to be assertive and influential in development of models of care (Benton 1999; O'Rourke 1994, 1996). Nurses have the opportunity to exercise their role authority and have the power to influence the direction of practice and the health care system at all levels in the system. Being acknowledged as an expert is essential if we are to take an active role in creating a better practice environment for the practitioner and patient. Expert power (O'Rourke 1979, 1980, 2003) is achieved when it can be demonstrated that the profession takes its obligation to evaluate seriously and creates ways to evaluate and monitor practice performance to ensure a best practice approach. It is from exercising these duties that a profession retains its position of power as an expert. Ultimately the key to expert power is the accumulation of scientific evidence and a demonstration of a standard of practice that strives for excellence and continual improvement.

To truly experience the value of professional expertise, the work environment in the practice setting must be conducive to collaboration and individual empowerment. Bieber and Swenson (2002) provide some interesting insights into the notion of empowerment. They define empowerment as the commitment nurses make to be involved in their practice and the decisions that drive it. This speaks to the issue of the need for the organisation to create a clinical governance structure so this commitment can be made operational. Through leadership, nurses exercise that power to meet the larger needs of society, generate science for practice, be involved in the decisions that guide their practice, and practise in a manner that ensures quality care. In this way, nurses can use the available knowledge, resources and experiences to improve practice. Each nurse is individually responsible for the work done, the service provided and their continued personal and professional growth and development. Porter-O'Grady (2001) identifies factors inherent in nursing culture that impede these processes, namely the failure to be involved in decision-making processes and a culture of co-dependent leadership instead of empowered leadership.

Nurses who are leaders have generally achieved excellence in their area of practice and possess the credibility, knowledge and confidence of their peers to guide nursing practice into the future. Implicit in effective leadership is vision and often this vision is a key to empowerment. O'Rourke (2001, 2003) defines a visionary leader as one who can accomplish four key elements in concert: These elements are:

▲ a vigilant focus on the goal of nursing—to promote health;

▲ the capacity to build teams capable of transitioning organisations from the known to unknown;

▲ a vision beyond the usual while managing intense pressure to produce immediate solutions; and

▲ the ability to quantify in word and deed what others cannot see.

These factors provide vision and direction, and facilitate successful strategies to implement structures to support professional practice. By participating in a defined decision-making process though a governance structure, nurses can enhance the ability to control nursing practice and generate successful patient outcomes. As professional nurses, we are more likely to have greater job satisfaction because we will be working in organisations that provide a system by which we can be active contributors in the decisions that guide our practice. Participation such as this has been identified as a key work environment satisfier (Aiken et al. 2001).

GOVERNANCE AND LEADERSHIP DEVELOPMENT

As nursing leaders we must engage in the mentoring and coaching of students and new graduates. We must provide opportunities that encourage and help them participate in clinical decision-making. All nurses must play an active role in keeping new graduates in the profession to build a strong workforce that will be able to secure a positive future of health care. Part of one's professional obligation is to participate in the activities that have the potential to impact our professional practice. Organisational involvement should occur at both the unit and system levels and may focus on such issues as compliance to standards, the impact of diversity on clinical practice, the need for education to develop knowledge and skill of the workforce and to create mechanisms to ensure standards-based practice. Through this work we are able to provide a sharp perspective based on our knowledge, education and experience in providing quality, effective patient care. As an active participant on these teams we aspire to experience personal fulfillment, mutual respect for each other and other members of the health care team, and ownership of our nursing practice. Leaders who coach and mentor new graduates by involving them early on in their career to engage in decision-making and shared-governance activities will help grow the profession. Nurses who are involved in committees contribute to decision-making, engage in leadership activities, and are provided the opportunity to share their expertise and influence system changes.

CLINICAL AND MANAGERIAL OBLIGATIONS FOR MEASURING PRACTICE PERFORMANCE AND OUTCOMES

For the most part, the measurement of outcomes in health has been limited to negative focus, such as morbidity, mortality and adverse events (Davidson & Elliott 2001; Elliot 1996; Lohr et al. 1998). A more dynamic, proactive measurement outcome approach focuses on patient-reported outcomes. Trends exist to include positive outcomes, such as improved health status, functional ability, patient satisfaction and quality of life (Davidson & Elliott 2001; Ingersol 2000). These data can provide guidance in how to develop and monitor services to better meet patient needs.

One of the barriers to outcome research and evaluation related to practice performance is the underlying assumption that it is difficult to quantify due to the discipline specific and individual variation in practice patterns. However, O'Rourke (2003) contends that this is not as difficult as it seems, believing that practice compliance can be measured when broken down into several levels. The first level relates to the degree to which the professional role across disciplines is successful in implementing the basic tenets of professional practice, as defined earlier in this chapter. The next level is to determine the degree to which the professional roles on the team are practising in a collaborative and interdisciplinary manner. The third level is the impact of interdisciplinary practice on clinical, service and financial outcomes. The two case studies that follow describe the work of one organisation to quantify more objectively these first three levels. The fourth level is the degree to which discipline-specific practice impacts on our outcomes, i.e. discipline-sensitive outcomes.

Recently, attention to outcomes research and evaluation has increased significantly as a consequence of the Institute of Medicine Report, *To err is human* (1999). This report, which showed an increase in medical error with adverse consequences for the patient, emphasises the need to scrutinise a number of variables including practice patterns. The results of the report underscore the need for organisations to firstly assist professionals meet their role obligation to monitor and evaluate practice in relation to practice standards, and secondly to examine the impact of that practice on patient outcomes. The purpose of the governance structure depicted in Figure 22.3 is to ensure there is accountability for monitoring and evaluating practice performance and to help clarify the extent to which that practice impacts on clinical, service and financial outcomes. According to Proenca (1995), the structure of an organisation will have an effect on communication, coordination and the manner in which the quality improvement efforts are integrated into the system. This supports the idea that there is a need for a defined patient care model and a governance structure for practice within an organisation to ensure there is a consistent and systematic approach to improving quality.

In the United States over the past ten years re-engineering attempts in the industry have further eroded workforce satisfaction levels that have occurred as a result of the decentralisation of nursing. Similar experiences have been reported internationally (Blythe et al. 2001). Organisations can counter the dissatisfaction by involving professional staff in governance structures that provide for the opportunity to make decision-making related to practice and by implementing patient care models that respect the role of the professional as decision-maker and leader of practice.

THE PROFESSIONAL PRACTICE MODEL IN ACTION

The following case studies provide operational insight into this model.

■ CASE STUDY 1

The Inter shift report and case review as structures for controlling practice

This case study describes an organisation's effort to restructure itself to an interdisciplinary professional practice model. The driving force behind the effort was to improve the clinical, service and financial outcomes of care delivery. This restructure not only quantified professional practice performance but linked that practice performance to outcomes (O'Rourke & Goeppinger 2000; O'Rourke & Parini 2001). This restructured patient care model was based on the model depicted in Figure 22.3, which in turn was based on a core clinical practice system, that sets the standard of care from which to measure performance.

As described above, the clinical practice system is an interdisciplinary professional practice model that aims to capture the intellectual capacity of the interdisciplinary team members, promote the unique contribution of the professional role in the decision process, and provide the practice framework for improving clinical, service and financial outcomes. This model established the role guidelines for the appropriate use of professional, technical and assisting roles as defined by scope of practice, licensure or regulation and professional association standards (American Nurses Association 2001; Australian Nursing Council 1998). It also supports clinical team/physician collaboration. The key element of the model is that accountability for determining the patient's condition and directing care activities in relation to the patient's changing status is viewed as a professional role responsibility.

The inter-shift report for nursing and the interdisciplinary case review were deemed to be so critical to improving the quality of the clinical conversation that restructuring and monitoring was instituted. The nine-step professional role decision-making process (Table 22.1) became the audit tool used to evaluate practice compliance to the professional practice process during the shift report and case reviews. A major challenge to improving outcomes is the need to change practice patterns of the professional staff and physicians. In this case study it was achieved by implementing an explicit, well-defined practice framework. This framework helped to demonstrate empirically that practice variation did exist across disciplines and that there was a need to improve the transfer of information about the patient condition within the clinical team and across departments. This organisation felt that by having a patient care model in place linking performance to the practice standards, the organisation was better able to coordinate its efforts to meet the challenge of improving outcomes. This was achieved by reducing practice variation across disciplines and improving the transfer of information about the patient condition, thus ensuring role and standards-based practice. Preliminary results indicate that the use of a defined protocol reinforcing the use of the nine steps of the professional decision-making process, has had a positive impact on length of stay. This case study demonstrates that practice based on a defined tool designed to capture professional practice decision-making behaviour has been a useful way to help professional staff in their practice and improve organisational outcomes.

■ CASE STUDY 2

Prevention of the sentinel event and potential adverse events

Risk reduction is a critical issue in every organisation and performance improvement departments are charged with helping organisations seek out what has caused errors. In this case study the organisation implemented an interdisciplinary clinical governance structure similar to the one depicted in Figure 22.3. O'Rourke (2003) assisted with the use of the nine-step professional practice decision-making process as a tool for evaluating the cause of sentinel events. The audit included all disciplines and their respective contributions to the decision-making process. By using the nine steps as indicators it was possible to more precisely pinpoint where in the decision-making process insufficient attention was paid to a particular element, therefore reducing the effectiveness of the decision-making across the disciplines. As an example, in a review of four sentinel events using the nine-core element of the professional practice process there was a consistent pattern: Step 7—the dynamic integration of steps one to six, traditionally referred to in nursing as the nursing process; Step 8, the determination of the stability of the patient condition; and Step 9, the dynamic integration of steps 7 and 8, were weak or non-existent. In another review of 60 cases, there was no evidence of steps 7, 8 and 9, and Step 5 Evaluation showed evidence of lack of follow-up on patient conditions considered to be 'near misses'. This analysis helped the Clinical Council define the problem and begin to understand how to solve it through appropriate corrective action; action that would be a fundamental change not just expedient. It also showed increased awareness that simply measuring whether the patient chart is complete is not a measure of whether there was coordination of care and follow-through on care requirements. In both case studies the organisation supported the hypothesis that if professional staff practise according to a professional practice model then patient outcomes would be optimised.

Both these case studies aimed to quantify the extent to which the professional staff were implementing the nine-step professional decision-making process and to see the effect of that practice on outcomes such as sentinel events. This is a first step towards generating data that supports the value of the professional role and interdisciplinary practice. Research suggests that governance models for practice are best served by examining the professional practice compliance of all disciplines prior to examining discipline specific ones.

Case studies from the literature

There are many opportunities and forums to enhance our professional practice. Nurses should continually be critically evaluating practice in relation to patient outcomes and asking if what they are doing is best for the patient. There is also an important agenda for systematic research and evaluation of practice. Implicit in the definition of a profession is the commitment of each individual nurse to being involved in enhancing professional practice. There is a role for every nurse, whether it is as a member of a local quality committee, discussing ideas about nursing practice with members at handover or participation in a national committee. The need to help identify issues and offer potential solutions and feedback is the responsibility of every nurse. The more nurses are involved in the decision-making process, the more supported the decision will be. Bieber and Swenson (2002) believe that empowered nurses make the commitment to being responsible, accountable and dedicated to patients and practice. Participation in the clinical decision-making process is pivotal to achieving this goal. In the literature you will find many examples of collaboration of health professionals which improve patient outcomes. Publishing experiences is a way to share valuable lessons learnt with our colleagues. One example can be seen in the paper discussed below. As you read this case study try and identify key strategies that can be used to improve patient care in your place of clinical practice.

Critical care bug team: A multidisciplinary team approach to reducing ventilator-associated pneumonia[*]

These investigators determined that ventilator-associated pneumonia rates in the medical-surgical intensive care unit exceeded the ninetieth percentile in September 1997 and were significantly ($P < .05$) higher when they benchmarked their data against a National Nosocomial Infections Surveillance System. Their Infection Control Committee convened a multidisciplinary 'Critical Care Bug Team' to review 1997 National Nosocomial Infections Surveillance System data for four adult intensive care units in a 583-bed tertiary care hospital.

Members of this committee included clinical nurse specialists, a dietitian, a pharmacist, a respiratory therapist, an infection control professional, a research specialist and a physician adviser. The authors state that having the team report directly to the hospital's Infection Control and Adult Critical Care committees maximised support for recommendations and provided a direct link from patient care to hospital administration. The 'Critical Care Bug Team' undertook a wide process of consultation, systematic literature review and a process of monitoring compliance. The team subsequently implemented interventions, including policy and procedure changes, equipment changes, and educational programs.

These efforts produced the intended outcome of decreasing ventilator-associated pneumonia rates. This study illustrates the effectiveness of a collaborative, inter-disciplinary team approach devised to reduce and stabilise ventilator-associated pneumonia rates in a medical-surgical intensive care unit. The authors concluded that a team approach was successful in obtaining significant support from administration. It was also useful in achieving a multifaceted approach from a variety of health professionals. This interdisciplinary approach also led to creativity in solutions and represented an efficient and successful strategy to improve patient care at their institution.

GOVERNANCE OF PRACTICE: A KEY TO THE RECRUITMENT AND RETENTION OF NURSES

Theories abound to explain the current shortage of nurses in our health care systems (Aiken et al. 2000; Bednash 2000; Flynn & Aiken 2002). There are common denomi-nators internationally, which may include: an agency workforce, chronic disease burden, older and sicker patients increasing demand, young women choosing other careers, low demand for nursing education and stressful work conditions. Hatmaker (2002) believes that in light of declining interest in nursing, employers must examine the workplace and strive to focus on employee satisfaction if they are to recruit and retain the caregivers they need to care for patients. It has been demonstrated that high levels of professional satisfaction are related to recruitment and retention. O'Rourke and Goeppinger (2000) reported preliminary findings including a positive trend in recruitment when a professional practice model was used. Hatmaker (2002) also believes that it is equally important for nurses to be responsible and accountable for their professional practice and be willing to embrace the responsibility and implications of governance of practice.

CONCLUSION

A wide range of knowledge, skills and professional behaviours are required to effectively manage the comprehensive needs of patients and populations, particularly in the context of an ageing society (Gortner 2000). Health care delivery systems increasingly depend on interdisciplinary and collaborative practice to achieve optimal individual and organisational outcomes. This trend is a two-edged sword. In many ways nurses are compelled to blend and compromise in their skills and practice and at the same time demonstrate leadership and advocacy for the unique professional role of nursing and the patients for whom they care. Models for practice governance provide a framework by which nurses can be empowered and motivated to direct professional practice. This empowerment combines vision, commitment to quality and dynamism to direct professional practice. Professional practice within a governance model is a commitment to excellence in care of patients and their families and the key to nurses' representation in decision-making in health at both a policy and practice level.

Reflective exercise

1 Identify an issue in your clinical practice that needs to be addressed to improve patient care at your institution.

2 Can you measure this factor and relate it to the effect of interventions as the investigators did above?

3 Who are the key stakeholders contributing to this area of patient care?

4 What are the key administrative processes for this aspect of patient care?

5 Who can you enlist to help you to do this project?

6 Can you identify an individual in power to help you deal with this issue?

7 What do you think is the best way to approach this issue using a governance of practice model?

8 How do you think you can develop a mechanism of governance and professional practice at your institution?

RECOMMENDED READINGS

Aiken, L., Havens, D. S., & Sloane, D. M. (2000). The magnet nursing service recognition program: A comparison of two groups of magnet hospitals. *American Journal of Nursing, 100* (3), 26–36.

American Association of Colleges of Nursing Task Force. (January 2002). *Hallmarks of the professional nursing practice environment.* Washington, DC: AACN.

Hinshaw, A. S. (2000). Nursing knowledge for the 21st century: Opportunities and challenges. *Journal of Nursing Scholarship 32* (2), 117–24.

Institute of Medicine, Committee on Quality Health Care in America (1999). *To err is human: Building a safer health system.* Kohn, Corrigan & Donaldson (eds). Washington, DC: National Academy Press.

Needleman, J., Buerhaus, P., Mattke, S., Stewart, M., & Zelevinsky, K. (2001). Nurse staffing and patient outcomes in hospitals. Final Report, US Department of Health and Human Services, Health Resources and Service Administration, Contract No.230–99–0021, February 28, 2001, Rockville, MD.

O'Rourke, M. (1980). *Expert power: The basis for political strength.* New York: National League for Nursing.

Wilson, R. M., Harrison, B. T., Gibberd, R. W., & Hamilton, J. D. (1999). An analysis of the causes of adverse events from the quality in Australian health care study. *Medical Journal of Australia, 170,* 411–15.

ENDNOTE

★ Kaye, J., Ashline, V., Erickson, D., Zeiler, K., Gavigan, D., Gannon, L., Wynne, P., Cooper, J., Kittle, W., Sharma, K., & Morton, J. (2000). Practice forum. Critical care bug team: a multidisciplinary team approach to reducing ventilator-associated pneumonia. *American Journal of Infection Control,* 28(2), 197–200.

CHAPTER TWENTY-THREE

Nursing leadership:
Trust and reciprocity

Judith Clare & Anne Hofmeyer

LEARNING OBJECTIVES

At the completion of this chapter, the reader will be able to:

- understand the debates about nursing leadership in complex organisations;

- develop a broader perspective of emerging ideas and theorising about trust-based approaches to leadership; and

- have insight into the implications of these ideas for current nursing education, practice and research.

KEY WORDS

Nursing, leadership, trust, organisational culture, transformation, governance

INTRODUCTION

This chapter explores the norms that leadership takes in the contemporary nursing context and the usefulness of traditional hierarchical 'top down' leadership in current health care contexts. It then goes on to explore other theories of leadership that have the capacity to build ethical, effective, creative and harmonious workplaces. The issue of trust is significant to nursing leadership and governance, as it underpins the development of respect for individual contributions to organisational practices.

THE AUSTRALIAN NURSING CONTEXT

In the last two decades the context of nursing practice has increased in complexity, pace and workload levels; there are shortages of skilled nurses, diminishing discipline boundaries and increasing managerialism. Moreover, the acuity of patients in general wards and nursing homes is increasing, and there is an imperative towards discharge of patients to the community as early as possible (DETYA 2001). Of specific interest too is the mode of delivery of health care and conditions of practice in the nursing workplace that are shaped by corporate neo-liberal values and measurement of progress and profit. Also of concern are equity issues in resource allocation for patient care and processes of inclusion and exclusion of nurses within health care teams and decision-making bodies.

Since the Reid (1994) review of nurse education in Australia, subsequent to the transfer of registered nurse education into the higher education sector in 1993, a number of national reviews and research studies have been conducted into aspects of nurse education and practice, and into workforce issues of supply and demand. Three recent reviews of issues in nursing education and practice in Australia have demonstrated what many previous nursing workforce reports confirmed; that is, the changing context of nursing and the increasing complexity of health care since the early 1980s (Clare et al. 2002; DETYA 2001; Heath 2002). Of significance are two particular areas identified in many of the reports reviewed in these recent studies.

First, is the need for 'family friendly and flexible work environments' because nurses report 'dissatisfaction with conditions of work—shift-work, frequent changes, overloads, lack of appreciation by superiors and colleagues, lack of child care' (Clare et al. 2002; DETYA 2001; Heath 2002). Second, is the issue of workforce strategies related to the difficulties in recruitment and retention of qualified nurses, specifically the cohort of registered nurses who leave the profession. Evidence confirms that pay levels are not the prime reason for qualified nurses leaving the workplace, but rather nurses report unacceptable levels of 'poor management practice and a general lack of appreciation' (Clare et al. 2002; DETYA 2001, p.7; Heath 2002).

Of specific concern is the number of nurses who leave the profession during their first year of employment, apparently due to unreasonable expectations by employers (Clare et al. 2002; DETYA 2001; Heath 2002). These are significant moral and professional issues for health care decision-makers to urgently consider. It seems incongruous that nurses feel they are not respected and valued in the workplace, because these elements of caring are purported to form the basis of nurse/patient relationships. Also of concern are the numerous reports reviewed in the recent research (Clare et al. 2002) which all failed to address crucial issues of leadership development, management and interpersonal relations (see, for example, Gerrish 2000; Greenwood 2000; Hart & Rotem 1995; Hegney et al. 1997).

CORPORATE VALUES OF NEO-LIBERALISM AND MANAGERIALISM

Contemporary heath care systems are characterised by modern managerial theories and practices. Managerialism is predicated on the assumption that markets should control society and governments should minimise their involvement in public services. In capitalist societies there has been a burgeoning of privatisation of public services in recent years, with claims of better services for consumers or customers. Corporate managerialism has been promoted globally as a set of values informing the management strategy of organisations since the early 1980s. Human productivity in these systems is viewed as a 'commodity' and the 'organisation's financial accountability is the criterion to measure performance' (Rees 1995, p.16). Corporate managerialism has resulted in profound changes in the health sector through greater efficiency, maximising productivity, cost cutting and increasing profits. The goal for managers is to manage people efficiently to meet organisational productivity and financial targets, with little scope for active participation in these decisions by workers. In more developed countries, health care systems are predicated upon neo-liberal capitalist values of competition, individual success and the consequent changes in public health policies. In this regard, we contend there is a crucial agenda for nursing leadership to meld political activism and organisational reform.

Nursing recognises that the life options and opportunity for people to enjoy an authentic existence free from unequal economic, gender or racial oppression, is dependent on access to health sustaining resources and social change (Stevens 1989). Moreover, Moccia (1988, p.32) stated 'social conditions, therefore, call for nurses' attention if caring work is to be allowed, recognised, acknowledge, and valued'. With the increasing attrition of registered nurses from the Australian (and worldwide) workforce, health administrators are beginning to acknowledge nurses who take this standpoint (see for example, Aiken et al. 2002).

VALUES SHAPING THE CURRENT HEALTH CARE CONTEXT

The nursing workplace has not escaped unscathed amid market-driven trends. Corporate language and markers of efficiency and outcomes call for a keen focus on rules and regulations, protocols and procedures, necessitating regular surveillance regimes. These systems have been widely embraced by administrators in nursing workplaces to ensure regularity and to manage risk. However, these limited corporate measures of efficiency and fiscal outcomes have often clashed with sets of values that underpin caring and other 'invisible' nursing work, because such measures lack the capacity to comprehensively and accurately account for the *processes* of nursing.

As a consequence of managerialism in the health sector, research from the 1960s to the present day demonstrates that nurses report moral constraint and distress in caring for patients, where workplace structures and measurements of efficiency and progress are shaped by managerialism and neo-liberalist policies (Clare et al. 2002; Corley 1995; Heath 2002; Hiraki 1998; Hutchinson 1990; Ketefian 1985, 1981; Komesaroff 1999; Liaschenko 1993, 1998; Menzies 1960; Rodney & Starzomski 1993;

Starzomski & Rodney 1997; Varcoe 1998; Varcoe & Rodney 2002; Wilkinson 1988, 1989). When a society is defined in economic terms, economic indicators primarily measure success and productivity, with little consideration of the social and environmental costs. Such an approach diminishes trust, social relationships and reciprocity.

We suggest nursing leadership is crucial because the leader is a 'driver' in the process of embedding concepts into policy and core organisational culture, rather than such concepts simply existing as unfulfilled statements in annual reports. Clearly, trust is fundamental in this long-term process. That being the case, what constitutes profit in broader social and ecological terms needs to be redefined, rather than defined in purely fiscal outcomes. For example, what constitutes social profit could be conceptualised in terms of the health levels of individuals and populations, and in work practice and relationships among nurses. These advances are predicated on the assumptions that trust and cooperation may work better than competition and that building social networks and reducing environmental degradation is as important as the aggregation of financial capital.

LEADERSHIP STYLES

Traditional leadership styles can be characterised as being based on hierarchical structures, commands, coercion and control activities such as constant surveillance of staff and checking systems for monitoring performance, risk, production and output. Porter-O'Grady (1996, p.6) noted 'vertical integration in organisations relates to the essentials of control'. To meet the challenges of leadership in health care in the twenty-first century, Porter-O'Grady (2001, p.182) asserted, 'much profound and personal transformation must be undertaken if good leadership is to continue and effective results are to be obtained'.

In view of the pressures being exerted from the external environment and the critical re-visioning of organisations, research suggests that senior management needs to establish a flexible and adaptive infrastructure that should assist contemporary and complex organisations to reach optimum levels of performance (Appelbaum et al. 1998). These authors conclude that the largest barrier to 'change' is not changes to technologies and work processes but those involving people. People usually want to understand changes in direction and how the changes will affect their working lives. Ray, Turkel and Marino (2002) argue that 'a loss of trust underscores employees' decreased loyalty to hospital organisations and herald their increasing disillusionment' with nursing education, practice and management of health care. Employees and the public need to trust the ability of managers to move the organisation in new directions without decreasing people's ability to derive satisfaction from their employment or from the services they receive.

Traditional leadership styles are not designed to be responsive or inclusive, and therefore do not necessarily build trust or collective valuing in teams and groups (Handy 1997; Porter-O'Grady 1997). However, models of shared governance are predicated on collaborative leadership, open communication and transparency (Blumgart 1997). Antrobus and Kitson (1999, p.746) claim 'effective nursing leadership currently is a vehicle through which both nursing practice and health policy can be influenced and shaped'. Leaders need to have the flexibility to 'live in permanent transition, to accommodate ambiguity, and to mentor and facilitate others in their struggle to redefine and renew themselves and their new roles' (Porter-O'Grady 1997, p. viii). This leadership style is based on mutual respect and recognition of contributions that all workers make to the whole organisation (Trofino 1995). Many nursing leaders are caught between the need to support traditional hierarchical management styles expected in organisations and the need to demonstrate more current attributes of leadership, as explained above. This dichotomy may mean that leaders can espouse one set of values about the direction and style of the organisation, while at the same time exhibiting behaviours that are inconsistent with them. In other words, actions and behaviours are manifestations of a different value-set to those espoused to colleagues and workers. This leads to a lack of trust in the organisation, which results in low levels of motivation, harmful conflict and waste of all types (see 12 Key Principles of Business Excellence, Australian Quality Council, 2000, for further explanation).

LEADERSHIP AND GOVERNANCE

A range of economic, social, political and environmental forces and technological complexities have interacted to create communities, workplaces and health care services that are rapidly and dramatically changing, and affront the wellbeing of many people (Hofmeyer 2002). In these environments of accelerated change, nursing leaders need to 'focus on the changes and translate them in ways that provide meaning and direction for the future' (Porter-O'Grady 1996, p.5). Responsive nursing leaders will work collaboratively to develop ethical learning organisations driven by clear mission statements and core values, rather than by rules and coercion, and build empowering health relationships that are defined by communities, rather than only delivering services. Collaboration between nursing organisations and education sectors will be led by nurses who are confident in embracing change, who are proactive, innovative, visionary and risk-takers. Such leaders will, in turn, empower other nurses to enhance their skills and confidence in leadership and build organisational capacity through social and political action to improve the health and wellbeing of all in society.

In contemporary society greater involvement by nursing into debates about societal responsibilities for the health of all in society is essential, thus promoting the common good, social justice and ultimately building a civil society. However, the achievement of health and wellbeing for all in society seems to be a somewhat elusive goal in the current neo-liberal climate and increasing widespread health inequalities (Leeder 2000).

NURSING IN VIRTUAL ORGANISATIONS

Another challenge to the enactment of new theories of leadership in current nursing contexts is the development of *virtual organisations*. This is due in part to advances in information technology, which is a major influence in changing the nature of society, how people live, communicate and how work is organised. For example, the expansion of technological advancements in computers, mobile phones, and electronic transfer of information have made it possible for people to work from their cars, from planes, or from home to best meet the core business of organisations. As a consequence, there are inevitable changes in the traditional institutional structures and the way in which work is organised.

Moreover, Bausch (1998, p.231) argued that 'virtual organisations' will be the main form of organisation of the future, because 'definitions of place, assets, ownership, and stakeholder are changing and calling for something other than the traditional hierarchical model of leadership'. Nurses too are involved in these changes, as early discharge of people from hospitals into the community requires new forms of communication, monitoring and caring practice. Of interest are the implications for district and rural and remote nurses, who largely work from their cars or clinics, managing caseloads through a call centre and accessing client records using hand–held computers. Clearly, the functioning of virtual organisations challenges traditional hierarchical management structures, resource allocation and human management, and requires a new form of leadership in nursing organisations. Different forms of leadership involving trust and individual professional accountability are required in the workplace rather than traditional surveillance models.

POWER RELATIONS AND LEADERSHIP

Issues of the use and misuse of power shape relations in workplace environments and the nature of care relationships with patients. Since nursing has historical links to the military and religious orders, nurses have traditionally been influenced by societal sanctions against women who openly assert their power. Thus, nurses have expressed uneasiness about the use of power for change in organisations and have shown a reluctance to acknowledge and use their own professional and personal power. In this context, Rafael (1996, p.3) suggests nursing has considered caring incongruent with the exercise of power in their practice, but argues the concepts can be intertwined to achieve 'empowered caring'. Critical social science research in nursing has uncovered some of the coercive misuses of power in the nursing workplace and society through making visible oppressive social structures and conditions (Clare 1993a, b; Stevens 1989; Varcoe & Rodney 2002). Understandings of ourselves in relation to others and our circumstances can, according to Stevens (1989, p.61), set 'the stage for conscienitised collective action to change oppressive constraints'. It is timely that leaders in nursing promote change through the development of emancipatory knowledge in the macro area of public health policy in order to mitigate health inequalities. Nurses need to promote change at the micro level in the nursing workplace to expose for critique oppressive structural conditions and processes at the organisational level.

Social activism by nursing leaders calls for a re-focus and engagement with a wider critique of the complex socio–political and cultural context of health, health services and factors that influence the health of a society. Collaboration requires disciplines to have sufficient trust to cooperate with each other. In addition, Moccia (1988) calls for better understanding of the societal context of health behaviours and nursing's role in re-directing the focus from short–term individual-based interventions to a macro or upstream view where the unequal structural conditions originate. Notably, the upstream view considers society as the locus of change, rather than the individual. Moreover, Butterfield (1990, p.2) notes, 'upstream endeavours focus on modifying economic, political, and environmental factors that have been shown to be precursors of poor health throughout the world'.

The conundrum facing those concerned about changing dominant neo-liberal ideologies is one of shaping a society that finds ways to respect people while ensuring economic prosperity for all. A shift in values would be required for a society to have such a relational capacity. Creating environments of hospitality, healing and stewardship are underpinned by confidence in trusting relationships, trust in health care providers and in the delivery of equitable services. As well, health agencies would need to be interested in trust and governance in the structures and processes shaping the nursing workplace and the capacities and capabilities underpinning 'leadership as collaborative practice' (Magendanz 2001, p.10). There is a clear imperative to consider how the role of trust and cooperation resonates with nursing leadership and governance in health care organisations.

PERSPECTIVES ON TRUST IN THE NURSE/PATIENT RELATIONSHIP AND IN THE NURSING WORKPLACE

The nursing literature broadly explores the concept of trust from two main perspectives. First, trust is conceptualised as an important aim and dimension of the clinical and ethical relationship between nurses and patients. Second, trust is considered crucial in relation with others in the workplace environment, and the concept of trust is connected with outcomes and levels of effectiveness (Gilbert 1998; Johns 1996). Trust can be viewed as confidence that one's expectations will be met. Defining attributes of trust include 'consistency, reliability, confidence, and fragility' (Meize-Grochowski 1984, p.567). But there remains a vagueness and lack of prudent conceptual analysis and definition of trust in the nursing literature, prompting calls for further conceptualisation and research (Johns 1996; Meize-Grochowski 1984; Thorne & Robinson 1988).

Trust has long been viewed as central to nurse–patient relationships and creating effective and successful caregiving relationships (Johns 1996; Meize-Grochowski 1984; Peter & Morgan 2001; Thorne & Robinson 1988; Wilson Morse & Penrod 1998). Of note, Hicks (2000) argued that nurses need to be trusted by patients to provide effective health care and that the caring relationship is dependent on respect and veracity. A common contention is that caring nurse–patient relationships are the moral foundation of nursing practice (Bishop & Scudder 1999; Fry 1989; Gadow 1985; Yarling & McElmurry 1986).

The second perspective considers trust as crucial in developing cooperative relationships between nurses, and in collaborative relationships between nurses and other health care disciplines to ensure effective team functioning in the workplace (Henneman et al. 1995; Peter & Morgan 2001). However, Johns (1996, p.76) noted there is a paucity of nursing literature that links 'nurses, trust, the work environment, co-workers, management and other work-related factors'. In an organisation, Kerfoot (1998, p.59) claimed, an important criterion of success is the level of trust created by the leader, and 'the level of trust is the foundation upon which financial and quality success can be built'. In the current era of incessant change, where health care services are increasingly adopting neo-liberal market values of economic restraint and outcome measures of productivity, widespread dissatisfaction and concern has escalated among nurses (Clare et al. 2002; Thorne & Robinson 1988). In health care workplaces, trust is a crucial component in patient care and in the process of restructuring work structures and practice (Johns 1996). Gilbert (1998) claimed that mistrust is the functional opposite of trust, and explained that it is abuse that provides the antithesis to trust in health care relationships and workplaces. This evidence is interesting in the light of recent research into bullying and other forms of abuse suffered by nurses in the nursing workplace (Jackson et al. 2002).

However, trust does not automatically exist between individuals, between nurses and patients, or between nurses and others in the workplace. Rather, it is built within social relationships that have the inherent power to restrict or provide access to life resources and opportunities in various ways and to various individuals (Gilbert 1998). From this perspective, scrutiny of the moral intentions of the co-workers is necessary to uncover the potential for maldistributions of power and other problems in a work relationship (Peter & Morgan 2001).

TWO SETS OF INSTITUTIONALISED TRUST NORMS

Different understandings of the social world and collective action can be analysed through the concept of values—specifically, value systems that further the ideas of security and harmony. These values shape expectations of others, and are linked to the criteria used to identify others as trustworthy, so are called trust norms. Braithwaite (1998 p.46) identifies two sets of trust norms. First, exchange trust norms, which are concerned with the regularity and predictability of action, and second, communal trust norms, which are concerned with an awareness of and capacity to act in the interests of others.

Exchange trust norms: Security values

Exchange trust norms are concerned with the regularity and predictability of action and are linked with security values. As Braithwaite (1998, p.65) explains, 'exchange trust norms are built on behaviours that reflect competence, predictability, consistency, and cautious decision-making'. This approach entails the ongoing collection and assessment of data to justify one's decision and prediction to risk trusting others. Exchange trust norms do not incorporate a feeling of particular responsibility for the wellbeing of others.

Trust based on exchange norms is intrinsically conservative, dependent on the established status, knowledge and the track record of others, and being able to reasonably predict their future behaviours and actions. In this way, exchange trust norms present difficulties for newcomers or marginalised groups who have not been able to establish a track record in trustworthiness, thus privileging elites or established groups. Not surprisingly, Braithwaite (1998, p.69) asserted: 'Exchange trust, therefore, might be expected to privilege past leaders who have done their job steadfastly and reliably but not necessarily with imagination or energy to find new modes of adaptation to meet the challenges of the future'.

Communal trust norms: Harmony values

Communal trust norms are based on perceptions of need and feelings of responsibility for others and promote trust through harmony in social relations with others. The awareness of the interests of the other and the capacity to act to promote the common good reflects high levels of generalised reciprocity and trust. The harmony value system combines values at a personal and social level that aim to build peace, respect, human dignity, cooperation, and greater resource sharing and ecological preservation. Harmony values for the individual include 'self-insight, inner harmony, the pursuit of knowledge, self-respect, and wisdom as well as being tolerant, generous, forgiving, helpful, and loving' (Braithwaite 1998, p.49). These harmony values are linked with communal trust norms.

We can expect to see societal relationships in less antagonist terms from those for whom harmony values dominate, where trust is given to individuals known to us and also to strangers. Benefits are given to others in response to their needs or to increase their happiness, and there is no expectation of repayment or debt accrued. The notion of trust can be expressed as 'I will trust you, and continue to trust you, unless you prove you are untrustworthy'. Hence, trustworthiness is generated through the communication that one is trusted in the first instance (Hofmeyer 2002).

LEADERSHIP AND TRUST

We contend that nursing leaders need to have a willingness to inculcate *communal* trust norms that engender trust with employees. Nursing leaders ought to be trustworthy and credible. They need to trust their nursing staff and also allow them to make mistakes because that is characteristic of a trusting environment. Nursing staff need to reflect on their relations with their nursing leaders and consider whether they take opportunities to affirm their leadership and actively contribute to a collegial and trusting workplace. Indeed, as Provis (2001) claims, trust is a key concern for leaders seeking to replace antagonistic relationships with partnership forms of relationships in the workplace.

POLICY DEVELOPMENT

Nursing is well placed with its historical and ethical lineage of caring in social spheres and in hospital and community settings to have firsthand knowledge of the impact of health inequalities and public health policies that are not inclusive of all citizens and limit life options. Thus, there is an ethical responsibility for nurses to become educated in the aforementioned areas and become 'politically savvy' (Johnstone 1999, p.429) in order to become effective influential contributors in areas of health law and public health policy reform and to improve our collective and individual futures.

There is scope for leadership in nursing in the ways in which difference and diversity are confronted in the community and the nursing workplace and the process by which some nurses are positioned by elite and powerful individuals. Difference poses issues of voice and representation, so it is crucial to question who is authorised to speak for whom, and whose views are marginalised and thus absent from the debates, such as in interdisciplinary exchanges and decision-making, or in discussions with patients and relatives, or in community consultation. Structures and processes in the nursing workplace and communities need to accommodate all voices being heard and valued, not only the powerful, popular or confident. Powerful interests coerce many nurses into silence (Hofmeyer, 2002).

We argue that nursing leadership incorporating trust is key in this process of challenging the construction of 'otherness' (Grosz 1993, p. i) and in the creation of trust for all nurses, in particular newcomers in the workplace. In order for that to happen, the power structures supporting such constructions must be changed and replaced with respectful and inclusive social relations and environments of trust, cooperation and connection across groups. Grosz (1993, p. i) argued there is a need to 'engage with the complexities and contradictions that otherness poses in a culture and in knowledges that pose themselves as singular, unified and universally representative'. Nurses depend on nursing leaders to create opportunities in which they can bring the organisational vision to a reality. In effect, a leader best leads through trusting themselves first. In addition, Handy (1997, p.190) argued 'organizations which rely on trust as their principal means of control are more effective, more creative, more fun and cheaper to operate'. Links between social trust, health, wellbeing and prosperity have been well established (Braithwaite 1998; Cox 1995; World Bank 1998).

VALUES IN THE WORKPLACE

Values are clearly evident in current public health policy in Australia, which allocates only 5 per cent of national health funding towards strategies to promote health. The minimal funding resources currently being directed towards health promotion, preventative care and strategies to reduce health inequalities are inadequate and represent a crucial area for research and political action by nursing. Nurse researchers can collaborate with individuals and groups to identify leadership issues, thus raising consciousness and generating nursing knowledge. We contend that nursing leadership in social and political activism and research is paramount to uncover 'oppressive social structures that constrain a person's health, limit their life possibilities, and restrict their equal and fully conscious participation in society' (Stevens 1989, p.63).

CONCLUSION

In this chapter traditional leadership values and practices have been contrasted with current notions of leadership involving trust and reciprocity. Nursing leadership is in the best position to lead the way in effective leadership reform in health care organisations. The nursing workforce is the largest component of the health workforce and nurses daily coordinate care for people in hospitals and in the community. We need to recognise the unique opportunity we have to influence health policy and the development of caring, ethical organisations that promote excellent standards of health care and health care management.

Reflective exercise

1   Think about your relationships with immediate colleagues and those in leadership positions in your workplace or university. What values are expressed in those relationships?

2   Write down five practical ways that you have supported colleagues in their leadership positions in the last year.

3   What do you understand by the word 'power'? In which ways do you act powerfully? Does your enactment of power affect your colleagues positively or negatively?

4   What is (or will be) your attitude and contribution to the decision-making processes in your workplace or team?

RECOMMENDED READINGS

Appelbaum, S. H., St-Pierre, N., & Glavas, W. (1998). Strategic organizational change: The role of leadership, learning, motivation and productivity. *Management Decision, 36*(5), 289–301.

Gilbert, A. (1998). Towards a politics of trust. *Journal of Advanced Nursing, 27,* 1010–16.

Henneman, E. A., Lee, J. L., & Cohen, J. I.. (1995). Collaboration: A concept analysis. *Journal of Advanced Nursing, 21,* 103–9.

Kerfoot, K. (1998). Creating trust on leadership. *Dermatology Nursing, 10*(1), 59–60.

Komesaroff, P. (1999). Ethical implications of competition policy in healthcare. *Medical Journal of Australia, 170,* 266–8.

References

Abbasi, S. M., & Hollman, K. W. (2000). Hanging on or fading out? Job satisfaction and the long-term worker. *Public Personnel Management, 29*(3), 333–43.

Ackroyd, S., & Thompson, P. (1999). *Organizational misbehaviour.* London: Sage.

Adams, A., & Bray, F. (1992). Holding out against workplace harassment and bullying. *Personnel Management, 24* (10), 48–50.

Aiken, L. H. (2002). Superior outcomes for magnet hospitals: The evidence base. In M. L. McClure, & A. S. Hinshaw (eds). *Magnet hospitals revisited: Attraction and retention of professional nurses.* Washington DC: American Nurses Publishing.

Aiken, L. H., Clarke, S. P., & Sloane, D. M. (2000). Hospital restructuring. Does it adversely affect care and outcomes? *Journal of Nursing Administration, 10,* 457–65.

Aiken, L. H., Clarke, S. P., Sloane, D. M., Sochalski, J. A, Busse R., Clarke H., Giovannetti, P., Hunt, J. Rafferty, A. M. & Shamian J. (2001). Nurses' reports on hospital care in five countries. *Health Affairs, 20*(3), 43–53.

Aiken, L. H., Clarke, S. P., Sloan, D. M., Sochalski, J. A., & Silber, J. (2002). Hospital nurse staffing and patient mortality, nurse burnout and job dissatisfaction. *JAMA, 288*(16). hhtp://jama.ama-assn.org/issues/v288n16/rfull/joc20547.html

Aiken, L. H., Havens, D. S., & Sloane, D. M. (2000). The magnet nursing service recognition program: A comparison of two groups of magnet hospitals. *Americal Journal of Nursing, 100*(3), 26–36.

Aiken, L. H., Sloane, D. M., & Sochalski J. (1998). Hospital organisation and outcomes. *Quality in Health Care, 7,* 222–6.

Aiken, L. H., Sochalski, J., & Andersen, G. (1996). Downsize the hospital nursing workforce. *Health Affairs, 15*(4), 88–92.

Aitken, D. (1997). Australia's universities: Present and retrospect. In *Crossing the divide: The future of post-compulsory education* (pp. 5–13). Melbourne, Australia: NTEU.

Alderman, M. C. (2001); Nursing in the new millenium: Challenges and opportunities. *Dermatology Nursing (13)1,* 44–9.

Alexander, V. (1998). Participative nursing management: A necessity for survival. *Kansas-Nurse, 73*(9), 4–5.

Alfano, G. J. (1971). Healing or care taking—Which will it be? *Nursing Clinics of North America, 6,* 273–80.

Alvesson, M., & Billing, Y. D. (1997). *Understanding gender and organizations.* London: Sage.

American Association of Colleges of Nursing Task Force. (2001). *Hallmarks of the professional nursing practice environment.* AACN. Washington, DC.

American Nurses Association. (2001a). Health & Safety Survey, September. www.NursingWorld.org.

American Nurses Association (2001b). *Scope and standards of nursing informatics practice.* Washington, DC: American Nurses Publishing.

American Nurses Association. (2001c). *Standards of Clinical Nursing Practice* (2nd edn). Washington, DC: American Nurses Publishing.

American Nurses Association. (1997). *Implementing nursing's report card: A study of RN staffing, length of stay and patient outcomes.* Washington, DC: American Nurses Association.

American Organizations of Nurse Executives (AONE) (2001) cited in Goode, C. Advancing quality patient care through research. *Journal of Nursing Administration, 31*(5), 221–2.

Andersson, L., & Pearson, C. M. (1999). Tit for tat? The spiralling effect of incivility in the workplace. *Academy of Management Review, 24*(3), 452–4.

Andrews, M. (1996). Using reflection to develop clinical expertise. *British Journal of Nursing 1996, 5*(8), 508–13.

Antrobus, S., & Kitson, A. (1999). Nursing leadership: Influencing and shaping health policy and nursing practice. *Journal of Advanced Nursing, 29*(3), 746–53.

Appelbaum, S. H., St-Pierre, N., & Glavas, W. (1998). Strategic organizational change: The role of leadership, learning, motivation and productivity. *Management Decision. 36*(5), 289–301.

Arbuthnot, S. (2002). Relational leadership. *Management Today. Sept. edition,* 20–2.

Argyris, C. (1964). *Integrating the individual and the organization.* New York: John Wiley and Sons.

Arnold, L. (2000). Letting go and taking on. In F. Bower, *Nurses taking the lead: Personal qualities of effective leadership,* pp. 277–96. Philadelphia: W.B. Saunders.

Ash, M. (1996). *Shaving the inside of your skull.* New York: G. P. Putnam & Sons.

Ashforth, B. E. (1994). Petty tyranny in organizations. *Human Relations, 47*(7), 755–78.

Ashforth, B. E. & Mael, F. A. (1998). The power of resistance: Sustaining valued identities. In R. M. Kramer, & M. A. Neale (eds). *Power and influence in organizations.* Thousand Oaks, California: Sage.

Ashley, J. A. (1980). Power in structured misogyny. *Advances in Nursing Science, 2*(3) 3–22.

Atsalos, C., & Greenwood, J. (2001). The lived experience of clinical development unit (nursing) leadership in Western Sydney, Australia. *Journal of Advanced Nursing, 34,* 408–16.

Attridge, C., & Callahan, M. (1990). Nurses' perspective of quality work environments. *Canadian Journal of Nursing Administration, 13*(3), 19.

Audit Commission for Local Authorities and the National Health Service in England and Wales. (2001). *Brief encounters—getting the best from temporary nursing staff.* http://www.audit-commission.gov.uk

Australian Bureau of Statistics. (2002). *Australian Social Trends 2002,* Retrieved 3 March 2003, at http://www.abs.gov.au/ausstats/abs.

Australian College of Critical Care Nurses [ACCCN] (2002). Retrieved 3 March 2003, at http://www.acccn.com.au.

Australian Institute of Health and Welfare. (1999). *Nursing labour force.* (AIHW Cat. no. HWL 20). Canberra.

Australian Nursing Council Incorporated. *National competency standards for the Registered Nurse* (2nd edn). Dickson, ACT: ANCI, 1998.

Australian Quality Council. (2000). *Business excellence: An overview.* St Leonards, Sydney: Australian Quality Council.

Axtell, R. E. (1990). *Do's and don'ts of hosting international visitors.* Sydney, Australia: John Wiley & Sons.

Baird, R., Cadenhead, S., & Schmele, J. A. (1993). The implementation of total quality. In A. F. Al-Assaf, & J. A. Schmele (eds), *The textbook of total quality in healthcare* (pp. 91–101). Delray Beach Fla: St Lucie Press.

Balfour, M., & Clarke, C. (2001). Searching for sustainable change. *Journal of Clinical Nursing, 10*(1), 44–50.

Ball, R. (2000). Nurse case managers and the internet. *Lippincott's Case Management, 5*(5), 174–83.

Bandura, A. (1986). *Social foundation of thought and action.* New Jersey, USA: Prentice-Hall.

Barr, B.J. (2002). Managing change during an information systems transition. *AORN Journal, 75*(6), 1085–8, 1090–2.

Barrett, E. A. M. (2002). What is nursing science? *Nursing Science Quarterly, 15,* 51–60.

Barrick, M. R. & Mount, M. K. (1993). Autonomy as a moderator of the relationship between the 'Big Five' personality dimensions and job performance. *Journal of Applied Psychology, 78*(1), 111–18.

Bartol, K., Martin, D., Tein, M., & Matthews, G. (1995). *Management: A Pacific Rim focus.* Sydney, Australia: McGraw-Hill Book Company.

REFERENCES

Bass, B. M. (1990a). *Bass & Stogdill's handbook of leadership: Theory, research and managerial applications*. (3rd edn). New York: The Free Press.

Bass, B. M. (1990b). From transactional to transformational leadership: Learning to share the vision. *Organizational Dynamics, 18*(3), 19–36.

Bass, B. M. (1985). *Leadership and performance beyond expectations*. New York: Free Press.

Bass, B. M. & Avolio, B. J. (1997). Shatter the glass ceiling: Women may make better managers. In Grint, K. (ed.) *Leadership: Classical, contemporary, and critical approaches*. Oxford: Oxford University Press.

Batalden, P. B. (1993). Organisation wide quality improvement in health care. In A. F. Al-Assaf, & J. A. Schmele (eds), *The textbook of total quality in healthcare* (pp. 60–73). Delray Beach, Fla: St Lucie Press.

Batalden, P. B., Nelson, E. C., & Roberts, J. S. (1994). Linking outcomes measurement to continual improvement: The serial 'V' way of thinking about improving clinical care. *Journal on Quality Improvement, 20*(4), 167–77.

Baumann, A., Giovanetti, P., O'Brien-Pallas, L., Mallette, C., Deber, R., Blythe, J., Hibberd, J., & DiCenso, A. (2001). Health care restructuring: the impact of job change. *Canadian Journal of Nursing Leadership, 14*(1), 14–20.

Bausch, T. A. (1998). Servant-leaders making human new models of work and organisation. In L. Spears, (ed.) *Insights on leadership: Service, stewardship, spirit, and servant-leadership* (pp. 230–45). The Greenleaf Center, USA: John Wiley & Sons.

Beardwood, B., Walters, V., Eyles, J., & French, S. (1999). Complaints against nurses: A reflection of 'the new managerialism' and consumerism in health care? *Social Science & Medicine, 48*(3), 363–74.

Beauchamp, T., & Childress, J. (2001). *Principles of biomedical ethics*. (5th edn). New York: OUP.

Bednash, G. (2000). The decreasing supply of registered nurses: Inevitable future or call to action. *JAMA, 283*(22), 2985–7.

Beech, M. (2002). Leaders or managers: The drive for effective leadership. *Nursing Standard, 16*(30), 35–6.

Begun, J. W., & White, K. R. (1995). Altering nursing's dominant logic: Guidelines from complex adaptive systems theory. *Complexity and Chaos in Nursing, 2*(1), 5–15.

Behling, O. (1998). Employee selection: Will intelligence and conscientiousness do the job? *Academy of Management Executive, 12*(1), 77–86.

Bennis, W., & Nanus, B. (1985). *Leaders: The strategies for taking charge*. New York: Harper & Row.

Bent, K. N. (1993). Perspectives on critical and feminist theory in developing nursing praxis. *Journal of Professional Nursing, 9*(5), 296–303.

Benton, D. (1999). Assertiveness, power and influence. *Nursing Standard, 13* (52), 48–52.

Bernstein, A. J. (1995). Quality vs quantity. In K. M. Shelton (ed.), *In search of quality. The business consultant's perspective*. Utah: Executive Excellence Publishing.

Bero, L. A., Grilli, R., Grimshaw, J. M., Harvet, E. M., & Oxman, A. D., & Thomson, M. A. (1998). Closing the gap between research and practice: An overview of systematic reviews of interventions to promote the implementation of research findings. *British Medical Journal 317,* 465–8.

Berry, D. C., & Dienes, Z. (1993). *Implicit learning: Theoretical and empirical issues*. Hove, Sussex: Lawrence Erlbaum Associates Ltd.

Berwick, D. M. (1998). Crossing the boundary: Changing mental models in the service of improvement. *International Journal for Quality in Health Care 10,* 435–41.

Berwick, D. M. (1989). Continuous improvement as an idea in health care. *New England Journal of Medicine, 320*(1), 53–4.

Beyers, M. (2001). Nursing workforce: A perspective for now and the future. *JONA'S Healthcare Law, Ethics, and Regulation, 3*(4), 109–13.

Bieber, B. L., Swenson, L. L., MS. (2002) http://nursingworld.org/tan/99novdec/asiseeit.htm Accessed 20 August 2002.

Bies, R. J., & Tripp, T. M. (1998). Two faces of the powerless: Coping with tyranny in organizations. In R. M. Kramer, & M. A. Neale (eds). *Power and influence in organizations.* Thousand Oaks, California: Sage.

Biscoe, G. & Lewis, B. (1996). *Strategic planning.* Geneva: World Health Organisation.

Bishop, A., & Scudder, J. (1999). A philosophical interpretation of nursing. *Scholarly Inquiry for Nursing Practice, 13*(1), 17–27.

Bixler, G., & Bixler, R. (1966). The professional status of nursing. *Issues in Nursing,* New York: Springer Publishing.

Blancett, S. S. (1995). *Re-engineering nursing and health care: The handbook for organisational transformation.* Meryland: Aspen Publishers.

Blanchard, K. (1999). *The heart of a leader.* Tulsa, OK: Books.

Blegen, M. A., Goode, C. J., & Reed, L. (1998). Nurse staffing and patient outcomes. *Nursing Research, 47*(1), 43–50.

Blue, L., Lang, E., McMurray, J. J., Davie, A. P., McDonagh, T. A., Murdoch D. R., et al. (2001). Randomised controlled trial of specialist nurse intervention in heart failure. *British Medical Journal, 323*(7315), 715–18.

Blumenthal, D. (1996a). Quality of health care. Part 1: Quality of care. What is it? *New England Journal of Medicine, 19,* 891–4.

Blumenthal, D. (1996b). Quality of health care. Part 4: The origins of the quality-of-care debate. *New England Journal of Medicine, 335*(15), 1146–9.

Blumgart, D. (1997). Collaborative leadership. *Journal of Shared Governance, 3*(1), 11–14.

Blythe, J., Baumann, A., & Giovannetti, P. (2001). Nurses' experiences of restructuring in three Ontario hospitals. *Journal of Nursing Scholarship 33*(1), 61–8.

Bohm, D. (1989). Meaning and information. In P. Pylkkanen (ed.). *The search for meaning: The new spirit in science and philosophy* (pp. 43–85). Wellingborough, Northamptonshire, UK: Crucible.

Bond, M., & Holland, S. (1998). *Skills of clinical supervision for nurses: A practical guide for supervisees, clinical supervisors and managers.* Buckingham: Open University Press.

Bond, S., & Thomas, L. H. (1991). Issues in measuring outcomes of nursing. *Journal of Advanced Nursing, 16,* 1492–502.

Bongers P. M., de Winter, C. R., Kompier, M. A., & Hildebrandt, V. H. (1993). Psychosocial factors at work and musculoskeletal disease. *Scandinavian Journal of Work, Environment & Health, 19*(5), 297–312.

Borbasi, S. & Gaston, C. (2002). Nursing and the 21st century: What's happened to leadership? *Collegian, 9(1),* pp. 31–5.

Borman, J., & Biordi, D. (1992). Female nurse executives, finally at an advantage? *Journal of Nursing Administration, 22*(9), 37–41.

Borthwick, C., & Galbally R. (2001). Nursing leadership and health sector reform. *Nursing Inquiry, 8*(2), 75–81.

Bostock, W. W. (2000). The quiet revolution in Australian higher education. *Policy, organisation & society, 19*(2), 59–80.

Bourantas, D., & Papelexandris, N. (1990). Sex differences in leadership: Leadership styles and subordinate satisfaction. *Journal of Managerial Psychology 5*(5), 7–10.

Bournes, D. A., & DasGupta, T. L. (1997). Professional practice leader: A transformational role that addresses human diversity. *Nursing Administration Quarterly, 21*(4), 61–86.

Bournes, D. A., & Mitchell, G. J. (2002). Waiting: The experience of persons in a critical care waiting room. *Research in Nursing & Health, 25,* 58–67.

Bova, B. (1987). Mentoring as a learning experience. In V. J. Marsick (ed.). *Learning in the workplace.* (pp. 119–33). London: Croom Helm.

Bower, F. (2000). *Nurses taking the lead: Personal qualities of effective leadership.* Philadelphia: W. B. Saunders.

Bowles, A., & Bowles, N. B. (2000). A comparative study of transformational leadership in nursing development units and conventional clinical settings. *Journal of Nursing Management, 8,* 69–76.

REFERENCES

Bowles, B.A., & Teale, R.(1994). Communications services in support of collaborative health care. *British Telecommunications Technology Journal, 12*(3), 29–44.

Boyd, E. M., & Fales, A. W. (1983). Reflective learning: A key to learning from experience. *Journal of Humanistic Psychology. 23*(2), 99–117.

Boyer, E. L. (1990). *Scholarship reconsidered. Priorities of the professoriate.* San Francisco: Carnegie Foundation, Jossey-Bass.

Boynton, D., & Rothman, L. (1996). Charge nurses: Critical change agents for successful restructuring. *Recruitment, Retention, and Restructuring Report, 9*(2), 2–5.

Bradford, D. L., & Cohen, A. R. (1998). *Power up: Transforming organizations through shared leadership.* New York: John Wiley & Sons.

Braithwaite, V. (1998). Communal and exchange trust norms: Their value base and relevance to institutional trust. In V. Braithwaite, & M. Levi (eds.) *Trust and governance* (pp. 46–74). New York: Russell Sage Foundation.

Brewis, J., Hampton, M., & Linstead, S. (1997). Unpacking Priscilla: Subjectivity and identity in the organisation of gendered appearance. *Human Relations, 50*(10) 1275–304.

Bridges, W. (1998). *The boundryless organization.* Upper Saddle River, PA: Prentice Hall.

Brink, P. (1999). Transcultural versus cross-cultural. *Journal of Transcultural Nursing, 10* (7).

Brook, R. H., McGlynn, E. A., & Cleary, P. D. (1996). Quality in health care. Part 2: Measuring quality of care. *New England Journal of Medicine, 335*(13), 966–70.

Brotheridge, C. M., & Grandey, A. A. (2002). Emotional labor and burnout: Comparing two perspectives of 'people work'. *Journal of Vocational Behavior, 60,* 17–39.

Brown, C. R. (1998). *Gender segmentation in the paid workforce: The case of nursing.* Unpublished PhD thesis, Griffith University.

Bryar, R. M., Closs, J. C., Baum, G., Cooke, J., Griffiths, J., Hostick, T., Kelly, S., Knight, S., Marshall, K., & Thompson, D. R. (2003). The Yorkshire BARRIERS project: Diagnostic analysis of barriers to research utilisation. *International Journal of Nursing Studies 40.*

Buchan, J. (1999). The 'greying' of the United Kingdom nursing workforce: Implications for employment policy and practice. *Journal of Advanced Nursing, 30,* 818–26.

Buchanan, D., & Badham, R. (1999a). *Power, politics and organizational change: Winning the game.* London: Sage.

Buchanan, D., & Badham, R. (1999b). *Winning the game: Power, politics and organizational change.* London: Paul Bass.

Buchanan, J., & Considine, G. (2002). *Stop telling us to cope.* Australian Centre for Industrial Relations Research and Training. Sydney, New South Wales: University of Sydney.

Budman, C., Lipson, J., & Meleis, A. (1992). The cultural consultant in mental health care: The case of an Arab adolescent. *American Journal of Orthopsychiatry, 62,* 359–70.

Buerhaus, P. I., Staiger, D. O., & Auerbach, D. I. (2000). Implications of an aging registered nurse workforce. *Journal of the American Medical Association, 283*(22), 2948–54.

Buetow, S. A., & Roland, M. (1999). Clinical governance: Bridging the gap between managerial and clinical approaches to quality of care. *Quality in Health Care, 8,* 184–90.

Bunkers, S. S. (1999). Emerging discoveries and possibilities in nursing. *Nursing Science Quarterly (12)1,* 26–31.

Buresh, B., & Gordon, S. (2000). *From silence to voice: What nurses know and must communicate to the public.* Ottawa: Canadian Nurses Association.

Burleson, C. W. (1990). *Effective team meetings: The complete guide.* New York, USA: John Wiley & Sons.

Burns, J. M. (1978). *Leadership.* New York: Harper & Row.

Burrows, D. E. (1995). The nurse teacher's role in the promotion of reflective practice. *Nurse Education Today; 15*(5), 346–50.

Butterfield, P. G. (1990). Thinking upstream: Nurturing a conceptual understanding of the societal context of health behaviour. *Advances in Nursing Science, 12*(2), 1–8.

Byers, J. F. (2001). Research abstract. *Nursing Administration Quarterly (25)4,* 87–90.

Cabban, P.T., & Caswell, J. R. (1997). *Hospital quality control: A user's manual.* (3rd edn). Sydney: Community Systems Foundation.

Cameron, G., & Wren, A. M. (1999). Reconstructing organizational culture: A process using multiple perspectives. *Public Health Nursing, 16*, 96–101.

Campbell, I., & Burgess, J. (1997). *National patterns of temporary employment: The distinctive case of casual employment in Australia.* (National Key Centre in Industrial Relations Working Paper no. 53). Melbourne, Victoria: Monash University.

Campbell, P. T., & Rudisill, P. (1999). Nursing in the next millennium: Leadership skills for surviving and thriving. *AWHONN, 3*(5), 56–8.

Campinha-Bacote, J. (1998). The process of cultural competence in the delivery of health care services. *Journal of Transcultural Nursing, 10,* 290–1.

Campinha-Bacote, J. (1994). Cultural competence in psychiatric-mental health nursing: A conceptual model. *Nursing Clinics of North America, 29*, 8–11.

Canadian Nursing Advisory Committee (2002). *Our health, our future 2002.* Ottawa, Canada: Advisory Committee on Human Resources http://www.hc-sc.gc.ca.

Caplan, A. (ed). (1992). *When medicine went mad: Bioethics and the holocaust.* Totowa, New Jersey: Humana Press.

Capowski, G. (1994). Where are the leaders of tomorrow?. *Management Review (83)3,* 10–17.

Carew, D. K., Parisi-Carew, E., & Blanchard, K. H. (1986). Group development and situational leadership: A model for managing groups. *Training and Development Journal, June 1986,* 48–49.

Carney, M. (2000). The development of a model to manage change: reflection on a critical incident in a focus group setting. An innovative approach. *Journal of Nursing Management, 8*, 265–272.

Carson, G, M., & Mitchell, G. J. (1998). The experience of living with persistent pain. *Journal of Advanced Nursing, 28*, 1242–8.

Cavers, K., & Livers, A. (2002). 'Dear White Boss . . .' *Harvard Business Review, November 2002,* 76–81.

Cebulski-Alexander, C. (1997). The nurse executive in the 21st century: How do we prepare? *Nursing Administration Quarterly, 22*(1), 76–82.

Cerner (2003). http://www.cerner.com/aboutcerner/default.asp Accessed April, 2003.

Champy, J. (2002). The residue of leadership: Why ambition matters. In F. Hesselbein, & R. Johnston (eds). *On creativity, innovation and renewal: A leader to leader guide,* (pp. 111–22). San Fransisco: Jossey-Bass.

Chassin, M. R. (1996). Quality of health care. Part 3: Improving the quality of care. *New England Journal of Medicine, 335*(14), 1060–3.

Cheater, F. M., & Keane, M. (1998). Nurses' participation in audit: A regional study. *Quality in Health Care, 7, 27*–36.

Checkland, P. B. (1981). *Systems thinking, systems practice.* Chichester: John Wiley & Sons.

Checkland, P. B., & Scholes, J. (1999). *Soft systems methodology in action.* Chichester: John Wiley & Sons.

Chen, C. H. (2002). *The current issues in advanced nursing practice in Taiwan.* International Council of Nurses. Retrieved 16 September 2002 at http://www.icn.ch/NPTaiwan.pdf.

Cherry, B. (2002). Nursing leadership and management. In B. Cherry, & S. Jacob (eds) pp. 351–83. *Contemporary nursing: Issues, trends, & management.* St. Louis: Mosby.

Chiu, L. (1999). Psychiatric liaison nursing in Taiwan. *Clinical Nurse Specialist, 13*, 311–14.

Chomsky, N. (1959). A review of Skinner's verbal behaviour. *Language, 35,* 26–58.

Ciulla, J. B. (ed). (1998a). *Ethics, the heart of leadership.* Westport, Connecticut: Praeger.

Ciulla, J. B. (1998b). Introduction. In J. B. Ciulla.(ed.). *Ethics, the heart of leadership* (pp. xv–xix). Westport, Connecticut: Praeger.

Ciulla, J. B. (1998c). Leadership ethics: Mapping the territory. In J. B. Ciulla (ed.). *Ethics, the heart of leadership* (pp. 3–25). Westport, Connecticut: Praeger.

Clare, J. (1991). Professional disunity: The effects on preparation for practice. *Nursing Praxis in New Zealand, 6*(3) 10–13.

Clare, J. (1993a). A challenge to the rhetoric of emancipation: Recreating a professional culture. *Journal of Advanced Nursing, 18,* 1033–8.

REFERENCES

Clare, J. (1993b). Changing the curriculum—or transforming the conditions of practice? *Nurse Education Today, Summer, 13,* 282–6.

Clare, J., Jackson, D., & Walker, M. (2001). The gendered world that is nursing practice, In, E. Chang, & J. Daly (eds), *Transitions in nursing: Preparing for professional practice.* Sydney: MacLennan & Petty.

Clare, J., White, J., Edwards, H., & van Loon, A. (2002). *Curriculum, clinical education, recruitment, transition and retention in nursing, AUTC Final Report.* Adelaide: Flinders University.

Clay, T. (1987). *Nurses, power and politics.* London: Heinemann Nursing.

Cleary, P. D. & Edgman-Levitan, S. (1997). Health care quality. Incorporating consumer perspectives. *Journal American Medical Association, 278*(19), 1608–12.

Cody, W. K. (2001). Interdisciplinarity and nursing: 'Everything is everything,' or is it? *Nursing Science Quarterly, 14,* 274–80.

Cody, W. K. (1995). The meaning of grieving for families living with AIDS. *Nursing Science Quarterly, 8,* 104–14.

Cody, W. K. (1991). Grieving a personal loss. *Nursing Science Quarterly, 4,* 61–8.

Cody, W. K., Bunkers, S. S., & Mitchell, G. J. (2000). The human becoming theory in practice, research, administration, and education. In M. Parker (ed.), *Nursing theories and nursing practice* (pp. 238–62). Philadelphia, PA: F. A. Davis.

Cody, W. K., & Mitchell, G. J. (2002). Nursing knowledge and human science revisited: Practical and political considerations. *Nursing Science Quarterly, 15,* 4–13.

Cody, W. K., & Mitchell, G. J. (1992). Parse's theory as a model for practice: The cutting edge. *Advances in Nursing Science, 15*(2), 52–65.

Coghlan, D. (1994). Managing organisational change through teams and groups. *Leadership and Organisational Development Journal, 15*(2) 18–23.

Cogin, J. A. (2002). The effect of sexual harassment on the work performance of nurses, *Proceedings of International Employment Relations Association Conference, July 2002,* Queensland, Australia.

Cohen, M. M., O'Brien-Pallas, L. L., Copplestone, C., Wall, R., Porter, J., & Rose, D. K. (1999). Nursing workload associated with adverse events in the post anaesthesia care unit. *Anaesthesiology, 1*(6), 1882–90.

Coiera, E. (2001). Maximising the uptake of evidence into clinical practice: an information economics approach. *Medical Journal of Australia, 174*(9), 467–70.

Coiera, E. (2000). When conversation is better than computation. *Journal of the American Medical Informatics Association, 7* (3), 277–86.

Coiera, E. (1998). Four myths about the information revolution in healthcare. In J. L. Lenagahan (ed) *Rethinking IT and health* (pp. 16–29). London: Institute of Public Policy Research.

Coiera, E. (1995). Recent advances: Medical informatics. *The British Medical Journal, 310* (6991) (May), 1381–1387.

Coile, R. C. (1999). Nursing case management in the millennium: Two perspectives. *Nursing Case Management, 4*(6), 244–54.

Collins, R., & McLaughlin, Y. (1996). *Effective management.* (2nd edn). CCH Australia Limited.

Collinson, D. L. (1994). Strategies of resistance: Power, knowledge and subjectivity in the workplace. In J. M. Jermier, D. Knights, & W. R. Nord (eds). *Resistance and Power in Organizations.* London: Routledge.

Collinson, D. L. (1992). *Managing the shopfloor: Subjectivity, masculinity and workplace culture.* Berlin: William de Gruyer.

Collinson, D. L., & Hearn, J. (1994). Naming men as men: Implications for work, organization and management. *Gender, Work and Organization, 1* (1), 2–22.

Commonwealth of Australia. (2001). National Review of Nursing Education Discussion Paper.

Concise Oxford Dictionary. (1982). Oxford: Clarendon Press.

Cook, M. J. (2001). The renaissance of clinical leadership. *International Nursing Review, 48,* 38–46.

Cope, B., & Kalantzis, M. (1997). *Productive diversity: A new Australian model for work and management.* Annandale, NSW: Pluto Press Australia.

Coppa, D. (1993). Chaos theory suggests a new paradigm for nursing science. *Journal of Advanced Nursing, 18,* 985–991.

Corley, M. C. (1995). Moral distress of critical care nurses. *American Journal of Critical Care,* 4(4), 280–5.

Cornel, A. (1998). Westpac benefits from teamwork. *Australian Financial Review, 14 September 1998.*

Cottingham, C. (1994). Transformational leadership: A strategy for nursing. In E. C. Hein, & M. J. Nicholson (eds) *Contemporary leadership behaviour* (Selected Readings 4th edn) (87–91). Philadelphia: J. B. Lippincott Co.

Cotton, J. L., & Vollrath, D. A. (1988). Employee participation: Diverse forms and different outcomes. *Academy of Management Review, 13,* 8–22.

Courtney, M. (ed.). (1998). *Financial management in health services.* Sydney: MacLennan & Petty.

Covey, S. (1998). Foreword, In L. Spears (ed.). *Insights on leadership: Service, stewardship, spirit and servant-leadership* (pp. X1–1). New York: John Wiley.

Covey, S. (1992). *Principle-centered leadership: Strategies for personal and professional effectiveness.* New York: Simon & Schuster.

Cox, E. (1995). A *truly civil society.* Australian Broadcasting Commission (ABC) Annual Boyer Lectures. Sydney, Australia: ABC Books.

Cox, H., Hickson, P., & Taylor, B. (1991). Exploring reflection: Knowing and constructing practice. In G. Gray, & R. Pratt (eds) *Towards a discipline of nursing* (pp. 373–90). Melbourne: Churchill Livingstone.

Crane, J. (1985). Research utilisation: Theoretical perspectives. *Western Journal of Nursing Research,* 7(2), 261–7.

Cranny, C. J., Smith, P. C., & Stone, E. F. (1992). *Job satisfaction: How people feel about their jobs and how it affects their performance.* New York, USA: Lexington Books.

Creegan, R., Duffield, C., & Forrester, K. (2003). Casualisation of the nursing workforce in Australia: Driving forces and implications. *Australian Health Review, 26* (1), 210–8.

Crisp, J., & Taylor, C. (2001). *Potter and Perry's fundamentals of nursing,* pp. 74–5. Sydney: Mosby.

Crookes, P. A., & Bradshaw, P. L. (2002). Developing scholarship in nursing: Steps within a strategy. *Journal of Nursing Management.* 10(3), 177–81.

Crookes, P. A., & Davies, S. (eds). (1998). *Research into practice.* Edinburgh: Baillière Tindall.

Crookes, P., & Knight, S. (2001). Processes of change in bureaucratic environments. In E. Chang & J. Daly (eds). *Transitions in nursing: Preparing for professional practice* (pp. 91–106). Sydney: MacLennan & Petty.

Cross, T., Bazron, B., Dennis, K., & Isaacs, M. (1989). *Towards a culturally competent system of care, Volume I.* Washington, DC: Georgetown University Child Development Center, CASSP Technical Assistance Center.

Cullen, J. (1998). The needle and the damage done: Research, action research and the organizational and social construction of health in the 'information society'. *Human Relations, 51*(12), 1543–64.

Curtain, L. L. (2000). Hot issues in health care: Safety, quality and professional discipline. *Seminars for Nurse Managers, 8*(4), 239–42.

Cutcliffe, J., & Bassett, C. (1997). Introducing change in nursing: the case of research. *Journal of Nursing Management, 5*(4), 241–7.

Cuthbert, M., Duffield, C., & Hope, J. (1992). *Management in nursing.* Sydney: Harcourt Brace Jovanovich (Australia).

Daft, R. (1997). *Management.* (4th edn). Fort Worth, TX: The Drydan Press.

Daft, R. L. (1998). *Organisational theory and design.* (6th edn). Cincinnati: Ohio.

Dakin, S., Nilakant, V., & Jensen, R. (1994). The role of personality in testing in managerial selection. *Journal of Managerial Psychology, 9*(5) 3–11.

Dale, C. (1998). Gender differences. *Nursing Management, 5*(7) 11.

Daly, J., & Jackson, D. (1999). On the use of nursing theory in nursing education, nursing practice, and nursing research in Australia. *Nursing Science Quarterly, 12,* 342–5.

REFERENCES

Daly, J., Mitchell, G. J., & Jonas-Simpson, C. M. (1996). Quality of life and the human becoming theory: Exploring discipline-specific contributions. *Nursing Science Quarterly, 9,* 170–6.

Darley, J. (1998). Trust in organizations. *Business Ethics Quarterly, 8*(2), 319–36.

Davenport, D., Pearce, S., & Kearsley, H. (1998). Studies in change. In S. G. Wright (ed.). *Changing nursing practice* (2nd edn). London: Arnold.

David, B. A. (2000). Nursing's gender politics: Reformulating the footnotes. *Advances in Nursing Science, 32*(1), 83–94.

Davidhizar, R., & Shearer, R. (1995). Dilemma for the nurse manager: The stress of caring 'too much'. *Today's O.R. Nurse, 17*(2), 36–38.

Davidhizar, R., Shearer, R., & Dowd, S. B. (1999). When the nurse manager must help staff cope with change. *Seminars for Nurse Managers, 7*(2), 81–5.

Davidson, M. J. and Cooper, C. L. (1987). Female managers in Britain—a comparative perspective. *Human Resource Management, 26,* 217–42.

Davidson, P., & Elliott, D. (2001). Managing approaches to nursing care delivery. In: E. Chang, & J. Daly (eds.). *Preparing for professional nursing practice,* pp. 120–36. Sydney: MacLennan and Petty.

Davies, H. T. O., Nutley, S. M., & Mannion, R. (2000). Organisational culture and quality of health care. *Quality in Health Care, 9,* 111–19.

Davis, E., & Lansbury, R. (1996). *Managing together: Consultation and participation in the workplace.* Melbourne, Australia: Longman.

Davis, L., Dumas, R., Ferketich, S., Flaherty, M., Isenberg, M., Koerner, J., Lacey, B., Stern, P., Valente, S. & Meleis, A. (1992). AAN Expert panel report: Culturally competent health care. *Nursing Outlook, 40,* 227–83.

Davis, R & Thurecht, R. (2001). Care planning and case conferencing. Building effective multidisciplinary teams. *Australian Family Physician, 30*(1), 78–81.

Dawson, S. (1986). *Analysing organisations.* London: Macmillan.

De Maria, W. (1996). Open spaces, secret places: Workplace violence towards whistleblowers. In E. J. Dwyer (ed.). *Beyond Bullying Association Inc.* New South Wales: Millennium Books.

De Pree, M. (1989). *Leadership Jazz.* New York: Dell Publishing.

Deans, C. (2002). Nurses under siege. *Campus Review, August.*

Department of Education, Science and Training. (2002). *Our duty of care.* Canberra, Australian Capital Territory: DEST.

Department of Education, Science and Training. (2001). *National review of nursing education.* Canberra, Australian Capital Territory: DEST.

Department of Education, Training and Youth Affairs (DETYA). (2001). *An overview of issues in nursing education.* Evaluations and Investigations Programme Higher Education Division. Commonwealth of Australia, Canberra.

Department of Health (2000). *Towards a strategy for nursing research and development: Proposals for action.* London: Department of Health.

Department of Human Services. (2001). *Nurse Recruitment and Retention Committee final report.* Melbourne, Victoria http://www.dhs.vic.gov.au

Derry, R. (1991). How can an organization support and encourage ethical behaviour? In R. Freeman (ed). *Business ethics: The state of the art* (pp. 121–36). New York: Oxford University Press.

Dettmer, H. (1998). *Breaking the constraints to world class performance.* Milwaukee, WI: ASQ Quality Press.

DiMaggio, P., & Powell, W. W. (1983). The iron cage revisited; Institutional isomorphism and collective rationality in organizational fields. *American Sociological Review (48),* 147–60.

Diers, D., & Pelletier, D. (2001). Seeding information management capacity to support operational management in hospitals. *Australian Health Review, 24*(2), 74–81.

Diers, D., Torre, C., Heard, D., Bozzo, J & O'Brien, W. (2000). Bringing decision support to nurse managers. *Computers in Nursing, 18* (3), 137–44, 146.

Dixon, D. (1999). Achieving results through transformational leadership. *Journal of Nursing Administration, 29*(12), 17–21.

Dollard, M., & Winefield, T. (2002). Mental health: Overemployment, underemployment, unemployment and healthy jobs. In L. Morrow, I. Verins, & E. Willis (eds). (pp. 3–41) *Mental health and work. Issues and perspectives.* Commonwealth of Australia.

Donabedian, D. (1988). The quality of care, how can it be assessed. *JAMA, 260* (2), 1743–48.

Douglass, L. M. (1996). Change, stress, and conflict resolution. *The effective nurse, leader and manager,* 217–23.

Draper, M., & Hill, S. (1996). Feasibility of national benchmarking of patient satisfaction with Australian hospitals. *International Journal for Quality in Health Care, 8*(5), 457–66.

DuBrin, A. (2000). *The complete idiot's guide to leadership.* (2nd edn). Indianopolis: Alpha Books, Macmillan.

Dubrin, A. J. and Dalglish, C. (2003). *Leadership: An Australian focus.* Brisbane: John Wiley & Sons.

Duckett, S. J. (2002). Australian hospital services: An overview. *Australian Health Review, 25*(1), 2–18.

Dufault, M. A., Bielecki, C., Collins, E., & Willey, C. (1995). Changing nurses' pain assessment practice: A collaborative research utilization approach. *Journal of Advanced Nursing, 21,* 634–45.

Duffield, C., & Franks, H. (2002). Qualifications and experience: How well prepared are nurse managers compared to health service executives? *Australian Health Review, 25*(2), 182–90.

Duffield, C., & Franks, H. (2001). The role and preparation of first-line nurse managers in Australia: Where are we going and how do we get there? *Journal of Nursing Management, 9,* 78–91.

Duffield, C., & O'Brien-Pallas, L. (*in press*). The causes and consequences of nursing shortages: A helicopter view of the research. *Australian Health Review.*

Duffield, C., & O'Brien-Pallas, L. (2002). The nursing workforce in Canada and Australia: Two sides of the same coin. *Australian Health Review, 25,* 136–44.

Duffin, C. (2001). Sexist, outdated . . . matron rejected for modern NHS. *Nursing Standard, 5*(37) 7.

Duffy, E. (1995). Horizontal violence: A condundrum for nursing. *Collegian, 2*(2) 5–17.

Dunn, S., & Yates, P. (2000). The roles of Australian chairs in clinical nursing. *Journal of Advanced Nursing, 31,* 165–71.

Durgahee, T. (1996). Reflective practice: Linking theory and practice in palliative care nursing. *International Journal of Palliative Nursing, 2*(1), 22–5.

Duxbury, L., & Higgins, C. (2001). Work-life balance in the new millenium: Where are we? Where do we need to go? (Canadian Policy Research Networks Discussion Paper No. W/12). http://www.cprn.org

Dyer, W. G. (1987). *Team building: Issues and alternatives,* 2nd edn. USA: Addison-Wesley.

Eastaugh, S. R. (2002). Hospital nurse productivity. *Journal of Health Care Finance, 29*(1) 14–22.

Edman, S. (1996). Coping with cataclysmic change. *Journal of Contemporary Nurse, 13,* 5–12.

Elangovan, A. R. & Shapiro, D. L. (1998). Betrayal of trust in organizations. *Academy of Management Review, 23*(3), 547–67.

Elliot, R. L. (1996). Double loop learning and the quality of quality improvement. *Journal of Quality Improvement, 22*(1), 59–66.

Elliott, D. (1997). A conjoint appointment involving a nursing research management role. *International Journal of Nursing Practice, 3,* 47–52.

Ellis, B. & Brockbank, B.K. (1993). Changing competition in health care marketing: A method for analysis and strategic planning. *Health Marketing Quarterly, 10,* 5–22.

Ellis, J. & Hartley, C. (2000). Health care finance and control. In J. Ellis, & C. Hartley (eds). *Nursing in today's world: Challenges, issues and trends.* (7th edn). Philadelphia: Lippincott.

Ellyard, P. (1998). *Ideas for the new millennium.* Australia: Melbourne University Press.

Emden, C. (1991). Becoming a reflective practitioner. In G. Gray, & R. Pratt (eds). *Towards a discipline of nursing* (pp. 335–54).

REFERENCES

Engebretson, J., & Littleton, L. (2001). Cultural negotiation: A constructivist-based model for nursing practice. *Nursing Outlook, 49,* 223–30.

England, G. W. (1978). Managers and their value system. *Columbia Journal of World Business,* 7–11.

Erbin-Rosemann, M. A., & Simms, L. M. (1997). Work locus of control: The intrinsic factor behind empowerment and work excitement. *Nursing Economic 15*(4), 1–10. aleph@metalib.lib.uts.edu.au .

Esterman, A. J., & Ben-Tovim, D. I. (2002). The Australian coordinated care trials: Success or failure? *Medical Journal of Australia.* Retrieved 9 December, 2002 at http://www.mja.com.au/public/issues/177_09_041102/est10526_fm.html

Evans, D., & Haines, M. (2000). *Implementing evidence-based changes in healthcare.* Oxford: Radcliffe.

Evans, J. (1997). Men in nursing: Issues of gender segregation and hidden advantage. *Journal of Advanced Nursing, 26*(2) 226–231.

Executive director nurses fear isolation and lack of authority. (1995). *Nursing Management, 2*(2) 4.

Fadiman, A. (1997). *The spirit catches you and you fall down.* New York: Farrar, Straus, and Giroux.

Fagin, C. M. (2001). *When care becomes a burden: Diminishing access to adequate nursing.* Milbank Memorial Fund. at www://milbank.org/010216fagin.html

Farley, S. (1999). Leadership. In R. C. Swansburg, & R. J. Swansburg (eds). *Introductory management and leadership for nurses: An interactive text.* (2nd edn). Boston: Jones & Bartlett.

Farrell, G. (1999). Aggression in clinical settings: Nurses' views—A follow-up study. *Journal of Advanced Nursing, 29*(3) 532–41.

Fawcett, J. (2002). On science and human science: A conversation with Marilyn M. Rawnsley. *Nursing Science Quarterly, 15,* 41–5.

Fayol, H. (1925). *General and industrial management.* London: Pittman and Sons.

Fedoruk, M., & Pincombe, J. (2000). The nurse executive: Challenges for the 21st century. *Journal of Nursing Management (8)1,* 13–20.

Feldman, D. C. (1984). The development of enforcement of group norms. *Academy of Management Review, 9*(1), 47–53.

Fierman, J. (1990). Do women manage differently? *Fortune, 122*(15), 115–18.

Finkler, S. & Kovner, C. (2000). *Financial management for nurse managers and executives.* Philadelphia: W. B. Saunders.

Firth, K. (2001). Developing nurse leaders of the future. *Professional Nurse Supplement, 16*(8), s.5–s.6.

Fisher, A., & Mitchell, G. J. (1998). Quality of life research: Transforming knowledge. *Clinical Nurse Specialist, 12*(3), 99–105.

Flam, H. (1993). Fear, loyalty and greedy organizations. In S. Fineman (ed.). *Emotion in Organizations.* London: Sage.

Flynn, L., & Aiken, L. H. (2002). Does international nurse recruitment influence practice values in U.S. hospitals? *Journal of Nursing Scholarship, 34*(1), 67–73.

Folger R., & Cropanzano, R. (1998). *Organizational justice and human resource management.* Thousand Oaks, California: Sage.

Follett, M. P. (1926). The giving of orders. In HC Metcalf (ed.), *Scientific foundations of business administration.* Baltimore: William and Wilkins.

Ford, P., & Walsh, M. (1994). *New rituals for old. Nursing through the looking glass.* London: Butterworth Heinemann.

Foreman, J. (2001). Organizational change. In E. Wilson (ed.). *Organizational behaviour reassessed: The impact of gender.* London: Sage.

Fox, S., & Spector, P. E. (1999). A model of work frustration-aggression. *Journal of Organizational Behaviour, 20,* 915–31.

Fox, S., Spector, P. E., & Miles, D. (2001). Counterproductive work behaviour (CWB) in response to job stressors and organizational justice: Some mediator and moderator tests for autonomy and emotions. *Journal of Vocational Behaviour, 59,* 291–309.

Fralic, M. F. (2000). What is leadership? *Journal of Nursing Administration, 30,* 340–1.

French, J. R. P., & Raven, B. (1960). The bases of social power. In Cartwright, D. & Zander, A. F. (eds). *Group dynamics: Research and theory.* New York: Harper and Row.

Friedman, C.P., & Wyatt, J.C. (1997). *Evaluation methods in medical informatics*. New York: Springer.

Frost, P. J. (1999). Why compassion counts! *Journal of Management Inquiry, 8*(2), 127–33.

Fry, M. (2001). Triage nurses order X-rays for patients with isolated distal limb injuries: A 12-month ED study. *Journal of Emergency Nursing, 27*(1), 17–22, 100–6.

Fry, M., Borg, A., Jackson, S., & McAlpine, A. (1999). The advanced clinical nurse—a new model of practice: Meeting the challenge of peak activity periods. *Australian Emergency Nursing Journal, 2*(3), 26–8.

Fry, S. (1989). The role of caring in a theory of nursing ethics. *Hypatia: A Journal of Feminist Philosophy, 4*(2), 88–103.

Fukuyama, F. (2002). *Our post human future: Consequences of the biotechnology revolution*. New York: Farrar, Strauss and Giroux.

Fulop, L., & Linstead, S. (1999). *Management: A critical text*. Melbourne: Macmillan Business.

Funk, S. G., Champagne, M. T., Wiese, R. A., & Tornquist, E. M. (1991a). BARRIERS: The barriers to research utlization scale. *Applied Nursing Research 4*, 39–45.

Funk, S. G., Champagne, M. T., Wiese, R. A., & Tornquist, E. M. (1991b). Barriers to using research findings in practice: The clinician's perspective. *Applied Nursing Research 4*, 90–5.

Funk, S. G., Tornquist, E. M., & Champagne, M. T. (1989). A model for improving the dissemination of research. *Western Journal of Nursing Research 11*, 361–7.

Gadow, S. (1990). Existential advocacy: philosophical foundations of nursing. In T. Pence, & J. Cantrall, *Ethics in nursing: An anthology* (pp. 41–51). NY: National League for Nursing.

Gadow, S. (1985). Nurse and patient: The caring relationship. In A. Bishop, & J. Scudder (eds.) *Caring, curing, coping: Nurse, physician, patient relationships* (pp. 31–43). Birmingham, Alabama: University of Alabama Press.

Gagliardi, P. (1986). The creation and change of organizational cultures: A conceptual framework. *Organization Studies, 7*(2), 117–34.

Gardener, H. (1993). *Frames of mind*. (2nd edn). USA: Fontana.

Gardner, J. W. (1986a). *The nature of leadership: Introductory considerations*. Washington DC: The Independent Sector.

Gardner, J. W. (1986b). *The tasks of leadership (Leadership Paper No. 2)*. Washington DC: Independent Sector.

Garnham, A., & Oakhill, J. (1994). *Thinking and reasoning*. Oxford: Blackwell Publishers.

Garside, P. (1998). Organisational context for quality: Lessons from the fields of organisational development and change management. *Quality in Health Care, 7* (Suppl.), S8–S15.

Gaston, C. (2003). Oration, Department of Clinical Nursing. Adelaide: Adelaide University.

Geboers, H., Horst, van der M., Mokkink, H., Monfort, van P., Bosch, van den W., Hoogen, van den H., & Grol, R. (1999). Setting up improvement projects in small scale primary care practice: Feasibility of a model for continuous quality improvement. *Quality in Health Care, 8,* 36–42.

Generational Health Review of South Australian Health System, Discussion Paper (2002) at www.dhs.sa.gov.au/generational-health-review.

Gergen, K. (1994). *Realities and relationships: Soundings in social construction*. Cambridge, Mass: Harvard University Press.

Gerrish, K. (2000). 'Still fumbling along? A comparative study of the newly qualified nurse's perception of the transition from student to qualified nurse', *Journal of Advanced Nursing, 32*(2), 473–80.

'Get ready for new breed' (2003). In Corporate Talk: Careers Section—*The Weekend Advertiser*, 4 January 2003, p. 3.

Gherardi, S. (1995). *Gender, symbolism and organizational cultures*. London: Sage.

Giacalone, R. A., & Knouse, S. B. (1990). Justifying wrongful employee behaviour: The role of personality in organizational sabotage. *Journal of Business Ethics, 9*(1), 55–62.

Giger, J. N., & Davidhizar, R. (1999). *Transcultural nursing: Assessment and intervention*. 3rd edn, St. Louis, MO: Mosby.

Gilbert, A. (1998). Towards a politics of trust. *Journal of Advanced Nursing, 27*, 1010–16.

Gillham, D. (2001). An approach to international internet based delivery. *AEJNE, 7*(1), 2–9.

REFERENCES

Gillies, D. A. (1994). *Nursing management: A systems approach.* (3rd edn). W. B. Saunders Company.

Gilloran, A. (1995). Gender differences in care delivery and supervisory relationship: The case of psychogeriatric nursing. *Journal of Advanced Nursing, 21*(4) 652–8.

Gillotti, C., Thompson, T., & McNeilis, K. (2002). Communicative competence in the delivery of bad news. *Social Science and Medicine, 54,* 1011–23.

Gilmartin, M. J. (1999). Creativity: The fuel of innovation. *Nursing Administration Quarterly (23)*2, 1–8.

Goffee, R., Scheele, N., & Pitman, B. (2000). Send out the right signals. *People Management (8)*21, 32–6.

Goleman, D. (1998). *Working with emotional intelligence.* London: Bloomsbury.

Goleman, D. (1996). *Emotional intelligence.* USA: Bloomsbury.

Goode, C. (2001). Advancing quality patient care through research. *Journal of Nursing Administration, 31*(5), 221–2.

Goold, S. (2001). Transcultural nursing: Can we meet the challenge of caring for the Australian indigenous person? *Journal of Transcultural Nursing, 12,* 94–9.

Goosen, W. T. F. (1996). Nursing information management and processing: A framework and definition for systems analysis, design and evaluation. *International Journal of Biomedical Computing, 40,* 187–95.

Gopee, N. (2000). Education. Self-assessment and the concept of the lifelong learning nurse. *British Journal of Nursing, 9*(11), 724–9.

Gordon, J., & Clout, P. (2002). Section 3 principles and practice of budgeting. *External financial management package.* NSW College of Nursing. Sydney. 1–19.

Gordon, J., & Newman, S. (2001). *Resource management.* Unpublished seminar paper, Greater Western Sydney Alliance for Nursing Advancement, Sydney. 1–7.

Gortner, S. R. (2000). Knowledge development in nursing: Our historical roots and future opportunities. *Nursing Outlook, 48*(2), 60–67.

Gould, D., Kelly, D., Goldstone, L., & Maidwell, A. (2001). The changing training needs of clinical nurse managers: Exploring issues for continuing professional development. *Journal of Advanced Nursing, 34*(1), 7–17.

Graetz, F., Rimmer, M., Lawrence, A. and Smith, A. (2002). *Managing organisational change.* Brisbane: John Wiley & Sons.

Grant-Mackie, D. (2002). Nursing leadership: Looking beyond the lamplight. *Kai Tiaki: Nursing New Zealand, 8*(4):20–1.

Graves, J. R., & Corcoran, S. (1989). The study of nursing informatics. *Image: Journal of Nursing Scholarship. 21*(4), 227–31. http://www.nih.gov/ninr/research/vol4/Overview.html Accessed April, 2003.

Graves, J.R., & Corcoran, S. (1988). Design of nursing information systems: conceptual and practice elements. *Journal of Professional Nursing,* 4(3), 168–177.

Gray, A. M., Phillips, V. L., & Normand, C. (1996). The costs of nursing turnover: evidence from the British National Health Service. *Health Policy, 3,* 117–28.

Gray, J. (1995). Survey confirms that women take longer to reach top jobs. *Nursing Standard, 9*(31) 7.

Gray, J. A. M. (2001). *Evidence-based healthcare.* (2nd edn). Edinburgh: Churchill Livingstone.

Graybill-D'ercole, P. (1998). Dare to break the glass ceiling: How to meet the challenges. *AORN Journal.* 67(6) 1152–1153.

Grealish, L. (2000). The skills of coach are an essential element in clinical learning. *Research Brief, 39*(5), 231–3.

Green, M. E. (2000). Beware and prepare: The government workforce of the future. *Public Personnel Management, 29*(4), 435–43.

Green, L., Parkin, W., & Hearn, J. (2001). Power. In E. Wilson (ed.). *Organizational behaviour reassessed: The impact of gender.* London: Sage.

Greenberg, J., & Baron, R. A. (1995). *Behavior in organizations: Understanding and managing the human side of work.* Englewood Cliffs, New Jersey: Prentice Hall.

Greenberg, L., & Barling, J. (1999). Predicting employee aggression against coworkers, subordinates and supervisors: The roles of person behaviours and perceived workplace factors. *Journal of Organizational Behaviour, 20*, 897–913.

Greene, J., & Nordhause-Bike, A. M. (1998). Nurse shortage: where have all the RNs gone? *Hospitals & Health Networks, 72*(15/16), 78–80.

Greenwood, J. (2001). Writing nursing, writing ourselves. In E. Chang, & J. Daly (eds) *Preparing for professional nursing practice: An introduction.* Sydney, Australia: MacLennan & Petty.

Greenwood, J. (2000). Critique of the graduate nurse: An international perspective. *Nurse Education Today, 20*(1), 17–23.

Greenwood, J. (1999a). Generative leadership. *Private Hospital*, October/November, 25.

Greenwood, J. (1999b). All saints or nurse as enquirer? An irritable polemic. *Contemporary Nurse, 8*, 128–35.

Greenwood, J. (1993). Reflective practice: A critique of the work of Argyris and Schon. *Journal of Advanced Nursing, 19*, 1183–7.

Greenwood, J. (1990). *Learning to care: Thought and action in the education of nurses.* Unpublished PhD thesis. Leeds University.

Greenwood, J., & Gray, G. (1998). Developing a nursing research culture in the university and health sectors in Western Sydney, Australia. *Nurse Education Today, 18*, 642–8.

Grint, K. (1997). *Leadership: Classical, contemporary, and critical approaches.* Oxford: Oxford University Press.

Grobe, S.J. (1988). Competencies for nurse educators and researchers. In H.E. Peterson, & U. Gerdin-Jeiger (eds) *Preparing nurses for using information systems: recommended informatics competencies* (pp. 25–40). New York: National League for Nursing.

Grossman, S., & Valiga, T. (2000). *The new leadership challenge: Creating the future of nursing.* Philadelphia: F.A. Davis.

Grosz, E. (1993). *Volatile bodies: Towards a corporeal feminism.* St Leonards, NSW: Allen & Unwin.

Grove, A. S. (1986). Tapping into the leader who lies within us. *Wall Street Journal, 22 col 3.*

Gulick, L. (1937). Notes on the theory of the organization. In L. Gulick, & L. Urwick (eds). *Papers on the science of administration,* (pp. 3–13). New York: Institute of Public Administration.

Gutek, B. A. (1992). Sexuality in the workplace: Key issues in social research and organizational practice. In J. Hearn, D. L. Sheppard, P. Tacred-Sheriff, & G. Burrell (eds). *The Sexuality of Organization.* London: Sage.

Guyatt, G., Rennie, D. (eds) (2002). *Users' guide to the medical literature: A manual for evidence-based clinical practice.* Chicago: AMA Press.

Hall, E.T. (1966). *The Hidden Dimension.* Garden City, NY: Doubleday Books.

Hall, P., & Weaver, L. (2001). Interdisciplinary education and teamwork: A long and winding road. *Medical Education, 35*, 867–75.

Hall-Taylor, B. (1997). The construction of women's management skills and the marginalization of women in senior management. *Women in Management Review, 12*(7), 255–63.

Hancock, C. (2001). Nursing, the modern profession. *Nursing Management, 8*(3) 23–7.

Handy, C. (1997). *The hungry spirit: Beyond capitalism—A quest for purpose in the modern world.* UK: Hutchinson Random House.

Hannah, K. J. (1985), Current trends in nursing informatics. In K. J. Hannah, E. J. Guillemin, & D. N. Conklin (eds), *Nursing uses of computers and information science* (pp.181–7), Amsterdam, Netherlands: Elsevier Science Publishing Ltd.

Hannan, M., & Freeman, J. (1977). The population ecology of organisations. *American Journal of Sociology (82)*, 929–64.

Hansen, M.T., & Von Oetinger, B. (2001). Introducing T-shaped managers, knowledge management's next generation. *Harvard Business Review. March.* 107–16.

Harlos, K. P., & Pinder, C. C. (2000). Emotion and injustice in the workplace. In S. Fineman (ed.). *Emotion in Organizations.* London: Sage.

Harlow, E., Hearn, J., & Parkin, W. (1995). Organizations and the silence and din of domination. In C. Itzen, & J. Newman (eds). *Gender, culture and organizational change.* London: Sage.

REFERENCES

Harris, M. R., & Warren, J. J. (1995). Patient outcomes: Assessment issues for the CNS. *Clinical Nurse Specialist, 9*(2), 82–6.

Harrow, D., Foster, J., & Greenwood, J. (2001). Evidence and leadership: The tools for change. *Contemporary Nurse, 11*(1), 9–17.

Hart, G., & Rotem, A. (1995). The clinical learning environment: Nurse's perceptions of professional development in clinical settings. *Nurse Education Today, 15*(1), 3–10.

Hase, S., Davies, A. T., & Dick, B. (1999). *The dark side of organisations: The Johari window.* Ultibase, RMIT, Melbourne. [http://ultibase.rmit.edu.au/Articles/aug99/hase1.htm].

Hatmaker, D. Message From the President—February 2002 Georgia Nurses Association. http://www.georgianurses.org/pm_It's_all_about.htm. Accessed 25 August 2002

Havelock, R. G. (1973). *The change agent's guide to innovation in education.* Englewood Cliffs, NJ: Educational Technology Publications.

Hawkins, J. (1999a). *American business management.* Honolulu, HI: The Directions Corporation.

Hawkins, J. (1999b). *Leadership in the customer's environment.* Honolulu, HI: The Directions Corporation.

Hearn, J. (1994). The organization(s) of violence: Men, gender relations, organizations, and violences. *Human Relations, 47*(6), 707–30.

Hearn, J. (1993). Emotive subjects: Organizational men, organizational masculinities and the (de)construction of emotions. In S. Fineman (ed.). *Emotion in organizations.* London: Sage.

Hearn, J., & Parkin, W. (2001). *Gender, sexuality and violence in organizations.* London: Sage.

Heath, P. (2001). *National review of nursing education: Discussion paper.* Canberra: AGPS

Heath, P. (2002). *National review of nursing education 2002: Our duty of care.* Canberra: Department of Education, Science and Training.

Hegney, D., Pearson, A., & McCarthy, A. (1997). The role and function of the rural nurse in Australia. Canberra: Royal College of Nursing Australia.

Heifetz, R. (1994). *Leadership without easy answers.* Cambridge, Mass: The Belknap Press of Harvard University Press.

Hein, E. C. (1998). *Contemporary leadership behaviour—selected readings.* (5th edn). Philadelphia: Lippincott-Raven.

Heller, R. (1999). *Achieving excellence.* New York: DK Publishing.

Hellriegel, D., Slocum, J. W., & Woodman, R. W. (1998). *Organisational behaviour.* (8th edn). UK: South-Western Publishing.

Henderson, E. (2000). Managers are made not born. *Nursing Management, 7*(1), 20–2.

Henneman, E. A., Lee, J. L., & Cohen, J. I.. (1995). Collaboration: A concept analysis. *Journal of Advanced Nursing, 21,* 103–9.

Hersey, P., Blanchard, K., & Johnson, D. (2001). *Management of organisational behaviour.* (8th edn). Upper Saddle River, NJ, USA: Prentice Hall.

Hicks, T. J. (2000). Ethical implications of pain management in a nursing home: A discussion. *Nursing Ethics, 7*(5), 392–8.

Hill, D. (1994). Women leaders doing it their way. *New Woman,* 78.

Hinshaw, A. S. (2000). Nursing knowledge for the 21st century: Opportunities and challenges. *Journal of Nursing Scholarship 32*(2), 117–24.

Hinshaw, A. S. (1999). Evolving nursing research traditions: Influencing factors. In A. S. Hinshaw, S. L. Feetham, & J. L. F. Shaver (eds), *Handbook of clinical nursing research* (pp. 19–30). Thousand Oaks, CA: Sage.

Hinshaw, A. S., Heinrich, J., & Bloch, D. (1988). Evolving clinical nursing research priorities: A national endeavor. *Journal of Professional Nursing 4,* 398, 458–9.

Hiraki, A. (1998). Corporate language and nursing practice. *Nursing Outlook, 46,* 115–19.

Hofmeyer, A. (2002). The relationship between nursing and the concept of social capital: A critical philosophical inquiry. Unpublished PhD thesis, School of Nursing & Midwifery, Flinders University, Australia.

Hofstede, G. (1980). *Culture's consequences.* London, UK: Sage Books.

Hollander, E. (1998). Ethical challenges in the leader-follower relationship. In J. B. Ciulla (ed.). *Ethics, the heart of leadership* (pp. 49–61). Westport, Connecticut: Praeger.

Holly, M. (1984). *Keeping a personal-professional journal*. Victoria, Australia: Deakin University Press.

Hooper, A., & Potter, J. (2000). *Intelligent leadership: Creating a passion for change*. London, UK: Random House/Business Books.

Horsley, J. A., Crane, J., & Bingle, J. D. (1978). Reseach utlization as an organizational process. *Journal of Administration 8*, 4–6.

Horsley, J. A., Crane, J., Crabtree, M. K., & Wood, D. J. (1983). *Using research to improve nursing practice: A guide*. New York: Grune and Stratton.

Hough, L. (1992). The 'Big Five' personality variables—construct confusion: Description versus prediction. *Human Performance 5*(1–2), 139–155.

Houkes, I., Janssen, P. M., de Jonge, J., & Bakker, A. B. (2003). Personality, work characteristics, and employee wellbeing: A longitudinal analysis of additive and moderating effects. *Journal of Occupational Health Psychology, 8*(1), 20–38.

Hovenga, E. (1994). Information and infrastructure requirements to measure outcomes. *Informatics in Healthcare-Australia, 3* (5), 197–202.

Hovenga, E., & Hay, D. (2000). The role of informatics to support evidence-based practice and clinical education. *Australian Health Review, 23* (3), 186–92.

Hovenga, E., Kidd, M., &Cesnick, B. (eds) (1998). *Health informatics: an overview*. Melbourne: Churchill Livingstone.

Howell, J. (2000). *A style of leadership that really delivers* at http://www.ivey.uwo.ca/publications/impact/vol1_31.htm.

Huber, D. (2000). *Leadership and nursing care management*. (2nd edn). Philadelphia: W. B. Saunders.

Hughes, R. L., Ginnett, R. C., & Curphy, G. J. (1999). *Leadership: Enhancing the lessons of experience*. Boston: Irwin McGraw-Hill.

Hunter, J. C. (1998). *The servant: A simple story about the true essence of leadership*. Rocklin, CA: Prima.

Hutchinson, S. A. (1990). Responsible subversion: A study of rule-bending among nurses. *Scholarly Inquiry for Nursing Practice, 4*(1), 3–17.

Ingersol, G. L. (2000). Evidence-based nursing: What it is and what isn't. *Nursing Outlook, 48*(1), 151–2.

Institute of Medicine, Committee on Quality Health care in America (1999). *To err is human: Building a safer health system*. Kohn, Corrigan & Donaldson (eds). Washington, DC: National Academy Press.

International Council of Nurses (ICN) (2002). *ICN definition of nursing*. http://www.icn.ch/def. .htm

Ireland, R., & Hill, M. A. (1992). Achieving and maintaining strategic competitiveness in the 21st century: The role of strategic leadership. *Academy of Management Executive (13)1*, 43–57.

Irvine, D., Sidani, S., & Hall, L. M. (1998). Linking outcomes to nurses' roles in health care. *Nursing Economics, 16*(2), 58–64.

Itzen, C., & Newman, J. (1995). *Gender, culture and organizational change*. London: Sage.

Ivancevich, J., Olekalns, M., & Matteson, M. (1997). *Organisational behaviour and management*. Boston: McGraw-Hill.

Jackson, D. (2003). Personal communication.

Jackson, D., Clare, J., & Mannix, J. (2001). Who would want to be a nurse? Violence in the workplace—a factor in recruitment and retention. *Journal of Nursing Management 101*, 13–20.

Jackson, D., Mannix, J., & Daly, J. (2001). Retaining a viable workforce: A critical challenge for nursing. *Contemporary Nurse, 11*, 163–72.

Jackson, D., & Raftos, M. (1997). In uncharted waters: Confronting the culture of silence in a residential care institution. *International Journal of Nursing Practice, 3*, 34–9.

Jacox, A., Suppe, F., Campbell, J., & Stashink, E. (1999). Diversity in philosophical approaches. In A. S. Hinshaw, S. L. Feetham, & J. L. F. Shaver (eds). *Handbook of clinical nursing research*. (pp. 3–17). Thousand Oaks, CA: Sage.

REFERENCES

Jacques, E. (1995). Why the psychoanalytical approach to understanding organizations is dysfunctional. *Human Relations, 48*(4), 343–50.

Jarvis, P. (1992). Reflective practice and nursing. *Nurse Education Today 12*(3), 174–81.

Javidan, M. (1995). Leading a high commitment high performance organization. In P. Sadler (ed.) *Strategic change: Building a high performance organization* (pp. 33–48). Oxford: Elsevier Science.

Jenkins-Clarke, S. (1999). Does nursing need 'the dismal science'? The case for economic evaluations in nursing. *Nursing Times Research 4*, 448–57.

Jezewski, M. (1993). Culture brokering as a model for advocacy. *Nursing and Health Care, 14*, 78–85.

Johns, C. (1995). Framing learning through reflection within Carper's fundamental ways of knowing in nursing. *Journal of Advanced Nursing, 22*, 226–34.

Johns, C. (1994). Guided reflection. In A. Palmer, S. Burns, & C. Bulman. (eds.) *Reflective practice in nursing: The growth of the professional practitioner.* (pp. 110–29). Oxford: Blackwell Scientific.

Johns, J. L. (1996). A concept analysis of trust. *Journal of Advanced Nursing, 24*, 76–83.

Johnson, C., & Nolan, M. T. (2000). A guide to choosing technology to support the measurement of patient outcomes. *Journal of Nursing Administration, 30*(1), 21–6.

Johnson, M. J., & Griffiths, R. (2001). Developing evidence-based clinicians. *International Journal of Nursing Practice, 7*, 109–18.

Johnson, M. J., Noble, C., Matthews, C., & Aguilar, N. (1999). Bilingual communicators within the health care setting. *Qualitative Health Research, 9*, 329–43.

Johnstone, M. J. (2002a). Poor working conditions and the capacity of nurses to provide moral care. *Contemporary Nurse*, February.

Johnstone, M. J. (2002b). The changing focus of health care ethics: Implications for health care professionals. *Contemporary Nurse, 12*(3), 213–24.

Johnstone, M. J. (2002c). Taking moral action. In S. Fry, & M. Johnstone. *Ethics in nursing practice: A guide to ethical decision making*, (rev. edn) (pp. 173–9). London, UK: Blackwell Science/International Council of Nurses, London UK/Geneva.

Johnstone, M. J. (1999). *Bioethics: A nursing perspective.* (3rd edn). NSW: Harcourt Saunders.

Johnstone, M. J.(1998). *Determining and responding effectively to ethical professional misconduct in nursing: A report to the Nurses Board of Victoria*, Melbourne.

Johnstone, M. J. (1996). Ethical decision making in nursing management. In. J. Anderson (ed.). *Thinking management: focusing on people* (pp. 214–31). Melbourne: Ausmed Publications.

Johnstone, M. J. (1994). *Nursing and the injustices of the law.* Sydney: W. B. Saunders /Baillière Tindall.

Johnstone, P. L. (2002). Nurse manager turnover and retention in New South Wales during the 1990s. *School of Public Health Monograph*, no. 1. Charles Sturt University, Bathurst.

Joint Commission on Accreditation of Healthcare Organisations (2002). *Health care at the crossroads, strategies for addressing the evolving nursing crisis.* Washington, DC: JCAHO.

Jonas-Simpson, C. J. (2001). From silence to voice: Knowledge, values, and beliefs guiding healthcare practices with persons living with dementia. *Nursing Science Quarterly, 14*, 304–10.

Jones, G. R., & George, J. M. (1998). The experience and evolution of trust: Implications for cooperation and teamwork. *Academy of Management Review, 23*(3), 531–47.

Jones, J., & Cheek, J. (2003). The scope of nursing in Australia. A snapshot of the challenges and skills needed. *Journal of Nursing Management, 11*, 1–9.

Jopling, R., Lucas, P., & Norton, G. (1998). *Accounting for business: A non-accountant's guide.* Sydney: McGraw-Hill Co. Inc.

Jordan, P. (2002). Uncontrolled emotions in organizations: Coercion and bullying in the workplace. Paper presented at the Third Conference on Emotions and Organizational Life, Bond University, Gold Coast.

Joyce, E. (2001). Leadership perceptions of nurse practitioners. Lippincott's *Case-Management, 6*(1), 24–30.

Kahn, W. A. (1993). Caring for the caregivers: Patterns of organizational caregiving. *Administrative Science Quarterly, 38*(4), 539–64.

Katz, J., & Green, E. (1992). *Managing quality: A guide to monitoring & evaluating nursing services.* St. Louis: Mosby Year Book.

Kaye, J. (1996). Sexual harassment and hostile environments in the perioperative area. *AORN Journal, 63*(2) 443–449.

Kaye, J., Ashline, V., Erickson, D., Zeiler, K., Gavigan, D., Gannon, L., Wynne, P., Cooper, J., Kittle, W., Sharma, K., & Morton, J. (2000). Practice forum. Critical care bug team: a multidisciplinary team approach to reducing ventilator-associated pneumonia. *American Journal of Infection Control, 28*(2), 197–200.

Kemmis, S., & McTaggart, R. (1988). *The action research planner.* (3rd edn). Geelong: University Press.

Kenney, P. A. (2001). Maintaining quality care during a nurse shortage using licenced practical nurses in acute care. *Journal of Nursing Care Quality, 15,* 60–8.

Kerfoot, K. (2001a). Leading from the inside out. *Dermatology Nursing (13)*1, 42–3.

Kerfoot, K. M. (2001b). Leadership in transition. In J. McCloskey Dochterman, & H. Kennedy Grace (eds). *Current issues in nursing.* (6th edn). (pp. 289–92). St. Louis: Mosby.

Kerfoot, K. (1998). Creating trust on leadership. *Dermatology Nursing, 10*(1), 59–60.

Ketefian, S. (1985). Professional and bureaucratic role conceptions and moral behaviour among nurses. *Nursing Research, 34*(4), 248–53.

Ketefian, S. (1981). Moral reasoning and moral behaviour among selected groups of practising nurses. *Nursing Research, 30*(2), 171–6.

Kets de Vries, M. F. R., & Balazs, K. (1997). The downside of downsizing. *Human Relations, 50*(1), 11–50.

Kets de Vries, M. F. R., & Miller, D. (1984). *The neurotic organization.* San Francisco: Jossey-Bass.

Kieffer, C. (1984). Citizen empowerment: A developmental perspective. *Prevention in Human Sciences, 3,* 201–26.

Kirk, R. (1997). *Managing outcomes, process and cost in a managed care environment.* Aspen: Gaithersburg Md.

Kitson, A. L., Ahmed, L. B., Harvey, G., Seers, K., & Thompson, D. R. (1996). From research to practice: One organisational model for promoting research-based practice. *Journal of Advanced Nursing 23,* 430–40.

Kitson, A., Harvey, G., & McCormack, B. (1998). Enabling the implementation of evidence based practice: a conceptual framework. *Quality in Health Care, 7,* 149–58.

Kitson, A., McMahon, A., Rafferty, A. M., & Scott, E. J. C. (1997). On developing an agenda to influence policy in health care research: A description of a national R & D priority-setting exercise. *Nursing Times Research 2,* 323–34.

Klein, R. (1998). Can policy drive quality? *Quality in health care, 7* (Suppl.), S512–S53.

Kluckhohn, F., & Strodbeck, F. (1961). *Variations in value orientations.* Evanston, IL: Row Petersen.

Knight, S., Bowman, G., & Thompson, D. R. (1997). A strategy for developing research in practice. *Nursing Times Research 2,* 119–26.

Knox, S., & Irving, J. (1997). Nurse managers' perceptions of health-care executive behaviours during organizational change. *Journal of Nursing Administration, 27*(11), 37.

Kobert, L. J. (1995). In our own voices: Journalling as a teaching/learning technique for nurses. *Journal of Nursing Education. 34*(3), 140–2.

Koehoorn, M., Lowe, G., Rondeau, K., Schellenberg, G., & Wagar, T. (2002). *Creating high-quality health care workplaces. Discussion paper No. W/14.* Ottawa, Canada: Canadian Policy Research Networks & The Canadian Health Services Research Foundation.

Komesaroff, P. (1999). Ethical implications of competition policy in healthcare. *Medical Journal of Australia, 170,* 266–8.

Kotter, J. P. (2001). What leaders really do: Breakthrough leadership. *Best of Harvard Business Review. December.* 85–96.

Kouzes, J. M., & Posner, B. Z. (1987). *The leadership challenge: How to get extraordinary things done in organisations.* San Francisco: Jossey Bass.

Kovner, C., & Gergen, P. J. (1998). Nurse staffing levels and adverse events following surgery in U.S. hospitals. *IMAGE: Journal of Nursing Scholarship, 30,* 389–93.

REFERENCES

Kramer, M., & Schmalenberg, C. (1988). Magnet hospitals: Institutions of excellence. Part I. *Journal of Nursing Administration, 18*(1), 13–24.

Kramer, R. M., & Neale, M. A. (eds). (1998). *Power and influence in organizations.* Thousand Oaks: SAGE Publications.

Krause, D. (1997). *The way of the leader.* London, UK: Nicholas Brealey Publishing.

Kriegel, R., & Brandt, D. (1997). *Sacred cows make the best burgers: Developing change-ready people and organizations.* New York: Warner Brothers.

Kummerow, J. M., Barger, N. J., & Kirby, L. K. (1997). *Work types: Understand your work personality and how it helps you and holds you back, and what you can do to understand it.* New York: Warner Books.

Kuokkanen, L., & Leino-Kilpi, H. (2000). Power and empowerment in nursing: Three theoretical approaches. *Journal of Advanced Nursing, 31*(1) 235–41.

Kupperschmidt, B. R. (2000). Multigeneration employees: Strategies for effective management. *The Health Care Manager, 19*(1), 65–76.

Landeen, J., Byrne, C., & Brown, B. (1995). Journal keeping as an educational strategy in teaching psychiatric nursing. *Journal of Advanced Nursing. 17,* 347–55.

Lansbury, R. D., & Spillane, R. (1983). *Organisational behaviour in the Australian context.* Melbourne, Australia: Longman Cheshire.

Lanser, E. G. (2001). Fulfilling the promise: Technology's role in improving patient safety. *Healthcare Executive, 16*(5), 6–11.

LaNuez, D., & Jermier, J. M. (1994). Sabotage by managers and technocrats: neglected patterns of resistance at work. In M. M. Jermier, D. Knights, & W. R. Nord (eds). *Resistance and power in organizations.* London: Routledge.

Larrabee, J. H., Engle, V. F., & Tolley, E. A. (1995). Predictors of patient-perceived quality. *Scandinavian Journal of Caring Sciences. 9,* 153–64.

Larson, M. S. (1977). *The rise of professionalism: A sociological analysis.* Berkeley, CA: University of California Press.

Latane, B., Williams, K., & Harkins, S. (1979). Many hands make light the work: The causes and consequences of social loafing. *Journal of Applied Personality and Social Psychology, 37,* 822–32.

Leatherman, S., & Sutherland, K. (1998). Evolving quality in the new NHS: Policy, process and pragmatic considerations. *Quality in Health Care, 7* (Suppl.), S54–S61.

Ledington, P., & Donaldson, J. (1997). Soft OR and management practice: a study of the adoption and use of soft systems methodology. *Journal of Operational Research Society, 48,* 229–40.

Leeder, S. R. (2000). Clinical and ethical considerations in health care in Australia. *Calvary Hospital Centenary Ethics Conference, 12 December 2000,* Adelaide, Australia. Notes taken by A. Hofmeyer.

Leininger, M. (1991). *Culture care diversity and universality: A theory of nursing.* New York: National League for Nursing Press.

Lenburg, C. B. (2002). The influence of contemporary trends and issues on nursing education. In B. Cherry, & S. Jacob (eds). *Contemporary nursing: Issues, trends & management.* (pp. 65–94). St. Louis: Mosby.

Leob, M., & Kindel, S. (1999). *Leadership for dummies.* Philadelphia, PA.: John Wiley & Sons.

Leonard, D. & Strauss, S. (1997). Putting your company's whole brain to work. *Harvard Business Review, July/August,* 111–21.

Lett, M. (2002). The concept of clinical leadership. *Contemporary Nurse, 12*(1), 16–21.

Lett, M. (1999). The need for leadership. *Contemporary Nurse, 8,* 136–41.

Levy, V. (1985). *Financial management of hospitals.* (3rd edn). Sydney: Law Book Co. Ltd.

Lewicki, R. J., McAllister, D. J., & Bies, R. J. (1998). Trust and distrust: New relationships and realities. *Academy of Management Review, 23*(3), 438–59.

Lewin, K. (1951). *Field theory in social science: Selected theoretical papers.* New York: Harper & Row.

Lewin, R., & Regine, B. (2000). *The soul at work. Listen. Respond. Let go.* New York: Simon and Schuster.

Lewis, (1998). Lifelong learning: Why professionals must have the desire for and the capacity to continue learning throughout life. *Health Information Management, 28*(2), 62–6.

Liaschenko, J. (1998). Moral evaluation and concepts of health and health promotion. *Advanced Practice Nursing Quarterly, 4*(2), 71–7.

Liaschenko, J. (1993). Feminist ethics and cultural ethos: Revisiting a nursing debate. *Advances in Nursing Science, 15*(4), 71–81.

Lifton, R. (1986). *The Nazi doctors: A study of the psychology of evil.* London, UK: Macmillan.

Linscott, J., Spee, R., Flint, F., & Fisher, A. (1999). Creating a culture of patient focused care through a learner-centered philosophy. *Canadian Journal of Nursing Leadership, 12*(4), 5–10.

Lippitt, R., Watson, J., & Westley, B. (1958). *The dynamics of planned change.* New York: Harcourt. Brace and Company.

Lipson, H., & Rogers, J. (2000). Cultural aspects of disability. *Journal of Transcultural Nursing, 11,* 212–19.

Lipson, J., & Meleis, A. (1985). Culturally appropriate care: The case of immigrants. *Topics in Clinical Nursing 7,* 48–56.

Lipson, J., & Steiger, N. (1996). *Self-care nursing in multi-cultural context.* Thousand Oaks, CA: Sage Publications.

Liu, Y., & Perrene, P. (2002). The role of emotion in employee counterproductive work behavior (CWB): Integrating the psychoevolutionary and constructivist perspectives. Paper presented at the Third Conference on Emotions and Organizational Life, Bond University, Gold Coast.

Lloyd, P., & Boyce, R. A. (1998). Management theory and practice. In M. Clinton, & D. Scheiwe (eds), *Management in the Australian health care industry.* (2nd edn). pp. 140–71, Melbourne: Longman.

Locke, E. A. (1966). The contradiction of epiphenomenalism. *British Journal of Psychology, 57,* 203–4.

Lohr, K. N., Donaldson, M. S., & Harris-Wehling, J. (1992). Medicare: A strategy for quality assurance v. quality of care in a changing health care environment. *Quality Review Bulletin, 18,* 120–6.

Lohr, K. N., Eleazer, K., & Mauskopf, J. (1998). Health policy issues and applications for evidence-based medicine and clinical practice guidelines. *Health Policy. 46*(1), 1–19.

Louv, R. (2002). Mapping the new world of leadership. The second in a series of essays on leadership from Leadership for a Changing World, a program of the Ford Foundation in partnership with the Advocacy Institute and the Robert F. Wagner Graduate School of Public Service, New York University at http://leadershipforchange.org/papers/mapping.php3 accessed online 6.1.03.

Lowe, G. (2002). High-quality healthcare workplaces: A vision and action plan. *Hospital Quarterly.* http://www.longwoods.com/hq/summer02/index.html

Lowe, G. S., & Schellenberg, G. (2001). *What's a good job? The importance of employment relationships.* Canadian Policy Research Networks Inc., http://www.renoufbooks.com

Luker, K. A. (1999). The dilemma concerning the nurse's role in a multidisciplinary research agenda. *Nursing Times Research 4,* 85–6.

Lusky, K. (2000). Is a personal digital assistant in your future? These palm-sized devices could give you immediate access to patient information at the bedside. Here's what you need to know about these tiny titans at http://www.nurses.com/content/news/article.asp?docid={d729d42d-bf95-11d4-8c7f-009027de0829} Accessed April, 2003.

Lusky, K., Crotty, G., Strong, P., Inman, D., Markham, S., Robertson, K., Koch, R., Whitehead, V., Preston, J., Bone, K., & Briggs, C. (2002). Meeting the challenges of a changing profession. *Tennessee Nurse, 65*(4), 10–17.

Machiavelli, N. (2002). (*The Prince,* 1513, Chapter 6) http://www.the-prince-by-machiavelli.com Accessed November, 2002.

Mackay, H. (1999). *Turning point: Australians choosing their future.* Sydney: Macmillan.

Mackay, H., & Blanchard, K. (1999). *Swim with the sharks without being eaten alive: Outsell, outmanage, outnegotiate your competition.* (Released edition). New York, N.Y.: Fawceet Books.

REFERENCES

Mackenzie, J. (1993). Effects of change on sisters/charge nurses. *Nursing Standard, 26,* 25–7.

Maehling, J., & Badger, K. (1996). Information systems tools available to the case manager. *Nurse Case Manager, 1*(1), 35–40.

Magendanz, D. (2001). Principles of ethical leadership. *Living Ethics, Newsletter of The St James Ethics Centre, Summer,* p. 10, Sydney, NSW.

Magnussen, L. (2001). The use of the cognitive behavior survey to assess nursing student learning. *Research Brief, 40*(1), 43–5.

Mahoney, J. (2001). Leadership skills for the 21st century. *Journal of Nursing Management (9),* 269–71.

Major, F. A., Pepin, J. I., & Légault, A. J. (2001). Nursing knowledge in a mostly French-speaking Canadian province: From past to present. *Nursing Science Quarterly, 14,* 355–68.

Malinski, V. (2002). Nursing research and the human sciences. *Nursing Science Quarterly, 15,* 14–20.

Mallick, M. (1998). The role of nurse educators in the development of reflective practitioners: A selective case study of the Australian and United Kingdom experience. *Nurse Education Today, 18,* 52–63.

Malone, B. L. (2001). Nurses in non-nursing leadership positions. In J. McCloskey Dochterman, & H. Kennedy Grace (eds) *Current issues in nursing.* (6th edn). (pp. 293–8). St Louis: Mosby.

Mangan, J., & Williams, C. (1999). *Casual employment in Australia: A further analysis.* Economic Research Papers in Australia at http://www.oesr.qld.gov.au/data/research/casaus/casaus.htm

Manion, J. (1994). Managing change: The leadership challenge of the 1990s. *Seminars for Nurse Managers, 2,* 203–8.

Manley, K. (2000). Organisational culture and consultant nurse outcomes: part 1 organisational culture, *Nursing Standard, 14*(36), 34–8.

Mann, J. (2002). Futurists vs planners. *The Futurist,* July–August, p. 68.

Mann, R. (1996). Psychological abuse in the workplace. In E. J. Dwyer (ed.). *Beyond Bullying Association Inc.* New South Wales: Millennium Books.

Mantas, J., & Hasman, A. (eds) (2002). *Textbook in health informatics a nursing informatics perspective.* Amsterdam: Vol. 65, IOS Press.

Markham, G. (1996). Gender in leadership. *Nursing Management, 3*(1) 18–19.

Marquis, B. L., & Huston, C. J. (2000). *Leadership roles and management functions in nursing: Theory and Application.* (3rd edn). Philadelphia: Lippincott, Williams & Wilkins.

Marquis, B. L., & Huston, C. J. (1996). *Leadership roles and management functions in nursing.* (2nd edn). Philadelphia: Lippincott–Raven Publishers.

Marriner Tomey, A. (2000). *Guide to nursing management and leadership.* (6th edn). St. Louis: Mosby.

Marriner-Tomey, A. (1996). *Guide to nursing management and leadership.* Mosby-Year Book, Inc: St Louis, 171.

Martin, C. R., Bowman, G. S., Knight, S., & Thompson, D. R. (1998). Progress with a strategy for developing research in practice. *Nursing Times Research 3,* 28–34.

Martin, C. R., & Thompson, D. R. (2000). *Design and analysis of clinical nursing research studies.* London: Routledge.

Martin, J., & Myerson, D. (1998). Women and power: Conformity, resistance and disorganized coaction. In R. M. Kramer, & M. A. Neale (eds). *Power and influence in organizations.* Thousand Oaks, California: Sage.

Martin, K. (2002). *The missing link: Management and employee retention.* The National Healthcare Cost and Quality Association http://www.cost-quality.com/restpast/v7i2a3.html

Maslen, G. (2002). UWS PhD researcher points to new approach to combat school bullying. *Campus Review,* August/September.

Matthews, P., & Newell, L. M. (1999). Clinical information systems: Paving the way for clinical information management. *Journal of Healthcare Information Management, 13*(3), 97–111.

Maxwell, J.C (1998). *The 21 irrefutable laws of leadership. Follow them and people will follow you.* Nashville: Nelson Publishers.

Mayo, E. (1953). *The human problems of an industrialized ciivilization*. New York: MacMillan.

McAlister, F. A., Lawson, F. M. E., Teo, K. K. & Armstrong, P. W. (2001). A systematic review of randomized trials of disease management programs in congestive heart failure. *American Journal of Medicine, 110*, 378–84.

McCarthy, M. (2000). Practical aspects. Computers and the internet: Tools for lifelong learning. *Journal of Renal Nutrition, 10*(1), 44–8.

McCarthy, P. (1996). When the mask slips: Inappropriate coercion in organisations undergoing restructuring. In E. J. Dyer (ed.). *Beyond Bullying Association Inc.* New South Wales: Millennium Books.

McCaughan, D., Thompson, C., Cullum, N., Sheldon, T. A., & Thompson, D. R. (2002). Acute nurses' perceptions of barriers to using research information in clinical decision-making. *Journal of Advanced Nursing.*

McClelland, D. C. (1975). *Power: The inner experience*. New York: Irvington.

McClelland, D. C., & Boyatzis, R. E. (1982). Leadership motive pattern and long-term success in management. *Journal of Applied Psychology, 67*, 737–43.

McCloskey, J. C., & Maas, M. (1998). Interdisciplinary team: The nursing perspective is essential. *Nursing Outlook, 46*(4), 157–63.

McCormack, B., & Hopkins, E. (1995). The development of clinical leadership through supported reflective practice. *Journal of Clinical Nursing, 4*, 161–8.

McCormack, B., Kitson, A., Harvey, G., Rycroft-Malone, J., Tichen, A., & Seers, K. (2002). Getting evidence into practice: The meaning of context. *Journal of Advanced Nursing, 38*, 94–104.

McCormack, M. (1988). *What they don't teach you in Harvard Business School.* New York, N.Y.: Bantam Doubleday Dell Publishers.

McCrae, R. R., & Costa, P. T. (1997). Personality trait structure. *American Psychologist, 52*, 509–16.

McDaniel, C., & Wolf, G. (1992). Transformational leadership in nursing service: A test of a theory, *Journal of Nursing Administration (22)2*, 60–5.

McElmurry, B. J., Kim, S. A. L., & Gasseer, N. (2000). Global nursing leadership: A professional imperative. *Seminars for Nurse Managers, 8*, 232–8.

McFarlane, F. (1999). The expanded importance and expectations for lifelong learning and continuing education in rehabilitation. *Rehabilitation Education, 13*(1), 3–12.

McGillis Hall, L., Doran, D. I., Baker, G. R., Pink, G. H., Sidani, S., O'Brien-Pallas, L., & Donner, G. J. (2001). *The impact of nursing staff mix models and organisational change strategies on patient, system and nurse outcomes.* Toronto: University of Toronto.

McGregor, D. (1960). *The human side of enterprise.* New York: McGraw-Hill.

McKee, M., Aiken, L., Rafferty A. M., & Sochalski, J. (1998). Organisational change and quality of health care: an evolving international agenda. *Quality in Health Care, 7*, 37–41.

McKenna, H., & Hsu, H. (1998). Quality and evidence in nursing. *Quality in Health Care, 7*, 179–80.

McKenna, R. (1999). *New management*. Australia: McGraw–Hill Companies.

McMillan, I. (1995). Losing control. *Nursing Times. 91*(15), 40.

McMillan, M., & Conway, J. (2002). Exploring nursing leadership. Editorial in *Australian Journal of Advanced Nursing, 19*(4), 5–6.

McPhail, G. (1997). Management of change: An essential skill for nursing in the 1990s. *Journal of Nursing Management, 5*, 199–205.

McTaggart, D., Findlay, C. & Parkin, M. (1996). *Microeconomics.* Sydney: Addison–Wesley Publishing Company.

Mead, D. (1991). An evaluation tool for primary nursing. *Nursing Standard, 6*(1), 37–9.

Meize-Grochowski, R. (1984). An analysis of the concept of trust. *Journal of Advanced Nursing, 9*, 563–72.

Meleis, A. (1999). Culturally competent care. *Journal of Transcultural Nursing, 10*, 12.

Meleis, A., Davis, L., Dumas, R., Ferketich, S., Flaherty, M., Isenberg, M., Koerner, J., Lacey, B., Stern, P., & Valente, S. (1992). American Academy of Nursing. Expert panel report: culturally competent health care. *Washington: American Academy of Nursing, 1992.*

REFERENCES

Meleis, A., Isenberg, M., Koerner, & Stern, P. (1995). *Diversity, marginalization, and culturally competent health care: Issues in knowledge development.* Washington, DC: American Academy of Nursing.

Meleis, A., & Jonsen, A. (1983). Ethical crises and cultural differences. *The Western Journal of Medicine, 138,* 889–93.

Meleis, A., Lipson, J., Muecke, M., & Smith, G. (1998). *Immigrant women and their health: An olive paper.* Indianapolis, IN: Sigma Theta Tau International Center Press.

Melohn, T. (1994). *The new partnership.* Philadelphia: John Wiley & Sons.

Menix, K. D. (2000). Educating to manage the accelerated change environment effectively: part 1. *Journal for Nurses in Staff Development, 16*(6), 282–8.

Menix, K. (2001). Educating to manage the accelerated change environment effectively: Part 2. *Journal for Nurses in Staff Development, 17*(1), 44–53.

Menzies, I. (1960). *A case study in the functioning of social systems as a defence against anxiety.* Great Britain: Tavistock Institute of Human Relations.

Merry, M. D. (1993). Total quality management for physicians: Translating the new paradigm. In A. F. Al-Assaf, & J. A. Schmele (eds), *The textbook of total quality in healthcare.* (pp. 51–9). Delray Beach, Fla: St Lucie Press.

Messias, D. K. H. (2001). World health. Globalization, nursing and health for all. *Journal of Nursing Scholarship, 33*(1), 9–11.

Messick, D. H., & Ohme, R. K. (1998). Some ethical aspects of the social psychology of social influence. In R. M. Kramer, & M. A. Neale (eds). *Power and influence in organizations.* Thousand Oaks, California: Sage.

Meurier, C. E., & Vincent, C. A. (1997). Learning from errors in nursing practice. *Journal of Advanced Nursing, 26*(1), 111–19.

Middleton, S., & Lumby, J. (1998). Outcome evaluation in nursing in Australia: 1960–80. *Australian Health Review, 21,* 72–9.

Miflin, B., Campbell, C., & Price, D. (2000). A conceptual framework to guide the development of self-directed, lifelong learning in problem-based medical curricula. *Medical Education, 34*(4), 299–306.

Miller, L. (1995). Customer focus: Key to total quality. In K. M. Shelton (ed.), *In search of quality. The Business consultant's perspective* (pp. 293–302). Utah: Executive Excellence Publishing.

Milton, C. L. (1999). Ethical codes and principles: The link to nursing theory. *Nursing Science Quarterly, 12,* 290–1.

Mintzberg, H. (1994). Managing as blended care. *Journal of Nursing Administration, 24,* 29–36.

Mintzberg, M. (2002). Managing care and cure—up and down, in and out. *Health Services Management Research, 15,* 193–206.

Mitchell, G. J. (2001). Pictures of paradox: Technology, nursing and human science. In R. C. Locsin, *Advancing technology, caring and nursing* (pp. 22–40). Westport, Conneticut: Auburn House.

Mitchell, G. J. (1999). Evidence based practice: Critique and alternative view. *Nursing Science Quarterly, 12,* 30–5.

Mitchell, G. J. (1998). Standards of nursing and the winds of change. *Nursing Science Quarterly, 11,* 97–8.

Mitchell, G. J. (1994). Discipline-specific inquiry: The hermeneutics of theory-guided nursing research. *Nursing Outlook, 42,* 224–8.

Mitchell, G. J. (1991). Nursing diagnosis: An ethical analysis. *IMAGE, 23*(2), 99–103.

Mitchell, G. J. (1990). Struggling in change: From the traditional approach to Parse's theory-based practice. *Nursing Science Quarterly, 3,* 170–6.

Mitchell, G. J. (1988). Man-living-health: The theory in practice. *Nursing Science Quarterly, 1,* 120–7.

Mitchell, G. J., & Bournes, D. A. (2000). Nurse as patient advocate? In search of straight thinking. *Nursing Science Quarterly, 13,* 204–9.

Mitchell, G. J., & Bournes, D. A. (1998). *Finding the way.* Toronto: Sunnybrook Health Sciences Centre.

Mitchell, G. J., Closson, T., Coulis, N., Flint, F., & Gray, B. (2000). Patient focused care and human becoming thought: Connecting the right stuff. *Nursing Science Quarterly, 13*, 216–24.

Mitchell, G. J., & Cody, W. K. (2002). Ambiguous opportunity: Toiling for truth of nursing art and science. *Nursing Science Quarterly, 15*, 71–9.

Mitchell, G. J., & Cody, W. K. (1999). Human becoming theory: A complement to medical science. *Nursing Science Quarterly, 12*, 304–10.

Mitchell, G. J., & Lawton, C. (2000). Living with the consequences of personal choices for persons with diabetes: Implications for educators and practitioners. *Canadian Journal of Diabetes Care, 24*(2), 23–30.

Mitchell, G. J., & Pilkington, F. B. (2000). Comfort-discomfort with ambiguity: Flight and freedom in nursing practice. *Nursing Science Quarterly, 13*, 31–6.

Mitchell, P. H., Ferketich, S., & Jennings, B. M. (1998). Health policy: Quality health outcomes model. *Image—the Journal of Nursing Scholarship, 30*, 43–6.

Moccia, P. (1988). At the faultline: Social activism and caring. *Nursing Outlook, 36*(1), 30–3.

Morgan, G. (1986). *Images of organization*. London: Sage.

Morrison, E. W., & Robinson, S. L. (1997). When employees feel betrayed: A model of how psychological contract violation develops. *Academy of Management Review, 22*(2), 226–56.

Morrison, R., Jones, L., & Fuller, B. (1997). The relation between leadership style and empowerment on job satisfaction of nurses. *Journal of Nursing Administration, 2*, 27–34.

Muihead, B., & Simon, W. (1999). *High velocity leadership: The Mars pathfinder approach to—faster, better, cheaper.* New York, N.Y.: Harper Business.

Mulholland, J. (1994). Competency-based learning applied to nursing management. *Journal of Nursing Management, 2*, 161–6.

Mullins, L. J. (1999). *Management and organisational behaviour*. UK: Pearson Education Limited.

Mullins, L. J. (1993). *Management and organisational behaviour.* London: Pitman Publishing.

Murdoch Perra, B. (2001). Leadership: The key to quality outcomes. *Journal of Nursing Care Quality (15)*2, 68–73.

Murray, D. (1997). *Ethics in organizations*. London, UK: Kogan Page.

Naish, J. (1995). Who are the new leaders? *Nursing Management, 2*(3) 6–7.

Namus, B. & Bennis, W. (1997). *Leaders' strategies for taking change.* (2nd edn). New York, N.Y.: Harper Business.

Nay, R., & Pearson, A. (2001). Educating nurses to protect the past or to advanced health care: A polemic. *Australian Journal of Advanced Nursing, 18*(4), 37–41.

Needleman, J., Buerhaus, P., Mattke, S., Stewart, M., & Zelevinsky. (2002). Nurse staffing levels and the quality of care in hospitals. *The New England Journal of Medicine, 346*(22), 1715–22.

Needleman, J., Buerhaus, P., Mattke, S., Stewart, M., & Zelevinsky, K. (2001). Nurse staffing and patient outcomes in hospitals. Final Report, US Department of Health and Human Services, Health Resources and Service Administration, Contract No. 230-99-0021, February 28, 2001, Rockville, MD.

Nelson, J. W. (2000). Models of nursing care: A century of vacillation. *Journal of Nursing Administration, 30*, 156, 184.

New South Wales Anti-Discrimination Act. (1997). No. 48. http://www.legislation.nsw.gov.au

New South Wales Occupational Health and Safety Act. (2000). No. 40. http://legislation.nsw.gov.au

New South Wales Privacy and Personal Information Act. (1998). No. 133. http://www.legislation.nsw.gov.au

Newman, K., & Maylor, U. (2002). The NHS plan: Nurse satisfaction, commitment and retention strategies, *Health Services Management Research, 15*, 93–105.

Newman, K., Maylor, U., & Chansarkar, B. (2001). The nurse retention chain, quality of care and patient satisfaction chain. *International Journal of Health, 14*(2), 57–69.

Newton, T., Handy, J., & Fineman, S. (1995). *'Managing' stress: Emotion and power at work.* London: Sage.

NHS Centre for Reviews and Dissemination (1999). Getting evidence into practice. *Effective Health Care 5*, 1–16.

REFERENCES

Nicholson, N. (2002). Gene politics and the natural selection of leaders. In F. Hesselbein, & R. Johnston (eds). (pp. 29–41). *On creativity, innovation and renewal: A leader to leader guide.* San Fransisco: Jossey-Bass.

Nichter, M., Trockman, G., & Grippin, J. (1985). Clinical anthropologist as therapy facilitator: Role development and clinician evaluation in a psychiatric training program. *Human Organization, 44,* 72–80.

Nicklin, P. J. (1996). Providing a quality service. In N. Kenworthy, G. Snowley, & C. Gilling (eds). *Common Foundations Studies in Nursing.* (2nd edn). (pp. 215–34). New York: Churchill-Livingston.

Nicolson, P. (1996). *Gender, power and organisation: A psychological perspective.* London: Routledge.

Nolan, M. T. (2000). Improving patient care through data competence. *Nurs Econ., 18*(5), 250–4.

Nolan, M. T., Johnson, C., Coleman, J., Patterson, S., & Dang, D. (2000). Unifying organisational approaches to measuring and managing patient outcomes. *Journal of Nursing Administration, 30*(1), 27–33.

Norman, L. (1997). Continuous improvement in nursing education. *Qual Connection, 6*(20), 4.

Norris, T. (2002). Making the transition from student to professional nurse. In B. Cherry, & S. Jacob (eds). (pp. 497–516). *Contemporary nursing: Issues, trends, & management.* St. Louis: Mosby.

NSW Health Department (2002) *Information Management and Technology Education, Training and Development Strategy—A Strategy for NSW Healthcare Workers. NSW Government Action Plan. Better Health Centre.* Publications Warehouse, Gladesville.

NSW Health Department (2001). *Improving health care for people with chronic illness: A blueprint for change 2001–2003.* Sydney: NSW Government Action Plan, NSW Health. Retrieved 28 January, 2003, at http://www.health.nsw.gov.au/policy/gap/chronic/chronic.pdf.

Nursing and Midwifery Council, United Kingdom (2002). Retrieved 16 December, 2002, at http://www.nmc-uk.org/cms/content/home

Nursing Council of New Zealand (2001). KPMG Strategic Review of Undergraduate Nursing Education. Retrieved 28 January, 2003, at http://www.nursingcouncil.org.nz/kpmgfinalreport.pdf .

O'Bannon, G. (2001). Managing our future: The Generation X Factor. *Public Personnel Management, 30*(1), 95–107.

O'Brien-Pallas, L. L., Baumann, A., & Lochhaas-Gerlach, J. (1998). *Health human resources: A preliminary analysis of nursing personnel in Ontario.* Toronto, Canada: Ontario Ministry of Health Nursing Task Force.

O'Brien-Pallas, L., & Baumann, A. (2000). Toward evidence-based policy decisions: A case study of nursing health human resources in Ontario, Canada. *Nursing Enquiry, 7,* 248–57.

O'Brien-Pallas, L., Thomson, D., Alksnis, C., & Bruce, S. (2001). The economic impact of nurse staffing decisions: Time to turn down another road? *Hospital Quarterly, 4,* 42–50.

O'Connell, B., Young, J., Brooks, J., Hutchings, J., & Lofthouse, J. (2000). Nurses' perceptions of the nature and frequency of aggression in general ward settings and high dependency areas. *Journal of Clinical Nursing, 9*(4), 602–10.

O'Hara, D. A., & Carson, N. J. (1997). Reporting of adverse events in hospitals in Victoria, 1994–1995. *Medical Journal of Australia, 166,* 460–3.

O'Leary-Kelly, A. M., Griffin, F. W., & Glew, D. J. (1996). Organization-motivated aggression: a research framework. *Academy of Management Review, 21*(1), 225–54.

O'May, F., & Buchan, J. (1999). Shared governance: A literature review. *International Journal of Nursing Studies, 36,* 281–300.

O'Rourke, M. W. (2003). Rebuilding a professional practice model: The return of role based practice accountability. *Nursing Administration Quarterly, Spring,* Leah Curtain (ed). *In press.*

O'Rourke, M. W. (2001). Building organisations to succeed beyond 2000 takes conviction. *Seminars for Nurse Managers, 9*(1), 16–32.

O'Rourke, M. W. (1996). Who holds the keys to the future of health care? *Nurse Week, Jan. 8,* 1–2.

O'Rourke, M. W. (1994). Professional practice and collaboration for care team redesign. *Nursing Horizons.* (December), Long Beach Memorial Medical Center, Division of Nursing.

O'Rourke, M.W. (1989). Generic professional behaviors: Implications for the CNS role. *Clinical Nurse Specialist, 3*(3), 128–32.

O'Rourke, M.W. (1985). Generic professional behaviors of registered nurses: A descriptive study. Paper presented at the National Symposium of Nursing Research, Palo Alto, CA.

O'Rourke, M.W. (1980). *Expert power: The basis for political strength.* New York, New York: National League for Nursing.

O'Rourke, M.W. (1979). *A coalition for health care: Bridge between individual accountability and public policy.* New York, New York: National League for Nursing.

O'Rourke, M.W. (1976). *California Nursing Practice Act: A model for implementation.* San Francisco, California: California Nurses' Association.

O'Rourke, M.W, & Goeppinger, S. (2000). Interdisciplinary professional practice: Good for patients, good for business. Peer reviewed poster session American Academy of Nursing, Annual Conference, San Diego CA.

O'Rourke, M., & Parini, S. (2001). Interdisciplinary professional practice: Good for patients, good for business. Paper presented at Health care Forum Annual Conference. Philadelphia PA.

Oakley, E. & Krug, D. (1991). *Enlightened leadership: Getting to the heart of change.* New York: Simon & Schuster.

Ospina, S., & Schall, E. (2001). Perspectives on leadership: Our approach to research and documentation for the leadership for a changing world program. *The first in a series of essays on leadership from Leadership for a Changing World, a program of the Ford Foundation in partnership with the Advocacy Institute and the Robert F. Wagner Graduate School of Public Service, New York University.* http://leadershipforchange.org/papers/mapping.php3 *6.1.03.*

Ospina, S., Godsoe, B. & Schall, E. (2002). Co-producing knowledge: Practitioners and scholars working together to understand leadership, Paper based on a round table presentation given at the 2001 International Leadership Association Conference, Miami, at http://leadershipforchange.org/research/papers/knowledge.pho3 – accessed 21 March 2003.

Ovretveit, J. (1999). A team quality improvement sequence for complex problems. *Quality in Health Care, 8,* 239–46.

Owen, G. M. (1985). Innovation in nursing—the role of higher education in relation to nursing practice. *Journal of Advanced Nursing, 10,* 179–83.

Pace, R.W., & Faules, D. F. (1994). *Organizational communication.* Englewood Cliffs, New Jersey: Prentice Hall.

Palmer, I., & Hardy, C. (2000). *Thinking about management: Implications of organizational debates for practice.* London: Sage.

Parkin, W. (1993). The public and the private: Gender, sexuality and emotion. In S. Fineman (ed.). *Emotion in organizations.* London: Sage.

Parry, K.W. (2001). Could leadership theory be generalised? In Wiesner, R. and Millett, B. (eds) (2001). *Management and organisational behaviour.* Brisbane: John Wiley & Sons.

Parry, K. (1996). *Transformational leadership.* Melbourne, Australia: Pitman Publishing.

Parse, R. R. (2001a). Nursing: Still in the shadow of medicine. *Nursing Science Quarterly, 14,* 181.

Parse, R. R. (2001b). Language and the sow-reap rhythm. *Nursing Science Quarterly, 14,* 273.

Parse, R. R. (2001c). *Qualitative inquiry: The path of sciencing.* Sudbury, MA: Jones and Bartlett.

Parse, R.R. (1998). *The human becoming school of thought: A perspective for nurses and other health professionals.* Thousand Oaks, CA: Sage.

Parse, R. R. (1997). The human becoming theory: The was, is, and will be. *Nursing Science Quarterly, 10,* 32–8.

Parse, R. R. (ed.) (1995). *Illuminations: The human becoming theory in practice and research.* New York: National League for Nursing Press.

Parse, R. R. (1993). Nursing and medicine: Two different disciplines. *Nursing Science Quarterly, 6,* 109.

Parse, R. R. (1992). Human becoming: Parse's theory of nursing. *Nursing Science Quarterly, 5,* 35–42.

REFERENCES

Parse, R. R. (1987). *Nursing science: Major paradigms, theories, and critiques*. Philadelphia: Saunders.

Parse, R. R. (1981). *Man-living-health: A theory of nursing*. New York: Wiley.

Paterson, B., McComish, A., & Aitken, I. (1997). Abuse and bullying. *Nursing Management, 3*(10) 8–9.

Pearcy, P., & Draper, P. (1996). Using the diffusion of innovation model to influence practice: A case study. *Journal of Advanced Nursing, 23*(4), 714–21.

Pearson, A & Borbasi, S. (1996). In praise of tall poppies—Nursing's need for leadership. In J. Anderson (ed.) *Thinking management: Focusing on people*. Melbourne: Ausmed Publications.

Pelled, L. H., Eisenhardt, K. M., & Xin, K. R. (1999). Exploring the black box: An analysis of work group diversity, conflict and performance. *Administrative Science Quarterly, 44*(1) 1–28.

Pelletier, D., Donoghue, J., Duffield, C., Adams, A., & Brown, D. (1999). Why undertake higher degrees in nursing? *Journal of Nursing Education (USA), 37*(9), 422–42.

Peter, E., & Morgan, K. P. (2001). Explorations of a trust approach for nursing ethics. *Nursing Inquiry, 8*(1), 3–10.

Pierce, J. L., & Newstrom, J. W. (2000). *Leaders and the leadership process: Readings, self-assessments and applications*. Boston: Irwin McGraw-Hill.

Pilkington, F. B. (1993). The lived experience of grieving the loss of an important other. *Nursing Science Quarterly, 6*, 130–9.

Poggenpoel, M. (1992). Managing change. *Nursing RSA Verplegin 7*, 28–31.

Porter-O'Grady, T. (2001a). Is shared governance still relevant? *Journal of Nursing Administration, 31*, 468–73.

Porter-O'Grady, T. (2001b). Profound change: 21st century nursing. *Nursing Outlook, 49*(4), 182–6.

Porter-O'Grady, T. (1999). Quantum leadership: New roles for a new age. *Journal of Nursing Administration, 29*(10), 37–42.

Porter-O'Grady, T. (1998). The seven basic rules for successful redesign. In E. C. Heim (ed.), *Contemporary Leadership Behaviour* (Selected Readings 5th edn, pp. 226–35). New York: Lippincott.

Porter-O'Grady, T. (1997a). Guest editorial. *Nursing Administration Quarterly, 22*(2), vii–viii.

Porter-O'Grady, T. (1997b). Quantum mechanics and the future of healthcare leadership. *Journal of Nursing Administration (27)*, 15–20.

Porter-O'Grady, T. (1996). Into the new paradigm: Writing the script for the future of health care. *Collegian, 3*(4), 5–10.

Porter-O'Grady, T. (1995). From principle to practice: Whole systems shared governance. *Journal of Shared Governance 1*(3), 21–6.

Porter-O'Grady, T., & Malloch, K. (2002). *Quantum leadership: A textbook of new leadership*. Aspen: Gatersburgh.

Posner, B., & Kouzes, J. (1993). Values congruence and differences between the interplay of personal and organisational values. *Journal of Business Ethics, 12*, 341–47.

Powell, W. W., & DiMaggio, P. (1991). *The new institutionalism in organisational analysis*. Chicago: Chicago University Press.

Prebble, K. (2001). On the brink of change? Implications of the review of undergraduate education in New Zealand for mental health nursing. *Australian and New Zealand Journal of Mental Health Nursing, 10*, 136–44.

Prenkert, F., & Ehnfors, M. (1997). A measure of organisational effectiveness in nursing management in relation to transformational and transactional leadership: A study in a Swedish county hospital. *Journal of Nursing Management (5)*, 279–87.

Prince, S. (1997). Shared governance: Sharing power and opportunity. *Journal of Nursing Administration, 18*, 37–43.

Procter, P. (1992). *Nurses, computers and information technology*. London: Chapman and Hall.

Proenca, E. J. (1995). Why outcomes management doesn't always work: An organisational perspective. *Quality Management in Health Care, 3*(4), 1–9.

Provis, C. (2001). Why is trust important? *Reason in Practice, 1*(2), 31–41.

Prusak, L., & Cohen, D. (2001). How to invest in social capital. *Harvard Business Review.* June, 86–93.

Purnell, L. (2000). A description of the Purnell Model for cultural competence. *Journal of Transcultural Nursing, 11,* 40–6.

Purnell, L., & Paulanka, B. (2002). *Transcultural health care: A culturally competent approach,* 2nd edn. Philadelphia, PA: F.A. Davis.

Putman, L. L., & Mumby, D. K. (1993). Organizations, emotion and the myth of rationality. In S. Fineman (ed.). *Emotion in organizations.* London: Sage.

Pylkkanen, P. (ed.). (1989). *The search for meaning: The new spirit in science and philosophy.* Wellingborough, Northamptonshire, UK: Crucible.

Queensland Department of Industrial Relations. (2001). *Creating safe and fair workplaces: Strategies to address workplace harassment in Queensland.* Brisbane, Queensland: Queensland Workforce Bullying Taskforce. http://www.whs.qld.gov.au/taskforces/bullying/bullyingreport.pdf

Rafael, A. R. F. (1996). Power and caring: A dialectic in nursing. *Advances in Nursing Science, 19*(1), 3–17.

Ray, M. A., Turkel, M. C. & Marino, N. (2002). The transformative process for nursing in workplace redevelopment. *Nursing Administration Quarterly, 26*(2), 1–5.

Ray, R. G. (1999). *The facilitative leader: Behaviours that enable success.* New York: Prentice Hall.

Reardon, K. K. (1995). *They just don't get it, do they? Communication in the workplace—closing the gap between women and men.* Boston: Little, Brown & Company.

Redfern, S., & Stevens, W. (1998). Nursing development units: Their structure and orientation. *Journal of Clinical Nursing, 7,* 218–26.

Reed, J., & Ground, I. (1997). *Philosophy for nursing.* London: Arnold Publications.

Rees, S. (1995). The fraud and the fiction. In S. Rees, & G. Rodley (eds.) *The human costs of managerialism: Advocating the recovery of humanity* (pp. 15–27). Australia: Pluto Press.

Reid, B. (1993). But we're doing it already! Exploring a response to the concept of reflective practice in order to improve its facilitation. *Nurse Education Today, 13,* 305–9.

Reid, J. (1994). *Nursing education in Australian universities: Report of the national review of nurse education in the higher education sector, 1994 and beyond.* Canberra, Australia: AGPS.

Reid, J. (1994). *The Reid review nursing education in Australian universities report of the national review of nurse education in the higher education sector—1994 and beyond.* AGPS.

Reiter-Tetel, J. (2002). The impact of restructuring on professional nursing practice. *Journal of Nursing Administration, 32,* 31–41.

Rigby, E. (1993). The Yale cost model and cost centres: Servant or master? *Australian Health Review 16*(1) 89–102.

Rigby, K. (2002). *A meta-evaluation of methods and approaches to reducing bullying in pre-schools and early primary school in Australia.* Attorney-General's Department, Commonwealth of Australia, Canberra.

Rigby, K. D., & Litt, J. C. B. (2000). Errors in health care management: What do they cost? *Quality in Health Care, 9,* 216–21.

Ritter-Teitel, J. (2002). The impact of restructuring on professional nursing practice. *The Journal of Nursing Administration, 32*(1), 31–9.

Robbins, S. P., Bergman, R., Stagg, I., & Coulter, M. (2000). *Management.* (2nd edn). Sydney: Prentice Hall.

Robbins, S. P., Millett, B., Cacioppe, R., & Waters-Marsh, T. (1998). *Organisational behaviour: Leading and managing in Australia and New Zealand.* Sydney: Prentice Hall.

Robbins, S., & Mukerji, D. (1998). *Managing organisations: New challenges and perspectives.* Sydney, Australia: Prentice-Hall.

Robertson, I. T. (1998). Personality and organisational behaviour. *Selection and Development Review, 14*(4), 11–15.

Robinson, S. L., & Bennett, R. J. (1995). A typology of deviant workplace behaviours: A multidimensional scaling study. *Academy of Management Journal, 38*(2), 555–72.

REFERENCES

Robinson, S., Kraatz, S. L., & Rousseau, M. S. (1994). Changing obligations and the psychological contract: A longitudinal study. *Academy of Management Journal, 37*(1), 137–52.

Robinson-Walker, C. (1999). *Women and leadership in health care: The journey to authenticity and power.* San Fransisco: Jossey-Bass Publishers.

Rodney, P., & Starzomski, R. (1993). Constraints on the moral agency of nurses. *Canadian Nurse, 89*(9), 23–6.

Rogers, E. M. (1995). *Diffusion of innovation* (4th edn). New York: The Free Press.

Rogers, E. M. (1983). *Diffusion of innovation* (3rd edn). New York: The Free Press.

Rokeach, M. (1973). *The nature of human values.* New York, USA: Free Press.

Rolfe, R. (2002). Faking a difference: Evidence-based nursing and the illusion of diversity. *Nurse Education Today 22,* 3–12.

Romme, G. (1998). Antisocial behaviour in organizations. *Organization Studies, 19*(5), 894–6.

Rorie, J., Paine, L., & Berger, M. (1996). Primary care for women: Cultural competence in primary care issues. *Journal of Nurse Midwifery, 41*(2), 92–100.

Rose, J. (1999). A soft systems approach to the evaluation of complex interventions in the public sector. *Journal of Applied Management Studies,* 8(2), 199–216.

Rosener, J. (1990). Ways women lead. *Harvard Business Review (Nov–Dec),* 119–25.

Ross, J. R. (1997). A paradigm shift: What a difference a day makes! *Perspectives, 21*(4), 2–6.

Rost, J. (1993). *Leadership for the 21st century.* Praeger: Westport.

Rothschild, J., & Miethe, T. D. (1994). Whistleblowing as resistance in modern work organizations: The politics of revealing organizational deception and abuse. In M. M. Jermier, D. Knights, & W. R. Nord (eds). *Resistance and power in organizations.* London: Routledge.

Rowland, H., & Rowland, B. (1985). *Nursing administration handbook.* (2nd edn). Aspen, USA.

Rubin, H. (1997). *The Princessa: Machiavelli for women.* New York: Dell Books.

Rubotzky, A. (2000). Nursing participation in health care reform efforts of 1993–1994: advocating for the national community. *Advances in Nursing Science, 23*(2) 12–33.

Saltmarche, A., Kolodny, V., & Mitchell, G. J. (1998). An educational approach for patient focused care: Shifting attitudes and practice. *Journal of Nursing Staff Development, 14*(2), 81–6.

Sampson, E. E., & Marthas, M. (1990). *Group process for the health professions,* 3rd edn. New York: Delmar.

Schon, D. A. (1987). *Educating the reflective practitioner.* San Francisco: Jossey Bass.

Schon, D. A. (1983). *The reflective practitioner.* New York: New York.

Senate Community Affairs Committee (2002). *The patient profession: Time for action. Report on the inquiry into nursing.* Retrieved 17 September, 2002, at http://www.aph.gov.au/Senate/committee/clac_ctte/nursing/report/index.htm

Senge, P. (1995). *The fifth discipline—the art & practice of the learning organisation.* Sydney, Australia: Random House.

Senge, P. (1990). *The Fifth Discipline: The Art and Practice of the Learning Organisation.* New York: Doubleday.

Senge, P. M. (1992). The leader's new work: Building learning organizations. http://www.courses.bus.Alberta.ca/oa-central/articles/senge.htm

Shah, C., & Burke, G. (2001). *Job growth and replacement needs in nursing occupations* (Report 01/18 to the Evaluations and Investigations Program, Higher Education Division, Department of Education, Science and Training, Canberra).

Shalala, D. E. (1995). Quality education. In K. M. Shelton (ed.), *In search of quality. The business consultant's perspective* (pp. 287–91). Utah: Executive Excellence Publishing.

Shamian, J., O'Brien-Pallas, L., Kerr, M., Koehoorn, M., Thomson, D., & Alksnis, C. (2001). *Effects of job strain, hospital organisational factors and individual characteristics on work-related disability among nurses.* Workplace Safety and Insurance Board, Canada.

Shapiro, M. (1998). A career ladder based on Benner's model—an analysis of expected outcomes. *Journal of Nursing Administration, 28*(3), 13–19.

Sharman, E. (1998). *The glass elevator: How men overtake women in the nursing higher education workforce in Australia.* Unpublished PhD thesis, University of NSW.

Shaw, M. E. (1981). *Group dynamics: The social psychology of small group behaviour.* New York, USA: McGraw Hill.

Sheehan, M. (1996). Case studies in organisational restructuring. In E. J. Dyer (ed.). *Beyond Bullying Association Inc.* New South Wales: Millennium Books.

Sheppard, B. H. (1992). *Organizational justice: The search for fairness.* New York: Lexington Books.

Sheppard, B. H., & Sherman, D. A. (1998). The grammars of trust: A model and general implications. *Academy of Management Review, 23*(3), 422–38.

Shortell, S. M., & Kaluzny, A. D. (1997). Organization theory and health services management. In S. M. Shortell, & A. D. Kaluzny (eds), *Essentials of health care management.* New York: Delmar.

Shortell, S. M., Gillies, R. R., Anderson, D. A., Mitchell, J. B., & Morgan, K. L. (1993). Creating organised delivery systems: The barriers and the facilitators. *Hospital and Health Services Administration. (38)*4, 447–66.

Sigma Theta Tau. (2002) Retrieved 17 September, 2002, at http://www.nursingsociety.org/about/overview.html#overview

Simmons, M. (1996). *New leadership for women and men: Building an inclusive organization.* Hampshire: Gower.

Sinclair, A. (1998). *Doing Leadership Differently: Gender, power and sexuality in a changing business culture.* Melbourne: Melbourne University Press.

Skarlicki, D. P., Folger, R., & Tesluk, P. (1999). Personality as a moderator in the relationship between fairness and retaliation. *Academy of Management Journal, 42*(1), 100–8.

Smaltz, D.H.(2002) The elevation of CIO roles: Organisational barriers and organisational enablers. *Journal of Healthcare Information Management, 15*(2), 22–8.

Smith, A., Russell, J. (1991). Using critical incidents in nurse education. *Nurse Education Today, 11*(4), 284–91.

Smyth, J. (1989). Developing and sustaining critical reflection in teacher education. *Journal of Teacher Education, 40*(2), 2–9.

Snyder, M. (1987). *Public appearances/private realities: The psychology of self-monitoring.* New York: W.H. Freeman.

Southon, G. (1999). IT, change and evaluation: an overview of the role of evaluation in health services. *International Journal of Medical Informatics, 56*(1–3), 125–33.

Southon, G. (1997). Strategic constraints in health informatics: are expectations realistic? *International Journal of Health Planning and Management, 12*(1), 3–13.

Sparbel, K. J., & Anderson, M. A. (2000). A continuity of care integrated literature review, Part 2: Methodological issues. *Journal of Nursing Scholarship, 32*, 131–5.

Speedy, S. (2000). Gender issues in Australian nursing. In J. Daly, S. Speedy, & D. Jackson (eds.), *Contexts of nursing: An introduction.* Sydney: MacLennan & Petty.

Spencer, E., Mills, A., Rorty, M., & Erhane, P. (2000). *Organization ethics in health care.* New York: Oxford University Press.

Stace, D., & Dunphy, D. (1996). Translating business strategy into action: Transitions, transformations and turnarounds. In D. Stace, & D. Dunphy (eds). *Beyond the boundaries: Leading and creating the successful enterprise* (p. 91–22). Sydney: McGraw-Hill.

Staiger, D. O., Auerbach, D. A., & Buerhaus, P. I. (2000). Expanding career opportunities for women and the declining interest in nursing as a career. *Nursing Economics (18)*5, 230–36.

Staring, S., & Taylor, C. (1997). A guide to managing workforce transitions. *Nursing management, Dec,* 31–2.

Starzomski, R., & Rodney, P. (1997). Nursing inquiry for the common good. In S. E. Thorne, & V. E. Hayes (eds) *Nursing praxis: Knowledge and action* (pp. 219–36). Thousand Oaks, California, USA: Sage Publications.

Steers, R. M. (1989). *An introduction to organisational behaviour.* Englewood Cliffs, USA: Prentice Hall.

Steinbrook, R. (2002). Nursing in the crossfire. *New England Journal of Medicine, 346*(22), 1757–66.

Stemberg, R. L. & Kaufman, J. C. (1998). Human abilities. *Annual Review of Psychology, 49,* 479–502.

REFERENCES

Stephenson, C. (1997). Toward a female model of leadership. *Vital Speeches of the Day, 63*(7), 202–5.

Stevens, P. E. (1989). A critical social reconceptualisation of environment in nursing: Implications for methodology. *Advances in Nursing Science, 11*(4), 56–68.

Stewart, S., Vandenbroek, A. J., Pearson, B. A., & Horowitz, J. D. (1999). Prolonged beneficial effects of home-based intervention on unplanned readmission and mortality among patients with congestive heart failure. *Archives of Internal Medicine, 159*(3), 257–61.

Stout-Shaffer, S., & Larrabee, J. (1992). Everyone can be a visionary leader. *Nursing Management* (23)12, 54–8.

Strachan, H. (2002). Defining nursing informatics. http://www.nursing-informatics.net/strachan.htm. Accessed April, 2003.

Stringer, E. (1996). *Action research: A handbook for practitioners.* Sage.

Sullivan, T. J. (1998). Transformational leadership. In T. J. Sullivan (ed.). *Collaboration: A health care imperative* (pp. 467–98). New York: McGraw Hill.

Summer, J. & Nowicki, M. (2002). Managing organisational improvement in a resource-challenged environment. *Healthcare Financial Management 56*(7) 60–2.

Swage, T. (2000). *Clinical governance in health care practice.* Oxford: Butterworth Heineman.

Swan, J., & MacVicar, B. (1992). The rough guide to change. *Nursing Times, 88*(13), 48–49.

Swansburg, R. (1997). *Budgeting and financial management for nurse managers.* Sudbury: Jones & Bartlett.

Tallon, D., Chard, J., & Dieppe, P. (2000). Relation between agendas of the research community and the research consumer. *Lancet 355*, 2037–40.

Tannen, D. (1994). *Gender and discourse.* New York: Oxford University Press.

Tannen, D. (1990). *You just don't understand: Women and men in conversation.* New York: Ballantine Books.

Tannen, D. (1986). *That's not what I meant!: How conversational style makes or breaks relationships.* New York: Ballantine Books.

Tappen, R. (2001). *Nursing leadership and management: Concepts and practice.* (4th edn). Philadelphia: F.A. Davis Company.

Tappen, R. (1995). *Nursing leadership and management: Concepts and practice.* (3rd edn). Philadelphia: F.A. Davis Company.

Tappen, R., Weiss, S., & Whitehead, D. (2001). *Essentials of nursing leadership and management.* (2nd edn). Philadelphia: F.A.Davis.

Tarnow-Mordi, W. O., Hau, C., Warden, A., & Shearer, A. J. (2000). Hospital mortality in relation to staff workload: A 4-year study in an adult intensive care unit. *Lancet, 356* (922), 185–9.

Taylor, F. W. (1911). *The principles of scientific management.* New York: Harper & Row.

Taylor, S., White, B., & Muncer, S. (1999). Nurses' cognitive structural models of work-based stress. *Journal of Advanced Nursing, 29*(4) 974–983.

The New Shorter Oxford Dictionary (1993). (5th edn). Oxford: Clarendon Press.

Thomas, B. (1995). Risky business. *Nursing Times, 91*(7) 52–4.

Thompson, A. A. Jr., & Strickland, A. J. III (1995). *Strategic management: Concepts and cases.* (8th edn). Chicago: Irwin.

Thompson, C., McCaughan, D., Cullum, N., Sheldon, T. A., Mulhall, A., & Thompson, D. R. (2001a). The accessibility of research-based knowledge for nurses in United Kingdom acute care settings. *Journal of Advanced Nursing 36*, 11–22.

Thompson, C., McCaughan, D., Cullum, N., Sheldon, T. A., Mulhall, A., & Thompson, D. R. (2001b). Research information in nurses' clinical decision-making: What is useful? *Journal of Advanced Nursing 36*, 376–88.

Thompson, D. R. (2002). A response to Gary Rolfe. *Nurse Education Today 22*,

Thompson, D. R. (2000a). An exploration of knowledge development in nursing—a personal perspective. *Nursing Times Research 5*, 391–4.

Thompson, D. R. (2000b). The practitioner-researcher in nursing. (Commentary). *Nurse Education Today 20*, 39–40.

Thompson, D. R. (1998a). The development of a programme of research in cardiac rehabilitation. *International Journal of Nursing Studies 1998, 35*, 72–8.

Thompson, D. R. (1998b). The art and science of research in clinical nursing. In B. Roe, & C. Webb (eds), *Research and development in clinical nursing practice* (pp. 13–18). London: Whurr.

Thompson, D. R., Daly, J., Elliott, D., & Chang, E. (2002). Research in nursing. In J. Daly, S. Speedy, D. Jackson, & P. Darbyshire (eds), *Contexts of nursing.* Oxford: Blackwell Science.

Thorne, S. E., & Robinson, C. A. (1988). Reciprocal trust in health care relationships. *Journal of Advanced Nursing, 13,* 782–9.

Tichy, N. M., & Devanna, M. A. (1986). *The transformational leader.* New York: Wiley & Sons.

Tierney, A. J., & Taylor, J. (1991). Research in practice: An 'experiment' in researcher-practitioner collaboration. *Journal of Advanced Nursing 16,* 506–10.

Tilley, H., & Tilley, I. G. (1999). External change and its impact on nurse management: A case study. *Journal of Nursing Management, 7,* 3–11.

Tong, R. (1998). *Feminist thought: A more comprehensive introduction.* Boulder: Westview Press.

Tonkin, A. M., Bauman, A. E., Bennet, S., Dobson, A. J., Hankey, G. J., & Ring, I. T. (1999). Cardiovascular health in Australia: Current state and future directions. *Asia Pacific Heart Journal, 8*(3), 183–7.

Tornabeni, J. (2001). The competency game: My take on what it really takes to lead. *Nursing Administration Quarterly (25)4,* 1–13.

Tranbarger, R. (1988). The nurse executive in a community hospital. In M. Johnson (ed.), *Series on Nursing Administration,* vol. 1. Menlo Park, CA: Addison-Wesley.

Trevelyan, R. (2001). *Unit 11 Organisational transformation in Managing people and organisations Part B,* (11–1, 11–48). Sydney: Australian Graduate School of Management.

Tripp-Reimer, T., & Brink, P. (1985). Cultural brokerage. In G. Bulechek & J. McCloskey (eds) *Nursing interventions: Treatment for nursing diagnoses* (pp. 352–62). Philadelphia: Saunders.

Trofino, (2000). Transformational leadership: Moving total quality management to world-class organisations. *International Nursing Review, 47*(4), 232–42.

Trofino, J. (1995). Transformational leadership in health care. *Nursing Management, 26*(8), 42–7.

Trompenaars, F. (1993). *Riding the waves of culture—understanding cultural diversity in business.* London, UK: Economist Books.

Trott, M., & Windsor, K. (1999). Leadership effectiveness: How do you measure up? *Nursing Economics, 17*(3), 127–30.

Tuckman, B. W. (1965). Developmental sequence in small groups. *Psychological Bulletin, 63,* pp. 384–99. In Hellriegel, D., Slocum, J. W., & Woodman, R. W. (1989). *Organisational behaviour,* 8th edn. UK: South-Western Publishing.

Turney, L. (2002). Mental health and workplace bullying: the role of power, professions and 'on the job' training. In L. Morrow, I. Verins, & E. Willis (eds). (pp. 135–48). *Mental health and work. Issues and perspectives.* Commonwealth of Australia.

Turnley, W. H., & Feldman, D. C. (1999). The impact of psychological contract violations on exit, voice, loyalty and neglect. *Human Relations, 52*(7), 895–7.

Tushman, M. L., & O'Reilly, C. A. III (1997). *Winning through innovation: A practical guide to leading organisational change and renewal.* Boston: Harvard Business Press.

U.S. Department of Health and Human Services (USDHHS). (1997). *The registered nurse population.* Rockville, MD: Author.

U.S. Department of Health and Human Services, Office of Minority Health (2000). Assuring Cultural Competence in Health Care: Recommendations for National Standards and an Outcomes-Focused Research Agenda. Washington, DC: Federal Register: December 22, 2000 (Volume 65, Number 247) pp. 80865–79; www.OMHRC.gov/CLAS

Urden, L. (1996). Development of a nurse executive decision support database: a model for outcomes evaluation. *Journal of Nursing Administration,, 26*(10), 15021.

Urden, L. D., & Walston, S. L. (2001). Outcomes of hospital restructuring and re-engineering: How is success or failure being measured? *Journal of Nursing Administration, 31,* 203–9.

Vaill, P. (1989). *Management as a performing art.* San Francisco: Jossey Bass.

REFERENCES

Valentine, N. M. (2001). Quality measures essential to the transformation of the Veterans Health Administration: Implications for nurses as co-creators of change. *Journal of Nursing Care Quality, 15*(4), 48–59.

Van Manen, M. (1977). Linking ways of knowing with ways of being. *Curriculum Inquiry, 6*(3), 205–28.

Varcoe, C. (1998). An ideology of scarcity: Working with/in austerity, *Ninth Annual International Critical and Feminist Perspectives in Nursing Conference*, Flinders University, Adelaide, 24–26 June.

Varcoe, C., & Rodney, P. (2002). Constrained agency: The social structure of nurses' work. In B. S. Bolaria, & H. Dickinson (eds). *Health, illness, and health care in Canada* (3rd edn) (pp. 102–28). Toronto: Harcourt Brace.

Vecchio, R. N., Hearn, G., & Southey, G. (1992). *Organisational behaviour: Life at work in Australia*. Sydney, Australia: Harcourt Brace Jovanovich.

Victorian Health Department. (2002). *Nursing in Victoria: Nurse recruitment and retention*. Retrieved 17 September, 2002, at http://nursing.health.gov.au/links.htm

Vilkinas, T., & Cartan, G. (1993). Competencies of Australian women in management. *Women in Management Review, 8*(3), 31–5.

Vleeming, R. G. (1979). Machiavellianism: A preliminary review. *Psychological Reports, February*, 295–310.

Vroom, V., & Jago, G. (1998). *The new leadership*. Englewood Cliffs, CA: Prentice Hall.

Warden, A., & McKenna, E. (1998). Managing change: Introduction of team primary nursing. *Managing Clinical Nursing, 2*, 12–18.

Warden, G. L. (1999). Leadership: Some things to think about. *Journal of Healthcare Management, 44*(2), 85–6.

Waters-Marsh, T. F. (2001). Exploiting differences: the exercise of power and politics in organisations. In R. Wiesner, & B. Millett (eds). *Management and organisational behaviour: Contemporary challenges and future directions*. Brisbane: John Wiley and Sons, Aust. Ltd.

Watson, W. E., Kumar, K., & Michaelsen, L. K. (1993). Cultural diversity's impact on interaction process and performance: Comparing homogeneous and diverse task groups. *Academy of Management Journal, 36*(3), 590–601.

Wells, J. (1995). Discontent without focus? An analysis of nurse management and activity on a psychiatric in-patient facility using a 'soft systems' approach. *Journal of Advanced Nursing, 21*(2), 214–21.

West, E. (2000). Organisational sources of safety and danger: Sociological contributions to the study of adverse events. *Quality in Health Care, 9*, 120–6.

Western Australia Auditor General. (2002). *A critical resource: Nursing shortages and the use of agency nurses*. Perth, Western Australia: Auditor General's Department.

Wheeler, R. (2000). Being proactive, not reactive. In F. Bower, F. (2000). *Nurses taking the lead: Personal qualities of effective leadership.*, pp. 199–222, Philadelphia: W. B. Saunders.

White, G. (2001). The code of ethics for nurses: Responding to new challenges in a new century. *American Journal of Nursing, 101*(10), 73–5.

Whitecross, L. (1999). Collaboration between GPs and nurse practitioners: The overseas experience and lessons for Australia. *Australian Family Physician, 28*, 349–53.

Whitener, E. M., Brodt, S. E., Korsgaard, A., & Werner, J. M. (1998). Managers as initiators of trust: An exchange relationship framework for understanding managerial trustworthy behavior. *Academy of Management Review, 23*(3), 513–31.

Whitfield, J. M., Anthony, W. P., & Kacmar, K. M. (1995). Evaluation of team-based management: A case study. *Journal of Organisation Change Management, 8*(2) 17–28.

Whittemore, R. (2000). Consequences of not 'knowing the patient'. *Clinical Nurse Specialist, 14*(2), 75–81.

Wiles, V., & Daffurn, K. (2002). *There's a bird in my hand and a bear by the bed, I must be in ICU: The pivotal years of Australian critical care nursing*. Carlton South, Victoria: Australian College of Critical Care Nurses Ltd.

Wilkie, W. (1996). Understanding the behaviour of victimised people. In E. J. Dyer (ed.). *Beyond Bullying Association Inc.* New South Wales: Millennium Books.

Wilkinson, J. M. (1989). Moral distress: A labor and delivery nurse's experience. *JOGNN, 18*(6), 513–19.

Wilkinson, J. M. (1988). Moral distress in nursing practice: Experience and effect. *Nursing Forum, 23*(1), 16–29.

Williams, G. F., Chaboyer, W., & Patterson, E. (2000). International perspectives. Australia's nursing workforce in perspective. *Journal of Nursing Administration, 30*(6), 304–8.

Williams, S. (1998). Computerised documentation of case management: from diagnosis to outcomes. *Nursing Case Management, 3*(6), 247–54.

Willmot, M. (1998). The new ward manager: An evaluation of the changing role of the charge nurse. *Journal of Advanced Nursing, 28*(2), 419–27.

Wilson, L. L., & Goldschmidt, P. (1995). *Quality management in health care.* Sydney: McGraw-Hill.

Wilson, R. M., Harrison, B. T., Gibberd, R. W., & Hamilton, J. D. (1999). An analysis of the causes of adverse events from the quality in Australian health care study. *Medical Journal of Australia, 170,* 411–15.

Wilson, S., Morse, J., & Penrod, J. (1998). Developing reciprocal trust in the caregiving relationship. *Qualitative Health Research, 8*(4), 446–5.

Winskill, R. (2000). Is competency based training/education useful for workplace training? *Contemporary Nurse 9*(2), 115–19.

Wolpe, A., Quinlan, O., & Martinez, L. (1997). *Gender equity in education.* Pretoria: Department of Education, South Africa.

Wood, J. M., Wallace, J., & Zeffane, R. M. (2001). *Organisational behaviour,* 2nd edn. Brisbane: John Wiley and Sons.

Wood, J., Wallace, J., Zeffane, R. M., Schermerhorn, J. R., Hunt, J.G., & Osborn, R. N. (2001). *Organisational Behaviour: A global perspective.* (2nd edn). Brisbane: John Wiley and Sons, Aust. Ltd.

World Bank 1998, http://www.worldbank.org/poverty/scapital/

World Health Organisation (2002). *World report on violence and health.* E. G. Krung, L. L. Dahlberg, J. A. Mercy, A. B. Zwi, & R. Lozano (eds). Geneva: WHO.

World Health Organisation. 54th World Health Assembly (2001) at www.who.int/health-services-delivery/nursing/background.htm

World Health Organisation. Acting on non-communicable diseases. An advocacy guide for the Western Pacific. Draft document 2002.

Wright, S. (1993). The standard guide to achieving change quietly. *Nursing Standard, 7*(26), 52–4.

Wright, S. G. (1998). *Changing nursing practice.* (2nd edn). London: Arnold.

Wyatt, J.C. (1995). Hospital information management: the need for clinical leadership. *BMJ 311* (175–180).

Wyatt, J., & Hare, C. (1997). *Work abuse: How to recognise and survive it.* Rochester, Vermont: Schenkman Books.

Yarling, R. R., & McElmurry, B. J. (1986). The moral foundation of nursing. *Advances in Nursing Science, 8*(2), 63–73.

Yiannis, G. (1998). Psychoanalytic contributions to the study of the emotional life of organizations. *Administration and Society.* 30 (3): 291–314.

Yin, T. J. C., Hsu, N., Tsai, S. L., Wang, B. W., Shaw, F. L., Shih, F. J., & Henry, B. (2000). Priority-setting for nursing research in the Republic of China. *Journal of Advanced Nursing, 32,* 19–27.

Yin, T. J. C., Tsai, J., & Chang, W. (1997). International perspectives: Health and nursing leadership in Taiwan, Republic of China. *Journal of Nursing Administration, 27,* 10–12.

Yoder-Wise, P. S. (1999). *Leading and managing in nursing,* 2nd edn., St Louis: Mosby.

Young, K.M. (2000). *Informatics for healthcare professionals.* Philadelphia: F.A. Davis Company.

Young-Mason, J. (2001). The caring ethic. *Clinical Nurse Specialist, 15*(3), 103–4.

Zaleznik, A. (1981). Managers and leaders: Are they different? *Journal of Nursing Administration, 11*(7), 25–31.

REFERENCES

Zerull, L. M. (1999). Community nurse case management: Evolving over time to meet new demands. *Family and Community Health, 22*(3), 12–29.

Zohar, D., & Marshall, I. (2000). *Spirtual intelligence: The ultimate intelligence.* London: Bloomsbury Publishing.

Index